Modernism and Literature

This volume offers a comprehensive representation of the exciting, pivotal, and urgent nature of literary modernism, as well as more recent approaches including the "global turn." Modernism can be difficult to understand without an awareness of contemporary concerns, so Mia Carter and Alan Friedman incorporate texts from a wide variety of disciplines such as art, politics, science, medicine, and philosophy.

This volume's thoroughly explained, informative, and interesting discussions provide:

- An extensive introduction to the history and debates surrounding modernism
- Numerous foundational texts of modernism such as Darwin, Duncan, Einstein, Freud, Hughes, Luxemburg, Nietzsche, Stein, Zola
- Full texts and extracts representing modernist writers – including Anand, Conrad, Eliot, James, Hurston, Lawrence, Wilde, Woolf, and Yeats – as critics of themselves and their contemporaries
- A chronology of key historical events and publications
- A glossary of key terms, people, theories, and themes
- A detailed bibliography offering advice on further study and research
- A companion website (www.routledge.com/cw/carter) featuring an interactive timeline with dates and images that contextualize the literature of the period, as well as author biographies and links to additional resources and videos

Addressing current as well as historical debates about modernism, this book includes discussion of the Harlem Renaissance, feminism and women's writing, international and global movements, and anti-imperialism, while acknowledging the variety of competing modernisms. This is the ideal guide for anyone seeking an overview and an in-depth treatment of this complex cultural turn and its foundational texts.

Mia Carter is a University Distinguished Teaching Associate Professor of Literature at the University of Texas at Austin, USA.

Alan Warren Friedman is Thaman Professor of English and Comparative Literature at the University of Texas at Austin, USA.

Modernism and Literature

An Introduction and Reader

Edited by

Mia Carter and Alan Warren Friedman

Routledge
Taylor & Francis Group

LONDON AND NEW YORK

First published 2013
by Routledge
2 Park Square, Milton Park, Abingdon, Oxon OX14 4RN

Simultaneously published in the USA and Canada
by Routledge
711 Third Avenue, New York, NY 10017

Routledge is an imprint of the Taylor & Francis Group, an informa business

British Library Cataloguing in Publication Data
A catalogue record for this book is available from the British Library

Library of Congress Cataloging-in-Publication Data
  Carter, Mia.
  Modernism and literature : an introduction and reader / Mia Carter and Alan Warren Friedman.
      p. cm.
  Includes bibliographical references and index.
  1. Modernism (Literature) I. Friedman, Alan Warren. II. Title.
  PN56.M54C37 2013
  809'.9112—dc23
                                                                    2012029496

ISBN13: 978–0–415–58163–9 (hbk)
ISBN 13: 978–0–415–58164–6 (pbk)

Typeset in Perpetua and Bell Gothic
by RefineCatch Limited, Bungay, Suffolk

Printed and bound in the United States of America
by Edwards Brothers, Inc.

For Liz and Brian

Contents

Acknowledgments

Our primary and deepest debt is to the staff at Routledge, who worked closely with us every step of the way to bring this book to fruition. Polly Dodson, who believed that such a book was worthwhile, perhaps even necessary, was in at the start, and played a significant role in transforming the initial, inadequate conception into a far deeper, richer, more comprehensive compendium. Jill D'Urso, our assiduous and infinitely patient and insightful overseer, interrogator, encourager, and guide, kept us firmly on track, answered all our questions, and negotiated the concerns and progress of those handling permissions and copyright matters, production, and marketing. The book also benefited enormously from the dozens of professional readings that Routledge generously contracted for several times along the way. They were intelligent and constructive, honest and forthright, highly detailed, both sharply critical and generous-spirited – critiques that became a major part of the process and go a long way to explain why this book is far better than it started out to be.

We are also fortunate to be members of the highly nurturing Department of English at the University of Texas at Austin, which is chaired by Elizabeth Cullingford, who encouraged and supported this project. The excellent staff at the Harry Ransom Center (HRC) provided crucial assistance, resources, and support. Several colleagues – including Brian Bremen, Jean Cannon, Ben Cohen, Layne Craig, Don Graham, Linda Henderson, David Kornhaber, Melvin Oakes, Susannah Hollister, Snehal Shingavi, and Dean Young – offered helpful suggestions and advice. Our research assistant, Emily Bloom, worked tirelessly with us to learn and explore the field, produce copy, coordinate materials, and shape the final product. Ashley Miller took the lead in creating the web site for the book. And Jennifer Harger assisted us during the final stages of our complicated and fascinating journey.

Mia would also like to thank her most revered and highly appreciated teachers at the University of Wisconsin-Milwaukee's Modern Studies Program: Herbert Blau, Ihab Hassan, the late, great Sheila Roberts, and *especially* the philosophical jazzman, Bernard Gendron. Some gifts keep on giving and, on the rarest occasions, they increase in value over time; such were each of yours to me.

Permissions

Mulk Raj Anand, "Muhammad Iqbal." *The Golden Breath: Studies in Five Poets of the New India*. New York: Dutton, 1933. 61–85.

Légitime Défense Manifesto (1932). Austin: University of Texas Press. Reprinted with permission of Black Swan Press.

Ezra Pound, "A Few Don'ts by an Imagiste," copyright © 1991 by The Trustees of the Ezra Pound Literary Property Trust. Used by permission of New Directions Publishing Corporation, agents for the heirs of Ezra Pound.

T.S. Eliot, "Tradition and the Individual Talent." *The Dial* 75 (November 1923). Used with permission from the Publisher Faber and Faber Ltd.

Excerpt from "Modern Fiction" from *The Common Reader* by Virginia Woolf, copyright 1925 by Houghton Mifflin Harcourt Publishing Company and renewed 1953 by Leonard Woolf, reprinted by permission of the publisher.

George Bernard Shaw, "The Technical Novelty in Ibsen's Plays" (1913). *Major Critical Essays*. London: Constable, 1948. 135–46. Reproduced with permission from The Society of Authors, on behalf of the Bernard Shaw Estate.

Ezra Pound, "Dubliners and Mr. James Joyce," copyright © 1991 by The Trustees of the Ezra Pound Literary Property Trust. Used by permission of New Directions Publishing Corporation, agents for the heirs of Ezra Pound.

T.S. Eliot, "Ulysses, Order and Myth" (1923). *The Dial* 75 (1923): 480–83. Used with permission from the publisher Faber and Faber Ltd.

"Modern Poetry" by Mina Loy is reprinted from *The Lost Lunar Baedeker*, edited by Roger L. Conover (New York: Farrar, Straus and Giroux, 1996) by permission of the editor.

Virginia Woolf, "How It Strikes a Contemporary." *The Common Reader* (1925). New York: Harcourt, Brace, 1953. 236–46. Used with permission from The Society of Authors as the Literary Representative of the Estate of Virginia Woolf.

"The Leaning Tower" from *The Moment And Other Essays* by Virginia Woolf, copyright 1948 by Harcourt, Inc. and renewed 1976 by Marjorie T. Parsons, reprinted by permission of Houghton Mifflin Harcourt Publishing Company.

E.M. Forster, "Virginia Woolf" (1942). *Two Cheers for Democracy*. New York: Harcourt, Brace, 1951. 242–58. Used with permission from the Provost and Scholars of King's College, Cambridge and The Society of Authors as the Literary Representative of the Estate of E.M. Forster.

Louis MacNeice, "The Tower That Once." *Folios of New Writing*. London: Hogarth Press, 1941. 37–41, reproduced with permission.

From *Shadow and Act* by Ralph Ellison, copyright 1953, 1964 and renewed 1981, 1992 by Ralph Ellison. Used by permission of Random House, Inc.

H.D., "Tribute to Freud." New York: Pantheon Books, 1956. (pgs. 14–18). Reproduced by permission of Pollinger Limited and New Directions.

Every effort has been made to trace and contact copyright holders. The publishers would be pleased to hear from any copyright holders not acknowledged here, so that this acknowledgement page may be amended at the earliest opportunity.

Timeline of modernisms

TEXTS AND CONTEXTS

Date	Literary texts	Other arts	Historic contexts
1870–71			Franco-Prussian War
1872		Claude Monet, *Impression: soleil levant* ("Impression: Sunrise"), displayed in first impressionist exhibition, Paris (1874)	
1873	Arthur Rimbaud, *A Season in Hell*; Walter Pater, *The Renaissance*		
1877		Helena Petrovna Blavatsky, *Isis Unveiled*	
1879	Henrik Ibsen, *A Doll's House*		
1881	Henry James, *The Portrait of a Lady*		
1882			Married Woman's Property Act: British women gain equal rights regarding control of private income, property, and inheritance; Cairo occupied by British troops; control of Suez Canal at issue
1883	Henrik Ibsen, *An Enemy of the People*		Ilbert Bill passes: admits Indians to Civil Service and allows Indian magistrates to judge Europeans; slavery banned throughout British Empire

Date	Literary texts	Other arts	Historic contexts
1884	Henrik Ibsen, *The Wild Duck*		Foundation of Fabian Society (British Socialists); gold discovered on the Rand, South Africa (harbinger of Boer War)
1884–85			Berlin Conference and New Imperialism (the Scramble for Africa); carved up – with no native representation – all of Africa and distributed it among European nations
1886	Jean Moréas, *The Symbolist Manifesto*; Henrik Ibsen, *Rosmersholm*		First meeting of Indian National Congress
			Statue of Liberty dedicated
1887			National Union of Women's Suffrage Societies founded in U.K.
1888	August Strindberg, *Miss Julie*; Helena Petrovna Blavatsky, *The Secret Doctrine*		George Eastman develops "Kodak" box camera; Heinrich Hertz confirms existence of electromagnetic waves
1889			Paris Exposition (which drew 28 million visitors), for which Eiffel Tower was built
1890	Henrik Ibsen, *Hedda Gabler*; William James, *Principles of Psychology*		Daimler produces first automobile
1891	Thomas Hardy, *Tess of the D'Urbervilles*; Oscar Wilde, *Salomé; The Picture of Dorian Gray*		Free Education Act passes, U.K.
1892	Henrik Ibsen, *The Master Builder*		
1893			New Zealand becomes first nation to grant women full voting rights
1894–95			Sino-Japanese War
1894–97	*The Yellow Book*		
1894–1906			Dreyfus affair
1895	Thomas Hardy, *Jude the Obscure*		French brothers Louis and Auguste Lumière present first projected, moving pictures to a paying audience; Guglielmo Marconi invents telegraphy; Wilhelm Roentgen discovers X-rays; trials of Oscar Wilde
1896	Anton Chekhov, *The Seagull*		

Date	Literary texts	Other arts	Historic contexts
1897	Joseph Conrad, *The Nigger of the "Narcissus"*; Henry James, *What Maisie Knew*; Bram Stoker, *Dracula*; H.G. Wells, *The Invisible Man*		Workmen's Compensation Act, U.K.; Magnus Hirschfield establishes Scientific-Humanitarian Committee; it later organizes a petition — signed by Rilke, Einstein, Tolstoy, Mann *et al.* — to protest Paragraph 175, a law that deemed sex between men a crime
1898	Émile Zola, *J'accuse*		Curies discover radium; Spanish–American War
1899	Joseph Conrad, *Heart of Darkness*	Sigmund Freud, *The Interpretation of Dreams* (Germany)	Great Britain signs Hague Convention establishing international rules of war
1899–1902			Boer War
1900	Joseph Conrad, *Lord Jim*		Women allowed to compete in Olympics for first time; Max Planck proposes quantum theory; Boxer Rebellion (China), suppressed by European and Japanese troops
1901			Queen Victoria dies; Robert Baden-Powell forms pro-imperialist Boy Scouts Organization
1901–10			Reign of King Edward VII
1902	Henry James, *The Wings of a Dove*		
1903	W.E.B. Du Bois, *The Souls of Black Folks*; Henry James, *The Ambassadors*; George Bernard Shaw, *Man and Superman*; *Protocols of the Elders of Zion*		Wilbur and Orville Wright, first successful airplane flight; Frank Lloyd Wright, Larkin Building; first silent movie, *The Great Train Robbery*
1904	Anton Chekhov, *The Cherry Orchard*; Joseph Conrad, *Nostromo*; Henry James, *The Golden Bowl*		
1904–05			Russo-Japanese War
1905	George Bernard Shaw, *Major Barbara*; Edith Wharton, *The House of Mirth*		Albert Einstein, special theory of relativity
1907	Henry Adams, *The Education of Henry Adams*; Joseph Conrad, *The Secret Agent: A Simple Tale*	Pablo Picasso, *Les demoiselles d'Avignon*	
1908–15			Ford Motor Company develops assembly line, first mass-produced cars

Date	Literary texts	Other arts	Historic contexts
1909	Ezra Pound, *Personae*; Gertrude Stein, *Three Lives*	Filippo Marinetti, *The Futurist Manifesto*	National Association for the Advancement of Colored People (NAACP) founded; plastic invented
1910	E.M. Forster, *Howards End*; William Butler Yeats, *The Green Helmet and Other Poems*	First post-impressionist exhibition, London	Beginning of Mexican Revolution
1910–13		Bertrand Russell and Alfred North Whitehead, *Principia Mathematica*	
1910–14		Futurism	
1912	Thomas Mann, *Death in Venice*	Arnold Schönberg, *Pierrot Lunaire*	
1912–44	H.D. (Hilda Doolittle), *Collected Poems* (1983)		
1913		Igor Stravinsky, *The Rite of Spring*; New York International Exhibition of Modern Art (the Armory Show)	Natives' Land Act, South Africa: restricts natives to certain areas
1913–27	Marcel Proust, *A la recherche du temps perdu*		
1914	James Joyce, *Dubliners*; Franz Kafka, "In the Penal Colony"; Amy Lowell, *Sword Blade and Poppy Seed*; W.B. Yeats, *Responsibilities*		Assassination of Archduke Franz Ferdinand, heir to Austro-Hungarian throne leads to outbreak of World War I
1914–15	Wyndham Lewis edits *Blast*		
1914–18			World War I
1915	Ford Madox Ford, *The Good Soldier*; Franz Kafka, *The Metamorphosis*; D.H. Lawrence, *The Rainbow*	D.W. Griffith, *Birth of a Nation*	First transcontinental telephone call: New York to San Francisco
1915–16		Constantin Brancusi, *Princess X*	
1915–17			Armenian Genocide under Ottoman Empire (1.5 million Armenians killed)
1915–67	Dorothy Richardson, *Pilgrimage*		
1916	H.D. (Hilda Doolittle), *Sea Garden*; James Joyce, *A Portrait of the Artist as a Young Man*; Amy Lowell, *Men, Women and Ghosts*		Easter Rising in Ireland; conscription begins in England; Albert Einstein, general theory of relativity; Margaret Sanger opens first birth control clinic in U.S., arrested for distributing contraception

Date	Literary texts	Other arts	Historic contexts
1917	T.S. Eliot, *Prufrock and Other Observations*; Edna St. Vincent Millay, *Renascence and Other Poems*; Luigi Pirandello, *Right You Are, If You Think You Are*	Marcel Duchamp, *Fountain*	Balfour Declaration; first use of mustard gas on the Western Front; Russian Revolution
c. 1917–35		Harlem Renaissance	
1918	Amy Lowell, *Can Grande's Castle*	Marie Stopes, *Married Love* (best-selling sex and contraception manual)	Women 30 and older obtain vote in U.K. (extended to those over 21 in 1928)
1918–19			Influenza pandemic kills three times as many people as World War I in one-third the time
1918–22		Oswald Spengler, *The Decline of the West*	
1919	Sherwood Anderson, *Winesburg, Ohio*; George Bernard Shaw, *Heartbreak House*		Amritsar (or Jallianwala Bagh) Massacre; first commercial Paris–London flight; Treaty of Versailles; Weimar Republic established; women obtain vote in U.S.
1919–33		Bauhaus school	
1920	D.H. Lawrence, *Women in Love*; Ezra Pound, *Hugh Selwyn Mauberley*		Gandhi begins nonviolent campaign for Indian independence; League of Nations holds first meeting, Geneva
1920–33			Prohibition in U.S.
1921	H.D. (Hilda Doolittle), *Hymen*; Marianne Moore, *Poems*; Luigi Pirandello, *Six Characters in Search of an Author*	Ludwig Wittgenstein, *Tractatus Logico-Philosophicus*	
1921–24			Irish Civil War
1922	T.S. Eliot, *The Waste Land*; James Joyce, *Ulysses*; Katherine Mansfield, *The Garden Party and Other Stories*; Luigi Pirandello, *Henry IV*; Wallace Stevens, *Harmonium*; Virginia Woolf, *Jacob's Room*; Constantin Brancusi, *Bird in Space* series		
1923	Louise Bogan, *Body of This Death*; Elmer Rice, *The Adding Machine*; Jean Toomer, *Cane*		

Date	Literary texts	Other arts	Historic contexts
1924	First *Surrealist Manifesto* (2nd issued 1929) by André Breton *et al.*; E.M. Forster, *A Passage to India*; Thomas Mann, *The Magic Mountain*; Eugene O'Neill, *The Emperor Jones*	Death of Vladimir Ilyich Lenin	
1924–28	Ford Madox Ford, *Parade's End*		
1925	Alain Locke, ed., *The New Negro*; F. Scott Fitzgerald, *The Great Gatsby*; Ernest Hemingway, *In Our Time*; Franz Kafka, *The Trial*; Amy Lowell, *The Complete Poetical Works*; *What's O'Clock*; Gertrude Stein, *The Making of Americans: The Hersland Family*; Virginia Woolf, *Mrs. Dalloway*	Sergei Eisenstein, *Battleship Potemkin*	Scopes (Monkey) trial (Creationism vs. Darwin's Theory of Evolution); Werner Heisenberg, quantum mechanics
1925–64	Ezra Pound, *The Cantos*		
1926	Alberto Giacometti, *The Couple*; *Spoon Woman*; Ernest Hemingway, *The Sun Also Rises*; Langston Hughes, *The Weary Blues*; Franz Kafka, *The Castle*		General Strike in U.K.
1926–29		Frank Lloyd Wright, Graycliff Estate	
1927	Virginia Woolf, *To the Lighthouse*		BBC begins broadcasting (radio); Charles Lindbergh, first solo non-stop flight across Atlantic Ocean; Werner Heisenberg, uncertainty principle
1928	Bertolt Brecht, *The Threepenny Opera*; D. H. Lawrence, *Lady Chatterley's Lover*; Claude McKay, *Home to Harlem*; Eugene O'Neill, *Strange Interlude*; William Butler Yeats, *The Tower*		Alexander Fleming discovers penicillin; suffrage for all women over 21, U.K.; Kellogg–Briand Pact outlawing war and prohibiting its use as "an instrument of national policy"
1929	Elizabeth Bowen, *The Last September*; William Faulkner, *The Sound and the Fury*; Luigi Pirandello, *Tonight We Improvise*; Gertrude Stein, *Four Saints in Three Acts*; William Butler Yeats, *The Winding Stairs*		Wall Street stock market crash followed by Great Depression
1929–59	William Faulkner, *The Yoknapatawpha Saga*		

Date	Literary texts	Other arts	Historic contexts
1930	Hart Crane, *The Bridge*; Jean Cocteau, *The Blood of a Poet*; William Faulkner, *As I Lay Dying*; Jean Rhys, *After Leaving Mr. Mackenzie*		
1931	Eugene O'Neill, *Mourning Becomes Electra*; Virginia Woolf, *The Waves*; Edmund Wilson, *Axel's Castle: A Study in the Imaginative Literature of 1870–1930*		
1931–36			Scottsboro Boys' trials
1932	William Faulkner, *Light in August*	Etienne Léro initiates revolutionary journal, *Légitime Défense*	
1932–33		Alberto Giacometti, "Walking Woman"	
1933			C.L.R. James, *The Case for West Indian Self-Government*; Franklin Delano Roosevelt becomes U.S. president; Adolf Hitler named German chancellor; Nazis open Dachau concentration camp; Reichstag fire enables Hitler to ban Communist Party; U.S. Customs seizes copies of *Ulysses* imported by Random House; resulting trial found it not to contravene obscenity laws and it was published in U.S.
1933–43	Thomas Mann, *Joseph and His Brothers*		
1934	Nancy Cunard, ed., *Negro: An Anthology*		
1935	Marianne Moore, *Selected Poems*; Wallace Stevens, *Ideas of Order*		
1935–39		Frank Lloyd Wright, Fallingwater	
1936	Djuna Barnes, *Nightwood*; William Faulkner, *Absalom, Absalom!*	Charlie Chaplin, *Modern Times*	
1936–38			Stalin's "Great Purge"
1936–39			Spanish Civil War

Date	Literary texts	Other arts	Historic contexts
1936–42	T.S. Eliot, *Four Quartets*		
1937	Zora Neale Hurston, *Their Eyes Were Watching God*; Wallace Stevens, *The Man with the Blue Guitar & Other Poems*	Picasso, *Guernica*	
1938			*Kristallnacht* (Crystal Night) across Germany
1939	James Joyce, *Finnegans Wake*; Katherine Anne Porter, *Pale Horse, Pale Rider*; Jean Rhys, *Good Morning, Midnight*		Deaths of W.B. Yeats and Sigmund Freud
1939–45			World War II
1940	Ernest Hemingway, *For Whom the Bell Tolls*	Charlie Chaplin, *The Great Dictator*	
1941	Virginia Woolf, *Between the Acts*		Deaths of James Joyce and Virginia Woolf

Mia Carter and Alan Warren Friedman

INTRODUCTION: LITERARY MODERNISMS

*M*ODERNISM AND LITERATURE: *An Introduction and Reader* grows out of our long engagement with teaching and researching the literature and culture of the first half of the twentieth century. It includes some of the materials that we have found to be most useful in contextualizing and historicizing the subject, offers many of the field's disciplinary foundations and ongoing debates, and reflects current redefinitions as well. Like all "isms," "modernism" is a controversial term and concept, richly ambiguous, reductive, and highly contested. At issue are its practitioners, techniques, locations, politics, intentions, and consequences. Thomas Kuhn notes that while sharp demarcations between eras, like those between the colors of a prism, can be difficult to discern and define, conflicting paradigms may coexist more or less peacefully, and consensus may be impossible to establish; nevertheless, a new era begins to establish itself, at least retrospectively, when a qualitative critical mass is achieved.[1] Even more than analogous labels, "modernism" is especially problematic because the word is commonly used in at least three very different ways: to designate certain qualities in art and culture that resist or transcend temporal limits; in contradistinction to "postmodernism"; and as a synonym for "contemporary." The term also has different meanings and implications when used in the contexts of religion, art history, architecture, music, and so on. And every age deems itself modern in at least some sense, but the era known as "modernist" remains so labeled, especially when viewed through the lens of the "postmodernist" era that followed.

Difficulties and debates arise in defining the temporal markers of modernist art movements, and modernity, the denomination of a specific temporal era, has been associated with the Industrial Revolution, World War I, the Russian Revolution, and the Suffrage Movement. Scientific discoveries – Charles Darwin's theories of evolution, for example – and philosophical declarations, like Friedrich Nietzsche's "God is Dead," have also been deemed clarions of modernity. The dates we have chosen are, admittedly, somewhat arbitrary; it would take more than one volume to encompass the current breadth of global modernism and the various socio-political, economic, and historical parameters of modernity. As we represent it in our Timeline, our arc of modernism dates from the Franco-Prussian War (1870) and the beginnings of impressionist painting to the beginning of World War II (1939), although we extend it to 1941 in order to encompass the deaths of two central figures – James Joyce and Virginia Woolf – and slightly beyond 1945 to foreshadow the anti-colonial movements and upheavals that would reshape the modern world. Our Foundational Readings include many of the traditional works that contextualized European modernism, as well as international and global literary and political texts that intersected with it. For example, we represent the Afro-Caribbean, Latin American, and South Asian anti-colonial and independence movements with writers – poets, essayists, and novelists – like Mulk Raj Anand and Munshi Premchand, who were members of the Pan-South Asian All-India Progress Writers Association (PWA), and European-educated intellectuals and Third World nationalists like José Martí, Muhammad Iqbal, and the Francophone signers of the "*Légitime Défense Manifesto*." The modernist journeys of the James Joyce-loving Anand connected him to Indian and Irish nationalists (Iqbal, Annie Besant, Gandhi), Bloomsbury (Virginia and Leonard Woolf at the Hogarth Press, T.S. Eliot and E.M. Forster at The Criterion), the International Brigades of the Spanish Civil War, and the BBC, where he befriended George Orwell during World War II. Dilip Parameshwar Gaonkar argues that any periodization of modernity and description of cultural modernism that fails to account for these global and political movements and changes would be blind to some of the monumental realities of modernity: "to announce the general end of modernity even as an epoch . . . seems premature, if not patently ethnocentric, at a time when non-Western people everywhere began to engage critically their own hybrid modernities."[2]

In the West, modernism was marked by the waning or weakening of certain pre-modern (Victorian) concepts and institutions – including duty, patriarchal structures, rigid class and gender constraints, environmental determinism, linear time, Newtonianism, Utilitarianism, materialism – and by a sense of historic crisis and rupture that coincided with the undermining of "progress," which had been the culture's dominant trope for several centuries. Critics like Edward Said and the editors of *Modernism and Empire* note the simultaneity of changing values and modernist epistemological crises and doubts with the collapse of imperial colonialism.[3] What caused these transformations? Terry Eagleton proposes that,

> If one were asked to provide a single explanation" for this radical change, "one could do worse than reply: 'the failure of religion'. By the mid-Victorian period, this traditionally reliable, immensely powerful ideological form was in deep trouble. It was no longer winning the hearts and minds of the masses, and under the twin impacts of scientific discovery and social change its previous unquestioned dominance was in danger of evaporating.[4]

For some modernists, the secular orientation was familial and cultural; Virginia Woolf's parents, Sir Leslie Stephen and Julia Duckworth Stephen, were both committed agnostics and they encouraged their children's secular worldview. Leslie Stephen helped to popularize agnosticism with his books, *An Agnostic's Apology and Other Essays* (1893) and the posthumously published *Essays on Freethinking and Plainspeaking* (1907). The range of writings contained in this Reader also suggest that habits and acts of reading and writing – changing forms and styles; the cross-pollination of experimentation and tradition; the mobility of writers, artists, and intellectuals; the creation of new audiences with small presses, pamphlets, and little magazines; new technologies like film and radio; cheap and affordable book editions; the accessibility of translations – were both shaped by and influenced the dynamic changes associated with modernist expressions and forms.

Modernity had been anticipated with an ambiguity that itself became a hallmark of the new age: some viewed its coming with delight and optimism; others with pessimism verging on despair; some, like Baudelaire and Nietzsche, managed to do both.[5] In the middle of the nineteenth century, Matthew Arnold hailed contemporary culture as a kind of antithesis and antidote to Victorian constraints when he declared: "I am a Liberal, yet I am a Liberal tempered by experience, reflection, and renunciation, and I am, above all, a believer in culture." Arnold's view of culture in what he called "our modern world" was expansive – rational, civilized, tolerant – and predicated on amelioration and progress: "Now, then, is the moment for culture to be of service, culture which believes in making reason and the will of God prevail, believes in perfection, is the study and pursuit of perfection, and is no longer debarred, by a rigid invincible exclusion of whatever is new, from getting acceptance for its ideas, simply because they are new."[6] In contrast, Thomas Hardy has his doomed heroine in *Tess of the D'Urbervilles* experience "feelings which might almost have been called those of the age – the ache of modernism," a sense of alienation and nihilism, of "look[ing] upon it as a mishap to be alive" that she associates with John Bunyan's Pilgrim in the Valley of Humiliation and with Job's longing for death.[7] Both of these strains were fully realized in the modern era: Arnoldian optimism ultimately seemed validated in the lessening of class and religious constraints, increased civil, social, and sexual liberty and opportunities, extraordinary technical and medical advancements that dramatically improved basic living conditions and standards for many (perhaps most notably in such areas as hygiene and health care), enhanced communication and mobility, and so on. At the same time, the dark side of modernity – in some ways an outgrowth of enduring aspects of certain pernicious and constricting Victorian mores, the horrific toll exacted by the Industrial Revolution on its workers and victims, and then World War I followed by the flu pandemic of 1918–19 – produced, as Albert Einstein remarked in 1917, extraordinary technical advances with no moral constraints.[8] It also exacerbated imperialist and anti-democratic strains as well as class prejudice and conflict that often manifested themselves as widespread anti-Semitism, racism, eugenics, as well as political fascism that seems in some ways analogous to, even descended from, Victorian patriarchy, as Woolf would provocatively argue in her long essay *Three Guineas* (1938).

Capitalism, industrialism, consumerism, class relations, hygiene and health care, women's roles in society, intellectual discourse, culture itself, were all in dramatic transition. Were these transformations greater than they were for other ages? As Kuhn suggests, such changes are hard to quantify and to speak of definitively, but the case could certainly be made. Certain "isms" inherited from the nineteenth century – communism, socialism, social Darwinism, feminism, imperialism, impressionism – came into their own in the early decades of the twentieth, and restless experimentation spawned an age of proliferating "isms" that were often proclaimed in manifestos: symbolism, cubism, post-impressionism, fauvism, expressionism, futurism, orphism, vorticism, suprematism, constructivism, surrealism, spiritualism, spatialism, perspectivism, dadaism, imagism, primitivism, Russian formalism, among many others, including enlivened skepticism.[9] Victorian certitude was upended by radical changes in cultural and social thinking and practice; political, religious, and scientific challenges, crises, and revolutions; rapidly advancing technology for both peaceful and wartime use; major innovations in medical and funeral practices; shifting global and cultural relationships and interactions; transformations in gender and sexual relationships as women entered the workplace in large numbers and gained the vote, to name just a few.

Underlying some of modernism's numerous manifestoes that sought to break with the past was the self-conscious Poundian behest to "Make it new" – and in a new, often obscure, way – and the term morphed into, among others, the New Architecture, the New Dwelling, the New Photography, the New Typography, and soon the New Criticism. Artists with divergent aesthetic and political agendas practiced the ethos of Pound's motto differently. For example, the dadaists and surrealists wanted to make it strange by liberating the imagination; they sought to reveal the restrictiveness of rationalism and bourgeois society. Négritude poets aimed to make it revolutionary; capitalism and colonialism were unsustainable, oppressive foundations of the old world that must be confronted in order to liberate the bodies and minds of peoples whose communities and culture had been destroyed or denigrated. The playwright Bertolt Brecht wanted to expose illusion and reveal the making, to critically arouse audiences in order to combat fascism and awaken new communal affiliations. And Gertrude Stein sought to plumb the depths of the new by exploring processes of making itself; her writing was in conversation with modernist painting and the plastic arts. Meanings could be explored by means of resonance, association, and juxtaposition.

One useful way to think about these reorientations is as ideological assaults on Victorian culture and bourgeois values; they were also aesthetic attacks on entrenched realism and naturalism, though it's not that the modernists were, at least in their own view, less realists than their predecessors were. Rather, as Virginia Woolf put it after viewing the first post-impressionist exhibition in London, reality itself (like "human character" and "all social relations") had changed (or so it seemed) "on or about December, 1910."[10] Woolf may have been speaking more literally – and presciently – than she knew. During a time of radical discovery and innovation, light was shown to confound all expectations by behaving as waves or photons depending on how the experiment was conducted; experimental outcomes turned out to be significantly impacted by how measuring devices were set up; time slowed down as velocity increased; either the velocity or position of sub-atomic particles could be determined, but not both, at least not simultaneously; time – reality, generally – came to seem a matter of perspective and one's subjective state. Such technologies of mechanical reproduction as X-rays, photography, film, sound recording, and radio offered radically new methods for representing visual images and sounds that also challenged artists in traditional media to develop new styles to address changing sensory experiences. Literary techniques became analogously disorienting: stream of consciousness (in Joyce, Dorothy Richardson, and Gertrude Stein, for example); unreliable narrators such as Ford Madox Ford's John Dowell in *The Good Soldier* and most of Conrad's and Faulkner's; perspectival complexity and ambiguity (Stephen Crane's "The Open Boat," Henry James's *What Maisie Knew*); unstable irony and open-endedness (Joyce's *Portrait of the Artist*); imagism and allusiveness in poetry (Pound, Eliot, Stevens); destabilized theatrical representation (Chekhov, Pirandello, O'Neill, Brecht), and so on.

In chapter 1 of their foundational collection, *Modernism: 1890–1930*, Malcolm Bradbury and James McFarlane address the ahistorical, qualitative aspect of modernism: "one claims as 'modern' Catullus (but not Virgil), Villon (but not Ronsard), Donne (but not Spenser), Clough (but not Tennyson), and when one does the same for one's own time (Conrad, but not Galsworthy), the semantic instability of the term becomes obvious."[11] Similarly addressing the vexed issue of what defines and characterizes modernism, Ricardo Quinones' *Mapping Literary Modernism* raises some fundamental, but not easily answerable, questions: is modernism reactionary or liberal? Is it primarily Dionysian or formal and reflexive?[12] Overly intellectual or devoid of ideas? "Formalistic and devoted to the Word" or "erotic, primitivistic, and given over to the unconscious"? Heroic elitist or common? Attached to self or mythseeking?[13] Or is it somehow all of these?

The late nineteenth and early twentieth centuries also saw the emergence of the disciplines that have evolved into what became the social sciences – anthropology, linguistics, psychology, sociology, among others. James George Frazer, Claude Lévi-Strauss, Sigmund Freud, Franz Boas, and Margaret Mead studied so-called primitive people in order to understand both those from whom urbanized Westerners evolved and also the origins and vestigial primitivism (meaning savagery, barbarism) that still existed within those commonly deemed civilized. James Joyce, who referred to himself as an "amateur sociologist,"[14] made Leopold Bloom, the protagonist of *Ulysses*, a dabbler in many of the emerging social sciences. As an anthropologist (and despite having been baptized three times), Bloom avidly plays the Margaret Mead role when he observes the religious rituals of Irish natives in church and at funerals (*U* 5.322–441, 6.595–630). Anticipating the emergence of funeral studies, he is curious about such social customs as Irish burial practice (6.764–72, 815–23). He empathetically imagines the inner workings and psychology of Dlugacz the butcher (4.186–87), Simon Dedalus (6.74–75), the blind stripling (8.1092–1102), Gerty MacDowell (13.774–79), and many others. And he gamely tries to satisfy Molly's linguistic curiosity by providing her with the etymology and definition of "metempsychosis": "It's Greek: from the Greek. That means the transmigration of souls" or "Reincarnation: that's the word. . . . They used to believe you could be changed into an animal or a tree" (4.341–76) – the word's very slipperiness and complexity making it a key concept for modernism itself.

The task of the artist who would keep faith with modernity's radically altered realities, therefore, also had to change. As Woolf notes,

> The accent falls differently from of old; the moment of importance came not here but there; so that if a writer were a free man and not a slave, if he could write what he chose, not what he must, if he could base his work upon his own feeling and not upon convention, there would be no plot, no comedy, no tragedy, no love interest or catastrophe in the accepted style, and perhaps not a single button sewn on as the Bond Street tailors would have it. Life is not a series of gig lamps symmetrically arranged; but a luminous halo, a semi-transparent envelope surrounding us from the beginning of consciousness to the end.[15]

Reflecting the age, many works of modernist literature became psychological, epistemological, open-ended, uncertain. In a world predicated on post-impressionism, Einsteinian relativity, Freudian psychology, Bergsonian duration, and "the death of God," where one stood seemed to define its very essence. For Oscar Wilde, speaking as Vivian in "The Decay of Lying," artifice determined reality:

> Life imitates Art far more than Art imitates Life. . . . Where, if not from the Impressionists, do we get those wonderful brown fogs that come creeping down our streets, blurring the gas-lamps and changing the houses into monstrous shadows? . . . The extraordinary change that has taken place in the climate of London during the last ten years is entirely due to a particular school of Art. . . . Things are because we see them, and what we see, and how we see it, depends on the Arts that have influenced us. . . . They did not exist till Art had invented them.[16]

Other writers concurred. In his memoir of Joseph Conrad, for example, Ford Madox Ford speaks of the truth of impression as superior to the truth of fact,[17] while Woolf calls facts "a very inferior form of fiction."[18]

Earlier literary texts that are qualitatively "modern" tend to be unstable and interrogative, in part because they foreground the perception and judgment of untrustworthy protagonists. In her novel *The House in Paris* (1935), Elizabeth Bowen writes, "sight . . . starts up emotion. . . . no object is mysterious. The mystery is your eye."[19] In *Oedipus Rex* Oedipus begins his quest for truth by asking who has murdered Laius, his predecessor as king and husband of Jocasta; gradually, inexorably, he is forced to ask a far more fundamental question: "Who am I?" *Hamlet*, which T.S. Eliot called the Mona Lisa of literature, begins with seven questions in the first twenty lines (most of which go unanswered), uses the word "question" (and variations on it) more than any other play of Shakespeare's, and remains in the interrogative mood throughout. Robert Browning's dramatic poem *The Ring and the Book* (1868–69) seems modernist in dramatizing several voices (including "Half-Rome," "The Other Half-Rome," and "Tertium Quid") that bear witness at a murder trial, but it remains a Victorian work since Browning has first the Pope and then an authorial voice cut through the conflicting testimony to pronounce the truth of what happened.

Other modernists, however, embraced epistemological certainty as a means of addressing and often confronting the world's social, material, and ideological conditions. For artists like the South Asian writers who signed the All-India Progressive Writers Alliance manifesto and for consciously politically engaged artists like Bertolt Brecht, the Négritude poets, the Harlem Renaissance writers, inherited traditions might be critiqued or rejected, representation thoroughly investigated or exposed, but meaning *mattered* and provided opportunities for transformational new ways of knowing and being. For many of the global modernist writers, accessibility and immediacy were aesthetic priorities; while the Négritude poet Aimé Césaire embraced an Antillean surrealism, his colleague Leopold Senghor wanted to create a direct, rhythmic, and forcefully expressive poetry that maintained a connection to the African conti-nent's oral traditions. And Mulk Raj Anand and Munshi Premchand, in their different ways, used the traditions of realism and naturalism to document the cruel realities of the caste system and cultural traditions that oppressed women and the poor.

In the West literary modernism is commonly seen as beginning by rejecting what it consid-ered the dead end of naturalism, with its pseudo-scientific emphasis on reportage as expressive of human life. For Arthur Symons, modernism was a "revolt against exteriority, against rhet-oric, against a materialistic tradition," a spiritual liberation that assumed "the duties and responsibilities of . . . sacred ritual,"[20] and it climaxed in the triumphant "blend of realism and symbolism pioneered by James and Conrad."[21] The consensus place to start is probably with the French symbolist poets: Charles Baudelaire (especially *Les fleurs du mal* [*The Flowers of Evil*], 1857), Stéphane Mallarmé (*Hérodiade*, 1869 and *L'après-midi d'un faune* [*The Afternoon of a Faun*], 1876), Arthur Rimbaud (*Le bateau ivre* [*The Drunken Boat*], 1871), and Paul Verlaine (*Romances sans paroles* [*Romances without Words*], 1874).[22] The term Symbolist was first applied to these writers by Jean Moréas in an 1885 essay in the journal *Le XIXe siècle* in which he championed their writings. The symbolists were concerned with moods and sensations rather than lucid statements and descriptions; they sought to penetrate surfaces in order to express the inscrutable essences of life, an hermetic subjectivity, and an interest in the morbid or esoteric. Like their contemporaries the Decadents, symbolist poets rejected conventional religious, social, and moral values, embracing instead a world-negating escapism, exoticism, and a radical individualism. Repudiating the work of the naturalists, who sought to depict human life in terms of physical and biological forces using an uncomplicated, journalistic prose, they also rejected traditional techniques, rigid forms, and objective repre-sentation. Seeking instead to express inward experience, the symbolists produced works that were often intentionally obscure and highly personal. Hence, the common notion that literary modernism offers complex challenges that either seduce or repel readers, a kind of initiation that confers an elite status on those few who manage to participate in the rites of its "mysteries."

The French symbolists directly influenced the writings of many of the so-called "high modernists," beginning with Oscar Wilde, the late novels of Henry James, Ford Madox Ford, Joseph Conrad, James Joyce, and Virginia Woolf. Global modernist writers as varied as the Martinican Négritude poet Aimé Césaire and the Japanese modern "father of the short story," Ryosuke Akutagawa, also claimed the symbolists as literary predecessors and major influ-ences. To varying degrees, and sometimes even somewhat contradictorily, modernist literary texts share many of the same qualities: an obsession with the autonomy of art ("art for art's sake"); the rejection of social convention, especially sexual; an interpretation of the artist as a kind of technician concerned with form and style rather than a social commentator; an emphasis on perspective and "impression," and therefore on unreliability, rather than on objective, chronological narration; a new concept of time as subjective and psychological; a sense of crisis and rupture in culture and history; an international or global orientation; and the notion of the artist as a spiritual (and often physical) exile, a stranger in a strange land. Some of the global modernists refract further these modernist rejections and contradictions. The legally and philosophically trained Iqbal, for example, studied in Great Britain and Germany and was an admirer of Goethe, Henri Bergson, and other modern European philoso-phers. His poetic tributes to Nietzsche embrace the will but stringently reject the ethos of individualism, which he sees as part of the West's corruption and decline. The poem "Selfhood Can Demolish the Magic of this World" (*Baal-i-Jibril* [*Gabriel Wing*], 1935) critically assesses what he calls the West's "faded light" as well as the East's misdirected spirituality; for Iqbal, collective strength can combat the static nature of spiritualism and generate revolutionary potential. The Nietzschean will is translated, subverted, and envisioned as a generator of a colonized people's collective will: "A sleepy ripple awaits, to swell into a wave/A wave that will swallow up monsters of the sea./What is slavery but a loss of the sense of beauty?/What the free call beautiful, is beautiful indeed."

Modernist texts are often slippery and indeterminate, epistemologically uncertain and shifting with each reading or reader. Conrad's *Heart of Darkness*, for example, demonstrates for Chinua Achebe that "Conrad was a thoroughgoing racist," while Frances B. Singh proclaims "that *Heart of Darkness* is one of the most powerful indictments of colonialism ever written." Seeking to reconcile such opposition, C.P. Sarvan views Conrad as both a man of his time and place and also a visionary: Conrad "was not entirely immune to the infection of the beliefs and attitudes of his age, but he was ahead of most in trying to break free."[23] Wayne Booth, a critic who is uncomfortable with modernist multiplicity, protests that Joyce's *A Portrait of the Artist as a Young Man* refuses to be unambiguous as to whether it depicts "the artistic soul battling through successfully to his necessary freedom, or that of the child of God, choosing, like Lucifer, his own damnation."[24] What Booth seems to fear most is that *Portrait* may somehow succeed in being both of these contradictory things. John Dowell, the narrator of Ford Madox Ford's *The Good Soldier*, feels adrift in his own plotless life: "no current . . . inevitable end . . . no nemesis, no destiny."[25] Failing to live or narrate his life, Dowell deems it all a darkness about which he understands nothing, a mystery that numerous critics have attempted to solve: John Reichert, for one, implies that Dowell murdered his wife, while Dewey Ganzel considers the book to be about the incestuous love of Edward Ashburnham, whom he views as the titular protagonist, for his ward Nancy, whom Ganzel insists is his daughter.[26] Of Faulkner, R.W.B. Lewis writes, "The difficulty of any Faulkner story lies in the order of its telling. . . What happens in a Faulkner story is more important than anything else; but it is the last thing we understand – we are let in on it gradually, from many different viewpoints and at different times,"[27] and we usually come to understand it only indirectly, tenuously, uncertainly. "No other American writer," Lewis adds, "engages his readers so strenuously."[28]

In F. Scott Fitzgerald's short story "Benjamin Button," the titular character lives his life backwards, growing younger instead of older. Ford's protagonist narrator in *The Good Soldier* lives in what he calls blissful ignorance until a sudden revelation causes him to reconceive his life in totally different terms, certain that he now understands all even as he contradicts and undercuts himself so that he unwittingly reveals yet a third reality of which he remains largely ignorant. Limited, unreliable characters who yet assert a compelling if disorienting perspective also narrate Conrad's *Heart of Darkness* and *Lord Jim*, Fitzgerald's *The Great Gatsby*, Hemingway's *The Sun Also Rises*, and Faulkner's *As I Lay Dying* and *Absalom, Absalom!* In *The Search for Lost Time*, Proust depicts multifaceted characters who not only seem but are different in different circumstances, and time that variously speeds and crawls by depending on a character's psychological state. And collections that read more like fragmented novels – Joyce's *Dubliners*, Anderson's *Winesburg, Ohio*, Hemingway's *In Our Time*, and, on a far larger scale, the fourteen volumes that comprise Faulkner's Yoknapatawpha Saga, as well as fragmented long poems or mixed genres such as Eliot's *The Waste Land*, Pound's *Cantos*, and Jean Toomer's *Cane* – create mosaic realities that are far richer and more complex than the sum of their parts or perspectives.

Modern novelists, like their Victorian forebears, often represented and investigated everyday reality, but they did so in rather different ways. Virginia Woolf dismissively refers to her most eminent predecessors – Bennett, Wells, and Galsworthy – as materialists because, she maintains, while they constructed rooms and edifices in painstaking detail, the characters who inhabit their meticulously mapped and catalogued rooms fail to come to life. Yet Woolf herself, although she could write dismissively of facts, greatly valued material specificity: "We may enjoy our room in the tower, with ... the commodious bookcases, but down in the garden there is a man digging who buried his father this morning, and it is he and his like who live the real life and speak the real language."[29] The modernist concern with the evolving present and the reconceiving of time as "always now,"[30] as spatial as well as linear,[31] led to another new fictional form – the Circadian novel – which, though a few had appeared in the nineteenth century, came into its own in the twentieth. Modernist novels that take place over 24 or fewer hours include Joyce's *Ulysses* (1922), Liam O'Flaherty's *The Informer* (1925), Woolf's *Mrs Dalloway* (1925) and *Between the Acts* (1941), Louis Bromfield's *Twenty-Four Hours* (1930), Nathaniel West's *The Dream Life of Balso Snell* (1931), Mulk Raj Anand's *Untouchable* (1935), and Henry Green's *Party Going* (1939). Variants include Elizabeth Bowen's *The House in Paris* (1935), whose first and third sections, both called "The Present," bookend "The Past," the central section which is a flashback within which characters both imagine and produce the present, and Woolf's *To the Lighthouse* (1927), whose first and third sections occupy single days separated and connected by a brief middle section, "Time Passes," that both separates and bridges the intervening ten years and contains, usually within parentheses, events that used to be central to fiction: the publication of a book of poems, a birth, several deaths, and World War I. Joyce's *Ulysses* also depends on temporal and structural disorientation. The first three chapters, for example, depict Stephen Dedalus at 8, 10, and 11 a.m., while in the next three, Leopold Bloom has similar or analogous experiences at the same times; in chapter 10, "The Wandering Rocks," fragments of scenes intrude into other scenes that occur simultaneously but miles away. All of these works detail the minutiae and vitality of everyday life, while simultaneously creating an impression of a spiritual reality that aestheticizes and transcends them.

The task assumed by the modern artist, then, was to represent the new reality honestly and faithfully. An age obsessed with perspective, human psychology, and ways of knowing fostered an epistemological literature that often verges on detective fiction[32] and challenges readers to tease out what texts like *What Maisie Knew, Heart of Darkness,*[33] *Lord Jim,* and *The Good Soldier* only imply, or to follow the allusive workings of human consciousness as depicted by writers such as Proust, Joyce, Richardson, and Woolf. A fragmented age produced the fragmented, cubistic art of Picasso and Braque, and made art, as Eliot has it, of fragments shorn against the culture's ruins. The form of the well-made novel was being broken and then reassembled like a mosaic, just as dramatists like Ibsen, Chekhov, Shaw, Brecht, Marita Bonner, and Langston Hughes were breaking the form of the well-made play. Pirandello's *Six Characters in Search of an Author*, for example, depicts a dysfunctional family whose members can't even agree on the story they are desperate to have performed. And writers like Amy Lowell, Wallace Stevens, Ezra Pound, H.D., Eliot, Hart Crane, e.e. cummings, Rabindranath Tagore, Muhammad Iqbal, and the Négritude poets challenged traditional forms of poetry, sometimes combining and reconceiving metric and vernacular traditions. Eliot's *The Waste Land*, for example, is an elegy for the dead of the recently-ended World War I; a celebration of ancient cultures, myths, and literature; an account of how civilizations die; an outpouring of nihilism and despair; and a plea for spiritual renewal. Yet the literature often scrupulously detailed bodily functions like sex and excretion, while being peopled by cuckolded, impotent, or emasculated protagonists incapable of functioning sexually.

Many of these works self-consciously foreground artistic failure, the inability to construct a coherent and meaningful narrative in the modern world out of the "fragments" (in Eliot's word) of history, memory, and experience; others celebrate fragmentation and uncertainty. A world in motion offers the possibilities, however, perhaps even the certainties, of meaningful change. For Sergei Eisenstein, the Soviet Russian theorist of revolutionary cinema, montage (the plastic and dynamic process of editing) "is conflict. At the basis of every art is conflict (an 'imagist' transformation of the dialectical principle)."[34] Several of the global modernists in this collection were actively involved with anti-colonial and independence movements; the poetic works of Rabindranath Tagore, Leopold Senghor, José Marti, and Muhammad Iqbal celebrated heroic nationalism – each poet's work was adapted into his nation's post-independence national anthem. For groups as distinct as Wyndham Lewis' vorticists, the Gaelic Revivalists, and the members of the Harlem Renaissance, the Modern also held the promise of new democratic affiliations, refashioned modes of self- and collective identification, and a forceful – even virile – energy with which to face the future. In "The Negro Artist and the Racial Mountain" (1926), Langston Hughes confronts black American audiences' cultural conservatism and white audiences' fascination with the exotic. Hughes embraces all that is beautiful and ugly in the history of race and representation as the grounds for a modernist aesthetic; acknowledging the historical and social messiness of contemporary culture, he declares, "We build our temples for tomorrow, strong as we know how, and we stand on top of the mountain, free within ourselves."[35]

What modernist literature does, among many other things, is to adumbrate and confront the changes that were occurring in the culture. For example, in *The Rainbow* (1916) D.H. Lawrence depicts the mid-nineteenth-century death of Tom Brangwen in a flood caused by an overflowing industrial canal he had allowed to bisect his farm; near the end of Forster's *Howards End* (1910), a novel set in the first decade of the twentieth century, the discussion turns to Margaret's having transformed "a house, ready furnished and empty" into a "permanent home," a living thing, even as the threatening "rust-red" of London itself, modernism's growing urbanization, looms on the horizon, encroaching upon and destroying the English countryside. "Logically," Margaret thinks, such country estates as Howards End "had no right to be alive. One's hope was in the weakness of logic."[36] Of *Ulysses*, Joyce (perhaps somewhat misleadingly) said, "I want . . . to give a picture of Dublin so complete that if the city one day suddenly disappeared from the earth it could be reconstructed out of my book,"[37] but while *Ulysses* depicts the vivid texture and impression of 1904 Dublin, it provides far less physical description of its places (and people) than Joyce promises, or that it seems at first to do; what it does offer is almost invariably from someone's unique perspective. Analogously, the decaying house in the "Time Passes" section of Woolf's *To the Lighthouse* (126), with its remarkable negative and undetailed description and its "furniture confounded," nearly tips into the abyss for the lack of human presence, for the family doesn't come for ten years, a period that includes the cataclysmic destruction of World War I. But then "Slowly and painfully, with broom and pail, mopping, scouring, Mrs McNab, Mrs Bast, stayed the corruption and the rot; rescued from the pool of Time that was fast closing over them now a basin, now a cupboard; fetched up from oblivion all the Waverley novels and a tea-set one morning. . . " What results is a resuscitation, what Woolf calls "some rusty laborious birth" (139), as the house again becomes animate, a site for human occupation that occurs in the novel's last section.

So the accent does indeed, as Woolf writes in "Modern Fiction," "fall differently from of old" and modernism – in its perspectivism, impressionism, encyclopedism, fragmentation, disorder, utopianism, difficulty, radicalism, and the like – disorients and challenges its readers, viewers, and listeners in ways that often seem startling and incomprehensible. For some, like the poet Philip Larkin, the price for an art that was deliberately obscure and user unfriendly was too high to pay, the rewards minimal if they existed at all: "This is my essential criticism of modernism, whether perpetrated by Parker, Pound, or Picasso: it helps us neither to enjoy nor endure."[38] But even a "high modernist" like Virginia Woolf considered that she was writing for someone she called "the common reader," and, according to an anonymous reviewer in *The Scotsman*, in Ulysses Joyce celebrated " 'the commonness of the common man.' "[39] Whether that "common man" – or woman – ever actually reads *Ulysses* remains an open question, but enough people do (or at least say they do) to keep placing it at the top of the lists of greatest twentieth-century novels.

At the turn of the twentieth century, Eagleton persuasively argues, English literature appeared ready to take its place not only as the sacred texts of a secular age, but also as what he calls "the poor man's Classics" and then as a fit subject for women who were just being admitted to universities.[40] But first it had to be deemed difficult and unpleasant, which it was thanks to modernism, and then rendered at least ostensibly comprehensible, which followed when the modernists themselves, as we suggest in Parts VIII and IX, implicitly and self-consciously acknowledging the difficulty and unfriendliness of their writings, offered explications and guides to their own work and that of their contemporaries. Becoming their own first critics, they produced a great deal of explanatory literature concerning what they and their contemporaries were about: James's prefaces to his novels and Shaw's to his plays; Joyce's charts for *Ulysses*; Eliot's notes for *The Waste Land*; Woolf's diaries and letters; critical essays and books by Eliot, Ford, Forster, Lawrence, Pound, Woolf, among many others. In the process, and presumably as an unintended consequence, they helped to make English a fit (and perhaps necessary) subject of academic study and to create the academic industry now known as Literary Criticism.

Since its incorporation into university curricula, the study of literary modernism has undergone numerous important revisions and rehabilitations. In "Making It New: Innovative Approaches to Teaching Modernism," a special forum of the Modernist Studies Association (MSA) published in the organization's scholarly journal *Modernism/Modernity*, a group of scholars tackled the challenges of defining and teaching modernism. In her essay "Modernism in Black and White," Suzanne W. Churchill examines the possibilities of New Modernist Studies and the pedagogical and intellectual goals of diversifying disciplines, the academic curricula, and scholarly communities, as well. Churchill points out that, despite years of critical conversation about "toppling the hierarchies of high modernism," ideas about canonical modernism have remained fixed, and instructive representations of modernism leave visible borders and biases intact.[41] She notes, for example, that Lawrence Rainey's 1,181-page *Modernism: An Anthology* (2005) fails to include a single African American writer and that even the MSA, despite its commitment to New Modernist Studies, publishes more articles on well-established canonical high modernists than it does on, say, Harlem Renaissance writers. Churchill, who teaches at Davidson College in North Carolina, a campus at which diversity is a "challenge and goal," developed a course on modernism that she hoped would "bridge the divide between modernism and the Harlem Renaissance."[42] Called "Modernism in Black and White," the course was a collaborative research forum in which undergraduate and graduate students worked together on canonical high modernist and Harlem Renaissance authors by conducting archival research on periodical magazines: modernist little magazines and contemporary social justice-oriented African American magazines like the NAACP's *The Crisis* and The Urban League's *Opportunity*. Churchill's periodical studies recuperated trans-racial modernist collaborative works in periodicals like Claude McKay and Mike Gold's co-edited *The Liberator*. The periodicals displayed networks of social, artistic, and political relationships, and also desacralized the works of notoriously "difficult" and intimidating writers like T.S. Eliot. Churchill discovered, for example, that students found *The Waste Land* more accessible in its original periodical form, nestled between reviews, visual artwork, and "ads for cigarettes and soap."[43] Such recovered situating reduced the strangeness of modernist literature, and made it more accessible and familiar. Churchill's essay also succinctly makes the point that "We are products of our educations"[44]; thus, one's ideas about and definitions of modernism are shaped by disciplinary ideologies, pedagogical practices, and the historical era in which one was educated. The periodicals in their original forms display one level of literary modernism's dynamism and complexity; the magazines materialize historical evidence in graphic and illuminating ways. As we worked to create *Modernism and Literature*, we were well aware that excellent modernist compilations of various kinds already exist (see our "Bibliography of literary modernisms"). But we believe that this work will uniquely meet the needs of modernist courses for both undergraduates and graduates by assisting them in the process of understanding the complex age and movements that make up the modern era.

Following this Introduction, two sections make up the heart and bulk of this Reader. The first section, "Readings in Foundational Texts of Modernism," includes introductions to significant concepts and disciplines – "Culture and aesthetics"; "Philosophy and religion"; "Medicine, science, and technology"; "Politics and war"; "Gender and sexuality"; "Race and ethnicity"; "Global modernisms" – plus a generous sampling of "Foundational readings" from the major, influential thinkers from the nineteenth and early twentieth centuries who, collectively, helped to create the historical and cultural context for those concerns and subjects in the modernist era. We also include "Suggested further readings" for each part. The second section, "Readings in Literary Criticism by Modernist Writers," discusses and exemplifies how modernists themselves explicated modernism, thereby both demonstrating and satisfying its initial needs for such critique. At the end of the book, the Glossary offers brief definitions of key modernist terms and concepts, while the Bibliography lists "Essential modernist literature" and then offers an annotated bibliography of collections and anthologies of modernism and critical commentary on that literature, and "Multimedia resources for literary modernisms."

No single work can pretend to comprehend such a vast and multifaceted subject as Modernism and Literature, but we hope that our introductions, the selected readings, and the apparatus we include effectively illustrate and represent a way into the rich interplay between and among traditional/canonical discussions of modernism and, for example, Marxist, renegade, global, and "New Modernist Studies," and that *Modernism and Literature: An Introduction and Reader* will be a valuable resource for both graduate and undergraduate courses, one that will enhance students' understanding of this complex and endlessly fascinating and contested material and period.

Notes

1   Kuhn xi.
2   Gaonkar, "On Alternative Modernities" 14.
3   Said, *Culture and Imperialism*; Booth and Rigby, eds., *Modernism and Empire*.
4   Eagleton, *Literary Theory* 22–23.
5   Quinones discusses how Baudelaire and Nietzsche manage to have it both ways (14–15).
6   Arnold 56–61.
7   Hardy 105–6.
8   See Clark 370.
9   Caws brings some 200 together in her invaluable collection, *Manifesto: A Century of Isms*.
10 Woolf, "Mr. Bennett and Mrs. Brown," *The Captain's Death Bed* 96.
11 Bradbury and McFarlane 22.
12 In *The Birth of Tragedy*, Nietzsche distinguishes the Dionysian (flamboyant, anarchic, emotional) from the Apollonian (calm, ordered, dispassionate) in modernism.
13 Quinones 14.
14 Joyce, "Ireland: Island of Saints and Sages" 125.
15 Woolf, "Modern Fiction," *The Common Reader* 154.
16 Wilde, "The Decay of Lying" 26–27.
17 Ford, *Joseph Conrad* 6.
18 Somewhat contradictorily (but perhaps "modernly"), Woolf also writes: "No fact is too little to let it slip through one's fingers, and besides the interest of facts themselves, there is the strange power we have of changing facts by the force of the imagination" ("Montaigne," *The Common Reader* 68).
19 Bowen, *The House in Paris* 126.
20 Symons 5.
21 Lawrence, "Why the Novel Matters," *Phoenix* 145.
22 See, especially, Wilson, *Axel's Castle*, and Bowra, *Heritage of Symbolism*.

23   In Conrad, *Heart of Darkness*, Norton 257, 268, 285.
24   Booth, *Rhetoric of Fiction* 327–28.
25   Ford, *The Good Soldier* 164.
26   Reichert 173; Ganzel 287–88.
27   Lewis 644.
28   Lewis 646.
29   Woolf, "Montaigne," *The Common Reader* 68.
30   Higdon 57.
31   See Frank.
32   Poe, Dickens, Wilkie Collins, and Conan Doyle, among others, laid the groundwork for detective fiction. Modernists who put epistemological questions and doubts at the center of their conception and representation of reality raise detective-like questions in their writings. Postmodernism's focus on ontology and multiple realities, on the other hand, seems grounded in science fiction, whose origins are also in the nineteenth century: Mary Shelley's *Frankenstein* and *The Last Man*, Jules Verne, H.G. Wells, among others.
33   Ford praises *Heart of Darkness* for its use of "detective story" technique (*The March of Literature* 771).
34   Eisenstein, "The Cinematographic Principle and the Ideogram" 38 (emphasis added).
35   Hughes 694.
36   Forster, *Howards End* 389.
37   Quoted in Budgen 67–68. In a review accusing *Ulysses* of being "low minded and inartistic," purposely obscure, dull, and indecent, Arnold Bennett unironically criticizes Joyce for having "no geographical sense, little sense of environment" (220–21).
38   Larkin, Introduction, Part 2, *All What Jazz*.
39   *The Scotsman* (26 April 1969), 10; quoted in McCleery 69.
40   Eagleton 22–23, 27.
41   Churchill 489.
42   Churchill 489.
43   Churchill 490.
44   Churchill 488.

Works cited

Achebe, Chinua. "An Image of Africa: Racism in Conrad's *Heart of Darkness*." In Joseph Conrad, *Heart of Darkness*. 251–62.

Arnold, Matthew. *Culture and Anarchy* (1869). Cambridge: Cambridge UP, 1993.

Bender, Todd K., Nancy Armstrong, Sue M. Briggum, and Frank A. Knobloch, eds. *Modernism in Literature*. New York: Holt, Reinhart and Winston, 1977.

Bennett, Arnold. "James Joyce's *Ulysses*." *Outlook* (London; 29 April 1922): 337–39. Reprinted in *James Joyce: The Critical Heritage*, vol. 1, 1907–27, ed. Robert H. Deming. New York: Routledge, 1997. 219–22.

Booth, Howard, and Nigel Rigby, eds. *Modernism and Empire*. Manchester: Manchester UP, 2000.

Booth, Wayne C. *The Rhetoric of Fiction*. Chicago and London: U of Chicago P, 1963.

Bowen, Elizabeth. *The House in Paris* (1935). New York: Anchor, 2002.

Bowra, Maurice. *Heritage of Symbolism*. London: Macmillan, 1943.

Bradbury, Malcolm, and James McFarlane, eds. *Modernism: A Guide to European Literature 1890–1930* (1976). New York: Penguin, 1991.

Budgen, Frank. *James Joyce and the Making of* Ulysses. New York: Harrison Smith and Robert, 1934.

Caws, Mary Ann, ed. *Manifesto: A Century of Isms*. Lincoln: U of Nebraska P, 2000.

Churchill, Suzanne W. "Modernism in Black and White." *Modernism/Modernity* 16.3 (Sept. 2009): 489–92.

Clark, Ronald W. *Einstein: The Life and Times*. New York: World, 1971.

Conrad, Joseph. *Heart of Darkness* (1899). Norton Critical Edition, 3rd edn. Ed. Robert Kimbrough. New York: Norton, 1988.

——. "Preface." *The Nigger of the "Narcissus": A Tale of the Sea* (1897). New York: Norton, 1979.

Eagleton, Terry. *Literary Theory: An Introduction*. Minneapolis: U of Minnesota P, 1983.

Eisenstein, Sergei. "The Cinematographic Principle and the Ideogram" (1929). *Film Form: Essays in Film Theory*. New York: Harvest/Harcourt, 1977.

Ellmann, Richard, and Charles Feidelson, Jr., eds. *The Modern Tradition: Backgrounds of Modern Literature*. New York: Oxford UP, 1965.

Faulkner, Peter, ed. *A Modernist Reader: Modernism in England 1910–1930*. London: B.T. Batsford, 1986.

Ford, Ford Madox. *The Good Soldier* (1916). New York: Vintage, 1955.

——. *The March of Literature: From Confucius to Modern Times* (1938). London: Allen and Unwin, 1947.

——. *Joseph Conrad: A Personal Remembrance*. London: Duckworth, 1924.

Forster, E.M. *Two Cheers for Democracy*. New York: Harcourt, Brace, 1938.

——. *Howards End* (1910). New York: Vintage, 1921.

Frank, Joseph. *The Idea of Spatial Form* (1945). New Brunswick: Rutgers UP, 1991.

Ganzel, Dewey. "What the Letter Said: Fact and Inference in *The Good Soldier*." *Journal of Modern Literature* 11.2 (July 1984): 277–90.

Gaonkar, Dilip Parameshwar. *Alternative Modernities*. Durham, NC: Duke UP, 2001.

——. "On Alternative Modernities." *Public Culture* 11.1 (1999): 1–18.

Gross, John, ed. *A TLS Companion: The Modern Movement*. London: HarperCollins, 1992.

Hardy, Thomas. *Tess of the D'Urbervilles* (1891). New York: Norton, 1965.

Higdon, David Leon. "A First Census of the Circadian or One-Day Novel." *Journal of Narrative Technique* 22.1 (Winter 1992): 57–64.

Howe, Irving, ed. *Literary Modernism*. Greenwich, CT: Fawcett, 1967.

Hughes, Langston. "The Negro Artist and the Racial Mountain." *The Nation* (23 June 1926): 692–94.

Iqbal, Muhammad Allama. "To the Saqi," from *Baal-i-Jibreel*. Trans. Naeem Siddiqui, from (site) *Poetry Chaikhana: Sacred Poetry from Around the World*: http://www.poetry-chaikhana.com/I/IqbalAllamaM/ToSaqifromBa.htm.

Iqbal, Muhammad. *Baal-i-Jibril* [*Gabriel's Wing*] (1935). Trans. Naeem Siddiqui.

Joyce, James. "Ireland: Island of Saints and Sages." *Occasional, Critical, and Political Writing of James Joyce*, ed. Kevin Barry. Oxford: Oxford UP, 2008.

——. *Ulysses* (1922). New York: Random House, 1986.

Keating, Peter. *The Haunted Study: A Social History of the English Novel 1875–1914*. London: Secker, 1989.

Kiely, Robert, ed. *Modernism Reconsidered*. Cambridge, MA: Harvard UP, 1983.

Kolocotroni, Vassiliki, Jane Goldman, and Olga Taxidou, eds. *Modernism: An Anthology of Sources and Documents* (1998). Edinburgh: Edinburgh UP, 2007.

Kuhn, Thomas. *The Structure of Scientific Revolution*. Chicago: U of Chicago P, 1962.

Larkin, Philip. Introduction, Part 2, *All What Jazz: A Record Diary 1961–1971* (1970). London: Faber, 1985.

Lawrence, D.H. *The Rainbow* (1915). Cambridge and New York: Cambridge UP, 1989.

——. *Phoenix: The Posthumous Papers of D.H. Lawrence* (1936). New York: Viking, 1972.

Levenson, Michael. *The Cambridge Companion to Modernism*. Cambridge and New York: Cambridge UP, 2003.

Lewis, R.W.B. "The Hero in the New World: William Faulkner's *The Bear*." *The Kenyon Review* 13.4 (Autumn 1951): 641–60.

Lief, Leonard, and James F. Light, eds. *The Modern Age: Literature*, 3rd edn. New York: Holt, Rinehart and Winston, 1976.

McCleery, Alistair. "The 1969 Edition of *Ulysses*: The Making of a Penguin Classic." *James Joyce Quarterly* 46.1 (Fall 2008): 55–73.

Nietzsche, Friedrich. *The Birth of Tragedy from the Spirit of Music* (1872). Trans. Douglas Smith. Oxford: Oxford UP, 2008

Quinones, Ricardo J. *Mapping Literary Modernism: Time and Development*. Princeton: Princeton UP, 1985.

Rainey, Lawrence, ed. *Modernism: An Anthology*. Hoboken, NJ: Wiley-Blackwell, 2005.

Reichert, John. "Poor Florence Indeed! or *The Good Soldier* Retold." *Studies in the Novel* 14.2 (Summer 1982): 161–79.

Said, Edward. *Culture and Imperialism*. New York: Knopf/Random House, 1993.

Schorer, Mark, ed. *Modern British Fiction: Essays in Criticism*. New York: Oxford UP, 1961.

Scott, Bonnie Kime, ed. *Refiguring Modernism, vol. 1, Women of 1928; vol. 2, Postmodern Feminist Readings of Woolf, West, and Barnes*. Bloomington: Indiana UP, 1995.

—— ed. *The Gender of Modernism: A Critical Anthology*. Bloomington: Indiana UP, 1990.

Shakespeare, William. *Hamlet* (1601). Ed. Ann Thompson and Neil Taylor. London: Arden, 2006.

Sophocles. *Oedipus Rex* (c. 429 BC).

Stromberg, Roland M., ed. *Realism, Naturalism, and Symbolism: Modes of Thought and Expression in Europe, 1848–1914*. New York, Evanston, and London: Harper and Row, 1968.

Symons, Arthur. *The Symbolist Movement in Literature* (1899). London: Constable, 1908.

Wilde, Oscar. "The Decay of Lying: An Observation" (1889). *Selected Writings of Oscar Wilde*, ed. Richard Ellmann. London and New York: Oxford UP, 1961. 1–37.

Wilson, Edmund. *Axel's Castle: A Study in the Imaginative Literature of 1870 to 1930*. New York: Scribner's, 1931.

Woolf, Virginia. *To The Lighthouse* (1927). New York: Harcourt, Brace, 1989.

——. *The Common Reader: First Series* (1925). New York: Harcourt, Brace, 1953.

——. *The Captain's Death Bed and Other Essays*. New York: Harcourt, Brace, 1950.

READINGS IN
FOUNDATIONAL TEXTS
OF MODERNISM

PART I

Culture and aesthetics

"A Century of Isms," the subtitle to Mary Ann Caws' *Manifesto* (2000), an edited collection of modernist manifestos, effectively illuminates modernity's diverse, international, and ideologically distinct range of artistic movements. Charles Baudelaire's *The Painter of Modern Life* (*Le peintre de la vie moderne*, 1859) opens this section; his tribute to the illustrator Constantin Guys is also a celebration of the *flâneur*, the wandering, observing man of the city and the world, a childlike organic historicist. Baudelaire, who is frequently credited for coining the term modernity (*modernité*), praised Guys for visually capturing the textures, movement and speed of modern life. Guys, who worked for the *Illustrated London News* and *Punch*, sketched impressionistic scenes from France's 1848 revolution, from Balaclava and other Crimean War battlegrounds, and famously captured Paris's cafés, brothels, streets, and social scene. Baudelaire's exuberant art criticism glorifies the new, curiosity, and the delirium of spectacle; *The Painter of Modern Life* is a harbinger of the coming art movements and artists' zeal for the re-examination of society and expressive cultures.

Symbolism, surrealism, dadaism, German expressionism, impressionism and post-impressionism, realism, formalism, futurism, vorticism, primitivism, the Gaelic Revival, the Harlem Renaissance, Négritude – these are just a few of the modern era's many discrete and cooperative artistic movements. At stake in the discussions about modern aesthetics and culture are two additional isms: individualism and collectivism. Modern artists and critics were speculating about art's social and philosophical possibilities and the artist's role as a cultural producer at a time when popular cultural forms such as film, radio, and blues and jazz music were becoming increasingly important. While some modernists defined their aesthetics against this popular culture, writing for an audience that they imagined as a small elite capable of understanding increasingly allusive and elusive works, others utilized popular and folk forms and, in so doing, blurred the lines between "highbrow" and "lowbrow" art. For Louise Bogan, the artist capable of evading the barricade lines drawn between "high," formalist art and folk and popular art was rare indeed. In her view, Federico García Lorca and Yeats were poets who uncommonly mingled forms; the Spanish poet's incorporation of flamenco, the Irish poet's intimacy with peasant culture, and both artists' vivid connection to music enabled expressive poetic forms that transgressed the great cultural divides ("Folk Art" 284 (see also Chapter 12 of this volume)).

Debates about modernist aesthetics also reflect artists' and intellectuals' engagements with tradition. In "Tradition and the Individual Talent" (1919), T.S. Eliot argues that literature advances in conversation with tradition: the artist serves as an impersonal catalyst that communes with inherited literary forms while representing contemporary concerns. Arthur Symons' discussion of the symbolist poets (Arthur Rimbaud, Paul Verlaine, Stéphane Mallarmé) reflects a similar notion of inheritance, mediation, and influence. In his "Introduction" to *The Symbolist Movement in Literature* (1919), Symons links the poets to the Romantics and the Decadents, and to the earliest utterances of man, as well. God is the first symbol-maker, he who "named the world into being." The symbolists, Symons argues, restore the spiritual to language in their poetry of concealment and revelation; what distinguishes modern symbolism from symbolism of the past is its self-consciousness. The modern poets revive the tradition of mystery in expressive language; they attempt to "evade the old bondage of rhetoric, the old bondage of exteriority. Description is banished that beautiful things may be evoked, magically." In revolting against a "materialistic tradition," symbolism makes "the soul of things visible"; the poets make words conjure rather than represent. The desire for the ethereal observed in Symons' tribute to the symbolist poets is, in part, a rejection of realism and a concrete faith in language's practical function; "the regular beat" of poetic verse is "broken in order that words may fly, upon subtler wings."[1] Walter Pater's "Conclusion" to *The Renaissance* (1868), though of an earlier date, further illuminates the aspects of modernist aesthetics that accentuate the fluid, permeable, mobile world and its apprehension, as well as the individual's refined aesthetic sensibility. He notes in the essay's opening that, "To regard all things and principles of things as instant modes or fashions has more and more become the tendency of modern thought."[2] The world is in perpetual motion, as is the body itself; its cells, blood, tissues, sense organs are in constant movement and modification. Pater's description of the constant flux of life and our vision and understanding of the objective world aims to expose the illusions of coherent, solidity, and stability:

> . . . when reflexion begins to play upon these objects they are dissipated under its influence; the cohesive force seems suspended like some trick of magic; each object is loosed into a group of impressions — colour, odour, texture — in the mind of the observer. And if we continue to dwell in thought on this world, not of objects in the solidity with which language invests them, but of impressions, unstable, flickering, inconsistent, which burn and are extinguished with our consciousness of them, it contracts still further.[3]

The impressions of reality and the physical world are myriad and individual, Pater argues, and the recognition and understanding of this constantly moving stream of impressions is an ecstatic process and the very substance and foundation of philosophy: "Philosophy is the microscope of thought."

William James's "The Stream of Consciousness" identifies the fundamental principles of human psychology, principles that highlight the unique, highly individual nature of consciousness. "The first and foremost concrete fact which everyone will affirm to belong to his inner experience," James writes, "is the fact that *consciousness of some sort goes on*. 'States of mind' succeed each other in him. . . . Within each personal consciousness states [of mind] are always changing. . . . Each personal consciousness . . . is interested in some parts of its object to the exclusion of others, and welcomes or rejects — *chooses* from among them. . . . — all the while."[4] Thought and sensibility are selective and continually altering processes. James points out that our senses perceive differently and distinctly; the same object does not give the same sensation every time that we encounter or experience it. A distinct musical note, bird's song, or a shade of color can be enjoyed on one occasion and can become tiresome or displeasing on another; our perception creates the difference. These notions of life as barely perceptible and constant streams of impressions can be linked to modernist visual culture and impressionist and post-impressionist experiments in painting, like pointillism and cubism, expressive work that aims to make the viewer look more consciously, to be conscious of what seeing might mean, to see through and beyond the surface of the thing or the conceptual idea of the word that denotes the object. In "Modern Fiction" (1919), Virginia Woolf describes this dynamic sense of reality, the stream-of-consciousness, when she writes, "The mind receives a myriad impressions – trivial, fantastic, evanescent, or engraved with the sharpness of steel. From all sides they come, an incessant shower of innumerable atoms."[5] The modern artist's quest is to avoid conventions – or habits or stereotypes, as Walter Pater describes them – in an attempt to perceive and reveal the living world.

Oscar Wilde's essay in play form, "The Decay of Lying" (1889), is defiantly unconcerned with an understanding of the nature of reality or accurate perception or reflection of the real. Its championing of art for art's sake is a rejection of Victorian moralism and utilitarianism. Wilde's double in the piece is Vivian, a shameless aesthete who enthusiastically embraces Lying – a human impulse worthy of capitalization – and the artifice of poetry as essential arts. He attributes the dreary commonplaceness of contemporary literature to "The Decay of Lying" in the arts, sciences, and in social life, as well. The "monstrous worship of facts" is destroying art, which is, in Vivian/Wilde's view, a form of exaggeration, a mode of exuberant expression wholly unconcerned with truth, morality, facts, or reflecting the real world. The return to life and nature in art, Vivian declares, has always reduced art and made it "vulgar, common, and uninteresting," and realism as an aesthetic method is always "a complete failure."[6] The young man's natural gift of exaggeration is educated and civilized out of him and he falls into "careless habits of accuracy."[7] Wilde, like James, Pater, Woolf, Isadora Duncan, and the vorticists, calls attention to the child's or adolescent's perspective and youthful and as yet undisciplined body and habits of perception. Vivian/Wilde depicts William Shakespeare and Émile Zola, artists separated by culture, language, and a great span of time, as having succumbed to the siren song of life, "calling for an echo of her own voice;"[8] realism threatens the health and vibrancy of the artist's gifts. In Wilde's view, art should be unconcerned with the representation or reproduction of its age; the object of art is "not simple truth" but the expression of "complex beauty."[9]

Modernists drew upon an eclectic range of aesthetic traditions from ancient Greek tragedy to Japanese haiku poetry and Noh drama, from Chinese calligraphy to medieval Irish illuminated manuscripts, from Renaissance painting to African masks. Sergei Eisenstein's theories of cinematic montage (editing) were inspired by Asian language and culture, especially the Chinese ideogram, Japanese pictorial arts, *haiku* poetry, and Noh theatre. Eisenstein's sense of cinema's aesthetic and political possibilities was also inspired by the Russian Revolution and the very idea of collision. He interwove the semiotic dynamics of Asian linguistic and representational cultures with Marxist dialectical materialism to theorize a dynamic, kinetic, revolutionarily agitational method of constructing film by using opposition as a plastic methodology. Juxtaposed images or objects, spaces, cinematic tempos could have a "copulative" function, could produce meaning through form. Here, for example, is his reading of how the Chinese ideogram conceptually produces meaning:

From separate hieroglyphs has been fused – the ideogram. By the combination of two "depictables" is achieved the representation of something that is graphically undepictable.

For example: the picture for water and the picture of an eye signifes "to weep"; the picture of an ear near the drawing of a door = "to listen"; a dog + a mouth = "to bark";

a mouth + a child = "to scream";
a mouth + a bird = "to sing";
a knife + a heart = "sorrow" . . . But this is – montage![10]

Eisenstein locates cinema's artistic potential in its anti-realist technological malleability: "Absolute realism is by no means the correct form of perception," he notes. "It is simply the function of a certain form of social structure. Following a state monarchy, a state uniformity of thought is implanted." For Eisenstein, "the basis of every art is conflict";[11] cinematic montage could embrace and productively put this theory into practice. Film's leftist revolutionary potential would be celebrated by Frankfurt School critic Walter Benjamin in his seminal essay, "The Work of Art in the Age of Its Mechanical Reproducibilty" (1936). Leni Riefenstahl's *The Triumph of the Will* (1935) would captivatingly utilize many of Eisenstein's methods of montage in order to seduce, spectacularly, its audience to support Hitler and National Socialism. Yet the ideological intent of Riefenstahl's film was completely opposite that of Eisenstein's *Battleship Potemkin* (1925) and *October* (1928).

Isadora Duncan's celebrated modern dance had evolutionary roots, as she describes them, in Greek art and culture and primitive culture, as well. The ideals of her modern dance theories, however, extoll an intelligent, willed reconnection with nature and the past: "Man, arrived at the end of civilization, will have to return to nakedness, not to the unconscious nakedness of the savage, but to the conscious and acknowledged nakedness of the mature Man."[12] Duncan describes a deracinated primitivism. Her modern dance featured bare feet – the human foot is a "triumph" of evolution; Duncan rejected ballet's "deformation" of the feet and body, and particularly the female dancer's form. Her dance would embrace religious ecstatic tradition, natural sensuality, eugenic health, and a new embodiment of womanhood; the modern dancer, restored to her relation with nature, would "help womankind to a new knowledge of the possible strength and beauty of their bodies and the relation of their bodies to the earth nature and to the children of the future."[13] Émile Jacques Dalcroze, a Swiss modernist dance and music theorist, created Eurythmics, another anti-classical and non-balletic form of dance, one that would inspire Serge Diaghilev and create one of modernist art's revolutionary shocks to the audience's taste and sensibility. Diaghilev, the director of the Ballet Russes, incorporated the rhythmic and percussive dance movements into Igor Stravinsky's *The Rite of Spring* (1913), which was infamously and sensationally performed by Vaslav Nijinsky.

More experimental, radical, and avant-garde artists conversely embraced a credo of rupture, rejecting tradition and notions of continuity to seek artistic expressions that would explore new modes and perceptions of being and belonging. Such artists envisioned themselves as engaged and ideologically invested visionaries, champions of the new and often outrageous. The century's technological and scientific advances, for example in physics, cinema, and psychology, expanded notions of time, space, and movement; the era's armed conflicts would lend additional urgency to the conversations about continuity and change, order and invention. In "The Negro Artist and the Racial Mountain" (1926), Langston Hughes articulates with manifesto-like verve his view of the modern "Negro" artist and his avant-garde vision and collective responsibility. Hughes notes the cultural conservatism of "high class" black Americans, the Negro bourgeoisie who disdain the expressive culture of urban America and over-value "Nordic manners, Nordic faces, Nordic art." He celebrates "truly racial culture," black folk art and wisdom, Jean Toomer's rural and cosmopolitan racial poetics, Negro spirituals, jazz music – "the eternal tom-tom beating in the Negro soul" – the bawdy sassiness of Bessie Smith, and the revolutionary soulfulness of Paul Robeson. Hughes worries about the dominance and ubiquity of American popular culture and oppressive influence of mainstream white American values. The Negro artist must fight the impulse toward racial abnegation and resist "the desire to pour racial individuality into the mold of American standardization."[14]

Wyndham Lewis and the vorticists' "*Blast* Manifesto" (1914) also bemoans standardization; popular art is the "art of the individuals," those who violently and energetically fight modern civilization's domesticating tendencies. The "*Blast* Manifesto" shouts "WE ONLY WANT THE WORLD TO LIVE, and to feel it's crude energy flowing through us." The grammatical errors ("it's" instead of "its"), like the dynamic graphics and casually spelled name, proclaim the vulgar, the immediate, the spontaneous and unconscious energy of "Individuals" – "the Primitive Mercenaries in the Modern World." The vorticists' aesthetic and political perspective mirrors the "violent structure of adolescent clearness" between the two extremes of "Action and Reaction." Staid Victorian conventions, continental aestheticism, and high-brow snobbishness are assailed, along with what the vorticists identify as the programmatic arrogance and sentimentality of other modernist manifesto movements. Filippo Marinetti and the futurists are a favorite target; they are "BLASTED" along with numerous other targets, including the "ART-PIMP," "Rhabindraneth" (Rabindranath) Tagore, the post office, Henri Bergson, the socialist and reformer "Sydney" (Sidney) Webb, "Clan Strachey," and the years "1837–1900." Lewis and company "BLESS" Shakespeare, Jonathan Swift, the "vast planetary abstraction of the OCEAN," and English humor. The "*Blast* Manifesto" also characterizes "Anglo-Saxon genius" as having the greatest *potential* for unleashing a revolutionary modern spirit; "The Latins are . . . in their 'discovery' of sport, their futuristic gush over machines, aeroplanes, etc., the most romantic and sentimental 'moderns' to be found," the manifesto claims.

Modernist artists' war with or negotiation of convention and tradition can be found in their notable individual essays. For example, in "Drama and Life" (1900) James Joyce defends the works of Henrik Ibsen and portrays modern theatre as the Dionysian expressive form that can speak to a broad audience and locate art in the ordinary and the everyday. Young Joyce considered literature too convention-bound to modernize successfully, adapt and transform; both the insistently democratic ethos and passionate commitment to theater articulated in "Drama and Life" evolved as Joyce, in embracing fiction, enjoyed and satirized the role of the artist as genius-visionary. D.H. Lawrence's "Surgery for the Novel – Or a Bomb" (1923) is a thinly veiled attack on *Ulysses* (1922) and what Lawrence views as a too self-consciously experimental, hyper-intellectual, and effete modernism. Even Virginia Woolf, a more selective and moderate excavator of tradition than many of her contemporaries, depicts the noise of crashing and destruction as the prevailing sounds of the "Georgian" modern age in "Mr. Bennett and Mrs. Brown" (1923).

The uncertain ideological uses and implications of modernist aesthetics and artistic and propagandistic uses of technological media like film and radio are illustrated by the Italian futurist Filippo Tomasso Marinetti's artistic and political life. In the "Futurist Manifesto" (written in 1908 and published in the Parisian newspaper *Le Figaro* in February 1909), Marinetti announces that the futurists' war is with "pastism"; he enthusiastically and anarchically celebrated technology, speed, the automobile, machine gun fire, and war. The opening line of the manifesto proclaims "the love of danger, the habit of energy, and rashness." Literature has "induced slumber and pensive immobility," the futurists declare; "Beauty exists only in struggle. There is no masterpiece that is not an aggressive character." Futurism declared war on tradition, the professions, morality, and feminism; libraries and museums would be devoured by the rapacious energy of the machine age. In "La Radia" (1933) Marinetti outlines the possibilities for using the radio as a new, unbound, anti-theatrical, narrative-resistant, sonic forcefield. "La Radia" is "A pure organism of radio sensations," a time and space expanding cosmic utopia in which language can be "recharged" with "essential and totalitarian" power. The essay unleashes the force of its purified rhetoric in its list of things that futurism has already "overcome": "Overcome patriotism 'with a more fervent patriotism thus transformed into authentic religion of the Fatherland warning to

Semites that they should identify with their various fatherlands if they do not wish to disappear.'" By 1919, Marinetti had approached Benito Mussolini to initiate a fascist-futurist allegiance.

The spread of European fascism would lead some cultural critics and artists to seek more urgently cultural expressions and artistic modes that would critically awaken the audience's consciousness and make them aware of the power of ideology and myth, as well as the seductive power of representation. Bertolt Brecht's Epic Theatre and its "alienation effects" were designed to disrupt the audience's passive observation or absorption. Brecht wanted to strip the theatre of its traditional uses of illusion, psychology, naturalistic familiarity, and affect. The "A-effect" would appeal to the audience's intellect and inherent knowledge of historicism and the social world. Brecht's theories addressed all aspects of the theatre – its physical space and use of the proscenium and beyond; acting theory and bodily performance; and narrative and linguistic semantics. Conventional modes of speech, gesture, and even rehearsal would stress the gradual alienation of resolved meaning and psychological and emotional transparency; Brecht was highly influenced by the Soviet constructivist theatre director Vsevolod Meyerhold. In rehearsing a part, the actor should remember the process of discovering the character's complexities and contradictions; this reactivated dialectical energy would force the actor to show and not become the character. The audience would be awakened as observers of the actor's performance and of the play's modes of representation, instead of emotionally identifying with the character, per se. Empathy would be created by the dynamic between actor, audience, space, and the recognizability of dynamic social situations. Brecht's theories, like Sergei Eisenstein's, were shaped by Asian theatrical traditions; his dramaturgical theories were also influenced by Eisenstein's theories of montage. His modernist ethos was also explicitly urban; the very movement and chaos of the city immersed men and women in an intricate reality which had prepared them for new modes of observation. Actors and artists should remind the audience of their shared experience of modernity. In the poem "On the Everyday Theatre," Brecht extolled "Actors/You who perform plays in great houses/Under false suns and before silent faces/Look sometimes at/The theatre whose stage is the street." Brecht's work has influenced contemporary theatre, film, and television; the now familiar violation of the invisible fourth wall between the actors and the audience, a domesticated satirical standard, is one of Brecht's inherited alienation effects.

In 1944, near the end of World War II, Theodor Adorno and Max Horkheimer cautioned against the ever-growing power of "the Culture Industry," whose allegedly standardized products, whether popular or jazz music, film, or consumer goods like automobiles, could superficially dazzle, while lacking complex form, containing no substance or meaning, and producing only the desire for the next new thing. Elizabeth Bowen's "Why I Go to the Cinema" contrasts Adorno and Horkheimer's dark views of popular culture, ones that were understandably influenced by Hitler's Ministry of Propaganda's appropriating of popular, folk, and avant-garde genres and aesthetics. Bowen, who saw value in distraction, spectacle, and entertainment, valued the common pleasures of mass experience. She shared with Walter Benjamin the notion that standards of taste and critical assessment could be stimulated by the cinema, and that perceptive faculties could be sharpened. Bowen's appreciation of cinema and the moviegoing experience foreshadowed feminist discussion of visual pleasure and contemporary star studies. Other parts in this *Reader* further complicate this introduction to "Culture and Aesthetics"; for example, several of the writers in Part VII "Global modernisms" embrace social realism as a vibrant and accessible aesthetic with which to speak to a broad audience about recognizable, material experiences of their lives. Critics like Antonio Gramsci, the Italian communist, maintained faith in people's art and organic intellectual tradition, while bemoaning the modernist aesthetics of elitism, self-referentiality, textual density and difficulty, and ironic distance. The writings by modernists on their own and others' works also illuminate what are, to date, the still-expanding cultural, temporal, and geographical parameters of modernist literature and art.

Notes

1   Symons 5. (See Chapter 5 of this volume, p. 56.)
2   Pater 194. (See Chapter 2 of this volume, p. 30.)
3   Pater 195. (See Chapter 2 of this volume, p. 31.)
4   William James 152–53. (See Chapter 4 of this volume, p. 42.)
5   Woolf, "Modern Fiction." (See Chapter 58 of this volume, p. 474.)
6   Wilde, "The Decay of Lying" 31, 30. (See Chapter 3 of this volume, p. 39.)
7   Wilde 14. (See also p. 34 of this volume.)
8   Wilde 29. (See also p. 36 of this volume.)
9   Wilde 28. (See also p. 36 of this volume.)
10   Eisenstein 30. (See Chapter 10 of this volume, p. 113.)
11   Eisenstein 35, 38. (See also p. 117 of this volume.)
12   Duncan 11. (See Chapter 6 of this volume, p. 58.)
13   Duncan 21. (See also p. 61 of this volume.)
14   Hughes: http://www.english.illinois.edu/maps/poets/g_l/hughes/mountain.htm (accessed 9 August 2011).

Suggested further readings

Adorno, Theodor, and Max Horkheimer. "The Culture Industry: Enlightenment as Mass Deception" (1944). *The Dialectic of Enlightenment*. Stanford: Stanford UP, 2007.

Adorno, Theodor, Walter Benjamin, Ernst Bloch, Bertolt Brecht, and Georg Lukács. *Aesthetics and Politics*. New York: Verso, 2010.

Arnold, Matthew. "On the Modern Element in Literature" (1857). *Essays by Matthew Arnold*. London: Oxford UP, 1914. 454–72.

Bell, Clive. "Art and Significant Form." *Art*. 1913. http://www.denisdutton.com/bell.htm (accessed: 08/10/11).

Benjamin, Walter. "Theory of Distraction" (1935–36). *Walter Benjamin: Selected Writings, vol. 3, 1935–1938*. Cambridge, MA: Belknap/Harvard UP, 2002. 141–42.

——. "The Work of Art in the Age of Its Technological Reproducibility" (1935–36), also known as "The Work of Art in the Age of Mechanical Reproduction." *Walter Benjamin: Selected Writings, vol. 3, 1935–1938*. Cambridge, MA: Belknap/Harvard UP, 2002. 101–33.

——. "Mickey Mouse" (1931). *Walter Benjamin: Selected Writings, vol. 2, 1927–1934*. Cambridge, MA: Belknap/Harvard UP, 1999. 545–46.

——. "A Child's View of Color" (1914–15). *Walter Benjamin: Selected Writings, vol. 1, 1913–1926*. Cambridge, MA: Belknap/Harvard UP, 1996. 50–51.

Bogan, Louise. "Folk Art" (1943). *A Poet's Prose: Selected Writings of Louise Bogan*, ed. Mary Kinzie. Athens, OH: Swallow Press/Ohio UP, 2005.

Brecht, Bertolt. *Brecht on Film and Radio*. Trans. and ed. Mac Silberman. London: Methuen, 2000.

——. *Poems on the Theatre*. Trans. John Berger and Anna Bostock. Lowestoft, Suffolk: Scorpion Press, 1961.

Caws, Mary Ann, ed. *Manifesto: A Century of Isms*. Lincoln: U of Nebraska P, 2000.

Dickstein, Morris. *A Cultural History of the Great Depression*. New York: Norton, 2009.

Eisenstein, Sergei. "A Dialectical Approach to Film Form" (1929). *Film Form: Essays in Film Theory*. New York: Harcourt, 1969.

Fry, Roger. "Negro Sculpture" (1920). *Vision and Design*. London: Chatto & Windus, 1920.

Gramsci, Antonio. "Concept of 'National-Popular,' " "Various Types of Popular Novels," "The Operatic Conception of Life," "Popular Literature. Operatic Taste" (1930). *A Gramsci Reader: Selected Writings, 1916–1935*. London: Lawrence and Wishart, 2000. 364–74.

Huysmans, Joris-Karl. *L'art moderne* (1883). Charleston, SC: BiblioBazaar, 2009.

James, Henry. "The Art of Fiction" (1894). *The Art of Criticism: Henry James on the Theory and Practice of Fiction*, ed. William Veeder and Susan M. Griffin. Chicago: U of Chicago P, 1986.

Jacques, Geoffrey. *Change in the Weather: Modernist Imagination, African American Imaginary*. Amherst: U of Massachusetts P, 2009.

Loy, Mina. "Aphorisms on Futurism." *Camera Work* 45 (1914).

McLuhan, Marshall. *Understanding Media: The Extensions of Man*. New York: Routledge, 2001.

Maerhofer, John W. *Rethinking the Vanguard: Aesthetic and Political Positions in the Modernist Debate*. Cambridge: Cambridge Scholars Publishing, 2009.

Mallarmé, Stéphane. "Crisis in Poetry" (1886). *Toward the Open Field: Poets on the Art of Poetry 1800–1950*, ed. Melissa Kwasny. Middletown, CT: Wesleyan UP, 2004. 151–59.

Marcus, Laura. *The Tenth Muse: Writing about Cinema in the Modernist Period*. Oxford: Oxford UP, 2010.

Marinetti, Filippo. "La Radia." Trans. Stephen Sartarelli. *Wireless Imagination: Sound Radio and the Avant-Garde*, ed. Douglas Kahn and Gregory Whitehead. Cambridge, MA: MIT Press, 1992.

Marx, Karl. "Estranged Labour." *Economic and Philosophic Manuscripts of 1844. The Marx-Engels Reader*, ed. Robert C. Tucker. New York: Norton, 1978. 70–81.

Matz, Jesse. *Literary Impressionism and Modernist Aesthetics*. Cambridge: Cambridge UP, 2007.

Pells, Richard H. *Modernist America: Art, Music, Movies, and the Globalization of American Culture*. New Haven: Yale UP, 2011.

Teukolsky, Rachel. *The Literate Eye: Victorian Art Writing and Modernist Aesthetics*. Oxford: Oxford UP, 2009.

Vertov, Dziga. *Kino-Eye: The Writings of Dziga Vertov*. Berkeley: U of California P, 1985.

Wilde, Oscar. "Preface," *The Picture of Dorian Gray* (1891). Norton: New York and London, 1988. 3–4.

——. "Mr. Pater's Appreciations." *Speaker* (22 March 1890): 471–81.

Woolf, Leonard. "Hunting the Highbrow" (1927). *The Hogarth Essays*, compiled by Leonard S. Woolf and Virginia Woolf. Freeport, NY: Books for Libraries, 1970. 135–59.

Chapter 1

Charles Baudelaire (1821–67)

THE PAINTER OF MODERN LIFE (1863)

I N 1841, THE PARIS-BORN BAUDELAIRE was sent to India by his parents, who wanted to prevent his further corruption by the city's bohemian influences. Baudelaire escaped and returned to the city where he became an exuberant dandy and flâneur, art critic, translator of Edgar Allen Poe, barricade fighter during the 1848 revolution, frequenter of cafes and brothels, and writer. Baudelaire lived in the city's Latin Quarter for most of his life and became one of the first poets of urban life; his sensational experiences of Paris are captured in his best-known collection of poems, *Les fleurs du mal* (1857). Baudelaire's social observations of *modernité* in formation and his writings were frequently enhanced by his consumption of opium and hashish. His aesthetic was rooted in all of the decadent, exotic, sensual, dark, and erotic experiences that Paris could offer; his privileged artist was a *specialist*, a man of the city and the world, a childlike man of unlimited curiosity and experience. This artist-hero is a fascinated watcher and observer who is unafraid of letting himself become possessed by the surrounding world and its forms; Baudelaire championed this distinctly modern artist, a figure influenced by Poe's "Man of the Crowd." He had little interest in coterie artists or aesthetic connoisseurs; they were "pure artisans, village intellects, cottage brains" (27). Baudelaire's favored painters included Eugene Delacroix, Goya, and Edouard Manet. His poetry and art criticism influenced his descendants, the modern symbolist poets Stephane Mallarmé, Arthur Rimbaud, and Paul Verlaine; Baudelaire was a major influence on Walter Benjamin, whose *Arcades Project* and essays on modernity and childhood sensuality and perception owe much to the epicurean renegade poet.

Charles Baudelaire, "The Artist, Man of the World, Man of the Crowd, and Child" (1863). *The Painter of Modern Life and Other Essays*. Trans. Jonathan Mayne. London: Phaidon Press, 1964: 5–12.

The artist, man of the world, man of the crowd, and child

Today I want to discourse to the public about a strange man, a man of so powerful and so decided an originality that it is sufficient unto itself and does not even seek approval. Not a single one of his drawings is signed, if by signature you mean that string of easily forgeable characters which spell a name and which so many other artists affix ostentatiously at the foot of their least important trifles. Yet all his works are signed—with his dazzling *soul*; and art-lovers who have seen and appreciated them will readily recognize them from the description that I am about to give.

A passionate lover of crowds and Monsieur C. G. [Constantine Guys] (1802–92) carries originality to the point of shyness. Mr. Thackeray, who, as is well known, is deeply inter-ested in matters of art, and who himself executes the illustrations to his novels, spoke one day of Monsieur G. in the columns of a London review. The latter was furious, as though at an outrage to his virtue. Recently again, when he learnt that I had it in mind to write an appre-ciation of his mind and his talent, be begged me—very imperiously, I must admit—to suppress his name, and if I must speak of his works, to speak of them as if they were those of an anonymous artist. I will humbly comply with this singular request. The reader and I will preserve the fiction that Monsieur G. does not exist, and we shall concern ourselves with his drawings and his watercolours (for which he professes a patrician scorn) as though we were scholars who had to pronounce upon precious historical documents, thrown up by chance, whose author must remain eternally unknown. And finally, to give complete reassurance to my conscience, it must be supposed that all that I have to say of his strangely and mysteriously brilliant nature is more or less justly suggested by the works in question—pure poetic hypothesis, conjecture, a labour of the imagination.

Monsieur G. is an old man. Jean-Jacques is said to have reached the age of forty-two before he started writing. It was perhaps at about the same age that Monsieur G., obsessed by the throng of pictures which teemed in his brain, was first emboldened to throw ink and colours on to a white sheet of paper. Truth to tell, he drew like a barbarian, or a child, impa-tient at the clumsiness of his fingers and the disobedience of his pen. I have seen a large number of these primitive scribbles, and I must own that the majority of those who are, or claim to be, connoisseurs in this matter, might well have been pardoned for failing to discern the latent genius which abode in such murky daubs. Today, after discovering by himself all the little tricks of his trade and accomplishing, without advice, his own education, Monsieur G. has become a powerful master in his own way, and of his early artlessness he has retained no more than what was needed to add an unexpected seasoning to his rich gifts. When he comes across one of those early efforts of his, he tears it up or burns it with a most comical show of bashfulness and indignation.

For ten years I had wanted to get to know Monsieur G., who is by nature a great trav-eller and cosmopolitan. I knew that for some time he had been on the staff of an English illustrated journal, and that engravings after his travel-sketches, made in Spain, Turkey and the Crimea, had been published there. Since then I have seen a considerable quantity of those drawings, hastily sketched on the spot, and thus I have been able to *read*, so to speak, a detailed account of the Crimean campaign which is much preferable to any other that I know. The same paper had also published, always without signature, a great number of his illustra-tions of new ballets and operas. When at last I ran him to earth, I saw at once that it was not precisely an *artist*, but rather a *man of the world* with whom I had to do. I ask you to understand the word *artist* in a very restricted sense, and *man of the world* in a very broad one. By the second I mean a man of the whole world, a man who understands the world and the myste-rious and lawful reasons for all its uses; by the first, a specialist, a man wedded to his palette like the serf to the soil. Monsieur G. does not like to be called an artist. Is he not perhaps a little right? His interest is the whole world; he wants to know, understand and appreciate everything that happens on the surface of our globe. The artist lives very little, if at all, in the world of morals and politics. If he lives in the Bréda district, he will be unaware of what is going on in the Faubourg Saint-Germain. Apart from one or two exceptions whom I need not name, it must be admitted that the majority of artists are no more than highly skilled animals, pure artisans, village intellects, cottage brains. Their conversation, which is necessarily limited to the narrowest of circles, becomes very quickly unbearable, to the *man of the world*, to the spiritual citizen of the universe.

And so, as a first step towards an understanding of Monsieur G., I would ask you to note at once that the mainspring of his genius is *curiosity*.

Do you remember a picture (it really is a picture!), painted—or rather written—by the most powerful pen of our age, and entitled *The Man of the Crowd*? In the window of a coffee-house there sits a convalescent, pleasurably absorbed in gazing at the crowd, and mingling, through the medium of thought, in the turmoil of thought that surrounds him. But lately returned from the valley of the shadow of death, he is rapturously breathing in all the odours and essences of life; as he has been on the brink of total oblivion, he remembers, and fervently desires to remember, everything. Finally he hurls himself headlong into the midst of the throng, in pursuit of an unknown, half-glimpsed countenance that has, on an instant, bewitched him. Curiosity has become a fatal, irresistible passion!

Imagine an artist who was always, spiritually, in the condition of that convalescent, and you will have the key to the nature of Monsieur G.

Now convalescence is like a return towards childhood. The convalescent, like the child, is possessed in the highest degree of the faculty of keenly interesting himself in things, be they apparently of the most trivial. Let us go back, if we can, by a retrospective effort of the imagination, towards our most youthful, our earliest, impressions, and we will recognize that they had a strange kinship with those brightly coloured impressions which we were later to receive in the aftermath of a physical illness, always provided that that illness had left our spiritual capacities pure and unharmed. The child sees everything in a state of newness; he is always *drunk*. Nothing more resembles what we call inspiration than the delight with which a child absorbs form and colour. I am prepared to go even further and assert that inspiration has something in common with a convulsion, and that every sublime thought is accompanied by a more or less violent nervous shock which has its repercussion in the very core of the brain. The man of genius has sound nerves, while those of the child are weak. With the one, Reason has taken up a considerable position; with the other, Sensibility is almost the whole being. But genius is nothing more nor less than *childhood recovered* at will—a childhood now equipped for self-expression with manhood's capacities and a power of analysis which enables it to order the mass of raw material which it has involuntarily accumulated. It is by this deep and joyful curiosity that we may explain the fixed and animally ecstatic gaze of a child confronted with something new, whatever it be, whether a face or a landscape, gilding, colours, shimmering stuffs, or the magic of physical beauty assisted by the cosmetic art. A friend of mine once told me that when he was quite a small child, he used to be present when his father dressed in the mornings, and that it was with a mixture of amazement and delight that he used to study the muscles of his arms, the gradual transitions of pink and yellow in his skin, and the bluish network of his veins. The picture of external life was already filling him with awe and taking hold of his brain. He was already being obsessed and possessed by form. Predestination was already showing the tip of its nose. His sentence was sealed. Need I add that today that child is a well-known painter?

I asked you a moment ago to think of Monsieur G. as an eternal convalescent. To complete your idea, consider him also as a man-child, as a man who is never for a moment without the genius of childhood—a genius for which no aspect of life has become *stale*.

I have told you that I was reluctant to describe him as an artist pure and simple, and indeed that he declined this title with a modesty touched with aristocratic reserve. I might perhaps call him a dandy, and I should have several good reasons for that; for the word 'dandy' implies a quintessence of character and a subtle understanding of the entire moral mechanism of this world; with another part of his nature, however, the dandy aspires to insensitivity, and it is in this that Monsieur G., dominated as he is by an insatiable passion— for seeing and feeling—parts company decisively with dandyism. '*Amabam amare*' said St. Augustine. 'I am passionately in love with passion,' Monsieur G. might well echo. The dandy is blasé, or pretends to be so, for reasons of policy and caste. Monsieur G. has a horror of blasé people. He is a master of that only too difficult art—sensitive spirits will understand me—of being sincere without being absurd. I would bestow upon him the title of philosopher, to which he has more than one right, if his excessive love of visible, tangible things, condensed to their plastic state, did not arouse in him a certain repugnance for the things that form the impalpable kingdom of the metaphysician. Let us be content therefore to consider him as a pure pictorial moralist, like La Bruyère.

The crowd is his element, as the air is that of birds and water of fishes. His passion and his profession are to become one flesh with the crowd. For the perfect *flâneur*, for the passionate spectator, it is an immense joy to set up house in the heart of the multitude, amid the ebb and flow of movement, in the midst of the fugitive and the infinite. To be away from home and yet to feel oneself everywhere at home; to see the world, to be at the centre of the world, and yet to remain hidden from the world—such are a few of the slightest pleasures of those independent, passionate, impartial natures which the tongue can but clumsily define. The spectator is a *prince* who everywhere rejoices in his incognito. The lover of life makes the whole world his family, just like the lover of the fair sex who builds up his family from all the beautiful women that he has ever found, or that are—or are not—to be found; or the lover of pictures who lives in a magical society of dreams painted on canvas. Thus the lover of universal life enters into the crowd as though it were an immense reservoir of electrical energy. Or we might liken him to a mirror as vast as the crowd itself; or to a kaleidoscope gifted with consciousness, responding to each one of its movements and reproducing the multiplicity of life and the flickering grace of all the elements of life. He is an 'I' with an insatiable appetite for the 'non-I', at every instant rendering and explaining it in pictures more living than life itself, which is always unstable and fugitive. 'Any man,' he said one day, in the course of one of those conversations which he illumines with burning glance and evocative gesture, 'any man who is not crushed by one of those griefs whose nature is too real not to monopolize all his capacities, and who can yet be *bored in the heart of the multitude*, is a blockhead! a blockhead! and I despise him!'

When Monsieur G. wakes up and opens his eyes to see the boisterous sun beating a tattoo upon his window-pane, he reproaches himself remorsefully and regretfully: 'What a peremptory order! what a bugle-blast of life! Already several hours of light—everywhere— lost by my sleep! How many *illuminated* things might I have seen and have missed seeing!' So out he goes and watches the river of life flow past him in all its splendour and majesty. He marvels at the eternal beauty and the amazing harmony of life in the capital cities, a harmony so providentially maintained amid the turmoil of human freedom. He gazes upon the landscapes of the great city—landscapes of stone, caressed by the mist or buffeted by the sun. He delights in fine carriages and proud horses, the dazzling smartness of the grooms, the expertness of the footmen, the sinuous gait of the women, the beauty of the children, happy to be alive and nicely dressed—in a word, he delights in universal life. If a fashion or the cut of a garment has been slightly modified, if bows and curls have been supplanted by cockades, if *bavolets* have been enlarged and *chignons* have dropped a fraction towards the nape of the neck, if waists have been raised and skirts have become fuller, be very sure that his eagle eye will already have spotted it from however great a distance. A regiment passes, on its way, as it may be, to the ends of the earth, tossing into the air of the boulevards its trumpet-calls as winged and stirring as hope; and in an instant Monsieur G. will already have seen, examined and analysed the bearing and external aspect of that company. Glittering equipment, music, bold determined glances, heavy, solemn moustaches—he absorbs it all pell-mell; and in a few moments the resulting 'poem' will be virtually composed. See how his soul lives with the soul of that regiment, marching like a single animal, a proud image of joy in obedience!

But now it is evening. It is that strange, equivocal hour when the curtains of heaven are drawn and cities light up. The gas-light makes a stain upon the crimson of the sunset. Honest men and rogues, sane men and mad, are all saying to themselves, 'The end of another day!' The thoughts of all, whether good men or knaves, turn to pleasure, and each one hastens to the place of his choice to drink the cup of oblivion. Monsieur G. will be the last to linger wherever there can be a glow of light, an echo of poetry, a quiver of life or a chord of music; wherever a passion can *pose* before him, wherever natural man and conventional man display themselves in a strange beauty, wherever the sun lights up the swift joys of the *depraved animal*! 'A fine way to fill one's day, to be sure,' remarks a certain reader whom we all know so well. 'Which one of us has not every bit enough genius to fill it in the same way?' But no! Few men are gifted with the capacity of seeing; there are fewer still who possess the power of expression. So now, at a time when others are asleep, Monsieur G. is bending over his table, darting on to a sheet of paper the same glance that a moment ago he was directing towards external things, skirmishing with his pencil, his pen, his brush, splashing his glass of water up to the ceiling, wiping his pen on his shirt, in a ferment of violent activity, as though afraid that the image might escape him, cantankerous though alone, elbowing himself on. And the external world is reborn upon his paper, natural and more than natural, beautiful and more than beautiful, strange and endowed with an impulsive life like the soul of its creator. The phantasmagoria has been distilled from nature. All the raw materials with which the memory has loaded itself are put in order, ranged and harmonized, and undergo that forced idealization which is the result of a childlike perceptiveness—that is to say, a perceptiveness acute and magical by reason of its innocence!

Chapter 2

Walter Pater (1839–94)

"CONCLUSION," *THE RENAISSANCE – STUDIES IN ART AND POETRY* (1868)

PATER WAS, IN MANY WAYS, an unlikely forefather of the aesthetic movement in England. An Oxford tutor, he lived a secluded intellectual life that gave few outward clues to the ecstatic worldview that would find expression in his conclusion to *The Renaissance*, a study of the major paintings of the period. Influenced by art historians such as Johann Joachim Winckelmann (1717–68) and John Ruskin (1819–1900), Pater's study and, particularly, his conclusion, espouses a view of "art for its own sake" that would become a cornerstone of aestheticism. Of *The Renaissance*, Wilde wrote, "[Pater] shows us how, behind the perfection of a man's style, must lie the passion of a man's soul" ("Mr. Pater's Appreciations"). Yeats was so taken with the lyricism of Pater's prose that he translated the Mona Lisa section from *The Renaissance* into verse form and included it as the first entry in his poetry anthology, *The Oxford Book of Modern Verse* (1936). After the publication of *The Renaissance,* Pater became closely associated with the Pre-Raphaelite Movement in the arts and published a novel titled *Marius the Epicurean* (1885), in which the titular hero attempts to lead an aesthetic life.

Walter Pater, "Conclusion," *The Renaissance – Studies in Art and Poetry.* New York: Boni and Liveright, 1919. 194–99.

Conclusion[1]

Δέγει που ῾ΗράΚλειτος ὅτι πάντα χωρεῖ καὶ οὐδὲν μένει

To regard all things and principles of things as inconstant modes or fashions has more and more become the tendency of modern thought. Let us begin, with that which is without— our physical life. Fix upon it in one of its more exquisite intervals, the moment, for instance, of delicious recoil from the flood of water in summer heat. What is the whole physical life in that moment but a combination of natural elements to which science gives their names? But those elements, phosphorus and lime and delicate fibres, are present not in the human body alone: we detect them in places most remote from it. Our physical life is a perpetual motion

of them—the passage of the blood, the waste and repairing of the lenses of the eye, the modification of the tissues of the brain under every ray of light and sound—processes which
science reduces to simpler and more elementary forces. Like the elements of which we are
composed, the action of these forces extends beyond us: it rusts iron and ripens corn. Far out
on every side of us those elements are broadcast, driven in many currents; and birth and
gesture and death and the springing of violets from the grave are but a few out of ten thousand
resultant combinations. That clear, perpetual outline of face and limb is but an image of ours,
under which we group them—a design in a web, the actual threads of which pass out beyond
it. This at least of flame-like our life has, that it is but the concurrence, renewed from moment
to moment, of forces parting sooner or later on their ways.

Or, if we begin with the inward world of thought and feeling, the whirlpool is still more
rapid, the flame more eager and devouring. There it is no longer the gradual darkening of the
eye, the gradual fading of colour from the wall—movements of the shore-side, where the
water flows down indeed, though in apparent rest—but the race of the mid-stream, a drift of
momentary acts of sight and passion and thought. At first sight experience seems to bury us
under a flood of external objects, pressing upon us with a sharp and importunate reality,
calling us out of ourselves in a thousand forms of action. But when reflexion begins to play
upon those objects they are dissipated under its influence; the cohesive force seems suspended
like some trick of magic; each object is loosed into a group of impressions—colour, odour,
texture—in the mind of the observer. And if we continue to dwell in thought on this world,
not of objects in the solidity with which language invests them, but of impressions, unstable,
flickering, inconsistent, which burn and are extinguished with our consciousness of them, it
contracts still further: the whole scope of observation is dwarfed into the narrow chamber of
the individual mind. Experience, already reduced to a group of impressions, is ringed round
for each one of us by that thick wall of personality through which no real voice has ever
pierced on its way to us, or from us to that which we can only conjecture to be without.
Every one of those impressions is the impression of the individual in his isolation, each mind
keeping as a solitary prisoner its own dream of a world. Analysis goes a step farther still and
assures us that those impressions of the individual mind to which, for each one of us, experience dwindles down, are in perpetual flight; that each of them is limited by time, and that as
time is infinitely divisible, each of them is infinitely divisible also; all that is actual in it being
a single moment, gone while we try to apprehend it, of which it may ever be more truly said
that it has ceased to be than that it is. To such a tremulous wisp constantly re-forming itself
on the stream, to a single sharp impression, with a sense in it, a relic more or less fleeting, of
such moments gone by, what is real in our life fines itself down. It is with this movement,
with the passage and dissolution of impressions, images, sensations, that analysis leaves off—
that continual vanishing away, that strange, perpetual weaving and unweaving of ourselves.

Philosophiren, says Novalis, *ist dephlegmatisiren, vivificiren*. The service of philosophy, of
speculative culture, towards the human spirit, is to rouse, to startle it to a life of constant and
eager observation. Every moment some form grows perfect in hand or face; some tone on
the hills or the sea is choicer than the rest; some mood of passion or insight or intellectual
excitement is irresistibly real and attractive to us,—for that moment only. Not the fruit of
experience, but experience itself, is the end. A counted number of pulses only is given to us
of a variegated, dramatic life. How may we see in them all that is to be seen in them by the
finest senses? How shall we pass most swiftly from point to point, and be present always at
the focus where the greatest number of vital forces unite in their purest energy?

To burn always with this hard, gemlike flame, to maintain this ecstasy, is success in life.
In a sense it might even be said that our failure is to form habits: for, after all, habit is relative
to a stereotyped world, and meantime it is only the roughness of the eye that makes any two
persons, things, situations, seem alike. While all melts under our feet, we may well grasp at

any exquisite passion, or any contribution to knowledge that seems by a lifted horizon to set the spirit free for a moment, or any stirring of the senses, strange dyes, strange colours, and curious odours, or work of the artist's hands, or the face of one's friend. Not to discriminate every moment some passionate attitude in those about us, and in the very brilliancy of their gifts some tragic dividing of forces on their ways, is, on this short day of frost and sun, to sleep before evening. With this sense of the splendour of our experience and of its awful brevity, gathering all we are into one desperate effort to see and touch, we shall hardly have time to make theories about the things we see and touch. What we have to do is to be for ever curiously testing new opinions and courting new impressions, never acquiescing in a facile orthodoxy of Comte, or of Hegel, or of our own. Philosophical theories or ideas, as points of view, instruments of criticism, may help us to gather up what might otherwise pass unregarded by us. "Philosophy is the microscope of thought." The theory or idea or system which requires of us the sacrifice of any part of this experience, in consideration of some interest into which we cannot enter, or some abstract theory we have not identified with ourselves, or of what is only conventional, has no real claim upon us.

One of the most beautiful passages of Rousseau is that in the sixth book of the *Confessions*, where he describes the awakening in him of the literary sense. An undefinable taint of death had clung always about him, and now in early manhood he believed himself smitten by mortal disease. He asked himself how he might make as much as possible of the interval that remained; and he was not biassed by anything in his previous life when he decided that it must be by intellectual excitement, which he found just then in the clear, fresh writings of Voltaire. Well! we are all *condamnés* as Victor Hugo says: we are all under sentence of death but with a sort of indefinite reprieve—*les hommes sont tous condamnés à mort avec des sursis indéfinis*: we have an interval, and then our place knows us no more. Some spend this interval in listlessness, some in high passions, the wisest, at least among "the children of this world," in art and song. For our one chance lies in expanding that interval, in getting as many pulsations as possible into the given time. Great passions may give us this quickened sense of life, ecstasy and sorrow of love, the various forms of enthusiastic activity, disinterested or otherwise, which come naturally to many of us. Only be sure it is passion—that it does yield you this fruit of a quickened, multiplied consciousness. Of such wisdom, the poetic passion, the desire of beauty, the love of art for its own sake, has most. For art comes to you proposing frankly to give nothing but the highest quality to your moments as they pass, and simply for those moments' sake.

Note

1   This brief "Conclusion" was omitted in the second edition of this book, as I conceived it might possibly mislead some of those young men into whose hands it might fall. On the whole, I have thought it best to reprint it here, with some slight changes which bring it closer to my original meaning. I have dealt more fully in *Marius the Epicurean* with the thoughts suggested by it.

Chapter 3

Oscar Wilde (1854–1900)

"THE DECAY OF LYING" (1889)

WITH MAJOR THEATRICAL SUCCESSES AT the end of the nineteenth-century such as *An Ideal Husband* (1894) and *The Importance of Being Earnest* (1895), Wilde brought aestheticism to a wide audience and became the embodiment of the Edwardian aesthete. Through figures such as Vivian in "The Decay of Lying," Wilde articulated an anti-realist worldview in which the pursuit of beauty and artifice reigned supreme. Born and raised in Ireland, Wilde began his university education at Trinity College, Dublin before moving on to Oxford University where he purged himself of his Irish brogue and was renowned as a gifted talker. While at Oxford, two of his tutors were John Ruskin and Walter Pater who greatly influenced his approach to art. Wilde rose to fame and noteriety through lecture tours, editorships, commercially successful plays, his novel *The Picture of Dorian Gray*, and, eventually, the three trials for "acts of gross obscenity" that resulted in his imprisonment. These trials resulted from an escalating feud between Wilde and the father of his lover, Alfred Douglas. After Douglas's father, the Marquess of Queensbury, sent a letter calling Wilde a "posing somdomite [*sic*]," Wilde sued for libel. In the following trials, Wilde was not only prosecuted for homosexual acts, but his aesthetic theories were also cited against him as signs of his dissipation and moral corruption.

Oscar Wilde, "The Decay of Lying," *The Works of Oscar Wilde. Intentions.* New York: Lamb Publishing, 1909. 7–8, 12–15, 23–29, 30–31, 37, 38–41, 46–51, 60–63.

Cyril (coming in through the open window from the terrace). My dear Vivian, don't coop yourself up all day in the library. It is a perfectly lovely afternoon. The air is exquisite. There is a mist upon the woods, like the purple bloom upon a plum. Let us go and lie on the grass, and smoke cigarettes, and enjoy Nature.

Vivian. Enjoy Nature! I am glad to say that I have entirely lost that faculty. People tell us that Art makes us love Nature more than we loved her before; that it reveals her secrets to us; and that after a careful study of Corot and Constable we see things in her that had escaped our observation. My own experience is that the more we study Art, the less we care for Nature. What Art really reveals to us is Nature's lack of design, her curious crudities, her extraordinary monotony, her absolutely unfinished condition. Nature has good intentions, of course, but, as Aristotle once said, she cannot carry them out. When I look at a landscape I cannot help seeing all its defects. It is fortunate for us, however, that Nature is so imperfect, as otherwise we should have had no art at all. Art is our spirited protest, our gallant attempt to teach Nature her proper place. As for the infinite variety of Nature, that is a pure myth. It is not to be found in Nature herself. It resides in the imagination, or fancy, or cultivated blindness of the man who looks at her. . . .

Vivian (*reading in a very clear, musical voice*). "The Decay of Lying: A Protest.—One of the chief causes that can be assigned for the curiously commonplace character of most of the literature of our age is undoubtedly the decay of Lying as an art, a science, and a social pleasure. The ancient historians gave us delightful fiction in the form of fact; the modern novelist presents us with dull facts under the guise of fiction. The Blue-Book is rapidly becoming his ideal both for method and manner. He has his tedious '*document humain,*' his miserable little '*coin de la création,*' into which he peers with his microscope. He is to be found at the Librairie Nationale, or at the British Museum, shamelessly reading up his subject. He has not even the courage of other people's ideas, but insists on going directly to life for everything, and ultimately, between encyclopaedias and personal experience, he comes to the ground, having drawn his types from the family circle or from the weekly washerwoman, and having acquired an amount of useful information from which never, even in his most meditative moments, can he thoroughly free himself.

"The loss that results to literature in general from this false ideal of our time can hardly be over-estimated. People have a careless way of talking about a 'born liar,' just as they talk about a 'born poet.' But in both cases they are wrong. Lying and poetry are arts—arts, as Plato saw, not unconnected with each other—and they require the most careful study, the most disinterested devotion. Indeed, they have their technique, just as the more material arts of painting and sculpture have, their subtle secrets of form and colour, their craft-mysteries, their deliberate artistic methods.

"As one knows the poet by his fine music, so one can recognise the liar by his rich rhythmic utterance, and in neither case will the casual inspiration of the moment suffice. Here, as elsewhere, practice must precede perfection. But in modern days while the fashion of writing poetry has become far too common, and should, if possible, be discouraged, the fashion of lying has almost fallen into disrepute. Many a young man starts in life with a natural gift for exaggeration which, if nurtured in congenial and sympathetic surroundings, or by the imitation of the best models, might grow into something really great and wonderful. But, as a rule, he comes to nothing. He either falls into careless habits of accuracy—"

Cyril. My dear fellow!

Vivian. Please don't interrupt in the middle of a sentence. "He either falls into careless habits of accuracy, or takes to frequenting the society of the aged and the well-informed. Both things are equally fatal to his imagination, as indeed they would be fatal to the imagination of anybody, and in a short time he develops a morbid and unhealthy faculty of truth-telling, begins to verify all statements made in his presence, has no hesitation in contradicting people who are much younger than himself, and often ends by writing novels which are so like life that no one can possibly believe in their probability. This is no isolated instance that we are giving. It is simply one example out of many; and if something cannot be done to check, or at least to modify, our monstrous worship of facts, Art will become sterile, and Beauty will pass away from the land. . . ."

. . .

Vivian. The public imagine that, because they are interested in their immediate surroundings, Art should be interested in them also, and should take them as her subject-matter. But the mere fact that they are interested in these things makes them unsuitable subjects for Art. The only beautiful things, as somebody once said, are the things that do not concern us. As long as a thing is useful or necessary to us, or affects us in any way, either for pain or for pleasure, or appeals strongly to our sympathies, or is a vital part of the environment in which we live, it is outside the proper sphere of art. To art's subject-matter we should be more or less indifferent. We should, at any rate, have no preferences, no prejudices, no partisan feeling of any kind. It is exactly because Hecuba is nothing to us that her sorrows are such an admirable motive for a tragedy. I do not know anything in the whole history of literature sadder than the artistic career of Charles Reade. He wrote one beautiful book, *The Cloister and the Hearth*, a book as much above *Romola* as *Romola* is above *Daniel Deronda*, and wasted the rest of his life in a foolish attempt to be modern, to draw public attention to the state of our convict prisons, and the management of our private lunatic asylums. Charles Dickens was depressing enough in all conscience when he tried to arouse our sympathy for the victims of the poor-law administration; but Charles Reade, an artist, a scholar, a man with a true sense of beauty, raging and roaring over the abuses of contemporary life like a common pamphleteer or a sensational journalist, is really a sight for the angels to weep over. Believe me, my dear Cyril, modernity of form and modernity of subject-matter are entirely and absolutely wrong. We have mistaken the common livery of the age for the vesture of the Muses, and spend our days in the sordid streets and hideous suburbs of our vile cities when we should be out on the hillside with Apollo. Certainly we are a degraded race, and have sold our birthright for a mess of facts.

Cyril. There is something in what you say, and there is no doubt that whatever amusement we may find in reading a purely modern novel, we have rarely any artistic pleasure in re-reading it. And this is perhaps the best rough test of what is literature and what is not. If one cannot enjoy reading a book over and over again, there is no use reading it at all. But what do you say about the return to Life and Nature? This is the panacea that is always being recommended to us.

Vivian. I will read you what I say on that subject. The passage comes later on in the article, but I may as well give it to you now:

> "The popular cry of our time is 'Let us return to Life and Nature; they will recreate Art for us, and send the red blood coursing through her veins; they will shoe her feet with swiftness and make her hand strong.' But, alas we are mistaken in our amiable and well-meaning efforts. Nature is always behind the age. And as for Life, she is 'the solvent that breaks up Art, the enemy that lays waste her house."

Cyril. What do you mean by saying that Nature is always behind the age?

Vivian. Well, perhaps that is rather cryptic. What I mean is this. If we take Nature to mean natural simple instinct as opposed to self-conscious culture, the work produced under this influence is always old-fashioned, antiquated, and out of date. One touch of Nature may make the whole world kin, but two touches of Nature will destroy any work of Art. If, on the other band, we regard Nature as the collection of phenomena external to man, people only discover in her what they bring to her. She has no suggestions of her own. Wordsworth went to the lakes, but he was never a lake poet. He found in stones the sermons he had already hidden there. He went moralising about the district, but his good work was produced when he returned, not to Nature but to poetry. Poetry gave him "Laodamia," and the fine sonnets, and the great Ode, such as it is. Nature gave him "Martha Ray" and "Peter Bell," and the address to Mr. Wilkinson's spade.

Cyril. I think that view might be questioned. I am rather inclined to believe in the "impulse from a vernal wood," though of course the artistic value of such an impulse depends entirely on the kind of temperament that receives it, so that the return to Nature would come to mean simply the advance of a great personality. You would agree with that, I fancy. However, proceed with your article.

Vivian (reading). "Art begins with abstract decoration with purely imaginative and pleasurable work dealing with what is unreal and non-existent. This is the first stage. Then Life becomes fascinated with this new wonder, and asks to be admitted into the charmed circle. Art takes life as part of her rough material, recreates it, and refashions it in fresh forms, is absolutely indifferent to fact, invents, imagines, dreams, and keeps between herself and reality the impenetrable barrier of beautiful style, of decorative or ideal treatment. The third stage is when Life gets the upper hand, and drives Art out into the wilderness. That is the true decadence, and it is from this that we are now suffering.

"Take the case of the English drama. At first in the hands of the monks Dramatic Art was abstract, decorative, and mythological. Then she enlisted Life in her service, and using some of life's external forms, she created an entirely new race of beings, whose sorrows were more terrible than any sorrow man has ever felt, whose joys were keener than lover's joys, who had the rage of the Titans and the calm of the gods, who had monstrous and marvellous sins, monstrous and marvellous virtues. To them she gave a language different from that of actual use, a language full of resonant music and sweet rhythm, made stately by solemn cadence, or made delicate by fanciful rhyme, jewelled with wonderful words, and enriched with lofty diction. She clothed her children in strange raiment and gave them masks, and at her bidding the antique world rose from its marble tomb. A new Cæsar stalked through the streets of risen Rome, and with purple sail and flute-led oars another Cleopatra passed up the river to Antioch. Old myth and legend and dream took shape and substance. History was entirely re-written, and there was hardly one of the dramatists who did not recognise that the object of Art is not simple truth but complex beauty. In this they were perfectly right. Art itself is really a form of exaggeration; and selection, which is the very spirit of art, is nothing more than an intensified mode of over-emphasis.

"But Life soon shattered the perfection of the form. Even in Shakespeare we can see the beginning of the end. It shows itself by the gradual breaking up of the blank-verse in the later plays, by the predominance given to prose, and by the over-importance assigned to characterisation. The passages in Shakespeare—and they are many—where the language is uncouth, vulgar, exaggerated, fantastic, obscene even, are entirely due to Life calling for an echo of her own voice, and rejecting the intervention of beautiful style, through which alone should Life be suffered to find expression. Shakespeare is not by any means a flawless artist. He is too fond of going directly to life, and borrowing life's natural utterance. He forgets that when Art surrenders her imaginative medium she surrenders everything. . . .

"What is true about the drama and the novel is no less true about those arts that we call the decorative arts. The whole history of these arts in Europe is the record of the struggle between Orientalism, with its frank rejection of imitation, its love of artistic convention, its dislike to the actual representation of any object in Nature, and our own imitative spirit. Wherever the former has been paramount, as in Byzantium, Sicily, and Spain, by actual contact, or in the rest of Europe by the influence of the Crusades, we have had beautiful and imaginative work in which the visible things of life are transmuted into artistic conventions, and the things that Life has not are invented and fashioned for her delight. But wherever we have returned to Life and Nature, our work has always become vulgar, common, and uninteresting. . . .

"Art finds her own perfection within, and not outside of, herself. She is not to be judged by any external standard of resemblance. She is a veil, rather than a mirror. She has flowers that no forests know of, birds that no woodland possesses. She makes and unmakes many worlds, and can draw the moon from heaven with a scarlet thread. Hers are the 'forms more real than living man,' and hers the great archetypes of which things that have existence are but unfinished copies. Nature has, in her eyes, no laws, no uniformity. She can work miracles at her will, and when she calls monsters from the deep they come. She can bid the almond tree blossom in winter, and send the snow upon the ripe cornfield. . . ."

Cyril. Well, before you read it to me, I should like to ask you a question. What do you mean by saying that life, "poor, probable, uninteresting human life," will try to reproduce the marvels of art? I can quite understand your objection to art being treated as a mirror. You think it would reduce genius to the position of a cracked looking-glass. But you don't mean to say that you seriously believe that Life imitates Art, that Life in fact is the mirror, and Art the reality?

Vivian. Certainly I do. Paradox though it may seem—and paradoxes are always dangerous things—it is none the less true that Life imitates art far more than Art imitates life. We have all seen in our own day in England how a certain curious and fascinating type of beauty, invented and emphasised by two imaginative painters, has so influenced Life that whenever one goes to a private view or to an artistic salon one sees, here the mystic eyes of Rossetti's dream, the long ivory throat, the strange square-cut jaw, the loosened shadowy hair that he so ardently loved, there the sweet maidenhood of "The Golden Stair," the blossom-like mouth and weary loveliness of the "Laus Amoris," the passion-pale face of Andromeda, the thin hands and lithe beauty of the Vivien in "Merlin's Dream." And it has always been so. A great artist invents a type, and Life tries to copy it, to reproduce it in a popular form, like an enterprising publisher. Neither Holbein nor Vandyck found in England what they have given us. They brought their types with them, and Life with her keen imitative faculty set herself to supply the master with models. The Greeks, with their quick artistic instinct, understood this, and set in the bride's chamber the statue of Hermes or of Apollo, that she might bear children as lovely as the works of art that she looked at in her rapture or her pain. They knew that Life gains from Art not merely spirituality, depth of thought and feeling, soul-turmoil or soul-peace, but that she can form herself on the very lines and colours of art, and can reproduce the dignity of Phidias as well as the grace of Praxiteles. Hence came their objection to realism. They disliked it on purely social grounds. They felt that it inevitably makes people ugly, and they were perfectly right. We try to improve the conditions of the race by means of good air, free sunlight, wholesome water, and hideous bare buildings for the better housing of the lower orders. But these things merely produce health, they do not produce beauty. For this, Art is required, and the true disciples of the great artist are not his studio-imitators, but those who become like his works of art, be they plastic as in Greek days, or pictorial as in modern times; in a word, Life is Art's best, Art's only pupil.

As it is with the visible arts, so it is with literature. The most obvious and the vulgarest form in which this is shown is in the case of the silly boys who, after reading the adventures of Jack Sheppard or Dick Turpin, pillage the stalls of unfortunate apple-women, break into sweet-shops at night, and alarm old gentlemen who are returning home from the city by leaping out on them in suburban lanes, with black masks and unloaded revolvers. This interesting phenomenon, which always occurs after the appearance of a new edition of either of the books I have alluded to, is usually attributed to the influence of literature on the imagination. But this is a mistake. The imagination is essentially creative and always seeks for a new form. The boy-burglar is simply the inevitable result of life's imitative instinct. He is Fact, occupied as Fact usually is, with trying to reproduce Fiction, and what we see in him is repeated on an extended scale throughout the whole of life. Schopenhauer has analysed the pessimism that characterises modern thought, but Hamlet invented it. . . .

Cyril. The theory is certainly a very curious one, but to make it complete you must show that Nature, no less than Life, is an imitation of Art. Are you prepared to prove that?

Vivian. My dear fellow, I am prepared to prove anything.

Cyril. Nature follows the landscape painter then, and takes her effects from him?

Vivian. Certainly. Where, if not from the Impressionists, do we get those wonderful brown fogs that come creeping down our streets, blurring the gas-lamps and changing the houses into monstrous shadows? To whom, if not to them and their master, do we owe the lovely silver mists that brood over our river, and turn to faint forms of fading grace, curved bridge and swaying barge? The extraordinary change that has taken place in the climate of London during the last ten years is entirely due to this particular school of Art. You smile. Consider the matter from a scientific or a metaphysical point of view, and you will find that I am right. For what is Nature? Nature is no great mother who has borne us. She is our creation. It is in our brain that she quickens to life. Things are because we see them, and what we see, and how we see it, depends on the Arts that have influenced us. To look at a thing is very different from seeing a thing. One does not see anything until one sees its beauty. Then, and then only, does it come into existence. At present, people see fogs, not because there are fogs, but because poets and painters hare taught them the mysterious loveliness of such effects. There may have been fogs for centuries in London. I dare say there were. But no one saw them, and so we do not know anything about them. They did not exist till Art had invented them. Now, it must be admitted, fogs are carried to excess. They have become the mere mannerism of a clique, and the exaggerated realism of their method gives dull people bronchitis. Where the cultured catch an effect, the uncultured catch cold. And so, let us be humane, and invite Art to turn her wonderful eyes elsewhere. She has done so already, indeed. That white quivering sunlight that one sees now in France, with its strange blotches of mauve, and its restless violet shadows, is her latest fancy, and, on the whole, Nature reproduces it quite admirably. Where she used to give us Corots and Daubignys, she gives us now exquisite Monets and entrancing Pisaros. Indeed, there are moments, rare, it is true, but still to be observed from time to time, when Nature becomes absolutely modern. Of course she is not always to be relied upon. The fact is that she is in this unfortunate position: Art creates an incomparable and unique effect, and, having done so, passes on to other things. Nature, upon the other hand, forgetting that imitation can be made the sincerest form of insult, keeps on repeating this effect until we all become absolutely wearied of it. Nobody of any real culture, for instance, ever talks nowadays about the beauty of a sunset. Sunsets are quite old-fashioned. They belong to the time when Turner was the last note in art. To admire them is a distinct sign of provincialism of temperament. Upon the other hand they go on. Yesterday evening Mrs. Arundel insisted on my going to the window, and looking at the glorious sky, as she called it. Of course I had to look at it. She is one of those absurdly pretty Philistines, to whom one can deny nothing. And what was it? It was simply a very second-rate Turner, a Turner of a bad period, with all the painter's worst faults exaggerated and over-emphasised. Of course, I am quite ready to admit that Life very often commits the same error. She produces her false Renés and her sham Vautrins, just as Nature gives us, on one day a doubtful Cuyp, and on another a more than questionable Rousseau. Still, Nature irritates one more when she does things of that kind. It seems so stupid, so obvious, so unnecessary. A false

Vautrin might be delightful. A doubtful Cuyp is unbearable. However, I don't want to be too hard on Nature. I wish the Channel, especially at Hastings, did not look quite so often like a Henry Moore, grey pearl with yellow lights, but then, when Art is more varied, Nature will, no doubt, be more varied also. That she imitates Art, I don't think even her worst enemy would deny now. It is the one thing that keeps her in touch with civilised man. But have I proved my theory to your satisfaction?

Cyril. You have proved it to my dissatisfaction, which is better. But even admitting this strange imitative instinct in Life and Nature, surely you would acknowledge that Art expresses the temper of its age, the spirit of its time, the moral and social conditions that surround it, and under whose influence it is produced.

Vivian. Certainly not! Art never expresses anything but itself. This is the principle of my new aesthetics; and it is this, more than that vital connection between form and substance, on which Mr. Pater dwells, that makes music the type of all the arts. Of course, nations and individuals, with that healthy natural vanity which is the secret of existence, are always under the impression that it is of them that the Muses are talking, always trying to find in the calm dignity of imaginative art some mirror of their own turbid passions, always forgetting that the singer of life is not Apollo, but Marsyas. Remote from reality, and with her eyes turned away from the shadows of the cave, Art reveals her own perfection, and the wondering crowd that watches the opening of the marvellous, many-petalled rose fancies that it is its own history that is being told to it, its own spirit that is finding expression in a new form. But it is not so. The highest art rejects the burden of the human spirit, and gains more from a new medium or a fresh material than she does from any enthusiasm for art, or from any great awakening of the human consciousness. She develops purely on her own lines. She is not symbolic of any age. It is the ages that are her symbols. . . .

Cyril. Then we must certainly cultivate it at once. But in order to avoid making any error, I want you to tell me briefly the doctrines of the new æsthetics.

Vivian. Briefly, then, they are these. Art never expresses anything but itself. It has an independent life, just as Thought has, and develops purely on its own lines. It is not necessarily realistic in an age of realism, nor spiritual in an age of faith. So far from being the creation of its time, it is usually in direct opposition to it, and the only history that it preserves for us is the history of its own progress. Sometimes it returns upon its footsteps, and revives some antique form, as happened in the archaistic movement of late Greek Art, and in the pre-Raphaelite movement of our own day. At other times it entirely anticipates its age, and produces in one century work that it takes another century to understand, to appreciate, and to enjoy. In no case does it reproduce its age. To pass from the art of a time to the time itself is the great mistake that all historians commit.

The second doctrine is this. All bad art comes from returning to Life and Nature, and elevating them into ideals. Life and Nature may sometimes be used as a part of Art's rough material, but before they are of any real service to art they must be translated into artistic conventions. The moment Art surrenders its imaginative medium it surrenders everything. As a method, Realism is a complete failure, and the two things that every artist should avoid are modernity of form and modernity of subject-matter. To us, who live in the nineteenth century, any century is a suitable subject for art except our own. The only beautiful things are the things that do not concern us. It is, to have the pleasure of quoting myself, exactly because Hecuba is nothing to us that her sorrows are so suitable a motive for a tragedy. Besides, it is only the modern that ever becomes old-fashioned. M. Zola sits down to give us a picture of the Second Empire. Who cares for the Second Empire now? It is out of date. Life goes faster than Realism, but Romanticism is always in front of Life.

The third doctrine is that Life imitates Art far more than Art imitates Life. This results not merely from Life's imitative instinct, but from the fact that the self-conscious aim of Life is to find expression, and that Art offers it certain beautiful forms through which it may realise that energy. It is a theory that has never been put forward before, but it is extremely fruitful, and throws an entirely new light upon the history of Art.

It follows, as a corollary from this, that external Nature also imitates Art. The only effects that she can show us are effects that we have already seen through poetry, or in paintings. This is the secret of Nature's charm, as well as the explanation of Nature's weakness.

The final revelation is that Lying, the telling of beautiful untrue things, is the proper aim of Art. But of this I think I have spoken at sufficient length. And now let us go out on the terrace, where "droops the milk-white peacock like a ghost," while the evening star "washes the dusk with silver." At twilight nature becomes a wonderfully suggestive effect, and is not without loveliness, though perhaps its chief use is to illustrate quotations from the poets. Come! We have talked long enough.

Chapter 4

William James (1842–1910)

"THE STREAM OF CONSCIOUSNESS" (1892)

BORN INTO A PROMINENT New England family that included younger brother Henry James, William James was a pioneer in the field of psychology and an advocate of pragmatism in philosophy. His descriptions of the "stream of thought" as a highly individualized and constantly changing state of perception would influence the modernist stream of consciousness technique. Taking "thought" as his object of inquiry, James shows the centrality and the fluidity of the "personal mind" to the experience of consciousness. This representation of consciousness initiated a shift in the novel from the unifying vision of the cosmos offered by the Victorian omniscient narrator to that of either a first-person or a third-person indirect narrator chronicling a chaotic flow of thoughts. As James writes, "Neither contemporaneity, nor proximity in space, nor similarity of quality and content are able to fuse thoughts which are sundered by this barrier of belonging to different personal minds. The breaches between such thoughts are the most absolute breaches in nature" (226 (see p. 42 of this volume)). Representing these breaches and, perhaps, their moments of near-transcendence became a central concern for modernist novelists.

William James, "The Stream of Consciousness," *Writings 1878–1899*. New York: The Library of America, 1992. 152–73.

The order of our study must be analytic. We are now prepared to begin the introspective study of the adult consciousness itself. Most books adopt the so-called synthetic method. Starting with 'simple ideas of sensation,' and regarding these as so many atoms, they proceed to build up the higher states of mind out of their 'association,' 'integration,' or 'fusion,' as houses are built by the agglutination of bricks. This has the didactic advantages which the synthetic method usually has. But it commits one beforehand to the very questionable theory that our higher states of consciousness are compounds of units; and instead of starting with what the reader directly knows, namely his total concrete states of mind, it starts with a set of supposed 'simple ideas' with which he has no immediate acquaintance at all, and concerning whose alleged interactions he is much at the mercy of any plausible phrase. On every ground, then, the method of advancing from the simple to the compound exposes us to illusion. All pedants and abstractionists will naturally hate to abandon it. But a student who loves the fulness of human nature will prefer to follow the 'analytic' method, and to begin with the most concrete facts, those with which he has a daily acquaintance in his own inner life. The analytic method will discover in due time the elementary parts, if such exist, without danger of precipitate assumption. The reader will bear in mind that our own chapters on sensation have dealt mainly with the physiological conditions thereof. They were put first as a mere matter of convenience, because incoming currents come first. *Psychologically* they might better have come last. . . .

The Fundamental Fact.—The first and foremost concrete fact which everyone will affirm to belong to his inner experience is the fact that *consciousness of some sort goes on*. '*States of mind*' *succeed each other in him*. If we could say in English 'it thinks,' as we say 'it rains' or 'it blows,' we should be stating the fact most simply and with the minimum of assumption. As we cannot, we must simply say that *thought goes on*.

Four Characters in Consciousness.—How does it go on? We notice immediately four important characters in the process, of which it shall be the duty of the present chapter to treat in a general way:

1)   Every 'state' tends to be part of a personal consciousness.
2)   Within each personal consciousness states are always changing.
3)   Each personal consciousness is sensibly continuous.
4)   It is interested in some parts of its object to the exclusion of others, and welcomes or rejects—*chooses* from among them, in a word—all the while.

In considering these four points successively, we shall have to plunge *in medias res* as regards our nomenclature and use psychological terms which can only be adequately defined in later chapters of the book. But everyone knows what the terms mean in a rough way; and it is only in a rough way that we are now to take them. This chapter is like a painter's first charcoal sketch upon his canvas, in which no niceties appear.

When I say *every 'state'* or *'thought' is part of a personal consciousness*, 'personal consciousness' is one of the terms in question. Its meaning we know so long as no one asks us to define it, but to give an accurate account of it is the most difficult of philosophic tasks. This task we must confront in the next chapter; here a preliminary word will suffice.

In this room—this lecture-room, say—there are a multitude of thoughts, yours and mine, some of which cohere mutually, and some not. They are as little each-for-itself and reciprocally independent as they are all-belonging-together. They are neither: no one of them is separate, but each belongs with certain others and with none beside. My thought belongs with *my* other thoughts, and your thought with *your* other thoughts. Whether anywhere in the room there be a *mere* thought, which is nobody's thought, we have no means of ascertaining, for we have no experience of its like. The only states of consciousness that we naturally deal with are found in personal consciousnesses, minds, selves, concrete particular I's and you's.

Each of these minds keeps its own thoughts to itself. There is no giving or bartering between them. No thought even comes into direct *sight* of a thought in another personal consciousness than its own. Absolute insulation, irreducible pluralism, is the law. It seems as if the elementary psychic fact were not *thought* or *this thought* or *that thought*, but *my thought*, every thought being *owned*. Neither contemporaneity, nor proximity in space, nor similarity of quality and content are able to fuse thoughts together which are sundered by this barrier of belonging to different personal minds. The breaches between such thoughts are the most absolute breaches in nature. Everyone will recognize this to be true, so long as the existence of *something* corresponding to the term 'personal mind' is all that is insisted on, without any particular view of its nature being implied. On these terms the personal self rather than the thought might be treated as the immediate datum in psychology. The universal conscious fact is not 'feelings and thoughts exist,' but 'I think' and 'I feel.' No psychology, at any rate, can question the *existence* of personal selves. Thoughts connected as we feel them to be connected are *what we mean* by personal selves. The worst a psychology can do is so to interpret the nature of these selves as to rob them of their *worth*.

Consciousness is in constant change. I do not mean by this to say that no one state of mind has any duration—even if true, that would be hard to establish. What I wish to lay stress on is this, that *no state once gone can recur and be identical with what it was before*. Now we are seeing, now hearing; now reasoning, now willing; now recollecting, now expecting; now loving, now hating; and in a hundred other ways we know our minds to be alternately engaged. But all these are complex states, it may be said, produced by combination of simpler ones;— do not the simpler ones follow a different law? Are not the *sensations* which we get from the same object, for example, always the same? Does not the same piano-key, struck with the same force, make us hear in the same way? Does not the same grass give us the same feeling of green, the same sky the same feeling of blue, and do we not get the same olfactory sensation no matter how many times we put our nose to the same flask of cologne? It seems a piece of metaphysical sophistry to suggest that we do not; and yet a close attention to the matter shows that *there is no proof that an incoming current ever gives us just the same bodily sensation twice*.

What is got twice is the same OBJECT. We hear the same *note* over and over again; we see the same *quality* of green, or smell the same objective perfume, or experience the same *species* of pain. The realities, concrete and abstract, physical and ideal, whose permanent existence we believe in, seem to be constantly coming up again before our thought, and lead us, in our carelessness, to suppose that our 'ideas' of them are the same ideas. When we come, some time later, to the chapter on Perception, we shall see how inveterate is our habit of simply using our sensible impressions as stepping-stones to pass over to the recognition of the realities whose presence they reveal. The grass out of the window now looks to me of the same green in the sun as in the shade, and yet a painter would have to paint one part of it dark brown, another part bright yellow, to give its real sensational effect. We take no heed, as a rule, of the different way in which the same things look and sound and smell at different distances and under different circumstances. The sameness of the *things* is what we are concerned to ascertain; and any sensations that assure us of that will probably be considered in a rough way to be the same with each other. This is what makes off-hand testimony about the subjective identity of different sensations well-nigh worthless as a proof of the fact. The entire history of what is called Sensation is a commentary on our inability to tell whether two sensible qualities received apart are exactly alike. What appeals to our attention far more than the absolute quality of an impression is its *ratio* to whatever other impressions we may have at the same time. When everything is dark a somewhat less dark sensation makes us see an object white. Helmholtz calculates that the white marble painted in a picture representing an architectural view by moonlight is, when seen by daylight, from ten to twenty thousand times brighter than the real moonlit marble would be, yet the latter looks white.

Such a difference as this could never have been *sensibly* learned; it had to be inferred from a series of indirect considerations. These make us believe that our sensibility is altering all the time, so that the same object cannot easily give us the same sensation over again. We feel things differently accordingly as we are sleepy or awake, hungry or full, fresh or tired; differently at night and in the morning, differently in summer and in winter; and above all, differently in childhood, manhood, and old age. And yet we never doubt that our feelings reveal the same world, with the same sensible qualities and the same sensible things occupying it. The difference of the sensibility is shown best by the difference of our emotion about the things from one age to another, or when we are in different organic moods. What was bright and exciting becomes weary, flat, and unprofitable. The bird's song is tedious, the breeze is mournful, the sky is sad.

To these indirect presumptions that our sensations, following the mutations of our capacity for feeling, are always undergoing an essential change, must be added another presumption, based on what must happen in the brain. Every sensation corresponds to some cerebral action. For an identical sensation to recur it would have to occur the second time *in an unmodified brain*. But as this, strictly speaking, is a physiological impossibility, so is an unmodified feeling an impossibility; for to every brain-modification, however small, we suppose that there must correspond a change of equal amount in the consciousness which the brain subserves.

But if the assumption of 'simple sensations' recurring in immutable shape is so easily shown to be baseless, how much more baseless is the assumption of immutability in the larger masses of our thought!

For there it is obvious and palpable that our state of mind is never precisely the same. Every thought we have of a given fact is, strictly speaking, unique, and only bears a resemblance of kind with our other thoughts of the same fact. When the identical fact recurs, we *must* think of it in a fresh manner, see it under a somewhat different angle, apprehend it in different relations from those in which it last appeared. And the thought by which we cognize it is the thought of it-in-those-relations, a thought suffused with the consciousness of all that dim context. Often we are ourselves struck at the strange differences in our successive views of the same thing. We wonder how we ever could have opined as we did last month about a certain matter. We have outgrown the possibility of that state of mind, we know not how. From one year to another we see things in new lights. What was unreal has grown real, and what was exciting is insipid. The friends we used to care the world for are shrunken to shadows; the women once so divine, the stars, the woods, and the waters, how now so dull and common!—the young girls that brought an aura of infinity, at present hardly distinguishable existences; the pictures so empty; and as for the books, what *was* there to find so mysteriously significant in Goethe, or in John Mill so full of weight? Instead of all this, more zestful than ever is the work, the work; and fuller and deeper the import of common duties and of common goods.

I am sure that this concrete and total manner of regarding the mind's changes is the only true manner, difficult as it may be to carry it out in detail. If anything seems obscure about it, it will grow clearer as we advance. Meanwhile, if it be true, it is certainly also true that no two 'ideas' are ever exactly the same, which is the proposition we started to prove. The proposition is more important theoretically than it at first sight seems. For it makes it already impossible for us to follow obediently in the footprints of either the Lockian or the Herbartian school, schools which have had almost unlimited influence in Germany and among ourselves. No doubt it is often *convenient* to formulate the mental facts in an atomistic sort of way, and to treat the higher states of consciousness as if they were all built out of unchanging simple ideas which 'pass and turn again.' It is convenient often to treat curves as if they were composed of small straight lines, and electricity and nerve-force as if they were fluids. But in the one case as in the other we must never forget that we are talking symbolically, and that there is nothing in nature to answer to our words. *A permanently existing 'Idea' which makes its appearance before the footlights of consciousness at periodical intervals is as mythological an entity as the Jack of Spades.*

Within each personal consciousness, thought is sensibly continuous. I can only define 'continuous' as that which is without breach, crack, or division. The only breaches that can well be conceived to occur within the limits of a single mind would either be *interruptions*, *time*-gaps during which the consciousness went out; or they would be breaks in the content of the thought, so abrupt that what followed had no connection whatever with what went before. The proposition that consciousness feels continuous, means two things:

a.   That even where there is a time-gap the consciousness after it feels as if it belonged together with the consciousness before it, as another part of the same self;

b.   That the changes from one moment to another in the quality of the consciousness are never absolutely abrupt.

The case of the time-gaps, as the simplest, shall be taken first.

 a.   When Paul and Peter wake up in the same bed, and recognize that they have been asleep, each one of them mentally reaches back and makes connection with but *one* of the two streams of thought which were broken by the sleeping hours. As the current of an electrode buried in the ground unerringly finds its way to its own similarly buried mate, across no matter how much intervening earth; so Peter's present instantly finds out Peter's past, and never by mistake knits itself on to that of Paul. Paul's thought in turn is as little liable to go astray. The past thought of Peter is appropriated by the present Peter alone. He may have a *knowledge*, and a correct one too, of what Paul's last drowsy states of mind were as he sank into sleep, but it is an entirely different sort of knowledge from that which he has of his own last states. He *remembers* his own states, whilst he only *conceives* Paul's. Remembrance is like direct feeling; its object is suffused with a warmth and intimacy to which no object of mere conception ever attains. This quality of warmth and intimacy and immediacy is what Peter's *present* thought also possesses for itself. So sure as this present is me, is mine, it says, so sure is anything else that comes with the same warmth and intimacy and immediacy, me and mine. What the qualities called warmth and intimacy may in themselves be will have to be matter for future consideration. But whatever past states appear with those qualities must be admitted to receive the greeting of the present mental state, to be owned by it, and accepted as belonging together with it in a common self. This community of self is what the time-gap cannot break in twain, and is why a present thought, although not ignorant of the time-gap, can still regard itself as continuous with certain chosen portions of the past.

 Consciousness, then, does not appear to itself chopped up in bits. Such words as 'chain' or 'train' do not describe it fitly as it presents itself in the first instance. It is nothing jointed; it flows. A 'river' or a 'stream' are the metaphors by which it is most naturally described. *In talking of it hereafter, let us call it the stream of thought, of consciousness, or of subjective life.*

 b.   But now there appears, even within the limits of the same self, and between thoughts all of which alike have this same sense of belonging together, a kind of jointing and separateness among the parts, of which this statement seems to take no account. I refer to the breaks that are produced by sudden *contrasts in the quality* of the successive segments of the stream of thought. If the words 'chain' and 'train' had no natural fitness in them, how came such words to be used at all? Does not a loud explosion rend the consciousness upon which it abruptly breaks, in twain? No; for even into our awareness of the thunder the awareness of the previous silence creeps and continues; for what we hear when the thunder crashes is not thunder *pure*, but thunder-breaking-upon-silence-and-contrasting-with-it. Our feeling of the same objective thunder, coming in this way, is quite different from what it would be were the thunder a continuation of previous thunder. The thunder itself we believe to abolish and exclude the silence; but the *feeling* of the thunder is also a feeling of the silence as just gone; and it would be difficult to find in the actual concrete consciousness of man a feeling so limited to the present as not to have an inkling of anything that went before.

 'Substantive' and 'Transitive' States of Mind.—When we take a general view of the wonderful stream of our consciousness, what strikes us first is the different pace of its parts. Like a bird's life, it seems to be an alternation of flights and perchings. The rhythm of language expresses this, where every thought is expressed in a sentence, and every sentence closed by a period. The resting-places are usually occupied by sensorial imaginations of some sort, whose peculiarity is that they can be held before the mind for an indefinite time, and contemplated without changing; the places of flight are filled with thoughts of relations, static or dynamic, that for the most part obtain between the matters contemplated in the periods of comparative rest.

Let us call the resting-places the 'substantive parts,' and the places of flight the 'transitive parts,' of the stream of thought. It then appears that our thinking tends at all times towards some other substantive part than the one from which it has just been dislodged. And we may say that the main use of the transitive parts is to lead us from one substantive conclusion to another.

Now it is very difficult, introspectively, to see the transitive parts for what they really are. If they are but flights to a conclusion, stopping them to look at them before the conclusion is reached is really annihilating them. Whilst if we wait till the conclusion *be* reached, it so exceeds them in vigor and stability that it quite eclipses and swallows them up in its glare. Let anyone try to cut a thought across in the middle and get a look at its section, and he will see how difficult the introspective observation of the transitive tracts is. The rush of the thought is so headlong that it almost always brings us up at the conclusion before we can arrest it. Or if our purpose is nimble enough and we do arrest it, it ceases forthwith to be itself. As a snowflake caught in the warm hand is no longer a flake but a drop, so, instead of catching the feeling of relation moving to its term, we find we have caught some substantive thing, usually the last word we were pronouncing, statically taken, and with its function, tendency, and particular meaning in the sentence quite evaporated. The attempt at introspective analysis in these cases is in fact like seizing a spinning top to catch its motion, or trying to turn up the gas quickly enough to see how the darkness looks. And the challenge to *produce* these transitive states of consciousness, which is sure to be thrown by doubting psychologists at anyone who contends for their existence, is as unfair as Zeno's treatment of the advocates of motion, when, asking them to point out in what place an arrow *is* when it moves, he argues the falsity of their thesis from their inability to make to so preposterous a question an immediate reply.

The results of this introspective difficulty are baleful. If to hold fast and observe the transitive parts of thought's stream be so hard, then the great blunder to which all schools are liable must be the failure to register them, and the undue emphasizing of the more substantive parts of the stream. Now the blunder has historically worked in two ways. One set of thinkers have been led by it to *Sensationalism*. Unable to lay their hands on any substantive feelings corresponding to the innumerable relations and forms of connection between the sensible things of the world, finding no *named* mental states mirroring such relations, they have for the most part denied that any such states exist; and many of them, like Hume, have gone on to deny the reality of most relations *out* of the mind as well as in it. Simple substantive 'ideas,' sensations and their copies, juxtaposed like dominoes in a game, but really separate, everything else verbal illusion,—such is the upshot of this view. The *Intellectualists*, on the other hand, unable to give up the reality of relations *extra mentem*, but equally unable to point to any distinct substantive feelings in which they were known, have made the same admission that such feelings do not exist. But they have drawn an opposite conclusion. The relations must be known, they say, in something that is no feeling, no mental 'state,' continuous and consubstantial with the subjective tissue out of which sensations and other substantive conditions of consciousness are made. They must be known by something that lies on an entirely different plane, by an *actus purus* of Thought, Intellect, or Reason, all written with capitals and considered to mean something unutterably superior to any passing perishing fact of sensibility whatever.

But from our point of view both Intellectualists and Sensationalists are wrong. If there be such things as feelings at all, *then so surely as relations between objects exist* in rerum naturâ, *so surely, and more surely, do feelings exist to which these relations are known.* There is not a conjunction or a preposition, and hardly an adverbial phrase, syntactic form, or inflection of voice, in human speech, that does not express some shading or other of relation which we at some moment actually feel to exist between the larger objects of our thought. If we speak objectively, it is the real relations that appear revealed; if we speak subjectively, it is the stream of consciousness that matches each of them by an inward coloring of its own. In either case the relations are numberless, and no existing language is capable of doing justice to all their shades.

We ought to say a feeling of *and*, a feeling of *if*, a feeling of *but*, and a feeling of *by*, quite as readily as we say a feeling of *blue* or a feeling of *cold*. Yet we do not: so inveterate has our habit become of recognizing the existence of the substantive parts alone, that language almost refuses to lend itself to any other use. Consider once again the analogy of the brain. We believe the brain to be an organ whose internal equilibrium is always in a state of change—the change affecting every part. The pulses of change are doubtless more violent in one place than in another, their rhythm more rapid at this time than at that. As in a kaleidoscope revolving at a uniform rate, although the figures are always rearranging themselves, there are instants during which the transformation seems minute and interstitial and almost absent, followed by others when it shoots with magical rapidity, relatively stable forms thus alternating with forms we should not distinguish if seen again; so in the brain the perpetual rearrangement must result in some forms of tension lingering relatively long, whilst others simply come and pass. But if consciousness corresponds to the fact of rearrangement itself, why, if the rearrangement stop not, should the consciousness ever cease? And if a lingering rearrangement brings with it one kind of consciousness, why should not a swift rearrangement bring another kind of consciousness as peculiar as the rearrangement itself?

The object before the mind always has a 'Fringe.' There are other unnamed modifications of consciousness just as important as the transitive states, and just as cognitive as they. Examples will show what I mean.

Suppose three successive persons say to us: 'Wait!' 'Hark!' 'Look!' Our consciousness is thrown into three quite different attitudes of expectancy, although no definite object is before it in any one of the three cases. Probably no one will deny here the existence of a real conscious affection, a sense of the direction from which an impression is about to come, although no positive impression is yet there. Meanwhile we have no names for the psychoses in question but the names hark, look, and wait.

Suppose we try to recall a forgotten name. The state of our consciousness is peculiar. There is a gap therein; but no mere gap. It is a gap that is intensely active. A sort of wraith of the name is in it, beckoning us in a given direction, making us at moments tingle with the sense of our closeness, and then letting us sink back without the longed-for term. If wrong names are proposed to us, this singularly definite gap acts immediately so as to negate them. They do not fit into its mould. And the gap of one word does not feel like the gap of another, all empty of content as both might seem necessarily to be when described as gaps. When I vainly try to recall the name of Spalding, my consciousness is far removed from what it is when I vainly try to recall the name of Bowles. There are innumerable consciousnesses of *want*, no one of which taken in itself has a name, but all different from each other. Such a feeling of want is *toto cœlo* other than a want of feeling: it is an intense feeling. The rhythm of a lost word may be there without a sound to clothe it; or the evanescent sense of something which is the initial vowel or consonant may mock us fitfully, without growing more distinct. Everyone must know the tantalizing effect of the blank rhythm of some forgotten verse, restlessly dancing in one's mind, striving to be filled out with words.

What is that first instantaneous glimpse of someone's meaning which we have, when in vulgar phrase we say we 'twig' it? Surely an altogether specific affection of our mind. And has the reader never asked himself what kind of a mental fact is his *intention of saying a thing* before he has said it? It is an entirely definite intention, distinct from all other intentions, an absolutely distinct state of consciousness, therefore; and yet how much of it consists of definite sensorial images, either of words or of things? Hardly anything! Linger, and the words and things come into the mind; the anticipatory intention, the divination is there no more. But as the words that replace it arrive, it welcomes them successively and calls them right if they agree with it, it rejects them and calls them wrong if they do not. The intention *to-say-so-and-so* is the only name it can receive. One may admit that a good third of our psychic life consists in these rapid premonitory perspective views of schemes of thought not yet articulate. How comes it about that a man reading something aloud for the first time is able immediately to emphasize all his words aright, unless from the very first he have a sense of at least the form of the sentence yet to come, which sense is fused with his consciousness of the present word, and modifies its emphasis in his mind so as to make him give it the proper accent as he utters it? Emphasis of this kind almost altogether depends on grammatical construction. If we read 'no more,' we expect presently a 'than'; if we read 'however,' it is a 'yet,' a 'still,' or a 'nevertheless,' that we expect. And this foreboding of the coming verbal and grammatical scheme is so practically accurate that a reader incapable of understanding four ideas of the book he is reading aloud can nevertheless read it with the most delicately modulated expression of intelligence.

It is, the reader will see, the reinstatement of the vague and inarticulate to its proper place in our mental life which I am so anxious to press on the attention. Mr. Galton and Prof. Huxley have, as we shall see in the chapter on Imagination, made one step in advance in exploding the ridiculous theory of Hume and Berkeley that we can have no images but of perfectly definite things. Another is made if we overthrow the equally ridiculous notion that, whilst simple objective qualities are revealed to our knowledge in 'states of consciousness,' relations are not. But these reforms are not half sweeping and radical enough. What must be admitted is that the definite images of traditional psychology form but the very smallest part of our minds as they actually live. The traditional psychology talks like one who should say a river consists of nothing but pailsful, spoonsful, quartpotsful, barrelsful, and other moulded forms of water. Even were the pails and the pots all actually standing in the stream, still between them the free water would continue to flow. It is just this free water of consciousness that psychologists resolutely overlook. Every definite image in the mind is steeped and dyed in the free water that flows round it. With it goes the sense of its relations, near and remote, the dying echo of whence it came to us, the dawning sense of whither it is to lead. The significance, the value, of the image is all in this halo or penumbra that surrounds and escorts it,—or rather that is fused into one with it and has become bone of its bone and flesh of its flesh, leaving it, it is true, an image of the same *thing* it was before, but making it an image of that thing newly taken and freshly understood.

Let us call the consciousness of this halo of relations around the image by the name of 'psychic overtone' *or* 'fringe.'

Cerebral Conditions of the 'Fringe.'—Nothing is easier than to symbolize these facts in terms of brain-action. Just as the echo of the *whence*, the sense of the starting point of our thought, is probably due to the dying excitement of processes but a moment since vividly aroused; so the sense of the *whither*, the foretaste of the terminus, must be due to the waxing excitement of tracts or processes whose psychical correlative will a moment hence be the vividly present feature of our thought. Represented by a curve, the neurosis underlying consciousness must at any moment be like this:

Let the horizontal in Fig. 4.1 be the line of time, and let the three curves beginning at *a*, *b*, and *c* respectively stand for the neural processes correlated with the thoughts of those three letters. Each process occupies a certain time during which its intensity waxes, culminates, and wanes. The process for *a* has not yet died out, the process for *c* has already begun, when that for *b* is culminating. At the time-instant represented by the vertical line all three

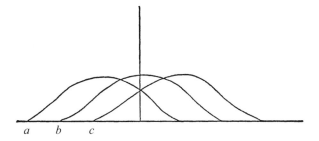

Figure 4.1

processes are *present,* in the intensities shown by the curve. Those before c's apex *were* more intense a moment ago; those after it *will be* more intense a moment hence. If I recite *a,b,c,* then, at the moment of uttering *b,* neither *a* nor *c* is out of my consciousness altogether, but both, after their respective fashions, 'mix their dim light' with the stronger *b,* because their processes are both awake in some degree.

It is just like 'overtones' in music: they are not separately heard by the ear; they blend with the fundamental note, and suffuse it, and alter it; and even so do the waxing and waning brain-processes at every moment blend with and suffuse and alter the psychic effect of the processes which are at their culminating point.

The 'Topic' of the Thought.—If we then consider the *cognitive function* of different states of mind, we may feel assured that the difference between those that are mere 'acquaintance' and those that are 'knowledges-*about*' is reducible almost entirely to the absence or presence of psychic fringes or overtones. Knowledge *about* a thing is knowledge of its relations. Acquaintance with it is limitation to the bare impression which it makes. Of most of its relations we are only aware in the penumbral nascent way of a 'fringe' of unarticulated affinities about it. And, before passing to the next topic in order, I must say a little of this sense of affinity, as itself one of the most interesting features of the subjective stream.

Thought may be equally rational in any sort of terms. *In all our voluntary thinking there is some* TOPIC *or* SUBJECT about which all the members of the thought revolve. Relation to this topic or interest is constantly felt in the fringe, and particularly the relation of harmony and discord, of furtherance or hindrance of the topic. Any thought the quality of whose fringe lets us feel ourselves 'all right,' may be considered a thought that furthers the topic. Provided we only feel its object to have a place in the scheme of relations in which the topic also lies, that is sufficient to make of it a relevant and appropriate portion of our train of ideas.

Now we may think about our topic mainly in words, or we may think about it mainly in visual or other images, but this need make no difference as regards the furtherance of our knowledge of the topic. If we only feel in the terms, whatever they be, a fringe of affinity with each other and with the topic, and if we are conscious of approaching a conclusion, we feel that our thought is rational and right. The words in every language have contracted by long association fringes of mutual repugnance or affinity with each other and with the conclusion, which run exactly parallel with like fringes in the visual, tactile and other ideas. The most important element of these fringes is, I repeat, the mere feeling of harmony or discord, of a right or wrong direction in the thought.

If we know English and French and begin a sentence in French, all the later words that come are French; we hardly ever drop into English. And this affinity of the French words for each other is not something merely operating mechanically as a brain-law, it is something we feel at the time. Our understanding of a French sentence heard never falls to so low an ebb that we are not aware that the words linguistically belong together. Our attention can hardly so wander that if an English word be suddenly introduced we shall not start at the change. Such a vague sense as this of the words belonging together is the very minimum of fringe that can accompany them, if 'thought' at all. Usually the vague perception that all the words we hear belong to the same language and to the same special vocabulary in that language, and that the grammatical sequence is familiar, is practically equivalent to an admission that what we hear is sense. But if an unusual foreign word be introduced, if the grammar trip, or if a term from an incongruous vocabulary suddenly appear, such as 'rat-trap' or 'plumber's bill' in a philosophical discourse, the sentence detonates as it were, we receive a shock from the incongruity, and the drowsy assent is gone. The feeling of rationality in these cases seems rather a negative than a positive thing, being the mere absence of shock, or sense of discord, between the terms of thought.

Conversely, if words do belong to the same vocabulary, and if the grammatical structure is correct, sentences with absolutely no meaning may be uttered in good faith and pass unchallenged. Discourses at prayer-meetings, reshuffling the same collection of cant phrases, and the whole genus of penny-a-line-isms and newspaper-reporter's flourishes give illustrations of this. "The birds filled the tree-tops with their morning song, making the air moist, cool, and pleasant," is a sentence I remember reading once in a report of some athletic exercises in Jerome Park. It was probably written unconsciously by the hurried reporter, and read uncritically by many readers.

We see, then, that it makes little or no difference in what sort of mind-stuff, in what quality of imagery, our thinking goes on. The only images *intrinsically* important are the halting-places, the substantive conclusions, provisional or final, of the thought. Throughout all the rest of the stream, the feelings of relation are everything, and the terms related almost naught. These feelings of relation, these psychic overtones, halos, suffusions, or fringes about the terms, may be the same in very different systems of imagery. A diagram may help to accentuate this indifference of the mental means where the end is the same. Let *A* be some experience from which a number of thinkers start. Let *Z* be the practical conclusion rationally inferrible from it. One gets to this conclusion by one line, another by another; one follows a course of English, another of German, verbal imagery. With one, visual images predominate; with another, tactile. Some trains are tinged with emotions, others not; some are very abridged, synthetic and rapid; others, hesitating and broken into many steps. But when the penultimate terms of all the trains, however differing *inter se*, finally shoot into the same conclusion, we say, and rightly say, that all the thinkers have had substantially the same thought. It would probably astound each of them beyond measure to be let into his neighbor's mind and to find how different the scenery there was from that in his own.

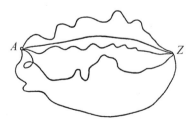

Figure 4.2

The last peculiarity to which attention is to be drawn in this first rough description of thought's stream is that—

Consciousness is always interested more in one part of its object than in another, and welcomes and rejects, or chooses, all the while it thinks.

The phenomena of selective attention and of deliberative will are of course patent examples of this choosing activity. But few of us are aware how incessantly it is at work in operations not ordinarily called by these names. Accentuation and Emphasis are present in every perception we have. We find it quite impossible to disperse our attention impartially over a number of impressions. A monotonous succession of sonorous strokes is broken up into rhythms, now of one sort, now of another, by the different accent which we place on different strokes. The simplest of these rhythms is the double one, tick-tóck, tick-tóck, tick-tóck. Dots dispersed on a surface are perceived in rows and groups. Lines separate into diverse figures. The ubiquity of the distinctions, *this* and *that*, *here* and *there*, *now* and *then*, in our minds is the result of our laying the same selective emphasis on parts of place and time.

But we do far more than emphasize things, and unite some, and keep others apart. We actually *ignore* most of the things before us. Let me briefly show how this goes on.

To begin at the bottom, what are our very senses themselves [...] but organs of selection? Out of the infinite chaos of movements, of which physics teaches us that the outer world consists, each sense-organ picks out those which fall within certain limits of velocity. To these it responds, but ignores the rest as completely as if they did not exist. Out of what is in itself an undistinguishable, swarming *continuum*, devoid of distinction or emphasis, our senses make for us, by attending to this motion and ignoring that, a world full of contrasts, of sharp accents, of abrupt changes, of picturesque light and shade.

If the sensations we receive from a given organ have their causes thus picked out for us by the conformation of the organ's termination, Attention, on the other hand, out of all the sensations yielded, picks out certain ones as worthy of its notice and suppresses all the rest. We notice only those sensations which are signs to us of *things* which happen practically or æsthetically to interest us, to which we therefore give substantive names, and which we exalt to this exclusive status of independence and dignity. But in itself, apart from my interest, a particular dust-wreath on a windy day is just as much of an individual *thing*, and just as much or as little deserves an individual name, as my own body does.

And then, among the sensations we get from each separate thing, what happens? The mind selects again. It chooses certain of the sensations to represent the thing most *truly*, and considers the rest as its appearances, modified by the conditions of the moment. Thus my table-top is named *square*, after but one of an infinite number of retinal sensations which it yields, the rest of them being sensations of two acute and two obtuse angles; but I call the latter *perspective* views, and the four right angles the *true* form of the table, and erect the attribute squareness into the table's essence, for æsthetic reasons of my own. In like manner, the real form of the circle is deemed to be the sensation it gives when the line of vision is perpendicular to its centre—all its other sensations are *signs* of this sensation. The real sound of the cannon is the sensation it makes when the ear is close by. The real color of the brick is the sensation it gives when the eye looks squarely at it from a near point, out of the sunshine and yet not in the gloom; under other circumstances it gives us other color-sensations which are but signs of this—we then see it looks pinker or bluer than it really is. The reader knows no object which he does not represent to himself by preference as in some typical attitude, of some normal size, at some characteristic distance, of some standard tint, etc., etc. But all these essential characteristics, which together form for us the genuine objectivity of the thing and are contrasted with what we call the subjective sensations it may yield us at a given moment, are mere sensations like the latter. The mind chooses to suit itself, and decides what particular sensation shall be held more real and valid than all the rest.

Next, in a world of objects thus individualized by our mind's selective industry, what is called our 'experience' is almost entirely determined by our habits of attention. A thing may be present to a man a hundred times, but if he persistently fails to notice it, it cannot be said to enter into his experience. We are all seeing flies, moths, and beetles by the thousand, but to whom, save an entomologist, do they say anything distinct? On the other hand, a thing met only once in a lifetime may leave an indelible experience in the memory. Let four men make a tour in Europe. One will bring home only picturesque impressions—costumes and colors, parks and views and works of architecture, pictures and statues. To another all this will be non-existent; and distances and prices, populations, and drainage-arrangements, door- and window-fastenings, and other useful statistics will take their place. A third will give a rich account of the theatres, restaurants, and public balls, and naught beside; whilst the fourth will perhaps have been so wrapped in his own subjective broodings as to be able to tell little more than a few names of places through which he passed. Each has selected, out of the same mass of presented objects, those which suited his private interest and has made his experience thereby.

If now, leaving the empirical combination of objects, we ask how the mind proceeds *rationally* to connect them, we find selection again to be omnipotent. In a future chapter we shall see that all Reasoning depends on the ability of the mind to break up the totality of the phenomenon reasoned about, into parts, and to pick out from among these the particular one which, in the given emergency, may lead to the proper conclusion. The man of genius is he who will always stick in his bill at the right point, and bring it out with the right element— 'reason' if the emergency be theoretical, 'means' if it be practical—transfixed upon it.

If now we pass to the æsthetic department, our law is still more obvious. The artist notoriously selects his items, rejecting all tones, colors, shapes, which do not harmonize with each other and with the main purpose of his work. That unity, harmony, 'convergence of characters,' as M. Taine calls it, which gives to works of art their superiority over works of nature, is wholly due to *elimination*. Any natural subject will do, if the artist has wit enough to pounce upon some one feature of it as characteristic, and suppress all merely accidental items which do not harmonize with this.

Ascending still higher, we reach the plane of Ethics, where choice reigns notoriously supreme. An act has no ethical quality whatever unless it be chosen out of several all equally possible. To sustain the arguments for the good course and keep them ever before us, to stifle our longing for more flowery ways, to keep the foot unflinchingly on the arduous path, these are characteristic ethical energies. But more than these; for these but deal with the means of compassing interests already felt by the man to be supreme. The ethical energy *par excellence* has to go farther and choose which *interest* out of several, equally coercive, shall become supreme. The issue here is of the utmost pregnancy, for it decides a man's entire career. When he debates, Shall I commit this crime? choose that profession? accept that office, or marry this fortune?—his choice really lies between one of several equally possible future Characters. What he shall *become* is fixed by the conduct of this moment. Schopenhauer, who enforces his determinism by the argument that with a given fixed character only one reaction is possible under given circumstances, forgets that, in these critical ethical moments, what consciously *seems* to be in question is the complexion of the character itself. The problem with the man is less what act he shall now resolve to do than what being he shall now choose to become.

Taking human experience in a general way, the choosings of different men are to a great extent the same. The race as a whole largely agrees as to what it shall notice and name; and among the noticed parts we select in much the same way for accentuation and preference, or subordination and dislike. There is, however, one entirely extraordinary case in which no two men ever are known to choose alike. One great splitting of the whole universe into two halves is made by each of us; and for each of us almost all of the interest attaches to one of the halves; but we all draw the line of division between them in a different place. When I say that we all call the two halves by the same names, and that those names are '*me*' and '*not-me*' respectively, it will at once be seen what I mean. The altogether unique kind of interest which each human mind feels in those parts of creation which it can call *me* or *mine* may be a moral riddle, but it is a fundamental psychological fact. No mind can take the same interest in his neighbor's *me* as in his own. The neighbor's me falls together with all the rest of things in one foreign mass against which his own *me* stands out in startling relief. Even the trodden worm, as Lotze somewhere says, contrasts his own suffering self with the whole remaining universe, though he have no clear conception either of himself or of what the universe may be. He is for me a mere part of the world; for him it is I who am the mere part. Each of us dichotomizes the Kosmos in a different place.

Chapter 5

Arthur Symons (1865–1945)

"INTRODUCTION," *THE SYMBOLIST MOVEMENT IN LITERATURE* (1899)

I N DEFINING THE FRENCH SYMBOLIST movement for an English-speaking audience, Symons helped shape English and American modernism. French symbolists such as Paul Verlaine, Stéphane Mallarmé, Auguste Villiers de l'Isle-Adam, and Maurice Maeterlinck used expressive objects in their work not as representations of reality but, rather, to point to some larger truth or ideal. The prevalence of symbols in modernist literature – Virginia Woolf's lighthouse, Ernest Hemingway's Mount Kilimanjaro, Katherine Mansfield's pear tree – show the influence of the symbolist movement in endowing representations with mystique, ambiguity, and spiritualism. Symons was not only an influential critic, but also a poet who contributed work to the *The Yellow Book*, an important publication in the development of the Aesthetic movement. While symbolism is interrelated with Aestheticism, Symons differentiates it from the Decadent movement, which he considers inartistic in its pursuit of shock value for its own sake. Symons was a close friend of W.B. Yeats and, as Yeats acknowledges in his own essay on symbolism (see Chapter 55 below), introduced him to the symbolist movement.

Arthur Symons, "Introduction," *The Symbolist Movement in Literature*. New York: Dutton, 1958. 1–5.

Introduction

> "It is in and through Symbols that man, consciously or unconsciously, lives, works, and has his being: those ages, moreover, are accounted the noblest which can the best recognise symbolical worth, and prize it highest."
>
> Carlyle

Without symbolism there can be no literature; indeed, not even language. What are words themselves but symbols, almost as arbitrary as the letters which compose them, mere sounds of the voice to which we have agreed to give certain significations, as we have agreed to translate these sounds by those combinations of letters? Symbolism began with the first words uttered by the first man, as he named every living thing; or before them, in heaven, when God named the world into being. And we see, in these beginnings, precisely what Symbolism in literature really is: a form of expression, at the best but approximate, essentially but arbitrary, until it has obtained the force of a convention, for an unseen reality apprehended by the consciousness. It is sometimes permitted to us to hope that our convention is indeed the reflection rather than merely the sign of that unseen reality. We have done much if we have found a recognisable sign.

"A symbol," says Comte Goblet d'Alviella, in his book on *The Migration of Symbols,* "might be defined as a representation which does not aim at being a reproduction." Originally, as he points out, used by the Greeks to denote "the two halves of the tablet they divided between themselves as a pledge of hospitality," it came to be used of every sign, formula, or rite by which those initiated in any mystery made themselves secretly known to one another. Gradually the word extended its meaning, until it came to denote every conventional representation of idea by form, of the unseen by the visible. "In a Symbol," says Carlyle, "there is concealment and yet revelation: hence therefore, by Silence and by Speech acting together, comes a double significance." And, in that fine chapter of *Sartor Resartus,* he goes further, vindicating for the word its full value: "In the Symbol proper, what we can call a Symbol, there is ever, more or less distinctly and directly, some embodiment and revelation of the Infinite; the Infinite is made to blend itself with the Finite, to stand visible, and as it were, attainable there."

It is in such a sense as this that the word Symbolism has been used to describe a movement which, during the last generation, has profoundly influenced the course of French literature. All such words, used of anything so living, variable, and irresponsible as literature, are, as symbols themselves must so often be, mere compromises, mere indications. Symbolism, as seen in the writers of our day, would have no value if it were not seen also, under one disguise or another, in every great imaginative writer. What distinguishes the Symbolism of our day from the Symbolism of the past is that it has now become conscious of itself, in a sense in which it was unconscious even in Gérard de Nerval, to whom I trace the particular origin of the literature which I call Symbolist. The forces which mould the thought of men change, or men's resistance to them slackens; with the change of men's thought comes a change of literature, alike in its inmost essence and in its outward form: after the world has starved its soul long enough in the contemplation and the re-arrangement of material things, comes the turn of the soul; and with it comes the literature of which I write in this volume, a literature in which the visible world is no longer a reality, and the unseen world no longer a dream.

The great epoch in French literature which preceded this epoch was that of the offshoot of Romanticism which produced Baudelaire, Flaubert, the Goncourts, Taine, Zola, Leconte de Lisle. Taine was the philosopher both of what had gone before him and of what came immediately after; so that he seems to explain at once Flaubert and Zola. It was the age of Science, the age of material things; and words, with that facile elasticity which there is in them, did miracles in the exact representation of everything that visibly existed, exactly as it existed. Even Baudelaire, in whom the spirit is always an uneasy guest at the orgy of life, had a certain theory of Realism which tortures many of his poems into strange, metallic shapes, and fills them with imitative odours, and disturbs them with a too deliberate rhetoric of the flesh. Flaubert, the one impeccable novelist who has ever lived, was resolute to be the novelist of a world in which art, formal art, was the only escape from the burden of reality, and in which the soul was of use mainly as the agent of fine literature. The Goncourts caught at Impressionism to render the fugitive aspects of a world which existed only as a thing of flat spaces, and angles, and coloured movement, in which sun and shadow were the artists; as moods, no less flitting, were the artists of the merely receptive consciousness of men and women. Zola has tried to build in brick and mortar inside the covers of a book; he is quite sure that the soul is a nervous fluid, which he is quite sure some man of science is about to catch for us, as a man of science has bottled the air; a pretty, blue liquid. Leconte de Lisle turned the world to stone, but saw, beyond the world, only a pause from misery in a Nirvana never subtilised to the Eastern ecstasy. And, with all these writers, form aimed above all things at being precise, at saying rather than suggesting, at saying what they had to say so completely that nothing remained over, which it might be the business of the reader to divine. And so they have expressed, finally, a certain aspect of the world; and some of them have carried style to a point beyond which the style that says, rather than suggests, cannot go. The whole of that movement comes to a splendid funeral in Heredia's sonnets, in which the literature of form says its last word, and dies.

Meanwhile, something which is vaguely called Decadence had come into being. That name, rarely used with any precise meaning, was usually either hurled as a reproach or hurled back as a defiance. It pleased some young men in various countries to call themselves Decadents, with all the thrill of unsatisfied virtue masquerading as uncomprehended vice. As a matter of fact, the term is in its place only when applied to style; to that ingenious deformation of the language, in Mallarmé, for instance, which can be compared with what we are accustomed to call the Greek and Latin of the Decadence. No doubt perversity of form and perversity of matter are often found together, and, among the lesser men especially, experiment was carried far, not only in the direction of style. But a movement which in this sense might be called Decadent could but have been a straying aside from the main road of literature. Nothing, not even conventional virtue, is so provincial as conventional vice; and the desire to "bewilder the middle classes" is itself middle-class. The interlude, half a mock-interlude, of Decadence, diverted the attention of the critics while something more serious was in preparation. That something more serious has crystallised, for the time, under the form of Symbolism, in which art returns to the one pathway, leading through beautiful things to the eternal beauty.

In most of the writers whom I have dealt with as summing up in themselves all that is best in Symbolism, it will be noticed that the form is very carefully elaborated, and seems to count for at least as much as in those writers of whose over-possession by form I have complained. Here, however, all this elaboration comes from a very different motive, and leads to other ends. There is such a thing as perfecting form that form may be annihilated. All the art of Verlaine is in bringing verse to a bird's song, the art of Mallarmé in bringing verse to the song of an orchestra. In Villiers de l'Isle-Adam drama becomes an embodiment of spiritual forces, in Maeterlinck not even their embodiment, but the remote sound of their voices. It is all an attempt to spiritualise literature, to evade the old bondage of rhetoric, the old bondage of exteriority. Description is banished that beautiful things may be evoked, magically; the regular beat of verse is broken in order that words may fly, upon subtler wings. Mystery is no longer feared, as the great mystery in whose midst we are islanded was feared by those to whom that unknown sea was only a great void. We are coming closer to nature, as we seem to shrink from it with something of horror, disdaining to catalogue the trees of the forest. And as we brush aside the accidents of daily life, in which men and women imagine that they are alone touching reality, we come closer to humanity, to everything in humanity that may have begun before the world and may outlast it.

Here, then, in this revolt against exteriority, against rhetoric, against a materialistic tradition; in this endeavour to disengage the ultimate essence, the soul, of whatever exists and can be realised by the consciousness; in this dutiful waiting upon every symbol by which the soul of things can be made visible; literature, bowed down by so many burdens, may at last attain liberty, and its authentic speech. In attaining this liberty, it accepts a heavier burden; for in speaking to us so intimately, so solemnly, as only religion had hitherto spoken to us, it becomes itself a kind of religion, with all the duties and responsibilities of the sacred ritual.

Chapter 6

Isadora Duncan (1877–1927)

THE DANCE OF THE FUTURE (1903)

U PENDING THE TRADITIONS OF CLASSICAL ballet, Duncan set out as an innovator and educator, creating a new style of modern dance that aimed to represent the
universal laws of nature as well as the individuality of the dancer. Duncan's techniques
sought to revolutionize not only dance, but also gender paradigms; in the three dance
schools that she founded in Germany, France, and post-revolutionary Russia, she trained
her students to embody the free spirit of the new woman through emphasizing natural,
relatively unconstricted movement. Her own life represented a shirking of conventionality
– as a young dancer in America, she rejected various schools and approaches before leaving
for Europe where she would live the rest of her life, taking on many lovers, giving birth to
two children who would die in a tragic car accident, and finally dying in another car accident when her scarf became caught in the vehicle. Drawing on a wide range of modernist
influences, Duncan's *Dance of the Future* cites evolutionary theory, primitivism, spiritualism, Schopenhauer's theory of the Will, and Greek art as influences on her dance.

Isadora Duncan, *The Dance of the Future*. New York: Forest Press, 1909. 11–21.

I am asked to speak upon the "Dance of the Future,"—yet how is it possible? In fifty years. I
may have something to say. Besides, I have always found it indiscreet for me to speak on my
dance. The people who are in sympathy with me understand what I am trying to do better
than myself; the people who are not in sympathy understand better than I why they are not.

A woman once asked me why I dance with bare feet and I replied, "Madam, I believe in
the religion of the beauty of the human foot"—and the lady replied, "But I do not," and I said,
"Yet you must, Madam, for the expression and intelligence of the human foot is one of
the greatest triumphs of the evolution of man." "But," said the lady, "I do not believe in the
evolution of man." At this said I, "My task is at an end. I refer you to my most revered
teachers, Mr. Charles Darwin and Mr. Ernest Haeckel"—"But," said the lady, "I do not
believe in Darwin and Haeckel"—. At this point I could think of nothing more to say. So you
see that, to convince people, I am of little value and ought not to speak.

But I am brought from the seclusion of my study trembling and stammering before a
public and told to lecture on the dance of the future.

If we seek the real source of the dance, if we go to nature, we find that the dance of the future is the dance of the past, the dance of eternity, and has been and will always be the same.

The movement of waves, of winds, of the earth is ever in the same lasting harmony. We do not stand on the beach and inquire of the ocean what was its movement of the past and what will be its movement in the future. We realize that the movement peculiar to its nature is eternal to its nature. The movement of the free animals and birds remains always in correspondence to their nature, the necessities and wants of that nature and its correspondence to the earth nature. It is only when you put free animals under false restrictions that they lose the power pf moving in harmony with nature and adopt a movement expressive of the restrictions placed about them. So it has been with civilized man. The movements of the savage, who lived in freedom, in constant touch with Nature, were unrestricted, natural and beautiful. Only the movements of the naked body can be perfectly natural. Man, arrived at the end of civilization, will have to return to nakedness, not to the unconscious nakedness of the savage, but to the conscious and acknowledged nakedness of the mature Man, whose, body will be the harmonious expression of his spiritual being.

And the movements of this Man will be natural and beautiful like those of the free animals.

The movement of the universe concentrating in an individual becomes what is termed the will; for example, the movement of the earth, being the concentration of surrounding forces, gives to the earth its individuality, its will of movement; as creatures of the earth receiving in turn these concentrating forces in their different relations, as transmitted to them through their ancestors and to those by the earth, in themselves evolve the movement of individuals which is termed the will.

The dance should simply be then the natural gravitation of this will of the individual, which in the end is no more nor less than a human translation of the gravitation of the universe.

—It is noticed that I speak in the terms and views of Schopenhauer. His terms are more convenient for what I intend to express.—

The school of the ballet of to-day vainly striving against the natural laws of gravitation or the natural will of the individual, and working in discord in its form and movement with the form and movement of nature, produces a sterile movement which gives no birth to future movements, but dies as it is made.

The expression of the modern school of ballet wherein each action is an end, and no movement, pose, or rhythm is successive or can be made to evolve succeeding action, is an expression of degeneration, of living death. All the movements of our modern ballet school are sterile movements because they are unnatural; their purpose is to create the delusion that the law of gravitation does not exist for them.

The primary or fundamental movements of the new school of the dance must have within them the seeds from which will evolve all other movements, each in turn to give birth to others in unending sequence of still higher and greater expressions, thoughts and ideas.

To those who nevertheless still enjoy the movements from historical or choreographic or whatever other reasons, to those I answer: They see no farther than the skirts and tights. But look—under the skirts, under the tights are dancing deformed muscles. —Look still farther—underneath the muscles are deformed bones: a deformed skeleton is dancing before you. This deformation through incorrect dress and incorrect movement is the result of the training necessary to the ballet.

The ballet condemns itself by enforcing the deformation of the beautiful woman's body! No historical, no choreographic reasons can prevail against that!

It is the mission of all art to express the highest and most beautiful ideals of man. What ideal does the ballet express?

No—the dance was once the most noble of all arts—and it shall be again. From the great depth to which it has fallen it shall be raised. The dancer of the future shall attain so great a height that all other arts shall be helped thereby.

To express what is the most moral, healthful and beautiful in art—this is the mission of the dancer, and to this I dedicate my life.

These flowers before me contain the dream of a dance; it could be named: "The light falling on white flowers." A dance that would be a subtle translation of the light and the whiteness—so pure, so strong, that people would say, "It is a soul we see moving, a soul that has reached the light and found the whiteness. We are glad it should move so." Through its human medium we have a satisfying sense of the movement of light and glad things. Through this human medium, the movement of all nature runs also through us, is transmitted to us from the dancer. We feel the movement of light intermingled with the thought of whiteness. It is a prayer, this dance, each movement reaches in long undulation to the heavens and becomes a part of the eternal rhythm of the spheres.

To find those primary movements for the human body from which shall evolve the movements of the future dance in ever varying natural, unending sequences, that is the duty of the new dancer of to-day.

To give an example of this, we might take the pose of the Hermes. He is represented as flying on the wind. If the artist had pleased to pose his foot in a vertical position he might have done so; as the god, flying on the wind, is not touching the earth; but realizing that no movement is true unless suggesting sequence of movements the sculptor placed the Hermes with the ball of his foot resting on the wind, giving the movement an eternal quality.

In the same way I might make examples of each pose and gesture in the thousands of figures we have left to us on the Greek vases and bas-reliefs; there is not one which in its movement does not presuppose another movement.

This is because the Greeks were the greatest students of the laws of nature, wherein all is the expression of unending, ever increasing evolution, wherein are no ends and no beginnings.

Such movements will always have to depend upon and correspond to the form that is moving. The movements of a beetle correspond to its form. So do those of the horse. Even so the movements of the human body must correspond to its form. They should even correspond to its individual form. The dance of no two persons should be alike.

People have thought that so long as one danced in rhythm, the form and design did not matter; but no—one must perfectly correspond to the other. The Greeks understood this very well.

There is a little dancing Cupid by Donatello. It is a child's dance. The movements of the plump little feet and arms are perfectly suited to its form. The sole of the foot rests flat on the ground, a position which might be ugly in a more developed person, but is natural in a child trying to keep its balance. One of the legs is half raised: if it were outstretched it would irritate us, because the movement would be unnatural.

The Greeks in all their painting, sculpture, architecture, literature, dance and tragedy evolved their movements from the movement of nature, as we plainly see expressed in all representations of the Greek gods, who, being no other than the representatives of natural forces, are always designed in a pose expressing the concentration and evolution of these forces. This is why the art of the Greeks is not a national or characteristic art, but has been and will be the art of all humanity for all time.

Therefore, dancing naked upon the earth, I naturally fall into Greek positions, for Greek positions are only earth positions.

The noblest in art is the nude. This truth is recognized by all, and followed by painters, sculptors and poets; only the dancer has forgotten it, who should most remember it, as the instrument of her art is the human body itself.

Man's first conception of beauty is gained from the form and symmetry of the human body. The new school of the dance should be that movement which is in harmony with, and which will develop, the highest form of the human body.

I intend to work for this dance of the future. I do not know whether I have the necessary qualities: I may have neither genius nor talent, nor temperament, but I know, that I have a Will; and will and energy are sometimes greater than either genius or talent or temperament.

Let me anticipate all that can be said against my qualification for my work in the following little fable:

The Gods looked down through the glass roof of my studio and Athena said: "She is not wise, she is not wise; in fact, she is remarkably stupid."

And Demeter looked and said: "She is a weakling small thing—not like my deep breasted daughters who play in the fields of Eleusis; one can see each rib; she is not worthy to dance on my broadswayed Earth." And Iris looked down and said: "See how heavily she moves— does she guess nothing of the swift and gracious movement of a winged being?" And Pan looked and said: "What! Does she think she knows aught of the movements of my satyrs, splendid twi-horned fellows who have within them all the fragrant life of the woods and waters?" And then Terpsichore gave one scornful glance: "And—she calls that dancing! Why, her feet move more like the lazy steps of a deranged turtle."

And all the Gods laughed; but I looked bravely up through the glass roof and said:

"O ye immortal Gods, who dwell in high Olympus and live on Ambrosia and Honey-Cakes and pay no studio rent nor bakers' bills thereof, do not judge me so scornfully. It is true, O Athena, that I am not wise, and my head is a rattled institution; but I do occasionally read a word of those who have gazed into the infinite blue of thine eyes and I bow my empty gourd head very humbly before thine altars. And, O Demeter of the Holy Garland," I continued, "it is true that the beautiful maidens of your broadswayed Earth would not admit me of their company; still I have thrown aside my sandals that my feet may touch your life-giving Earth more reverently and I have had your sacred Hymn sung before the present day Barbarians and I have made them to listen and to find it good.

"And, O Iris of the Golden Wings, it is true that mine is but a sluggish movement;—others of my profession have luted more violently against the laws of gravitation, from which laws, O glorious one, you are alone exempt. Yet the wind from your wings has swept through my poor earthy spirit, and I have often brought prayers to your courage-inspiring image.

"And, O Pan, you who were pitiful and gentle to simple Psyche in her wanderings, think more kindly of my little attempts to dance in your woody places.

"And you most exquisite one, Terpsichore, send to me a little comfort and strength that I may proclaim your power on Earth during my life; and afterwards, in the shadowy Hades my wistful spirit shall dance dances better yet in thine honour—."

Then came the voice of Zeus the thunderer: "Continue your way and rely upon the eternal justice of the immortal Gods: if you work well they shall know of it and be pleased thereof."

In this sense, then, I intend to work, and if I could find in my dance a few or even one single position that the sculptor could transfer into marble so that it might be preserved, my work would not have been in vain; this one form would be a gain; it would be a first step for the future.

This may seem a question of little importance, a question of differing opinions on the ballet and the new dance. But it is a great question. It is not only a question of true art, it is a question of race, of the development, of the female sex to beauty and health, of the return to the original strength and to natural movements of woman's body. It is a question of the development of perfect mothers and the birth of healthy and beautiful children. The dancing school of the future is to develop and to show the ideal form of woman. It will be, as it were, a museum of the living beauty of the period.

Travellers coming into a country and seeing the dancers should find in them that country's ideal of the beauty of form and movement. But strangers who to-day come to any country and there see the dancers of the ballet school would get a strange notion indeed of the ideal of beauty in this country. More than that dancing, like any art of any time, should reflect the highest point the spirit of mankind has reached in that special period. Does anybody think that the present-day ballet school expresses this?

Why are its positions in such a contrast to the beautiful positions of the antique sculptures which we preserve in our museums and which are constantly represented to us as perfect models of ideal beauty? Have our museums only been founded but of historical and archeological interest and not for the sake of the beauty of the objects which they contain?

The ideal of beauty of the human body cannot change with fashion, but only with evolution. Remember the story of the beautiful sculpture of a Roman girl which was found during the reign of Pope Innocent VIII, and which, by its beauty, created such a sensation that the men thronged to see it and made pilgrimages to it as to a holy shrine, so that the pope, troubled by the movement which it originated, finally had it buried again.

And here I want to avoid a misunderstanding that might easily arise. From what I have said you might conclude that my intention is to return to the dances of the old Greeks or that I think that the dance of the future will be a revival of the antique dances or even of those of the primitive tribes. No, the dance of the future will be a new movement, a consequence of the entire evolution which mankind has passed through. To return to the dances of the Greeks would be as impossible as it is unnecessary. We are not Greeks and cannot therefore dance Greek dances. But the dance of the future will have to become again a high religious art, as it was with the Greeks. For art which is not religious is not art; it is mere merchandise.

The dancer of the future will be one whose body and soul have grown so harmoniously together that the natural language of that soul will have become the movement of the body. The dancer will not belong to a nation but to all humanity. She will dance not in the form of nymph, nor fairy, nor coquette, but in the form of woman in its greatest and purest expression. She will realize the mission of woman's body and the holiness of all its parts. She will dance the changing life of nature, showing how each part is transformed into the other. From all parts of her body shall shine radiant intelligence, bringing to the world the message of the thoughts and aspirations of thousands of women. She shall dance the freedom of woman. Oh, what a field is here awaiting her! Do you not feel that she is near, that she is coming, this dancer of the future? She will help womankind to a new knowledge of the possible strength and beauty of their bodies and the relation of their bodies to the earth nature and to the children of the future. She will dance the body emerging again from centuries of civilized forgetfulness, emerging not in the nudity of primitive man, but in a new nakedness, no longer at war with spirituality and intelligence, but joining itself forever with his intelligence in a glorious harmony.

This is the mission of the dancer of the future. Oh, do you not feel that she is near, do you not long for her coming as I do? Let us prepare the place for her. I would build for her a temple to await her. Perhaps she is yet unborn; perhaps she is now a little child; perhaps—O blissful!—it may be my holy mission to guide her first steps, to watch the progress of her movements day by day until, far outgrowing my poor teaching, her movements will become godlike, mirroring in themselves the movement of growing things, the flight of birds, the passing of clouds and finally the thought of man in his relation to the universe.

Oh, she is coming, the dancer of the future: the free spirit, who will inhabit the body of new women; more glorious than any woman that has yet been; more beautiful than the Egyptian, than the Greek, the early Italian, than all women of past centuries—the highest intelligence in the freest body!

Chapter 7

Wyndham Lewis *et al.* (1882–1957)

BLAST: REVIEW OF THE GREAT ENGLISH VORTEX (1914)

A S A WRITER AND PAINTER, LEWIS was and is a polarizing figure for his outspoken, flamboyant antagonism to literary, artistic, and political establishments and for the right-wing political views that led him to write a book supporting Hitler (later recanted). Born in Canada and raised in England, Lewis achieved fame as the founder of vorticism, a visual arts movement so-labelled by Ezra Pound. The little magazine, *Blast*, edited by Lewis with Pound's help and running for only two issues in 1914–15, was the voice of vorticism. Representing a fusion of cubist form and futurist ideology, vorticism offered a home-grown English alternative to continental art movements. Notable for its typographic experimentalism, *Blast* published works by modernists including Ford Madox Ford and Rebecca West. In its last issue in 1915, *Blast* published the death notice for the young vorticist and war enthusiast, Henri Gaudier-Brzeska (see Chapter 29 below), and came to an end.

Lewis Wyndham, *et al.*, *Blast: Review of the Great English Vortex* (20 June 1914). 9–42.

Long Live the Vortex!

Long live the great art vortex sprung up in the centre of this town !

We stand for the Reality of the Present—not for the sentimental Future, or the sacripant Past.

We want to leave Nature and Men alone.

We do not want to make people wear Futurist Patches, or fuss men to take to pink and sky-blue trousers.

We are not their wives or tailors.

The only way Humanity can help artists is to remain independent and work unconsciously.

WE NEED THE UNCONSCIOUSNESS OF HUMANITY—their stupidity, animalism and dreams.

We believe in no perfectibility except our own.

Intrinsic beauty is in the Interpreter and Seer, not in the object or content.

We do not want to change the appearance of the world, because we are not Naturalists, Impressionists or Futurists (the latest form of Impressionism), and do not depend on the appearance of the world for our art.

WE ONLY WANT THE WORLD TO LIVE, and to feel it's crude energy flowing through us.

It may be said that great artists in England are always revolutionary, just as in France any really fine artist had a strong traditional vein.

Blast sets out to be an avenue for all those vivid and violent ideas that could reach the Public in no other way.

Blast will be popular, essentially. It will not appeal to any particular class, but to the fundamental and popular instincts in every class and description of people, TO THE INDIVIDUAL. The moment a man feels or realizes himself as an artist, he ceases to belong to any milieu or time. Blast is created for this timeless, fundamental Artist that exists in everybody.

The Man in the Street and the Gentleman are equally ignored.

Popular art does not mean the art of the poor people, as it is usually supposed to. It means the art of the individuals.

Education (art education and general education) tends to destroy the creative instinct. Therefore it is in times when education has been non-existant that art chiefly flourished.

But it is nothing to do with " the People."

It is a mere accident that that is the most favourable time for the individual to appear.

To make the rich of the community shed their education skin, to destroy politeness, standardization and academic, that is civilized, vision, is the task we have set ourselves,

We want to make in England not a popular art, not a revival of lost folk art, or a romantic fostering of such unactual conditions, but to make individuals, wherever found.

We will convert the King if possible.

A VORTICIST KING! WHY NOT?

DO YOU THINK LLOYD GEORGE HAS THE VORTEX IN HIM?

MAY WE HOPE FOR ART FROM LADY MOND?

We are against the glorification of " the People," as we are against snobbery. It is not necessary to be an outcast bohemian, to be unkempt or poor, any more than it is necessary to be rich or handsome, to be an artist. Art is nothing to do with the coat you wear. A top-hat can well hold the Sixtine. A cheap cap could hide the image of Kephren.

AUTOMOBILISM (Marinetteism) bores us. We don't want to go about making a hullo-bulloo about motor cars, anymore than about knives and forks, elephants or gas-pipes.

Elephants are VERY BIG. Motor cars go quickly.

Wilde gushed twenty years ago about the beauty of machinery. Gissing, in his romantic delight with modern lodging houses was futurist in this sense.

The futurist is a sensational and sentimental mixture of the aesthete of 1890 and the realist of 1870.

The " Poor " are detestable animals ! They are only picturesque and amusing for the sentimentalist or the romantic ! The " Rich " are bores without a single exception, *en tant que riches !*
We want those simple and great people found everywhere.

Blast presents an art of Individuals.

MANIFESTO.

BLAST First (from politeness) **ENGLAND**

CURSE ITS CLIMATE FOR ITS SINS AND INFECTIONS

DISMAL SYMBOL, SET round our bodies, of effeminate lout within.

VICTORIAN VAMPIRE, the LONDON cloud sucks the TOWN'S heart.

A 1000 MILE LONG, 2 KILOMETER Deep

BODY OF WATER even, is pushed against us

from the Floridas, TO MAKE US MILD.

OFFICIOUS MOUNTAINS keep back DRASTIC WINDS

SO MUCH VAST MACHINERY TO PRODUCE

THE CURATE of "Eltham"
BRITANNIC ÆSTHETE
WILD NATURE CRANK
DOMESTICATED
                    POLICEMAN
LONDON COLISEUM
  SOCIALIST-PLAYWRIGHT
DALY'S MUSICAL COMEDY
GAIETY CHORUS GIRL
TONKS

CURSE

the flabby sky that can manufacture no snow, but can only drop the sea on us in a drizzle like a poem by Mr. Robert Bridges.

CURSE

the lazy air that cannot stiffen the back of the SERPENTINE, or put Aquatic steel half way down the MANCHESTER CANAL.

But ten years ago we saw distinctly both snow and ice here.

May some vulgarly inventive, but useful person, arise, and restore to us the necessary BLIZZARDS.

LET US ONCE MORE WEAR THE ERMINE OF THE NORTH.

WE BELIEVE IN THE EXISTENCE OF THIS USEFUL LITTLE CHEMIST IN OUR MIDST!

2

OH BLAST FRANCE

pig plagiarism
BELLY
SLIPPERS
POODLE TEMPER
BAD MUSIC

SENTIMENTAL GALLIC GUSH
SENSATIONALISM
FUSSINESS.

PARISIAN PAROCHIALISM. Complacent young man,
so much respect for Papa
and his son !—Oh !—Papa
is wonderful : but all papas
are !

BLAST

APERITIFS (Pernots, Amers picon)
Bad change
Naively seductive Houri salon-
picture Cocottes
Slouching blue porters (can
carry a pantechnicon)
Stupidly rapacious people at
every step
Economy maniacs
Bouillon Kub (for being a bad
pun)

PARIS. Clap-trap Heaven of amative German professor.

Ubiquitous lines of silly little trees.

Arcs de Triomphe.

Imperturbable, endless prettiness.

Large empty cliques, higher up.

Bad air for the individual.

BLAST

MECCA OF THE AMERICAN

because it is not other side of Suez Canal, instead of an afternoon's ride from London.

CURSE 3

WITH EXPLETIVE OF WHIRLWIND

THE BRITANNIC ÆSTHETE

CREAM OF THE SNOBBISH EARTH

**ROSE OF SHARON OF GOD-PRIG
OF SIMIAN VANITY**

**SNEAK AND SWOT OF THE SCHOOL-
ROOM**

IMBERB (or Berbed when in Belsize)-**PEDANT**

> PRACTICAL JOKER
> DANDY
> CURATE

BLAST all products of phlegmatic cold
Life of **LOOKER-ON.**

CURSE

SNOBBERY
(disease of femininity)
FEAR OF RIDICULE
(arch vice of inactive, sleepy)
PLAY
STYLISM
SINS AND PLAGUES
of this **LYMPHATIC** finished
(we admit in every sense
finished)
VEGETABLE HUMANITY.

BLAST

THE SPECIALIST
" PROFESSIONAL "
" GOOD WORKMAN "
" GROVE-MAN "
ONE ORGAN MAN

BLAST THE

AMATEUR
SCIOLAST
ART-PIMP
JOURNALIST
SELF MAN
NO-ORGAN MAN

5

BLAST HUMOUR

Quack ENGLISH drug for stupidity and sleepiness.
Arch enemy of REAL, conventionalizing like

gunshot, freezing supple
REAL in ferocious chemistry
of laughter.

BLAST SPORT

HUMOUR'S FIRST COUSIN AND ACCOMPLICE.

Impossibility for Englishman to be
grave and keep his end up,
psychologically.

Impossible for him to use Humour
as well and be persistently
grave.

Alas! necessity for big doll's show
in front of mouth.

Visitation of Heaven on
English Miss

gums, canines of FIXED GRIN
Death's Head symbol of Anti-Life.

CURSE those who will hang over this
Manifesto with SILLY CANINES exposed.

6

BLAST

years **1837** to **1900**

Curse abysmal inexcusable middle-class
(also Aristocracy and Proletariat).

BLAST

pasty shadow cast by gigantic **Boehm**
(imagined at introduction of **BOURGEOIS VICTORIAN VISTAS**).

WRING THE NECK OF all sick inventions born in that progressive white wake.

BLAST their weeping whiskers—hirsute
RHETORIC of EUNUCH and STYLIST—
SENTIMENTAL HYGIENICS
ROUSSEAUISMS (wild Nature cranks
FRATERNIZING WITH MONKEYS
DIABOLICS—raptures and roses
of the erotic bookshelves
culminating in
PURGATORY OF PUTNEY.

CHAOS OF ENOCH ARDENS

laughing Jennys
Ladies with Pains
good-for-nothing Guineveres.

SNOBBISH BORROVIAN running after
GIPSY KINGS and ESPADAS

bowing the knee to
wild Mother Nature,
her feminine contours,
Unimaginative insult to
MAN.

DAMN

all those to-day who have taken on that Rotten Menagerie,
and still crack their whips and tumble in Piccadilly Circus,
as though London were a provincial town.

WE WHISPER IN YOUR EAR A GREAT SECRET.

LONDON IS NOT A PROVINCIAL TOWN.

We will allow Wonder Zoos. But we do not want the
GLOOMY VICTORIAN CIRCUS in
Piccadilly Circus.

IT IS PICCADILLY'S CIRCUS !

NOT MEANT FOR MENAGERIES trundling out of Sixties **DICKENSIAN CLOWNS, CORELLI LADY RIDERS, TROUPS OF PERFORMING GIPSIES** (who complain besides that 1/6 a night does not pay fare back to Clapham).

BLAST

The Post Office   Frank Brangwyn   Robertson Nicol

Rev. Pennyfeather   Galloway Kyle
(Bells)   (Cluster of Grapes)

Bishop of London and all his posterity

Galsworthy   Dean Inge   Croce   Matthews

Rev Meyer   Seymour Hicks

Lionel Cust   C. B. Fry   Bergson   Abdul Bahaï

Hawtrey   Edward Elgar   Sardlea

Filson Young   Marie Corelli   Geddes

Codliver Oil   St. Loe Strachey   Lyceum Club

Rhabindraneth Tagore   Lord Glenconner of Glen

Weiniger   Norman Angel   Ad. Mahon

Mr. and Mrs. Dearmer   Beecham   Ella

A. C. Benson   (Pills, Opera, Thomas)   Sydney Webb

British Academy   Messrs. Chapell

Countess of Warwick   George Edwards

Willie Ferraro   Captain Cook   R. J. Campbell

Clan Thesiger   Martin Harvey   William Archer

George Grossmith   R. H. Benson

Annie Besant   Chenil   Clan Meynell

Father Vaughan   Joseph Holbrooke   Clan Strachey

1

BLESS ENGLAND !

BLESS ENGLAND

FOR ITS SHIPS

which switchback on **Blue, Green and Red SEAS** all around the **PINK EARTH-BALL,**

BIG BETS ON EACH.

BLESS ALL SEAFARERS.

THEY exchange not one **LAND** for another, but one **ELEMENT** for **ANOTHER.** The **MORE** against the **LESS ABSTRACT.**

BLESS the vast planetary abstraction of the **OCEAN.**

BLESS THE ARABS OF THE **ATLANTIC.**

THIS ISLAND MUST BE CONTRASTED WITH THE BLEAK WAVES.

BLESS ALL PORTS.

PORTS, RESTLESS MACHINES of

- scooped out basins
- heavy insect dredgers
- monotonous cranes
- stations
- lighthouses, blazing through the frosty starlight, cutting the storm like a cake
- beaks of infant boats, side by side,
- heavy chaos of wharves,
- steep walls of factories
- womanly town

BLESS these **MACHINES** that work the little boats across clean liquid space, in beelines.

BLESS the great **PORTS**

- HULL
- LIVERPOOL
- LONDON
- NEWCASTLE-ON-TYNE
- BRISTOL
- GLASGOW

BLESS ENGLAND,

Industrial island machine, pyramidal

workshop, its apex at Shetland, discharging itself on the sea.

BLESS | cold
| magnanimous
| delicate
| gauche
| fanciful
| stupid

ENGLISHMEN.

BLESS the HAIRDRESSER.

He attacks Mother Nature for a small fee.

Hourly he ploughs heads for sixpence,

Scours chins and lips for threepence.

He makes systematic mercenary war on this
WILDNESS.

He trims aimless and retrograde growths
into CLEAN ARCHED SHAPES and
ANGULAR PLOTS.

BLESS this HESSIAN (or SILESIAN) EXPERT

correcting the grotesque anachronisms
of our physique.

BLESS ENGLISH HUMOUR

It is the great barbarous weapon of
the genius among races.
The wild **MOUNTAIN RAILWAY** from **IDEA**
to **IDEA,** in the ancient Fair of **LIFE.**

BLESS SWIFT for his solemn bleak
wisdom of laughter.

SHAKESPEARE for his bitter Northern
Rhetoric of humour.

BLESS ALL ENGLISH EYES
that grow crows-feet with their
FANCY and **ENERGY.**

BLESS this hysterical **WALL** built round
the **EGO.**

BLESS the solitude of **LAUGHTER.**

BLESS the separating, ungregarious
BRITISH GRIN.

4

BLESS FRANCE

for its **BUSHELS** of **VITALITY**

to the square inch.

HOME OF MANNERS (the Best, the **WORST** and interesting mixtures).

MASTERLY PORNOGRAPHY (great enemy of progress).

COMBATIVENESS

GREAT HUMAN SCEPTICS

DEPTHS OF ELEGANCE

FEMALE QUALITIES

FEMALES

BALLADS of its **PREHISTORIC APACHE**

Superb hardness and hardiesse of its

Voyou type, rebellious adolescent.

Modesty and humanity of many there.

GREAT FLOOD OF LIFE pouring out

of wound of **1797.**

Also bitterer stream from **1870.**

STAYING POWER, like a cat.

BLESS

Bridget   Berrwolf   Bearline   Cranmer Byng
Frieder Graham   The Pope   Maria de Tomaso
Captain Kemp   Munroe   Gaby   Jenkins
R. B. Cuningham Grahame   Barker
(not his brother)   (John and Granville)
Mrs. Wil Finnimore   Madame Strindberg   Carson
Salvation Army   Lord Howard de Walden
Capt. Craig   Charlotte Corday   Cromwell
Mrs. Duval   Mary Robertson   Lillie Lenton
Frank Rutter   Castor Oil   James Joyce
Leveridge   Lydia Yavorska   Preb. Carlyle   Jenny
Mon. le compte de Gabulis   Smithers   Dick Burge
33 Church Street   Sievier   Gertie Millar
Norman Wallis   Miss Fowler   Sir Joseph Lyons
Martin Wolff   Watt   Mrs. Hepburn
Alfree   Tommy   Captain Kendell   Young Ahearn
Wilfred Walter   Kate Lechmere   Henry Newbolt
Lady Aberconway   Frank Harris   Hamel
Gilbert Canaan   Sir James Mathew Barry
Mrs. Belloc Lowdnes   W. L. George   Rayner
George Robey   George Mozart   Harry Weldon
Chaliapine   George Hirst   Graham White
Hucks   Salmet   Shirley Kellogg   Bandsman Rice
Petty Officer Curran   Applegarth   Konody
Colin Bell   Lewis Hind   LEFRANC
Hubert   Commercial Process Co.

Newcastle.   Edward Wadsworth.

MANIFESTO.

I.

1. Beyond Action and Reaction we would establish ourselves.

2. We start from opposite statements of a chosen world. Set up violent structure of adolescent clearness between two extremes.

3. We discharge ourselves on both sides.

4. We fight first on one side, then on the other, but always for the SAME cause, which is neither side or both sides and ours.

5. Mercenaries were always the best troops.

6. We are Primitive Mercenaries in the Modern World.

7 Our <u>Cause</u> is NO-MAN'S.

8 We set Humour at Humour's throat.
Stir up Civil War among peaceful apes.

9 We only want Humour if it has fought like Tragedy.

10 We only want Tragedy if it can clench its side-muscles like hands on it's belly, and bring to the surface a laugh like a bomb.

II.

1. We hear from America and the Continent all sorts of disagreeable things about England: " the unmusical, anti-artistic, unphilosophic country."

2. We quite agree.

3. Luxury, sport, the famous English "Humour," the thrilling ascendancy and idée fixe of Class, producing the most intense snobbery in the World; heavy stagnant pools of Saxon blood, incapable of anything but the song of a frog, in home-counties :—these phenomena give England a peculiar distinction in the wrong sense, among the nations.

4. This is why England produces such good artists from time to time.

5. This is also the reason why a movement towards art and imagination could burst up here, from this lump of compressed life, with more force than anywhere else.

6   To believe that it is necessary for or conducive to art, to "improve" life, for instance—make architecture, dress, ornament, in "better taste," is absurd.

7   The Art-instinct is permanently primitive.

8   In a chaos of imperfection, discord, etc., it finds the same stimulus as in Nature.

9   The artist of the modern movement is a savage (in no sense an "advanced," perfected, democratic, Futurist individual of Mr. Marinetti's limited imagination): this enormous, jangling, journalistic, fairy desert of modern life serves him as Nature did more technically primitive man.

10   As the steppes and the rigours of the Russian winter, when the peasant has to lie for weeks in his hut, produces that extraordinary acuity of feeling and intelligence we associate with the Slav; so England is just now the most favourable country for the appearance of a great art.

III.

1 We have made it quite clear that there is nothing Chauvinistic or picturesquely patriotic about our contentions.

2 But there is violent boredom with that feeble Europeanism, abasement of the miserable "intellectual" before anything coming from Paris, Cosmopolitan sentimentality, which prevails in so many quarters.

3 Just as we believe that an Art must be organic with its Time,

So we insist that what is actual and vital for the South, is ineffectual and unactual in the North.

4 Fairies have disappeared from Ireland (despite foolish attempts to revive them) and the bull-ring languishes in Spain.

5 But mysticism on the one hand, gladiatorial instincts, blood and asceticism on the other,

will be always actual, and springs of Creation for these two peoples.

6 | The English Character is based on the Sea.

7 | The particular qualities and characteristics that the sea always engenders in men are those that are, among the many diagnostics of our race, the most fundamentally English.

8 | That unexpected universality as well, found in the completest English artists, is due to this.

IV.

1 We assert that the art for these climates, then, must be a northern flower.

2 And we have implied what we believe should be the specific nature of the art destined to grow up in this country, and models of whose flue decorate the pages of this magazine.

3 It is not a question of the characterless material climate around us.

Were that so the complication of the Jungle, dramatic Tropic growth, the vastness of American trees, would not be for us.

4 But our industries, and the Will that determined, face to face with its needs, the direction of the modern world, has reared up steel trees where the green ones were lacking ; has exploded in useful growths, and found wilder intricacies than those of Nature.

V.

1. We bring clearly forward the following points, before further defining the character of this necessary native art.

2. At the freest and most vigorous period of ENGLAND'S history, her literature, then chief Art, was in many ways identical with that of France.

3. Chaucer was very much cousin of Villon as an artist.

4. Shakespeare and Montaigne formed one literature.

5. But Shakespeare reflected in his imagination a mysticism, madness and delicacy peculiar to the North, and brought equal quantities of Comic and Tragic together.

6. Humour is a phenomenon caused by sudden pouring of culture into Barbary.

7 It is intelligence electrified by flood of Naivety.

8 It Is Chaos invading Concept and bursting it like nitrogen.

9 It is the Individual masquerading as Humanity like a child in clothes too big for him.

10 Tragic Humour is the birthright of the North.

11 Any great Northern Art will partake of this insidious and volcanic chaos.

12 No great ENGLISH Art need be ashamed to share some glory with France, to-morrow it may be with Germany, where the Elizabethans did before it.

13 But it will never be French, any more than Shakespeare was, the most catholic and subtle Englishman.

1. The Modern World is due almost entirely to Anglo-Saxon genius,—its appearance and its spirit.

2. Machinery, trains, steam-ships, all that distinguishes externally our time, came far more from here than anywhere else.

3. In dress, manners, mechanical inventions, LIFE, that is, ENGLAND, has influenced Europe in the same way that France has in Art.

4. But busy with this LIFE-EFFORT, she has been the last to become conscious of the Art that is an organism of this new Order and Will of Man.

5. Machinery is the greatest Earth-medium: incidentally it sweeps away the doctrines of a narrow and pedantic Realism at one stroke.

6. By mechanical inventiveness, too, just as Englishmen have spread themselves all over the

Earth, they have brought all the hemispheres about them in their original island.

7 It cannot be said that the complication of the Jungle, dramatic tropic growths, the vastness of American trees, is not for us.

8 For, in the forms of machinery, Factories, new and vaster buildings, bridges and works, we have all that, naturally, around us.

VII.

1. Once this consciousness towards the new possibilities of expression in present life has come, however, it will be more the legitimate property of Englishmen than of any other people in Europe.

2. It should also, as it is by origin theirs, inspire them more forcibly and directly.

3. They are the inventors of this bareness and hardness, and should be the great enemies of Romance.

4. The Romance peoples will always be, at bottom, its defenders.

5. The Latins are at present, for instance, in their "discovery" of sport, their Futuristic gush over machines, aeroplanes, etc., the most romantic and sentimental "moderns" to be found.

6. It is only the second-rate people in France or Italy who are thorough revolutionaries.

7 In England, on the other hand, there is n
vulgarity in revolt.

8 Or, rather, there is no revolt, it is the norma
state.

9 So often rebels of the North and the South ar
diametrically opposed species.

10 The nearest thing in England to a great traditiona
French artist, is a great revolutionary Englis
one.

Signatures for Manifesto

R. Aldington

Arbuthnot

L. Atkinson

Gaudier Brzeska

J. Dismorr

C. Hamilton

E. Pound

W. Roberts

H. Sanders

E. Wadsworth

Wyndham Lewis

Langston Hughes (1902–67)

"THE NEGRO ARTIST AND THE RACIAL MOUNTAIN" (1926)

HUGHES began writing poetry in elementary school and published his first "jazz poem" while in high school. "The Negro Artist and the Great Racial Mountain," Hughes's manifesto for a popular, urban black people's art, was published when he was just twenty-four years old. Hughes's work was disparaged by his intellectual and bourgeois Harlem Renaissance contemporaries, who felt that his stories, plays, and poems celebrated the "lowlife." Hughes's accessible, direct and rhythmic poems unashamedly celebrated everyday experiences – the hardships and delights – of workers, neighbors, recognizable and familiar regular folk; his beloved character Jesse B. Semple/Simple represented the wit and wisdom of the black everyman. Hughes claimed Carl Sandburg, Paul Laurence Dunbar, and Walt Whitman as influences; his own poetry inspired the international circle of African and Caribbean poets who modeled their Négritude poetry after Hughes's embrace of black expressive cultures and all facets of the black experience. Hughes was a foreign correspondent for the *Baltimore Afro-American* and other newspapers during the Spanish Civil War; he also wrote operas and juvenile literature, like *Popo and Fifinia* (1932; with Arna Bontemps) and *The Sweet Flypaper of Life* (1955), a children's story illustrated with photographs by the Harlem photographer Roy DeCarava. Some of his best-known poetry collections include *The Weary Blues* (1926), *Fine Clothes to the Jew* (1927), and *Scottsboro Limited: Five Poems and a Play* (1932).

Langston Hughes, "The Negro Artist and the Racial Mountain," *The Nation* (1926)

One of the most promising of the young Negro poets said to me once, "I want to be a poet—not a Negro poet," meaning, I believe, "I want to write like a white poet"; meaning subconsciously, "I would like to be a white poet"; meaning behind that, "I would like to be white." And I was sorry the young man said that, for no great poet has ever been afraid of being himself. And I doubted then that, with his desire to run away spiritually from his race, this boy would ever be a great poet. But this is the mountain standing in the way of any true Negro art in America—this urge within the race toward whiteness, the desire to pour racial individuality into the mold of American standardization, and to be as little Negro and as much American as possible.

But let us look at the immediate background of this young poet. His family is of what I suppose one would call the Negro middle class: people who are by no means rich yet never uncomfortable nor hungry—smug, contented, respectable folk, members of the Baptist church. The father goes to work every morning. He is a chief steward at a large white club. The mother sometimes does fancy sewing or supervises parties for the rich families of the town. The children go to a mixed school. In the home they read white papers and magazines. And the mother often says "Don't be like niggers" when the children are bad. A frequent phrase from the father is, "Look how well a white man does things." And so the word white comes to be unconsciously a symbol of all virtues. It holds for the children beauty, morality, and money. The whisper of "I want to be white" runs silently through their minds. This young poet's home is, I believe, a fairly typical home of the colored middle class. One sees immediately how difficult it would be for an artist born in such a home to interest himself in interpreting the beauty of his own people. He is never taught to see that beauty. He is taught rather not to see it, or if he does, to be ashamed of it when it is not according to Caucasian patterns.

For racial culture the home of a self-styled "high-class" Negro has nothing better to offer. Instead there will perhaps be more aping of things white than in a less cultured or less wealthy home. The father is perhaps a doctor, lawyer, landowner, or politician. The mother may be a social worker, or a teacher, or she may do nothing and have a maid. Father is often dark but he has usually married the lightest woman he could find. The family attend a fashionable church where few really colored faces are to be found. And they themselves draw a color line. In the North they go to white theaters and white movies. And in the South they have at least two cars and house "like white folks." Nordic manners, Nordic faces, Nordic hair, Nordic art (if any), and an Episcopal heaven. A very high mountain indeed for the would-be racial artist to climb in order to discover himself and his people.

But then there are the low-down folks, the so-called common element, and they are the majority—may the Lord be praised! The people who have their hip of gin on Saturday nights and are not too important to themselves or the community, or too well fed, or too learned to watch the lazy world go round. They live on Seventh Street in Washington or State Street in Chicago and they do not particularly care whether they are like white folks or anybody else. Their joy runs, bang! into ecstasy. Their religion soars to a shout. Work maybe a little today, rest a little tomorrow. Play awhile. Sing awhile. O, let's dance! These common people are not afraid of spirituals, as for a long time their more intellectual brethren were, and jazz is their child. They furnish a wealth of colorful, distinctive material for any artist because they still hold their own individuality in the face of American standardizations. And perhaps these common people will give to the world its truly great Negro artist, the one who is not afraid to be himself. Whereas the better-class Negro would tell the artist what to do, the people at least let him alone when he does appear. And they are not ashamed of him—if they know he exists at all. And they accept what beauty is their own without question.

Certainly there is, for the American Negro artist who can escape the restrictions the more advanced among his own group would put upon him, a great field of unused material ready for his art. Without going outside his race, and even among the better classes with their "white" culture and conscious American manners, but still Negro enough to be different, there is sufficient matter to furnish a black artist with a lifetime of creative work. And when he chooses to touch on the relations between Negroes and whites in this country, with their innumerable overtones and undertones surely, and especially for literature and the drama, there is an inexhaustible supply of themes at hand. To these the Negro artist can give his racial individuality, his heritage of rhythm and warmth, and his incongruous humor that so often, as in the Blues, becomes ironic laughter mixed with tears. But let us look again at the mountain.

A prominent Negro clubwoman in Philadelphia paid eleven dollars to hear Raquel Meller sing Andalusian popular songs. But she told me a few weeks before she would not think of going to hear "that woman," Clara Smith, a great black artist, sing Negro folksongs. And many an upper-class Negro church, even now, would not dream of employing a spiritual in its services. The drab melodies in white folks' hymnbooks are much to be preferred. "We want to worship the Lord correctly and quietly. We don't believe in 'shouting.' Let's be dull like the Nordics," they say, in effect.

The road for the serious black artist, then, who would produce a racial art is most certainly rocky and the mountain is high. Until recently he received almost no encouragement for his work from either white or colored people. The fine novels of Chesnutt go out of print with neither race noticing their passing. The quaint charm and humor of Dunbar's dialect verse brought to him, in his day, largely the same kind of encouragement one would give a sideshow freak (A colored man writing poetry! How odd!) or a clown (How amusing!).

The present vogue in things Negro, although it may do as much harm as good for the budding artist, has at least done this: it has brought him forcibly to the attention of his own people among whom for so long, unless the other race had noticed him beforehand, he was a prophet with little honor.

The Negro artist works against an undertow of sharp criticism and misunderstanding from his own group and unintentional bribes from the whites. "Oh, be respectable, write about nice people, show how good we are," say the Negroes. "Be stereotyped, don't go too far, don't shatter our illusions about you, don't amuse us too seriously. We will pay you," say the whites. Both would have told Jean Toomer not to write Cane. The colored people did not praise it. The white people did not buy it. Most of the colored people who did read Cane hate it. They are afraid of it. Although the critics gave it good reviews the public remained indifferent. Yet (excepting the work of Du Bois) Cane contains the finest prose written by a Negro in America. And like the singing of Robeson, it is truly racial.

But in spite of the Nordicized Negro intelligentsia and the desires of some white editors we have an honest American Negro literature already with us. Now I await the rise of the Negro theater. Our folk music, having achieved world-wide fame, offers itself to the genius of the great individual American composer who is to come. And within the next decade I expect to see the work of a growing school of colored artists who paint and model the beauty of dark faces and create with new technique the expressions of their own soul-world. And the Negro dancers who will dance like flame and the singers who will continue to carry our songs to all who listen—they will be with us in even greater numbers tomorrow.

Most of my own poems are racial in theme and treatment, derived from the life I know. In many of them I try to grasp and hold some of the meanings and rhythms of jazz. I am as sincere as I know how to be in these poems and yet after every reading I answer questions like these from my own people: Do you think Negroes should always write about Negroes? I wish you wouldn't read some of your poems to white folks. How do you find anything interesting in a place like a cabaret? Why do you write about black people? You aren't black. What makes you do so many jazz poems?

But jazz to me is one of the inherent expressions of Negro life in America; the eternal tom-tom beating in the Negro soul—the tom-tom of revolt against weariness in a white world, a world of subway trains, and work, work, work; the tom-tom of joy and laughter, and pain swallowed in a smile. Yet the Philadelphia clubwoman is ashamed to say that her race created it and she does not like me to write about it, The old subconscious "white is best" runs through her mind. Years of study under white teachers, a lifetime of white books, pictures, and papers, and white manners, morals, and Puritan standards made her dislike the spirituals. And now she turns up her nose at jazz and all its manifestations—likewise almost everything else distinctly racial. She doesn't care for the Winold Reiss' portraits of Negroes because they are "too Negro." She does not want a true picture of herself from anybody. She wants the artist to flatter her, to make the white world believe that all negroes are as smug and as near white in soul as she wants to be. But, to my mind, it is the duty of the younger Negro artist, if he accepts any duties at all from outsiders, to change through the force of his art that old whispering "I want to be white," hidden in the aspirations of his people, to "Why should I want to be white? I am a Negro—and beautiful"?

So I am ashamed for the black poet who says, "I want to be a poet, not a Negro poet," as though his own racial world were not as interesting as any other world. I am ashamed, too, for the colored artist who runs from the painting of Negro faces to the painting of sunsets after the manner of the academicians because he fears the strange unwhiteness of his own features. An artist must be free to choose what he does, certainly, but he must also never be afraid to do what he must choose.

Let the blare of Negro jazz bands and the bellowing voice of Bessie Smith singing the Blues penetrate the closed ears of the colored near intellectuals until they listen and perhaps understand. Let Paul Robeson singing "Water Boy," and Rudolph Fisher writing about the streets of Harlem, and Jean Toomer holding the heart of Georgia in his hands, and Aaron Douglas's drawing strange black fantasies cause the smug Negro middle class to turn from their white, respectable, ordinary books and papers to catch a glimmer of their own beauty. We younger Negro artists who create now intend to express our individual dark-skinned selves without fear or shame. If white people are pleased we are glad. If they are not, it doesn't matter. We know we are beautiful. And ugly too. The tom-tom cries and the tom-tom laughs. If colored people are pleased we are glad. If they are not, their displeasure doesn't matter either. We build our temples for tomorrow, strong as we know how, and we stand on top of the mountain, free within ourselves.

Chapter 9

Gertrude Stein (1874–1946)

"COMPOSITION AS EXPLANATION" (1926)

GERTRUDE STEIN was an American-born writer, salon hostess, and art collector who lived most of her life as an expatriate in France. She collected the extraordinary art of many of her contemporaries who were on the verge of great acclaim: Renoir, Cézanne, Matisse, Picasso, among others. Her major work includes *Three Lives* (1909; independent stories of three women set in the same fictional town); *Tender Buttons* (1914; poetry); *The Making of Americans: Being a History of a Family's Progress* (1925; modernist novel focused on a single family); and *The Autobiography of Alice B. Toklas* (1933; a novel thinly disguised as a memoir). Despite her playful and radical use of language, Stein was a political conservative who opposed Roosevelt and the New Deal and supported Hitler (at least during his early years in power), Franco during the Spanish Civil War, and the French Vichy leader Pétain. As exemplified by "Composition as Explanation," Stein's writings, of which it was commonly said that they were far more concerned with sound than sense ("A rose is a rose is a rose"; "There is no there there"), were among the most experimental of the modernists, a version of stream of consciousness that was so extreme that it seemed to many a kind of "automatic writing," though she viewed it, rather, as an "excess of consciousness." While it's difficult to summarize this piece, it contemplates that differences "from one time to another [depend on] what is seen," that composition occurs in what she calls "the continuous present," and that "nothing changes except composition."

Gertrude Stein, "Composition as Explanation," *What Are Masterpieces*? Los Angeles: The Conference Press, 1940. 25–38. Originally delivered by the author as a lecture at Cambridge and Oxford, this essay was first published by the Hogarth Press in London in 1926.

There is singularly nothing that makes a difference a difference in beginning and in the middle and in ending except that each generation has something different at which they are all looking. By this I mean so simply that anybody knows it that composition is the difference which makes each and all of them then different from other generations and this is what makes everything different otherwise they are all alike and everybody knows it because everybody says it.

It is very likely that nearly every one has been very nearly certain that something that is interesting is interesting them. Can they and do they. It is very interesting that nothing inside in them, that is when you consider the very long history of how every one ever acted or has felt, it is very interesting that nothing inside in them in all of them makes it connectedly different. By this I mean this. The only thing that is different from one time to another is what is seen and what is seen depends upon how everybody is doing everything. This makes the thing we are looking at very different and this makes what those who describe it make of it, it makes a composition, it confuses, it shows, it is, it looks, it likes it as it is, and this makes what is seen as it is seen. Nothing changes from generation to generation except the thing seen and that makes a composition. Lord Grey remarked that when the generals before the war talked about the war they talked about it as a nineteenth century war although to be fought with twentieth century weapons. That is because war is a thing that decides how it is to be when it is to be done. It is prepared and to that degree it is like all academies it is not a thing made by being made it is a thing prepared. Writing and painting and all that, is like that, for those who occupy themselves with it and don't make it as it is made. Now the few who make it as it is made, and it is to be remarked that the most decided of them usually are prepared just as the world around them is preparing, do it in this way and so I if you do not mind I will tell you how it happens. Naturally one does not know how it happened until it is well over beginning happening.

To come back to the part that the only thing that is different is what is seen when it seems to be being seen, in other words, composition and time-sense.

No one is ahead of his time, it is only that the particular variety of creating his time is the one that his contemporaries who also are creating their own time refuse to accept. And they refuse to accept it for a very simple reason and that is that they do not have to accept it for any reason. They themselves that is everybody in their entering the modern composition and they do enter it, if they do not enter it they are not so to speak in it they are out of it and so they do enter it; but in as you may say the non-competitive efforts where if you are not in it nothing is lost except nothing at all except what is not had, there are naturally all the refusals, and the things refused are only important if unexpectedly somebody happens to need them. In the case of the arts it is very definite. Those who are creating the modern composition authentically are naturally only of importance when they are dead because by that time the modern composition having become past is classified and the description of it is classical. That is the reason why the creator of the new composition in the arts is an outlaw until he is a classic, there is hardly a moment in between and it is really too bad very much too bad naturally for the creator but also very much too bad for the enjoyer, they all really would enjoy the created so much better just after it has been made than when it is already a classic, but it is perfectly simple that there is no reason why the contemporaries should see, because it would not make any difference as they lead their lives in the new composition anyway, and as every one is naturally indolent why naturally they don't see. For this reason as in quoting Lord Grey it is quite certain that nations not actively threatened are at least several generations behind themselves militarily so aesthetically they are more than several generations behind themselves and it is very much too bad, it is so very much more exciting and satisfactory for everybody if one can have contemporaries, if all one's contemporaries could be one's contemporaries.

There is almost not an interval. For a very long time everybody refuses and then almost without a pause almost everybody accepts. In the history of the refused in the arts and literature the rapidity of the change is always startling. Now the only difficulty with the *volte-face* concerning the arts is this. When the acceptance comes, by that acceptance the thing created becomes a classic. It is a natural phenomena a rather extraordinary natural phenomena that a thing accepted becomes a classic. And what is the characteristic quality of a classic. The characteristic quality of a classic is that it is beautiful. Now of course it is perfectly true that a more or less first rate work of art is beautiful but the trouble is that when that first rate work of art becomes a classic because it is accepted the only thing that is important from then on to the majority of the acceptors the enormous majority, the most intelligent majority of the acceptors is that it is so wonderfully beautiful. Of course it is wonderfully beautiful, only when it is still a thing irritating annoying stimulating then all quality of beauty is denied to it.

Of course it is beautiful but first all beauty in it is denied and then all the beauty of it is accepted. If every one were not so indolent they would realise that beauty is beauty even when it is irritating and stimulating not only when it is accepted and classic. Of course it is extremely difficult nothing more so than to remember back to its not being beautiful once it has become beautiful. This makes it so much more difficult to realise its beauty when the work is being refused and prevents every one from realising that they were convinced that beauty was denied, once the work is accepted. Automatically with the acceptance of the time-sense comes the recognition of the beauty and once the beauty is accepted the beauty never fails any one.

Beginning again and again is a natural thing even when there is a series. Beginning again and again and again explaining composition and time is a natural thing.

It is understood by this time that everything is the same except composition and time, composition and the time of the composition and the time in the composition.

Everything is the same except composition and as the composition is different and always going to be different everything is not the same. Everything is not the same as the time when of the composition and the time in the composition is different. The composition is different, that is certain.

The composition is the thing seen by every one living in the living they are doing, they are the composing of the composition that at the time they are living in the composition of the time in which they are living. It is that that makes living a thing they are doing. Nothing else is different, of that almost any one can be certain. The time when and the time of and the time in that composition is the natural phenomena of that composition and of that perhaps every one can be certain.

No one thinks these things when they are making when they are creating what is the composition, naturally no one thinks, that is no one formulates until what is to be formulated has been made.

Composition is not there, it is going to be there and we are here. This is some time ago for us naturally.

The only thing that is different from one time to another is what is seen and what is seen depends upon how everybody is doing everything. This makes the thing we are looking at very different and this makes what those who describe it make of it, it makes a composition, it confuses, it shows, it is, it looks, it likes it as it is, and this makes what is seen as it is seen. Nothing changes from generation to generation except the thing seen and that makes a composition.

Now the few who make writing as it is made and it is to be remarked that the most decided of them are those that are prepared by preparing, are prepared just as the world around them is prepared and is preparing to do it in this way and so if you do not mind I will again tell you how it happens. Naturally one does not know how it happened until it is well over beginning happening.

Each period of living differs from any other period of living not in the way life is but in the way life is conducted and that authentically speaking is composition. After life has been conducted in a certain way everybody knows it but nobody knows it, little by little, nobody knows it as long as nobody knows it. Any one creating the composition in the arts does not know it either, they are conducting life and that makes their composition what it is, it makes their work compose as it does.

Their influence and their influences are the same as that of all of their contemporaries only it must always be remembered that the analogy is not obvious until as I say the composition of a time has become so pronounced that it is past and the artistic composition of it is a classic.

And now to begin as if to begin. Composition is not there, it is going to be there and we are here. This is some time ago for us naturally. There is something to be added afterwards.

Just how much my work is known to you I do not know. I feel that perhaps it would be just as well to tell the whole of it.

In beginning writing I wrote a book called *Three Lives* this was written in 1905. 1 wrote a negro story called Melanctha. In that there was a constant recurring and beginning there was a marked direction in the direction of being in the present although naturally I had been accustomed to past present and future, and why, because the composition forming around me was a prolonged present. A composition of a prolonged present is a natural composition in the world as it has been these thirty years it was more and more a prolonged present. I created then a prolonged present naturally I knew nothing of a continuous present but it came naturally to me to make one, it was simple it was clear to me and nobody knew why it was done like that I did not myself although naturally to me it was natural.

After that I did a book called *The Making of Americans* it is a long book about a thousand pages.

Here again it was all so natural to me and more and more complicatedly a continuous present. A continuous present is a continuous present. I made almost a thousand pages of a continuous present.

Continuous present is one thing and beginning again and again is another thing. These are both things. And then there is using everything.

This brings us again to composition this the using everything. The using everything brings us to composition and to this composition. A continuous present and using everything and beginning again. In these two books there was elaboration of the complexities of using everything and of a continuous present and of beginning again and again and again.

In the first book there was a groping for a continuous present and for using everything by beginning again and again.

There was a groping for using everything and there was a groping for a continuous present and there was an inevitable beginning of beginning again and again and again.

Having naturally done this I naturally was a little troubled with it when I read it. I became then like the others who read it. One does, you know, excepting that when I reread it myself I lost myself in it again. Then I said to myself this time it will be different and I began. I did not begin again I just began.

In this beginning naturally since I at once went on and on very soon there were pages and pages and pages more and more elaborated creating a more and more continuous present including more and more using of everything and continuing more and more beginning and beginning and beginning.

I went on and on to a thousand pages of it.

In the meantime to naturally begin I commenced making portraits of anybody and anything. In making these portraits I naturally made a continuous present an including everything and a beginning again and again within a very small thing. That started me into composing anything into one thing. So then naturally it was natural that one thing an enormously long thing was not everything an enormously short thing was also not everything nor was it all of it a continuous present thing nor was it always and always beginning again. Naturally I would then begin again. I would begin again I would naturally begin. I did naturally begin. This brings me to a great deal that has been begun.

And after that what changes what changes after that, after that what changes and what changes after that and after that and what changes and after that and what changes after that.

The problem from this time on became more definite. It was all so nearly alike it must be different and it is different, it is natural that if everything is used and there is a continuous present and a beginning again and again if it is all so alike it must be simply different and everything simply different was the natural way of creating it then.

In this natural way of creating it then that it was simply different everything being alike it was simply different, this kept on leading one to lists. Lists naturally for a while and by lists I mean a series. More and more in going back over what was done at this time I find that I naturally kept simply different as an intention. Whether there was or whether there was not a continuous present did not then any longer trouble me there was or there was not, and using everything no longer troubled me if everything is alike using everything could no longer trouble me and beginning again and again could no longer trouble me because if lists were inevitable if series were inevitable and the whole of it was inevitable beginning again and again could not trouble me so then with nothing to trouble me I very completely began naturally since everything is alike making it as simply different naturally as simply different as possible. I began doing natural phenomena what I call natural phenomena and natural phenomena naturally everything being alike natural phenomena are making things be naturally simply different. This found its culmination later, in the beginning it began in a center confused with lists with series with geography with returning portraits and with particularly often four and three and often with five and four. It is easy to see that in the beginning such a conception as everything being naturally different would be very inarticulate and very slowly it began to emerge and take form of anything, and then naturally if anything that is simply different is simply different what follows will follow.

So far then the progress of my conceptions was the natural progress entirely in accordance with my epoch as I am sure is to be quite easily realised if you think over the scene that was before us all from year to year.

As I said in the beginning, there is the long history of how every one ever acted or has felt and that nothing inside in them in all of them makes it connectedly different. By this I mean all this.

The only thing that is different from one time to another is what is seen and what is seen depends upon how everybody is doing everything.

It is understood by this time that everything is the same except composition and time, composition and the time of the composition and the time in the composition.

Everything is the same except composition and as the composition is different and always going to be different everything is not the same. So then I as a contemporary creating the composition in the beginning was groping toward a continuous present, a using everything a beginning again and again and then everything being alike then everything very simply everything was naturally simply different and so I as a contemporary was creating everything being alike was creating everything naturally being naturally simply different, everything being alike. This then was the period that brings me to the period of the beginning of 1914. Everything being alike everything naturally would be simply different and war came and everything being alike and everything being simply different brings everything being simply different brings it to romanticism.

Romanticism is then when everything being alike everything is naturally simply different, and romanticism.

Then for four years this was more and more different even though this was, was everything alike. Everything alike naturally everything was simply different and this is and was romanticism and this is and was war. Everything being alike everything naturally everything is different simply different naturally simply different.

And so there was the natural phenomena that was war, which had been, before war came, several generations behind the contemporary composition, because it became war and so completely needed to be contemporary became completely contemporary and so created the completed recognition of the contemporary composition. Every one but one may say every one became consciously became aware of the existence of the authenticity of the modern composition. This then the contemporary recognition, because of the academic thing known as war having been forced to become contemporary made every one not only contemporary in act not only contemporary in thought but contemporary in self-consciousness made every one contemporary with the modem composition. And so the art creation of the contemporary composition which would have been outlawed normally outlawed several generations more behind even than war, war having been brought so to speak up to date art so to speak was allowed not completely to be up to date, but nearly up to date, in other words we who created the expression of the modem composition were to be recognized before we were dead some of us even quite a long time before we were dead. And so war may be said to have advanced a general recognition of the expression of the contemporary composition by almost thirty years.

And now after that there is no more of that in other words there is peace and something comes then and it follows coming then.

And so now one finds oneself interesting oneself in an equilibration, that of course means words as well as things and distribution as well as between themselves between the words and themselves and the things and themselves, a distribution as distribution. This makes what follows what follows and now there is every reason why there should be an arrangement made. Distribution is interesting and equilibration is interesting when a continuous present and a beginning again and again and using everything and everything alike and everything naturally simply different has been done.

After all this, there is that, there has been that that there, is a composition and that nothing changes except composition the composition and the time of and the time in the composition.

The time of the composition is a natural thing and the time in the composition is a natural thing it is a natural thing and it is a contemporary thing.

The time of the composition is the time of the composition. It has been at times a present thing it has been at times a past thing it has been at times a future thing it has been at times an endeavour at parts or all of these things. In my beginning it was a continuous present a beginning again and again and again and again, it was a series it was a list it was a similarity and everything different it was a distribution and an equilibration. That is all of the time some of the time of the composition.

Now there is still something else the time-sense in the composition. This is what is always a fear a doubt and a judgement and a conviction. The quality in the creation of expression the quality in a composition that makes it go dead just after it has been made is very troublesome.

The time in the composition is a thing that is very troublesome. If the time in the composition is very troublesome it is because there must even if there is no time at all in the composition there must be time in the composition which is in its quality of distribution and equilibration. In the beginning there was the time in the composition that naturally was in the composition but time in the composition comes now and this is what is now troubling every one the time in the composition is now a part of distribution and equilibration. In the beginning there was confusion there was a continuous present and later there was romanticism which was not a confusion but an extrication and now there is either succeeding or failing there must be distribution and equilibration there must be time that is distributed and equilibrated. This is the thing that is at present the most troubling and if there is the time that is at present the most troublesome the time-sense that is at present the most troubling is the thing that makes the present the most troubling. There is at present there is distribution, by this I mean expression and time, and in this way at present composition is time that is the reason that at present the time-sense is troubling that is the reason why at present the time-sense in the composition is the composition that is making what there is in composition.

And afterwards. Now that is all.

Chapter 10

Sergei Eisenstein (1898–1948)

"THE CINEMATOGRAPHIC PRINCIPLE AND THE IDEOGRAM" (1929)

EISENSTEIN WAS THE SON OF an architect and himself a student of architecture and civil engineering. His technological interests were enriched by his passions for Renaissance art, philosophy, avant-garde theatre and cinema, expressionism, Japanese visual and performing arts, and Marxist and formalist theories. The filmmaker's theatrical roots influenced his vision of cinema as a revolutionary and transformational art; in the 1920s, he served as assistant stage director and, eventually, co-director of Moscow's Theatre of the People (*Proletkult Theatre*), which embraced folk and popular "low" cultural expressions. Eisenstein's vision of kinetic filmmaking was inspired by Vsevolod Meyerhold's biomechanical acting, a style influenced by Ivan Pavlov's experiments on conditioned reflexes; for example, Eisenstein's notion of "metric montage" aligned film editing to the tempo of the body's heart beat. His best-known films, *Strike* (1924), *The Battleship Potemkin* (1925), and *October: Ten Days that Shook the World* (1927), aestheticized agitation with the goal of communally awakening the audience. He was eventually spurned by the Soviet Union's Communist Party and the Hollywood film industry for his works' theoretical formalism.

Sergei Eisenstein, "The Cinematographic Principle and the Ideogram," *Film Form: Essays in Film Theory*. Trans. Jay Leyda. San Diego, New York, and London: Harcourt, 1977. 28–44.

It is a weird and wonderful feat to have written a pamphlet on something that in reality does not exist. There is, for example, no such thing as a cinema without cinematography. And yet the author of the pamphlet preceding this essay[1] has contrived to write a book about the *cinema* of a country that has no *cinematography*. About the cinema of a country that has, in its culture, an infinite number of cinematographic traits, strewn everywhere with the sole exception of—its cinema.

This essay is on the cinematographic traits of Japanese culture that lie outside the Japanese cinema, and is itself as apart from the preceding pamphlet as these traits are apart from the Japanese cinema.

Cinema is: so many corporations, such and such turnovers of capital, so and so many stars, such and such dramas.

Cinematography is, first and foremost, montage.

The Japanese cinema is excellently equipped with corporations, actors, and stories. But the Japanese cinema is completely unaware of montage. Nevertheless the principle of montage can be identified as the basic element of Japanese representational culture.

Writing—for their writing is primarily representational.

The hieroglyph.

The naturalistic image of an object, as portrayed by the skilful Chinese hand of Ts'ang Chieh 2650 years before our era, becomes slightly formalized and, with its 539 fellows, forms the first "contingent" of hieroglyphs. Scratched out with a stylus on a slip of bamboo, the portrait of an object maintained a resemblance to its original in every respect.

But then, by the end of the third century, the brush is invented. In the first century after the "joyous event" (A.D.)—paper. And, lastly, in the year 220—India ink.

A complete upheaval. A revolution in draughtsmanship. And, after having undergone in the course of history no fewer than fourteen different styles of handwriting, the hieroglyph crystallized in its present form. The means of production (brush and India ink) determined the form.

The fourteen reforms had their way. As a result:

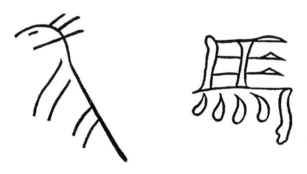

In the fierily cavorting hieroglyph *ma* (a horse) it is already impossible to recognize the features of the dear little horse sagging pathetically in its hindquarters, in the writing style of Ts'ang Chieh, so well-known from ancient Chinese bronzes.

But let it rest in the Lord, this dear little horse, together with the other 607 remaining *hsiang cheng* symbols—the earliest extant category of hieroglyphs.

The real interest begins with the second category of hieroglyphs—the *huei-i*, i.e., "copulative."

The point is that the copulation (perhaps we had better say, the combination) of two hieroglyphs of the simplest series is to be regarded not as their sum, but as their product, i.e., as a value of another dimension, another degree; each, separately, corresponds to an *object*, to a fact, but their combination corresponds to a *concept*. From separate hieroglyphs has been fused—the ideogram. By the combination of two "depictables" is achieved the representation of something that is graphically undepictable.

For example: the picture for water and the picture of an eye signifies "to weep"; the picture of an ear near the drawing of a door = "to listen";

a dog + a mouth = "to bark";

a mouth + a child = "to scream";

a mouth + a bird = "to sing";

a knife + a heart = "sorrow," and so on.

But this is—montage!

Yes. It is exactly what we do in the cinema, combining shots that are *depictive*, single in meaning, neutral in content—into *intellectual* contexts and series.

This is a means and method inevitable in any cinematographic exposition. And, in a condensed and purified form, the starting point for the "intellectual cinema."

For a cinema seeking a maximum laconism for the visual representation of abstract concepts.

And we hail the method of the long-lamented Ts'ang Chieh as a first step along these paths.

We have mentioned laconism. Laconism furnishes us a transition to another point. Japan possesses the most laconic form of poetry: the *haikai* (appearing at the beginning of the thirteenth century and known today as "haiku" or "hokku") and the even earlier *tanka* (mythologically assumed to have been created along with heaven and earth).

Both are little more than hieroglyphs transposed into phrases. So much so that half their quality is appraised by their calligraphy. The method of their resolution is completely analogous to the structure of the ideogram.

As the ideogram provides a means for the laconic imprinting of an abstract concept, the same method, when transposed into literary exposition, gives rise to an identical laconism of pointed imagery.

Applied to the collision of an austere combination of symbols this method results in a dry definition of abstract concepts. The same method, expanded into the luxury of a group of already formed verbal combinations, swells into a splendor of *imagist* effect.

The concept is a bare formula; its adornment (an expansion by additional material) transforms the formula into an image—a finished form.

Exactly, though in reverse, as a primitive thought process—imagist thinking, displaced to a definite degree, becomes transformed to conceptual thinking.

But let us turn to examples.

The *haiku* is a concentrated impressionist sketch:

> A lonely crow
>   On leafless bough,
>   One autumn eve.
>
>   BASHŌ

> What a resplendent moon!
>   It casts the shadow of pine boughs
>   Upon the mats.
>
>   KIKAKU

> An evening breeze blows.
>   The water ripples
>   Against the blue heron's legs.
>
>   BUSON

> It is early dawn.
>   The castle is surrounded
>   By the cries of wild ducks.
>
>   KYOROKU

The earlier *tonka* is slightly longer (by two lines):

> O mountain pheasant
> long are the feathers trail'st thou
>   on the wooded hill-side—
> as long the nights seem to me
> on lonely couch sleep seeking.
>   HITOMARO[?]

From our point of view, these are montage phrases. Shot lists. The simple combination of two or three details of a material kind yields a perfectly finished representation of another kind—psychological.

And if the finely ground edges of the intellectually defined concepts formed by the combined ideograms are blurred in these poems, yet, in *emotional quality*, the concepts have blossomed forth immeasurably. We should observe that the emotion is directed towards the reader, for, as Yone Noguchi has said, "it is the readers who make the *haiku's* imperfection a perfection of art."

It is uncertain in Japanese writing whether its predominating aspect is as a system of characters (denotative), or as an independent creation of graphics (depictive). In any case, born of the dual mating of the depictive by method, and the denotative by purpose, the ideogram continued both these lines (not consecutive historically but consecutive in principle in the minds of those developing the method).

Not only did the denotative line continue into literature, in the *tanka*, as we have shown, but exactly the same method (in its depictive aspect) operates also in the most perfect examples of Japanese pictorial art.

Sharaku—creator of the finest prints of the eighteenth century, and especially of an immortal gallery of actors' portraits. The Japanese Daumier. Despite this, almost unknown to us. The characteristic traits of his work have been analyzed only in our century. One of these critics, Julius Kurth, in discussing the question of the influence on Sharaku of sculpture, draws a parallel between his wood-cut portrait of the actor Nakayama Tomisaburō and an antique mask of the semi-religious Nō theater, the mask of a Rozo.

The faces of both the print and the mask wear an *identical expression* . . . Features and masses are similarly arranged although the mask represents an old priest, and the print a young woman. This relationship is striking, yet these two works are otherwise totally dissimilar; this in itself is a demonstration of Sharaku's originality. While the carved mask was constructed according to fairly accurate anatomical proportions, the proportions of the portrait print are simply impossible. The space between the eyes comprises a width that makes mock of all good sense. The nose is almost twice as long in relation to the eyes as any normal nose would dare to be, and the chin stands in no sort of relation to the mouth; the brows, the mouth, and every feature—is hopelessly misrelated. *This observation may be made in all the large heads by Sharaku.* That the artist was unaware that all these proportions are false is, of course, out of the question. It was with a full awareness that he repudiated normalcy, and, while the drawing of the separate features depends on severely concentrated naturalism, their proportions have been subordinated to purely intellectual considerations. *He set up the essence of the psychic expression as the norm for the proportions of the single features.*

Is not this process that of the ideogram, combining the independent "mouth" and the dissociated symbol of "child" to form the significance of "scream"?

Is this not exactly what we of the cinema do temporally, just as Sharaku in simultaneity, when we cause a monstrous disproportion of the parts of a normally flowing event, and suddenly dismember the event into "close-up of clutching hands," "medium shots of the struggle," and "extreme close-up of bulging eyes," in making a montage disintegration of the event in various planes? In making an eye twice as large as a man's full figure?! By combining these monstrous incongruities we newly collect the disintegrated event into one whole, but in *our* aspect. According to the treatment of our relation to the event.

The disproportionate depiction of an event is organically natural to us from the beginning. Professor Luriya, of the Psychological Institute in Moscow, has shown me a drawing by a child of "lighting a stove." Everything is represented in passably accurate relationship and with great care. Firewood. Stove. Chimney. But what are those zigzags in that huge central rectangle? They turn out to be—matches. Taking into account the crucial importance of these matches for the depicted process, the child provides a proper scale for them.[2]

The representation of objects in the actual (absolute) proportions proper to them is, of course, merely a tribute to orthodox formal logic. A subordination to an inviolable order of things.

Both in painting and sculpture there is a periodic and invariable return to periods of the establishment of absolutism. Displacing the expressiveness of archaic disproportion for regulated "stone tables" of officially decreed harmony.

Absolute realism is by no means the correct form of perception. It is simply the function of a certain form of social structure. Following a state monarchy, a state uniformity of thought is implanted. Ideological uniformity of a sort that can be developed pictorially in the ranks of colors and designs of the Guards regiments. . . .

Thus we have seen how the principle of the hieroglyph—"denotation by depiction"—split in two: along the line of its purpose (the principle of "denotation"), into the principles of creating literary imagery; along the line of its method of realizing this purpose (the principle of "depiction"), into the striking methods of expressiveness used by Sharaku.[3]

And, just as the two outspreading wings of a hyperbola meet, as we say, at infinity (though no one has visited so distant a region!), so the principle of hieroglyphics, infinitely splitting into two parts (in accordance with the function of symbols), unexpectedly unites again from this dual estrangement, in yet a fourth sphere—in the theater.

Estranged for so long, they are once again—in the cradle period of the drama—present in a *parallel* form, in a curious dualism.

The *significance* (denotation) of the action is effected by the reciting of the *Jōruri* by a voice behind the stage—the *representation* (depiction) of the action is effected by silent marionettes on the stage. Along with a specific manner of movement this archaism migrated into the early Kabuki theater, as well. To this day it is preserved, as a partial method, in the classical repertory (where certain parts of the action are narrated from behind the stage while the actor mimes).

But this is not the point. The most important fact is that into the technique of acting itself the ideographic (montage) method has been wedged in the most interesting ways.

However, before discussing this, let us be allowed the luxury of a digression—on the matter of the shot, to settle the debated question of its nature, once and for all.

A shot. A single piece of celluloid. A tiny rectangular frame in which there is, organized in some way, a piece of an event.

"Cemented together, these shots form montage. When this is done in an appropriate rhythm, *of course!*"

This, roughly, is what is taught by the old, old school of film-making, that sang:

> "Screw by screw,
> Brick by brick . . ."

Kuleshov, for example, even writes with a brick:

> If you have an idea-phrase, a particle of the story, a link in the whole dramatic chain, then that idea is to be expressed and accumulated from shot-ciphers, just like bricks.

"The shot is an element of montage. Montage is an assembly of these elements." This is a most pernicious make-shift analysis.

Here the understanding of the process as a whole (connection, shot-montage) derives only from the external indications of its flow (a piece cemented to another piece). Thus it would be possible, for instance, to arrive at the well-known conclusion that street-cars exist in order to be laid across streets. An entirely logical deduction, if one limits oneself to the external indications of the functions they performed during the street-fighting of February, 1917, here in Russia. But the materialist conception of history interprets it otherwise.

The worst of it is that an approach of this kind does actually lie, like an insurmountable street-car, across the potentialities of formal development. Such an approach overrules dialectical development, and dooms one to mere evolutionary "perfecting," in so far as it gives no bite into the dialectical substance of events.

In the long run, such evolutionizing leads either through refinement to decadence or, on the other hand, to a simple withering away due to stagnation of the blood.

Strange as it may seem, a melodious witness to both these distressing eventualities, simultaneously, is Kuleshov's latest film, *The Gay Canary* [1929].

The shot is by no means an *element* of montage.

The shot is a montage *cell*.

Just as cells in their division form a phenomenon of another order, the organism or embryo, so, on the other side of the dialectical leap from the shot, there is montage.

By what, then, is montage characterized and, consequently, its cell—the shot?

By collision. By the conflict of two pieces in opposition to each other. By conflict. By collision.

In front of me lies a crumpled yellowed sheet of paper. On it is a mysterious note:

> "Linkage-P" and "Collision-E."

This is a substantial trace of a heated bout on the subject of montage between P (Pudovkin) and E (myself).

This has become a habit. At regular intervals he visits me late at night and behind closed doors we wrangle over matters of principle. A graduate of the Kuleshov school, he loudly defends an understanding of montage as a *linkage* of pieces. Into a chain. Again, "bricks." Bricks, arranged in series to *expound* an idea.

I confronted him with my viewpoint on montage as a *collision*. A view that from the collision of two given factors *arises* a concept.

From my point of view, linkage is merely a possible *special* case.

Recall what an infinite number of combinations is known in physics to be capable of arising from the impact (collision) of spheres. Depending on whether the spheres be resilient, non-resilient, or mingled. Amongst all these combinations there is one in which the impact is so weak that the collision is degraded to an even movement of both in the same direction.

This is the one combination which would correspond with Pudovkin's view.

Not long ago we had another talk. Today he agrees with my point of view. True, during the interval he took the opportunity to acquaint himself with the series of lectures I gave during that period at the State Cinema Institute. . . .

So, montage is conflict.

As the basis of every art is conflict (an "imagist" transformation of the dialectical principle). The shot appears as the *cell* of montage. Therefore it also must be considered from the viewpoint of *conflict*.

Conflict within the shot is potential montage, in the development of its intensity shattering the quadrilateral cage of the shot and exploding its conflict into montage impulses *between* the montage pieces. As, in a zigzag of mimicry, the *mise-en-scène* splashes out into a spatial zigzag with the *same* shattering. As the slogan, "All obstacles are vain before Russians," bursts out in the multitude of incident of *War and Peace*.

If montage is to be compared with something, then a phalanx of montage pieces, of shots, should be compared to the series of explosions of an internal combustion engine, driving forward its automobile or tractor: for, similarly, the dynamics of montage serve as impulses driving forward the total film.

Conflict within the frame. This can be very varied in character: it even can be a conflict in—the story. As in that "prehistoric" period in films (although there are plenty of instances in the present, as well), when entire scenes would be photographed in a single, uncut shot. This, however, is outside the strict jurisdiction of the film-form.

These are the "cinematographic" conflicts within the frame:

Conflict of graphic directions.

> *(Lines—either static or dynamic)*

Conflict of scales.
Conflict of volumes.
Conflict of masses.

> *(Volumes filled with various intensities of light)*

Conflict of depths.

And the following conflicts, requiring only one further impulse of intensification before flying into antagonistic pairs of pieces:

Close shots and long shots.

Pieces of graphically varied directions. Pieces resolved in volume, with pieces resolved in area.

Pieces of darkness and pieces of lightness.

And, lastly, there are such unexpected conflicts as:

Conflicts between an object and its dimension—and conflicts between an event and its duration.

These may sound strange, but both are familiar to us. The first is accomplished by an optically distorted lens, and the second by stop-motion or slow-motion.

The compression of all cinematographic factors and properties within a single dialectical formula of conflict is no empty rhetorical diversion.

We are now seeking a unified system for methods of cinematographic expressiveness that shall hold good for all its elements. The assembly of these into series of common indications will solve the task as a whole.

Experience in the separate elements of the cinema cannot be absolutely measured.

Whereas we know a good deal about montage, in the theory of the shot we are still floundering about amidst the most academic attitudes, some vague tentatives, and the sort of harsh radicalism that sets one's teeth on edge.

To regard the frame as a particular, as it were, molecular case of montage makes possible the direct application of montage practice to the theory of the shot.

And similarly with the theory of lighting. To sense this as a collision between a stream of light and an obstacle, like the impact of a stream from a fire-hose striking a concrete object, or of the wind buffeting a human figure, must result in a usage of light entirely different in comprehension from that employed in playing with various combinations of "gauzes" and "spots."

Thus far we have one such significant principle of conflict: *the principle of optical counterpoint.*

And let us not now forget that soon we shall face another and less simple problem in counterpoint: *the conflict in the sound film of acoustics and optics.*

Let us return to one of the most fascinating of optical conflicts: the conflict between the frame of the shot and the object!

The camera position, as a materialization of the conflict between organizing logic of the director and the inert logic of the object, in collision, reflects the dialectic of the camera-angle.

In this matter we are still impressionistic and lacking in principle to a sickening degree. Nevertheless, a sharpness of principle can be had in the technique of this, too. The dry quadrilateral, plunging into the hazards of nature's diffuseness. . . .

And once again we are in Japan! For the cinematographic method is used in teaching drawing in Japanese schools.

What is our method of teaching drawing? Take any piece of white paper with four corners to it. Then cram onto it, usually even without using the edges (mostly greasy from the long drudgery!), some bored caryatid, some conceited Corinthian capital, or a plaster Dante (not the magician performing at the Moscow Hermitage, but the other one—Alighieri, the comedy writer).

The Japanese approach this from a quite different direction:

Here's the branch of a cherry-tree. And the pupil cuts out from this whole, with a square, and a circle, and a rectangle – compositional units:

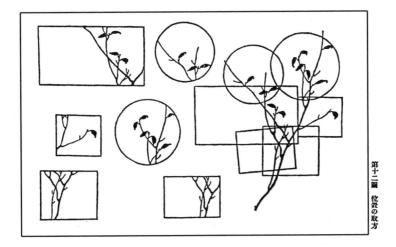

He frames a shot!

These two ways of teaching drawing can characterize the two basic tendencies struggling within the cinema of today. One—the expiring method of artificial spatial organization of an event in front of the lens. From the "direction" of a sequence, to the erection of a Tower of Babel in front of the lens. The other—a "picking-out" by the camera: organization by means of the camera. Hewing out a piece of actuality with the ax of the lens.

However, at the present moment, when the center of attention is finally beginning, in the intellectual cinema, to be transferred from the materials of cinema, as such, to "deductions and conclusions," to "slogans" based on the material, both schools of thought are losing distinction in their differences and can quietly blend into a synthesis.

Several pages back we lost, like an overshoe in a street-car, the question of the theater. Let us turn back to the question of methods of montage in the Japanese theater, particularly in acting.

The first and most striking example, of course, is the purely cinematographic method of "acting without transitions." Along with mimic transitions carried to a limit of refinement, the Japanese actor uses an exactly contrary method as well. At a certain moment of his performance he halts; the black-shrouded *kurogo* obligingly conceals him from the spectators. And lo!—he is resurrected in a new make-up. And in a new wig. Now characterizing another stage (degree) of his emotional state.

Thus, for example, in the Kabuki play *Narukami*, the actor Sadanji must change from drunkenness to madness. This transition is solved by a mechanical cut. And a change in the arsenal of grease-paint colors on his face, emphasizing those streaks whose duty it is to fulfill the expression of a higher intensity than those used in his previous make-up.

This method is organic to the film. The forced introduction into the film, by European acting traditions, of pieces of "emotional transitions" is yet another influence forcing the cinema to mark time. Whereas the method of "cut" acting makes possible the construction of entirely new methods. Replacing one changing face with a whole scale of facial types of varying moods affords a far more acutely expressive result than does the changing surface, too receptive and devoid of organic resistance, of any single professional actor's face.

In our new film [*Old and New*] I have eliminated the intervals between the sharply contrasting polar stages of a face's expression. Thus is achieved a greater sharpness in the "play of doubts" around the new cream separator. Will the milk thicken or no? Trickery?

Wealth? Here the psychological process of mingled faith and doubt is broken up into its two extreme states of joy (confidence) and gloom (disillusionment). Furthermore, this is sharply emphasized by light—illumination in no wise conforming to actual light conditions. This brings a distinct strengthening of the tension.

Another remarkable characteristic of the Kabuki theater is the principle of "disintegrated" acting. Shocho, who played the leading female rôles in the Kabuki theater that visited Moscow, in depicting the dying daughter in *Yashaō (The Mask-Maker)*, performed his rôle in pieces of acting completely detached from each other: Acting with only the right arm. Acting with one leg. Acting with the neck and head only. (The whole process of the death agony was disintegrated into solo performances of each member playing its own rôle: the rôle of the leg, the rôle of the arms, the rôle of the head.) A breaking-up into shots. With a gradual shortening of these separate, successive pieces of acting as the tragic end approached.

Freed from the yoke of primitive naturalism, the actor is enabled by this method to fully grip the spectator by "rhythms," making not only acceptable, but definitely attractive, a stage built on the most consecutive and detailed flesh and blood of naturalism.

Since we no longer distinguish in principle between questions of shot-content and montage, we may here cite a third example:

The Japanese theater makes use of a slow tempo to a degree unknown to our stage. The famous scene of hara-kiri in *Chushingura* is based on an unprecedented slowing down of all movement—beyond any point we have ever seen. Whereas, in the previous example, we observed a disintegration of the transitions between movements, here we see disintegration of the process of movement, viz., slow-motion. I have heard of only one example of a thorough application of this method, using the technical possibility of the film with a compositionally reasoned plan. It is usually employed with some purely pictorial aim, such as the "submarine kingdom" in *The Thief of Bagdad*, or to represent a dream, as in *Zvenigora*. Or, more often, it is used simply for formalist jackstraws and unmotivated camera mischief as in Vertov's *Man with the Movie-Camera*. The more commendable example appears to be in Jean Epstein's *La chute de la Maison Usher*—at least according to the press reports. In this film, normally acted emotions filmed with a speeded-up camera are said to give unusual emotional pressure by their unrealistic slowness on the screen. If it be borne in mind that the effect of an actor's performance on the audience is based on its identification by each spectator, it will be easy to relate both examples (the Kabuki play and the Epstein film) to an identical causal explanation. The intensity of perception increases as the didactic process of identification proceeds more easily along a disintegrated action.

Even instruction in handling a rifle can be hammered into the tightest motor-mentality among a group of raw recruits if the instructor uses a "break-down" method.

The most interesting link of the Japanese theater is, of course, its link with the sound film, which can and must learn its fundamentals from the Japanese—the reduction of visual and aural sensations to a common physiological denominator.

So, it has been possible to establish (cursorily) the permeation of the most varied branches of Japanese culture by a pure cinematographic element—its basic nerve, montage.

And it is only the Japanese cinema that falls into the same error as the "leftward drifting" Kabuki. Instead of learning how to extract the principles and technique of their remarkable acting from the traditional feudal forms of their materials, the most progressive leaders of the Japanese theater throw their energies into an adaptation of the spongy shapelessness of our own "inner" naturalism. The results are tearful and saddening. In its cinema Japan similarly pursues imitations of the most revolting examples of American and European entries in the international commercial film race.

To understand and apply her cultural peculiarities to the cinema, this is the task of Japan! Colleagues of Japan, are you really going to leave this for us to do?

Notes

1   Eisenstein's essay was originally published as an "afterword" to N. Kaufman's pamphlet, *Japanese Cinema* (Moscow, 1929).

2   It is possible to trace this particular tendency from its ancient, almost pre-historical source (". . . in all ideational art, objects are given size according to their importance, the king being twice as large as his subjects, or a tree half the size of a man when it merely informs us that the scene is out-of-doors. Something of this principle of size according to significance persisted in the Chinese tradition. The favorite disciple of Confucius looked like a little boy beside him and the most important figure in any group was usually the largest.") through the highest development of Chinese art, parent of Japanese graphic arts: ". . . natural scale always had to bow to pictorial scale . . . size according to distance never followed the laws of geometric perspective but the needs of the design. Foreground features might be diminished to avoid obstruction and overemphasis, and far distant objects, which were too minute to count pictorially, might be enlarged to act as a counterpoint to the middle distance or foreground."

3   It has been left to James Joyce to develop in *literature* the depictive line of the Japanese hieroglyph. Every word of Kurth's analysis of Sharaku may be applied, neatly and easily, to Joyce.

Chapter 11

Elizabeth Bowen (1899–1973)

"WHY I GO TO THE CINEMA" (1938)

BOWEN WAS FOND OF SAYING that she was born with the century; however, this statement was not strictly true since she was born in Ireland a year before, in 1899. Despite her factual infelicity, Bowen's identification with the twentieth century reflects her sense of her life as inexorably connected to the wars, revolutions, and social changes of her time. Born into privilege as the only daughter of a well-established Anglo-Irish family and heir to her ancestral home, Bowen's Court in County Cork, Ireland, Bowen became a keen observer of the cataclysmic changes that racked Ireland and England in the twentieth century. Her works bear particular witness to the experience of women, adolescents, and children, and, despite the lingering presence of the Irish War of Independence, World War I and World War II in her works, the plots that she explores are definitively domestic, with interior spaces looming larger than more public settings. Often considered a late-Bloomsbury writer, Bowen employs the dense, experimental flourishes of modernists such as Virginia Woolf, whom she knew and greatly admired, with a generic eclecticism that she seems to have drawn, in part, from her interests in popular media such as radio and film. In "Why I Go to the Cinema," Bowen revels in the communal experience of theatre-going while also expressing the hope that cinema will continue to develop as an art form capable of powerfully moving its viewers.

Elizabeth Bowen, "Why I Go to the Cinema," *Listening In: Broadcasts, Speeches, and Interviews by Elizabeth Bowen*, ed. Allan Hepburn. Edinburgh UP, 1938.

I go to the cinema for any number of different reasons – these I ought to sort out and range in order of their importance. At random, here are a few of them: I go to be distracted (or "taken out of myself"); I go when I don't want to think; I go when I do want to think and need stimulus; I go to see pretty people; I go when I want to see life ginned up, charged with unlikely energy; I go to laugh; I go to be harrowed; I go when a day has been such a mess of detail that I am glad to see even the most arbitrary, the most preposterous, pattern emerge; I go because I like bright light, abrupt shadow, speed; I go to see America, France, Russia; I go because I like wisecracks and slick behaviour; I go because the screen is an oblong opening into the world of fantasy for me; I go because I like story, with its suspense; I go because I like sitting in a packed crowd in the dark, among hundreds riveted on the same thing; I go to have my most general feelings played on.

These reasons, put down roughly, seem to fall under five headings: wish to escape, lassitude, sense of lack in my nature or my surroundings, loneliness (however passing) and natural frivolity. As a writer, I am probably subject during working hours to a slightly unnatural imaginative strain, which leaves me flat and depleted by the end of a day. But though the strain may be a little special in nature, I do not take it to be in any way greater than the strain, the sense of depletion, suffered by other people in most departments of life now. When I take a day off and become a person of leisure, I embark on a quite new method of exhausting myself; I amuse myself through a day, but how arduous that is: by the end of the day I am generally down on the transaction – unless I have been in the country.

I take it that for the professional leisured person things, in the long run, work out the same way. Writers, and other inventive workers, are wrong, I think, in claiming a special privilege, or in representing themselves as unfairly taxed by life: what is taken out of them in some ways is saved them in others; they work, for the most part, in solitude; they are not worn by friction with other people (unless they choose to seek this in their spare time); they have not to keep coming to terms with other people in order to get what they have to do done. They escape monotony; they are sustained in working by a kind of excitement; they are shut off from a good many demands. Their work *is* exhausting, and by human standards unnatural, but it cannot be more exhausting than routine work in office, shop or factory, teaching, running a family, hanging on to existence if one is in the submerged class, or amusing oneself. I make this point in order to be quite clear that my reasons for cinema-going are not unique or special: they would not be worth discussing if they were.

I am not at all certain, either, that the practice of one art gives one a point of vantage in discussing another. Where the cinema is concerned, I am a fan, not a critic. I have been asked to write on "Why I Go to the Cinema" because I do write, and should therefore do so with ease; I have not been asked to write, and am not writing, *as* a writer. It is not as a writer that I go to the cinema; like everyone else, I slough off my preoccupations there. The film I go to see is the product of a kind of art, just as a bottle of wine is the product of a kind of art. I judge the film as I judge the bottle of wine, in its relation to myself, by what it does to me. I sum up the pleasure it gives. This pleasure is, to an extent, an affair of my own palate, or temperament, but all palates and temperaments have something in common; hence general "taste," an accepted, objective standard in judgement of films or wine. Films, like wines, are differently good in their different classes; some of us prefer to seek one kind, some another, but always there is the same end – absolute pleasure – in view.

Cinemas draw all sorts. In factory towns they are packed with factory workers, in university cities with dons, at the seaside with trippers (who take on a strong though temporary character), in the West End with more or less moneyed people with time to kill, in country towns and villages with small tradespeople and with workers scrubbed and hard from the fields. Taste, with these different audiences, differs widely, but the degree of pleasure sought is the same. A film either hits or misses. So affectable are we that to sit through a film that is not pleasing the house, however much it may happen to please one personally, causes restless discomfort that detracts from one's pleasure. (Avoid, for instance, seeing the Marx Brothers in Cork city.) This works both ways: the success of a film with its house communicates a tingling physical pleasure – joining and heightening one's private exhilaration – a pleasure only the most weathered misanthrope could withstand – and your misanthrope is rarely a cinema-goer. There is no mistaking that tension all round in the dark, that almost agonised tension of a pleased house – the electric hush, the rapt immobility. The triumphantly funny film, hitting its mark, makes even laughter break off again and again, and the truly tragic suspends the snuffle.

The happily constituted cinema-goer learns to see and savour a positive merit in films that may do nothing to him personally, films whose subjects, stars or settings may to him, even, be antipathetic. To reject as any kind of experience a film that is acting powerfully on people round seems to me to argue poverty in the nature. What falls short as aesthetic experience may do as human experience: the film rings no bell in oneself, but one hears a bell ring elsewhere. This has a sort of value, like being in company with a very popular person one does not oneself dislike but who does not attract one. Popularity ought to confer a sort of hallmark, not have to be taken up as a challenge. I speak of the happily constituted cinema-goer – I mean, perhaps, the happily constituted, and therefore very rare, person. The generality of us, who hate jokes we cannot see and mysteries we are out of, may still hope to become sophisticates in at least this one pleasure by bringing with us, when we go to a cinema, something more active, more resourceful than tolerance. This is worthwhile: it doubles our chance of that fun for which we paid at the box-office. To my mind, any truly popular film is worth seeing – granted one happens to have the time and money to spare. I say, *truly* popular film, the film that after release has triumphantly stayed the course; not the *should-be* popular film, the film stuck with big names or inflated beforehand by misleading publicity. If nothing else, the popular film I don't like adds to my knowledge of what I don't like and don't want. One's own apathies are complex and interesting.

Films have – it is a truism of the trade – a predetermined destination. Every film made makes a bid for the favour of certain localities whose taste has been gauged in advance, correctly or not. Local appeal, at its strongest, is strongly delimited. If one is to go to a film for its popularity-interest, one should go to it in its own country – its areas may be social, not geographic, though largely they *are* geographic, for climate and occupation do condition an audience. For instance, my great respect for Miss Gracie Fields does not alter the fact that I would not willingly see, for its own sake, at my nearest London cinema, a film in which she appeared. But I should feel I had missed something if I missed seeing a Gracie Fields film in the Gracie Fields country. There she operates in full force, and I cannot fail to react – to the audience, if not to her. I see a great girl in play. The comedian's hold on his or her own public is hard to analyse: in some cases (such as Miss Fields') it has a strong moral element. Or it may have a healthily anti-moral element. The determining factor must, I think, be social: hard-living people like to have someone to admire; they like what is like themselves. The sophisticated are attracted, titillated, by what is foreign, outrageous, by what they may half deplore.

But it would be misleading, as well as precious, to overstress this rest-of-the-audience factor in my reaction to films. I do really only like what *I* like, I go to please myself, and when I sit opposite a film the audience is *me*. My faculties are riveted, my pleasure can only be a little damped down or my disappointment added to by the people cheek by jowl with me in the dark. I expect a good deal, when I go to the cinema: my expectations absorb me from the moment I enter. I am giving myself a treat – or being given a treat. I have little spare time or money, the cinema is my anodyne, not my subject, and my objective interest in its emotional mechanics is not really very great. Nine times out of ten, it is alert, exacting expectations of pleasure that carry me to the cinema. The tenth time I may go from abstract curiosity, or at random – as when I have hours to pass in a strange town where it is raining or there are no buildings to see. This tenth time I will discount; it is seldom serious – though it does some-times turn out to have started up a new fancy, or left a residue of interest behind.

I expect, then, to enjoy myself. This end I do all I can to further by taking as good a seat as my purse, that day, will allow – a seat giving room for my knees, in which I need not tip my head back or keep craning my neck round, and from which I have an undistorted view of the screen. (In the up-to-date cinema this last, of course, is all right in all seats.) Cramp or any other physical irritation militates quite unfairly against the best film: if a film is worth seeing at all they seem to me worth avoiding. Sometimes I can't avoid them: if a film is booming I'm lucky to get in at all, and have to sit where I can. But there is a good deal in waiting till the first rush is over, then seeing the film in comfort: a film, I try to remind myself, doesn't lose quality in the course of its run, and the urge to see it at once may be sheer vulgar topicality. Anyhow, I seek comfort – and how important smoking is. I start slightly against the best film in a foreign cinema where I am unable to smoke. Very great films (generally Russian) and moments in any good film do suspend my desire to smoke: this is the supreme test.

I have – like, I suppose every other cinema-goer – a physical affection for certain cinemas. In London the Empire is my favourite; when I settle down in there I feel I am back in the old home, and am predisposed to happiness. May it never come down. I suppose I could rationalise my feeling for the Empire by saying I like Metro-Goldwyn-Mayer films – but though I have enjoyed these all over Europe, the last drop of pleasure is added by being at the Empire. However, one must take films not only as but where one finds them. In the provinces, I have often had to desert my favourite cinema in order to see a promising film elsewhere: this gave the evening, though the film might prove excellent, an undertone of nostalgia: "I wish this were at the Such-and-such." The sentiment was absurd, and is only mentioned because I think it is general. Pleasure is at its best when it has in it some familiar element. And the pleasure-seeker has a difficult temperament; he is often as captious as a spoilt beauty, as whimsical as a child, and given to fretting against conditions not in his power to change. This may be because, in most cases, he goes to his pleasure tired. He does not know what he wants, but he knows when he does not get it. It is for him – myself – that the cinema caters; and how much the cinema has to overcome!

I hope never to go to the cinema in an entirely unpropitious mood. If I do, and am not amused, that is my fault, also my loss. As a rule, I go empty but hopeful, like someone bringing a mug to a tap that may not turn on. The approach tunes me up for pleasure. The enchantment that hung over those pre-war façades of childhood – gorgeously white stucco façades, with caryatids and garlands – has not dissolved, though the façades have been changed. How they used to beam down the street. Now concrete succeeds stucco and chromium gilt; foyers once crimson and richly stuffy are air-conditioned and dove-grey. But, like a chocolate-box lid, the entrance is still voluptuously promising: sensation of some sort seems to be guaranteed. How happily I tread the pneumatic carpet, traverse anterooms with their exciting muted vibration, and walk down the spotlit aisle with its eager tilt to the screen. I climb over those knees to the sticky velvet seat, and fumble my cigarettes out – as I used not to do.

I am not only home again, but am, if my choice is lucky, in ideal society. I am one of the millions who follow Names from cinema to cinema. The star system may be all wrong – it has implications I hardly know of in the titanic world of Hollywood, also it is, clearly, a hold-up to proper art – but I cannot help break it down. I go to see So-and-so. I cannot fitly quarrel with this magnification of personalities, while I find I can do with almost unlimited doses of anybody exciting, anybody with beauty (in my terms), verve, wit, style, *toupet* (nerve) and, of course, glamour. What do I mean by glamour? A sort of sensuous gloss: I know it to be synthetic, but it affects me strongly. It is a trick knowingly practised on my most fuzzy desires; it steals a march on me on my silliest side. But all the same, in being subject to glamour I experience a sort of elevation. It brings, if not into life at least parallel to it, a sort of fairy-tale element. It is a sort of trumpet call, mobilising the sleepy fancy. If a film is to get across, glamour somewhere, in some form – moral, if you like, for it can be moral – cannot be done without. The Russians break with the bourgeois-romantic conception of personality; they have scrapped sex-appeal as an annexe of singularising, anti-social love. But they still treat with glamour; they have transferred it to mass movement, to a heroicised pro-human emotion. I seek it, in any form.

To get back to my star: I enjoy, sitting opposite him or her, the delights of intimacy without the onus, high points of possession without the strain. This could be called inoperative love. Relationships in real life are made arduous by their reciprocities; one can too seldom simply sit back. The necessity to please, to shine, to make the most of the moment, overshadows too many meetings. And apart from this – how seldom in real life (or so-called real life) does acquaintanceship, much less intimacy, with dazzling, exceptional beings come one's way. How very gladly, therefore, do I fill the gaps in my circle of ideal society with these black-and-white personalities, to whom absence of colour has added all the subtleties of tone. Directly I take my place I am on terms with these Olympians; I am close to them with nothing at all at stake. Rapture lets me suppose that for me alone they display the range of their temperaments, their hesitations, their serious depths. I find them not only dazzling but sympathetic. They live for my eye. Yes, and I not only perceive them but *am* them; their hopes and fears are my own; their triumphs exalt me. I am proud for them and in them. Not only do I enjoy them; I enjoy in them a vicarious life.

Nevertheless, I like my stars well supported. If a single other character in the film beside them be unconvincing or tin-shape, the important illusion weakens; something begins to break down. I like to see my star played up to and played around by a cast that is living, differentiated and definite. The film must have background, depth, its own kind of validity. Hollywood, lately, has met this demand: small parts are being better and better played. Casts are smallish, characters clear-cut, action articulated. (Look at *It Happened One Night*, *She Married Her Boss*, *My Man Godfrey*.) There is family-feeling inside a good film – so that the world it creates is valid, water-tight, *probable*.

What a gulf yawns between improbability – which is desolating – and fantasy – which is dream-probability, likeliness on an august, mad plane. Comedy films show this fantasy element more strongly than tragedies, which attempt to approach life and fail too often through weakness and misrepresentation: comedies are thus, as a rule, better. A really good comic (a Laurel and Hardy, for instance) is never simply improbable: it suspends judgement on the workaday plane. Comedy-drama needs some verisimilitude.

When I say verisimilitude, I do not mean that I want the film to be exactly *like* life: I should seldom go to the cinema if it were. The effective film (other, of course, than the film that is purely documentary) must have at least a touch of the preposterous. But its distance from life, or from probability, should stay the same throughout: it must keep inside its pitch. The film that keeps in its pitch makes, and imposes, a temporary reality of its own.

Any cinema-goer, however anxious for peace and for his own pleasure, may detect in a film a *gaffe* that he cannot pass. I quarrel most, naturally, with misrepresentations of anything that I happen to know about. For instance, I have, being Irish, seen few films about Ireland, or set in Ireland, that did not insult and bore me. (*The Informer* was one remarkable exception.) But I could sit through a (no doubt) equally misrepresenting film about Scotland, which I do not know, without turning a hair. I know only a very small part of America – and that superficially – so that American films can take almost any licence with me. In fact, years of cinema-going probably did condition my first view of America: I felt as though I were stepping into the screen. Dreamlike familiarity in the streets and landscapes not only endeared the country but verified the cinema. But I cannot know how greatly Hollywood's representations, however idyllic, of New England small towns may offend New Englanders, or how cardboardy, to the Southerner, may seem the screen face of the Old Colonial Home. I cannot challenge falseness in setting, detail or manners past the point where my experience stops. As a woman, I am annoyed by improbability in clothes: English films offend rather badly in this way. Dressy at all costs, the English heroines hike, run down spies or reclaim lovers from storm-girt islands in their Kensington High Street Sunday bests. An equal unlikeliness blights the English film interior: I revolt from ancestral homes that are always Gothic, from

Louis Seize bedrooms in poverty-stricken manors, from back-street dwellings furnished by Mr. Drage. The frumpy and unsatirical flatness of the average English stage-set is almost always transferred by the English film to the screen. The French make *genre* films in which every vase, tassel and door-handle thickens the atmosphere, makes for verisimilitude and adds more to the story: why cannot we do the same?

Why are there so few English *genre* films? All over this country, indoors and out, a photographable drama of national temperament is going on, and every object has character. Bypasses, trees on skylines, small country town streets with big buses pushing along them, village Sundays, gasometers showing behind seaside towns, half-built new estates, Midland canals, the lounges of private hotels, stucco houses with verandas, rectory tea-tables, the suburban shopping rush, garden fêtes and the abstract perspectives of flyblown, semi-submerged London are all waiting the camera and are very dramatic. English interiors are highly characterised; English social routine is romantically diverse. As it is, the same few shots – which might, from their symbolic conventionality, have been made to be exported to Hollywood – drearily re-appear, to give English films their locality: Westminster Bridge, crazy gables stuck with oak beams, corners of (apparently) Oxford colleges masquerading as Great Homes, clotted orchards (that might be faked with a few rolls of crêpe paper), the spire of always the same church, and those desolating, unconvincing, always-the-same rooms. There are exceptions to this – Anthony Asquith shows feeling for landscape, and Hitchcock gets humour into interiors – but not nearly enough exceptions. Generally speaking, English films lack humour in the perceptive, sympathetic and wide sense. They lack sensibility; they do not know how to use objects. Are we blind to our country? Too many English films are, humanly speaking, dead. Character in them is tin-shape and two-dimensional. The whole effect is laborious, genteel, un-adult and fussy. Comedies, technically "clean," are unbearably vulgar; there is no fun, only knockabout and facetiousness. It is true that we are beginners, that we have admittedly much to learn, still, in the way of technique. But we fail in more than technique; we fail, flatly and fatally, in conception.

At present it appears, discouragingly enough, that to make outstanding films one must either be sophisticated, like some Americans; disabused and witty, like the French; vividly neurotic, like the Germans; or noble, like the Russians. One must know how to use convention, and when to break with it. One must either, like the Russians, take the heroic view, or else be iconoclastic, racy, though still know what to honour. One must have an eye for what is essential, telling, in action, scene or face. One must know how to hitch one's particular invention on to the general dream. Human fantasies are general; the film, to live, must discover, feed and command these.

I am discussing, throughout, the "story" (or "entertainment") film. That is the film I go to see; I go to the cinema for amusement only; my feeling for it may be exceptionally frivolous. I more than admire, I am often absorbed by, good "interest," or documentary films that may occur in a programme, but, as these are not the films I seek, I do not feel that I am qualified to discuss them. I go for what is untrue, to be excited by what is fantastic, to see what has never happened happen. I go for the fairy story. I state – I do not see why this should rank as a confession – that I would rather see a film in which a (probably doped) lion brings a tense plot to a close by eating a millionaire than the most excellent film about lions in their wild state, roving about and not furthering any plot. If I am to see a documentary film, I prefer what I can only describe with Lower-form vagueness as "films about foreign countries" – preferably, European countries. I like to get some idea how foreigners spend their day – and the incidental beauty of "interest" films is often very great, their rhythm admirable. But I have very little curiosity, and an inordinate wish to be entertained. If many more cinema-goers were as lazy-minded and fantasy-loving as I am what a pity it would be – but I take it that I am in a minority. I hope that the cinema may develop along all lines, while still giving me many more of the films I like – grown-up comedies, taut thrillers, finished period pieces and dashing Westerns. I want no more American tragedies, Russian comedies or crepitating Teutonic analysis. I should like still more dramatic use of landscape and architecture. I like almost any French film – perhaps I have been lucky. I have rather dreaded beforehand, as one dreads drastic experience, any Russian film I have seen; have later wished, while it lasted, to protract every moment, and finally found it, when it was over, more powerful than a memory – besides everything else, there had been so much more fun than one foresaw.

I am shy of the serious aspect of my subject, and don't want to finish on an unnaturally high note. It is, of course, clear to me that a film, like any other attempt on art, or work of art – all being tentative – can have in it germs of perfection. Its pretension to an aesthetic need be no less serious than that of a poem, picture or piece of music. Its medium, which is unique to it, is important: fluid pattern, variation of light, speed. In time, the cinema has come last of all the arts; its appeal to the racial child in us is so immediate that it should have come first. Pictures came first in time, and bore a great weight of meaning: "the pictures" date right back in their command of emotion: they are inherently primitive. A film can put the experience of a race or a person on an almost dreadfully simplified epic plane.

We have promise of great art here, but so far few great artists. Films have not caught up with the possibilities of the cinema: we are lucky when we get films that keep these in sight. Mechanics, the immense technical knowledge needed, have kept the art, as an art, unnaturally esoteric; its technical progress (more and more discoveries: sound, now colour) moves counter to its spiritual progress. An issue keeps on being obscured, a problem added to. Yet we have here, almost within our grasp, a means to the most direct communication possible between man and man. What might be a giant instrument is still a giant toy.

How much I like films I like – but I could like my films better. I like being distracted, flattered, tickled, even rather upset – but I should not mind something more; I should like something serious. I should like to be changed by more films, as art can change one: I should like something to happen when I go to the cinema.

Chapter 12

Louise Bogan (1897–1970)

"FOLK ART" (1943)

BOGAN WAS BORN IN LIVERMORE Falls, Maine; her family's misfortunes led to her and her brother's itinerant life in her home state and across New Hampshire and Massachusetts. The daughter of a millworker and unstable and frequently disappearing mother, she attended Boston's prestigious Girls' Latin High School, with a patron's assistance; there, her interest in poetry flourished. Deeply attached to poetic tradition and form, Bogan combined the intellectual ruminations of the metaphysical poets with metered and lyrical verse forms. The personal and emotional elements of her poetry are contained by spare, precise, elegant, and sculptured verse. An insistently individual poet, Bogan eschewed the fashionable modernist free-verse style and insisted upon full immersion in poetics and not politics. She grew more distant from friends like Edmund Wilson, whose leftward lean she considered a personal, artistic, and intellectual weakness. Bogan's best-known works include *Body of Death: Poems* (1923), *The Blue Estuaries, Poems, 1923–1959*, and her critical study, *Achievement in American Poetry, 1900–1950* (1951); she is also known for her translations of Goethe, Jules Renard, and Ernst Jünger. Bogan, whose favorite poets were W.B. Yeats and Rainer Maria Rilke, served as the *The New Yorker*'s poetry reviewer 1931–69.

Louise Bogan, "Folk Art," *A Poet's Prose: Selected Writings of Louise Bogan*, ed. Mary Kinzie. Athens, OH: Swallow Press/Ohio UP, 2005. 283–92.

Will folk art save us from creative and moral aridity if we can find and use it? The reiterated insinuation that formal art is fraudulent because it is difficult to understand and makes no effort to appeal to the majority—that it is, in fact, somehow treasonable to mankind's higher purposes and aims—is a typical bourgeois notion that has been around for a long time. That formal art cannot be put to any immediate use also lays it open to materialist denigration. The conviction that the simple is straight and pure and true, while the complex is concocted and double-dealing, is a partially moral one. It is a conviction which shares room, in the minds and emotions of many people, with an unconscious yearning for a lost rural world. In America, just enough time has elapsed since real urbanization set in for this yearning to roll up to its present proportions and to have acquired its present rationalizations. In spite of these desires and beliefs of the middle-class Subconscious, the fact remains that no civilization has ever produced a literature out of folk (either current or revived) alone. The formal artist cannot be outlawed. The whole question is muddled in the extreme. Let us examine it with as much detachment as possible.

It is true that the formal artist, at least twice within living memory, has succeeded in getting past modern barriers to a real folk tradition, and that remarkable literature has resulted in both cases from the intersection of the formal with the folk line. Lorca's genius was ignited in the most brilliant way by Flamenco tradition, and Yeats was fortified and refreshed from the beginning by his close knowledge of the Irish peasant. Both these poets received the experience of poetry still attached to music, at the improvisatory stage; and of an audience creatively involved (actually listeners, as distinguished from mere readers) in what they as poets produced.

But the fact is that only the most abnormal situations, political or otherwise, kept these two folk traditions alive so late in an industrial and urbanized Europe. The turning toward the folk, at the end of the eighteenth century, was not only preindustrial but prerevolutionary; and the same sort of ferments were present in Yeats's Ireland and Lorca's Spain. The current attempts in America to get back to primitive material are natural enough, but they are different. They are the desire of a far from revolutionary population to get back to some earlier fun, as well as some earlier integrity. Certainly the material is there. We can trace the line of the American folk song through the ballads of English, Irish, and Scotch origin (broken away from their original scene and transformed) through the work songs of all kinds (sea chanteys, songs of the plantation and the cattle-range), the hymns and spirituals, up to the beginning of town life. Then the culmination of the American folk song appears. Stephen Foster, the untrained and greatly gifted writer of "popular songs," managed to express fully the emotions common during this period of transition. On the one hand, through him the loneliness as well as the rough gaiety of a primitive society found its voice. On the other, Foster gave expression to something quite new: an emotion which was to become increasingly persistent in the American spirit—the sense of profound nostalgia for an already disappearing non-urban way of life. The strong sentimentalization of Foster by his modern audience proceeds from the holdover of this crucial though hidden nostalgia into our own time. Clearly, he was the end of one kind of American folk, the point beyond which no unadulterated development of his kind of material was possible.

We begin to get the production of the urbanized folk after the hymns and marching songs of the Civil War. The railroads building and having been built, we get the railroad songs. The cities once made, we get the hybrid genteel, and the barbershop ballads, and what is more vivid and interesting, the songs of the "underworld": brothel, saloon, dope joint, and prison. The earlier tradition fell into neglect as the way back to the farm became more and more closed. It was rediscovered and refurbished, along with hooked rugs and pine blanket chests, when the 1914 war broke up American Victorian and aroused, in some not quite understandable fashion, the middle-class enthusiasm for the American antique. The folk tradition, as a result, has become thoroughly "bourgeoizified." At present there is no way for the artist to get at it, for it has been dragged into a region where nothing living or nutritious for his purposes exists. It can be looked at and listened to, admired and imitated; but it cannot at the present time be called upon to do any truly important task. Only a writer thoroughly immersed in middle-class values, and soaked through and through with the sentimentality of the middle, could for a moment believe that this mummified and genteelized folk could contribute any spark of life to his purposes.

The English and French tradition of town-folk (with a head start of some forty or fifty years of true industrialism over the United States) channeled itself into the music hall. "The supreme embodiment of the surviving character of the English working people," writes one chronicler of the English nineteenth-century scene, "was the music hall. . . . Springing spontaneously out of the sing-song of the upper tavern room and the old out-of-door gardens of the artisans of the pastoral past, it became for a space of time a British institution. Its morality was to make the best of a bad job; its purpose to make everyone free and easy. . . ." The authenticity of this institution, created by the first articulate development of urban folk for its own enjoyment, soon impressed itself on the artists and writers of the time. Through it, they were able to skirt the middle, find excitement and restorative energy, and make a point of contact with "life." But the music hall decayed. It was based on that period of "proletarian" existence when the workers were stiffly encased in the tradition of knowing their place and imitating their betters. This tradition exploded in 1918; and we hear Eliot making a final tribute to Marie Lloyd, with added gloomy prognostications for the future:

> It was her capacity for expressing the soul of a people that made her unique. . . .
> It was her understanding of the people and sympathy with them, and the people's recognition of the fact that she embodied the virtues that they most genuinely respected in private life, that raised her to the position she occupied at her death. I have called her the expressive figure of the lower classes. There is no such expressive figure for any other classes. The middle classes have no such idol: the middle classes are morally corrupt . . . .

Eliot then goes on to express his fear that, with the disappearance of the music hall, and "the encroachment of the cheap and rapid-breeding cinema, the lower classes will drop to the same state of protoplasm as the bourgeoisie," and, moreover, when this state has overcome them, that they may die off from sheer boredom! This essay, written in 1923, closes with words of deep dismay as to the possibility of the hastening of this general disintegration by the development of another mechanical device for transmitting entertainment—the radio.

Eliot underestimated his "lower classes." The music hall disappeared only after it had reached a high point of breadth and elegance. Folk expression continually runs toward this elegance, contrary to the *idée reçue* of its being by necessity clumsy and "vulgar." (And this elegance is not to be confused with the empty slickness of the revue kind.) But as a rather stuffy set of prewar conventions broke, the urban crowd shifted toward a freer, less imitative and reverent habit of mind and manner. Something new began immediately; persistent energy released itself into new forms and new media.

The energy is now at a more primitive level than formerly; these shifts go back and forth, as this current of urban life or that is released and breaks; many reasons requiring specialized attention are here involved. But the fact remains that American folk has never been more vigorous than at this moment. In "hot jazz," words are attached to music, as in all primitive states of poetry and music. Improvisation (the "lick") is in every talented performer's power. The rhythm is the important matter; the music has all the harmonic tricks under control with which to surround and embellish the beat. The various mechanical devices which Eliot feared and deplored have served, as a matter of fact, to aid the development and dissemination of this folk art. The folk now gets exactly what it wants to listen to. If the radio does not give it what it needs in sufficient quantity, people have their records and juke boxes, and, of course, the live performers. The vigor of folk at present is shown by its tendency to raid over into "classical" and bring back whatever tunes please it. The juke-box repertoire is a thing in itself: there the hymn tune (disguised) shares popularity with the crooned ballad and with certain holdovers from the open spaces of the past. Compared to the songs of the upright piano and sheet music era, even the most naïve songs are less awkward and saccharine, more vitalized. And the imitation "folk song," such as the really remarkable "Blues in the Night," has taken on a finish which always characterizes folk in a good creative period *of its own*.

It is interesting to note that at this particular stage, "popular" interest in accident, sudden death, and the morbid in general (unlike American songs of an earlier day) has very nearly disappeared, along with the "topical song," that sister to the broadsheet.

A proposition could be drawn up:

Folk crosses formal art:

1.   When folk has reached a moment of comparative breadth and elegance (when it can express anything, from the grotesque through emotion and satire, well).
2.   When formal art has become easy and secular enough to recognize just where folk lies; and, having located folk, understands what is happening there.

A long period of time must elapse before, in America, the demands of this proposition can be fulfilled. But Eliot's fears were unjustified; just as the present middle-class hope that L. Stokowski can be crossed with Disney, or some genteel poet with the songs of pioneering backwoodsmen, is at once previous and misplaced.

Let us now take a brief glance at the American intellectual. The intellectual is a middle-class product; if he is not born into the class he must soon insert himself into it, in order to exist. He is the fine nervous flower of the bourgeoisie. His task, ideally, would be the close critical observation of the field in which he stands, while keeping his attention alert for new movement in the landscape as a whole. That the intellectual fails in this job is one reason for the wholesale mixture of genres, the unrebuked mistakes of prize committees, publishers, etc., the general insolence of entrepreneurs—in fact the general failure to understand what is going on which marks the small remaining section of American life still interested in literature.

The intellectual, being nervous, is subject to all the floating airs of modern religion (present in quantity, no matter how fogged and misted into the semblance of something else). One must not forget that religious enthusiasm (and intolerance) has always been inextricably mixed with every materialist idea; has been a concomitant of all material push since Calvin. Intellectuals range through the finest gradations of kind and quality: from those who are merely educated neurotics, usually with strong hidden reactionary tendencies, through mediocrities of all kinds, to men of real brains and sensibility, more or less stiffened into various respectabilities or substitutes for respectability. The number of Ignorant Specialists is large. The number of hysterics and compulsives is also large. It is natural that the truly sensitive intellectual should have spiritual needs; for such a person the necessity for those moments in life when one is forced to see reality without wraps and unrationalized is strong. This necessity leads to a real breakthrough into maturity on the part of some individuals. For the less sensitive, the spiritual necessity hardly exists; they require not steadying insight but emotional outlet. It is in this class that we find the hot-gospellers, the morally pretentious, the reformers, and the seekers of closed systems of salvation. These men and women are not entirely the products of an imperfect culture (for the type appeared in quantity in France in the nineteenth century) but of a culture somehow blocked and mixed; and of the impact of this curious situation upon natures more simply constituted than they themselves suppose Flaubert wrote down an approximation of the type in *Bouvard et Pécuchet*. He gave the two simple-minded copyists a set of manias which is still complete for the dislocated middle-class mind of our time; manias ranging from the collecting of antiques to an absorption in various forms of science and politics. These two prototypes of the middle-class yearner with a few retouches could represent not only the modern lecture-listening audience but many of "the experts who tend the complicated machinery of modern civilization."

One characteristic of the Bouvard-Pécuchet sort of enthusiasm is the violent repudiation after violent interest of one craze after another when the satiation point is reached. The revulsion shown by the intellectual towards the artist, during recent years, resembles this sort of compensating tendency. The too-great emphasis of emotion and hope placed upon the artist in the preceding period is lifted and placed at an opposite point. The D.H. Lawrence, Proust, Hart Crane kind of semi-worship went over, for a time, to Malraux; and then became transformed into something else. The very complexity of the artist's equipment became as much a target for the subsequent badgering and denigration as the non-material quality of his aim. It is moral blame of the most childish kind that we find most frequently expressed; and real puzzlement, also at a childish level. The atmosphere of former religious paroxysms and squabblings returns; the old fights between established religion and the sects and between the sects themselves; the old tiresome yet dangerous extremes of the persecutory centuries.

Now, one would think that the unstable intellectual should stand out against all these moral acrobatics and tergiversations: if not as judge, at least as arbiter. If he cannot remain firm, he should at least be in another part of the field, out of the melee and ahead of it. But as things turn out, he is either squarely in the mix-up, name-calling with the best or making motions of advancing, the while he has managed rapidly to retreat into something truly comforting in the way of pre-Copernican scholasticism, or has made a full flight back to Aristotle. And if he is of no real use in reconciling embattled sects, perhaps he could do a little simple journeyman's work in keeping entrepreneurism in its place. But here he rather fails us, too.

At this point it is necessary to remember that the middle class has produced, at the expense of much time and effort, a whole literature of its own. Its own writers, bred out of its own bone and flesh, educated in its own schools and amenable to its own scheme of manners and custom, have fanned out into the middle region; adapted in every way to express the middle intellect, temperament, grasp of reality, powers of analysis and emotion. Some of these poets, novelists, critics, biographers, and belletrists were born middle; some either rose or sank to where they at length find themselves. The complicated but smoothly oiled machinery of the publishing business, the general run of reviewers, the committees giving out literary awards, the more benumbed mass of academics: all these agents function, for the most part (and changing the figure), inside the same structure. During certain short periods, certain wild individuals stay outside and throw rocks, but since these intransigents tend to disappear for long intervals, the easiest supposition is that they are absorbed. And the periods of almost complete absorption present a very amusing spectacle indeed. These are the times when the book sections produce, week after week, month after month, serious judgments on books, but when everything judged and the judges themselves are cut out of the same piece of medium material. The commodity books are being dealt with by the commodity critics—a spectacle which would be purely funny if there were not elements of rather tragic irony in it.

The intellectual should at least know the difference between kinds, and have the courage to speak up when matters get really out of hand. He should make some admonishing gesture when a particularly startling piece of mutual aid comes through. He should know how the literary mechanism works: the way blurb-writing and prize-giving, journalists and literary impresarios engage with each other. He should be able to sense, watching the open pulls and twitches given reputations, all the subterranean maneuvering which must go on so that certain effects are produced at eye-level. What about the distinguished specialists who write blurbs for dust-jackets? Is this a harmless bit of fun, or a plan to get around the subsequent remarks of the book reviewer? What about the American prize committee (situated rather disadvantageously, one might suppose, for anyone not a journalist, in a school of journalism) which, having ignored brilliant talent, young and old, falls back ever again upon old standbys?

What about the extra-literary influences which manage, from time to time, to bring to laudatory view a book of gibberish? What about certain anthologists who teeter on the verge of being members of the vanity press: are all their contributors paid? Who is to deal with these matters but the intellectual?

Meanwhile, the cry rises that poetry has disappeared. This plaint often comes from the dead center, say from the core of the Sunday book section. It rises with particular sharpness during times of cataclysm. The middle wishes poetry to throb, as it were, under the historic processes without a break; to light up ambiguous terrain with continual succeeding flashes of "inspiration." But poetry cannot be counted upon to act as a sort of combination faith-healing and artificial thunder and lightning. Poetry of the lyric order disappears for a century at a time. It shifts. And when the formal line has in some manner been exhausted, the vigor goes back to the base. The middle must put up with what it has: their flabby little songs, their attempts at reviving the "golden" American past; and their more ambitious flights: those attempts to combine autobiography with *post hoc ergo propter hoc* comment on the world situation.

"The function of the great individual is to take up and transform what has been communally produced." For this function one must wait, when the folk material is in a transitional phase—unmalleable and too full of its own rough vigor to be handled, and when "great individuals" seem to be lacking. Even the artist may misjudge the time. In Eliot's "Sweeney Agonistes" and "Fragment of an Agon" the two lines—of formal treatment and "rough" material—are somehow artificially combined; the result cannot really move us. But there are times when the poet can deal with whatever comes to hand. And folk will not always remain ungraspable.

A few notes on the future direction of the poet:

The true hierarchic attitude as exemplified by some "inheritors of Symbolism" (Stefan George and to a lesser degree Valéry and Yeats) seems to be exhausted. George's "willed rationalism toward the antique, his aesthetic and individualist humanism . . . which seeks in the universe the exaltation of man"—this line we have seen warped and corrupted; it now leads nowhere. The lesser task of the poet at present is satire. But satire cannot be asked to bear all of the weight of the diversified and subtle modern spirit. There is another development of this century's early period of aesthetic experiment and moral explanation. This proceeds from Rilke. "In Rilke (as opposed to George)," writes Geneviève Bianquis, "exists the most absolute abandonment to the law of the inanimate; the need to unknot, to detach the bonds of the individual; the need to love everything, to absorb everything into himself and to absorb himself in all; to channel toward God or toward things all happiness, all sorrow and all emotion." This is the contrast between the will which builds Ages of Faith and the act of faith itself; between compulsion and serenity; arrogance and humility; between the raw act of force and the more complex refusal of force but openness to spiritual power.

The foundation material is ready for this tendency. The only really usable and incontrovertible modern discoveries are in the spiritual field; and these have their everyday diagnostic and therapeutic uses. Truth has been told, experience undergone, and movement undertaken—"forward" as Eliot says; but this forward has not its old "progressive" connotation. The number of individuals engaged in writing poetry of this order will not be large, and, as is so often the case, may be unseen by their generation. The forms will be kept clear and the tone uninflated. No more rhetoric; no more verbalizing; no more exhortations or elegies or eulogies. No more conscious and affected investigations of dark corridors and deserted strands; no more use of the universe as a backdrop against which one acts out hope or despair. No more dejected sitting about. No more searching nature for an answering mood . . .

This exploration and movement can go on without having to search out the folk for refreshment. The more complex tasks have been neglected for a long time; attention to them is overdue. Compared to these at once subtle and difficult necessities the reiterated standardized demands of the bourgeois yearner sound incredibly stupid and outdated.

> Is it possible that despite our discoveries and progress, despite our culture, religion, and world-wisdom, we still remain on the surface of life? Is it possible that we have even covered this surface which might still have been something, with an incredibly uninteresting stuff which makes it look like drawing-room furniture during the summer holidays?
>
> Yes, it is possible. . . .
>
> But if all this is possible . . . then surely, for all the world's sake, something must be done. The first comer, he who has had these disturbing thoughts, must begin to do some of the neglected things; even if he be just anybody, by no means the most suitable person: there is no one else at hand. This young insignificant foreigner, Brigge, will have to sit down in his room five flights up, and write, day and night. Yes, he will have to write; that will be the end of it.[1]

This was written at the beginning of the century; but nothing much seems to have been accomplished. Now that a good deal of the drawing-room furniture lies in ruins, there may be another beginning.

Note

1   From Rainer Maria Rilke's *Journal of My Other Self*, also known as *The Notebooks of Malte Laurids Brigge*, 1910.

Chapter 13

Bertolt Brecht (1898–1956)

"SHORT DESCRIPTION OF A NEW TECHNIQUE OF ACTING WHICH PRODUCES AN ALIENATION EFFECT" (1943–44)

ALTHOUGH BORN IN AUGSBURG, BAVARIA, Bertolt Brecht – playwright, theatre director, poet, and fiction writer – was most famously associated with Weimar-era Berlin, where his plays were greeted with enthusiastic critical acclaim and fervent Nazi protests. A nearly lifelong Marxist and anti-militarist – Brecht was threatened with expulsion from grammar school for his caustically unenthusiastic response to a patriotic essay exercise – Brecht aimed to agitate his audience and improve social relations; his was a transformational approach to culture, rather than an affirmative one. In his view, the Aristotelian cathartic tradition and conventional realist theatre hypnotized audiences and affirmed the bourgeois and capitalistic status quo. After he and his family escaped Germany in 1933, he lived in exile in various European cities, including Prague, Stockholm, and Helsinki. He, like Sergei Eisenstein, had a short and unsuccessful stint in Hollywood; both men's theoretical approaches to representation were too strangely European and unmarketable for Hollywood moguls. Brecht's most famous plays, which are explicitly anti-Nazi and anti-fascistic, include *Fear and Misery of the Third Reich* (1938), *Mother Courage and Her Children* (1941), *Galileo* (1943), and *The Caucasian Chalk Circle* (1945). Brecht's collaborations with the composer Kurt Weill, *The Threepenny Opera* (1928) and *The Rise and Fall of the City of Mahoganny* (1930), helped to revive serious musical theatre. Some of the German playwright's most famous theoretical essays include "The Modern Theatre is Epic Theatre" (1930), "The Street Scene: A Basic Model for Epic Theatre" (1938–40), and "On Experimental Theatre" (1939, 1961).

Bertolt Brecht, "Short Description of a New Technique of Acting which Produces an Alienation Effect," *Brecht on Theatre: The Development of an Aesthetic*. New York: Hill & Wang, 1964.

What follows represents an attempt to describe a technique of acting which was applied in certain theatres[1] with a view to taking the incidents portrayed and alienating them from the spectator. The aim of this technique, known as the alienation effect, was to make the spectator adopt an attitude of inquiry and criticism in his approach to the incident. The means were artistic.

The first condition for the A-effect's application to this end is that stage and auditorium must be purged of everything 'magical' and that no 'hypnotic tensions' should be set up. This ruled out any attempt to make the stage convey the flavour of a particular place (a room at evening, a road in the autumn), or to create atmosphere by relaxing the tempo of the conversation. The audience was not 'worked up' by a display of temperament or 'swept away' by acting with tautened muscles; in short, no attempt was made to put it in a trance and give it the illusion of watching an ordinary unrehearsed event. As will be seen presently, the audience's tendency to plunge into such illusions has to be checked by specific artistic means.[2]

The first condition for the achievement of the A-effect is that the actor must invest what he has to show with a definite gest of showing. It is of course necessary to drop the assumption that there is a fourth wall cutting the audience off from the stage and the consequent illusion that the stage action is taking place in reality and without an audience. That being so, it is possible for the actor in principle to address the audience direct.

It is well known that contact between audience and stage is normally made on the basis of empathy. Conventional actors devote their efforts so exclusively to bringing about this psychological operation that they may be said to see it as the principal aim of their art.[3] Our introductory remarks will already have made it clear that the technique which produces an A-effect is the exact opposite of that which aims at empathy. The actor applying it is bound not to try to bring about the empathy operation.

Yet in his efforts to reproduce particular characters and show their behaviour he need not renounce the means of empathy entirely. He uses these means just as any normal person with no particular acting talent would use them if he wanted to portray someone else, i.e. show how he behaves. This showing of other people's behaviour happens time and again in ordinary life (witnesses of an accident demonstrating to newcomers how the victim behaved, a facetious person imitating a friend's walk, etc.), without those involved making the least effort to subject their spectators to an illusion. At the same time they do feel their way into their characters' skins with a view to acquiring their characteristics.

As has already been said, the actor too will make use of this psychological operation. But whereas the usual practice in acting is to execute it during the actual performance, in the hope of stimulating the spectator into a similar operation, he will achieve it only at an earlier stage, at some time during rehearsals.

To safeguard against an unduly 'impulsive', frictionless and uncritical creation of characters and incidents, more reading rehearsals can be held than usual. The actor should refrain from living himself into the part prematurely in any way, and should go on functioning as long as possible as a reader (which does not mean a reader-aloud). An important step is memorizing one's first impressions.

When reading his part the actor's attitude should be one of a man who is astounded and contradicts. Not only the occurrence of the incidents, as he reads about them, but the conduct of the man he is playing, as he experiences it, must be weighed up by him and their peculiarities understood; none can be taken as given, as something that 'was bound to turn out that way', that was 'only to be expected from a character like that'. Before memorizing the words he must memorize what he felt astounded at and where he felt impelled to contradict. For these are dynamic forces that he must preserve in creating his performance.

When he appears on the stage, besides what he actually is doing he will at all essential points discover, specify, imply what he is not doing; that is to say he will act in such a way that the alternative emerges as clearly as possible, that his acting allows the other possibilities to be inferred and only represents one out of the possible variants. He will say for instance 'You'll pay for that', and not say 'I forgive you'. He detests his children; it is not the case that he loves them. He moves down stage left and not up stage right. Whatever he doesn't do must be contained and conserved in what he does. In this way every sentence and every gesture signifies a decision; the character remains under observation and is tested. The technical term for this procedure is 'fixing the "not . . . but"'.

The actor does not allow himself to become completely transformed on the stage into the character he is portraying. He is not Lear, Harpagon, Schweik; he shows them. He reproduces their remarks as authentically as he can; he puts forward their way of behaving to the best of his abilities and knowledge of men; but he never tries to persuade himself (and thereby others) that this amounts to a complete transformation. Actors will know what it means if I say that a typical kind of acting without this complete transformation takes place when a producer or colleague shows one how to play a particular passage. It is not his own part, so he is not completely transformed; he underlines the technical aspect and retains the attitude of someone just making suggestions.

Once the idea of total transformation is abandoned the actor speaks his part not as if he were improvising it himself but like a quotation.[4] At the same time he obviously has to render all the quotation's overtones, the remark's full human and concrete shape; similarly the gesture he makes must have the full substance of a human gesture even though it now represents a copy.

Given this absence of total transformation in the acting there are three aids which may help to alienate the actions and remarks of the characters being portrayed:

1.   Transposition into the third person.
2.   Transposition into the past.
3.   Speaking the stage directions out loud.

Using the third person and the past tense allows the actor to adopt the right attitude of detachment. In addition he will look for stage directions and remarks that comment on his lines, and speak them aloud at rehearsal ('He stood up and exclaimed angrily, not having eaten: . . .', or 'He had never been told so before, and didn't know if it was true or not', or 'He smiled, and said with forced nonchalance: . . .'). Speaking the stage directions out loud in the third person results in a clash between two tones of voice, alienating the second of them, the text proper. This style of acting is further alienated by taking place on the stage after having already been outlined and announced in words. Transposing it into the past gives the speaker a standpoint from which he can look back at his sentence. The sentence too is thereby alienated without the speaker adopting an unreal point of view; unlike the spectator, he has read the play right through and is better placed to judge the sentence in accordance with the ending, with its consequences, than the former, who knows less and is more of a stranger to the sentence.

This composite process leads to an alienation of the text in the rehearsals which generally persists in the performance too.[5] The directness of the relationship with the audience allows and indeed forces the actual speech delivery to be varied in accordance with the greater or smaller significance attaching to the sentences. Take the case of witnesses addressing a court. The underlinings, the characters' insistence on their remarks, must be developed as a piece of effective virtuosity. If the actor turns to the audience it must be a whole-hearted turn rather than the asides and soliloquizing technique of the old-fashioned theatre. To get the full A-effect from the poetic medium the actor should start at rehearsal by paraphrasing the verse's content in vulgar prose, possibly accompanying this by the gestures designed for the verse. A daring and beautiful handling of verbal media will alienate the text. (Prose can be alienated by translation into the actor's native dialect.)

Gesture will be dealt with below, but it can at once be said that everything to do with the emotions has to be externalized; that is to say, it must be developed into a gesture. The actor has to find a sensibly perceptible outward expression for his character's emotions, preferably some action that gives away what is going on inside him. The emotion in question must be brought out, must lose all its restrictions so that it can be treated on a big scale. Special elegance, power and grace of gesture bring about the A-effect.

A masterly use of gesture can be seen in Chinese acting. The Chinese actor achieves the A-effect by being seen to observe his own movements.

Whatever the actor offers in the way of gesture, verse structure, etc., must be finished and bear the hallmarks of something rehearsed and rounded-off. The impression to be given is one of ease, which is at the same time one of difficulties overcome. The actor must make it possible for the audience to take his own art, his mastery of technique, lightly too. He puts an incident before the spectator with perfection and as he thinks it really happened or might have happened. He does not conceal the fact that he has rehearsed it, any more than an acrobat conceals his training, and he emphasizes that it is his own (actor's) account, view, version of the incident.

Because he doesn't identify himself with him he can pick a definite attitude to adopt towards the character whom he portrays, can show what he thinks of him and invite the spectator, who is likewise not asked to identify himself, to criticize the character portrayed.

The attitude which he adopts is a socially critical one. In his exposition of the incidents and in his characterization of the person he tries to bring out those features which come within society's sphere. In this way his performance becomes a discussion (about social conditions) with the audience he is addressing. He prompts the spectator to justify or abolish these conditions according to what class he belongs to.[6]

The object of the A-effect is to alienate the social gest underlying every incident. By social gest is meant the mimetic and gestural expression of the social relationships prevailing between people of a given period.[7]

It helps to formulate the incident for society, and to put it across in such a way that society is given the key, if titles are thought up for the scenes. These titles must have a historical quality.

This brings us to a crucial technical device: historicization.

The actor must play the incidents as historical ones. Historical incidents are unique, transitory incidents associated with particular periods. The conduct of the persons involved in them is not fixed and 'universally human'; it includes elements that have been or may be overtaken by the course of history, and is subject to criticism from the immediately following period's point of view. The conduct of those born before us is alienated from us by an incessant evolution.

It is up to the actor to treat present-day events and modes of behaviour with the same detachment as the historian adopts with regard to those of the past. He must alienate these characters and incidents from us.

Characters and incidents from ordinary life, from our immediate surroundings, being familiar, strike us as more or less natural. Alienating them helps to make them seem remarkable to us. Science has carefully developed a technique of getting irritated with the everyday, 'self-evident', universally accepted occurrence, and there is no reason why this infinitely useful attitude should not be taken over by art.[8] It is an attitude which arose in science as a result of the growth in human productive powers. In art the same motive applies.

As for the emotions, the experimental use of the A-effect in the epic theatre's German productions indicated that this way of acting too can stimulate them, though possibly a different class of emotion is involved from those of the orthodox theatre.[9] A critical attitude on the audience's part is a thoroughly artistic one.[10] Nor does the actual practice of the A-effect seem anything like so unnatural as its description. Of course it is a way of acting that has nothing to do with stylization as commonly practised. The main advantage of the epic theatre with its A-effect, intended purely to show the world in such a way that it becomes manageable, is precisely its quality of being natural and earthly, its humour and its renunciation of all the mystical elements that have stuck to the orthodox theatre from the old days.

Notes

1   *Edward II* after Marlowe (Munich Kammerspiele).
Trommeln in der Nacht (Deutsches Theater, Berlin).
The Threepenny Opera (Theater am Schiffbauerdamm, Berlin).
Die Pioniere von Ingolstadt (Theater am Schiffbauerdamm).
Aufstieg und Fall der Stadt Mahagonny, opera (Aufricht's Kurfürstendammtheater, Berlin).
Mann ist Mann (Staatstheater, Berlin).
Die Massnahme (Grosses Schauspielhaus, Berlin).
The Adventures of the Good Soldier Schweik (Piscator's Theater am Nollendorfplatz, Berlin).
Die Plattköpfe und die Spitzköpfe (Riddersalen, Copenhagen).
Señora Carrar's Rifles (Copenhagen, Paris).
Furcht und Elend des Dritten Reiches (Paris).

2   E.g. such mechanical means as very brilliant illumination of the stage (since a half-lit stage plus a completely darkened auditorium makes the spectator less level-headed by preventing him from observing his neighbour and in turn hiding him from his neighbour's eyes) and also *making visible the sources of light*.

MAKING VISIBLE THE SOURCES OF LIGHT

> There is a point in showing the lighting apparatus openly, as it is one of the means of preventing an unwanted element of illusion; it scarcely disturbs the necessary concentration. If we light the actors and their performance in such a way that the lights themselves are within the spectator's field of vision we destroy part of his illusion of being present at a spontaneous, transitory, authentic, unrehearsed event. He sees that arrangements have been made to show something; something is being repeated here under special conditions, for instance in a very brilliant light. Displaying the actual lights is meant to be a counter to the old-fashioned theatre's efforts to hide them. No one would expect the lighting to be hidden at a sporting event, a boxing match for instance. Whatever the points of difference between the modern theatre's presentations and those of a sporting promoter, they do not include the same concealment of the sources of light as the old theatre found necessary.
>
> (Brecht: 'Der Bühnenbau des epischen Theaters')

3   Cf. these remarks by Poul Reumert, the best-known Danish actor:

> '. . . If I feel I am *dying*, and if I *really* feel it, then so does everybody else; if I act as though I had a dagger in my hand, and am entirely filled by the one idea of killing the child, then everybody shudders. . . . The whole business is a matter of mental activity being communicated by emotions, or by another way round if you prefer it: a feeling so strong as to be an obsession, which is translated into thoughts. If it comes off it is the most infectious thing in the world; anything external is then a matter of complete indifference . . . .'

And Rapaport, 'The Work of the Actor', *Theatre Workshop*, October 1936:

> '. . . On the stage the actor is surrounded entirely by fictions. . . . The actor must be able to regard all this as though it were true, as though he were convinced that all that surrounds him on the stage is a living reality and, along with himself, he must convince the audience as well. This is the central feature of our method of work on the part. . . . Take any object, a cap for example; lay it on the table or on the floor and try to regard it as though it were a rat; make believe that it is a rat, and not a cap. . . . Picture what sort of rat it is; what size, colour? . . . We thus commit ourselves to believe quite naïvely that the object before us is something other than it is and, at the same time, learn to compel the audience to believe . . . .'

This might be thought to be a course of instruction for conjurers, but in fact it is a course of acting, supposedly according to Stanislavsky's method. One wonders if a technique that equips an actor to make the audience see rats where there aren't any can really be all that suitable for disseminating the truth. Given enough alcohol it doesn't take acting to persuade almost anybody that he is seeing rats: pink ones.

4   QUOTATION

> Standing in a free and direct relationship to it, the actor allows his character to speak and move; he presents a report. He does not have to make us forget that the text is not spontaneous, but has been memorized, is a fixed quantity; the fact doesn't matter, as we anyway assume that the report is not about himself but about others. His attitude would be the same if he were simply speaking from his own memory.

5   The theatre can create the corresponding A-effect in the performance in a number of ways. The Munich production of *Edward II* for the first time had titles preceding the scenes, announcing the contents. The Berlin production of *The Three Penny Opera* had the titles of the songs projected while they were sung. The Berlin production of *Mann ist Mann* had the actors' figures projected on big screens during the action.

6   Another thing that makes for freedom in the actor's relationship with the audience is that he does not treat it as an undifferentiated mass. He doesn't boil it down to a shapeless dumpling in the stockpot of the emotions. He does not address himself to everybody alike; he allows the existing divisions within the audience to continue, in fact he widens them. He has friends and enemies in the audience; he is friendly to the one group and hostile to the other. He takes sides, not necessarily with his character but if not with it then against it. (At least, that is his basic attitude, though it too must be variable and change according to what the character may say at different stages. There may, however, also be points at which everything is in the balance and the actor must withhold judgment, though this again must be expressly shown in his acting.)

7   If *King Lear* (in Act I, scene i) tears up a map when he divides his kingdom between his daughters, then the act of division is alienated. Not only does it draw our attention to his kingdom, but by treating the kingdom so plainly as his own private property he throws some light on the basis of the feudal idea of the family. In *Julius Caesar* the tyrant's murder by Brutus is alienated if during one of his monologues accusing Caesar of tyrannical motives he himself maltreats a slave waiting on him. Weigel as *Maria Stuart* suddenly took the crucifix hanging round her neck and used it coquettishly as a fan, to give herself air.

8   THE A-EFFECT AS A PROCEDURE IN EVERYDAY LIFE

The achievement of the A-effect constitutes something utterly ordinary, recurrent; it is justly a widely-practised way of drawing one's own or someone else's attention to a thing, and it can be seen in education as also in business conferences of one sort or another. The A-effect consists in turning the object of which one is to be made aware, to which one's attention is to be drawn, from something ordinary, familiar, immediately accessible, into something peculiar, striking and unexpected. What is obvious is in a certain sense made incomprehensible, but this is only in order that it may then be made all the easier to comprehend. Before familiarity can turn into awareness the familiar must be stripped of its inconspicuousness; we must give up assuming that the object in question needs no explanation. However frequently recurrent, modest, vulgar it may be will now be labelled as something unusual.

A common use of the A-effect is when someone says: 'Have you ever really looked carefully at your watch?' The questioner knows that I've looked at it often enough, and now his question deprives me of the sight which I've grown used to and which accordingly has nothing more to say to me. I used to look at it to see the time, and now when he asks me in this importunate way I realize that I have given up seeing the watch itself with an astonished eye; and it is in many ways an astonishing piece of machinery. Similarly it is an alienation effect of the simplest sort if a business discussion starts off with the sentence: 'Have you ever thought what happens to the waste from your factory which is pumped into the river twenty-four hours a day?' This waste wasn't just swept down the river unobserved; it was carefully channelled into the river; men and machines have worked on it; the river has changed colour, the waste has flowed away most conspicuously, but just as waste. It was superfluous to the process of manufacture, and now it is to become material for manufacture; our eye turns to it with interest. The asking of the question has alienated it, and intentionally so. The very simplest sentences that apply in the A-effect are those with 'Not . . . But': (He didn't say 'come in' but 'keep moving'. He was not pleased but amazed). They include an expectation which is justified by experience but, in the event, disappointed. One might have thought that . . . but one oughtn't to have thought it. There was not just one possibility but two; both are introduced, then the second one is alienated, then the first as well. To see one's mother as a man's wife one needs an A-effect; this is provided, for instance, when one acquires a stepfather. If one sees one's teacher hounded by the bailiffs an A-effect occurs: one is jerked out of a relationship in which the teacher seems big into one where he seems small. An alienation of the motor-car takes place if after driving a modern car for a long while we drive an old model T Ford. Suddenly we hear explosions once more; the motor works on the principle of explosion. We start feeling amazed that such a vehicle, indeed any vehicle not drawn by animal-power, can move; in short, we understand cars, by looking at them as something strange, new, as a triumph of engineering and to that extent something unnatural. Nature, which certainly embraces the motor-car, is suddenly imbued with an element of unnaturalness, and from now on this is an indelible part of the concept of nature.

The expression 'in fact' can likewise certify or alienate. (He wasn't in fact at home; he said he would be, but we didn't believe him and had a look; or again, we didn't think it possible for him not to be at home; but don't actually agree'.) Similarly the Eskimo definition 'A car is a wingless aircraft that crawls along the ground' is a way of alienating the car.

In a sense the alienation effect itself has been alienated by the above explanation; we have taken a common, recurrent, universally-practised operation and tried to draw attention to it by illuminating its peculiarity. But we have achieved the effect only with those people who have truly ('in fact') grasped that it does 'not' result from every representation 'but' from certain ones: only 'actually' is it familiar.

9   ABOUT RATIONAL AND EMOTIONAL POINTS OF VIEW

The rejection of empathy is not the result of a rejection of the emotions, nor does it lead to such. The crude aesthetic thesis that emotions can only be stimulated by means of empathy is wrong. None the less a non-aristotelian dramaturgy has to apply a cautious criticism to the emotions which it aims at and incorporates. Certain artistic tendencies like the provocative behaviour of Futurists and Dadists and the icing-up of music point to a crisis of the emotions. Already in the closing years of the Weimar Republic the post-war German drama took a decisively rationalist turn. Fascism's grotesque emphasizing of the emotions, together perhaps with the no less important threat to the rational element in Marxist aesthetics, led us to lay particular stress on the rational. Nevertheless there are many contemporary works of art where one can speak of a decline in emotional effectiveness due to their isolation from reason, or its revival thanks to a stronger rationalist message. This will surprise no one who has not got a completely conventional idea of the emotions.

The emotions always have quite a definite class basis; the form they take at any time is historical, restricted and limited in specific ways. The emotions are in no sense universally human and timeless.

The linking of particular emotions with particular interests is not unduly difficult so long as one simply looks for the interests corresponding to the emotional effects of works of art. Anyone can see the colonial adventures of the Second Empire looming behind Delacroix's paintings and Rimbaud's 'Bateau Ivre'.

If one compares the 'Bateau Ivre' say, with Kipling's 'Ballad of East and West', one can see the difference between French mid-nineteenth century colonialism and British colonialism at the beginning of the twentieth. It is less easy to explain the effect that such poems have on ourselves, as Marx already noticed. Apparently emotions accompanying social progress will long survive in the human mind as emotions linked with interests, and in the case of works of art will do so more strongly than might have been expected, given that in the meantime contrary interests will have made themselves be felt. Every step forward means the end of the previous step forward, because that is where it starts and goes on from. At the same time it makes use of this previous step, which in a sense survives in men's consciousness as a step forward, just as it survives its effects in real life. This involves a most interesting type of generalization, a continual process of abstraction. Whenever the works of art handed down to us allow us to share the emotions of other men, of men of a bygone period, different social classes, etc., we have to conclude that we are partaking in interests which really were universally human. These men now dead represented the interests of classes that gave a lead to progress. It is a very different matter when Fascism today conjures up on the grandest scale emotions which for most of the people who succumb to them are not determined by interest.

10   IS THE CRITICIAL ATTITUDE AN INARTISTIC ONE?

An old tradition leads people to treat a critical attitude as a predominately negative one. Many see the difference between the scientific and artistic attitudes as lying precisely in their attitude to criticism.

People cannot conceive of contradiction and detachment as being part of artistic appreciation. Of course such appreciation normally includes a higher level, which appreciates critically, but the criticism here only applies to matters of technique; it is quite a different matter from being required to observe not a representation of the world but the world itself in a critical, contradictory, detached manner.

   To introduce this critical attitude into art, the negative element which it doubtless includes must be shown from its positive side: this criticism of the world is active, practical, positive. Criticizing the course of a river means improving it, correcting it. Criticism of society is ultimately revolution; there you have criticism taken to its logical conclusion playing an active part. A critical attitude of this type is an operative factor of productivity; it is deeply enjoyable to watch as such, and if we commonly use the term 'arts' for enterprises that improve people's lives why should art proper remain aloof from arts of this sort?

PART II

Philosophy and religion

Friedrich Nietzsche's "madman" in *The Gay Science* (1882) articulated a growing feeling (and fear, at least for some) when he proclaimed: "God is dead." Numerous scientific discoveries (including fossils that helped to establish that the earth originated billions of years ago rather than in 4004 BC as proclaimed by the seventeenth-century Anglican Archbishop James Ussher), the establishment of human-centered social sciences, Freud's work on the id and the ego, and secular humanism, among other forces and events, worked to weaken established religious orthodoxies in the latter part of the nineteenth century and the beginning of the twentieth. Some modernists, including Albert Einstein, did proclaim a more or less traditional faith despite traveling paths of intellectual inquiry that would seem to take them in a very different direction. T.S. Eliot, for one, in his Preface to his collection of critical essays entitled *For Lancelot Andrewes* (1928), declared that, "The general point of view [of the essays] may be described as classicist in literature, royalist in politics, and anglo-catholic in religion."[1] Yet Eliot was certainly at odds with Arnoldian liberal secularism as embodied by, for example, George Bernard Shaw and with that of Arnold's heir, E.M. Forster who, in "What I Believe," writes: "Faith, to my mind, is a stiffening process, a sort of mental starch, which ought to be applied as sparingly as possible. I dislike the stuff. I do not believe in it . . . My motto is: 'Lord, I disbelieve – help thou my unbelief.'" Speaking during and for what seemed an increasingly secular age, Forster sought to replace traditional faith with "tolerance, good temper and sympathy – they are what matter really, and if the human race is not to collapse they must come to the front before long."[2] Forster and many members of the Bloomsbury Circle were inspired by Cambridge philosopher G.E. Moore (1873–1958), whose *Principia Ethica* (1903) celebrated rigorous individual ethical inquiry and humanism; Leonard Woolf described the book as his generation's "bible" in his autobiography, *Growing* (1967). Also influential were William James (1842–1910), who considered true beliefs those that that were useful to the believer and who espoused a pragmatic view of truth in which thoughts and statements were coherent and corresponded with external reality; Bertrand Russell (1872–1970), a British philosopher, mathematician, historian, and social critic who was a founder of analytic philosophy, wrote prolifically on metaphysics, the logic and philosophy of mathematics, the philosophy of language, ethics, and epistemology, was an outspoken pacifist, and famously said, "No one can sit at the bedside of a dying child and still believe in God"; and Ludwig Wittgenstein (1889–1951), who founded one of the century's most important philosophical movements, logical positivism, which combines empiricism and epistemology. Yet Eliot's reactionary profession of faith was also of a piece with beliefs that persisted during the modern era, which, for all its revolutionary fervor, saw many (Lawrence, Yeats, Hemingway) espousing conservative values, including anti-Semitism and reactionary politics, long before the American priest Charles Edward Coughlin and Ezra Pound went over the edge and made treasonous radio broadcasts in support of Hitler and Mussolini.

Thus, while traditional religion may have declined in the West, the modern era was, in its way, as spiritually complex as its predecessor. James Joyce's *Ulysses* (1922), generally considered the greatest novel of the twentieth century, achieves an extraordinarily detailed representation of the quotidian, material doings of Dubliners on a single day, 16 June 1904. But it begins with a parodic mass (*"Introibo ad altare Dei"*) performed by Buck Mulligan, the housemate of Stephen Dedalus who, lapsing from his Catholicism in Joyce's *A Portrait of the Artist as a Young Man*, nonetheless admits that the language he speaks is that of the religion he rejects, for that's all he knows. Called a "fearful jesuit" by Mulligan and "a spoiled priest" by a prostitute he later encounters, Dedalus is haunted by his deceased mother, whose dying request for him to kneel down and pray he had refused; her anguished spirit finally appears to him in "a torn bridal veil, her face worn and noseless, green with grave mould." Leopold Bloom, Joyce's Odysseus, is an apostate Jew who has been baptized three times but still fails to understand much of what occurs in the Catholic services he witnesses, first in a church and then at a gravesite – speculating, for example, that INRI carved on a cross stands for "Iron Nails Ran In" rather than "Jesus of Nazareth King of the Jews." Yet Bloom, who has been obsessed with his own dead (his son Rudy who, though he lived for only eleven days, remains very much alive in his thoughts throughout the book), attains an apotheosis of sorts when, at the novel's climax, he stands up for his Jewish heritage against the anti-Semitic Citizen, proclaiming a gospel of justice and love, and then, like Elijah, "ascend[s] to heaven" where he is received by "clouds of angels." Like Stephen, he subsequently receives a visitation from his dead, but Rudy appears to him not as a ghoulish corpse but as the boy he might have been had he lived.

For all its emphasis on scientific achievement and great material advances in transportation, communication, medical science, and weaponry, modernism is, in fact, haunted by revenants, who appear throughout the literature and the culture. Though the word "spiritualist" seems especially inapposite for such an age and few of modernism's practitioners had any use for established religion, many of its painters, for example (Piet Mondrian, Wassily Kandinsky, Paul Gauguin, Constantin Brancusi, Robert Delauney, Paul Klee, among others), were theosophists influenced by Madame Blavatsky, whose *Isis Unveiled* positions spiritualism as a bridge between theology and science. Klee's "Angelus Novus" serves as the "Angel of History" in Walter Benjamin's "Theses on the Philosophy of History" (1940), an epistemological search for lasting meaning and value, written in the midst of the Nazi occupation of Paris. The Jewish-German cultural critic and philosopher's synthetic beliefs included ideological skepticism, inventive and unorthodox Marxist historical materialism, millenarianism, Jewish mysticism, and opium-inspired reverie. Pablo Picasso, an affirmed atheist, spent many hours reading tarot cards; and Amedeo Modigliani favored Ouija boards and attended seances. W.B. Yeats, who was devoted to automatic writing, and L. Frank Baum, the writer of *The Wizard of Oz*, also saw no necessary opposition between spiritualism and intellectual pursuits and eagerly participated in seances. For them, as for numerous others, "scientific epistemology would verify the materiality of the unseen world."[3]

The study of comparative religion emerged at this time. Sir James George Frazer's great comparatist study, *The Golden Bough* (1890–1915), found universal religious and mythical paradigms that made Christianity exemplary rather than unique, a conclusion that greatly enriched works, such as Eliot's *The Waste Land* and Pound's *Cantos*, that took many of their ideas and much of their inspiration and imagery from non-Western and non-contemporary cultures. Conflating spatiality with temporality, European modernists often looked to the non-Western world in hope of rediscovering a primitive spirituality from which they felt cut off by the forces of modernity. The narrative of religious decline in the West was often accompanied by a sense among European modernists that spirituality could be found elsewhere – perhaps in the East or in the ancient past. Influential gurus, often from Eastern Europe, such as the neo-Platonist Blavatsky and Georges Ivanovitch Gurdjieff, whose "esoteric Christianity" influenced Katherine Mansfield and Jean Toomer, captivated artists in search of a spiritual identity outside of organized religion and did so through a heady brew of global and ancient religious practices. These gurus and their close-knit circle of initiates may have been particularly attractive to modernists because of their esotericism, their heavy reliance on symbolism, and their promise of equality between souls that crossed lines of gender, color, and mortality. In her essay "On Being Young – A Woman – and Colored" (1925), Marita Bonner found respite from American racism in the calm, quiet image of the Buddha whom, she notes, is "brown like I am" and sits "entirely at ease, entirely sure of himself; motionless and knowing."[4] Alain Locke's vision of the "New Negro" included a willful combination of spiritual forces as a means of reaching "something like a spiritual emancipation" from racism and the psychology of victimization and dependence. He found foundations for the New Negro's self-reinvention in a variety of sources, including Emersonian self-reliance and a modified version of Mohandas Gandhi's *satyagraha* (truth-force or passive resistance); "mental passive resistance," self-respect and American ideals fulfilled could enable the New Negro's "spiritual Coming of Age."[5] The pronounced eastward glance of much modernist spiritualism led to chains of influence and collaborations between writers from Europe, India, China, Japan, and the Middle East. Pound's Confucianism, H.D.'s Egyptology, Eliot's studies of the Sanskrit *Upanishads*, and Yeats's studies of Japanese Noh theatre to name a few, directly influenced the theory and practice of their writing. An increasingly secular view of religion also enabled writers, artists, and intellectuals from different religions, sects, and castes to reimagine a collective identity beyond rigidly defined and sometimes explosively violent divisions; the All-India Progressive Writers Alliance Pan-South Asian orientation privileged socialism and communism over the tenets of Indian religion. Muhammad Iqbal, who studied Western philosophy in Germany, combined Islamic Sufism, radical anti-materialism and Nietzschean will; for Iqbal only a new, syncretic religious outlook could lead to the "reconstruction" of religious thought in Islam. These cross-cultural influences were not always consigned to the past; in the 1920s, Yeats translated and, with intermittent help from Pound, promoted the works of the contemporary Indian writer Rabindranath Tagore, who won the Nobel Prize for Literature in 1913. Yeats considered Tagore's poetry to be representative of a "tradition, where poetry and religion are the same thing."[6] Although Tagore wrote in various genres, the European craze for his religious poetry in *Gitanjali* ("Song Offerings") shows the spiritual bent toward which European writers and readers inclined in their acceptance of non-Western writers.

   In addition, advances in science and technology, rather than vanquishing spiritualism, became the tools for new, modern forms of spiritual inquiry. Organizations such as the Society for Psychical Research (founded in London in 1882) emerged using modern technologies to conduct empirical research on paranormal phenomena. For some, in fact, such developments as X-rays and radio waves seemed to imply a possible convergence of science and religion, with technology increasingly able to access the immaterial, perhaps even the spiritual, realm. Thus, intellectuals like Sir Arthur Conan Doyle, a lapsed Catholic, and Yeats, a lapsed Protestant (though he never took established religion seriously) – both haunted by a sense of the supernatural and seeking scientific means to investigate paranormal phenomena such as extra-sensory perception and automatic writing – participated in seances, while other of their contemporaries sought to photograph the evoked spirits or to quantify the soul by placing dying persons on scales in order to measure the loss that occurs at the moment of death. And just as Charles Lyell, Edmund Gosse, and Einstein sought to reconcile faith and scientific knowledge, so too, in its own way, did literary modernism take upon itself the task of filling a great cultural breach.

Modernist writers like Virginia Woolf and D.H. Lawrence consciously sought to fill the spiritual vacuum by assuming the serious and significant role of redefining and depicting the intersection of the material and the intangible. Woolf's dismissal of her popular Edwardian predecessors – H.G. Wells, Arnold Bennett, and John Galsworthy – was prompted by what she saw as their thorough-going materiality, "because they are concerned not with the spirit but with the body," and the lifelessness of their characters. In Woolf's view, certain Victorians – Thomas Hardy, Joseph Conrad, and to a lesser degree W.H. Hudson – anticipated Joyce, who (though she found his writings often indecent) "is spiritual; he is concerned at all costs to reveal the flickerings of that innermost flame which flashes its messages through the brain, and in order to preserve it he disregards with complete courage whatever seems to him adventitious, whether it be probability, or coherence or any other of these signposts which for generations have served to support the imagination of a reader when called upon to imagine what he can neither touch nor see."[7] For Lawrence, the waning of religious orthodoxy meant that the novel, which he called "the one bright book of life," would replace the Bible, "a great confused novel" that was irrelevant to contemporary life, as the twentieth-century's sacred text. What matters in both the original and the modernist Bible, Lawrence insisted, is neither merely material nor transcendent, but that "the characters . . . do nothing but *live* . . . [by] an instinct of the whole consciousness in a man, bodily, mental, spiritual at once,"[8] though with a focus reoriented on this world. Hence, rewriting the story of the slain and reborn Christ in *The Man Who Died* (originally called *The Escaped Cock*), Lawrence emphasizes that Christ's resurrection is very much in and of the material world and the healing erotic touch.

So while Eliot took his spiritual journey into high Anglicanism, Joyce's Stephen Dedalus flees his Catholic upbringing, driven away in part by the fire and brimstone sermon at the heart of *A Portrait of the Artist*, rejecting service to that in which he no longer believes. Also spiritually haunted, Jake Barnes in Hemingway's *The Sun Also Rises* (1926), rendered impotent by the wound he received in World War I, seeks higher meaning in a world bereft of it, claiming that "I'm pretty religious." But he repeatedly comes up empty: he's a "lousy" Catholic whose praying is "not much of a success"; he seeks the equivalent as an *aficion* in the brotherhood of the bullfighting into which he is accepted but then betrays by introducing the bullfighter Romero to Brett Ashley, who seduces him; and he rejects her view that "deciding not to be a bitch" is the equivalent of having God: "Some people have God. . . . Quite a lot."[9] But the notion of having "God. . . . Quite a lot" is one that Sinclair Lewis satirizes in his novel *Elmer Gantry* (1927), in which a cynical evangelical preacher wields religion to gull others and serve his own interests. (The book was denounced by the evangelist Billy Sunday as the work of the devil and banned in Boston.) Finding spirituality in the quotidian, Woolf's Mrs. Ramsay in *To the Lighthouse* (1926) experiences isolated moments that partake of eternity: "Of such moments, she thought, the thing is made that endures"; and the painter Lily Briscoe has a revelation that enables her to declare "I have had my vision."[10] And at the end of the twenties, the decade of the "lost generation" (according to Hemingway's quoting of Gertrude Stein in his epigraph to *The Sun Also Rises*), Faulkner published his end-of-culture novel, *The Sound and the Fury* (1929), that seems both to sum up and challenge many of its predecessors – with what seems a *reductio ad absurdum* parodic sermon of Joyce's in *Portrait*; its impotent and childless male scions (Benjy, Quentin, Jason) of the once aristocratic Compsons; and the comprehensive vision and faith of Dilsey (Faulkner's favorite of all his characters because she was "much more brave and honest and generous than I am"[11]) who "seed de first en de last," but who nonetheless endures.[12]

Notes

1   Eliot, *For Lancelot Andrewes*.
2   Forster, "What I Believe," *Two Cheers* 67. (See Chapter 17 of this volume, p. 178).
3   See Owen, *Darkened Room* xvii.
4   Bonner, "On Being Young – A Woman – and Colored" 7. (See Chapter 41 of this volume, p. 362.)
5   Locke, "Introduction," *The New Negro* 16. (See Chapter 42 of this volume, p. 370.)
6   Yeats, "Introduction," *Gitanjali* 11.
7   Woolf, "Modern Fiction" (1919), *The Common Reader* 151–55.
8   Lawrence, "Why the Novel Matters" (1925), *Phoenix* 145.
9   Hemingway, *The Sun Also Rises* 209, 208, 245.
10   Woolf, *To the Lighthouse* 158, 310.
11   Faulkner, *Lion in the Garden* 224.
12   Faulkner, *The Sound and the Fury* 297, 348.

Suggested further readings

Barth, Karl. *The Knowledge of God and the Service of God*. Trans. J.L.M. Haire and Ian Henderson. London: Hodder and Stoughton, 1938.

Blavatsky, Helena Petrovna. *Isis Unveiled: A Master-Key to the Mysteries of Ancient and Modern Science and Technology* (1910). Pasadena: Theosophical, 1998.

——. *The Key to Theosophy* (1889). Pasadena: Theosophical, 1946.

Buber, Martin. *I and Thou* (1923). Eastford, CT: Martino Fine Books, 2010.

Doyle, Arthur Conan. *The Case for Spirit Photography*. New York: George H. Doran Company, 1923.

Eagleton, Terry. *Literary Theory: An Introduction*. Minneapolis: U of Minnesota P, 1983.

Eliot, T.S. *For Lancelot Andrewes: Essays on Style and Order*. Garden City, NY: Doubleday, Doran, 1929.

Faulkner, William. *The Sound and the Fury* (1929). New York: Modern Library, 1992.

——. *Lion in the Garden: Interviews with William Faulkner 1926–1962*. Ed. James B. Meriwether and Michael Millgate. Lincoln, NE and London: U of Nebraska P, 1980.

Freud, Sigmund. *Civilization and Its Discontents*. New York: Norton, 1961.

Handelman, Susan A. *Fragments of Redemption: Jewish Thought and Literary Theory in Benjamin, Scholem, and Levinas*. Bloomington: Indiana UP, 1991.

Hemingway, Ernest. *The Sun Also Rises* (1926). New York: Scribner's, 1987.

Hoffman, Frederick J. *The Mortal No: Death and the Modern Imagination*. Princeton: Princeton UP, 1964.

James, William. *The Meaning of Truth: A Sequel to "Pragmatism"* (1909). Buffalo, NY: Prometheus Books, 1997.

——. *Pragmatism: A New Name for Some Old Ways of Thinking* (1907). Cambridge, MA: Hackett Publishing, 1981; New York: Dover, 1995.

——. *The Varieties of Religious Experience: A Study in Human Nature* (1902). New York: Modern Library, 1994.

Kierkegaard, Søren. *The Point of View for My Work as an Author* (1859). Trans. Walter Lowrie. New York: Harper, 1962.

——. *Concluding Unscientific Postscript to Philosophical Fragments* (1846). Trans. David F. Swanson. Princeton: Princeton UP, 1941.

Lawrence. D.H. *Phoenix: The Posthumous Papers of D.H. Lawrence* (1936). Ed. Edward D. McDonald. New York: Viking, 1968.

Lewis, Pericles. *Religious Experience and the Modernist Novel*. Leiden: Cambridge UP, 2010.

Marx, Karl. *The Economic and Philosophic Manuscripts of* 1844; "The Coming Upheaval," from *The Poverty of Philosophy* (1847); "Manifesto of the Communist Party" (1848); "The Eighteenth Brumaire of Louis Bonaparte" (1852). *The Marx-Engels Reader.* Ed. Robert C. Tucker. New York: Norton, 1978. 218–19, 473–91, 594–98.

Moore, G. E. *Principia Ethica* (1903). New York: Barnes and Noble, 2005.

Nietzsche, Friedrich. "Eternal Recurrence." *Thus Spoke Zarathustra: A Book for All and None* (1883). Trans. Walter Kaufmann. New York: Modern Library, 1995.

——. *The Antichrist* (1895). Trans. R.J. Hollingdale. New York: Penguin Books, 1990.

——. *Beyond Good and Evil* (1886). Trans. Helen Zimmern. Buffalo, NY: Prometheus Books, 1989.

——. *The Gay Science* (1882). Trans. Walter Kaufmann. New York: Vintage, 1974.

——. *The Birth of Tragedy and the Genealogy of Morals* (1872, 1887). Trans. Francis Golffing. Garden City, NY: Doubleday, 1956.

Owen, Alex. The *Darkened Room: Women, Power and Spiritualism in Late Victorian England.* London: Virago, 1989.

Russell, Bertrand. *Why I Am Not a Christian.* London: Watts, 1927.

——. *What I Believe.* London: Kegan Paul, Trench, Trubner, 1925.

——. *The Problems of Philosophy.* London: Williams and Norgate, 1912.

Shaw, George Bernard. "Preface on the Prospects of Christianity." *Androcles and the Lion: A Fable Play* (1913). London: Constable, 1918.

Spengler, Oswald. *The Decline of the West* (1918–22). Trans. Charles Francis Atkinson. New York: Knopf, 1980.

Wittgenstein, Ludwig. *Tractatus Logico-Philosophicus* (1921). Trans. D.F. Pears and B.F. McGuinness. London and New York: Routledge, 2001.

——. *Philosophical Investigations* (1953). Trans. G.E.M. Anscombe. Oxford: Blackwell, 1976.

Woolf, Leonard. *Growing.* London: Hogarth Press, 1961.

Woolf, Virginia. *To the Lighthouse* (1927). New York: Harcourt, 1955; Harmondsworth: Penguin, 1969.

——. *The Common Reader* (1925). New York: Harcourt, Brace and World, 1953.

Yeats, W.B. *A Vision.* London: Macmillan, 1962.

——. "Introduction." Rabindranath Tagore, *Gitanjali.* Boston: Four Seas Company Publishers, 1919.

Chapter 14

Friedrich Nietzsche (1844–1900)

THE GAY SCIENCE (1882), "UPON THE BLESSED ISLES" (1885), AND "ATTEMPT AT A CRITIQUE OF CHRISTIANITY" (1895)

A GERMAN PHILOSOPHER, CRITIC, AND CLASSICIST, Friedrich Nietzsche challenged prevailing nineteenth-century views of morality, epistemology, and religion, especially Christianity, which he considered decadent, life-denying, nihilistic, and morbid. Questioning and challenging all traditional doctrines, Nietzsche focused on individual and cultural health – what he called "life-affirmation" – and he sought to release creativity and power within this world rather than the next. Along with Søren Kierkegaard (1813–55), Nietzsche is commonly viewed as one of the first existentialist philosophers.

Friedrich Nietzsche, from *The Gay Science*. Trans. Walter Kaufmann. New York: Vintage, 1974. 181–82.

———, "Upon the Blessed Isles" *Thus Spoke Zarathustra: A Book for All and None* (1885). Trans. Walter Kaufmann. New York: Penguin, 1978. 85–88.

———, "Attempt at a Critique of Christianity," *The Antichrist* (1895) from *The Portable Nietzsche*. Trans. Walter Kaufmann. New York: Viking, 1968. 569–74, 581–86.

From *The Gay Science*

The madman.—Have you not heard of that madman who lit a lantern in the bright morning hours, ran to the market place, and cried incessantly: "I seek God! I seek God!"—As many of those who did not believe in God were standing around just then, he provoked much laughter. Has he got lost? asked one. Did he lose his way like a child? asked another. Or is he hiding? Is he afraid of us? Has he gone on a voyage? emigrated?—Thus they yelled and laughed.

The madman jumped into their midst and pierced them with his eyes. "Whither is God?" he cried; "I will tell you. *We have killed him*—you and I. All of us are his murderers. But how did we do this? How could we drink up the sea? Who gave us the sponge to wipe away the entire horizon? What were we doing when we unchained this earth from its sun? Whither is it moving now? Whither are we moving? Away from all suns? Are we not plunging continually? Backward, sideward, forward, in all directions? Is there still any up or down? Are we not straying as through an infinite nothing? Do we not feel the breath of empty space? Has it not become colder? Is not night continually closing in on us? Do we not need to light lanterns in the morning? Do we hear nothing as yet of the noise of the gravediggers who are burying God? Do we smell nothing as yet of the divine decomposition? Gods, too, decompose. God is dead. God remains dead. And we have killed him.

"How shall we comfort ourselves, the murderers of all murderers? What was holiest and mightiest of all that the world has yet owned has bled to death under our knives: who will wipe this blood off us? What water is there for us to clean ourselves? What festivals of atonement, what sacred games shall we have to invent? Is not the greatness of this deed too great for us? Must we ourselves not become gods simply to appear worthy of it? There has never been a greater deed; and whoever is born after us—for the sake of this deed he will belong to a higher history than all history hitherto."

Here the madman fell silent and looked again at his listeners; and they, too, were silent and stared at him in astonishment. At last he threw his lantern on the ground, and it broke into pieces and went out. "I have come too early," he said then; "my time is not yet. This tremendous event is still on its way, still wandering; it has not yet reached the ears of men. Lightning and thunder require time; the light of the stars requires time; deeds, though done, still require time to be seen and heard. This deed is still more distant from them than the most distant stars—*and yet they have done it themselves*."

It has been related further that on the same day the madman forced his way into several churches and there struck up his *requiem aeternam deo*. Led out and called to account, he is said always to have replied nothing but: "What after all are these churches now if they are not the tombs and sepulchers of God?"

[. . .]

"Upon the Blessed Isles", from *Thus Spoke Zarathustra*

The figs are falling from the trees; they are good and sweet; and, as they fall, their red skin bursts. I am a north wind to ripe figs.

Thus, like figs, these teachings fall to you, my friends; now consume their juice and their sweet meat. It is autumn about us, and pure sky and afternoon. Behold what fullness there is about us! And out of such overflow it is beautiful to look out upon distant seas. Once one said God when one looked upon distant seas; but now I have taught you to say: overman.

God is a conjecture; but I desire, that your conjectures should not reach beyond your creative will. Could you *create* a god? Then do not speak to me of any gods. But you could well create the overman. Perhaps not you yourselves, my brothers. But into fathers and forefathers of the overman you could re-create yourselves: and let this be your best creation.

God is a conjecture; but I desire that your conjectures should be limited by what is thinkable. Could you *think* a god? But this is what the will to truth should mean to you: that everything be changed into what is thinkable for man, visible for man, feelable by man. You should think through your own senses to their consequences.

And what you have called world, that shall be created only by you: your reason, your image, your will, your love shall thus be realized. And verily, for your own bliss, you lovers of knowledge.

And how would you bear life without this hope, you lovers of knowledge? You could not have been born either into the incomprehensible or into the irrational.

But let me reveal my heart to you entirely, my friends: *if* there were gods, how could I endure not to be a god! *Hence* there are no gods. Though I drew this conclusion, now it draws me.

God is a conjecture; but who could drain all the agony of this conjecture without dying? Shall his faith be taken away from the creator, and from the eagle, his soaring to eagle heights?

God is a thought that makes crooked all that is straight, and makes turn whatever stands. How? Should time be gone, and all that is impermanent a mere lie? To think this is a dizzy whirl for human bones, and a vomit for the stomach; verily, I call it the turning sickness to conjecture thus. Evil I call it, and misanthropic—all this teaching of the One and the Plenum and the Unmoved and the Sated and the Permanent. All the permanent—that is only a parable. And the poets lie too much.

It is of time and becoming that the best parables should speak: let them be a praise and a justification of all impermanence.

Creation—that is the great redemption from suffering, and life's growing light. But that the creator may be, suffering is needed and much change. Indeed, there must be much bitter dying in your life, you creators. Thus are you advocates and justifiers of all impermanence. To be the child who is newly born, the creator must also want to be the mother who gives birth and the pangs of the birth-giver.

Verily, through a hundred souls I have already passed on my way, and through a hundred cradles and birth pangs. Many a farewell have I taken; I know the heartrending last hours. But thus my creative will, my destiny, wills it. Or, to say it more honestly: this very destiny—my will wills.

Whatever in me has feeling, suffers and is in prison; but my will always comes to me as my liberator and joy-bringer. Willing liberates: that is the true teaching of will and liberty— thus Zarathustra teaches it. Willing no more and esteeming no more and creating no more— oh, that this great weariness might always remain far from me! In knowledge too I feel only my will's joy in begetting and becoming; and if there is innocence in my knowledge, it is because the will to beget is in it. Away from God and gods this will has lured me; what could one create if gods existed?

But my fervent will to create impels me ever again toward man; thus is the hammer impelled toward the stone. O men, in the stone there sleeps an image, the image of my images. Alas, that it must sleep in the hardest, the ugliest stone! Now my hammer rages cruelly against its prison. Pieces of rock rain from the stone: what is that to me? I want to perfect it; for a shadow came to me—the stillest and lightest of all things once came to me. The beauty of the overman came to me as a shadow. O my brothers, what are the gods to me now?

Thus spoke Zarathustra.

[. . .]

"Attempt at a Critique of Christianity," from *The Antichrist*

1

Let us face ourselves. We are Hyperboreans; we know very well how far off we live. "Neither by land nor by sea will you find the way to the Hyperboreans"—Pindar already knew this about us. Beyond the north, ice, and death—*our* life, *our* happiness. We have discovered happiness, we know the way, we have found the exit out of the labyrinth of thousands of years. Who *else* has found it? Modern man perhaps? "I have got lost; I am everything that has got lost," sighs modern man.

This modernity was our sickness: lazy peace, cowardly compromise, the whole virtuous uncleanliness of the modern Yes and No. This tolerance and *largeur* of the heart, which "forgives" all because it "understands" all, is *sirocco* for us. Rather live in the ice than among modern virtues and other south winds!

We were intrepid enough, we spared neither ourselves nor others; but for a long time we did not know where to turn with our intrepidity. We became gloomy, we were called fatalists. *Our fatum*—the abundance, the tension, the damming of strength. We thirsted for lightning and deeds and were most remote from the happiness of the weakling, "resignation." In our atmosphere was a thunderstorm; the nature we are became dark—*for we saw no way*. Formula for our happiness: a Yes, a No, a straight line, a goal.

2

What is good? Everything that heightens the feeling of power in man, the will to power, power itself.

What is bad? Everything that is born of weakness.

What is happiness? The feeling that power is *growing*, that resistance is overcome.

Not contentedness but more power; not peace but war; not virtue but fitness (Renaissance virtue, *virtù*, virtue that is moraline[1] free).

The weak and the failures shall perish: first principle of *our* love of man. And they shall even be given every possible assistance.

What is more harmful than any vice? Active pity for all the failures and all the weak: Christianity.

3

The problem I thus pose is not what shall succeed mankind in the sequence of living beings (man is an *end*), but what type of man shall be *bred*, shall be *willed*, for being higher in value, worthier of life, more certain of a future.

Even in the past this higher type has appeared often—but as a fortunate accident, as an exception, never as something *willed*. In fact, this has been the type most dreaded—almost *the* dreadful—and from dread the opposite type was willed, bred, and *attained:* the domestic animal, the herd animal, the sick human animal—the Christian.

4

Mankind does *not* represent a development toward something better or stronger or higher in the sense accepted today. "Progress" is merely a modern idea, that is, a false idea. The European of today is vastly inferior in value to the European of the Renaissance: further development is altogether *not* according to any necessity in the direction of elevation, enhancement, or strength.

In another sense, success in individual cases is constantly encountered in the most widely different places and cultures: here we really do find a *higher type*, which is, in relation to mankind as a whole, a kind of overman. Such fortunate accidents of great success have always been possible and *will* perhaps always be possible. And even whole families, tribes, or peoples may occasionally represent such a *bull's-eye*.

5

Christianity should not be beautified and embellished: it has waged deadly war against this higher type of man; it has placed all the basic instincts of this type under the ban; and out of these instincts it has distilled evil and the Evil One: the strong man as the typically reprehensible man, the "reprobate." Christianity has sided with all that is weak and base, with all failures; it has made an ideal of whatever *contradicts* the instinct of the strong life to preserve itself; it has corrupted the reason even of those strongest in spirit by teaching men to consider the supreme values of the spirit as something sinful, as something that leads into error—as temptations. The most pitiful example: the corruption of Pascal, who believed in the corruption of his reason through original sin when it had in fact been corrupted only by his Christianity.

6

It is a painful, horrible spectacle that has dawned on me: I have drawn back the curtain from the *corruption* of man. In my mouth, this word is at least free from one suspicion: that it might involve a moral accusation of man. It is meant—let me emphasize this once more—*moraline-free*. So much so that I experience this corruption most strongly precisely where men have so far aspired most deliberately to "virtue" and "godliness." I understand corruption, as you will guess, in the sense of decadence: it is my contention that all the values in which mankind now sums up its supreme desiderata are *decadence-values*.

I call an animal, a species, or an individual corrupt when it loses its instincts, when it chooses, when it prefers, what is disadvantageous for it. A history of "lofty sentiments," of the "ideals of mankind"—and it is possible that I shall have to write it—would almost explain too *why* man is so corrupt. Life itself is to my mind the instinct for growth, for durability, for an accumulation of forces, for *power*: where the will to power is lacking there is decline. It is my contention that all the supreme values of mankind *lack* this will—that the values which are symptomatic of decline, *nihilistic* values, are lording it under the holiest names.

7

Christianity is called the religion of *pity*. Pity stands opposed to the tonic emotions which heighten our vitality: it has a depressing effect. We are deprived of strength when we feel pity. That loss of strength which suffering as such inflicts on life is still further increased and multiplied by pity. Pity makes suffering contagious. Under certain circumstances, it may engender a total loss of life and vitality out of all proportion to the magnitude of the cause (as in the case of the death of the Nazarene). That is the first consideration, but there is a more important one.

Suppose we measure pity by the value of the reactions it usually produces; then its perilous nature appears in an even brighter light. Quite in general, pity crosses the law of development, which is the law of *selection*. It preserves what is ripe for destruction; it defends those who have been disinherited and condemned by life; and by the abundance of the failures of all kinds which it keeps alive, it gives life itself a gloomy and questionable aspect.

Some have dared to call pity a virtue (in every *noble* ethic it is considered a weakness); and as if this were not enough, it has been made *the* virtue, the basis and source of all virtues. To be sure—and one should always keep this in mind—this was done by a philosophy that was nihilistic and had inscribed the *negation of life* upon its shield. Schopenhauer was consistent enough: pity negates life and renders it *more deserving of negation*.

Pity is the *practice* of nihilism. To repeat: this depressive and contagious instinct crosses those instincts which aim at the preservation of life and at the enhancement of its value. It multiplies misery and conserves all that is miserable, and is thus a prime instrument of the advancement of decadence: pity persuades men to *nothingness!* Of course, one does not say "nothingness" but "beyond" or "God," or "*true* life," or Nirvana, salvation, blessedness.

This innocent rhetoric from the realm of the religious-moral idiosyncrasy appears much less innocent as soon as we realize which tendency it is that here shrouds itself in sublime words: *hostility against life.* Schopenhauer was hostile to life; therefore pity became a virtue for him.

Aristotle, as is well known, considered pity a pathological and dangerous condition, which one would be well advised to attack now and then with a purge: he understood tragedy as a purge. From the standpoint of the instinct of life, a remedy certainly seems necessary for such a pathological and dangerous accumulation of pity as is represented by the case of Schopenhauer (and unfortunately by our entire literary and artistic decadence from St. Petersburg to Paris, from Tolstoi to Wagner)—to puncture it and make it *burst.*

In our whole unhealthy modernity there is nothing more unhealthy than Christian pity. To be physicians *here*, to be inexorable *here*, to wield the scalpel *here*—that is *our* part, that is *our* love of man, that is how *we* are philosophers, we *Hyperboreans.*[. . .]

15

In Christianity neither morality nor religion has even a single point of contact with reality. Nothing but imaginary *causes* ("God," "soul," "ego," "spirit," "free will"—for that matter, "unfree will"), nothing but imaginary *effects* ("sin," "redemption," "grace," "punishment," "forgiveness of sins"). Intercourse between imaginary *beings* ("God," "spirits," "souls"); an imaginary *natural* science (anthropocentric; no trace of any concept of natural causes); an imaginary *psychology* (nothing but self-misunderstandings, interpretations of agreeable or disagreeable general feelings—for example, of the states of the *nervus sympathicus*—with the aid of the sign language of the religio-moral idiosyncrasy: "repentance," "pangs of conscience," "temptation by the devil," "the presence of God"); an imaginary *teleology* ("the kingdom of God," "the Last Judgment," "eternal life").

This *world of pure fiction* is vastly inferior to the world of dreams insofar as the latter *mirrors* reality, whereas the former falsifies, devalues, and negates reality. Once the concept of "nature" had been invented as the opposite of "God," "natural" had to become a synonym of "reprehensible": this whole world of fiction is rooted in *hatred* of the natural (of reality!); it is the expression of a profound vexation at the sight of reality.

But this explains everything. Who alone has good reason to lie his way out of reality? He who suffers from it. But to suffer from reality is to be a piece of reality that has come to grief. The preponderance of feelings of displeasure over feelings of pleasure is the cause of this fictitious morality and religion; but such a preponderance provides the very formula for decadence.

16

A critique of the *Christian conception of God* forces us to the same conclusion. A people that still believes in itself retains its own god. In him it reveres the conditions which let it prevail, its virtues: it projects its pleasure in itself, its feeling of power, into a being to whom one may offer thanks. Whoever is rich wants to give of his riches; a proud people needs a god: it wants to *sacrifice.* Under such conditions, religion is a form of thankfulness. Being thankful for himself, man needs a god. Such a god must be able to help and to harm, to be friend and enemy—he is admired whether good or destructive. The *anti-natural* castration of a god, to make him a god of the good alone, would here be contrary to everything desirable. The evil god is needed no less than the good god: after all, we do not owe our own existence to tolerance and humanitarianism.

What would be the point of a god who knew nothing of wrath, revenge, envy, scorn, cunning, and violence? who had perhaps never experienced the delightful *ardeurs* of victory and annihilation? No one would understand such a god: why have him then?

To be sure, when a people is perishing, when it feels how its faith in the future and its hope of freedom are waning irrevocably, when submission begins to appear to it as the prime necessity and it becomes aware of the virtues of the subjugated as the conditions of self-preservation, then its god *has to* change too. Now he becomes a sneak, timid and modest; he counsels "peace of soul," hate-no-more, forbearance, even "love" of friend and enemy. He moralizes constantly, he crawls into the cave of every private virtue, he becomes god for everyman, he becomes a private person,[2] a cosmopolitan.

Formerly, he represented a people, the strength of a people, everything aggressive and power-thirsty in the soul of a people; now he is merely the good god.

Indeed, there is no other alternative for gods: *either* they are the will to power, and they remain a people's gods, *or* the incapacity for power, and then they necessarily become *good*.

17

Wherever the will to power declines in any form, there is invariably also a physiological retrogression, decadence. The deity of decadence, gelded in his most virile virtues and instincts, becomes of necessity the god of the physiologically retrograde, of the weak. Of course, they do not *call* themselves the weak; they call themselves "the good."

No further hint is required to indicate the moments in history at which the dualistic fiction of a good and an evil god first became possible. The same instinct which prompts the subjugated to reduce their god to the "good-in-itself" also prompts them to eliminate all the good qualities from the god of their conquerors; they take revenge on their masters by turning their god into the *devil*. The *good* god and the devil—both abortions of decadence.

How can anyone today still submit to the simplicity of Christian theologians to the point of insisting with them that the development of the conception of God from the "God of Israel," the god of a people, to the Christian God, the quintessence of everything good, represents *progress*? Yet even Renan does this. As if Renan had the right to be simple-minded! After all, the opposite stares you in the face. When the presuppositions of *ascending* life, when everything strong, brave, masterful, and proud is eliminated from the conception of God; when he degenerates step by step into a mere symbol, a staff for the weary, a sheet-anchor for the drowning; when he becomes the god of the poor, the sinners, and the sick par excellence, and the attribute "Savior" or "Redeemer" remains in the end as the one essential attribute of divinity—just *what* does such a transformation signify? what, such a *reduction* of the divine?

To be sure, "the kingdom of God" has thus been enlarged. Formerly he had only his people, his "chosen" people. Then he, like his people, became a wanderer and went into foreign lands; and ever since, he has not settled down anywhere—until he finally came to feel at home anywhere, this great cosmopolitan—until "the great numbers" and half the earth were on his side. Nevertheless, the god of "the great numbers," the democrat among the gods, did not become a proud pagan god: he remained a Jew, he remained a god of nooks, the god of all the dark corners and places, of all the unhealthy quarters the world over!

His world-wide kingdom is, as ever, an underworld kingdom, a hospital, a *souterrain* kingdom, a ghetto kingdom. And he himself: so pale, so weak, so decadent. Even the palest of the pale were able to master him: our honorable metaphysicians, those concept-albinos. They spun their webs around him until, hypnotized by their motions, he himself became a spider, another metaphysician. Now he, in turn, spun the world out of himself—*sub specie Spinozae*. Now he transfigured himself into something ever thinner and paler; he became an "ideal," he became "pure spirit," the "Absolute," the "thing-in-itself." The deterioration of a god: God became the "thing-in-itself."

18

The Christian conception of God—God as god of the sick, God as a spider, God as spirit—is one of the most corrupt conceptions of the divine ever attained on earth. It may even represent the low-water mark in the descending development of divine types. God degenerated into the *contradiction* of life, instead of being its transfiguration and eternal Yes! God as the declaration of war against life, against nature, against the will to live! God—the formula for every slander against "this world," for every lie about the "beyond"! God—the deification of nothingness, the will to nothingness pronounced holy![. . .]

Notes

1   The coinage of a man who neither smoked nor drank coffee.
2   Literal translation of the Greek *idiotes*.

Chapter 15

James George Frazer (1854–1941)

"SCAPEGOATS," *THE GOLDEN BOUGH* (1890–1915)

S IR JAMES GEORGE FRAZER was a Scottish social anthropologist who pioneered the modern study of mythology and comparative religion. Frazer posited that human belief progressed through three stages: primitive magic, religion, and science, a theory that has had great influence but which remains dubious. *The Golden Bough*, his magnum opus, analyzes the similarities in ancient cults, rites, and myths, including their parallels with early Christianity.

James George Frazer, "Scapegoats," *The Golden Bough* (1890–1915). New York: Criterion, 1959. 529–45, 648–51.

Evil expelled in a material vessel

We now come to the second class of expulsions, in which the evil influences are embodied in a visible form or are at least supposed to be loaded upon a material medium, which acts as a vehicle to draw them off from the people, village, or town. In spring, as soon as the willow-leaves were full grown on the banks of the river, the Mandan Indians celebrated their great annual festival, one of the features of which was the expulsion of the devil. A man, painted black to represent the devil, entered the village from the prairie, chased and frightened the women, and acted the part of a buffalo bull, in the buffalo dance, the object of which was to ensure a plentiful supply of buffaloes during the ensuing year. Finally he was chased from the village, the women pursuing him with hisses and gibes, beating him with sticks, and pelting him with dirt. The Mayas of Yucatan divided the year into eighteen months of twenty days each, and they added five supplementary days at the end of the year in order to make a total of three hundred and sixty-five days. These five supplementary days were deemed unlucky. In the course of them the people banished the evils that might threaten them in the year on which they were about to enter. For that purpose they made a clay image of the demon of evil Uuayayab, that is *u-uayab-haab*, "He by whom the year is poisoned," confronted it with the deity who had supreme power over the coming year, and then carried it out of the village in the direction of that cardinal point to which, on the system of the Mayan calendar, the particular year was supposed to belong. Having thus rid themselves of the demon, they looked forward to a happy New Year. Russian villagers seek to protect themselves against epidemics, whether of man or beast, by drawing a furrow with a plough right round the village. The plough is dragged by four widows and the ceremony is performed at night; all fires and lights must be extinguished while the plough is going the round. The people think that no unclean spirit can pass the furrow which has thus been traced. In the village of Dubrowitschi a puppet is carried before the plough with the cry, "Out of the village with the unclean spirit!" and at the end of the ceremony it is torn in pieces and the fragments scattered about. Sometimes in an Esthonian village a rumour will get about that the Evil One himself has been seen in the place. Instantly the entire population, armed with sticks, flails, and scythes, turns out to give him chase. They generally expel him in the shape of a wolf or a cat, occasionally, they brag that they have beaten the devil to death. At Carmona, in Andalusia, on one day of the year, boys are stripped naked and smeared with glue in which feathers are stuck. Thus disguised, they run from house to house, the people trying to avoid them and to bar their houses against them. The ceremony is probably a relic of an annual expulsion of devils.

More often, however, the expelled demons are not represented at all, but are understood to be present invisibly in the material and visible vehicle which conveys them away. Here, again, it will be convenient to distinguish between occasional and periodical expulsions. We begin with the former.

The vehicle which conveys away the demons may be of various kinds. A common one is a little ship or boat. Thus, in the southern district of the island of Ceram, when a whole village suffers from sickness, a small ship is made and filled with rice, tobacco, eggs, and so forth, which have been contributed by all the people. A little sail is hoisted on the ship. When all is ready, a man calls out in a very loud voice, "O all ye sicknesses, ye smallpoxes, agues, measles, etc., who have visited us so long and wasted us so sorely, but who now cease to plague us, we have made ready this ship for you and we have furnished you with provender sufficient for the voyage. Ye shall have no lack of food nor of betel-leaves nor of areca nuts nor of tobacco. Depart; and sail away from us directly; never come near us again; but go to a land which is far from here. Let all the tides and winds waft you speedily thither, and so convey you thither that for the time to come we may live sound and well, and that we may never see the sun rise on you again." Then ten or twelve men carry the vessel to the shore, and let it drift away with the land-breeze, feeling convinced that they are free from sickness for ever, or at least till the next time.

Similar ceremonies are commonly resorted to in other East Indian islands. Thus in Timor-laut, to mislead the demons who are causing sickness, a small proa, containing the image of a man and provisioned for a long voyage, is allowed to drift away with wind and tide. As it is being launched, the people cry, "O sickness, go from here; turn back! What do you here in this poor land?"

The plan of putting puppets in the boat to represent sick persons, in order to lure the demons after them, is not uncommon. For example, most of the pagan tribes on the coast of Borneo seek to drive away epidemic disease as follows. They carve one or more rough human images from the pith of the sago palm and place them on a small raft or boat or full-rigged Malay ship together with rice and other food. The boat is decked with blossoms of the areca palm and with ribbons made from its leaves, and thus adorned the little craft is allowed to float out to sea with the ebb-tide, bearing, as the people fondly think or hope, the sickness away with it.

In Selangor, one of the native states in the Malay Peninsula, the ship employed in the export of disease is, or used to be, a model of a special kind of Malay craft called a *lanchang*. This was a two-masted vessel with galleries fore and aft, armed with cannon, and used by

Malay rajahs on the coast of Sumatra. So gallant a ship would be highly acceptable to the spirits, and to make it still more beautiful in their eyes it was not uncommonly stained yellow with tumeric or saffron, for among the Malays yellow is the royal colour. Some years ago a very fine model of a *lanchang*, with its cargo of sickness, was towed down the river to the sea by the Government steam launch. A common spell uttered at the launching of one of these ships runs as follows:—

> "Ho, elders of the upper reaches,
> Elders of the lower reaches,
> Elders of the dry land,
> Elders of the river-flats,
> Assemble ye, O people, lords of hill and hill-foot,
> Lords of cavern and hill-locked basin,
> Lords of the deep primeval forest,
> Lords of the river-bends,
> Come on board this *lanchang*, assembling in your multitudes.
> So may ye depart with the ebbing stream,
> Depart on the passing breeze,
> Depart in the yawning earth,
> Depart in the red-dyed earth.
> Go ye to the ocean which has no wave,
> And the plain where no green herb grows,
> And never return hither.
> But if ye return hither,
> Ye shall be consumed by the curse.
> At sea ye shall get no drink,
> Ashore ye shall get no food,
> But gape in vain about the world."

When the Tagbanuas and other tribes of the Philippines suffered from epidemics, they used to make little models of ships, supply them with rice and fresh drinking water, and launch them on the sea, in order that the evil spirits might sail away in them. When the people of Tikopia, a small island in the Pacific, to the north of the New Hebrides, were attacked by an epidemic cough, they made a little canoe and adorned it with flowers. Four sons of the principal chiefs carried it on their shoulders all round the island, accompanied by the whole population, some of whom beat the bushes, while others uttered loud cries. On returning to the spot from which they had set out, they launched the canoe on the sea.

Evil expelled in animals

Often the vehicle which carries away the collected demons or ills of a whole community is an animal or scapegoat. When cholera rages among the Bhars, Mallans, and Kurmis of India, they take a goat or a buffalo—in either case the animal must be a female, and as black as possible—then having tied some grain, cloves, and red lead in a yellow cloth on its back they turn it out of the village. The animal is conducted beyond the boundary and not allowed to return. Sometimes the buffalo is marked with a red pigment and driven to the next village, where he carries the plague with him.

In 1886, during a severe outbreak of smallpox, the people of Jepur did reverence to a goat, marched it to the Ghats, and let it loose on the plains. In Southern Konkan, on the appearance of cholera, the villagers went in procession from the temple to the extreme boundaries of the village, carrying a basket of cooked rice covered with red powder, a wooden doll representing the pestilence, and a cock. The head of the cock was cut off at the village boundary, and the body was thrown away. When cholera had thus been transferred from one village to another, the second village observed the same ceremony and passed on the scourge to its neighbours, and so on through a number of villages. Again, if a murrain attacks their cattle, the Kharwars of Northern India take a black cock and put red lead on its head, antimony on its eyes, a spangle on its forehead, and a pewter bangle on its leg; thus arrayed they let it loose, calling out to the disease, "Mount on the fowl and go elsewhere into the ravines and thickets; destroy the sin." In 1857, when the Aymara Indians of Bolivia and Peru were suffering from a plague, they loaded a black llama with the clothes of the plague-stricken people, sprinkled brandy on the clothes, and then turned the animal loose on the mountains, hoping that it would carry the pest away with it.

Evil expelled in human beings

Occasionally the scapegoat is *a man*.

Some of the aboriginal tribes of China, for example, select a man of great muscular strength to act the part of a scapegoat as a protection against pestilence. Having smeared his face with paint, he performs many antics with the view of enticing all pestilential and noxious influences to attach themselves to him only. He is assisted by a priest. Finally the scapegoat, hotly pursued by men and women beating gongs and tom-toms, is driven with great speed out of the town or village. When disease breaks out among a herd, the Oraons take the herdsman, tie a wooden bell from one of the cows round his neck, beat him with sticks, and drive him out of the village to a cross-road, where the bell and sticks are deposited.

Periodic and divine scapegoats

The mediate expulsion of evils by means of a scapegoat or other material vehicle, like the immediate expulsion of them in invisible form, tends to become periodic, and for a like reason.

Every year, at the beginning of the dry season, the Nicobar Islanders carry the model of a ship through their villages. The devils are chased out of the huts, and driven on board the little ship, which is then launched and suffered to sail away with the wind. The ceremony has been described by a cathechist, who witnessed it at Car Nicobar in July 1897. For three days the people were busy preparing two very large floating cars, shaped like canoes, fitted with sails, and loaded with certain leaves, which possessed the valuable property of expelling devils. While the young people were thus engaged, the exorcists and the elders sat in a house singing songs by turns; but often they would come forth, pace the beach armed with rods, and forbid the devil to enter the village. The fourth day of the solemnity bore the name of *Intō-nga-Sīya*, which means "Expelling the Devil by Sails." In the evening all the villagers assembled, the women bringing baskets of ashes and bunches of devil-expelling leaves. These leaves were then distributed to everybody, old and young. When all was ready, a band of robust men, attended by a guard of exorcists, carried one of the cars down to the sea on the right side of the village graveyard, and set it floating in the water. As soon as they had returned, another band of men carried the other car to the beach and floated it similarly in the sea to the left of the graveyard. The demon-laden barks being now launched, the women threw ashes from the shore, and the whole crowd shouted, saying, "Fly away, devil, fly away, never come again!" The wind and the tide being favourable, the canoes sailed quickly away; and that night all the people feasted together with great joy, because the devil had departed in the direction of Chowra. A similar expulsion of devils takes place once a year in other Nicobar villages; but the ceremonies are held at different times in different places. On New Year's Day people in Korea seek to rid themselves of all their distresses by painting images on paper, writing against them their troubles of body or mind, and afterwards giving the papers to a boy to burn.

The scapegoat by means of which the accumulated ills of a whole year are publicly expelled is sometimes an animal.

On one day of the year the Bhotiyas of Juhar, in the Western Himalayas, take a dog, intoxicate him with spirits and bhang or hemp, and having fed him with sweetmeats, lead him round the village and let him loose. They then chase and kill him with sticks and stones, and believe that, when they have done so, no disease or misfortune will visit the village during the year. In Ulawa, one of the Solomon Islands, once a year a live dog is driven from the brow of a cliff into the sea. The dog is supposed to be laden with all the sicknesses of the people.

On the Day of Atonement, which was the tenth day of the seventh month, the Jewish high-priest laid both his hands on the head of a live goat, confessed over it all the iniquities of the Children of Israel, and, having thereby transferred the sins of the people to the beast, sent it away into the wilderness.

The periodic scapegoat may also be a human being. At Onitsha, on the Niger, two human beings used to be annually sacrificed to take away the sins of the land. The victims were purchased by public subscription. All persons who, during the past year, had fallen into gross sins, such as incendiarism, theft, adultery, witchcraft, and so forth, were expected to contribute 28 *ngugas*, or a little over £2. The money thus collected was taken into the interior of the country and expended in the purchase of two sickly persons "to be offered as a sacrifice for all these abominable crimes—one for the land and one for the river." A man from a neighbouring town was hired to put them to death.

In Siam it used to be the custom on one day of the year to single out a woman broken down by debauchery, and carry her on a litter through all the streets to the music of drums and hautboys. The mob insulted her and pelted her with dirt; and after having carried her through the whole city, they threw her on a dunghill or a hedge of thorns outside the ramparts, forbidding her ever to enter the walls again. They believed that the woman thus drew upon herself all the malign influences of the air and of evil spirits. There was formerly a practice at Asakusa in Tokio on the last day of the year for a man got up as a devil to be chased round the pagoda there by another wearing a mask. After this 3,000 tickets were scrambled for by the spectators. These were carried away and pasted up over the doors as a charm against pestilence.

Human scapegoats, as we shall see presently, were well known in classical antiquity, and even in mediaeval Europe the custom seems not to have been wholly extinct. In the town of Halberstadt, in Thüringen, there was a church said to have been founded by Charlemagne. In this church every year they chose a man, who was believed to be stained with heinous sins. On the first day of Lent he was brought to the church, dressed in mourning garb, with his head muffled up. At the close of the service he was turned out of the church. During the forty days of Lent he perambulated the city barefoot, neither entering the churches nor speaking to any one. The canons took it in turn to feed him. After midnight he was allowed to sleep in the streets. On the day before Good Friday, after the consecration of the holy oil, he was readmitted to the church and absolved from his sins. The people gave him money. He was called Adam, and was now believed to be in a state of innocence. At Entlebuch, in Switzerland, down to the close of the eighteenth century, the custom of annually expelling a scapegoat was preserved in the ceremony of driving "Posterli" from the village into the lands of the neighbouring village. "Posterli" was represented by a lad disguised as an old witch or as a goat or an ass. Amid a deafening noise of horns, clarionets, bells, whips, and so forth, he was driven out. Sometimes "Posterli" was represented by a puppet, which was drawn on a sledge and left in a corner of the neighbouring village. The ceremony took place on the Thursday evening of the last week but one before Christmas.

In Munich down to about a hundred years ago the expulsion of the devil from the city used to be annually enacted on Ascension Day. On the Eve of Ascension Day a man disguised as a devil was chased through the streets, which were then narrow and dirty in contrast to the broad, well-kept thoroughfares, lined with imposing buildings, which now distinguish the capital of Bavaria. His pursuers were dressed as witches and wizards and provided with the indispensable crutches, brooms, and pitchforks which make up the outfit of these uncanny beings. While the devil fled before them, the troop of maskers made after him with wild whoops and halloos, and when they overtook him they ducked him in puddles or rolled him on dunghills. In this way the demon at last succeeded in reaching the palace, where he put off his hideous and now filthy disguise and was rewarded for his vicarious sufferings by a copious meal. The devilish costume which he had thrown off was then stuffed with hay and straw and conveyed to a particular church (the Frauenkirche), where it was kept over night, being hung by a rope from a window in the tower. On the afternoon of Ascension Day, before the Vesper service began, an image of the Saviour was drawn up to the roof of the church, no doubt to symbolize the event which the day commemorates. Then burning tow and wafers were thrown on the people. Meantime the effigy of the devil, painted black, with a pair of horns and a lolling red tongue, had been dangling from the church tower, to the delight of a gaping crowd of spectators gathered before the church. It was now flung down into their midst, and a fierce struggle for possession of it took place among the rabble. Finally, it was carried out of the town by the Isar gate and burned on a neighbouring height, "in order that the foul fiend might do no harm to the city." The custom died out at Munich towards the end of the eighteenth century; but it is said that similar ceremonies are observed to this day in some villages of Upper Bavaria.

This quaint ceremony suggests that the pardoned criminal who used to play the principal part in a solemn religious procession on Ascension Day at Rouen may in like manner have originally served, if not as a representative of the devil, at least as a public scapegoat, who relieved the whole people of their sins and sorrows for a year by taking them upon himself. This would explain why the gaol had to be raked in order to furnish one who would parade with the highest ecclesiastical dignitaries in their gorgeous vestments through the streets of Rouen, while the church bells pealed out, the clergy chanted, banners waved, and every circumstance combined to enchance the pomp and splendour of the pageant. It would add a pathetic significance to the crowning act of the ceremony, when on a lofty platform in the public square, with the eyes of a great and silent multitude turned upon him, the condemned malefactor received from the Church the absolution and remission of his sins; for if the rite is to be interpreted in the way here suggested the sins which were thus forgiven were those not of one man only but of the whole people. No wonder, then, that when the sinner, now a sinner no more, rose from his knees and thrice lifted the silver shrine of St. Romain in his arms, the whole vast assembly in the square broke out into joyous cries of "*Noel! Noel! Noel!*" which they understood to signify, "God be with us!" In Christian countries no more appropriate season could be selected for the ceremony of the human scapegoat than Ascension Day, which commemorates the departure from earth of Him who, in the belief of millions, took away the sins of the world.

Sometimes the scapegoat is a divine animal. The people of Malabar share the Hindu reverence for the cow, to kill and eat which "they esteem to be a crime as heinous as homicide or wilful murder." Nevertheless the "Bramans transfer the sins of the people into one or more

Cows, which are then carry'd away, both the Cows and the Sins wherewith these Beasts are charged, to what place the Braman shall appoint." When the ancient Egyptians sacrificed a bull, they invoked upon its head all the evils that might otherwise befall themselves and the land of Egypt, and thereupon they either sold the bull's head to the Greeks or cast it into the river. It seems not improbable, too, that the lamb annually slain by the Madis of Central Africa is a divine scapegoat.

Lastly, the scapegoat may be a divine man. Thus, in November the Gonds of India worship Ghansyam Deo, the protector of the crops, and at the festival the god himself is said to descend on the head of one of the worshippers, who is suddenly seized with a kind of fit and, after staggering about, rushes off into the jungle, where it is believed that, if left to himself, he would die mad. However, they bring him back, but he does not recover his senses for one or two days. The people think that one man is thus singled out as a scapegoat for the sins of the rest of the village. In the temple of the Moon the Albanians of the Eastern Caucasus kept a number of sacred slaves, of whom many were inspired and prophesied. When one of these men exhibited more than usual symptoms of inspiration or insanity, and wandered solitary up and down the woods, like the Gond in the jungle, the high priest had him bound with a sacred chain and maintained him in luxury for a year. At the end of the year he was anointed with unguents and led forth to be sacrificed. A man whose business it was to slay these human victims and to whom practice had given dexterity, advanced from the crowd and thrust a sacred spear into the victim's side, piercing his heart. From the manner in which the slain man fell, omens were drawn as to the welfare of the commonwealth. Then the body was carried to a certain spot where all the people stood upon it as a purificatory ceremony. This last circumstance clearly indicates that the sins of the people were transferred to the victim, just as the Jewish priest transferred the sins of the people to the scapegoat by laying his hands on the animal's head; and since the man was believed to be possessed by the divine spirit, we have here an undoubted example of a man-god slain to take away the sins and misfortunes of the people.

In Tibet the ceremony of the scapegoat presents some remarkable features. The Tibetan new year begins with the new moon which appears about the fifteenth of February. For twenty-three days afterwards the government of Lhasa, the capital, is taken out of the hands of the ordinary rulers and entrusted to the monk of the Debang monastery who offers to pay the highest sum for the privilege. The successful bidder is called the Jalno, and he announces his accession to power in person, going through the streets of Lhasa with a silver stick in his hand. Monks from all the neighbouring monasteries and temples assemble to pay him homage. The Jalno exercises his authority in the most arbitrary manner for his own benefit, as all the fines which he exacts are his by purchase. The profit he makes is about ten times the amount of the purchase money. His men go about the streets in order to discover any conduct on the part of the inhabitants that can be found fault with. Every house in Lhasa is taxed at this time, and the slightest offence is punished with unsparing rigour by fines. This severity of the Jalno drives all working classes out of the city till the twenty-three days are over. But if the laity go out, the clergy come in. All the Buddhist monasteries of the country for miles round about open their gates and disgorge their inmates. All the roads that lead down into Lhasa from the neighbouring mountains are full of monks hurrying to the capital, some on foot, some on horseback, some riding asses or lowing oxen, all carrying their prayer-books and culinary utensils. In such multitudes do they come that the streets and squares of the city are encumbered with their swarms, and incarnadined with their red cloaks. The disorder and confusion are indescribable. Bands of the holy men traverse the streets chanting prayers or uttering wild cries. They meet, they jostle, they quarrel, they fight; bloody noses, black eyes, and broken heads are freely given and received. All day long, too, from before the peep of dawn till after darkness has fallen, these red-cloaked monks hold services in the dim incense-laden air of the great Machindranath temple, the cathedral of Lhasa; and thither they crowd thrice a day to receive their doles of tea and soup and money. The cathedral is a vast building, standing in the centre of the city, and surrounded by bazaars and shops. The idols in it are richly inlaid with gold and precious stones.

Twenty-four days after the Jalno has ceased to have authority, he assumes it again, and for ten days acts in the same arbitrary manner as before. On the first of the ten days the priests again assemble at the cathedral, pray to the gods to prevent sickness and other evils among the people, "and, as a peace-offering, sacrifice one man. The man is not killed purposely, but the ceremony he undergoes often proves fatal. Grain is thrown against his head, and his face is painted half white, half black." Thus grotesquely disguised, and carrying a coat of skin on his arm, he is called the King of the Years, and sits daily in the market-place, where he helps himself to whatever he likes and goes about shaking a black yak's tail over the people, who thus transfer their bad luck to him. On the tenth day, all the troops in Lhasa march to the great temple and form in line before it. The King of the Years is brought forth from the temple and receives small donations from the assembled multitude. He then ridicules the Jalno, saying to him, "What we perceive through the five senses is no illusion. All you teach is untrue," and the like. The Jalno, who represents the Grand Lama for the time being, contests these heretical opinions; the dispute waxes warm, and at last both agree to decide the questions at issue by a cast of the dice, the Jalno offering to change places with the scapegoat should the throw be against him. If the King of the Years wins, much evil is prognosticated; but if the Jalno wins, there is great rejoicing, for it proves that his adversary has been accepted by the gods as a victim to bear all the sins of the people of Lhasa. Fortune, however, always favours the Jalno, who throws sixes with unvarying success, while his opponent turns up only ones. Nor is this so extraordinary as at first sight it might appear; for the Jalno's dice are marked with nothing but sixes and his adversary's with nothing but ones. When he sees the finger of Providence thus plainly pointed against him, the King of the Years is terrified and flees away upon a white horse, with a white dog, a white bird, salt, and so forth, which have all been provided for him by the government. His face is still painted half white and half black, and he still wears his leathern coat. The whole populace pursues him, hooting, yelling, and firing blank shots in volleys after him. Thus driven out of the city, he is detained for seven days in the great chamber of horrors at the Samyas monastery, surrounded by monstrous and terrific images of devils and skins of huge serpents and wild beasts. Thence he goes away into the mountains of Chetang, where he has to remain an outcast for several months or a year in a narrow den. If he dies before the time is out, the people say it is an auspicious omen; but if he survives, he may return to Lhasa and play the part of scapegoat over again the following year.

This quaint ceremonial, still annually observed in the secluded capital of Buddhism—the Rome of Asia—is interesting because it exhibits, in a clearly marked religious stratification, a series of divine redeemers themselves redeemed, of vicarious sacrifices vicariously atoned for, of gods undergoing a process of fossilization, who, while they retain the privileges, have disburdened themselves of the pains and penalties of divinity. In the Jalno we may without undue straining discern a successor of those temporary kings, those mortal gods, who purchase a short lease of power and glory at the price of their lives. That he is the temporary substitute of the Grand Lama is certain; that he is, or was once, liable to act as scapegoat for the people is made nearly certain by his offer to change places with the real scapegoat—the King of the Years—if the arbitrament of the dice should go against him. It is true that the conditions under which the question is now put to the hazard have reduced the offer to an idle form. But such forms are no mere mushroom growths, springing up of themselves in a night. If they are now lifeless formalities, empty husks devoid of significance, we may be sure that they once had a life and a meaning; if at the present day they are blind alleys leading nowhere, we may be certain that in former days they were paths that led somewhere, if only to death. That death was the goal to which of old the Tibetan scapegoat passed after his brief period of licence in the market-place, is a conjecture that has much to commend it. Analogy suggests it; the blank shots fired after him, the statement that the ceremony often proves fatal, the belief that his death is a happy omen, all confirm it. We need not wonder then that the Jalno, after paying so dear to act as deputy-deity for a few weeks, should have preferred to die by deputy rather than in his own person when his time was up. The painful but necessary duty was accordingly laid on some poor devil, some social outcast, some wretch with whom the world had gone hard, who readily agreed to throw away his life at the end of a few days if only he might have his fling in the meantime. For observe that while the time allowed to the original deputy—the Jalno—was measured by weeks, the time allowed to the deputy's deputy was cut down to days, ten days according to one authority, seven days according to another. So short a rope was doubtless thought a long enough tether for so black or sickly a sheep; so few sands in the hour-glass, slipping so fast away, sufficed for one who had wasted so many precious years. Hence in the jack-pudding who now masquerades with motley countenance in the market-place of Lhasa, sweeping up misfortune with a black yak's tail, we may fairly see the substitute of a substitute, the vicar of a vicar, the proxy on whose back the heavy burden was laid when it had been lifted from nobler shoulders. But the clue, if we have followed it aright, does not stop at the Jalno; it leads straight back to the pope of Lhasa himself, the Grand Lama, of whom the Jalno is merely the temporary vicar. The analogy of many customs in many lands points to the conclusion that, if this human divinity stoops to resign his ghostly power for a time into the hands of a substitute, it is, or rather was once, for no other reason than that the substitute might die in his stead. Thus through the mist of ages unillumined by the lamp of history, the tragic figure of the pope of Buddhism—God's vicar on earth for Asia—looms dim and sad as the man-god who bore his people's sorrows, the Good Shepherd who laid down his life for the sheep.

Human scapegoats in classical antiquity

We are now prepared to notice the use of the human scapegoat in classical antiquity. Every year on the fourteenth of March a man clad in skins was led in procession through the streets of Rome, beaten with long white rods, and driven out of the city. He was called Mamurius Veturius, that is, "the old Mars," and as the ceremony took place on the day preceding the first full moon of the old Roman year (which began on the first of March), the skin-clad man must have represented the Mars of the past year, who was driven out at the beginning of a new one. Now Mars was originally not a god of war but of vegetation. For it was to Mars that the Roman husbandman prayed for the prosperity of his corn and his vines, his fruit-trees and his copses, it was to Mars that the priestly college of the Arval Brothers, whose business it was to sacrifice for the growth of the crops, addressed their petitions almost exclusively; and it was to Mars that a horse was sacrificed in October to secure an abundant harvest. Moreover, it was to Mars, under his title of "Mars of the woods" (*Mars Silvanus*), that farmers offered sacrifice for the welfare of their cattle. Thus the Roman custom of expelling the old Mars at the beginning of the new year in spring is identical with the Slavonic custom of "carrying out Death," if the view here taken of the latter custom is correct. The similarity of the Roman and Slavonic customs has been already remarked by scholars. In both, the representative of the god appears to have been treated not only as a deity of vegetation but also as a scapegoat.

The ancient Greeks were also familiar with the use of a human scapegoat. In Plutarch's native town of Chaeronea a ceremony of this kind was performed by the chief magistrate at the Town Hall, and by each householder at his own home. It was called the "expulsion of hunger." A slave was beaten with rods of the *agnus castus*, and turned out of doors with the words, "Out with hunger, and in with wealth and health." When Plutarch held the office of chief magistrate of his native town he performed this ceremony at the Town Hall, and he has recorded the discussion to which the custom afterwards gave rise.

But in civilized Greece the custom of the scapegoat took darker forms than the innocent rite over which the amiable and pious Plutarch presided. Whenever Marseilles, one of the busiest and most brilliant of Greek colonies, was ravaged by a plague, a man of the poorer classes used to offer himself as a scapegoat. For a whole year he was maintained at the public expense, being fed on choice and pure food. At the expiry of the year he was dressed in sacred garments, decked with holy branches, and led through the whole city, while prayers were uttered that all the evils of the people might fall on his head. He was then cast out of the city or stoned to death by the people outside of the walls. The Athenians regularly maintained a number of degraded and useless beings at the public expense; and when any calamity, such as plague, drought, or famine, befell the city, they sacrificed two of these outcasts as scapegoats. One of the victims was sacrificed for the men and the other for the women. The former wore round his neck a string of black, the latter a string of white figs. Sometimes, it seems, the victim slain on behalf of the women was a woman. They were led about the city and then sacrificed, apparently by being stoned to death outside the city. But such sacrifices were not confined to extraordinary occasions of public calamity; it appears that every year, at the festival of the Thargelia in May, two victims, one for the men and one for the women, were led out of Athens and stoned to death. The city of Abdera in Thrace was publicly purified once a year, and one of the burghers, set apart for the purpose, was stoned to death as a scapegoat or vicarious sacrifice for the life of all the others; six days before his execution he was excommunicated, "in order that he alone might bear the sins of all the people."

As practised by the Greeks of Asia Minor in the sixth century before our era, the custom of the scapegoat was as follows. When a city suffered from plague, famine, or other public calamity, an ugly or deformed person was chosen to take upon himself all the evils which afflicted the community. He was brought to a suitable place, where dried figs, a barley loaf, and cheese were put into his hand. These he ate. Then he was beaten seven times upon his genital organs with squills and branches of the wild fig and other wild trees, while the flutes played a particular tune. Afterwards he was burned on a pyre built of the wood of forest trees; and his ashes were cast into the sea.

Beating with squills, "Easter Smacks"

In the ritual just described the scourging of the victim with squills, branches of the wild fig, and so forth, cannot have been intended to aggravate his sufferings, otherwise any stick would have been good enough to beat him with. The true meaning of this part of the ceremony has been explained by Mannhardt. He points out that the ancients attributed to squills a magical power of averting evil influences, and that accordingly they hung them up at the doors of their houses and made use of them in purificatory rites. Hence the Arcadian custom of whipping the image of Pan with squills at a festival, or whenever the hunters returned empty-handed, must have been meant, not to punish the god, but to purify him from the harmful influences which were impeding him in the exercise of his divine functions as a god who should supply the hunter with game. Similarly the object of beating the human scapegoat on the genital organs with squills and so on, must have been to release his reproductive energies from any restraint or spell under which they might be laid by demoniacal or other malignant agency; and as the Thargelia at which he was annually sacrificed was an early harvest festival celebrated in May, we must recognize in him a representative of the creative and fertilizing god of vegetation. The representative of the god was annually slain for the purpose I have indicated, that of maintaining the divine life in perpetual vigour, untainted by the weakness of age; and before he was put to death it was not unnatural to stimulate his reproductive powers in order that these might be transmitted in full activity to his successor, the new god of new embodiment of the old god, who was doubtless supposed immediately to take the place of the one slain. Similar reasoning would lead to a similar treatment of the scapegoat on special occasions, such as drought or famine. If the crops did not answer to the expectation of the husbandman, this would be attributed to some failure in the generative powers of the god whose function it was to produce the fruits of the earth. It might be thought that he was under a spell or was growing old and feeble. Accordingly he was slain in the person of his representative, with all the ceremonies already described, in order that, born young again, he might infuse his own youthful vigour into the stagnant energies of nature. On the same principle we can understand why Mamurius Veturius was beaten with rods, why the slave at the Chaeronean ceremony was beaten with the *agnus castus* (a tree to which magical properties were ascribed), why the effigy of Death in some parts of Europe is assailed with sticks and stones, and why at Babylon the criminal who played the god was scourged.

In some parts of Eastern and Central Europe a similar custom is very commonly observed in spring. On the first of March the Albanians strike men and beast with cornel branches, believing that this is very good for their health. In March the Greek peasants of Cos switch their cattle, saying, "It is March, and up with your tail!" They think that the ceremony benefits the animals, and brings good luck. It is never observed at any other time of the year. In some parts of Mecklenburg it is customary to beat the cattle before sunrise on the morning of Good Friday with rods of buckthorn, which are afterwards concealed in some secret place where neither sun nor moon can shine on them. The belief is that though the blows light upon the animals, the pain of them is felt by the witches who are riding the beasts. In the neighbourhood of Iserlohn, in Westphalia, the herdsman rises at peep of dawn on May morning, climbs a hill, and cuts down the young rowan-tree which is the first to catch the beams of the rising sun. With this he returns to the farm-yard. The heifer which the farmer desires to "quicken" is then led to the dunghill, and the herdsman strikes it over the hind-quarters, the haunches, and the udders with a branch of the rowan-tree, saying,

"Quick, quick, quick!
Bring milk into the dugs.
The sap is in the birches.
The heifer receives a name.

"Quick, quick, quick!
Bring milk into the dugs.
The sap comes in the beeches,
The leaf comes on the oak.

"Quick, quick, quick!
Bring milk into the dugs.
In the name of the sainted Greta,
Gold-flower shall be thy name,"

and so on. The intention of the ceremony appears to be to make sure that the heifer shall in due time yield a plentiful supply of milk; and this is perhaps supposed to be brought about by driving away the witches, who are particularly apt to rob the cows of their milk on the morning of May Day. Certainly in the northeast of Scotland pieces of rowan-tree and wood-bine used to be placed over the doors of the byres on May Day to keep the witches from the cows; sometimes a single rod of rowan, covered with notches, was found to answer the purpose. An even more effectual guard against witchcraft was to tie a small cross of rowan-wood by a scarlet thread to each beast's tail; hence people said,

> "Rawn-tree in red-threed
> Pits the witches t' their speed."

In Germany also the rowan-tree is a protection against witchcraft; and Norwegian sailors and fishermen carry a piece of it in their boats for good luck. Thus the benefit to young cows of beating them with rowan appears to be not so much the positive one of pouring milk into their udders, as merely the negative one of averting evil influence; and the same may perhaps be said of most of the beatings with which we are here concerned.

On Good Friday and the two previous days people in Croatia and Slavonia take rods with them to church, and when the service is over they beat each other "fresh and healthy." In some parts of Russia people returning from the church on Palm Sunday beat the children and servants who have stayed at home with palm branches, saying, "Sickness into the forest, health into the bones." A similar custom is widely known under the name of *Schmeckostern* or "Easter Smacks" in some parts of Germany and Austria. The regions in which the practice prevails are for the most part districts in which the people either are or once were predominantly of Slavonic blood, such as East and West Prussia, Voigtland, Silesia, Bohemia, and Moravia. While the German population call the custom *Schmeckostern*, the Slavonic inhabitants give it, according to their particular language or dialect, a variety of names which signify to beat or scourge. It is usually observed on Easter Monday, less frequently on Easter Saturday or Easter Sunday.

In some parts of Germany and Austria a custom like that of "Easter Smacks" is observed at the Christmas holidays, especially on Holy Innocents' Day, the twenty-eighth of December. Young men and women beat each other mutually, but on different days, with branches of fresh green, whether birch, willow, or fir. Thus, for example, among the Germans of western Bohemia it is customary on St. Barbara's Day (the fourth of December) to cut twigs or branches of birch and to steep them in water in order that they may put out leaves or buds. They are afterwards used by each sex to beat the other on subsequent days of the Christmas holidays. In some villages branches of willow or cherry-trees or rosemary are employed for the same purpose. With these green boughs, sometimes tied in bundles with red or green ribbons, the young men go about beating the young women on the morning of St. Stephen's Day (the twenty-sixth of December) and also on Holy Innocents' Day (the twenty-eighth of December). The beating is inflicted on the hands, feet, and face; and in Neugramatin it is said that she who is not thus beaten with fresh green will not herself be fresh and green. As the blows descend, the young men recite verses importing that the beating is administered as a compliment and in order to benefit the health of the victim. For the service which they thus render the damsels they are rewarded by them with cakes, brandy, or money. Early in the morning of New Year's Day the lasses pay off the lads in the same kind. A similar custom is also observed in central and south-west Germany, especially in Voigtland. Thus in Voigtland and the whole of the Saxon Erz-gebirge the lads beat the lasses and women on the second day of the Christmas holidays with something green, such as rosemary or juniper; and if possible the beating is inflicted on the women as they lie in bed. As they beat them, the lads say

> "Fresh and green! Pretty and fine!
> Gingerbread and brandy-wine!"

The last words refer to the present of gingerbread and brandy which the lads expect to receive from the lasses for the trouble of thrashing them. Next day the lasses and women retaliate on the lads and men. In Thüringen on Holy Innocents' Day (the twenty-eighth of December) children armed with rods and green boughs go about the streets beating passers-by and demanding a present in return; they even make their way into the houses and beat the maid-servants. In Orlagau the custom is called "whipping with fresh green." On the second day of the Christmas holidays the girls go to their parents, godparents, relations, and friends, and beat them with fresh green branches of fir; next day the boys and lads do the same. The words spoken while the beating is being administered are "Good morning! fresh green! Long life! You must give us a bright thaler," and so on.

In these European customs the intention of beating persons, especially of the other sex, with fresh green leaves appears unquestionably to be the beneficent one of renewing their life and vigour, whether the purpose is supposed to be accomplished directly and positively by imparting the vital energy of the fresh green to the persons, or negatively and indirectly by dispelling any injurious influences, such as the machinations of witches and demons, by which the persons may be supposed to be beset. The application of the blows by the one sex to the other, especially by young men to young women, suggests that the beating is or was origi-nally intended above all to stimulate the reproductive powers of the men or women who received it; and the pains taken to ensure that the branches with which the strokes are given should have budded or blossomed out just before their services are wanted speak strongly in favour of the view that in these customs we have a deliberate attempt to transfuse a store of vital energy from the vegetable to the animal world . . .

Farewell to Nemi

We are at the end of our enquiry, but as often happens in the search after truth, if we have answered one question, we have raised many more; if we have followed one track home, we have had to pass by others that opened off it and led, or seemed to lead, to far other goals than the sacred grove at Nemi. Some of these paths we have followed a little way; others, if fortune should be kind, the writer and the reader may one day pursue together. For the present we have journeyed far enough together, and it is time to part. Yet before we do so, we may well ask ourselves whether there is not some more general conclusion, some lesson, if possible, of hope and encouragement, to be drawn from the melancholy record of human error and folly which has engaged our attention in these volumes.

If then we consider, on the one hand, the essential similarity of man's chief wants every-where and at all times, and on the other hand, the wide difference between the means he has adopted to satisfy them in different ages, we shall perhaps be disposed to conclude that the movement of the higher thought, so far as we can trace it, has on the whole been from magic through religion to science. In magic man depends on his own strength to meet the difficul-ties and dangers that beset him on every side. He believes in a certain established order of nature on which he can surely count, and which he can manipulate for his own ends. When he discovers his mistake, when he recognizes sadly that both the order of nature which he had assumed and the control which he had believed himself to exercise over it were purely imag-inary, he ceases to rely on his own intelligence and his own unaided efforts, and throws himself humbly on the mercy of certain great invisible beings behind the veil of nature, to whom he now ascribes all those far-reaching powers which he once arrogated to himself. Thus in the acuter minds magic is gradually superseded by religion, which explains the succession of natural phenomena as regulated by the will, the passion, or the caprice of spiritual beings like man in kind, though vastly superior to him in power.

But as time goes on this explanation in its turn proves to be unsatisfactory. For it assumes that the succession of natural events is not determined by immutable laws, but is to some extent variable and irregular, and this assumption is not borne out by closer observation. On the contrary, the more we scrutinize that succession the more we are struck by the rigid uniformity, the punctual precision with which, wherever we can follow them, the operations of nature are carried on. Every great advance in knowledge has extended the sphere of order and correspondingly restricted the sphere of apparent disorder in the world, till now we are ready to anticipate that even in regions where chance and confusion appear still to reign, a fuller knowledge would everywhere reduce the seeming chaos to cosmos. Thus the keener minds, still pressing forward to a deeper solution of the mysteries of the universe, come to reject the religious theory of nature as inadequate, and to revert in a measure to the older standpoint of magic by postulating explicitly, what in magic had only been implicitly assumed, to wit, an inflexible regularity in the order of natural events, which, if carefully observed, enables us to foresee their course with certainty and to act accordingly. In short, religion, regarded as an explanation of nature, is displaced by science.

But while science has this much in common with magic that both rest on a faith in order as the underlying principle of all things, readers of this work will hardly need to be reminded that the order presupposed by magic differs widely from that which forms the basis of science. The difference flows naturally from the different modes in which the two orders have been reached. For whereas the order on which magic reckons is merely an extension, by false analogy, of the order in which ideas present themselves to our minds, the order laid down by science is derived from patient and exact observation of the phenomena themselves. The abundance, the solidity, and the splendour of the results already achieved by science are well fitted to inspire us with a cheerful confidence in the soundness of its method. Here at last, after groping about in the dark for countless ages, man has hit upon a clue to the labyrinth, a golden key that opens many locks in the treasury of nature. It is probably not too much to say that the hope of progress—moral and intellectual as well as material—in the future is bound up with the fortunes of science, and that every obstacle placed in the way of scientific discovery is a wrong to humanity.

Yet the history of thought should warn us against concluding that because the scientific theory of the world is the best that has yet been formulated, it is necessarily complete and final. We must remember that at bottom the generalizations of science or, in common parlance, the laws of nature are merely hypotheses devised to explain that ever-shifting phantasmagoria of thought which we dignify with the high-sounding names of the world and the universe. In the last analysis magic, religion, and science are nothing but theories of thought; and as science has supplanted its predecessors, so it may hereafter be itself superseded by some more perfect hypothesis, perhaps by some totally different way of looking at the phenomena—of registering the shadows on the screen—of which we in this generation can form no idea. The advance of knowledge is an infinite progression towards a goal that for ever recedes. We need not murmur at the endless pursuit:—

"Fatti non foste a viver come bruti
Ma per seguir virtute e conoscenza."

Great things will come of that pursuit, though we may not enjoy them. Brighter stars will rise on some voyager of the future—some great Ulysses of the realms of thought—than shine on us. The dreams of magic may one day be the waking realities of science. But a dark shadow lies athwart the far end of this fair prospect. For however vast the increase of knowledge and of power which the future may have in store for man, he can scarcely hope to stay the sweep of those great forces which seem to be making silently but relentlessly for the destruction of all this starry universe in which our earth swims as a speck or mote. In the ages to come man may be able to predict, perhaps even to control, the wayward courses of the winds and clouds, but hardly will his puny hands have strength to speed afresh our slackening planet in its orbit or rekindle the dying fire of the sun. Yet the philosopher who trembles at the idea of such distant catastrophes may console himself by reflecting that these gloomy apprehensions, like the earth and the sun themselves, are only parts of that unsubstantial world which thought has conjured up out of the void, and that the phantoms which the subtle enchantress has evoked to-day she may ban to-morrow. They too, like so much that to common eyes seems solid, may melt into air, into thin air.

Without dipping so far into the future, we may illustrate the course which thought has hitherto run by likening it to a web woven of three different threads—the black thread of magic, the red thread of religion, and the white thread of science, if under science we may include those simple truths drawn from observation of nature, of which men in all ages have possessed a store. Could we then survey the web of thought from the beginning, we should probably perceive it to be at first a chequer of black and white, a patchwork of true and false notions, hardly tinged as yet by the red thread of religion. But carry your eye further along the fabric and you will remark that, while the black and white chequer still runs through it, there rests on the middle portion of the web, where religion has entered most deeply into its texture, a dark crimson stain, which shades off insensibly into a lighter tint as the white thread of science is woven more and more into the tissue. To a web thus chequered and stained, thus shot with threads of diverse hues, but gradually changing colour the farther it is unrolled, the state of modern thought, with all its divergent aims and conflicting tendencies, may be compared. Will the great movement which for centuries has been slowly altering the complexion of thought be continued in the near future? or will a reaction set in which may arrest progress and even undo much that has been done? To keep up our parable, what will be the colour of the web which the Fates are now weaving on the humming loom of time? will it be white or red? We cannot tell. A faint glimmering light illumines the backward portion of the web. Clouds and thick darkness hide the other end.

Our long voyage of discovery is over and our bark has drooped her weary sails in port at last. Once more we take the road to Nemi. It is evening, and as we climb the long slope of the Appian Way up to the Alban Hills, we look back and see the sky aflame with sunset, its golden glory resting like the aureole of a dying saint over Rome and touching with a crest of fire the dome of St. Peter's. The sight once seen can never be forgotten, but we turn from it and pursue our way darkling along the mountain side, till we come to Nemi and look down on the lake in its deep hollow, now fast disappearing in the evening shadows. The place has changed but little since Diana received the homage of her worshippers in the sacred grove. The temple of the sylvan goddess, indeed, has vanished and the King of the Wood no longer stands sentinel over the Golden Bough. But Nemi's woods are still green, and as the sunset fades above them in the west, there comes to us, borne on the swell of the wind, the sound of the church bells of Rome ringing the Angelus. *Ave Maria!* Sweet and solemn they chime out from the distant city and die lingeringly away across the wide Campagnan marshes. *Le roi est mort, vive le roi! Ave Maria!*

Chapter 16

Henri Bergson (1859–1941)

"THE EVOLUTION OF LIFE – MECHANISM AND TELEOLOGY," *CREATIVE EVOLUTION* (1907)

HENRI BERGSON WAS A FRENCH PHILOSOPHER who viewed evolution as a creative rather than a mechanistic process (or Darwinian "natural selection"), the product of an enduring "*elan vital*." His vitalist philosophy concerning time, memory, and experience – which are more meaningfully to be thought of as occurring subjectively than in ways measurable by clocks and calendars – influenced modernist thinking and writing, perhaps most especially what came to be called the psychological novel. He served as president (in 1913) of the Society for Psychical Research, whose mission was "to conduct organised scholarly research into human experiences that challenge contemporary scientific models," and was awarded the Nobel Prize in Literature in 1927 "in recognition of his rich and vitalizing ideas and the brilliant skill with which they have been presented."

Henri Bergson, "The Evolution of Life – Mechanism and Teleology," *Creative Evolution* (1907). New York: Henry Holt, 1911. 1–7.

The existence of which we are most assured and which we know best is unquestionably our own, for of every other object we have notions which may be considered external and superficial, whereas, of ourselves, our perception is internal and profound. What, then, do we find? In this privileged case, what is the precise meaning of the word "exist"? Let us recall here briefly the conclusion of an earlier work.

I find, first of all, that I pass from state to state. I am warm or cold, I am merry or sad, I work or I do nothing, I look at what is around me or I think of something else. Sensations, feelings, volitions, ideas—such are the changes into which my existence is divided and which color it in turns. I change, then, without ceasing. But this is not saying enough. Change is far more radical than we are at first inclined to suppose.

For I speak of each of my states as if it formed a block and were a separate whole. I say indeed that I change, but the change seems to me to reside in the passage from one state to the next: of each state, taken separately, I am apt to think that it remains the same during all the time that it prevails. Nevertheless, a slight effort of attention would reveal to me that there is no feeling, no idea, no volition which is not undergoing change every moment: if a mental state ceased to vary, its duration would cease to flow. Let us take the most stable of internal states, the visual perception of a motionless external object. The object may remain the same, I may look at it from the same side, at the same angle, in the same light; nevertheless the vision I now have of it differs from that which I have just had, even if only because the one is an instant older than the other. My memory is there, which conveys something of the past into the present. My mental state, as it advances on the road of time, is continually swelling with the duration which it accumulates: it goes on increasing—rolling upon itself, as a snowball on the snow. Still more is this the case with states more deeply internal, such as sensation, feelings, desires, etc., which do not correspond, like a simple visual perception, to an unvarying external object. But it is expedient to disregard this uninterrupted change, and to notice it only when it becomes sufficient to impress a new attitude on the body, a new direction on the attention. Then, and then only, we find that our state has changed. The truth is that we change without ceasing, and that the state itself is nothing but change.

This amounts to saying that there is no essential difference between passing from one state to another and persisting in the same state. If the state which "remains the same" is more varied than we think, on the other hand the passing from one state to another resembles, more than we imagine, a single state being prolonged; the transition is continuous. But, just because we close our eyes to the unceasing variation of every psychical state, we are obliged, when the change has become so considerable as to force itself on our attention, to speak as if a new state were placed alongside the previous one. Of this new state we assume that it remains unvarying in its turn, and so on endlessly. The apparent discontinuity of the psychical life is then due to our attention being fixed on it by a series of separate acts: actually there is only a gentle slope; but in following the broken line of our acts of attention, we think we perceive separate steps. True, our psychic life is full of the unforeseen. A thousand incidents arise, which seem to be cut off from those which precede them, and to be disconnected from those which follow. Discontinuous though they appear, however, in point of fact they stand out against the continuity of a background on which they are designed, and to which indeed they owe the intervals that separate them; they are the beats of the drum which break forth here and there in the symphony. Our attention fixes on them because they interest it more, but each of them is borne by the fluid mass of our whole psychical existence. Each is only the best illuminated point of a moving zone which comprises all that we feel or think or will—all, in short, that we are at any given moment. It is this entire zone which in reality makes up our state. Now, states thus defined cannot be regarded as distinct elements. They continue each other in an endless flow.

But, as our attention has distinguished and separated them artificially, it is obliged next to reunite them by an artificial bond. It imagines, therefore, a formless *ego,* indifferent and unchangeable, on which it threads the psychic states which it has set up as independent entities. Instead of a flux of fleeting shades merging into each other, it perceives distinct and, so to speak, *solid* colors, set side by side like the beads of a necklace; it must perforce then suppose a thread, also itself solid, to hold the beads together. But if this colorless substratum is perpetually colored by that which covers it, it is for us, in its indeterminateness, as if it did not exist, since we only perceive what is colored, or, in other words, psychic states. As a matter of fact, this substratum has no reality; it is merely a symbol intended to recall unceasingly to our consciousness the artificial character of the process by which the attention places clean-cut states side by side, where actually there is a continuity which unfolds. If our existence were composed of separate states with an impassive ego to unite them, for us there would be no duration. For an ego which does not change does not *endure,* and a psychic state which remains the same so long as it is not replaced by the following state does not *endure* either. Vain, therefore, is the attempt to range such states beside each other on the ego supposed to sustain them: never can these solids strung upon a solid make up that duration which flows. What we actually obtain in this way is an artificial imitation of the internal life, a static equivalent which will lend itself better to the requirements of logic and language, just because we have eliminated from it the element of real time. But, as regards the psychical life unfolding beneath the symbols which conceal it, we readily perceive that time is just the stuff it is made of.

There is, moreover, no stuff more resistant nor more substantial. For our duration is not merely one instant replacing another; if it were, there would never be anything but the present—no prolonging of the past into the actual, no evolution, no concrete duration. Duration is the continuous progress of the past, which gnaws into the future and which swells as it advances. And as the past grows without ceasing, so also there is no limit to its preservation. Memory, as we have tried to prove, is not a faculty of putting away recollections in a drawer, or of inscribing them in a register. There is no register, no drawer; there is not even, properly speaking, a faculty, for a faculty works intermittently, when it will or when it can, whilst the piling up of the past upon the past goes on without relaxation. In reality, the past is preserved by itself, automatically. In its entirety, probably, it follows us at every instant; all that we have felt, thought and willed from our earliest infancy is there, leaning over the present which is about to join it, pressing against the portals of consciousness that would fain leave it outside. The cerebral mechanism is arranged just so as to drive back into the unconscious almost the whole of this past, and to admit beyond the threshold only that which can cast light on the present situation or futher the action now being prepared—in short, only that which can give *useful* work. At the most, a few superfluous recollections may succeed in smuggling themselves through the half-open door. These memories, messengers from the unconscious, remind us of what we are dragging behind us unawares. But, even though we may have no distinct idea of it, we feel vaguely that our past remains present to us. What are we, in fact, what is our *character*, if not the condensation of the history that we have lived from our birth—nay, even before our birth, since we bring with us prenatal dispositions? Doubtless we think with only a small part of our past, but it is with our entire past, including the original bent of our soul, that we desire, will and act. Our past, then, as a whole, is made manifest to us in its impulse; it is felt in the form of tendency, although a small part of it only is known in the form of idea.

From this survival of the past it follows that consciousness cannot go through the same state twice. The circumstances may still be the same, but they will act no longer on the same person, since they find him at a new moment of his history. Our personality, which is being built up each instant with its accumulated experience, changes without ceasing. By changing, it prevents any state, although superficially identical with another, from ever repeating it in its very depth. That is why our duration is irreversible. We could not live over again a single moment, for we should have to begin by effacing the memory of all that had followed. Even could we erase this memory from our intellect, we could not from our will.

Thus our personality shoots, grows and ripens without ceasing. Each of its moments is something new added to what was before. We may go further: it is not only something new, but something unforeseeable. Doubtless, my present state is explained by what was in me and by what was acting on me a moment ago. In analyzing it I should find no other elements. But even a superhuman intelligence would not have been able to foresee the simple indivisible form which gives to these purely abstract elements their concrete organization. For to foresee consists of projecting into the future what has been perceived in the past, or of imagining for a later time a new grouping, in a new order, of elements already perceived. But that which has never been perceived, and which is at the same time simple, is necessarily unforeseeable. Now such is the case with each of our states, regarded as a moment in a history that is gradually unfolding: it is simple, and it cannot have been already perceived, since it concentrates in its indivisibility all that has been perceived and what the present is adding to it besides. It is an original moment of a no less original history.

The finished portrait is explained by the features of the model, by the nature of the artist, by the colors spread out on the palette; but, even with the knowledge of what explains it, no one, not even the artist, could have foreseen exactly what the portrait would be, for to predict it would have been to produce it before it was produced—an absurd hypothesis which is its own refutation. Even so with regard to the moments of our life, of which we are the artisans. Each of them is a kind of creation. And just as the talent of the painter is formed or deformed—in any case, is modified—under the very influence of the works he produces, so each of our states, at the moment of its issue, modifies our personality, being indeed the new form that we are just assuming. It is then right to say that what we do depends on what we are; but it is necessary to add also that we are, to a certain extent, what we do, and that we are creating ourselves continually. This creation of self by self is the more complete, the more one reasons on what one does. For reason does not proceed in such matters as in geometry, where impersonal premises are given once for all, and an impersonal conclusion must perforce be drawn. Here, on the contrary, the same reasons may dictate to different persons, or to the same person at different moments, acts profoundly different although equally reasonable. The truth is that they are not quite the same reasons, since they are not those of the same person, nor of the same moment. That is why we cannot deal with them in the abstract, from outside, as in geometry, nor solve for another the problems by which he is faced in life. Each must solve them from within, on his own account. But we need not go more deeply into this. We are seeking only the precise meaning that our consciousness gives to this word "exist," and we find that, for a conscious being, to exist is to change, to change is to mature, to mature is to go on creating oneself endlessly. Should the same be said of existence in general?

Chapter 17

E.M. Forster (1879–1970)

"WHAT I BELIEVE" (1939)

ALTHOUGH TRADITIONAL RELIGIOUS INSTITUTIONS had a weakening hold on modernist culture, the English novelist, essayist, and literary critic E.M. Forster asserted his lack of belief in Belief during what he considered "an age of faith." As a self-proclaimed heir of the liberal, humanist tradition personified by Erasmus and Montaigne (and Matthew Arnold), Forster valued "tolerance, good temper and sympathy," while acknowledging that they were insufficient "in a world which is rent by religious and racial persecution," one "battered beneath a military jack-boot." Forster was known primarily for his novels *Howards End* (with its humanistic epigraph, "Only connect" [1910]) and *A Passage to India* (1924); *Maurice*, a semi-autobiographical homosexual love story set in pre-Great War "greenwood England," was published posthumously (1971).

E.M. Forster, "What I Believe," *Two Cheers for Democracy*. New York: Harcourt, Brace, 1951. 67–76.

I do not believe in Belief. But this is an age of faith, and there are so many militant creeds that, in self-defence, one has to formulate a creed of one's own. Tolerance, good temper and sympathy are no longer enough in a world which is rent by religious and racial persecution, in a world where ignorance rules, and science, who ought to have ruled, plays the subservient pimp. Tolerance, good temper and sympathy—they are what matter really, and if the human race is not to collapse they must come to the front before long. But for the moment they are not enough, their action is no stronger than a flower, battered beneath a military jack-boot. They want stiffening, even if the process coarsens them. Faith, to my mind, is a stiffening process, a sort of mental starch, which ought to be applied as sparingly as possible. I dislike the stuff. I do not believe in it, for its own sake, at all. Herein I probably differ from most people, who believe in Belief, and are only sorry they cannot swallow even more than they do. My law-givers are Erasmus and Montaigne, not Moses and St. Paul. My temple stands not upon Mount Moriah but in that Elysian Field where even the immoral are admitted. My motto is: "Lord, I disbelieve—help thou my unbelief."

I have, however, to live in an Age of Faith—the sort of epoch I used to hear praised when I was a boy. It is extremely unpleasant really. It is bloody in every sense of the word. And I have to keep my end up in it. Where do I start?

With personal relationships. Here is something comparatively solid in a world full of violence and cruelty. Not absolutely solid, for Psychology has split and shattered the idea of a "Person," and has shown that there is something incalculable in each of us, which may at any moment rise to the surface and destroy our normal balance. We don't know what we are like. We can't know what other people are like. How, then, can we put any trust in personal relationships, or cling to them in the gathering political storm? In theory we cannot. But in practice we can and do. Though A is not unchangeably A or B unchangeably B, there can still be love and loyalty between the two. For the purpose of living one has to assume that the personality is solid, and the "self" is an entity, and to ignore all contrary evidence. And since to ignore evidence is one of the characteristics of faith, I certainly can proclaim that I believe in personal relationships.

Starting from them, I get a little order into the contemporary chaos. One must be fond of people and trust them if one is not to make a mess of life, and it is therefore essential that they should not let one down. They often do. The moral of which is that I must, myself, be as reliable as possible, and this I try to be. But reliability is not a matter of contract—that is the main difference between the world of personal relationships and the world of business relationships. It is a matter for the heart, which signs no documents. In other words, reliability is impossible unless there is a natural warmth. Most men possess this warmth, though they often have bad luck and get chilled. Most of them, even when they are politicians, *want* to keep faith. And one can, at all events, show one's own little light here, one's own poor little trembling flame, with the knowledge that it is not the only light that is shining in the darkness, and not the only one which the darkness does not comprehend. Personal relations are despised today. They are regarded as bourgeois luxuries, as products of a time of fair weather which is now past, and we are urged to get rid of them, and to dedicate ourselves to some movement or cause instead. I hate the idea of causes, and if I had to choose between betraying my country and betraying my friend, I hope I should have the guts to betray my country. Such a choice may scandalise the modern reader, and he may stretch out his patriotic hand to the telephone at once and ring up the police. It would not have shocked Dante, though. Dante places Brutus and Cassius in the lowest circle of Hell because they had chosen to betray their friend Julius Caesar rather than their country Rome. Probably one will not be asked to make such an agonising choice. Still, there lies at the back of every creed something terrible and hard for which the worshipper may one day be required to suffer, and there is even a terror and a hardness in this creed of personal relationships, urbane and mild though it sounds. Love and loyalty to an individual can run counter to the claims of the State. When they do—down with the State, say I, which means that the State would down me.

This brings me along to Democracy, "even Love, the Beloved Republic, which feeds upon Freedom and lives." Democracy is not a Beloved Republic really, and never will be. But it is less hateful than other contemporary forms of government, and to that extent it deserves our support. It does start from the assumption that the individual is important, and that all types are needed to make a civilisation. It does not divide its citizens into the bossers and the bossed—as an efficiency-regime tends to do. The people I admire most are those who are sensitive and want to create something or discover something, and do not see life in terms of power, and such people get more of a chance under a democracy than elsewhere. They found religions, great or small, or they produce literature and art, or they do disinterested scientific research, or they may be what is called "ordinary people," who are creative in their private lives, bring up their children decently, for instance, or help their neighbours. All these people need to express themselves; they cannot do so unless society allows them liberty to do so, and the society which allows them most liberty is a democracy.

Democracy has another merit. It allows criticism, and if there is not public criticism there are bound to be hushed-up scandals. That is why I believe in the Press, despite all its lies and vulgarity, and why I believe in Parliament. Parliament is often sneered at because it is a Talking Shop. I believe in it *because* it is a talking shop. I believe in the Private Member who makes himself a nuisance. He gets snubbed and is told that he is cranky or ill-informed, but he does expose abuses which would otherwise never have been mentioned, and very often an abuse gets put right just by being mentioned. Occasionally, too, a well-meaning public official starts losing his head in the cause of efficiency, and thinks himself God Almighty. Such officials are particularly frequent in the Home Office. Well, there will be questions about them in Parliament sooner or later, and then they will have to mind their steps. Whether Parliament is either a representative body or an efficient one is questionable, but I value it because it criticises and talks, and because its chatter gets widely reported.

So Two Cheers for Democracy: one because it admits variety and two because it permits criticism. Two cheers are quite enough: there is no occasion to give three. Only Love the Beloved Republic deserves that.

What about Force, though? While we are trying to be sensitive and advanced and affectionate and tolerant, an unpleasant question pops up: does not all society rest upon force? If a government cannot count upon the police and the army, how can it hope to rule? And if an individual gets knocked on the head or sent to a labour camp, of what significance are his opinions?

This dilemma does not worry me as much as it does some. I realise that all society rests upon force. But all the great creative actions, all the decent human relations, occur during the intervals when force has not managed to come to the front. These intervals are what matter. I want them to be as frequent and as lengthy as possible, and I call them "civilisation." Some people idealise force and pull it into the foreground and worship, it, instead of keeping it in the background as long as possible. I think they make a mistake, and I think that their opposites, the mystics, err even more when they declare that force does not exist. I believe that it exists, and that one of our jobs is to prevent it from getting out of its box. It gets out sooner or later, and then it destroys us and all the lovely things which we have made. But it is not out all the time, for the fortunate reason that the strong are so stupid. Consider their conduct for a moment in the Niebelung's Ring. The giants there have the guns, or in other words the gold; but they do nothing with it, they do not realise that they are all-powerful, with the result that the catastrophe is delayed and the castle of Walhalla, insecure but glorious, fronts the storms. Fafnir, coiled round his hoard, grumbles and grunts; we can hear him under Europe today; the leaves of the wood already tremble, and the Bird calls its warnings uselessly. Fafnir will destroy us, but by a blessed dispensation he is stupid and slow, and creation goes on just outside the poisonous blast of his breath. The Nietzschean would hurry the monster up, the mystic would say he did not exist, but Wotan, wiser than either, hastens to create warriors before doom declares itself. The Valkyries are symbols not only of courage but of intelligence; they represent the human spirit snatching its opportunity while the going is good, and one of them even finds time to love. Brünnhilde's last song hymns the recurrence of love, and since it is the privilege of art to exaggerate, she goes even further, and proclaims the love which is eternally triumphant and feeds upon freedom, and lives.

So that is what I feel about force and violence. It is, alas! the ultimate reality on this earth, but it does not always get to the front. Some people call its absences "decadence"; I call them "civilisation" and find in such interludes the chief justification for the human experiment. I look the other way until fate strikes me. Whether this is due to courage or to cowardice in my own case I cannot be sure. But I know that if men had not looked the other way in the past, nothing of any value would survive. The people I respect most behave as if they were immortal and as if society was eternal. Both assumptions are false: both of them must be accepted as true if we are to go on eating and working and loving, and are to keep open a few breathing holes for the human spirit. No millennium seems likely to descend upon humanity; no better and stronger League of Nations will be instituted; no form of Christianity and no alternative to Christianity will bring peace to the world or integrity to the individual; no "change of heart" will occur. And yet we need not despair, indeed, we cannot despair; the evidence of history shows us that men have always insisted on behaving creatively under the shadow of the sword; that they have done their artistic and scientific and domestic stuff for the sake of doing it, and that we had better follow their example under the shadow of the aeroplanes. Others, with more vision or courage than myself, see the salvation of humanity ahead, and will dismiss my conception of civilisation as paltry, a sort of tip-and-run game. Certainly it is presumptuous to say that we *cannot* improve, and that Man, who has only been in power for a few thousand years, will never learn to make use of his power. All I mean is that, if people continue to kill one another as they do, the world cannot get better than it is, and that since there are more people than formerly, and their means for destroying one another superior, the world may well get worse. What is good in people—and consequently in the world—is their insistence on creation, their belief in friendship and loyalty for their own sakes; and though Violence remains and is, indeed, the major partner in this muddled establishment, I believe that creativeness remains too, and will always assume direction when violence sleeps. So, though I am not an optimist, I cannot agree with Sophocles that it were better never to have been born. And although, like Horace, I see no evidence that each batch of births is superior to the last, I leave the field open for the more complacent view. This is such a difficult moment to live in, one cannot help getting gloomy and also a bit rattled, and perhaps short-sighted.

In search of a refuge, we may perhaps turn to hero-worship. But here we shall get no help, in my opinion. Hero-worship is a dangerous vice, and one of the minor merits of a democracy is that it does not encourage it, or produce that unmanageable type of citizen known as the Great Man. It produces instead different kinds of small men—a much finer achievement. But people who cannot get interested in the variety of life, and cannot make up their own minds, get discontented over this, and they long for a hero to bow down before and to follow blindly. It is significant that a hero is an integral part of the authoritarian stock-in-trade today. An efficiency-regime cannot be run without a few heroes stuck about it to carry off the dullness—much as plums have to be put into a bad pudding to make it palatable. One hero at the top and a smaller one each side of him is a favourite arrangement, and the timid and the bored are comforted by the trinity, and, bowing down, feel exalted and strengthened.

No, I distrust Great Men. They produce a desert of uniformity around them and often a pool of blood too, and I always feel a little man's pleasure when they come a cropper. Every now and then one reads in the newspapers some such statement as: "The coup d'état appears to have failed, and Admiral Toma's whereabouts is at present unknown." Admiral Toma had probably every qualification for being a Great Man—an iron will, personal magnetism, dash, flair, sexlessness—but fate was against him, so he retires to unknown whereabouts instead of parading history with his peers. He fails with a completeness which no artist and no lover can experience, because with them the process of creation is itself an achievement, whereas with him the only possible achievement is success.

I believe in aristocracy, though—if that is the right word, and if a democrat may use it. Not an aristocracy of power, based upon rank and influence, but an aristocracy of the sensitive, the considerate and the plucky. Its members are to be found in all nations and classes, and all through the ages, and there is a secret understanding between them when they meet.

They represent the true human tradition, the one permanent victory of our queer race over cruelty and chaos. Thousands of them perish in obscurity, a few are great names. They are sensitive for others as well as for themselves, they are considerate without being fussy, their pluck is not swankiness but the power to endure, and they can take a joke. I give no examples—it is risky to do that—but the reader may as well consider whether this is the type of person he would like to meet and to be, and whether (going farther with me) he would prefer that this type should *not* be an ascetic one. I am against asceticism myself. I am with the old Scotsman who wanted less chastity and more delicacy. I do not feel that my aristocrats are a real aristocracy if they thwart their bodies, since bodies are the instruments through which we register and enjoy the world. Still, I do not insist. This is not a major point. It is clearly possible to be sensitive, considerate and plucky and yet be an ascetic too, if anyone possesses the first three qualities, I will let him in! On they go—an invincible army, yet not a victorious one. The aristocrats, the elect, the chosen, the Best People—all the words that describe them are false, and all attempts to organise them fail. Again and again Authority, seeing their value, has tried to net them and to utilise them as the Egyptian Priesthood or the Christian Church or the Chinese Civil Service or the Group Movement, or some other worthy stunt. But they slip through the net and are gone; when the door is shut, they are no longer in the room; their temple, as one of them remarked, is the Holiness of the Heart's Affection, and their kingdom, though they never possess it, is the wide-open world.

With this type of person knocking about, and constantly crossing one's path if one has eyes to see or hands to feel, the experiment of earthly life cannot be dismissed as a failure. But it may well be hailed as a tragedy, the tragedy being that no device has been found by which these private decencies can be transmitted to public affairs. As soon as people have power they go crooked and sometimes dotty as well, because the possession of power lifts them into a region where normal honesty never pays. For instance, the man who is selling newspapers outside the Houses of Parliament can safely leave his papers to go for a drink and his cap beside them: anyone who takes a paper is sure to drop a copper into the cap. But the men who are inside the Houses of Parliament—they cannot trust one another like that, still less can the Government they compose trust other governments. No caps upon the pavement here, but suspicion, treachery and armaments. The more highly public life is organised the lower does its morality sink; the nations of today behave to each other worse than they ever did in the past, they cheat, rob, bully and bluff, make war without notice, and kill as many women and children as possible; whereas primitive tribes were at all events restrained by taboos. It is a humiliating outlook—though the greater the darkness, the brighter shine the little lights, reassuring one another, signalling: "Well, at all events, I'm still here. I don't like it very much, but how are you?" Unquenchable lights of my aristocracy! Signals of the invincible army! "Come along—anyway, let's have a good time while we can." I think they signal that too.

The Saviour of the future – if ever he comes—will not preach a new Gospel. He will merely utilise my aristocracy, he will make effective the good will and the good temper which are already existing. In other words, he will introduce a new technique. In economics, we are told that if there was a new technique of distribution, there need be no poverty, and people would not starve in one place while crops were being ploughed under in another. A similar change is needed in the sphere of morals and politics. The desire for it is by no means new; it was expressed, for example, in theological terms by Jacopone da Todi over six hundred years ago. "Ordina questo amore, O tu che m'ami," he said; "O thou who lovest me—set this love in order." His prayer was not granted, and I do not myself believe that it ever will be, but here, and not through a change of heart, is our probable route. Not by becoming better, but by ordering and distributing his native goodness, will Man shut up Force into its box, and so gain time to explore the universe and to set his mark upon it worthily. At present he only explores it at odd moments, when Force is looking the other way, and his divine creativeness appears as a trivial byproduct, to be scrapped as soon as the drums beat and the bombers hum.

Such a change, claim the orthodox, can only be made by Christianity, and will be made by it in God's good time: man always has failed and always will fail to organise his own goodness, and it is presumptuous of him to try. This claim—solemn as it is—leaves me cold. I cannot believe that Christianity will ever cope with the present world-wide mess, and I think that such influence as it retains in modern society is due to the money behind it, rather than to its spiritual appeal. It was a spiritual force once, but the indwelling spirit will have to be restated if it is to calm the waters again, and probably restated in a non-Christian form. Naturally a lot of people, and people who are not only good but able and intelligent, will disagree here; they will vehemently deny that Christianity has failed, or they will argue that its failure proceeds from the wickedness of men, and really proves its ultimate success. They have Faith, with a large F. My faith has a very small one, and I only intrude it because these are strenuous and serious days, and one likes to say what one thinks while speech is comparatively free: it may not be free much longer.

The above are the reflections of an individualist and a liberal who has found liberalism crumbling beneath him and at first felt ashamed. Then, looking around, he decided there was no special reason for shame, since other people, whatever they felt, were equally insecure. And as for individualism—there seems no way of getting off this, even if one wanted to. The dictator-hero can grind down his citizens till they are all alike, but he cannot melt them into a single man. That is beyond his power. He can order them to merge, he can incite them to mass-antics, but they are obliged to be born separately, and to die separately, and, owing to these unavoidable termini, will always be running off the totalitarian rails. The memory of birth and the expectation of death always lurk within the human being, making him separate from his fellows and consequently capable of intercourse with them. Naked I came into the world, naked I shall go out of it! And a very good thing too, for it reminds me that I am naked under my shirt, whatever its colour.

Chapter 18

Walter Benjamin (1892–1940)

"THESES ON THE PHILOSOPHY OF HISTORY" (1955)

A GERMAN-JEWISH LITERARY CRITIC, TRANSLATOR, freelance journalist and cultural critic, Walter Benjamin is renowned for his idiosyncratic scholarship and his affiliations with the intellectuals associated with the Frankfurt School for Social Research (Theodor Adorno, Bertolt Brecht, Siegfried Kracauer, Ernst Bloch, and others). He moved to Paris after Hitler's rise to power; subsequently fleeing France just ahead of the German invasion, he was believed to have committed suicide in despair at the French-Spanish border when it seemed likely that he would be captured by Franco's police. Most of the work Benjamin published in his lifetime was fragmentary and ephemeral, but abundant; the French writer Georges Bataille protected his unfinished magnum opus, *The Arcades Project* (*Passengenwerk*), in Paris's Bibliothèque Nationale; and Harvard University Press published a four-volume collection of his selected writings (1996–2003). In "The Work of Art in the Age of Mechanical Reproduction," perhaps his most influential study, Benjamin marks a shift in the auratic (original, proto-sacred) status of art as such technical means of reproduction as photography and film come to dominate the popular imagination.

Walter Benjamin, "Theses on the Philosophy of History," *Illuminations*. Trans. Harry Zohn. New York: Schocken, 1962. 253–64.

I

The story is told of an automaton constructed in such a way that it could play a winning game of chess, answering each move of an opponent with a countermove. A puppet in Turkish attire and with a hookah in its mouth sat before a chessboard placed on a large table. A system of mirrors created the illusion that this table was transparent from all sides. Actually, a little hunchback who was an expert chess player sat inside and guided the puppet's hand by means of strings. One can imagine a philosophical counterpart to this device. The puppet called "historical materialism" is to win all the time. It can easily be a match for anyone if it enlists the services of theology, which today, as we know, is wizened and has to keep out of sight.

II

"One of the most remarkable characteristics of human nature," writes Lotze, "is, alongside so much selfishness in specific instances, the freedom from envy which the present displays toward the future." Reflection shows us that our image of happiness is thoroughly colored by the time to which the course of our own existence has assigned us. The kind of happiness that could arouse envy in us exists only in the air we have breathed, among people we could have talked to, women who could have given themselves to us. In other words, our image of happiness is indissolubly bound up with the image of redemption. The same applies to our view of the past, which is the concern of history. The past carries with it a temporal index by which it is referred to redemption. There is a secret agreement between past generations and the present one. Our coming was expected on earth. Like every generation that preceded us, we have been endowed with a *weak* Messianic power, a power to which the past has a claim. That claim cannot be settled cheaply. Historical materialists are aware of that.

III

A chronicler who recites events without distinguishing between major and minor ones acts in accordance with the following truth: nothing that has ever happened should be regarded as lost for history. To be sure, only a redeemed mankind receives the fullness of its past—which is to say, only for a redeemed mankind has its past become citable in all its moments. Each moment it has lived becomes a *citation à l'ordre du jour*—and that day is Judgment Day.

IV

> Seek for food and clothing first, then
> the Kingdom of God shall be added unto you.
>
> —Hegel, 1807

The class struggle, which is always present to a historian influenced by Marx, is a fight for the crude and material things without which no refined and spiritual things could exist. Nevertheless, it is not in the form of the spoils which fall to the victor that the latter make their presence felt in the class struggle. They manifest themselves in this struggle as courage, humor, cunning, and fortitude. They have retroactive force and will constantly call in question every victory, past and present, of the rulers. As flowers turn toward the sun, by dint of a secret heliotropism the past strives to turn toward that sun which is rising in the sky of history. A historical materialist must be aware of this most inconspicuous of all transformations.

V

The true picture of the past flits by. The past can be seized only as an image which flashes up at the instant when it can be recognized and is never seen again. "The truth will not run away from us": in the historical outlook of historicism these words of Gottfried Keller mark the exact point where historical materialism cuts through historicism. For every image of the past that is not recognized by the present as one of its own concerns threatens to disappear irretrievably. (The good tidings which the historian of the past brings with throbbing heart may be lost in a void the very moment he opens his mouth.)

VI

To articulate the past historically does not mean to recognize it "the way it really was" (Ranke). It means to seize hold of a memory as it flashes up at a moment of danger. Historical materialism wishes to retain that image of the past which unexpectedly appears to man singled out by history at a moment of danger. The danger affects both the content of the tradition and its receivers. The same threat hangs over both: that of becoming a tool of the ruling classes. In every era the attempt must be made anew to wrest tradition away from a conformism that is about to overpower it. The Messiah comes not only as the redeemer, he comes as the subduer of Antichrist. Only that historian will have the gift of fanning the spark of hope in the past who is firmly convinced that *even the dead* will not be safe from the enemy if he wins. And this enemy has not ceased to be victorious.

VII

Consider the darkness and the great cold
In this vale which resounds with mysery.

—Brecht, *The Threepenny Opera*

To historians who wish to relive an era, Fustel de Coulanges recommends that they blot out everything they know about the later course of history. There is no better way of characterizing the method with which historical materialism has broken. It is a process of empathy whose origin is the indolence of the heart, *acedia*, which despairs of grasping and holding the genuine historical image as it flares up briefly. Among medieval theologians it was regarded as the root cause of sadness. Flaubert, who was familiar with it, wrote: *"Peu de gens devineront combien il a fallu être triste pour ressusciter Carthage."* ["Few will be able to guess how sad one had to be in order to resuscitate Carthage."] The nature of this sadness stands out more clearly if one asks with whom the adherents of historicism actually empathize. The answer is inevitable: with the victor. And all rulers are the heirs of those who conquered before them. Hence, empathy with the victor invariably benefits the rulers. Historical materialists know what that means. Whoever has emerged victorious participates to this day in the triumphal procession in which the present rulers step over those who are lying prostrate. According to traditional practice, the spoils are carried along in the procession. They are called cultural treasures, and a historical materialist views them with cautious detachment. For without exception the cultural treasures he surveys have an origin which he cannot contemplate without horror. They owe their existence not only to the efforts of the great minds and talents who have created them, but also to the anonymous toil of their contemporaries. There is no document of civilization which is not at the same time a document of barbarism. And just as such a document is not free of barbarism, barbarism taints also the manner in which it was transmitted from one owner to another. A historical materialist therefore dissociates himself from it as far as possible. He regards it as his task to brush history against the grain.

VIII

The tradition of the oppressed teaches us that the "state of emergency" in which we live is not the exception but the rule. We must attain to a conception of history that is in keeping with this insight. Then we shall clearly realize that it is our task to bring about a real state of emergency, and this will improve our position in the struggle against Fascism. One reason why

Fascism has a chance is that in the name of progress its opponents treat it as a historical norm. The current amazement that the things we are experiencing are "still" possible in the twentieth century is *not* philosophical. This amazement is not the beginning of knowledge—unless it is the knowledge that the view of history which gives rise to it is untenable.

IX

Mein Flügel ist zum Schwung bereit,
ich kehrte gern zurück,
denn blieb ich auch lebendige Zeit,
ich hätte wenig Glück.

—Gerhard Scholem, "Gruss vom Angelus"

[My wing is ready for flight,
I would like to turn back.
If I stayed timeless time,
I would have little luck.]

A Klee painting named "Angelus Novus" shows an angel looking as though he is about to move away from something he is fixedly contemplating. His eyes are staring, his mouth is open, his wings are spread. This is how one pictures the angel of history. His face is turned toward the past. Where we perceive a chain of events, he sees one single catastrophe which keeps piling wreckage upon wreckage and hurls it in front of his feet. The angel would like to stay, awaken the dead, and make whole what has been smashed. But a storm is blowing from Paradise; it has got caught in his wings with such violence that the angel can no longer close them. This storm irresistibly propels him into the future to which his back is turned, while the pile of debris before him grows skyward. This storm is what we call progress.

X

The themes which monastic discipline assigned to friars for meditation were designed to turn them away from the world and its affairs. The thoughts which we are developing here originate from similar considerations. At a moment when the politicians in whom the opponents of Fascism had placed their hopes are prostrate and confirm their defeat by betraying their own cause, these observations are intended to disentangle the political worldlings from the snares in which the traitors have entrapped them. Our consideration proceeds from the insight that the politicians' stubborn faith in progress, their confidence in their "mass basis," and, finally, their servile integration in an uncontrollable apparatus have been three aspects of the same thing. It seeks to convey an idea of the high price our accustomed thinking will have to pay for a conception of history that avoids any complicity with the thinking to which these politicians continue to adhere.

XI

The conformism which has been part and parcel of Social Democracy from the beginning attaches not only to its political tactics but to its economic views as well. It is one reason for its later breakdown. Nothing has corrupted the German working class so much as the notion that it was moving with the current. It regarded technological developments as the fall of the stream with which it thought it was moving. From there it was but a step to the illusion that the factory work which was supposed to tend toward technological progress constituted a political achievement. The old Protestant ethics of work was resurrected among German workers in secularized form. The Gotha Program already bears traces of this confusion, defining labor as "the source of all wealth and all culture." Smelling a rat, Marx countered that ". . . the man who possesses no other property than his labor power" must of necessity become "the slave of other men who have made themselves the owners. . . ." However, the confusion spread, and soon thereafter Josef Dietzgen proclaimed: "The savior of modern times is called work. The . . . improvement . . . of labor constitutes the wealth which is now able to accomplish what no redeemer has ever been able to do." This vulgar-Marxist conception of the nature of labor bypasses the question of how its products might benefit the workers while still not being at their disposal. It recognizes only the progress in the mastery of nature, not the retrogression of society; it already displays the technocratic features later encountered in Fascism. Among these is a conception of nature which differs ominously from the one in the Socialist utopias before the 1848 revolution. The new conception of labor amounts to the exploitation of nature, which with naïve complacency is contrasted with the exploitation of the proletariat. Compared with this positivistic conception, Fourier's fantasies, which have so often been ridiculed, prove to be surprisingly sound. According to Fourier, as a result of efficient cooperative labor, four moons would illuminate the earthly night, the ice would recede from the poles, sea water would no longer taste salty, and beasts of prey would do man's bidding. All this illustrates a kind of labor which, far from exploiting nature, is capable of delivering her of the creations which lie dormant in her womb as potentials. Nature, which, as Dietzgen puts it, "exists gratis," is a complement to the corrupted conception of labor.

XII

> We need history, but not the way a spoiled loafer in the garden of knowledge needs it.
>
> —Nietzsche, *Of The Use and Abuse of History*

Not man or men but the struggling, oppressed class itself is the depository of historical knowledge. In Marx it appears as the last enslaved class, as the avenger that completes the task of liberation in the name of generations of the downtrodden. This conviction, which had a brief resurgence in the Spartacist group, has always been objectionable to Social Democrats. Within three decades they managed virtually to erase the name of Blanqui, though it had been the rallying sound that had reverberated through the preceding century. Social Democracy thought fit to assign to the working class the role of the redeemer of future generations, in this way cutting the sinews of its greatest strength. This training made the working class forget both its hatred and its spirit of sacrifice, for both are nourished by the image of enslaved ancestors rather than that of liberated grandchildren.

XIII

> Every day our cause becomes clearer and people get smarter.
>
> —Wilhelm Dietzgen, *Die Religion der Sozialdemokratie*

Social Democratic theory, and even more its practice, have been formed by a conception of progress which did not adhere to reality but made dogmatic claims. Progress as pictured in the minds of Social Democrats was, first of all, the progress of mankind itself (and not just advances in men's ability and knowledge). Secondly, it was something boundless, in keeping with the infinite perfectibility of mankind. Thirdly, progress was regarded as irresistible, something that automatically pursued a straight or spiral course. Each of these predicates is controversial and open to criticism. However, when the chips are down, criticism must penetrate beyond these predicates and focus on something that they have in common. The concept of the historical progress of mankind cannot be sundered from the concept of its progression through a homogeneous, empty time. A critique of the concept of such a progression must be the basis of any criticism of the concept of progress itself.

XIV

> Origin is the goal.
>
> —Karl Kraus, *Worte in Versen*, Vol. I

History is the subject of a structure whose site is not homogeneous, empty time, but time filled by the presence of the now [*Jetztzeit*]. Thus, to Robespierre ancient Rome was a past charged with the time of the now which he blasted out of the continuum of history. The French Revolution viewed itself as Rome reincarnate. It evoked ancient Rome the way fashion evokes costumes of the past. Fashion has a flair for the topical, no matter where it stirs in the thickets of long ago; it is a tiger's leap into the past. This jump, however, takes place in an arena where the ruling class gives the commands. The same leap in the open air of history is the dialectical one, which is how Marx understood the revolution.

XV

The awareness that they are about to make the continuum of history explode is characteristic of the revolutionary classes at the moment of their action. The great revolution introduced a new calendar. The initial day of a calendar serves as a historical time-lapse camera. And, basically, it is the same day that keeps recurring in the guise of holidays, which are days of remembrance. Thus the calendars do not measure time as clocks do; they are monuments of a historical consciousness of which not the slightest trace has been apparent in Europe in the past hundred years. In the July revolution an incident occurred which showed this consciousness still alive. On the first evening of fighting it turned out that the clocks in towers were being fired on simultaneously and independently from several places in Paris. An eyewitness, who may have owed his insight to the rhyme, wrote as follows:

> Qui le croirait! on dit, qu'irrités contre l'heure
> De nouveaux Josués au pied de chaque tour,
> Tiraient sur les cadrans pour arrêter le jour.
>
> > [Who would have believed it! we are told that new Joshuas
> > at the foot of every tower, as though irritated with time itself,
> > fired at the dials in order to stop the day.]

XVI

A historical materialist cannot do without the notion of a present which is not a transition, but in which time stands still and has come to a stop. For this notion defines the present in which he himself is writing history. Historicism gives the "eternal" image of the past; historical materialism supplies a unique experience with the past. The historical materialist leaves it to others to be drained by the whore called "Once upon a time" in historicism's bordello. He remains in control of his powers, man enough to blast open the continuum of history.

XVII

Historicism rightly culminates in universal history. Materialistic historiography differs from it as to method more clearly than from any other kind. Universal history has no theoretical armature. Its method is additive; it musters a mass of data to fill the homogeneous, empty time. Materialistic historiography, on the other hand, is based on a constructive principle. Thinking involves not only the flow of thoughts, but their arrest as well. Where thinking suddenly stops in a configuration pregnant with tensions, it gives that configuration a shock, by which it crystallizes into a monad. A historical materialist approaches a historical subject only where he encounters it as a monad. In this structure he recognizes the sign of a Messianic cessation of happening, or, put differently, a revolutionary chance in the fight for the oppressed past. He takes cognizance of it in order to blast a specific era out of the homogeneous course of history—blasting a specific life out of the era or a specific work out of the lifework. As a result of this method the lifework is preserved in this work and at the same time canceled; in the lifework, the era; and in the era, the entire course of history. The nourishing fruit of the historically understood contains time as a precious but tasteless seed.

XVIII

"In relation to the history of organic life on earth," writes a modern biologist, "the paltry fifty millennia of *homo sapiens* constitute something like two seconds at the close of a twenty-four-hour day. On this scale, the history of civilized mankind would fill one-fifth of the last second of the last hour." The present, which, as a model of Messianic time, comprises the entire history of mankind in an enormous abridgment, coincides exactly with the stature which the history of mankind has in the universe.

A

Historicism contents itself with establishing a causal connection between various moments in history. But no fact that is a cause is for that very reason historical. It became historical post-humously, as it were, through events that may be separated from it by thousands of years. A historian who takes this as his point of departure stops telling the sequence of events like the beads of a rosary. Instead, he grasps the constellation which his own era has formed with a definite earlier one. Thus he establishes a conception of the present as the "time of the now" which is shot through with chips of Messianic time.

B

The soothsayers who found out from time what it had in store certainly did not experience time as either homogeneous or empty. Anyone who keeps this in mind will perhaps get an idea of how past times were experienced in remembrance—namely, in just the same way. We know that the Jews were prohibited from investigating the future. The Torah and the prayers instruct them in remembrance, however. This stripped the future of its magic, to which all those succumb who turn to the soothsayers for enlightenment. This does not imply, however, that for the Jews the future turned into homogeneous, empty time. For every second of time was the strait gate through which the Messiah might enter.

PART III

Medicine, science, and technology

The transformations occurring in science in the run-up to modernism are both illustrative and instructive of what was happening generally to Western notions of progress and melioration. The Newtonian Pierre Laplace (1749–1827) had conflated theology, philosophy, and mathematics when he posited a powerful intelligence capable of embracing "in the same formula the movements of the greatest bodies of the universe and those of the lightest atom; for it, nothing would be uncertain and the future, as the past, would be present to its eyes."[1] Laplace maintained that all events follow nature's immutable laws as necessarily as the sun's revolution,[2] so that the future can be depicted with certainty if the details of the present are fully known.

Yet nineteenth-century science increasingly told a different story from Laplace's. In 1857, two years before the publication of Darwin's *Origin of Species*, Philip Henry Gosse, an eminent marine biologist and Royal Society Fellow, was shaken to the depths of what he deemed his immortal soul by the evolution revolution: the work, for example, of Charles Lyell who, in his *Principles of Geology* (1830–33), maintained that the present is the key to the past and that, therefore, geological remains were best explained as products of processes that occurred slowly over many millennia and that were still occurring and observable. In reaction, Gosse, in *Omphalos: An Attempt to Untie the Geological Knot*, propounded an ingenious scheme for reconciling his fundamentalist beliefs with new geological findings that his scientific training would not let him deny.[3] Fossil evidence indubitably exists, Gosse acknowledged, but it was God who, following "the law of organic creation," fashioned plants and animals with the "retrospective marks [of their] specific identity." Just as "the absolute necessity of retrospective phenomena in newly-created organisms" required that the first tree have rings and the first man a navel as a relic of a birth that never occurred, so the world was "created with fossil skeletons in its crust" – skeletons of animals that never existed.[4] They were put there, according to the seventeenth-century Archbishop Ussher, at nine in the morning of 26 October 4004 BC, a moment determined by counting back through biblical genealogies.

Gosse was ridiculed both in his day and subsequently for treating the earth as God's great forgery. Yet Gosse, who anticipated and tried to disarm such attacks, was not alone in seeking a solution to a genuine problem: how to reconcile faith and scientific knowledge rather than abandon one or the other. A century after Laplace, and as Einstein was beginning his work in relativity theory, Laplace's scientific heir, Lord Kelvin (1824–1907), tried again, declaring that scientists like himself would soon be out of work because physics, a coherent system, a closed set brought into being by a "Creative Power [that] is the only feasible answer to the origin of life from a scientific perspective," was about to be wholly understood: "There is nothing new to be discovered in physics now. All that remains is more and more precise measurement."[5] (Kelvin also proclaimed, in 1895, that "Heavier-than-air flying machines are impossible.") Only two major areas of exploration seemed to remain: the Michelson–Morley experiment concerning the existence of the ether and blackbody radiation.[6] The results of these explorations, however, were astonishing and problematic rather than predictable and conclusive: the Michelson–Morley experiment led to Einstein's theory of special relativity, blackbody radiation to quantum mechanics and Heisenberg's uncertainty principle. In fact, according to Abraham Pais, Einstein's biographer, "In all the history of physics, there has never been a period of transition as abrupt, as unanticipated, and over as wide a front as the decade 1895–1905."[7] And, in the modernist period and beyond, scientific open-endedness was more and more the order of the day, for what followed were concepts like the general theory of relativity, the relativity of simultaneity, complementarity (some objects appear to have contradictory properties, depending on the measuring instruments), string theory, non-Euclidian geometry, Godel's proof, Bell's theories, chaos theory, fractal mathematics, complexity theory – all of which entered into and greatly impacted the literature.

Yet for all that Einsteinian relativity challenged Newtonian physics and helped to produce the culture of modernism, Einstein himself consistently adhered to Newton's belief that both knowledge and the universe were finite and increasingly within our understanding. Newtonian mechanics explained macrocosmic actions so well that the universe seemed manageable, comprehensible, divinely ordered. Einstein, in fact, considered relativity a natural development from, rather than a revolutionary break with, the physics he inherited. Einstein's quarrel was not with those who preceded him, or with God, but with successors like Bohr and Heisenberg, whose work led to quantum mechanics, which Einstein rejected because it relied on probabilistic uncertainty. Curiously, Einstein's antipathy toward quantum mechanics, which he first saw as logically inconsistent and then as an incomplete description of nature, was only strengthened by his inability to substantiate his opposition. In 1912 Einstein wrote that "The more success the quantum theory has, the sillier it looks"; and he never wavered from, or succeeded in, his quest for "a model of reality which shall represent events themselves and not merely the probability of their occurrence."[8] Einstein maintained faith in what he called objective reality "although, up to now, *success* is against it."[9] And he was especially upset because quantum mechanics rested on his own work, just as his rested on Newtonian mechanics, and so was as revolutionary *and* conservative as relativity.

Modern science was perhaps most revolutionary in its subversion of faith in an infinite, omnipotent deity, but also in a finite, knowable universe. It became increasingly a matter of scientific as well as literary knowledge – in the writings, for example, of Henry James, Ford Madox Ford, and Joseph Conrad – that what we "know" largely depends on where we stand; that some things are inherently unknowable; and that much of the rest, like light, accords with self-contradictory principles. In 1924 Einstein wrote unhappily that there are "now two theories of light, both indispensable, and – as one must admit today despite twenty years of tremendous effort on the part of theoretical physicists – without any logical connection."[10] Depending on the equipment used to measure it, light – like the subject of a Jamesian interpreting consciousness, Fordian impressionism, or Yeats's dancer and dance – proves to be a wave phenomenon or a stream of particles or, somehow, both. The ontological status of scientific knowledge consequently came under assault as experimental data seemed increasingly to represent not the "real" world, but the relationship of scientist, equipment, and cultural context. For Einstein, relativity meant that the world appeared different depending on where one stood, while Heisenbergian uncertainty and quantum mechanics meant that where one stood helped to determine reality itself, and that certitude and incertitude were not opposites but complementary. Of sub-atomic particles Heisenberg wrote, "The more precisely the position is determined, the less precisely the momentum is known in this instant, and vice versa."[11] The revolutionary idea represented here seems to be that to a significant extent we choose our truth, our reality, or at least what we can know of it.

The physicist Gerald Holton describes the transformation of the predominant scientific (and cultural) worldview that occurred during the latter part of the nineteenth century:

> a static, homocentric, hierarchically ordered, harmoniously arranged cosmos . . . a finite universe in time and space; a divine temple, God-given, God-expressing, God penetrated, knowable. . . . This representation was gradually supplanted by another. . . . The universe became unbounded, "restless," . . . a weakly coupled ensemble of infinitely many separate, individually sovereign parts and events. Though evolving, it is continually interrupted by random discontinuities on the cosmological scale as well as on the submicroscopic scale.[12]

What had seemed solidly anchored was suddenly cast adrift: nothing, it seemed to scientists such as Gosse, Kelvin, and Einstein, was possible without God, and God was increasingly impossible. In his place were random atoms and individuals, each the measure of its own reality, for, where classical Newtonian physics depended on universal laws that were independent of humans, relativity and quantum mechanics restored humans to the center of the universe. Hence, existentialism and anomie, empowerment and a sense of loss, independence and drift came to characterize modernist culture, literature, and thought.

Modernist fiction was moving along lines that paralleled those of science as so-called "omniscient narrators" or puppet masters (as Thackeray has it in *Vanity Fair*) yielded to limited, subjective narrators, who are doubly partial — having both limited knowledge and a personal perspective, in, for example, Conrad's *Heart of Darkness* and *Lord Jim*, Ford's *The Good Soldier*, Fitzgerald's *The Great Gatsby*, and Hemingway's *The Sun Also Rises*. Even more than the stories they tell, what Marlow, Dowell, Nick Carraway, and Jake Barnes know, and when and how they know it, becomes central to what their narratives — and their realities — are all about. Thus, the paradigmatic text of modernist writing, with its emphasis on perspectivism, partial understanding, and epistemological incertitude, is detective fiction — though the texts of that genre usually claim that the puzzling out process they depict leads to truth. (In contrast, the paradigmatic text of postmodernist writing, with its focus on alternative realities, ontological incertitude, and achronological history, is science fiction.) In his curious and remarkable autobiography, *The Education of Henry Adams*, Adams objectifies his subjectivity by alluding to himself in the third person throughout and enacts the rupture that he and Western culture experienced at the turn of the century. He dramatizes the tension between the quest for great scientific advancement and the creation of a Frankensteinian monster when, in "the great hall of dynamos" at the Paris Exposition of 1900, he prophetically envisaged the unleashing of an "infinite force" that he felt "as a moral force, much as the early Christians felt the Cross." But unlike the figure of the Virgin, which he took to be the great symbolic force of the Middle Ages, the dynamo represented chaos and historic discontinuity, so that "he found himself lying in the Gallery of Machines at the Great Exposition of 1900, his historical neck broken by the sudden irruption of forces totally new."[13] Like Filippo Marinetti in his "Futurist Manifesto" (1909), Adams envisaged mighty engines spinning out of control, technology developing in all sorts of unpredictable ways and directions, and society driven at an increasingly frenetic pace.

On a more mundane level, major scientific achievements, technological breakthroughs, and material advances had begun to transform lives and alter social reality. The standardization of time (which in the U.S. was primarily driven by the need of railroads for trustworthy and easily understandable schedules) and common scientific measures of, for example, weights, sizes, and electricity were crucial to modern production, communication, and transportation. Advances in household technology appeared in the culture and then in the literature. Eighteenth-century streets were treacherous for a number of reasons, including their being the place where chamber pots were often emptied, yet as late as 1865 John Ruskin describes the cities of his day as overcrowded places of darkness, disease, and despair:

> mere crowded masses of store, and warehouse, and counter, . . . cities in which the object of men is not life, but labor; . . . cities in which the streets are not the avenues for the passing and process of a happy people, but the drains for the discharge of a tormented mob, . . . in which existence becomes mere transition, and every creature is only one atom in a drift of human dust, and current of interchanging particles. . . .[14]

Sewers and indoor plumbing were being developed during the nineteenth century, with the flush toilet being patented in mid-century. The aptly named sanitary engineer Thomas Crapper heavily promoted sanitary plumbing and, in the 1880s, was hired by Prince Edward (later King Edward VII) to equip Sandringham House in Norfolk with thirty toilets. But they remained largely the privilege of the rich. James Joyce titled the collection of poems he published in 1907 *Chamber Music,* an apparent reference to the sound of urine tinkling in a chamber pot, which seems likely given the late addition to the collection of the poem "All Day I Hear the Noise of Waters"; and Leopold Bloom, in *Ulysses,* reflects, "Chamber music. Could make a kind of pun on that. It is a kind of music I often thought when she [his wife Molly (uses the chamber pot)]. Acoustics that is. Tinkling" (*U* 364). Set in 1904, the Dublin of *Ulysses* lacks indoor plumbing, so Bloom has to use an outhouse ("the jakes" [83–85]) and his wife, Molly, avails herself of a chamber pot in the middle of the night in the last chapter.

For a time, toilets, or at least latrines, became associated with World War I, or at least with one way of representing it. In *War Books,* Cyril Falls refers to *All Quiet on the Western Front* (1929), Erich Maria Remarque's great novel about the war, as "frank propaganda," attacking it (and German literature generally) for representing the intense sufferings of individual soldiers, rather than cheering for the larger cause, through its focus on representations of the body, including its natural functions. Falls maintains that "the latrine always had a fascination for the German soldier, and that during the War one used to find on postcards in prisoners' pockets pictures of this necessity of nature in use."[15] Influenced by the harshly negative and controversial review of *All Quiet* published by J.C. Squire in the *London Mercury* (January 1930), entitled "The Lavatory School of Literature," Falls attacks scatologically obsessed Germans as lovers of smut whose depictions of wartime experience he viewed as unpatriotic, hysterical, hyperbolical, and unreadable. An enormous popular success, *All Quiet* and its sequel, *The Road Back*, were among the books banned and burned in Nazi Germany.

Thereafter, Western literature tends to assume, usually without mentioning, the presence of indoor toilets, whereas Mulk Raj Anand's *Untouchable* (1935), about an Indian cleaner of communal latrines, ultimately suggests that liberation, the end of caste-based discrimination, may result from technology as the newly introduced flush system eliminates the need for untouchable toilet cleaners.

Representing the changes that were occurring in the culture, D.H. Lawrence's *The Rainbow*, published in 1916 though set in the mid-nineteenth century, depicts the death of Tom Brangwen in a flood caused by the overflowing of an industrial canal that he had allowed to run through his once edenic farmland; at the end of the novel his pregnant daughter Ursula encounters a herd of wild horses that – seemingly bent on revenge for the despoiling of the land – causes her to have a miscarriage. In *The Ambassadors* (1903), Henry James has Lambert Strether – who has been sent to Paris to bring back the wayward Chad Newsome to the stifling embrace of his New England family and to the family business that manufactures a "small domestic item" that is never named (and whose identity has sparked much critical debate) – instead cry out: "Live all you can; it's a mistake not to. . . . Live, live!" Here the late convert to romanticism rails against the encroaching capitalism of contemporary life.

Yet advances in manufacturing, transportation, communication, and medical science – with their consequences intended and otherwise – appeared at an ever-accelerating rate in both the culture, the domestic sphere, and in literary texts, and material advances were not always seen as being at odds with what Strether calls "freedom." In *The Years* (1937), a novel that follows a single family from 1880 to the "Present Day," Virginia Woolf traces her characters' experiences of and reactions to changing cultural and material circumstances: " 'A new world – a new world!' Sally had cried," responding to the appearance of cars, airplanes, the radio, indoor plumbing, hot water, and electric lights (*The Years* 329–30). Material advances, sometimes with malign as well as benign effects, became commonplace – and central plot devices – in modernist literature, as for example: cameras (Stoker, *Dracula*, 1897); typewriters (*Dracula*; Eliot, *The Waste Land*, 1922); phonographs (*Dracula*; Joyce, *Ulysses*, 1922); X-rays (Wells, *The Invisible Man*, 1897; Strindberg, *Ghost Sonata*, 1907; Mann, *The Magic Mountain*, 1924); telegraphy (*Dracula*; James, *In the Cage*, 1898; Ford, *The Good Soldier*, 1915; Hemingway, *The Sun Also Rises* 1926); automobiles (Shaw, *Man and Superman*, 1903; Grahame, *The Wind in the Willows*, 1908; *The Waste Land*; Dreiser, *An American Tragedy*, 1925; Fitzgerald, *The Great Gatsby*, 1925; Faulkner, *The Sound and the Fury*, 1929; Woolf, *The Years*, 1937); adding machines (Rice, *The Adding Machine*, 1923); telephones (*The Great Gatsby*); airplanes (Woolf, *Mrs. Dalloway*, 1925; Faulkner, *Pylon*, 1934); contraception (Waugh, *Black Mischief*, 1932; Faulkner, *The Wild Palms*, 1939); electricity (*The Years*); indoor plumbing (*The Years*); radio (*The Years*; Joyce, *Finnegans Wake*, 1939); TV (*Finnegans Wake*); sewing machines (Faulkner, *The Hamlet*, 1940). Science-gone-wrong literature had come to the fore in the nineteenth century with Mary Shelley's *Frankenstein* (1818), Robert Louis Stevenson's *Dr. Jekyll and Mr. Hyde* (1886), and H.G. Wells's *The Invisible Man*, but subsequent developments made the products of modern technology culturally far more pervasive – with consequences that were sometimes liberating (labor-saving devices, quicker and easier communication and travel), sometimes destructive (physically dangerous and soul-debilitating at times, as most memorably depicted, perhaps, in Charlie Chaplin's film, *Modern Times* [1936]), and sometimes both.

No moral reformation accompanied nineteenth- and twentieth-century technological advances. Producing both massive wealth and grinding poverty, the Industrial Revolution had a disproportionately class-based impact on urban mortality rates. By 1900 unchecked inventiveness, industrialization, and ruthless acquisitiveness had produced both healing and killing machines that gave those who were rich, white, and privileged greater control of life and death than ever before. Marx, who saw such contradictions as inherent in capitalism, would not have been surprised. According to Erich Fromm, "Capital for him was the manifestation of the past, of labor transformed and amassed into things; labor was the manifestation of *life*, of human energy applied to nature in the process of transforming it. . . . Who (what) was to rule over what (whom)? What is dead over what is alive, or what is alive over what is dead?" Paralleling Marx's thinking with Freud's death instinct, Fromm defines the "necrophilous" – or death-loving – person as someone for whom "only the past is experienced as quite real, not the present or the future. What has been, i.e., what is dead, rules his life: institutions, laws, property, traditions, and possessions. Briefly, *things* rule *man*; *having* rules *being*; *the dead* rule the *living*."[16] The consequence, as subsequent history has demonstrated, is a constant state of warfare, between and among both individuals and nations.

Medical practice also underwent a remarkable transformation in the modernist period. Superstition and deduction had held sway in medicine through the nineteenth-century, even though Hippocrates (460–377 BC), the "Father of Medicine," and Galen (129–203?), his great successor, had sought to base medical practice on observation, experimentation, the study of the human body, and reason. Despite the widespread acknowledgment of the basic medical premise "first, do no harm" and occasional breakthroughs like William Harvey's seventeenth-century discovery of the circulation of blood throughout the body, harm is what most doctors seem to have done until around the beginning of the twentieth century, which may help to explain why the profession was generally held in low esteem and its practitioners poorly remunerated. Beginning around the latter part of the nineteenth century, literary depictions of doctors hinted at significant changes to come in an evolving medical profession. In George Eliot's *Middlemarch* (1871–72), for example, the enlightened and altruistic Dr. Lydgate strives to determine the causes and cure of fever, but he receives little respect and less money for his work because, as he acknowledges, for some "the medical profession was an inevitable system of humbug" (251). He is apparently a skilled doctor who employs efficacious technique – "He not only used his stethoscope (which had not become a matter of course in practice at that time), but sat quietly by his patient and watched him" (414) – and achieves excellent results: "They say he cures every one" (375). Yet his attempts at reform create professional jealousy, antagonism from political reactionaries, and the animosity of his spoiled, extravagant wife. In Henrik Ibsen's *An Enemy of the People* (1882), the similarly advanced Dr. Stockmann discovers that the town baths, a great source of tourism and local pride, are contaminated by the town's tannery waste and causing serious illness. But his attempts to solve the problem are defeated by powerful political and financial leaders who persuade the people to turn against Stockmann, whom they denounce as a lunatic and an enemy of the people because the action he proposes would end their new prosperity.

George Bernard Shaw's Dr. Ridgeon in *The Doctor's Dilemma* (1906) has developed a new cure for tuberculosis, but he has only enough for one patient. His dilemma is that he must decide whether to treat a weak but honest colleague or a great artist who is a charming socio-path. Ridgeon determines to treat the former for totally defensible reasons: his colleague humbly serves the poor while the artist, who does personal harm, would have his reputation enhanced by his romantic death. But Ridgeon, whose moral position is compromised by his own desire to wed the artist's wife, seems more the model of modern-era doctors than the high-minded but ultimately ineffectual Lydgate and Stockmann. Shaw's extensive Preface (excerpted below), which discusses at length the inherent conflict of interest in a medical system in which doctors are rewarded in proportion to the extent of the treatment they prescribe for their patients (rather than their success in helping them), implicitly and presciently advo-cates a national health system in which doctors receive a salary rather than payments for services rendered. Virginia Woolf also depicts medical practitioners who exercise life and death authority, but more for the sake of power than money. In *Mrs. Dalloway* Sir William Bradshaw, Clarissa thinks, arrogantly and cruelly brings death into "the middle of my party" (279), and Woolf's personal doctor, the life-denying and aptly named Sir George Savage, kept her from all the things she loved: "my own home, and books, and pictures, and music, from all of which I have been parted since February now, – and I have never spent such a wretched 8 months in my life. And yet that tyrannical, and as I think, shortsighted Savage insists upon another two."[17]

Medical advances proceeded rapidly during the time when these works were written: lectures in medical schools began to give way to clinical experience; the germ theory of illness led to increased washing of hands (the one new medical practice that apparently did more to save lives than any other); and extraordinary scientific and technological advances like X-rays meant that, by the second decade of the twentieth century, and for the first time in history, doctors were more likely to help than harm their patients, and so being a medical practitioner was increasingly likely to be financially rewarding. As a consequence, and perhaps predictably, medical practice migrated from the female domestic sphere to male-dominated clinics and hospitals, with doctors increasingly arrogating to themselves a paternalistic authority symbolized by their coming to wear professionally imposing white lab coats. James Joyce adumbrates the transition in *Ulysses* (published in 1922 but set in 1904) when he has Stephen Dedalus, his would-be bard, silently mock the poor old milk woman, decrepit personification of Ireland who doesn't understand Irish, for serving the Englishman Haines and "her gay betrayer," the medical student Buck Mulligan: "She bows her old head to a voice that speaks to her loudly, her bonesetter, her medicineman: me she slights" (*U* 1.404–19). Later on Stephen sees a woman he takes for a midwife and thinks, "One of her sisterhood lugged me squealing into life" (in 1882 [3.35]); but in the present, when Leopold Bloom visits a woman in labor, the birth occurs in a maternity hospital presided over by the potently named doctor, "Of that house A. Horne is lord" (14.74), and, appalled by the boisterous medical students, he wonders how "the mere acquisition of academic titles should suffice to transform in a pinch of time these votaries of levity into exemplary practitioners of an art which most anywise eminent have esteemed the noblest" (14.899–902). Yet Woolf depicts a female doctor in *The Years* (1937), the last novel she published in her lifetime, thinking of herself in pre-modern terms as "merely a doctor," a drudge, socially awkward – "nothing that she did mattered" – even while being up to date in her ability "to make money" and grudgingly acknowledging that "People live longer than they used" and "They don't die so painfully" because doctors "have learned a few little tricks" (354–60).

Medical progress has followed a simple, linear, and upward path no more than other areas of science and technology, for instead of occupying opposite ends of a moral spectrum, healing and killing are often complementary: each requires and sustains the other. Modern politicians realized the need to harness healing in the service of killing in order to guarantee sufficient numbers of soldiers. Twenty-five years before World War I, the *Herald* of January 25, 1890 editorialized on the irony of this situation:

> The epidemic of influenza has the one advantage that it is a preserver of the public peace. War is out of the question when armies are suffering from the prostrating effects of the grippe. We can fancy an army, say, of 200,000 men receiving orders to march to attack. The attacking army would have to leave at least 150,000 men in the hospital, and the sneezing of the remaining 50,000 would warn the enemy of their approach. We may be quite sure that no European war will break out until the influenza has vanished, especially as the disease has shown a marked fondness for soldiers.

Yet break out of course the European war eventually did, with the virulent flu pandemic of 1918–19 immediately following its end, as if it had held off until World War I had completed *its* horrific work. At least that's how Katherine Anne Porter represents the impact of the war and the epidemic on her pair of young lovers in her remarkable novella, "Pale Horse, Pale Rider" (1939), for she has the innocent soldier Adam, whom she calls a "sacrificial lamb," survive the war; but his nursing of Miranda through her influenza nightmare ends with her awakening to both Armistice Day and Adam's death, and to what seems a posthumous world in which there would now, despite her utter indifference, "be time for everything."

Given the growing respect and status accorded doctors and their profession in the decades following the 1890 editorial, it was ironic as well as tragic that what may have been history's worst plague in terms of the most people dead in the shortest time was the catastrophic pandemic that began, apparently at a U.S. military base, just as the war was ending. In one-third the time, the flu killed an estimated three times as many people as the nine to ten million claimed by

World War I. Although influenza still lacks a cure, war-related health research produced many of the century's great medical advances: the first hospital in England devoted to plastic surgery was established in 1917 to repair, or recreate, faces disfigured by fire or shrapnel; "wonder drugs" were fortuitous by-products of political and military necessity. Writing in the 1950s about an analogous phenomenon, the philosopher Bertrand Russell dryly commented that atomic energy, which "has already proved itself very useful in medicine . . . may in time cure nearly as many people as it will kill."[18] Modern medicine's semi-triumphal march throughout the second half of the twentieth century and into the twenty-first was often accompanied by its dissociation from ethics. Doctors helped to further Hitler's racial and eugenics policies; experimented on marginalized or imprisoned populations in places like Tuskegee, Alabama as well as concentration camps; conducted the Milgram experiments at Yale; and often facilitated and professionalized torture and executions. Ironically, the very symbol of medical professionalism, the lab coats that many doctors still wear, is increasingly seen as a major source of the infections that still kill perhaps 100,000 hospital patients in the United States annually.

Notes

1   Both Gleick (*Chaos* 14) and Stewart (*Does God Play Dice?* 12) quote this statement.
2   Laplace 3.
3   Lyell, who was also a devout Christian, had difficulty reconciling his faith with the principle of natural selection.
4   Gosse, *Omphalos* 347–49.
5   Kelvin, address to the British Association for the Advancement of Science, 1900.
6   Michelson, however, agreed with Kelvin; see *Light Waves* 23–24.
7   Pais 26.
8   Einstein, *Theoretical Physics*, quoted in Pais, 460.
9   Quoted in Pais 319, 389, 461.
10   Quoted in Pais 414.
11   Heisenberg, uncertainty paper, 1927. (See also Chapter 23 of this volume.)
12   Holton 9.
13   Adams 380–82.
14   Ruskin, "The Study of Architecture in Our Schools" 137.
15   Falls, *War Books* 294.
16   Fromm 377.
17   Woolf, letter to Violet Dickinson, 30 Oct. 1904 (*Letters*, vol. 1, 147).
18   Russell, *Human Society* 208.

Suggested further readings

Adams, Henry. *The Education of Henry Adams: An Autobiography* (1907). New York: Modern Library, 1996.
Anand, Mulk Raj. *Untouchable* (1935). "Introduction" by E.M. Forster. London: Penguin, 1940.
Armstrong, Tim. *Modernism, Technology, and the Body: A Cultural Study*. Cambridge, U.K. and New York: Cambridge UP, 1998.
Belkin, Lisa. *First, Do No Harm*. New York: Simon, 1993.
Black, Douglas, *et al. Medicine Betrayed: The Participation of Doctors in Human Rights Abuses*. London: Zed, 1992.
Chaplin, Charlie. *Modern Times* (1936). Film.
Clark, Ronald W. *Einstein: The Life and Times*. New York: World, 1971.
Conrad, Joseph. *The Secret Agent* (1907). London: Penguin, 2007.
Darwin, Charles. *The Descent of Man* (1871). London: Penguin, 2007.
Dreiser, Theodore. *An American Tragedy* (1925). New York: Signet, 2010.
Einstein, Albert. The Annus Mirabilis Papers (1905).

——. *Relativity: The Special and General Theory*. Trans. Robert W. Lawson. New York: Henry Holt, 1920.

Eliot, George. *Middlemarch* (1871-2). Boston: Houghton, 1956.

Eliot, T.S. *The Waste Land* (1922). *The Complete Poems and Plays 1909–1950*. New York: Harcourt, 1962.

Falls, Cyril. *War Books*. London: Peter Davies, 1930.

Faulkner, William. *The Wild Palms* (1939). New York: Vintage, 1995.

——. *The Hamlet* (1938). New York: Vintage, 1994.

——. *Pylon* (1934). New York: Vintage, 1987.

——. *The Sound and the Fury* (1929). New York: Modern, 1956.

Fitzgerald, F. Scott *The Great Gatsby* (1925). New York: Scribner, 2004.

Ford, Ford Madox. *The Good Soldier* (1916) New York: Vintage, 1955.

Fromm, Erich. *The Anatomy of Human Destructiveness* (1973). Greenwich, CT: Fawcett, 1975.

Gleick, James. *Chaos: Making a New Science*. New York: Viking, 1987.

Gosse, Philip Henry. *Omphalos: An Attempt to Untie the Geological Knot*. London: Van Voorst, 1857.

Grahame, Kenneth. *The Wind in the Willows* (1908). New York: Signet, 1969.

Haley, Bruce. *The Healthy Body and Victorian Culture*. Cambridge, MA: Harvard UP, 1978.

Heisenberg, Werner. "Non-Objective Science and Uncertainty" (1955). *The Physicist's Conception of Nature*. Trans. Arnold J. Pomerans. New York: Greenwood, 1970.

Henderson, Linda Dalrymple. *The Fourth Dimension and Non-Euclidean Geometry in Modern Art*. Princeton: Princeton UP, 1983; Cambridge, MA: MIT Press, 2005.

Holton, Gerald. *Thematic Origins of Scientific Thought: Kepler to Einstein* (1973). Rev. edn, Cambridge, MA: Harvard UP, 1988.

James, Henry. "In the Cage" (1898). *Selected Tales*. New York: Penguin, 2001.

Joyce, James. *Finnegans Wake* (1939). New York: Viking, 1962.

Kafka, Franz. "In the Penal Colony" (1914). *The Complete Stories*. New York: Schocken, 1971.

Kenner, Hugh. *The Mechanic Muse*. New York: Oxford UP, 1987.

Laplace, Pierre Simon de. *A Philosophical Essay on Probabilities* (1796). Trans. Frederick Wilson Truscott and Frederick Lincoln Emory. New York: Dover, 1951.

Lawrence, D.H. "Odour of Chrysanthemums" (1911). London: Penguin, 2011.

Lifton, Robert Jay. *The Nazi Doctors: Medical Killing and the Psychology of Genocide*. New York: Basic, 1986.

Lyell, Charles. *Principles of Geology* (1830–33). London: Penguin, 1997.

Mann, Thomas. *The Magic Mountain*, 1924. Trans. John E. Woods. New York: Knopf, 1995.

Michelson, Albert A. *Light Waves and Their Uses*. Chicago: U of Chicago P, 1903.

Mitford, Jessica. *The American Way of Death*. New York: Simon, 1963.

Nicolson, Juliet. *The Great Silence: Britain from the Shadow of the First World War to the Dawn of the Jazz Age*. New York: Grove, 2010.

Pais, Abraham. *"Subtle is the Lord . . .": The Science and the Life of Albert Einstein* (1982). Oxford: Oxford UP, 1983.

Plock, Vike Martina. *Joyce, Medicine, and Modernity*. UP of Florida, 2010.

Porter, Katherine Anne. "Pale Horse, Pale Rider" (1939). *Pale Horse, Pale Rider: Three Short Novels*. New York, San Diego, and London: Harcourt, Brace, 1964.

Rice, Elmer. *The Adding Machine* (1923). New York: Samuel French, 1956.

Ruskin, John. "An Inquiry into the Conditions at Present Affecting the Study of Architecture in Our Schools". *Lectures on Architecture and Painting, Delivered at Edinburgh in November, 1853*. New York: John W. Lovell, [1885].

Russell, Bertrand. *ABC of Relativity* (1925). London: Routledge, 2001.

——. *Human Society in Ethics and Politics* (1954). London: Allen, 1972.

Shaw, George Bernard. *Man and Superman* (1903). London: Penguin, 2001.

——. *The Doctor's Dilemma* (1906). London: Penguin, 1957.

Shelley, Mary. *Frankenstein* (1818). New York: Modern, 1999.

Stevenson, Robert Louis. *Dr. Jekyll and Mr. Hyde* (1886).

Stewart, Ian. *Does God Play Dice? The Making of a New Science*. Oxford: Blackwell, 1989.

Stoker, Bram. *Dracula* (1897). New York: Barnes and Noble, 2004.

Strindberg, August. *Ghost Sonata* (1907). U of Chicago P, 2000.

Vargish, Thomas, and Delo E. Mook. *Inside Modernism: Relativity Theory, Cubism, Narrative*. New Haven and London: Yale UP, 1999.

Waugh, Evelyn. *Black Mischief* (1932). New York: Black Bay, 2002.

Wells, H.G. *The Invisible Man* (1897). New York: Signet, 2005.

Whitworth, Michael. *Einstein's Wake: Relativity, Metaphor, and Modernist Literature*. Oxford and New York: Oxford UP, 2001.

Williams, William Carlos. "The Use of Force" (1938). *The William Carlos Williams Reader*. New York: New Directions, 1966.

Woolf, Virginia. "Gas" (1929). *The Captain's Deathbed*. New York: Harcourt, Brace, 1978. 219–22.

——. *The Letters of Virginia Woolf*. 6 vols. Ed. Nigel Nicolson and Joanne Trautmann. New York: Harcourt, 1975–80.

——. *The Years* (1937). New York: Harcourt, Brace, 1965.

——. *Mrs. Dalloway* (1925). New York: Harcourt, Brace, 1953.

Chapter 19

Charles Darwin (1809–82)

"STRUGGLE FOR EXISTENCE," *THE ORIGIN OF SPECIES BY MEANS OF NATURAL SELECTION* (1859)

CHARLES DARWIN, the first evolutionary biologist, was the originator of the concept of natural selection. This excerpt from Chapter 3, "Struggle for Existence," of Darwin's classic work, *The Origin of Species by Means of Natural Selection*, is from the sixth edition (1872), the last published during Darwin's lifetime. Darwin significantly and substantially revised all the editions published in his lifetime, including, for example, using the phrase "survival of the fittest" for the first time in the fifth edition and dropping "On" from the title of the sixth. "Nature, red in tooth and claw," a phrase often associated with Darwin's concept of "natural selection" or the "survival of the fittest," actually appears in Canto 56 of *In Memoriam A.H.H.* (1849), a poem by Alfred, Lord Tennyson.

Charles Darwin, "Struggle for Existence," *The Origin of Species by Means of Natural Selection*, 6th edn, 1872. *Darwin: A Norton Critical Edition*, edn. Philip Appleman. New York: Norton, 1970. 114–19.

Variability is governed by many complex laws,—by correlated growth, compensation, the increased use and disuse of parts, and the definite action of the surrounding conditions. There is much difficulty in ascertaining how largely our domestic productions have been modified; but we may safely infer that the amount has been large, and that modifications can be inherited for long periods. As long as the conditions of life remain the same, we have reason to believe that a modification, which has already been inherited for many generations, may continue to be inherited for an almost infinite number of generations. On the other hand, we have evidence that variability when it has once come into play, does not cease under domestication for a very long period; nor do we know that it ever ceases, for new varieties are still occasionally produced by our oldest domesticated productions.

Variability is not actually caused by man; he only unintentionally exposes organic beings to new conditions of life, and then nature acts on the organisation and causes it to vary. But man can and does select the variations given to him by nature, and thus accumulates them in any desired manner. He thus adapts animals and plants for his own benefit or pleasure. He may do this methodically, or he may do it unconsciously by preserving the individuals most useful or pleasing to him without any intention of altering the breed. It is certain that he can largely influence the character of a breed by selecting, in each successive generation, individual differences so slight as to be inappreciable except by an educated eye. This unconscious process of selection has been the great agency in the formation of the most distinct and useful domestic breeds. That many breeds produced by man have to a large extent the character of natural species, is shown by the inextricable doubts whether many of them are varieties or aboriginally distinct species.

There is no reason why the principles which have acted so efficiently under domestication should not have acted under nature. In the survival of favoured individuals and races, during the constantly-recurrent Struggle for Existence, we see a powerful and ever-acting form of Selection. The struggle for existence inevitably follows from the high geometrical ratio of increase which is common to all organic beings. This high rate of increase is proved by calculation,—by the rapid increase of many animals and plants during a succession of peculiar seasons, and when naturalised in new countries. More individuals are born than can possibly survive. A grain in the balance may determine which individuals shall live and which shall die,—which variety or species shall increase in number, and which shall decrease, or finally become extinct. As the individuals of the same species come in all respects into the closest competition with each other, the struggle will generally be most severe between them; it will be almost equally severe between the varieties of the same species, and next in severity between the species of the same genus. On the other hand the struggle will often be severe between beings remote in the scale of nature. The slightest advantage in certain individuals, at any age or during any season, over those with which they come into competition, or better adaptation in however slight a degree to the surrounding physical conditions, will, in the long run, turn the balance.

With animals having separated sexes, there will be in most cases a struggle between the males for the possession of the females. The most vigorous males, or those which have most successfully struggled with their conditions of life, will generally leave most progeny. But success will often depend on the males having special weapons, or means of defense, or charms; and a slight advantage will lead to victory.

As geology plainly proclaims that each land has undergone great physical changes, we might have expected to find that organic beings have varied under nature, in the same way as they have varied under domestication. And if there has been any variability under nature, it would be an unaccountable fact if natural selection had not come into play. It has often been asserted, but the assertion is incapable of proof, that the amount of variation under nature is a strictly limited quantity. Man, though acting on external characters alone and often capriciously, can produce within a short period a great result by adding up mere individual differences in his domestic productions; and every one admits that species present individual differences. But, besides such differences, all naturalists admit that natural varieties exist, which are considered sufficiently distinct to be worthy of record in systematic works. No one has drawn any clear distinction between individual differences and slight varieties; or between more plainly marked varieties and sub-species, and species. On separate continents, and on different parts of the same continent when divided by barriers of any kind, and on outlying islands, what a multitude of forms exist, which some experienced naturalists rank as varieties, others as geographical races or sub-species, and others as distinct, though closely allied species!

If then, animals and plants do vary, let it be ever so slightly or slowly, why should not variations or individual differences, which are in any way beneficial, be preserved and accumulated through natural selection, or the survival of the fittest? If man can by patience select variations useful to him, why, under changing and complex conditions of life, should not variations useful to nature's living products often arise, and be preserved or selected? What limit can be put to this power, acting during long ages and rigidly scrutinising the whole constitution, structure, and habits of each creature,—favouring the good and rejecting the bad? I can see no limit to this power, in slowly and beautifully adapting each form to the most complex relations of life. The theory of natural selection, even if we look no farther than this, seems to be in the highest degree probable. I have already recapitulated, as fairly as I could, the opposed difficulties and objections: now let us turn to the special facts and arguments in favour of the theory.

On the view that species are only strongly marked and permanent varieties, and that each species first existed as a variety, we can see why it is that no line of demarcation can be drawn between species, commonly supposed to have been produced by special acts of creation, and varities which are acknowledged to have been produced by secondary laws. On this same view we can understand how it is that in a region where many species of a genus have been produced, and where they now flourish, these same species should present many varieties; for where the manufactory of species has been active, we might expect, as a general rule, to find it still in action; and this is the case if varieties be incipient species. Moreover, the species of the larger genera, which afford the greater number of varieties or incipient species, retain to a certain degree the character of varieties; for they differ from each other by a less amount of difference than do the species of smaller genera. The closely allied species also of the larger genera apparently have restricted ranges, and in their affinities they are clustered in little groups round other species—in both respects resembling varieties. These are strange relations on the view that each species was independently created, but are intelligible if each existed first as a variety.

As each species tends by its geometrical rate of reproduction to increase inordinately in number; and as the modified descendants of each species will be enabled to increase by as much as they become more diversified in habits and structure, so as to be able to seize on many and widely different places in the economy of nature, there will be a constant tendency in natural selection to preserve the most divergent offspring of any one species. Hence, during a long-continued course of modification, the slight differences characteristic of varieties of the same species, tend to be augmented into the greater differences characteristic of the species of the same genus. New and improved varieties will inevitably supplant and exterminate the older, less improved, and intermediate varieties; and thus species are rendered to a large extent defined and distinct objects. Dominant species belonging to the larger groups within each class tend to give birth to new and dominant forms; so that each large group tends to become still larger, and at the same time more divergent in character. But as all groups cannot thus go on increasing in size, for the world would not hold them, the more dominant groups beat the less dominant. This tendency in the large groups to go on increasing in size and diverging in character, together with the inevitable contingency of much extinction, explains the arrangement of all the forms of life in groups subordinate to groups, all within a few great classes, which has prevailed throughout all time. This grand fact of the grouping of all organic beings under what is called the Natural System, is utterly inexplicable on the theory of creation.

As natural selection acts solely by accumulating slight, successive, favourable variations, it can produce no great or sudden modifications; it can act only by short and slow steps. Hence, the canon of "Natura non facit saltum," which every fresh addition to our knowledge tends to confirm, is on this theory intelligible. We can see why throughout nature the same general end is gained by an almost infinite diversity of means, for every peculiarity when once acquired is long inherited, and structures already modified in many different ways have to be adapted for the same general purpose. We can, in short, see why nature is prodigal in variety, though niggard in innovation. But why this should be a law of nature if each species has been independently created no man can explain.

Many other facts are, as it seems to me, explicable on this theory. How strange it is that a bird, under the form of a woodpecker, should prey on insects on the ground; that upland geese which rarely or never swim, should possess webbed feet; that a thrush-like bird should dive and feed on sub-aquatic insects; and that a petrel should have the habits and structure fitting it for the life of an auk! and so in endless other cases. But on the view of each species constantly trying to increase in number, with natural selection always ready to adapt the slowly varying descendants of each to any unoccupied or ill-occupied place in nature, these facts cease to be strange, or might even have been anticipated.

We can to a certain extent understand how it is that there is so much beauty throughout nature; for this may be largely attributed to the agency of selection. That beauty, according to our sense of it, is not universal, must be admitted by every one who will look at some venomous snakes, at some fishes, and at certain hideous bats with a distorted resemblance to the human face. Sexual selection has given the most brilliant colours, elegant patterns, and other ornaments to the males, and sometimes to both sexes of many birds, butterflies, and other animals. With birds it has often rendered the voice of the male musical to the female, as well as to our ears. Flowers and fruit have been rendered conspicuous by brilliant colours in contrast with the green foliage, in order that the flowers may be readily seen, visited and fertilised by insects, and the seeds disseminated by birds. How it comes that certain colours, sounds, and forms should give pleasure to man and the lower animals,—that is, how the sense of beauty in its simplest form was first acquired,—we do not know any more than how certain odours and flavours were first rendered agreeable.

As natural selection acts by competition, it adapts and improves the inhabitants of each country only in relation to their co-inhabitants; so that we need feel no surprise at the species of any one country, although on the ordinary view supposed to have been created and specially adapted for that country, being beaten and supplanted by the naturalised productions from another land. Nor ought we to marvel if all the contrivances in nature be not, as far as we can judge, absolutely perfect, as in the case even of the human eye; or if some of them be abhorrent to our ideas of fitness. We need not marvel at the sting of the bee, when used against an enemy, causing the bee's own death; at drones being produced in such great numbers for one single act, and being then slaughtered by their sterile sisters; at the astonishing waste of pollen by our fir-trees; at the instinctive hatred of the queenbee for her own fertile daughters; at the ichneumonidæ feeding within the living bodies of caterpillars; or at other such cases. The wonder indeed is, on the theory of natural selection, that more cases of the want of absolute perfection have not been detected.

The complex and little known laws governing the production of varieties are the same, as far as we can judge, with the laws which have governed the production of distinct species. In both cases physical conditions seem to have produced some direct and definite effect, but how much we cannot say. Thus, when varieties enter any new station, they occasionally assume some of the characters proper to the species of that station. With both varieties and species, use and disuse seem to have produced a considerable effect; for it is impossible to resist this conclusion when we look, for instance, at the logger-headed duck, which has wings incapable of flight, in nearly the same condition as in the domestic duck; or when we look at the burrowing tucu-tucu, which is occasionally blind, and then at certain moles, which are habitually blind and have their eyes covered with skin; or when we look at the blind animals inhabiting the dark caves of America and Europe. With varieties and species, correlated variation seems to have played an important part, so that when one part has been modified other parts have been necessarily modified. With both varieties and species, reversions to long-lost characters occasionally occur. How inexplicable on the theory of creation is the occasional appearance of stripes on the shoulders and legs of the several species of the horse-genus and of their hybrids! How simply is this fact explained if we believe that these species are all descended from a striped progenitor, in the same manner as the several domestic breeds of the pigeon are descended from the blue and barred rock-pigeon!

On the ordinary view of each species having been independently created, why should specific characters, or those by which the species of the same genus differ from each other, be more variable than generic characters in which they all agree? Why, for instance, should the colour of a flower be more likely to vary in any one species of a genus, if the other species possess differently coloured flowers, than if all possessed the same coloured flowers? If species are only well-marked varieties, of which the characters have become in a high degree permanent, we can understand this fact; for they have already varied since they branched off from a common progenitor in certain characters, by which they have come to be specifically distinct from each other; therefore these same characters would be more likely again to vary than the generic characters which have been inherited without change for an immense period. It is inexplicable on the theory of creation why a part developed in a very unusual manner in one species alone of a genus, and therefore, as we may naturally infer, of great importance to that species, should be eminently liable to variation; but, on our view, this part has undergone, since the several species branched off from a common progenitor, an unusual amount of variability and modification, and therefore we might expect the part generally to be still variable. But a part may be developed in the most unusual manner, like the wing of a bat, and yet not be more variable than any other structure, if the part be common to many subordinate forms, that is, if it has been inherited for a very long period; for in this case, it will have been rendered constant by long-continued natural selection.

Chapter 20

John Tyndall (1820–93)

ESSAYS ON THE USE AND LIMIT OF THE IMAGINATION IN SCIENCE (1871)

A N EMINENT PHYSICIST WHO MADE several discoveries about atmospheric processes, Tyndall produced 17 books aimed at helping a general audience to understand experimental physics. In *Essays on the Use and Limit of the Imagination in Science*, he maintains that, "Bounded and conditioned by cooperant Reason, imagination becomes the mightiest instrument of the physical discoverer." Yet Tyndall's discussion of the concept of the ether ("an assemblage of vibrations" through which light was supposed to move), a belief widely held since it was first promulgated by Aristotle, unwittingly demonstrates both the power of the imagination and its limits since, contrary to expectations, the Michelson–Morley experiment of 1887 not only failed to verify the ether's existence, it ultimately led to Einstein's discovery of special relativity, which was dependent on the notion of "the constancy of the speed of light" and the non-existence of the ether. Nonetheless, the concept retained metaphorical force throughout the modernist period: Virginia Woolf in *The Waves*, for one, considered the fluid theories of Tyndall and other scientists to be useful explanations of such physical realities as sound and light waves; and numerous modern novels – for example, Kate Chopin's *The Awakening* (1899), Edith Wharton's *Ethan Frome* (1911), and D.H. Lawrence's *Women in Love* (1920) – employ the notion of the ether to represent forbidden passion, the lack of saving spirituality, and the attenuation of a solid, stable reality.

John Tyndall, *Essays on the Use and Limit of the Imagination in Science*, 2nd edn. London: Longmans, Green, 1871. 16–28, 42–44.

I should like to illustrate by a few simple instances the use that scientific men have already made of this power of imagination, and to indicate afterwards some of the further uses that they are likely to make of it. Let us begin with the rudimentary experiences. Observe the falling of heavy rain-drops into a tranquil pond. Each drop as it strikes the water becomes a centre of disturbance, from which a series of ring-ripples expand outwards. Gravity and inertia are the agents by which this wave-motion is produced, and a rough experiment will suffice to show that the rate of propagation does not amount to a foot a second. A series of slight mechanical shocks is experienced by a body plunged in the water as the wavelets reach it in succession. But a finer motion is at the same time set up and propagated. If the head and ears be immersed in the water, as in an experiment of Franklin's, the shock of the drop is communicated to the auditory nerve—the *tick* of the drop is heard. Now this sonorous impulse is propagated, not at the rate of a foot a second, but at the rate of 4,700 feet a second. In this case it is not the gravity, but the *elasticity* of the water that is the urging force. Every liquid particle pushed against its neighbour delivers up its motion with extreme rapidity, and the pulse is propagated as a thrill. The incompressibility of water, as illustrated by the famous Florentine experiment, is a measure of its elasticity, and to the possession of this property in so high a degree the rapid transmission of a sound-pulse through water is to be ascribed.

But water, as you know, is not necessary to the conduction of sound; air is its most common vehicle. And you know that when the air possesses the particular density and elasticity corresponding to the temperature of freezing water the velocity of sound in it is 1,090 feet a second. It is almost exactly one-fourth of the velocity in water; the reason being that though the greater weight of the water tends to diminish the velocity, the enormous molecular elasticity of the liquid far more than atones for the disadvantage due to weight. By various contrivances we can compel the vibrations of the air to declare themselves; we know the length and frequency of sonorous waves, and we have also obtained great mastery over the various methods by which the air is thrown into vibration. We know the phenomena and laws of vibrating rods, of organ-pipes, strings, membranes, plates, and bells. We can abolish one sound by another. We know the physical meaning of music and noise, of harmony and discord. In short, as regards sound we have a very clear notion of the external physical processes which correspond to our sensations.

In these phenomena of sound we travel a very little way from downright sensible experience. Still the imagination is to some extent exercised. The bodily eye, for example, cannot see the condensations and rarefactions of the waves of sound. We construct them in thought, and we believe as firmly in their existence as in that of the air itself. But now our experience has to be carried into a new region, where a new use is to be made of it. Having mastered the cause and mechanism of sound, we desire to know the cause and mechanism of light. We wish to extend our enquiries from the auditory nerve to the optic nerve. Now there is in the human intellect a power of expansion—I might almost call it a power of creation—which is brought into play by the simple brooding upon facts. The legend of the Spirit brooding over chaos may have originated in a knowledge of this power. In the case now before us it has manifested itself by transplanting into space, for the purposes of light, an adequately modified form of the mechanism of sound. We know intimately whereon the velocity of sound depends. When we lessen the density of a medium and preserve its elasticity constant we augment the velocity. When we heighten the elasticity and keep the density constant we also augment the velocity. A small density, therefore, and a great elasticity, are the two things necessary to rapid propagation. Now light is known to move with the astounding velocity of 185,000 miles a second. How is such a velocity to be obtained? By boldly diffusing in space a medium of the requisite tenuity and elasticity. Let us make such a medium our starting point, endowing it with one or two other necessary qualities; let us handle it in accordance with strict mechanical laws; give to every step of our deduction the surety of the syllogism; carry it thus, forth from the world of imagination to the world of sense, and see whether the final outcrop of the deduction be not the very phenomena of light which ordinary knowledge and skilled experiment reveal. If in all the multiplied varieties of these phenomena, including those of the most remote and entangled description, this fundamental conception always brings us face to face with the truth; if no contradiction to our deductions from it be found in external nature, but on all sides agreement and verification; if, moreover, as in the case of Conical Refraction and in other cases, it has actually forced upon our attention phenomena which no eye had previously seen, and which no mind had previously imagined, such a conception, which never disappoints us, but always lands us on the solid shores of fact, must, we think, be something more than a mere figment of the scientific fancy. In forming it that composite and creative unity in which reason and imagination are together blent, has, we believe, led us into a world not less real than that of the senses, and of which the world of sense itself is the suggestion and justification.

Far be it from me, however, to wish to fix you immovably in this or in any other theoretic conception. With all our belief of it, it will be well to keep the theory plastic and capable of change. You may, moreover, urge that although the phenomena occur *as if* the medium existed, the absolute demonstration of its existence is still wanting. Far be it from me to deny to this reasoning such validity as it may fairly claim. Let us endeavour by means of analogy to form a fair estimate of its force. You believe that in society you are surrounded by reasonable beings like yourself. You are perhaps as firmly convinced of this as of anything. What is your warrant for this conviction? Simply and solely this, your fellow-creatures behave as if they were reasonable; the hypothesis, for it is nothing more, accounts for the facts. To take an eminent example: you believe that our President is a reasonable being. Why? There is no known method of superposition by which any one of us can apply himself intellectually to another so as to demonstrate coincidence as regards the possession of reason. If, therefore, you hold our President to be reasonable, it is because he behaves *as if* he were reasonable. As in the case of the ether, beyond the '*as if*' you cannot go. Nay I should not wonder if a close comparison of the data on which both inferences rest, caused many respectable persons to conclude that the ether had the best of it.

This universal medium, this light-ether as it is called, is a vehicle, not an origin of wave-motion. It receives and transmits, but it does not create. Whence does it derive the motions it conveys? For the most part from luminous bodies. By this motion of a luminous body I do not mean its sensible motion, such as the flicker of a candle, or the shooting out of red prominences from the limb of the sun. I mean an intestine motion of the atoms or molecules of the luminous body. But here a certain reserve is necessary. Many chemists of the present day refuse to speak of atoms and molecules as real things. Their caution leads them to stop short of the clear, sharp, mechanically intelligible atomic theory enunciated by Dalton, or any form of that theory, and to make the doctrine of multiple proportions their intellectual bourne. I respect the caution, though I think it is here misplaced. The chemists who recoil form these notions of atoms and molecules accept without hesitation the Undulatory Theory of Light. Like you and me they one and all believe in an ether and its light producing waves. Let us consider what this belief involves. Bring your imaginations once more into play and figure a series of sound-waves passing through air. Follow them up to their origin, and what do you there find? A definite, tangible, vibrating body. It may be the vocal chords of a human being, it may be an organ-pipe, or it may be a stretched string. Follow in the same manner a train of ether waves to their source; remembering at the same time that your ether is matter, dense, elastic, and capable of motions subject to and determined by mechanical laws. What then do you expect to find as the source of a series of ether waves? Ask your imagination if it will accept a vibrating multiple proportion—a numerical ratio in a state of oscillation? I do not think it will. You cannot crown the edifice by this abstraction. The scientific imagination, which is here authoritative, demands as the origin and cause of a series of ether waves a particle of vibrating matter quite as definite, though it may be excessively minute, as that which gives origin to a musical sound. Such a particle we name an atom or a molecule. I think the seeking intellect when focussed so as to give definition without penumbral haze, is sure to realise this image at the last.

To preserve thought continuous throughout this discourse, to prevent either lack of knowledge or failure of memory from producing any rent in our picture, I here propose to run rapidly over a bit of ground which is probably familiar to most of you, but which I am anxious to make familiar to you all. The waves generated in the ether by the swinging atoms of luminous bodies are of different lengths and amplitudes. The amplitude is the width of swing of the individual particles of the wave. In water-waves it is the height of the crest above the trough, while the length of the wave is the distance between two consecutive crests. The aggregate of waves emitted by the sun may be broadly divided into two classes: the one class competent, the other incompetent, to excite vision. But the light-producing waves differ markedly among themselves in size, form, and force. The length of the largest of these waves is about twice that of the smallest, but the amplitude of the largest is probably a hundred times that of the smallest. Now the force or energy of the wave, which, expressed with reference to sensation, means the intensity of the light, is proportional to the square of the amplitude. Hence the amplitude being one-hundredfold, the energy of the largest light-giving waves would be ten-thousandfold that of the smallest. This is not improbable. I use these figures not with a view to numerical accuracy, but to give you definite ideas of the differences that probably exist among the light-giving waves. And if we take the whole range of solar radiation into account—its non-visual as well as its visual waves—I think it probable that the force or energy of the largest wave is a million times that of the smallest.

Turned into their equivalents of sensation, the different light-waves produce different colours. Red, for example, is produced by the largest waves, violet by the smallest, while green is produced by a wave of intermediate length and amplitude. On entering from air into more highly refracting substances, such as glass or water, or the sulphide of carbon, all the waves are retarded, but the smallest ones most. This furnishes a means of separating the different classes of waves from each other; in other words, of analysing the light. Sent through a refracting prism, the waves of the sun are turned aside in different degrees from their direct course, the red least, the violet most. They are virtually pulled asunder, and they paint upon a white screen placed to receive them 'the solar spectrum.' Strictly speaking, the spectrum embraces an infinity of colours, but the limits of language and of our powers of distinction cause it to be divided into seven segments: red, orange, yellow, green, blue, indigo, violet. These are the seven primary or prismatic colours. Separately, or mixed in various proportions, the solar waves yield all the colours observed in nature and employed in art. Collectively, they give us the impression of whiteness. Pure unsifted solar light is white; and if all the wave-constituents of such light be reduced in the same proportion, the light, though diminished in intensity, will still be white. The whiteness of Alpine snow with the sun shining upon it is barely tolerable to the eye. The same snow under an overcast firmament is still white. Such a firmament enfeebles the light by reflection, and when we lift ourselves above a cloud-field—to an Alpine summit, for instance, or to the top of Snowdon—and see, in the proper direction, the sun shining on the clouds, they appear dazzlingly white. Ordinary clouds, in fact, divide the solar light impinging on them into two parts—a reflected part and a transmitted part, in each of which the proportions of wave-motion which produce the impression of whiteness are sensibly preserved.

It will be understood that the conditions of whiteness would fail if all the waves were diminished *equally*, or by the same absolute quantity. They must be reduced *proportionately*, instead of equally. If by the act of reflexion the waves of red light are split into exact halves, then, to preserve the light white, the waves of yellow, orange, green, and blue must also be split into exact halves. In short, the reduction must take place, not by absolutely equal quantities, but by equal factional parts. In white light the preponderance as regards energy of the larger over the smaller waves must always be immense. Were the case otherwise, the physiological correlative, *blue,* of the smaller waves would have the upper hand in our sensations.

My wish to render our mental images complete causes me to dwell briefly upon these known points, and the same wish will cause me to linger a little longer among others. But here I am disturbed by my reflections. When I consider the effect of dinner upon the nervous system, and the relation of that system to the intellectual powers I am now invoking—when I remember that the universal experience of mankind has fixed upon certain definite elements of perfection in an after-dinner speech, and when I think how conspicuous by their absence these elements are on the present occasion, the thought is not comforting to a man who wishes to stand well with his fellow-creatures in general, and with the members of the British Association in particular. My condition might well resemble that of the ether, which is scientifically defined as an assemblage of vibrations. And the worst of it is that unless you reverse the general verdict regarding the effect of dinner, and prove in your own persons that a uniform experience need not continue uniform—which will be a great point gained for some people—these tremors of mine are likely to become more and more painful. But I call to mind the comforting words of an inspired though uncanonical writer, who admonishes us in the Apocrypha that fear is a bad counsellor. Let me then cast him out, and let me trustfully assume that you will one and all postpone that balmy sleep, of which dinner might under the circumstances be regarded as the indissoluble antecedent, and that you will manfully and womanfully prolong your investigations of the ether and its waves into regions which have been hitherto crossed by the pioneers of science alone.

Not only are the waves of ether reflected by clouds, by solids, and by liquids, but when they pass from light air to dense, or from dense air to light, a portion of the wave-motion is always reflected. Now our atmosphere changes continually in density from top to bottom. It will help our conceptions if we regard it as made up of a series of thin concentric layers, or shells of air, each shell being of the same density throughout, and a small and sudden change of density occurring in passing from shell to shell. Light would be reflected at the limiting surfaces of all these shells, and their action would be practically the same as that of the real atmosphere. And now I would ask your imagination to picture this act of reflection. What must become of the reflected light? The atmospheric layers turn their convex surfaces towards the sun, they are so many convex mirrors of feeble power, and you will immediately perceive that the light regularly reflected from these surfaces cannot reach the earth at all, but is dispersed in space.

But though the sun's light is not reflected in this fashion from the aërial layers to the earth, there is indubitable evidence to show that the light of our firmament is reflected light. Proofs of the most cogent description could be here adduced; but we need only consider that we receive light at the same time from all parts of the hemisphere of heaven. The light of the firmament comes to us across the direction of the solar rays, and even against the direction of the solar rays; and this lateral and opposing rush of wave-motion can only be due to the rebound of the waves from the air itself, or from something suspended in the air. It is also evident that, unlike the action of clouds, the solar light is not reflected by the sky in the proportions which produce white. The sky is blue, which indicates a deficiency on the part of the larger waves. In accounting for the colour of the sky, the first question suggested by analogy would undoubtedly be, is not the air blue? The blueness of the air has in fact been given as a solution of the blueness of the sky. But reason basing itself on observation, asks in reply, How, if the air be blue, can the light of sunrise and sunset, which travels through vast distances of air, be yellow, orange, or even red? The passage of the white solar light through a blue medium could by no possibility redden the light. The hypothesis of a blue air is therefore untenable. In fact the agent, whatever it is, which sends us the light of the sky, exercises in so doing a dichroitic action. The light reflected is blue, the light transmitted is orange or red. A marked distinction is thus exhibited between the matter of the sky and that of an ordinary cloud, which latter exercises no such dichroitic action.

By the force of imagination and reason combined we may penetrate this mystery also. The cloud takes no note of size on the part of the waves of ether, but reflects them all alike. It exercises no selective action. Now the cause of this may be that the cloud particles are so large in comparison with the size of the waves of ether as to reflect them all indifferently. A broad cliff reflects an Atlantic roller as easily as a ripple produced by a sea-bird's wing; and in the presence of large reflecting surfaces, the existing differences of magnitude among the waves of ether may disappear. But supposing the reflecting particles, instead of being very large, to be very small, in comparison with the size of the waves. In this case, instead of the whole wave being fronted and in great part thrown back, a small portion only is shivered off. The great mass of the wave passes over such a particle without reflection. Scatter then a handful of such minute foreign particles in our atmosphere, and set imagination to watch their action upon the solar waves. Waves of all sizes impinge upon the particles, and you see at every collision a portion of the impinging wave struck off by reflection. All the waves of the spectrum, from the extreme red to the extreme violet, are thus acted upon. But in what proportions will the waves be scattered? A clear picture will enable us to anticipate the experimental answer. Remembering that the red waves are to the blue much in the relation of billows to ripples, let us consider whether those extremely small particles are competent to scatter all the waves in the same proportion. If they be not—and a little reflection will make it clear to you that they are not—the production of colour must be an incident of the scattering. Largeness is a thing of relation; and the smaller the wave, the greater is the relative size of any particle on which the wave impinges·, and the greater also the ratio of the reflected portion to the total wave. A pebble placed in the way of the ring-ripples produced by our heavy rain-drops on a tranquil pond will throw back a large fraction of the ripple incident upon it, while the fractional part of a larger wave thrown back by the same pebble might be infinitesimal. Now we have already made it clear to our minds that to preserve the solar light white, its constituent proportions must not be altered; but in the act of division performed by these very small particles we see that the proportions *are* altered; an undue fraction of the smaller waves is scattered by the particles, and, as a consequence, in the scattered light, blue will be the predominant colour. The other colours of the spectrum must, to some extent, be associated with the blue. They are not absent but deficient. We ought, in fact, to have them all, but in diminishing proportions, from the violet to the red.

We have here presented a case to the imagination, and, assuming the undulatory theory to be a reality, we have, I think, fairly reasoned our way to the conclusion, that were particles, small in comparison to the size of the ether waves, sown in our atmosphere, the light scattered by those particles would be exactly such as we observe in our azure skies. When this light is analysed, all the colours of the spectrum are found; but they are found in the proportions indicated by our conclusion. . . .

In the case of Mr. Darwin, observation, imagination, and reason combined have run back with wonderful sagacity and success over a certain length of the line of biological succession. Guided by analogy, in his 'Origin of Species,' he placed at the root of life a primordial germ, from which he conceived the amazing richness and variety of the life that now is upon the earth's surface might be deduced. If this were true, it would not be final. The human imagination would infallibly look behind the germ, and enquire into the history of its genesis. Certainty is here hopeless, but the materials for an opinion may be attainable. In this dim twilight of conjecture the enquirer welcomes every gleam, and seeks to augment his light by indirect incidences. He studies the methods of nature in the ages and the worlds within his reach, in order to shape the course of speculation in the antecedent ages and worlds. And though the certainty possessed by experimental enquiry is here shut out, the imagination is not left entirely without guidance. From the examination of the solar system, Kant and Laplace came to the conclusion that its various bodies once formed parts of the same undislocated mass; that matter in a nebulous form preceded matter in a dense form; that as the ages rolled away, heat was wasted, condensation followed, planets were detached, and that finally the chief portion of the fiery cloud reached, by self-compression, the magnitude and density of our sun. The earth itself offers evidence of a fiery origin; and in our day the hypothesis of Kant and Laplace receives the independent countenance of spectrum analysis, which proves the same substances to be common to the earth and sun. Accepting some such view of the construction of our system as probable, a desire immediately arises to connect the present life of our planet with the past. We wish to know something of our remotest ancestry. On its first detachment from the central mass, life, as we understand it, could hardly have been present on the earth. How then did it come there? The thing to be encouraged here is a reverent freedom—a freedom preceded by the hard discipline which checks licentiousness in speculation—while the thing to be repressed, both in science and out of it, is dogmatism. And here I am in the hands of the meeting—willing to end, but ready to go on. I have no right to intrude upon you, unasked, the unformed notions which are floating like clouds, or gathering to more solid consistency in the modern speculative scientific mind. But if you wish me to speak plainly, honestly, and undisputatiously, I am willing to do so. On the present occasion—

You are ordained to call, and I to come.

Two views, then, offer themselves to us. Life was present potentially in matter when in the nebulous form, and was unfolded from it by the way of natural development, or it is a principle inserted into matter at a later date. With regard to the question of time, the views of men have changed remarkably in our day and generation; and I must say as regards courage also, and a manful willingness to engage in open contest, with fair weapons, a great change has also occurred. The clergy of England—at all events the clergy of London—have nerve enough to listen to the strongest views which any one amongst us would care to utter; and they invite, if they do not challenge, men of the most decided opinions to state and stand by those opinions in open court. No theory upsets them. Let the most destructive hypothesis be stated only in the language current among gentlemen, and they look it in the face. They forego alike the thunders of heaven and the terrors of the other place, smiting the theory, if they do not like it, with honest secular strength. In fact, the greatest cowards of the present day are not to be found among the clergy, but within the pale of science itself.

Chapter 21

George Bernard Shaw (1856–1950)

"PREFACE ON DOCTORS," *THE DOCTOR'S DILEMMA* (1909)

S HAW WAS A PROLIFIC IRISH dramatist who was also a leading music and theatre critic, an active member of the Fabian Society, a co-founder of the London School of Economics, and an outspoken advocate for numerous causes, including women's rights, pacifism, public ownership of all land, equal pay for everyone, vegetarianism, public sanitation and personal hygiene (as opposed to such medical treatment as vaccination), and spelling reform. In his lengthy "Preface on Doctors," which he wrote to contextualize and accompany his play *The Doctor's Dilemma*, Shaw summarized and critiqued the state of the medical profession, which he called "a murderous absurdity" because, at just the time when medical knowledge had sufficiently advanced that doctors, for the first time in history, were likely to do their patients more good than harm, a system of payment for their services was established (one that still operates in the United States) that paid doctors according to the extent and complexity of the procedures they performed regardless of the results, hence creating a conflict of interest that often ill serves patients. "The tragedy of illness at present," Shaw maintains, "is that it delivers you helplessly into the hands of a profession which you deeply mistrust [because doctors] have a strong pecuniary interest . . . [to] perform unnecessary operations and manufacture and prolong lucrative illnesses." Shaw won the Nobel Prize for Literature in 1925.

George Bernard Shaw, "Preface on Doctors," *The Doctor's Dilemma* (1906). New York: Brentano's, 1909. v–ix, xvxxii, lxxi–lxxii, lxxii–lxxvii, lxxix–lxxx, lxxxv–lxxxvi, xc–xcii.

It is not the fault of our doctors that the medical service of the community, as at present provided for, is a murderous absurdity. That any sane nation, having observed that you could provide for the supply of bread by giving bakers a pecuniary interest in baking for you, should go on to give a surgeon a pecuniary interest in cutting off your leg, is enough to make one despair of political humanity. But that is precisely what we have done. And the more appalling the mutilation, the more the mutilator is paid. He who corrects the ingrowing toe-nail receives a few shillings: he who cuts your inside out receives hundreds of guineas, except when he does it to a poor person for practice.

Scandalized voices murmur that these operations are necessary. They may be. It may also be necessary to hang a man or pull down a house. But we take good care not to make the hangman and the housebreaker the judges of that. If we did, no man's neck would be safe and no man's house stable. But we do make the doctor the judge, and fine him anything from sixpence to several hundred guineas if he decides in our favor. I cannot knock my shins severely without forcing on some surgeon the difficult question, "Could I not make a better use of a pocketful of guineas than this man is making of his leg? Could he not write as well—or even better—on one leg than on two? And the guineas would make all the difference in the world to me just now. My wife—my pretty ones—the leg may mortify—it is always safer to operate—he will be well in a fortnight—artificial legs are now so well made that they are really better than natural ones—evolution is towards motors and leglessness, &c., &c, &c."

Now there is no calculation that an engineer can make as to the behavior of a girder under a strain, or an astronomer as to the recurrence of a comet, more certain than the calculation that under such circumstances we shall be dismembered unnecessarily in all directions by surgeons who believe the operations to be necessary solely because they want to perform them. The process metaphorically called bleeding the rich man is performed not only metaphorically but literally every day by surgeons who are quite as honest as most of us. After all, what harm is there in it? The surgeon need not take off the rich man's (or woman's) leg or arm: he can remove the appendix or the uvula, and leave the patient none the worse after a fortnight or so in bed, whilst the nurse, the general practitioner, the apothecary, and the surgeon will be the better.

Doubtful character borne by the medical profession

Again I hear the voices indignantly muttering old phrases about the high character of a noble profession and the honor and conscience of its members. I must reply that the medical profession has not a high character: it has an infamous character. I do not know a single thoughtful and well-informed person who does not feel that the tragedy of illness at present is that it delivers you helplessly into the hands of a profession which you deeply mistrust, because it not only advocates and practises the most revolting cruelties in the pursuit of knowledge, and justifies them on grounds which would equally justify practising the same cruelties on yourself or your children, or burning down London to test a patent fire extinguisher, but, when it has shocked the public, tries to reassure it with lies of breath-bereaving brazenness. That is the character the medical profession has got just now. It may be deserved or it may not: there it is at all events, and the doctors who have not realized this are living in a fool's paradise. As to the honor and conscience of doctors, they have as much as any other class of men, no more and no less. And what other men dare pretend to be impartial where they have a strong pecuniary interest on one side? Nobody supposes that doctors are less virtuous than judges; but a judge whose salary and reputation depended on whether the verdict was for plaintiff or defendant, prosecutor or prisoner, would be as little trusted as a general in the pay of the enemy. To offer me a doctor as my judge, and then weight his decision with a bribe of a large sum of money and a virtual guarantee that if he makes a mistake it can never be proved against him, is to go wildly beyond the ascertained strain which human nature will bear. It is simply unscientific to allege or believe that doctors do not under existing circumstances perform unnecessary operations and manufacture and prolong lucrative illnesses. The only ones who can claim to be above suspicion are those who are so much sought after that their cured patients are immediately replaced by fresh ones. And there is this curious psychological fact to be remembered: a serious illness or a death advertizes the doctor exactly as a hanging advertizes the barrister who defended the person hanged. Suppose, for example, a royal personage gets something wrong with his throat, or has a pain in his inside. If a doctor effects some trumpery cure with a wet compress or a peppermint lozenge nobody takes the least notice of him. But if he operates on the throat and kills the patient, or extirpates an internal organ and keeps the whole nation palpitating for days whilst the patient hovers in pain and fever between life and death, his fortune is made: every rich man who omits to call him in when the same symptoms appear in his household is held not to have done his utmost duty to the patient. The wonder is that there is a king or queen left alive in Europe.

Doctor's consciences

There is another difficulty in trusting to the honor and conscience of a doctor. Doctors are just like other Englishmen: most of them have no honor and no conscience: what they commonly mistake for these is sentimentality. and an intense dread of doing anything that everybody else does not do, or omitting to do anything that everybody else does. This of course does amount to a sort of working or rule-of-thumb conscience; but it means that you will do anything, good or bad, provided you get enough people to keep you in countenance by doing it also. It is the sort of conscience that makes it possible to keep order on a pirate ship, or in a troop of brigands. It may be said that in the last analysis there is no other sort of honor or conscience in existence—that the assent of the majority is the only sanction known to ethics. No doubt this holds good in political practice. If mankind knew the facts, and agreed with the doctors, then the doctors would be in the right; and any person who thought otherwise would be a lunatic. But mankind does not agree, and does not know the facts. All that can be said for medical popularity is that until there is a practicable alternative to blind trust in the doctor, the truth about the doctor is so terrible that we dare not face it. Molière saw through the doctor; but he had to call them in just the same. Napoleon had no illusions about them; but he had to die under their treatment just as much as the most credulous ignoramus that ever paid sixpence for a bottle of strong medicine. In this predicament most people, to save themselves from unbearable mistrust and misery, or from being driven by their conscience into actual conflict with the law, fall back on the old rule that if you cannot have what you believe in you must believe in what you have. When your child is ill or your wife dying, and you happen to be very fond of them, or even when, if you are not fond of them, you are human enough to forget every personal grudge before the spectacle of a fellow creature in pain or peril, what you want is comfort, reassurance, something to clutch at, were it but a straw. This the doctor brings you. You have a wildly urgent feeling that something must be done; and the doctor does something. Sometimes what he does kills the patient; but you do not know that; and the doctor assures you that all that human skill could do has been done. And nobody has the brutality to say to the newly bereft father, mother, husband, wife, brother, or sister, "You have killed your lost darling by your credulity."

The craze for operations

Thus everything is on the side of the doctor. When men die of disease they are said to die from natural causes. When they recover (and they mostly do) the doctor gets the credit of curing them. In surgery all operations are recorded as successful if the patient can be out of the hospital or nursing home alive, though the subsequent history of the case may be such as would make an honest surgeon vow never to recommend or perform the operation again. The large range of operations which consist of amputating limbs and extirpating organs admits of no direct verification of their necessity. There is a fashion in operation as there is in sleeves and skirts: the triumph of some surgeon who has at last found out how to make a once desperate operation fairly safe is usually followed by a rage for that operation not only among the doctors, but actually among their patients. There are men and woman whom the operating table seems to fascinate: half-alive people who through vanity, or hypochondria, or a craving to be the constant objects of anxious attention or what not, lose such feeble sense as they ever had of the value of their own organs and limbs. They seem to care as little for mutilation as lobsters or lizards, which at least have the excuse that they grow new claws and new tails if they lose the old ones. Whilst this book was being prepared for the press a case was tried in the Courts of a man who sued a railway company for damages because a train had run over him and amputated both his legs. He lost his case because it was proved that he had deliberately contrived the occurrence himself for the sake of getting an idler's pension at the expense of the railway company, being too dull to realize how much more he had to lose than to gain by the bargain even if he had won his case and received damages above his utmost hopes.

This amazing case makes it possible to say, with some prospect of being believed, that there is in the classes who can afford to pay for fashionable operations a sprinkling of persons so incapable of appreciating the relative importance of preserving their bodily integrity (including the capacity for parentage) and the pleasure of talking about themselves and hearing themselves talked about as the heroes and heroines of sensational operations that they tempt surgeons to operate on them not only with huge fees, but with personal solicitation. Now it cannot be too often repeated that when an operation is once performed, nobody can ever prove that it was unnecessary. If I refuse to allow my leg to be amputated, its mortification and my death may prove that I was wrong; but if I let the leg go, nobody can ever prove that it would not have mortified had I been obstinate. Operation is therefore the safe side for the surgeon as well as the lucrative side. The result is that we hear of "conservative surgeons" as a distinct class of practitioners who make it a rule not to operate if they can possibly help it, and who are sought after by the people who have vitality enough to regard an operation as a last resort. But no surgeon is bound to take the conservative view. If he believes that an organ is at best a useless survival and that if he extirpates it the patient will be well and none the worse in a fortnight, whereas to await the natural cure would mean a month's illness, then he is clearly justified in recommending the operation even if the cure without operation is as certain is anything of the kind ever can be. Thus the conservative surgeon and the radical or extirpatory surgeon may both be right as far as the ultimate cure is concerned; so that their consciences do not help them out of their differences.

Credulity and chloroform

There is no harder scientific fact in the world than the fact that belief can be produced in practically unlimited quality and intensity, without observation or reasonings, and even in defiance of both, by the simple desire to believe founded on a strong interest in believing. Everybody recognizes this in the case of the amatory infatuation of the adolescents who see angels and heroes in obviously (to others) commonplace and even objectionable maidens and youth. But it holds good over the entire field of human activity. The hardest-headed materialist will become a consulter of table-rappers and slate-writers if he loses a child or a wife so beloved that the desire to revive and communicate with them becomes irresistible The cobbler believes that there is nothing like leather. The Imperialist who regards the conquest of England by a foreign power as the worst of political misfortunes believes that the conquest of a foreign power by England would be a boon to the conquered. Doctors are no more proof against such illusions than other men. Can anyone then doubt that under existing conditions a great deal of unnecessary and mischievous operating is bound to go on, and that patients are encouraged to imagine that modern surgery and anesthesia have made operations much less serious matters than they really are? When doctors write or speak to the public about operations, they imply, and often say in so many words, that chloroform has made surgery painless. People who have been operated on know better. The patient does not feel the knife, and the operation is therefore enormously facilitated for the surgeon; but the patient pays for the anesthesia with hours of wretched sickness; and when that is over there is the pain of the wound made by the surgeon, which has to heal like any other wound. This is why operating surgeons, who are usually out of the the house with their fee in their pocket before the patient has recovered consciousness, and who therefore see nothing of the suffering witnessed by the general practitioner and the nurse, occasionally talk of operations very much as the hangman in Barnaby Rudge talked of executions, as if being operated on were a luxury in sensation as well as in price.

Medical poverty

To make matters worse, doctors are hideously poor. The Irish gentleman doctor of my boyhood, who took nothing less than a guinea, though he might pay you four visits for it, seems to have no equivalent nowadays in English society. Better be a railway porter than an ordinary English general practitioner. A railway porter has from eighteen to twenty-three shillings a week from the Company merely as a retainer; and his additional fees from the public, if we leave the third-class twopenny tip out of account (and I am by no means sure that even this reservation need be made), are equivalent to doctor's fees in the case of second-class passengers, and double doctor's fees in the case of first. Any class of educated men thus treated tends to become a brigand class, and doctors are no exception to the rule. They are offered disgraceful prices for advice and medicine. Their patients are for the most part so poor and so ignorant that good advice would be resented as impracticable and wounding. When you are so poor that you cannot afford to refuse eighteenpence from a man who is too poor to pay you any more, it is useless to tell him that what he or his sick child needs is not medicine, but more leisure, better clothes, better food, and a better drained and ventilated house. It is kinder to give him a bottle of something almost as cheap as water, and tell him to come again with another eighteenpence if it does not cure him. When you have done that over and over again every day for a week, how much scientific conscience have you left? If you are weak-minded enough to cling desperately to your eighteenpence as denoting a certain social superiority to the sixpenny doctor, you will be miserably poor all your life; whilst the sixpenny doctor, with his low prices and quick turnover of patients, visibly makes much more than you do and kills no more people.

A doctor's character can no more stand out against such conditions than the lungs of his patient can stand out against bad ventilation. The only way in which he can preserve his self-respect is by forgetting all he ever learnt of science, and clinging to such help as he can give without cost merely by being less ignorant and more accustomed to sick-beds than his patients. Finally, he acquires a certain skill at nursing cases under poverty-stricken domestic conditions, just as women who have been trained as domestic servants in some huge institution with lifts, vacuum cleaners, electric lighting, steam heating, and machinery that turns the kitchen into a laboratory and engine house combined, manage, when they are sent out into the world to drudge as general servants, to pick up their business in a new way, learning the slatternly habits and wretched makeshifts of homes where even bundles of kindling wood are luxuries to be anxiously economized.

The successful doctor

The doctor whose success blinds public opinion to medical poverty is almost as completely demoralized. His promotion means that his practice becomes more and more confined to the idle rich. The proper advice for most of their ailments is typified in Abernethy's "Live on sixpence a day and earn it." But here, as at the other end of the scale, the right advice is neither agreeable nor practicable. And every hypochondriacal rich lady or gentleman who can be persuaded that he or she is a lifelong invalid means anything from fifty to five hundred pounds a year for the doctor. Operations enable a surgeon to earn similar sums in a couple of hours and if the surgeon also keeps a nursing home, he may make considerable profits at the same time by running what is the most expensive kind of hotel. These gains are so great that they undo much of the moral advantage which the absence of grinding pecuniary anxiety gives the rich doctor over the poor one. It is true that the temptation to prescribe a sham treatment because the real treatment is too dear for either patient or doctor does not exist for the rich doctor. He always has plenty of genuine cases which can afford genuine treatment and these provide him with enough sincere scientific professional work to save him from the ignorance, obsolescence, and atrophy of scientific conscience into which his poorer colleagues sink. But on the other hand his expenses are enormous. Even as a bachelor, he must, at London west end rates, make over a thousand a year before he can afford even to insure his life. His house, his servants, and his equipage (or autopage) must be on the scale to which his patients are accustomed, though a couple of rooms with a camp bed in one of them might satisfy his own requirements. Above all, the income which provides for these outgoings stops the moment he himself stops working. Unlike the man of business, whose managers, clerks, warehousemen and laborers keep his business going whilst he is in bed or in his club, the doctor cannot earn a farthing by deputy. Though he is exceptionally exposed to infection, and has to face all weathers at all hours of the night and day, often not enjoying a complete night's rest for a week, the money stops coming in the moment he stops going out; and therefore illness has special terrors for him, and success no certain permanence. He dare not stop making hay while the sun shines; for it may set at any time. Men do not resist pressure of this intensity. When they come under it as doctors they pay unnecessary visits; they write prescriptions that are as absurd as the rub of chalk with which an Irish tailor once charmed away a wart from my father's finger; they conspire with surgeons to promote operations; they nurse the delusions of the *malade imaginaire* (who is always really ill because, as there is no such thing as perfect health, nobody is ever really well); they exploit human folly, vanity, and fear of death as ruthlessly as their own health, strength, and patience are exploited by selfish hypochondriacs. They must do all these things or else run pecuniary risks that no men can fairly be asked to run. And the healthier the world becomes, the more they are compelled to live by imposture and the less by that really helpful activity of which all doctors get enough to preserve them from utter corruption. . . .

The reforms also come from the laity

In the main, then, the doctor learns that if he gets ahead of the superstition of his patients he is a ruined man; and the result is that he instinctively takes care not to get ahead of them. That is why all the changes come from the laity. It was not until an agitation had been conducted for many years by laymen, including quacks and faddists of all kinds, that the public was sufficiently impressed to make it possible for the doctors to open their minds and their mouths on the subject of fresh air, cold water, temperance, and the rest of the new fashions in hygiene. At present the tables have been turned on many old prejudices. Plenty of our most popular elderly doctors believe that cold tubs in the morning are unnatural, exhausting, and rheumatic; that fresh air is a fad and that everybody is the better for a glass or two of port wine every day; but they no longer dare say as much until they know exactly where they are; for many very desirable patients in country houses have lately been persuaded that their first duty is to get up at six in the morning and begin the day by taking a walk barefoot through the dewy grass. He who shows the least scepticism as to this practice is at once suspected of being "an old-fashioned doctor," and dismissed to make room for a younger man.

In short, private medical practice is governed not by science but by supply and demand; and however scientific a treatment may be, it cannot hold its place in the market if there is no demand for it; nor can the grossest quackery be kept off the market if there is a demand for it. . . .

The doctor's virtues

It will be admitted that this is a pretty bad state of things. And the melodramatic instinct of the public, always demanding that every wrong shall have, not its remedy, but its villain to be hissed, will blame, not its own apathy, superstition, and ignorance, but the depravity of the doctors. Nothing could be more unjust or mischievous. Doctors, if no better than other men, are certainly no worse. I was reproached during the performances of *The Doctor's Dilemma* at the Court Theatre in 1907 because I made the artist a rascal, the journalist an illiterate incapable, and all the doctors "angels." But I did not go beyond the warrant of my own experience. It has been my luck to have doctors among my friends for nearly forty years past (all perfectly aware of my freedom from the usual credulity as to the miraculous power and knowledge attributed to them); and though I know that there are medical blackguards as well as military, legal, and clerical blackguards (one soon finds that out when one is privileged to hear doctors talking shop among themselves), the fact that I was no more at a loss for private medical advice and attendance when I had not a penny in my pocket than I was later on when I could afford fees on the highest scale, has made it impossible for me to share that hostility to the doctor as a man which exists and is growing as an inevitable result of the present condition of medical practice. Not that the interest in disease and aberrations which turns some men and women to medicine and surgery is not sometimes as morbid as the interest in misery and vice which turns some others to philanthropy and "rescue work." But the true doctor is inspired by a hatred of ill-health, and a divine impatience of any waste of vital forces. Unless a man is led to medicine or surgery through a very exceptional technical aptitude, or because doctoring is a family tradition, or because he regards it unintelligently as a lucrative and gentlemanly profession, his motives in choosing the career of a healer are clearly generous. However actual practice may disillusion and corrupt him, his selection in the first instance is not a selection of a base character.

The doctor's hardships

A review of the counts in the indictment I have brought against private medical practice will show that they arise out of the doctor's position as a competitive private tradesman: that is, out of his poverty and dependence. And it should be borne in mind that doctors are expected to treat other people specially well whilst themselves submitting to specially inconsiderate treatment. The butcher and baker are not expected to feed the hungry unless the hungry can pay; but a doctor who allows a fellow-creature to suffer or perish without aid is regarded as a monster. Even if we must dismiss hospital service as really venal, the fact remains that most doctors do a good deal of gratuitous work in private practice all through their careers. And in his paid work the doctor is on a different footing to the tradesman. Although the articles he sells, advice and treatment, are the same for all classes, his fees have to be graduated like the income tax. The successful fashionable doctor may weed his poorer patients out from time to time, and finally use the College of Physicians to place it out of his own power to accept low fees; but the ordinary general practitioner never makes out his bills without considering the taxable capacity of his patients.

Then there is the disregard of his own health and comfort which results from the fact that he is, by the nature of his work, an emergency man. We are polite and considerate to the doctor when there is nothing the matter and we meet him as a friend or entertain him as a guest, but when the baby is suffering from croup, or its mother has a temperature of 104°, or its grandfather has broken his leg, nobody thinks of the doctor except as a healer and saviour. He may be hungry, weary, sleepy, run down by several successive nights disturbed by that instrument of torture, the night bell; but who ever thinks of this in the face of sudden sickness or accident? We think no more of the condition of a doctor attending a case than of the condition of a fireman at a fire. In other occupations night-work is specially recognized and provided for. The worker sleeps all day; has his breakfast in the evening; his lunch or dinner at midnight; his dinner or supper before going to bed in the morning; and he changes to day-work if he cannot stand night-work. But a doctor is expected to work day and night. In practices which consist largely of workmen's clubs, and in which the patients are therefore taken on wholesale terms and very numerous, the unfortunate assistant, or the principal if he has no assistant, often does not undress, knowing that he will be called up before he has snatched an hour's sleep. To the strain of such inhuman conditions must be added the constant risk of infection. One wonders why the impatient doctors do not become savage and unmanageable, and the patient ones imbecile. Perhaps they do, to some extent. And the pay is wretched, and so uncertain that refusal to attend without payment in advance becomes often a necessary measure of self-defence, whilst the County Court has long ago put an end to the tradition that the doctor's fee is an honorarium. Even the most eminent physicians, as such biographies as those of Paget shew, are sometimes, miserably, inhumanly poor until they are past their prime.

In short, the doctor needs our help for the moment much more than we often need his. The ridicule of Molière, the death of a well-informed and clever writer like the late Harold Frederic in the hands of Christian Scientists (a sort of sealing with his blood of the contemptuous disbelief in and dislike of doctors he had bitterly expressed in his books), the scathing and quite justifiable exposure of medical practice in the novel by Mr. Maarten Maartens entitled *The New Religion*: all these trouble the doctor very little, and are in any case well set off by the popularity of Sir Luke Fildes' famous picture and by the verdicts in which juries from time to time express their conviction that the doctor can do no wrong. The real woes of the doctor are the shabby coat, the wolf at the door, the tyranny of ignorant patients, the work-day of 24 hours, and the uselessness of honestly prescribing what most of the patients really need: that is, not medicine, but money.

The public doctor

What then is to be done?

Fortunately we have not to begin absolutely from the beginning: we already have, in the Medical Officer of Health, a sort of doctor who is free from the worst hardships, and consequently from the worst vices, of the private practitioner. His position depends, not on the number of people who are ill, and whom he can keep ill, but on the number of people who are well. He is judged, as all doctors and treatments should be judged, by the vital statistics of his district. When the death rate goes up his credit goes down. As every increase in his salary depends on the issue of a public debate as to the health of the constituency under his charge, he has every inducement to strive towards the ideal of a clean bill of health. He has a safe, dignified, responsible, independent position based wholly on the public health; whereas the private practitioner has a precarious, shabby-genteel, irresponsible, servile position, based wholly on the prevalence of illness.

It is true, there are grave scandals in the public medical service. The public doctor may be also a private practitioner eking out his earnings by giving a little time to public work for a mean payment. There are cases in which the position is one which no successful practitioner will accept, and where, therefore, incapables or drunkards get automatically selected for the post, *faute de mieux*; but even in these cases the doctor is less disastrous in his public capacity than in his private one: besides, the conditions which produce these bad cases are doomed, as the evil is now recognized and understood. A popular but unstable remedy is to enable local authorities, when they are too small to require the undivided time of such men as the Medical Officers of our great municipalities, to combine for public health purpose so that each may share the service of a highly paid official of the best class; but the right remedy is a larger area as the sanitary unit. . . .

The social solution of the medical problem

The social solution of the medical problem, then, depends on that large, slowly advancing, pettishly resisted integration of society called generally Socialism. Until the medical profession becomes a body of men trained and paid by the country to keep the country in health it will remain what it is at present: a conspiracy to exploit popular credulity and human suffering. Already our M.O.H.s (Medical Officers of Health) are in the new position: what is lacking is appreciation of the change, not only by the public but by the private doctors. For, as we have seen, when one of the first-rate posts becomes vacant in one of the great cities, and all the leading M.O.H.s compete for it, they must appeal to the good health of the cities of which they have been in charge, and not to the size of the incomes the local private doctors are making out of the ill-health of their patients. If a competitor can prove that he has utterly ruined every sort of medical private practice in a large city except obstetric practice and the surgery of accidents, his claims are irresistible; and this is the ideal at which every M.O.H should aim. But the profession at large should none the less welcome him and set its house in order for the social change which will finally be its own salvation. For the M.O.H. as we know him is only the beginning of that army of Public Hygiene which will presently take the place in general interest and honor now occupied by our military and naval forces. It is silly that an Englishman should be more afraid of a German soldier than of a British disease germ, and should clamor for more barracks in the same newspapers that protest against more school clinics, and cry out that if the State fights disease for us it makes us paupers, though they never say that if the State fights the Germans for us it make us cowards. Fortunately, when a habit of thought is silly it only needs steady treatment by ridicule from sensible and witty people to be put out of countenance and perish. Every year sees an increase in the number of persons employed in the Public Health Service, who would formerly have been mere adventurers in the Private Illness Service. To put it another way, a host of men and women who have now a strong incentive to be mischievous and even murderous rogues will have a much stronger, because a much honester, incentive to be not only good citizens but active benefactors to the community. And they will have no anxiety whatever about their incomes. . . .

And here we come to the danger that terrifies so many of us: the danger of having a hygienic orthodoxy imposed on us. But we must face that: in such crowded and poverty ridden civilizations as ours any orthodoxy is better than laisser-faire. If our population ever comes to consist exclusively of well-to-do, highly cultivated, and thoroughly instructed free persons in a position to take care of themselves, no doubt they will make short work of a good deal of official regulation that is now of life-and-death necessity to us; but under existing circumstances, I repeat, almost any sort of attention that democracy will stand is better than neglect. Attention and activity lead to mistakes as well as to successes; but a life spent in making mistakes is not only more honorable but more useful than a life spent doing nothing. The one lesson that comes out of all our theorizing and experimenting is that there is only one really scientific progressive method, and that is the method of trial and error. If you come to that, what is laisser-faire but an orthodoxy? the most tyrannous and disastrous of all the orthodoxies, since it forbids you even to learn. . . .

Science becomes dangerous only when it imagines that it has reached its goal. What is wrong with priests and popes is that instead of being apostles and saints, they are nothing but empirics who say "I know" instead of "I am learning," and pray for credulity and inertia as wise men pray for scepticism and activity. Such abominations as the Inquisition and the Vaccination Acts are possible only in the famine years of the soul, when the great vital dogmas of honor, liberty, courage, the kinship of all life, faith that the unknown is greater than the known and is only the As Yet Unknown, and resolution to find a manly highway to it, have been forgotten in a paroxysm of littleness and terror in which nothing is active except concupiscence and the fear of death, playing on which any trader can filch a fortune, any blackguard gratify his cruelty, and any tyrant make us his slaves.

Lest this should seem too rhetorical a conclusion for our professional men of science, who are mostly trained not to believe anything unless it is worded in the jargon of those writers who, because they never really understand what they are trying to say, cannot find familiar words for it, and are therefore compelled to invent a new language of nonsense for every book they write, let me sum up my conclusions as dryly as is consistent with accurate thought and live conviction.

1.   Nothing is more dangerous than a poor doctor: not even a poor employer or a poor landlord.
2.   Of all the anti-social vested interests the worst is the vested interest in ill-health.
3.   Remember that an illness is a misdemeanor; and treat the doctor as an accessory unless he notifies every case to the Public Health authority.
4.   Treat every death as a possible and under our present system a probable murder, by making it the subject of a reasonably conducted inquest; and execute the doctor, if necessary, *as* a doctor, by striking him off the register.
5.   Make up your mind how many doctors the community needs to keep it well. Do not register more or less than this number; and let registration constitute the doctor a civil servant with a dignified living wage paid out of public funds.
6.   Municipalize Harley Street.
7.   Treat the private operator exactly as you would treat a private executioner.
8.   Treat persons who profess to be able to cure disease as you treat fortune tellers.
9.   Keep the public carefully informed, by special statistics and announcements of individual cases, of all illnesses of doctors or in their families.
10. Make it compulsory for a doctor using a brass plate to have inscribed on it, in addition to the letters indicating his qualifications, the words "Remember that I too am mortal."
11. In legislation and social organization, proceed on the principle that invalids, meaning persons who cannnot keep themselves alive by their own activities, cannot, beyond reason, expect to be kept alive by the activity of others. There is a point at which the most energetic policeman or doctor, when called upon to deal with an apparently

drowned person, gives up artificial respiration, although it is never possible to declare with certainty, at any point short of decomposition, that another five minutes of the exercise would not effect resuscitation. The theory that every individual alive is of infinite value is legislatively impracticable. No doubt the higher the life we secure to the individual by wise social organization, the greater his value is to the community, and the more pains we shall take to pull him through any temporary danger or disablement. But the man who costs more than he is worth is doomed by sound hygiene as inexorably as by sound economics.

12.   Do not try to live for ever. You will not succeed.

13.   Use your health, even to the point of wearing it out. That is what it is for. Spend all you have before you die; and do not outlive yourself.

14.   Take the utmost care to get well born and well brought up. This means that your mother must have a good doctor. Be careful to go to a school where there is what they call a school clinic, where your nutrition and teeth and eyesight and other matters of importance to you will be attended to. Be particularly careful to have all this done at the expense of the nation, as otherwise it will not be done at all, the chances being about forty to one against your being able to pay for it directly yourself, even if you know how to set about it. Othewise you will be what most people are at present: an unsound citizen of an unsound nation, without sense enough to be ashamed or unhappy about it.

Chapter 22

Albert Einstein (1879–1955)

THE EVOLUTION OF PHYSICS FROM EARLY CONCEPTS TO RELATIVITY AND QUANTA (1938)

EINSTEIN WAS A GERMAN (LATER AMERICAN) theoretical physicist whose revolutionary discoveries, including the theory of general relativity and the law of the photoelectric effect, led to his being regarded as the father of modern physics. In *The Evolution of Physics from Early Concepts to Relativity and Quanta* (1938), Einstein helped to reconceptualize physics and to set physicists on previously unimagined paths when, echoing Tyndall, he maintained that "Physical concepts are free creations of the human mind, and are not . . . uniquely determined by the external world." Human thinking or psychology creates the concept of pure numbers, the subjective feeling of time, both Euclidean and non-Euclidean geometry, the electromagnetic field, the four-dimensional time-space continuum, quantum theory and probability laws, and numerous others. Einstein received the Nobel Prize for Physics in 1921.

Albert Einstein, *The Evolution of Physics from Early Concepts to Relativity and Quanta*, with Leopold Infeld. New York: Simon and Schuster, 1966. 31–35, 294–97.

Physical concepts are free creations of the human mind, and are not, however it may seem, uniquely determined by the external world. In our endeavor to understand reality we are somewhat like a man trying to understand the mechanism of a closed watch. He sees the face and the moving hands, even hears its ticking, but he has no way of opening the case. If he is ingenious he may form some picture of a mechanism which could be responsible for all the things he observes, but he may never be quite sure his picture is the only one which could explain his observations. He will never be able to compare his picture with the real mechanism and he cannot even imagine the possibility or the meaning of such a comparison. But he certainly believes that, as his knowledge increases, his picture of reality will become simpler and simpler and will explain a wider and wider range of his sensuous impressions. He may also believe in the existence of the ideal limit of knowledge and that it is approached by the human mind. He may call this ideal limit the objective truth.

One clew remains

When first studying mechanics one has the impression that everything in this branch of science is simple, fundamental and settled for all time. One would hardly suspect the existence of an important clew which no one noticed for three hundred years. The neglected clew is connected with one of the fundamental concepts of mechanics, that of *mass*.

Again we return to the simple idealized experiment of the cart on a perfectly smooth road. If the cart is initially at rest and then given a push, it afterwards moves uniformly with a certain velocity. Suppose that the action of the force can be repeated as many times as desired, the mechanism of pushing acting in the same way and exerting the same force on the same cart. However many times the experiment is repeated the final velocity is always the same. But what happens if the experiment is changed, if previously the cart was empty and now it is loaded? The loaded cart will have a smaller final velocity than the empty one. The conclusion is: if the same force acts on two different bodies, both initially at rest, the resulting velocities will not be the same. We say that the velocity depends on the mass of the body, being smaller if the mass is greater.

We know, therefore, at least in theory, how to determine the mass of a body or, more exactly, how many times greater one mass is than another. We have identical forces acting on two resting masses. Finding that the velocity of the first mass is three times greater than that of the second we conclude that the first mass is three times smaller than the second. This is certainly not a very practical way of determining the ratio of two masses. We can, nevertheless, well imagine having done it in this, or in some similar way, based upon the application of the law of inertia.

How do we really determine mass in practice? Not, of course, in the way just described. Everyone knows the correct answer. We do it by weighing on a scale.

Let us discuss in more detail the two different ways of determining mass.

The first experiment had nothing whatever to do with gravity, the attraction of the earth. The cart moves along a perfectly smooth and horizontal plane after the push. Gravitational force, which causes the cart to stay on the plane, does not change, and plays no role in the determination of the mass. It is quite different with weighing. We could never use a scale if the earth did not attract bodies, if gravity did not exist. The difference between the two determinations of mass is that the first has nothing to do with the force of gravity while the second is based essentially on its existence.

We ask: if we determine the ratio of two masses in both ways described above do we obtain the same result? The answer given by experiment is quite clear. The results are exactly the same! This conclusion could not have been foreseen, and is based on observation, not reason. Let us, for the sake of simplicity, call the mass determined in the first way the *inertial mass* and that determined in the second way the *gravitational mass*. In our world it happens that they are equal but we can well imagine that this should not have been the case at all. Another question arises immediately: is this identity of the two kinds of mass purely accidental, or does it have a deeper significance? The answer, from the point of view of classical physics, is: the identity of the two masses is accidental and no deeper significance should be attached to it. The answer of modern physics is just the opposite: the identity of the two masses is fundamental and forms a new and essential clew leading to a more profound understanding. This was, in fact, one of the most important clews from which the so-called general theory of relativity was developed.

A mystery story seems inferior if it explains strange events as accidents. It is certainly more satisfying to have the story follow a rational pattern. In exactly the same way a theory which offers an explanation for the identity of gravitational and inertial mass is superior to one which interprets their identity as accidental, provided, of course, that the two theories are equally consistent with observed facts.

Since this identity of inertial and gravitational mass was fundamental for the formulation of the theory of relativity we are justified in examining it a little more closely here. What experiments prove convincingly that the two masses are the same? The answer lies in Galileo's old experiment in which he dropped different masses from a tower. He noticed that the time required for the fall was always the same, that the motion of a falling body does not depend on the mass. To link this simple but highly important experimental result with the identity of the two masses needs some rather intricate reasoning.

A body at rest gives way before the action of an external force, moving and attaining a certain velocity. It yields more or less easily, according to its inertial mass, resisting the motion more strongly if the mass is large than if it is small. We may say, without pretending to be rigorous: the readiness with which a body responds to the call of an external force depends on its inertial mass. If it were true that the earth attracts all bodies with the same force, that of greatest inertial mass would move more slowly in falling than any other. But this is not the case: all bodies fall in the same way. This means that the force by which the earth attracts different masses must be different. Now the earth attracts a stone with the force of gravity and knows nothing about its inertial mass. The "calling" force of the earth depends on the gravitational mass. The "answering" motion of the stone depends on the inertial mass. Since the "answering" motion is always the same—all bodies dropped from the same height fall in the same way—it must be deduced that gravitational mass and inertial mass are equal.

More pedantically a physicist formulates the same conclusion: the acceleration of a falling body increases in proportion to its gravitational mass and decreases in proportion to its inertial mass. Since all falling bodies have the same constant acceleration, the two masses must be equal.

In our great mystery story there are no problems wholly solved and settled for all time. After three hundred years we had to return to the initial problem of motion, to revise the procedure of investigation, to find clews which had been overlooked, thereby reaching a different picture of the surrounding universe. . . .

During the last few years all the difficulties of quantum physics have been concentrated around a few principal points. Physics awaits their solution impatiently. But there is no way of foreseeing when and where the clarification of these difficulties will be brought about.

Physics and reality

What are the general conclusions which can be drawn from the development of physics indicated here in a broad outline representing only the most fundamental ideas?

Science is not just a collection of laws, a catalogue of unrelated facts. It is a creation of the human mind, with its freely invented ideas and concepts. Physical theories try to form a picture of reality and to establish its connection with the wide world of sense impressions. Thus the only justification for our mental structures is whether and in what way our theories form such a link.

We have seen new realities created by the advance of physics. But this chain of creation can be traced back far beyond the starting point of physics. One of the most primitive concepts is that of an object. The concepts of a tree, a horse, any material body, are creations gained on the basis of experience, though the impressions from which they arise are primitive in comparison with the world of physical phenomena. A cat teasing a mouse also creates, by thought, its own primitive reality. The fact that the cat reacts in a similar way toward any mouse it meets shows that it forms concepts and theories which are its guide through its own world of sense impressions.

"Three trees" is something different from "two trees." Again "two trees" is different from "two stones." The concepts of the pure numbers 2, 3, 4 . . . , freed from the objects from which they arose, are creations of the thinking mind which describe the reality of our world.

The psychological subjective feeling of time enables us to order our impressions, to state that one event precedes another. But to connect every instant of time with a number, by the use of a clock, to regard time as a one-dimensional continuum, is already an invention. So also are the concepts of Euclidean and non-Euclidean geometry, and our space understood as a three-dimensional continuum.

Physics really began with the invention of mass, force, and an inertial system. These concepts are all free inventions. They led to the formulation of the mechanical point of view. For the physicist of the early nineteenth century, the reality of our outer world consisted of particles with simple forces acting between them and depending only on the distance. He tried to retain as long as possible his belief that he would succeed in explaining all events in nature by these fundamental concepts of reality. The difficulties connected with the deflection of the magnetic needle, the difficulties connected with the structure of the ether, induced us to create a more subtle reality. The important invention of the electromagnetic field appears. A courageous scientific imagination was needed to realize fully that not the behavior of bodies, but the behavior of something between them, that is, the field, may be essential for ordering and understanding events.

Later developments both destroyed old concepts and created new ones. Absolute time and the inertial co-ordinate system were abandoned by the relativity theory. The background for all events was no longer the one-dimensional time and the three-dimensional space continuum, but the four-dimensional time-space continuum, another free invention, with new transformation properties. The inertial co-ordinate system was no longer needed. Every co-ordinate system is equally suited for the description of events in nature.

The quantum theory again created new and essential features of our reality. Discontinuity replaced continuity. Instead of laws governing individuals, probability laws appeared.

The reality created by modern physics is, indeed, far removed from the reality of the early days. But the aim of every physical theory still remains the same.

With the help of physical theories we try to find our way through the maze of observed facts, to order and understand the world of our sense impressions. We want the observed facts to follow logically from our concept of reality. Without the belief that it is possible to grasp the reality with our theoretical constructions, without the belief in the inner harmony of our world, there could be no science. This belief is and always will remain the fundamental motive for all scientific creation. Throughout all our efforts, in every dramatic struggle between old and new views, we recognize the eternal longing for understanding, the ever-firm belief in the harmony of our world, continually strengthened by the increasing obstacles to comprehension.

We summarize:

Again the rich variety of facts in the realm of atomic phenomena forces us to invent new physical concepts. Matter has a granular structure; it is composed of elementary particles, the elementary quanta of matter. Thus, the electric charge has a granular structure and—most important from the point of view of the quantum theory—so has energy. Photons are the energy quanta of which light is composed.

Is light a wave or a shower of photons? Is a beam of electrons a shower of elementary particles or a wave? These fundamental questions are forced upon physics by experiment. In seeking to answer them we have to abandon the description of atomic events as happenings in space and time, we have to retreat still further from the old mechanical view. Quantum physics formulates laws governing crowds and not individuals. Not properties but probabilities are described, not laws disclosing the future of systems are formulated, but laws governing the changes in time of the probabilities and relating to great congregations of individuals.

Chapter 23

Werner Heisenberg (1901–76)

"NON-OBJECTIVE SCIENCE AND UNCERTAINTY" (1955)

A GERMAN THEORETICAL PHYSICIST, HEISENBERG made foundational contributions to quantum mechanics; he is best known for formulating the Uncertainty Principle, which states that a particle's position and momentum cannot simultaneously both be known with a high degree of certainty. "Non-Objective Science and Uncertainty" from *The Physicist's Conception of Nature* sums up the movement from nineteenth-century physics – nature operated "as a set of laws in space and time," atoms "were the immutable building-stones of matter" – to twentieth, in which fields of force displaced matter as a fundamental explanation of nature, the laws of quantum theory concern observation and the effects of our measuring instruments, not "the behaviour of the elementary particles but only our knowledge of this behaviour," uncertainty is fundamental since it is "impossible to describe simultaneously both the position and the velocity of an atomic particle with any prescribed degree of accuracy," and the "concept of complementarity" obtains, whereby different pictures of atomic systems are both true for their appropriate contexts and mutually exclusive. All of these concepts found their way into modernist thinking and literature. Heisenberg received the Nobel Prize for Physics in 1932.

Werner Heisenberg, "Non-Objective Science and Uncertainty," *The Physicist's Conception of Nature*. Trans. Arnold J. Pomerans. New York: Greenwood, 1970. 11–16, 28–29, 33–42.

Changes in the meaning of the word 'nature'

. . . From the behaviour of matter during chemical changes, chemistry tried to fathom processes on the atomic scale. Experiments with the induction machine and the Voltaic cell provided the first common knowledge of electrical phenomena not yet understood. Thus, there took place a slow change in the significance of 'nature' as a subject for investigation by science. It became a collective concept for all those realms of experience into which man could penetrate by means of science and technology, regardless of whether or not they appeared as 'nature' to his immediate perception. Even the phrase 'description of nature' lost more and more of its original significance of a living and meaningful account of nature.

Increasingly it became to mean the mathematical description of nature, *i.e.*, an accurate and concise yet comprehensive collection of data about relations that hold in nature.

This semi-conscious extension of the concept of nature must not yet be considered a basic departure from the original aims of science, since, even in this wider field, the crucial concepts were still the same as those of ordinary experience. In the nineteenth century nature still appeared as a set of laws in space and time in which man and man's intervention in nature could be ignored in principle, if not in practice.

Matter was thought of in terms of its mass, which remained constant through all changes, and which required forces to move it. Because, from the eighteenth century onwards, chemical experiments could be classified and explained by the atomic hypothesis of ancient times, it appeared reasonable to take over the view of ancient philosophy that atoms were the real substance, the immutable building-stones of matter. Just as in the philosophy of Democritus, the differences in material qualities were considered to be merely apparent; smell or colour, temperature or viscosity, were not actual qualities of matter but resulted from the interaction of matter and our senses, and had to be explained by the arrangements and movements of atoms, and by the effect of these arrangements on our minds. It is thus that there arose the over-simplified world-view of nineteenth-century materialism: atoms move in space and time as the real and immutable substances, and it is their arrangement and motion that create the colourful phenomena of the world of our senses.

The crisis of the materialist conception

The first, but not yet very dangerous, incursion into this world-view took place in the second half of the last century with the development of the theory of electricity, in which not matter but fields of force were considered to be the real explanation. Interactions between fields of force without any matter to propagate the force were very much more difficult to understand than the materialist picture of atomic physics, and introduced an element of abstraction and a lack of clarity into what appeared otherwise to be so reasonable a world-view. Attempts were not lacking to return once more to the simpler concepts of materialist philosophy by way of the ether, which was supposed to be an elastic medium transmitting these fields of force; yet no such attempt had any real success. Even so, one could take comfort from the fact that changes in the fields of force could still be considered as processes in space and time, and that they could be described objectively, *i.e.*, without any reference to the manner in which they were observed, and thus in accordance with the generally held idealized view of laws of space and time. Furthermore, fields of force, *i.e.*, forces which can only be observed by their effect on atoms, could be considered as produced by atoms, and so as explaining atomic movements in some way. Thus atoms still remained as the actual essence, and between them there was empty space, real only inasmuch as it was a transmitter of fields of force.

In this world-view it did not matter overmuch that after the discovery of radio-activity at the end of the last century, the atoms of chemistry could no longer be considered as the ultimate indivisible building-stones of matter. These were now thought to consist of three kinds of basic units—the protons, neutrons and electrons of today. The practical consequences of this new knowledge have been the transmutation of elements and the rise of atomic physics, and they have thus become extremely important. Basically, however, nothing has been changed in principle by our acceptance of protons, neutrons and electrons as the smallest building-stones of matter, if we interpret these as the real essence. What is important for the materialistic world-view is simply the possibility that such small building-stones of elementary particles exist and that they may be considered the ultimate objective reality. Thus, the well-constructed world-view of the nineteenth and early twentieth centuries was preserved, and thanks to its simplicity it managed to retain its full power of conviction for a number of decades.

But in our century it is just in this sphere that fundamental changes have taken place in the basis of atomic physics which have made us abandon the world-view of ancient atomic philosophy. It has become clear that the desired objective reality of the elementary particles is too crude an over-simplification of what really happens, and that it must give way to very much more abstract conceptions. For if we wish to form a picture of the nature of these elementary particles, we can no longer ignore the physical processes through which we obtain our knowledge of them. While, in observing everyday objects, the physical process involved in making the observation plays a subsidiary role only, in the case of the smallest building particles of matter, every process of observation produces a large disturbance. We can no longer speak of the behaviour of the particle independently of the process of observation. As a final consequence, the natural laws formulated mathematically in quantum theory no longer deal with the elementary particles themselves but with our knowledge of them. Nor is it any longer possible to ask whether or not these particles exist in space and time objectively, since the only processes we can refer to as taking place are those which represent the interplay of particles with some other physical system, *e.g.*, a measuring instrument.

Thus, the objective reality of the elementary particles has been strangely dispersed, not into the fog of some new ill-defined or still unexplained conception of reality, but into the transparent clarity of a mathematics that no longer describes the behaviour of the elementary particles but only our knowledge of this behaviour. The atomic physicist has had to resign himself to the fact that his science is but a link in the infinite chain of man's argument with nature, *and that it cannot simply speak of nature 'in itself'*. Science always presupposes the existence of man and, as Bohr has said, we must become conscious of the fact that we are not merely observers but also actors on the stage of life. . . .

[W]e must not be misled into underestimating the firmness of the foundations of exact science. The concept of scientific truth, on which science is based, can apply to many different forms of knowledge. Thus, on it are based not only the sciences of the past centuries but modern atomic physics also, and this will make it clear why we can accept the fact that there are situations which no longer permit an objective understanding of natural processes, and yet use this realization to order our relationships with nature. When we speak of the picture of nature in the exact science of our age, we do not mean a picture of nature so much as a *picture of our relationships with nature*. The old division of the world into objective processes in space and time and the mind in which these processes are mirrored—in other words, the Cartesian difference between *res cogitans* and *res extensa*—is no longer a suitable starting point for our understanding of modern science. Science, we find, is now focused on the network of relationships between man and nature, on the framework which makes us as living beings dependent parts of nature, and which we as human beings have simultaneously made the object of our thoughts and actions. Science no longer confronts nature as an objective observer, but sees itself as an actor in this interplay between man and nature. The scientific method of analysing, explaining and classifying has become conscious of its limitations, which arise out of the fact that by its intervention science alters and refashions the object of investigation. In other words, method and object can no longer be separated. *The scientific world-view has ceased to be a scientific view in the true sense of the word*. . . .

The concept of causality

The use of the concept of causality for describing the law of cause and effect is of relatively recent origin. In previous philosophies the word *causa* had a very much more general significance than it has today. Thus scholasticism, following Aristotle, spoke of four kinds of 'causes': the *causa formalis* which might be considered as the form or the spiritual essence of a thing, the *causa materialis* which referred to the matter of which the thing consisted, the *causa finalis* or the purpose for which the thing was created, and finally, the *causa efficiens*. Only the *causa efficiens* corresponds to what is meant by the word 'cause' today.

The transformations of *causa* into the modern concept of cause have taken place in the course of centuries, in close connection with the changes in man's conception of reality and with the creation of science at the beginning of the modern age. As material processes became more prominent in man's conception of reality, the word *causa* was used increasingly to refer to the particular material event which preceded, and had in some way caused, the event to be explained. Thus even Kant, who frequently did what at root amounted to drawing philo-sophic consequences from the developments in science since Newton's time, already used the word 'causality' in a nineteenth-century sense. When we experience an event we always assume that there was another event preceding it from which the second has followed according to some law. Thus the concept of causality became narrowed down, finally, to refer to our belief that events in nature are uniquely determined, or, in other words, that an exact knowledge of nature or some part of it would suffice, at least in principle, to determine the future. Newton's physics was so constructed that the future motion of a system could be calculated from its particular state at a given time. The idea that nature really was like this was perhaps enunciated most generally and most lucidly by Laplace when he spoke of a demon, who at a given time, by knowing the position and motion of every atom, would be capable of predicting the entire future of the world. When the word 'causality' is interpreted in this very narrow sense, we speak of 'determinism', by which we mean that there are immutable natural laws that uniquely determine the future state of any system from its present state.

Statistical laws

From its very beginnings atomic physics evolved concepts which do not really fit this picture. True, they do not contradict it basically, but the approach of atomic physics was by its very character different from that of determinism. Even in the ancient atomic theory of Democritus and Leucippus it was assumed that large-scale processes were the results of many irregular processes on a small scale. That this is basically the case is illustrated by innumerable exam-ples in everyday life. Thus, a farmer need only know that a cloud has condensed and watered his fields. He does not bother about the path of each individual drop of rain. To give another example, we know precisely what is meant by the word 'granite', even when we are ignorant of the form, colour, and chemical composition of each small constituent crystal. Thus we always use concepts which describe behaviour on the large scale without in the least both-ering about the individual processes that take place on the small scale.

This notion of the statistical combination of many small individual events was already used in ancient atomic theory as the basis for an explanation of the world, and was general-ized in the concept that all the sensory qualities of matter were indirectly caused by the posi-tion and movements of the atoms. Thus Democritus wrote that things only *appeared* to be sweet or bitter, and only appeared to have colour, for in reality there existed only atoms and empty space. Now, if the processes which we can observe with our senses are thought to arise out of the interactions of many small individual processes, we must needs conclude that all natural laws may be considered to be only statistical laws. True, even statistical law can lead to statements with so high a degree of probability that they are almost certain, but there can always be exceptions in principle. The concept of statistical law is frequently thought to be contradictory. Thus it is contended that while it is possible to look upon natural processes either as determined by laws, or else as running their course without any order whatever, we cannot form any picture of processes obeying statistical laws.

Yet we must remind the reader that in everyday life all of us encounter statistical laws with every step we take, and make these laws the basis of our practical actions. Thus, when an engineer is constructing a dam he always bases his calculations on the average yearly rainfall, although he cannot have the faintest idea when it will rain and how much of it at a time. When speaking of statistical laws we generally mean that a particular physical system is known incompletely. The most common example is the throw of dice. Since no one side of a die is heavier than any other, and since it is thus impossible to predict which side will turn up, we can assume that in a large number of throws precisely one in six will turn up with five dots.

From the very beginning of modern times attempts have been made to explain both qualitatively and also quantitatively the behaviour of matter through the statistical behaviour of atoms. Robert Boyle demonstrated that we could understand the relations between the pressure and the volume of a gas if we looked upon pressure as the many thrusts of the individual atoms on the walls of the vessel. Similarly thermodynamical phenomena have been explained by the assumption that atoms move more violently in a hot body than in a cold one. This statement could be given a quantitative mathematical formulation and in this way the laws of heat could be understood.

This application of the concept of statistical laws was finally formulated in the second half of the last century as the so-called *statistical mechanics*. In this theory, which is based on Newton's mechanics, the consequences that spring from an incomplete knowledge of a complicated mechanical system are investigated. Thus in principle it is not a renunciation of determinism. While it is held that the details of events are fully determined according to the laws of Newton's mechanics, the condition is added that the mechanical properties of the *system* are not fully known.

Gibbs and Boltzmann managed to formulate this kind of incomplete knowledge mathematically, and Gibbs was able to demonstrate that, in particular, our conception of temperature is closely related to the incompleteness of our knowledge. When we know the temperature of a particular system, it means that the system must be considered to be only one out of a whole set of systems. This set of systems can be described accurately by mathematics, but not the particular system with which we are concerned. With this Gibbs had half-unconsciously taken a step which later on was to have the most important consequences. Gibbs was the first to introduce a physical concept which can only be applied to an object when our knowledge of the object is incomplete. If for instance the motion and position of each molecule in a gas were known, then it would be pointless to continue speaking of the temperature of the gas. The concept of temperature can only be used meaningfully when the system is not fully known and we wish to derive statistical conclusions from our incomplete knowledge.

The statistical character of quantum theory

Although the discoveries of Gibbs and Boltzmann made an incomplete knowledge of a system part of the formulation of physical laws, nevertheless determinism was still present in principle until Max Planck's famous discovery ushered in quantum theory. Planck, in his work on the theory of radiation, had originally encountered an element of uncertainty in radiation phenomena. He had shown that a radiating atom does not deliver up its energy continuously, but discretely in bundles. This assumption of a discontinuous and pulse-like transfer of energy, like every other notion of atomic theory, leads us once more to the idea that the emission of radiation is a statistical phenomenon. However, it took two and a half decades before it became clear *that quantum theory actually forces us to formulate these laws precisely as statistical laws* and to depart radically from determinism. Since the work of Einstein, Bohr and Sommerfeld, Planck's theory has proved to be the key with which the door to the entire sphere of atomic physics could be opened. Chemical processes could be explained by means of the Rutherford-Bohr atomic model, and since then, chemistry, physics and astrophysics have been fused into unity. With the mathematical formulation of quantum-theoretical laws pure determinism had to be abandoned.

Since I cannot speak of the mathematical methods here, I should merely like to mention some aspects of the strange situation confronting the physicist in atomic physics.

We can express the departure from previous forms of physics by means of the so-called uncertainty relations. It was discovered that it was impossible to describe simultaneously both the position and the velocity of an atomic particle with any prescribed degree of accuracy. We can either measure the position very accurately—when the action of the instrument used for the observation obscures our knowledge of the velocity, or we can make accurate measurements of the velocity and forego knowledge of the position. The product of the two uncertainties can never be less than Planck's constant. This formulation makes it quite clear that we cannot make much headway with the concepts of Newtonian mechanics, since in the calculation of a mechanical process it is essential to know simultaneously the position and velocity at a particular moment, and this is precisely what quantum theory considers to be impossible.

Another formulation is that of Niels Bohr, who introduced the *concept of complementarity*. By this he means that the different intuitive pictures which we use to describe atomic systems, although fully adequate for given experiments, are nevertheless mutually exclusive. Thus, for instance, the Bohr atom can be described as a small-scale planetary system, having a central atomic nucleus about which the external electrons revolve. For other experiments, however, it might be more convenient to imagine that the atomic nucleus is surrounded by a system of stationary waves whose frequency is characteristic of the radiation emanating from the atom. Finally, we can consider the atom chemically. We can calculate its heat of reaction when it becomes fused with other atoms, but in that case we cannot simultaneously describe the motion of the electrons. Each picture is legitimate when used in the right place, but the different pictures are contradictory and therefore we call them mutually complementary. The uncertainty that is attached to each of them is expressed by the uncertainty relation, which is sufficient for avoiding logical contradiction between the different pictures.

Even without entering into the mathematics of quantum theory these brief comments might have helped us to realize *that the incomplete knowledge of a system must be an essential part of every formulation in quantum theory*. Quantum theoretical laws must be of a statistical kind. To give an example: we know that the radium atom emits alpha-radiation. Quantum theory can give us an indication of the probability that the alpha-particle will leave the nucleus in unit time, but it cannot predict at what precise point in time the emission will occur, for this is uncertain in principle. We cannot even assume that new laws still to be discovered will allow us to determine this precise point in time; were this possible the alpha-particle could not also be considered to behave as a wave leaving the atomic nucleus, a fact which we can prove experimentally. The various experiments proving both the wave nature and also the particle nature of atomic matter create a paradox which forces us to devise a formulation of statistical laws.

In large-scale processes this statistical aspect of atomic physics does not arise, generally because statistical laws for large-scale processes lead to such high probabilities that to all intents and purposes we can speak of the processes as determined. Frequently, however, there arise cases in which a large-scale process depends on the behaviour of one or of a few atoms alone. In that case, the large-scale process also can only be predicted statistically. I should like to illustrate this by means of a well-known but unhappy example, that of the atom bomb. In an ordinary bomb the strength of the explosion can be predicted from the mass of the explosive material and its chemical composition. In the atom bomb we can still indicate an upper and a lower limit of the strength of the explosion but we cannot make exact calculations of this strength in advance. This is impossible in principle since it depends on the behaviour of only a few atoms at the moment of firing.

Similarly, there may be biological processes—and Jordan, especially, has drawn our attention to this—in which large-scale events are set off by processes in individual atoms; this would appear to be the case particularly in the mutation of genes during hereditary processes. These two examples were meant to illustrate the practical consequences of the statistical character of quantum theory. This development, too, was concluded over two decades ago, and we cannot possibly assume that the future will see any basic changes in this field.

PART IV

Politics and war

In 1917, in the midst of World War I, Albert Einstein denounced the schizophrenia in the West's use of its great material knowledge: "Our much vaunted progress in technology, generally of civilization, is like the axe in the hand of a pathological criminal." In 1932, hoping to forestall or prevent the next "great war," he proposed that, "if the workers of this world, men and women, decide not to manufacture and transport ammunition, it would stop war for all time."[1] But Einstein maintained his pacifist stance for only a little while longer: it ended with Hitler's rise to power in 1933 and the physicist's acknowledgment that an anti-war stance was unsustainable in the face of Nazi aggression, tyranny, and genocide.

The decades before 1914 were far from peaceful, though looking back through what was soon, and continues (in Europe), to be called the Great War, they may have come to seem so. There were numerous major conflicts with significant consequences in the years following the Napoleonic wars and the American Civil War. The Franco-Prussian War (1870–71) ended in France's total defeat and the unification of Germany, the downfall of Napoleon III, the transfer to Prussia of Alsace-Lorraine (which Germany retained until the Treaty of Versailles in 1919), and the Paris Commune uprising of 1871. In 1882 British troops occupied Cairo and seized control of the Suez Canal. In the Sino-Japanese War of 1894–95 Japan overwhelmed China and exacted heavy indemnities. The Spanish-American War (1898) resulted in temporary American control of Cuba and its indefinite colonial authority over Guam, Puerto Rico, and the Philippines. Britain fought the Boer War (1899–1902), in support of its citizens who were immigrants in the Transvaal (South Africa), against the Boer government run by Dutch settlers and supported by Germany; confronting successful guerrilla tactics, the British finally won only after they imprisoned Boer women and children under terrible conditions in what became the first concentration camps, where they died by the thousands. The Boxer Rebellion in China (1900) was harshly suppressed by European and Japanese troops. The Russo-Japanese War (1904–05), which resulted in a crushing defeat for Russia (the first ever of a European power – to the extent that Russia was one – by an Asian power), led to the abortive Russian revolution of 1905 and a peace conference, mediated by President Theodore Roosevelt, at which Japan gained significant influence in China and control of Korea (which it retained until 1945). In 1912 Italy defeated Turkey and seized control of its African holdings. The Balkan Wars of

1912–13 concerned shifting alliances and dominance. And throughout this period, the various powers jockeyed for position and allies, resulting in an intricate web of alliances and military commitments, so that when Archduke Franz Ferdinand, heir to the Austro-Hungarian Empire, was assassinated in Sarajevo on June 28, 1914 by the Black Hand, a secret Serbian nationalist society, the event led, as the treaty alliance system clicked into place like falling dominos, inexorably and tragically, to the outbreak of the Great War. On the battlefields of 1914–18, the deployment of such technology as tanks, machine guns, and poison gas produced what Ezra Pound called "wastage as never before."[2] Although there were opponents of it (among the most outspoken were members of the Bloomsbury Group, most notably perhaps Virginia Woolf and Lytton Strachey),[3] the War was largely welcomed by a generation of young men eager for adventure and to prove their manhood; it seemed likely to be such a lark that the common assumption was that it would be "over by Christmas" and the world would have a renewed and exhilarated sense of purpose. Rupert Brooke, in a poem paradoxically entitled "Peace" (1914), captured that exalted mood, thanking the deity for the outbreak of war that has aroused a people from lethargy. It begins, "Now, God be thanked who has matched us with His hour,/And caught our youth, and wakened us from sleeping." But the world was of course transformed in wholly unanticipated and largely undesired ways. In "Absolution" (1914), for example, Siegfried Sassoon wrote, "War is our scourge; yet war has made us wise,/And, fighting for our freedom, we are free," which expressed, as he later wrote in his autobiography, "the self-glorifying feelings of a young man about to go to the Front for the first time,"[4] but by 1917 his powerful statement denouncing the war, "Finished with the War: A Soldier's Declaration," was read out in the British House of Commons. (See Chapter 30 below.) Similarly, Rudyard Kipling, who was as chauvinistically pro-war and outspokenly anti-Germany as anyone, wrote very differently after his only son was killed in battle in 1915: "If any question why we died,/Tell them, because our fathers lied."[5]

For the first two years, the War was fought with volunteers, but their numbers eventually proved insufficient. Paul Fussell, who dates the beginning of modernism from Britain's institution of conscription in 1916, argues that, before the War, "The certainties were intact . . . the Great War was perhaps the last to be conceived as taking place within a seamless, purposeful 'history' involving a coherent stream of time running from past through present to future . . . where the values appeared stable and where the meanings of abstractions seemed permanent and reliable." The rupture, which was at first commonly misread as continuity or historically sanctioned change, was widely embraced in both Britain and Germany as likely to put an end to a complacent, stultifying culture and provide opportunities to sacrifice for, and achieve, a noble ideal. But it turned out that far more was at stake, and lost. For Fussell, the Great War was unique: "Every war is ironic because . . . worse than expected. . . . But the Great War was more ironic than any before or since. It was a hideous embarrassment to the prevailing Meliorist myth, which had dominated the public consciousness for a century. It reversed the idea of Progress."[6] With its estimated ten million deaths, the Great War not only destroyed a generation of young men, it inaugurated what Lawrence Langer calls "the age of atrocity," producing killing machines, fields, and graves that seemed to metastasize like cancer and make continuing mass death a central feature of Western civilization. In the first months of the War, the British, who brought over a million horses during its four years, attempted numerous cavalry charges, as if they were fighting the Crimean War again; but machine guns mowed the horses down as they did the men.

Thanks to the concept now known as "combat gnosticism,"[7] memoirs and semi-autobiographical literary works were generally assumed to represent war honestly and directly: for example, Erich Maria Remarque's novel *All Quiet on the Western Front* (1928), which depicts the terrible physical and mental suffering of German soldiers and was consequently banned and burned in Nazi Germany, and Frederic Manning's *The Middle Parts of Fortune*

(1929), which the author calls "a record of experience on the Somme and Ancre fronts . . . during the latter half of the year 1916 . . . the events described in it actually happened; the characters are fictitious." War plays out as both personal and macroscopic tragedy in R.C. Sheriff's play *Journey's End* (1928), which represents four days in the lives of British army officers in February 1918 and ends with the obliteration of a soldier by a mortar shell, and in Ernest Hemingway's *A Farewell to Arms* (1929), in which Lieutenant Henry and a British nurse, Catherine Barkley, try, and fail, to make a separate peace by fleeing the war. Many other works depict the world the soldiers left behind, the one that sent adolescent males off to the Great War, from which they often disappeared, leaving no trace of a body to bury or mourn. They were, instead, blown to bits (like Andrew Ramsay in Virginia Woolf's *To the Lighthouse* and O'Nine Morgan in Ford Madox Ford's *Parade's End*) or just inexplicably gone (like Jacob in Woolf's *Jacob's Room* and Adam in Katherine Anne Porter's *Pale Horse, Pale Rider*, though Adam dies from the great influenza pandemic of 1918–19 rather than in the War). Many of those who did return – to a world changed by their absence and the intervening experiences – came back shell-shocked, maimed physically or psychologically, or both, often with symptoms that had, before the war, been associated solely with female ailments; as a result the Victorian belief that hysteria was a consequence of possessing a womb could no longer be sustained, and modern medicine had to adjust its thinking. Having gone off to "become men," those who returned became the unmanned, sexually dysfunctional anti-heroes of modern literature: impotent Jake Barnes in Hemingway's *The Sun Also Rises*; shell-shocked and suicidal Septimus Smith in Woolf's *Mrs. Dalloway*; catatonic Lieutenant Donald Mahon in William Faulkner's *Soldier's Pay*; paralyzed Mark Tietjens in Ford's *Parade's End*, Clifford Chatterley in D.H. Lawrence's *Lady Chatterley's Lover*, and Joe Bonham in Dalton Trumbo's *Johnny Got His Gun* (astonishingly and grotesquely, Bonham somehow retains his mental capacity despite his loss of arms, legs, and face). It is unsurprising that sex and impotence (along with death and maiming) are interwoven themes in many of these works, for, as Fussell notes, the vocabulary of love and war is a shared one: "The language of military attack – assault, impact, thrust, penetration – has always overlapped with that of sexual importunity."[8]

Modernist literature commonly represents the era's conflicts with bodies, minds, and communities laid to waste or fractured and traumatized; landscapes are haunted by memories of loss and the inescapable realities of the costs of warfare, colliding worldviews, and violent conflict. Joseph Conrad has Stevie, unwittingly serving an anarchist plot, blown to bits in the pre-war industrialized London of *The Secret Agent* (1907), while cuckoldry and sexual incompetence largely define non-combatants such as Dowell in Ford's *The Good Soldier*, Eliot's Fisher King in *The Waste Land*, and Leopold Bloom in Joyce's *Ulysses*. Numerous other characters are said to die simply by disappearing – Mrs. Wilcox in E.M. Forster's *Howards End* and Mrs. Moore in his *A Passage to India*, Mrs. Ramsay in *To the Lighthouse*, Henry Bon in *Absalom! Absalom!* – while Joyce's deaths mostly occur outside his fictional confines (Parnell in "Ivy Day in the Committee Room"; Michael Furey in "The Dead"; Paddy Dignam, Rudy Bloom, and May Daedalus in *Ulysses*), but then, and perhaps rather surprisingly given the materiality of the modernist age, the deceased appear or are invoked as ghostly presences, revenants.

Combatant writers like Wilfred Owen, Siegfried Sassoon, Robert Graves, and David Jones were themselves revenants of a sort, embodying and depicting deathly experiences that the world mostly wanted to forget, and they did so by writing in a way that put them at odds with mainstream modernism, which, from the 1890s or so, had been creating an avant-garde aesthetic and cultural orientation that the war may have interrupted, but which resumed with greater intensity at its conclusion. As Samuel Hynes argues in *A War Imagined*, the war writers depicted and propounded both the history and the myth of the Great War, viewing it as representing a radical disjunction with progressive and meliorist views that had dominated the culture prior to its occurrence. Non-combatants often did what combatants could not: construct literary forms and techniques in reaction not only to the War but also to the chauvinistic rhetoric that produced and supported it. Some writers – like Ford in *The Good Soldier*, Lawrence in *Women in Love*, Forster in *Maurice*, and Joyce in *Ulysses* – wrote through and after the War about the time before it, re-imagining the world before it had gone off its tracks and into the trenches that they themselves had not experienced. In contrast, Katherine Mansfield imagines a father in her story "The Fly" who, representing the generation that sent men off to die in the war and unable to mourn his dead soldier son, replicates the conditions of his son's death in the muck of the trenches by, first, rescuing a fly that has fallen into his ink pot, and then sadistically killing it.

Writers like Mulk Raj Anand and C.L.R. James commemorated the war sacrifices made by men who were not themselves free and whose military efforts in the European wars were often omitted from the official histories of the conflicts. Anand's political trilogy and *Bildungsroman* follows Lai Sing from his upbringing as a boy from a village in the Punjab (*The Village*, 1939) and to his experiences as a sepoy on the battlefields of Flanders during the Great War (*Across the Black Waters*, 1940). The final volume of the trilogy, *The Sword and the Sickle* (1942), represents Sing's revolution in consciousness and his radicalized political worldview. As C.L.R. James makes clear with the pen name he borrowed from Richard Wright's recently published novel and selected for his 1940 political pamphlet, for "Native Sons" (and daughters) who were not yet full or equal citizens, the questions of patriotism, just causes, and national sacrifice continued to throw into high relief the limits of democratic affiliations during World War II. For many oppressed peoples, the injustices of the West and the contradictions of civilization legitimized the continuing relevance of Marxist, socialist, and communist oppositional beliefs and communal ideals, even in light of Stalinist atrocities. Gandhi was rumored to have remarked sardonically when asked what he thought of Western civilization, "I think it is a good idea." The century's legacy of war, civil and international conflict, would lead artists and thinkers to examine man's continuing cycles of destruction, the dark impulses obscured by ideals of civilization and social progress and made even more dreadful with the technological "advances" of modern warfare.

Writing in the aftermath of the "terrible war which has just ended,"[9] Sigmund Freud tried to reconcile the life-affirming "pleasure principle" with what he theorized as the "death instinct," both of which he viewed as equally fundamental to the "vacillating rhythm" of human life.[10] Freud, who had shared the optimistic vision that characterized Europe's middle class in the years leading up to the destructive event itself, proposed the repression theory – in which violent, primitive instincts remain under constraint as we enter society, but are always capable of bursting forth uncontrollably – as a way to explain the underlying mechanism of Western civilization's tragedy. And yet he joined with Einstein, who also believed that aggression had a biological basis, shortly after Hitler's accession to power in 1933 in a fruitless attempt to resuscitate a meliorist view of history. Maintaining that organic reasons oblige us to be pacifists who "have a constitutional intolerance of war," Freud prophesied "an end to the waging of war. By what paths or by what side-tracks this will come about we cannot guess. But one thing we can say: whatever fosters the growth of civilization works . . . against war."[11] Unfortunately this vision proved as invalid as the optimism that predominated before the Great War.

Ideological wars on the home front and in colonial territories created unrest and heightened anxieties about the maintenance of civil order and governmental status quo. Increasingly fractious and resistant activists, journalists, philosophers, and cultural theorists were questioning established systems of social and economic power and debating the legitimacy of capitalism and colonialism. In turn, socialists, communists, labor activists, and anarchists were targeted by state leaders and colonial administrators as "enemies within"; the growing threats of leftist political ideologies were viewed as viruses threatening the body politic, ones that needed to be repressed, often violently. In Europe, communists and socialists like Antonio Gramsci and Rosa Luxemburg were imprisoned for their leftist journalism and revolutionary political activities. Luxemburg continued to examine the possibilities of a communist society while writing in her diary and composing letters from her prison cell; she remained a committed agitator, although she also foresaw the dangers of ideological rigidity. Her essay "The Russian Revolution" sounds a cautionary alarm about the dangers of Bolshevik dictatorship that would soon become recognized as the realities of the Stalin regime. But Luxemburg was captured and murdered in 1919 by the armed forces of Germany's Social Democrats, the forerunners of Hitler's storm troopers. Gramsci, who had been arrested in 1926 under "emergency laws" imposed by Benito Mussolini's fascist government, gained a conditional release from prison due to his rapidly declining health in 1934; he died three years later.

In India, "emergency measures" like the British colonial administration's March 1919 Rowlatt Acts were designed to suppress anti-colonial protests and the growing political power of opposition parties like the Indian National Congress as well as communist and socialist anti-imperialist organizations. The Rowlatt Acts censored Indian publications and repressed freedom of movement and association; they also allowed the colonial administration to imprison political agitators and "terrorists" for up to two years without trial. Mohandas Gandhi and others organized peaceful "*hartals*" – strikes – to protest the injustices of the Rowlatt Acts; for Gandhi "satyagraha" – truth-force, passive resistance – was envisioned as the form of protest that could reveal the grotesque injustices of colonial domination. In the Punjab on April 13, 1919, British soldiers opened fire on peacefully protesting and unarmed Indian men, women, and children in what came to be known as the Jallianwala Bagh or Amritsar Massacre, thus unveiling the true nature of Britain's colonial mission.

The influences of Marxist and fascist theories interwove these social and political conflicts with what could be called the post- and interwar periods' culture wars, ones that would inspire expressions of refusal like dadaism and the vorticists' 1914 "*Blast* Manifesto," and which continued to appeal to revolutionary, class-rebellious young poets in the 1930s. Marx's base/superstructure analysis of capitalism influenced Gramsci's theory of political hegemony; he argued that capitalist societies maintained their social and economic power by means of bourgeois values. The social institutions and cultural products of capitalism – the church, the family, the military and state, educational institutions, as well as conventional, socially sanctioned literature and arts – celebrated and upheld the interests of the capitalist economic system; they made capitalist ideology common sense. Some artists accepted this politicized view of culture, as is evident in Lu Xun's belief that all art is propaganda and Sergei Eisenstein's theory of montage, which asserts that all forms of artistic production are based on conflict.

In England, the 1926 General Strike galvanized a generation, many of them Oxford-educated (including W.H. Auden, Stephen Spender, Cecil Day Lewis, and Louis MacNeice), but also many who were not (including Sean O'Casey, Hugh MacDiarmid, and Sorely Maclean), to write committed poetry in support of the political left. Virginia Woolf argued with these poets about their radical view of artistic creation and consumption in her "Letter to a Young Poet" (1932), and her "The Leaning Tower" (1940) essay would warn its original audience at Brighton's Workers' Educational Association about the dangers of revolutionary theories of culture. Woolf, a committed pacifist even in the run-up to World War II, insisted that literature maintained its power to unite readers and create what she called "common ground."

Others besides Woolf had opposed the War, including Julian Bell, her nephew, who compiled the collection *We Did Not Fight: 1914–18 Experiences of War Resisters*. The collection includes pieces by, among others, Woolf's brother Adrian Stephen, the suffragette and Irish nationalist Hanna Sheehy-Skeffington, the writer and publisher David Garnett, and the great philosopher and mathematician Bertrand Russell. Their efforts had little impact on the war effort itself, but they remained a force, perhaps culminating in "The Kellogg–Briand Pact" (1928) that sought to outlaw war. The Pact, of course, failed to accomplish its main goal, but it did succeed in making war a crime. (See Chapter 31 below.)

The Great War and its consequences – including the punitive Treaty of Versailles, the founding of the League of Nations and the U.S. refusal to join it, the establishment of the shaky and ill-fated Weimar Republic in Germany – cast a large shadow over a world that ineffectually mourned and inadequately understood it. Paul Fussell maintains that the "whole texture of British daily life" in the 1920s and 1930s "could be said to commemorate the war still," and that World War II and its literature self-consciously repeated events during and after the earlier war. He writes that "The way the data and usages of the Second War behave as if 'thinking in terms of' the First is enough almost to make one believe in a single continuing Great War running through the whole middle of the twentieth century."[12] As Fussell sees it, the Great War's casualties included patriotic rhetoric, what he calls the "system of 'high' diction." In 1908 Conrad could write unironically: "you cannot fail to see the power of mere words; such words as Glory, for instance, or Pity. . . . Shouted with perseverance, with ardour, with conviction, these two by their sound alone have set whole nations in motion and upheaved the dry, hard ground on which rests our whole social fabric. . . . Give me the right word and the right accent and I will move the world."[13] For Hemingway, like Fussell, the war debased such rhetoric: "There were many words that you could not stand to hear and finally only the names of places had dignity. . . . Abstract words such as glory, honor, courage, or hallow were obscene beside the concrete names of villages, the numbers of roads, the names of rivers, the numbers of regiments and the dates."[14] Ford's *The Good Soldier* (1915), a novel set before (but written in the early days of) the Great War, enacts this linguistic transformation. Ford's obtuse narrator, John Dowell, unintentionally caricatures the virile Edward Ashburnham who has apparently cuckolded him and whom he absurdly projects as his alter ego and eponymous hero: "For all good soldiers are sentimentalists – all good soldiers of that type. Their profession, for one thing, is full of the big words – 'courage,' 'loyalty,' 'honor,' 'constancy.' "[15] And yet William Faulkner, a writer who tried to participate in the war but got only as far as Canada, could in his 1950 Nobel Prize acceptance speech still unironically extol "the old verities and truths of the heart . . . the courage and honor and hope and pride and compassion and pity and sacrifice which have been the glory of [man's] past."[16] By World War II, the vast propaganda machines mobilized by mass media would make this crisis of rhetoric even more acute. Hitler's writing and, to a greater extent, his speeches relied on perverse versions of such "verities." The Nazi propaganda machine orchestrated by Joseph Goebbels was perceived as accomplishing a hitherto unknown scale of mass persuasion that Kenneth Burke's essay "The Rhetoric of Hitler's Battle" (Chapter 32) analyzes with deep foreboding, warning that America was not immune to the efficacy of fascist propaganda.

For some, the vast scale of man-made death is "the central moral as well as material fact of our time": the twentieth century, a "century of death," was distinguished, simultaneously, by a public commitment "to the preservation and care of life," but also to the replacement of disease and plague – which (despite the occasional flu epidemics, prior to AIDS and the return of tuberculosis) seemed increasingly under control – by mass slaughter. The apparent paradox results from the fact "that one area of public death has been tackled and secured by the forces of reason; the other has not."[17] Michel Foucault writes that, "For millennia, man remained what he was for Aristotle: a living animal with the additional capacity for a political existence; modern man is an animal whose politics places his existence . . . in question."[18] For the thanatologist Edwin Shneidman the twentieth was our "oxymoronic century": great efforts were expended in saving individual lives and improving mortality, at least for the well off, Caucasian, and Western. Yet "brutish wars, deliberate famines, planned starvations, police and government execution" have wiped out vast populations[19] – estimated to number

150–200 million. To the extent that modernism supported policies, principles, and actions that played a part in such policies and practices it has much to answer for. The Foundational Readings in Part IV of this volume offer a range of attitudes toward warfare and its consequences in the run-up to modernism.

Notes

1   Quoted in Clark, *Einstein* 370.
2   Pound, "E.P. Ode pour l'election de son sepulchre."
3   See Bell, *We Did Not Fight.*
4   Sassoon, *Siegfried's Journey* 17.
5   Kipling, "Common Form" (1918).
6   Fussell, *The Great War* 270. See Hays *The Limping Hero* for a full discussion of emasculated modern heroes and Sarah Cole's *Modernism, Male Friendship, and the First World War* for its treatment of the War and male intimacy.
7   See Campbell, "Combat Gnosticism."
8   Fussell, *The Great War* 270.
9   Freud, "Beyond the Pleasure Principle" 12.
10   Freud, "Beyond the Pleasure Principle" 41.
11   Freud and Einstein, "Why War?" 214–15.
12   Fussell, *The Great War* 315–26.
13   Conrad, *Personal Record* 6.
14   Hemingway, *Farewell to Arms* 185.
15   Ford, *The Good Soldier* 26–27.
16   Faulkner, "Address upon Receiving the Nobel Prize for Literature" (10 December 1950), in *The Portable Faulkner* 723–24.
17   Elliot, *Book of the Dead* 6–10.
18   Foucault, *History of Sexuality* 143.
19   Shneidman, *Death: Current Perspectives* 2.

Suggested further readings

Bagnold, Enid. *Diary without Dates*. London: Heinemann, 1918.
Bell, Julian, ed. *We Did Not Fight: 1914–18 Experiences of War Resisters*. London: Cobden-Sanderson, 1935.
Bergonzi, Bernard. *Heroes' Twilight: A Study of the Literature of the Great War*. London: Constable, 1965.
Booth, Allyson. *Postcards from the Trenches*. New York: Oxford UP, 1996.
Brecht, Bertolt. "Epitaph" (1919). *Bertolt Brecht: Poems, 1913–1956*. Ed. John Willett, Ralph Manheim, and Erich Fried. New York: Methuen, 1979.
Brittain, Vera. *Testament of Youth*. London: V. Gollancz, 1933.
Brooke, Rupert. "Peace" (1914), "The Soldier" (1914). *The Collected Poems of Rupert Brooke*, 3rd edn. London: Sidgwick and Jackson, 1942.
Campbell, James. "Combat Gnosticism: The Ideology of First World War Poetry Criticism." *New Literary History* 30.1 (Winter 1999): 203–15.
Celine, Louis-Ferdinand. *Journey to the End of the Night*. Boston: Little, Brown, 1934.
Clark, Ronald W. *Einstein: The Life and Times*. New York: World, 1971.
Cole, Sarah. *Modernism, Male Friendship, and the First World War*. Cambridge: Cambridge UP, 2003.
Conrad, Joseph. *A Personal Record* (1908–9). London: Thomas Nelson, 1912.
Cunard, Nancy, ed. *Authors Take Sides on the Spanish War*. London: Left Review, 1937.
Elliot, Gil. *Twentieth Century Book of the Dead*. London: Allen Lane, 1972.
Faulkner, William. *Soldier's Pay* (1926). New York: Signet, 1968.
——. *The Portable Faulkner*. Ed. Malcolm Cowley. New York: Viking, 1946.

Ford, Ford Madox. *Parade's End* (1924–28). New York: Knopf, 1961.

——. *The Good Soldier* (1915). New York: Vintage, 1955.

Foucault, Michel. *The History of Sexuality*, Vol. 1 (1976). Trans. Robert Hurley. New York: Vintage, 1980.

Freud, Sigmund. "Beyond the Pleasure Principle" (1920). *The Standard Edition of the Complete Psychological Works of Sigmund Freud (1886–1939)*, vol. 18, 7–64. Ed. and trans. James Strachey. London: Hogarth and the Institute of Psycho-Analysis, 1964.

——. "Thoughts for the Times on War and Death" (1915). *The Standard Edition of the Complete Psychological Works of Sigmund Freud (1886–1939)*, vol. 14, 273–300. Ed. and trans. James Strachey. London: Hogarth and the Institute of Psycho-Analysis, 1964.

Freud, Sigmund, and Albert Einstein. "Why War?" (1933). *The Standard Edition of the Complete Psychological Works of Sigmund Freud (1886–1939)*, vol. 22, 197–215. Ed. and trans. James Strachey. London: Hogarth and the Institute of Psycho-Analysis, 1964.

Friedrich, Ernst. *Krieg dem Krieg! (War against War!)* (1924). Seattle: Real Comet Press, 1987.

Fussell, Paul. *The Great War and Modern Memory* (1975). New York: Oxford UP, 1977.

Gilbert, Sandra M., and Susan Gubar. *No Man's Land: The Place of the Woman Writer in the Twentieth Century*. 3 vols. New Haven: Yale UP, 1988–94.

Goldman, Emma. "Anarchism: What It Stands For" (1916?). *Red Emma Speaks: Selected Writings and Speeches*. New York: Random, 1972. 61–77.

Gramsci, Antonio. "Utopia." *Avanti!* (25 July 1918). In *Gramsci Reader*. New York: New York UP, 2000.

Graves, Robert. *Good-bye to All That: An Autobiography* (1929). New York: Cape and Smith, 1930.

——. *Contemporary Techniques of Poetry*. London: Hogarth Press, 1925.

Hardy, Thomas. "Drummer Hodge" (1899); "Channel Firing" (1914). *The Complete Poems of Thomas Hardy*, ed. James Gibson. London: Macmillan, 1979.

Hays, Peter. *The Limping Hero: Grotesques in Literature*. New York: New York UP, 1971.

Hemingway, Ernest. *The Sun Also Rises* (1926). New York: Scribner's, 1987.

——. *A Farewell to Arms* (1929). New York: Scribner's, 1969.

——. *For Whom the Bell Tolls*. New York: Scribner's, 1940.

Hynes, Samuel. *A War Imagined: The First World War and English Culture*. New York: Atheneum, Maxwell Macmillan International, 1991.

Jones, David. *In Parenthesis*. London: Faber and Faber, 1937.

Kipling, Rudyard. "Common Form" (1918); "Recessional" (1897); "The White Man's Burden" (1899). *The Collected Poems of Rudyard Kipling*. Ware, Hertfordshire: Wordsworth Poetry Library, 1994.

Klein, Holger, ed. *The First World War in Literature*. London: Macmillan, 1976.

Langer, Lawrence L. *The Age of Atrocity: Death in Modern Literature*. Boston: Beacon, 1978.

Lawrence, D.H. *Women in Love* (1920). Ed. David Farmer. Cambridge: Cambridge UP, 1991.

——. *Lady Chatterley's Lover* (1928). New York: Modern, 1983.

Lenin, Vladimir. "Imperialism as a Special Stage of Capitalism." *Imperialism, the Highest Stage of Capitalism* (1916). Australia: Resistance Books, 1999. 91–9.

Lewis, C. Day. *Revolution in Writing*, Day-to-Day Pamphlet No. 29. London: Hogarth Press, 1935.

Mussolini, Benito. *The Political and Social Doctrine of Fascism*. London: Hogarth Press Day-to-Day Pamphlet (1933).

Owen, Wilfred. "Anthem for Doomed Youth" (1917); "Dulce et Decorum Est" (1917–18). *The Collected Poems of Wilfred Owen*. London: Chatto & Windus, 1963. 44, 55.

Peppis, Paul. *In Literature, Politics, and the English Avant-garde: Nation and Empire, 1901–1918*. Cambridge and New York: Cambridge UP, 2000.

Porter, Katherine Anne. *Pale Horse, Pale Rider* (1939). New York: NAL, 1967.

Pound, Ezra. "E.P. Ode pour l'election de son sepulchre," *Hugh Selwyn Mauberley*. London: Ovid Press, 1920.

Remarque, Erich Maria. *All Quiet on the Western Front* (1929). New York: Continuum, 2004.

Russell, Bertrand, and Ralph Barton Perry. *The Ethics of War*. New York: Garland, 1972.

Sassoon, Siegfried. *Memoirs of an Infantry Officer* (1930). London: Faber and Faber, 1995.

——. *Siegfried's Journey, 1916–20*. London, New York, White Lion, 1973.

Sherriff, R.C. *Journey's End: A Play in Three Acts* (1928). New York: Coward-McCann, 1940.

Sherry, Vincent. *The Great War and the Language of Modernism*. Oxford and New York: Oxford UP, 2003.

Shneidman, Edwin, ed. *Death: Current Perspectives* (1976, 1980). 3rd edn, Palo Alto: Mayfield, 1984.

Smith, Angela. *The Second Battlefield: Women, Modernism, and the First World War*. New York: Manchester UP, 2000.

Smith, Helen Zenna (Evadne Price). *Not So Quiet . . . Stepdaughters of War* (1930). New York: the Feminist Press, 1989.

Tate, Trudi. *Modernism, History, and the First World War* (1988). Manchester: Manchester UP, 1998.

Tratner, Michael. *Modernism and Mass Politics: Joyce, Woolf, Eliot, Yeats*. Stanford: Stanford UP, 1995.

Trumbo, Dalton. *Johnny Got His Gun* (1939). New York: Bantam, 1982.

Woolf, Virginia. *"Jacob's Room" and "The Waves"* (1922, 1931). New York: Harcourt, 1959.

——. *To the Lighthouse* (1927). New York: Harcourt, 1955.

——. *Mrs. Dalloway* (1925). New York: Harcourt, 1953.

——. "Thunder at Wembley" (1924). *The Captain's Deathbed and Other Essays*. London, Hogarth, 1950. 223–27.

——. "Thoughts on Peace in an Air Raid" (1940). *The Death of the Moth and Other Essays*. New York, Harcourt, Brace, 1942. 243–48.

Chapter 24

Friedrich Nietzsche (1844–1900)

"APHORISM #477," *HUMAN, ALL TOO HUMAN: A BOOK FOR FREE SPIRITS* (1878)

A GERMAN PHILOSOPHER, FRIEDRICH NIETZSCHE viewed Christianity and its attendant morality as death-oriented since it deemed this world as merely a stage in our journey to eternity in the next. He espoused the enhancement of individuals and cultural health, and affirmed life, creativity, power, and the reality of this world. Nietzsche's Aphorism exemplifies the common pre-war attitude that military conflict is cleansing, ennobling, and necessary for the health and vitality of mankind, for "Culture can in no way do without passions, vices, and acts of wickedness."

Friedrich Nietzsche, "Aphorism #477," *Human, All Too Human: A Book for Free Spirits, Vol. 1* Trans. R.J. Hollingdale. Cambridge: Cambridge UP, Reprint, 2005. 176.

War indispensable.—It is vain reverie and beautiful-soulism to expect much more (let alone only then to expect much) of mankind when it has unlearned how to wage war. For the present we know of no other means by which that rude energy that characterizes the camp, that profound impersonal hatred, that murderous coldbloodedness with a good conscience, that common fire in the destruction of the enemy, that proud indifference to great losses, to one's own existence and that of one's friends, that inarticulate, earthquake-like shuddering of the soul, could be communicated more surely or strongly than every great war communicates them: the streams and currents that here break forth, though they carry with them rocks and rubbish of every kind and ruin the pastures of tenderer cultures, will later under favourable circumstances turn the wheels in the workshops of the spirit with newfound energy. Culture can in no way do without passions, vices and acts of wickedness.

When the Romans of the imperial era had grown a little tired of war they tried to gain new energy through animal-baiting, gladiatorial combats and the persecution of Christians. Present-day Englishmen, who seem also on the whole to have renounced war, seize on a different means of again engendering their fading energies: those perilous journeys of discovery, navigations, mountain-climbings, undertaken for scientific ends as they claim, in truth so as to bring home with them superfluous energy acquired through adventures and perils of all kinds. One will be able to discover many other such surrogates for war, but they will perhaps increasingly reveal that so highly cultivated and for that reason necessary feeble humanity as that of the present-day European requires not merely war but the greatest and most terrible wars—thus a temporary relapse into barbarism—if the means to culture are not to deprive them of their culture and of their existence itself.

Chapter 25

J.A. Hobson (1858–1940)

"NATIONALISM AND IMPERIALISM," *IMPERIALISM: A STUDY* (1902)

FOR JOHN ATKINSON HOBSON, *laissez-faire*, the prevailing political and philosophical doctrine of Victorian England, was ill-equipped to address the problems of widespread poverty and inadequate education, as well as poor housing, health, and working conditions. He sought to improve social conditions through the work of progressive societies, journalism, and political campaigning. Comparing the workings of society to a biological organism, he viewed the health of the whole as dependent on the health of the parts. For him, the creation of "large strong national unities" in Europe "was the most definite achievement of the nineteenth century," but he hoped that nationalism was only a step on the way toward internationalism, while fearing that it would, instead, lead to its perversion: imperialism and political antagonism, as in the "scramble for Africa and Asia, . . . a retrograde step fraught with grave perils to the cause of civilization."

J.A. Hobson, "Nationalism and Imperialism," *Imperialism: A Study*. London: George Allen and Unwin, 1902. 3–13.

Amid the welter of vague political abstractions to lay one's finger accurately upon any "ism" so as to pin it down and mark it out by definition seems impossible. Where meanings shift so quickly and so subtly, not only following changes of thought, but often manipulated artificially by political practitioners so as to obscure, expand, or distort, it is idle to demand the same rigour as is expected in the exact sciences. A certain broad consistency in its relations to other kindred terms is the nearest approach to definition which such a term as Imperialism admits. Nationalism, internationalism, colonialism, its three closest congeners, are equally elusive, equally shifty, and the changeful, overlapping of all four demands the closest vigilance of students of modern politics.

During the nineteenth century the struggle towards nationalism, or establishment of political union on a basis of nationality, was a dominant factor alike in dynastic movements and as an inner motive in the life of masses of population. That struggle, in external politics, sometimes took a disruptive form, as in the case of Greece, Servia, Roumania, and Bulgaria breaking from Ottoman rule, and the detachment of North Italy from her unnatural alliance with the Austrian Empire. In other cases it was a unifying or a centralising force, enlarging the area of nationality, as in the case of Italy and the Pan-Slavist movement in Russia. Sometimes nationality was taken as a basis of federation of States, as in United Germany and in North America.

It is true that the forces making for political union sometimes went further, making for federal union of diverse nationalities, as in the cases of Austria-Hungary, Norway and Sweden, and the Swiss Federation. But the general tendency was towards welding into large strong national unities the loosely related States and provinces with shifting attachments and alliances which covered large areas of Europe since the break-up of the Empire. This was the most definite achievement of the nineteenth century. The force of nationality, operating in this work, is quite as visible in the failures to achieve political freedom as in the successes; and the struggles of Irish, Poles, Finns, Hungarians, and Czechs to resist the forcible subjection to or alliance with stronger neighbours brought out in its full vigour the powerful sentiment of nationality.

The middle of the century was especially distinguished by a series of definitely "nationalist" revivals, some of which found important interpretation in dynastic changes, while others were crushed, or collapsed. Holland, Poland, Belgium, Norway, the Balkans, formed a vast arena for these struggles of national forces.

The close of the third quarter of the century saw Europe fairly settled into large national States or federations of States, though in the nature of the case there can be no finality, and Italy continued to look to Trieste, as Germany still looks to Austria, for the fulfilment of her manifest destiny.

This passion and the dynastic forms it helped to mould and animate are largely attributable to the fierce prolonged resistance which peoples, both great and small, were called on to maintain against the imperial designs of Napoleon. The national spirit of England was roused by the tenseness of the struggle to a self-consciousness it had never experienced since "the spacious days of great Elizabeth." Jena made Prussia into a great nation; the Moscow campaign brought Russia into the field of European nationalities as a factor in politics, opening her for the first time to the full tide of Western ideas and influences.

Turning from this territorial and dynastic nationalism to the spirit of racial, linguistic, and economic solidarity which has been the underlying motive, we find a still more remarkable movement. Local particularism on the one hand, vague cosmopolitanism upon the other, yielded to a ferment of nationalist sentiment, manifesting itself among the weaker peoples not merely in a sturdy and heroic resistance against political absorption or territorial nationalism, but in a passionate revival of decaying customs, language, literature and art; while it bred in more dominant peoples strange ambitions of national "destiny" and an attendant spirit of Chauvinism.

The true nature and limits of nationality have never been better stated than by J. S. Mill.

"A portion of mankind may be said to constitute a nation if they are united among themselves by common sympathies which do not exist between them and others. This feeling of nationality may have been generated by various causes. Sometimes it is the effect of identity of race and descent. Community of language and community of religion greatly contribute to it. Geographical limits are one of the causes. But the strongest of all is identity of political antecedents, the possession of a national history and consequent community of recollections, collective pride and humiliation, pleasure and regret, connected with the same incidents in the past."[1]

It is a debasement of this genuine nationalism, by attempts to overflow its natural banks and absorb the near or distant territory of reluctant and unassimilable peoples, that marks the passage from nationalism to a spurious colonialism on the one hand, Imperialism on the other.

Colonialism, where it consists in the migration of part of a nation to vacant or sparsely peopled foreign lands, the emigrants carrying with them full rights of citizenship in the mother country, or else establishing local self-government in close conformity with her institutions and under her final control, may be considered a genuine expansion of nationality, a territorial enlargement of the stock, language and institutions of the nation. Few colonies in history have, however, long remained in this condition when they have been remote from the mother country. Either they have severed the connexion and set up for themselves as separate nationalities, or they have been kept in complete political bondage so far as all major processes of government are concerned, a condition to which the term Imperialism is at least as appropriate as colonialism. The only form of distant colony which can be regarded as a clear expansion of nationalism is the self-governing British colony in Australasia and Canada, and even in these cases local conditions may generate a separate nationalism based on a strong consolidation of colonial interests and sentiments alien from and conflicting with those of the mother nation. In other "self-governing" colonies, as in Cape Colony and Natal, where the majority of whites are not descended from British settlers, and where the presence of subject or "inferior" races in vastly preponderating numbers, and alien climatic and other natural conditions, mark out a civilization distinct from that of the "mother country," the conflict between the colonial and the imperial ideas has long been present in the forefront of the consciousness of politicians. When Lord Rosmead spoke of the permanent presence of the imperial factor as "simply an absurdity," and Mr. Rhodes spoke of its "elimination," they were championing a "colonialism" which is more certain in the course of time to develop by inner growth into a separate "nationalism" than in the case of the Australasian and Canadian colonies, because of the wider divergence, alike of interests and radical conditions of life, from the mother nation. Our other colonies are plainly representative of the spirit of Imperialism rather than of colonialism. No considerable proportion of the population consists of British settlers living with their families in conformity with the social and political customs and laws of their native land: in most instances, they form a small minority wielding political or economic sway over a majority of alien and subject people, themselves under the despotic political control of the Imperial Government or its local nominees. This, the normal condition of a British colony, was well-nigh universal in the colonies of other European countries. The "colonies" which France and Germany established in Africa and Asia were in no real sense plantations of French and German national life beyond the seas; nowhere, not even in Algeria, did they represent true European civilization; their political and economic structure of society is wholly alien from that of the mother country.

Colonialism, in its best sense, is a natural overflow of nationality; its test is the power of colonists to transplant the civilization they represent to the new natural and social environment in which they find themselves. We must not be misled by names; the "colonial" party in Germany and France is identical in general aim and method with the "imperialist" party in England, and the latter is the truer title. Professor Seeley well marked the nature of Imperialism. "When a State advances beyond the limits of nationality its power becomes precarious and artificial. This is the condition of most empires, and it is the condition of our own. When a nation extends itself into other territories the chances are that it cannot destroy or completely drive out, even if it succeeds in conquering, them. When this happens it has a great and permanent difficulty to contend with, for the subject or rival nationalities cannot be properly assimilated, and remain as a permanent cause of weakness and danger."[2]

The novelty of recent Imperialism regarded as a policy consists chiefly in its adoption by several nations. The notion of a number of competing empires is essentially modern. The root idea of empire in the ancient and mediæval world was that of a federation of States, under a hegemony, covering in general terms the entire known recognized world, such as was held by Rome under the so-called *pax Romana*. When Roman citizens, with full civic rights, were found all over the explored world, in Africa and Asia, as well as in Gaul and Britain, Imperialism contained a genuine element of internationalism. With the fall of Rome this conception of a single empire wielding political authority over the civilized world did not disappear. On the contrary, it survived all the fluctuations of the Holy Roman Empire. Even after the definite split between the Eastern and Western sections had taken place at the close of the fourth century, the theory of a single State, divided for administrative purposes, survived. Beneath every cleavage or antagonism, and notwithstanding the severance of many independent kingdoms and provinces, this ideal unity of the empire lived. It formed the conscious avowed ideal of Charlemagne, though as a practical ambition confined to Western Europe. Rudolph of Habsburg not merely revived the idea, but laboured to realize it through Central Europe, while his descendant Charles V gave a very real meaning to the term by gathering under the unity of his imperial rule the territories of Austria, Germany, Spain, the Netherlands, Sicily, and Naples. In later ages this dream of a European Empire animated the policy of Peter the Great, Catherine, and Napoleon. Nor is it impossible that Kaiser Wilhelm III held a vision of such a world-power.

Political philosophers in many ages, Vico, Machiavelli, Dante, Kant, have speculated on an empire as the only feasible security for peace, a hierarchy of States conforming on the larger scale to the feudal order within the single State.

Thus empire was identified with internationalism, though not always based on a conception of equality of nations. The break-up of the Central European Empire, with the weakening of nationalities that followed, evoked a new modern sentiment of internationalism which, through the eighteenth century, was a flickering inspiration in the intellectual circles of European States. "The eve of the French Revolution found every wise man in Europe—Lessing, Kant, Goethe, Rousseau, Lavater, Condorcet, Priestley, Gibbon, Franklin—more of a citizen of the world than of any particular country. Goethe confessed that he did not know what patriotism was, and was glad to be without it. Cultured men of all countries were at home in polite society everywhere. Kant was immensely more interested in the events of Paris than in the life of Prussia. Italy and Germany were geographical expressions; those countries were filled with small States in which there was no political life, but in which there was much interest in the general progress of culture. The Revolution itself was at bottom also human and cosmopolitan. It is, as Lamartine said, 'a date in the human mind,' and it is because of that fact that all the carping of critics like Taine cannot prevent us from seeing that the character of the men who led the great movements of the Revolution can never obliterate the momentous nature of the Titanic strife. The soldiers of the Revolution who, barefooted and ragged, drove the insolent reactionaries from the soil of France were fighting not merely for some national cause, but for a cause dimly perceived to be the cause of general mankind. With all its crudities and imperfections, the idea of the Revolution was that of a conceived body of Right in which all men should share."[3]

This early flower of humane cosmopolitanism was destined to wither before the powerful revival of nationalism which marked the next century. Even in the narrow circles of the cultured classes it easily passed from a noble and a passionate ideal to become a vapid sentimentalism, and after the brief flare of 1848 among the continental populace had been extinguished, little remained but a dim smouldering of the embers. Even the Socialism which upon the continent retains a measure of the spirit of internationalism is so tightly confined within the national limits, in its struggle with bureaucracy and capitalism, that "the international" expresses little more than a holy aspiration, and has little opportunity of putting into practice the genuine sentiments of brotherhood which its prophets have always preached.

Thus the triumph of nationalism seems to have crushed the rising hope of internationalism. Yet it would appear that there is no essential antagonism between them. A true strong internationalism in form or spirit would rather imply the existence of powerful self-respecting nationalities which seek union on the basis of common national needs and interests. Such a historical development would be far more conformable to laws of social growth than the rise of anarchic cosmopolitanism from individual units amid the decadence of national life.

Nationalism is a plain highway to internationalism, and if it manifests divergence we may well suspect a perversion of its nature and its purpose. Such a perversion is Imperialism, in which nations trespassing beyond the limits of facile assimilation transform the wholesome stimulative rivalry of varied national types into the cut-throat struggle of competing empires.

Not only does aggressive Imperialism defeat the movement towards internationalism by fostering animosities among competing empires; its attack upon the liberties and the existence of weaker or lower races stimulates in them a corresponding excess of national self-consciousness. A nationalism that bristles with resentment and is all astrain with the passion of self-defence is only less perverted from its natural genius than the nationalism which glows with the animus of greed and self-aggrandisement at the expense of others. From this aspect aggressive Imperialism is an artificial stimulation of nationalism in peoples too foreign to be absorbed and too compact to be permanently crushed. We welded Africanderdom into just such a strong dangerous nationalism, and we joined with other nations in creating a resentful nationalism until then unknown in China. The injury to nationalism in both cases consists in converting a cohesive, pacific internal force into an exclusive, hostile force, a perversion of the true power and use of nationality. The worst and most certain result is the retardation of internationalism. The older nationalism was primarily an inclusive sentiment; its natural relation to the same sentiment in another people was lack of sympathy, not open hostility; there was no inherent antagonism to prevent nationalities from growing and thriving side by side. Such in the main was the nationalism of the earlier nineteenth century, and the politicians of Free Trade had some foundation for their dream of a quick growth of effective, informal internationalism by peaceful, profitable intercommunication of goods and ideas among nations recognizing a just harmony of interests in free peoples.

The overflow of nationalism into imperial channels quenched all such hopes. While co-existent nationalities are capable of mutual aid involving no direct antagonism of interests, co-existent empires following each its own imperial career of territorial and industrial aggrandisement are natural necessary enemies. The full nature of this antagonism on its economic side is not intelligible without a close analysis of those conditions of modern capitalist production which compel an ever keener "fight for markets," but the political antagonism is obvious.

The scramble for Africa and Asia virtually recast the policy of all European nations, evoked alliances which cross all natural lines of sympathy and historical association, drove every continental nation to consume an ever-growing share of its material and human resources upon military and naval equipment, drew the great new power of the United States from its isolation into the full tide of competition; and, by the multitude, the magnitude, and the suddenness of the issues it had thrown on to the stage of politics, became a constant agent of menace and of perturbation to the peace and progress of mankind. The new policy exercised the most notable and formidable influence upon the conscious statecraft of the nations which indulge in it. While producing for popular consumption doctrines of national destiny and imperial missions of civilization, contradictory in their true import, but subsidiary to one another as supports of popular Imperialism, it evoked a calculating, greedy type of Machiavellianism, entitled "real-politik" in Germany, where it was made, which remodelled the whole art of diplomacy and erected national aggrandisement without pity or scruple as the conscious motive force of foreign policy. Earth hunger and the scramble for markets were responsible for the openly avowed repudiation of treaty obligations which Germany, Russia, and England had not scrupled to defend. The sliding scale of diplomatic language, hinterland, sphere of interest, sphere of influence, paramountcy, suzerainty, protectorate, veiled or open, leading up to acts of forcible seizure or annexation which sometimes continue to be hidden under "lease," "rectification of frontier," "concession," and the like, was the invention and expression of this cynical spirit of Imperialism. While Germany and Russia were perhaps more open in their professed adoption of the material gain of their country as the sole criterion of public conduct, other nations were not slow to accept the standard. Though the conduct of nations in dealing with one another has commonly been determined at all times by selfish and shortsighted considerations, the conscious, deliberate adoption of this standard at an age when the intercourse of nations and their interdependence for all essentials of human life grow ever closer, is a retrograde step fraught with grave perils to the cause of civilization.

Notes

1   *Representative Government*, chap. xvi.
2   "Expansion of England," lect. iii.
3   W. Clarke, *Progressive Review*, February, 1897.

Chapter 26

Filippo Tommaso Marinetti (1876–1944)

"THE FOUNDING AND MANIFESTO OF FUTURISM" (1909)

ITALIAN POET, NOVELIST, AND CRITIC, Marinetti was best known for "The Founding and Manifesto of Futurism," which proclaims the unity of art and life and the necessity of violence and cruelty in both in order to break definitively with the past. He advocated, for example, the destruction of museums, libraries, and "every type of academy," and became a leading voice in glorifying machines, speed, and war. Marinetti, who later became an active supporter of Benito Mussolini, had a significant impact on Wyndham Lewis' vorticist movement.

Filippo Tommaso Marinetti, "The Founding and Manifesto of Futurism." In *Manifesto: A Century of Isms,* ed. Mary Ann Caws. Lincoln, NE: U of Nebraska P, 2001. 185–89.

We had stayed up all night, my friends and I, under hanging mosque lamps with domes of filigreed brass, domes starred like our spirits, shining like them with the prisoned radiance of electric hearts. For hours we had trampled our atavistic ennui into rich oriental rugs, arguing up to the last confines of logic and blackening many reams of paper with our frenzied scribbling.

An immense pride was buoying us up, because we felt ourselves alone at that hour, alone, awake, and on our feet, like proud beacons or forward sentries against an army of hostile stars glaring down at us from their celestial encampments. Alone with stokers feeding the hellish fires of great ships, alone with the black specters who grope in the red-hot bellies of locomotives launched down their crazy courses, alone with drunkards reeling like wounded birds along the city walls.

Suddenly we jumped, hearing the mighty noise of the huge double-decker trams that rumbled by outside, ablaze with colored lights, like villages on holiday suddenly struck and uprooted by the flooding Po and dragged over falls and through gorges to the sea.

Then the silence deepened. But, as we listened to the old canal muttering its feeble prayers and the creaking bones of sickly palaces above their damp green beards, under the windows we suddenly heard the famished roar of automobiles.

"Let's go!" I said. "Friends, away! Let's go! Mythology and the Mystic Ideal are defeated at last. We're about to see the Centaur's birth and, soon after, the first flight of Angels! . . .

We must shake the gates of life, test the bolts and hinges. Let's go! Look there, on the earth, the very first dawn! There's nothing to match the splendor of the sun's red sword, slashing for the first time through our millennial gloom!"

We went up to the three snorting beasts, to lay amorous hands on their torrid breasts. I stretched out on my car like a corpse on its bier, but revived at once under the steering wheel, a guillotine blade that threatened my stomach.

The raging broom of madness swept us out of ourselves and drove us through streets as rough and deep as the beds of torrents. Here and there, sick lamplight through window glass taught us to distrust the deceitful mathematics of our perishing eyes.

I cried, "The scent, the scent alone is enough for our beasts."

And like young lions we ran after Death, its dark pelt blotched with pale crosses as it escaped down the vast violet living and throbbing sky.

But we had no ideal Mistress raising her divine form to the clouds, nor any cruel Queen to whom to offer our bodies, twisted like Byzantine rings! There was nothing to make us wish for death, unless the wish to be free at last from the weight of our courage!

And on we raced, hurling watchdogs against doorsteps, curling them under our burning tires like collars under a flatiron. Death, domesticated, met me at every turn, gracefully holding out a paw, or once in a while hunkering down, making velvety caressing eyes at me from every puddle.

"Let's break out of the horrible shell of wisdom and throw ourselves like pride-ripened fruit into the wide, contorted mouth of the wind! Let's give ourselves utterly to the Unknown, not in desperation but only to replenish the deep wells of the Absurd!!"

The words were scarcely out of my mouth when I spun my car around with the frenzy of a dog trying to bite its tail, and there, suddenly, were two cyclists coming toward me, shaking their fists, wobbling like two equally convincing but nevertheless contradictory arguments. Their stupid dilemma was blocking my way—damn! Ouch! . . . I stopped short and to my disgust rolled over into a ditch with my wheels in the air. . . .

Oh! Maternal ditch, almost full of muddy water! Fair factory drain! I gulped down your nourishing sludge; and I remembered the blessed black breast of my Sudanese nurse. . . . When I came up—torn, filthy, and stinking—from under the capsized car, I felt the white-hot iron of joy deliciously pass through my heart!

A crowd of fishermen with handlines and gouty naturalists were already swarming around the prodigy. With patient, loving care those people rigged a tall derrick and iron grapnels to fish out my car, like a big beached shark. Up it came from the ditch, slowly, leaving in the bottom like scales its heavy framework of good sense and its soft upholstery of comfort.

They thought it was dead, my beautiful shark, but a caress from me was enough to revive it; and there it was, alive again, running on its powerful fins!

And so, faces smeared with good factory muck—plastered with metallic waste, with senseless sweat, with celestial soot—we, bruised, our arms in slings, but unafraid, declared our high intentions to all the *living* of the earth:

Manifesto of futurism

1.   We intend to sing the love of danger, the habit of energy and fearlessness.
2.   Courage, audacity, and revolt will be essential elements of our poetry.
3.   Up to now literature has exalted a pensive immobility, ecstasy, and sleep. We intend to exalt aggressive action, a feverish insomnia, the racer's stride, the mortal leap, the punch and the slap.

4. We say that the world's magnificence has been enriched by a new beauty; the beauty of speed. A racing car whose hood is adorned with great pipes, like serpents of explosive breath—a roaring car that seems to ride on grapeshot—is more beautiful than the *Victory of Samothrace*.

5. We want to hymn the man at the wheel, who hurls the lance of his spirit across the Earth, along the circle of its orbit.

6. The poet must spend himself with ardor, splendor, and generosity, to swell the enthusiastic fervor of the primordial elements.

7. Except in struggle, there is no more beauty. No work without an aggressive character can be a masterpiece. Poetry must be conceived as a violent attack on unknown forces, to reduce and prostrate them before man.

8. We stand on the last promontory of the centuries! . . . Why should we look back, when what we want is to break down the mysterious doors of the Impossible? Time and Space died yesterday. We already live in the absolute, because we have created eternal, omnipresent speed.

9. We will glorify war—the world's only hygiene—militarism, patriotism, the destructive gesture of freedom-bringers, beautiful ideas worth dying for, and scorn for woman.

10. We will destroy the museums, libraries, academies of every kind, will fight moralism, feminism, every opportunistic or utilitarian cowardice.

11. We will sing of great crowds excited by work, by pleasure, and by riot; we will sing of the multicolored, polyphonic tides of revolution in the modern capitals; we will sing of the vibrant nightly fervor of arsenals and shipyards blazing with violent electric moons; greedy railway stations that devour smoke-plumed serpents; factories hung on clouds by the crooked lines of their smoke; bridges that stride the rivers like giant gymnasts, flashing in the sun with a glitter of knives; adventurous steamers that sniff the horizon; deep-chested locomotives whose wheels paw the tracks like the hooves of enormous steel horses bridled by tubing; and the sleek flight of planes whose propellers chatter in the wind like banners and seem to cheer like an enthusiastic crowd.

It is from Italy that we launch through the world this violently upsetting, incendiary manifesto of ours. With it, today, we establish *Futurism* because we want to free this land from its smelly gangrene of professors, archaeologists, ciceroni, and antiquarians. For too long has Italy been a dealer in secondhand clothes. We mean to free her from the numberless museums that cover her like so many graveyards.

Museums: cemeteries! . . . Identical, surely, in the sinister promiscuity of so many bodies unknown to one another. Museums: public dormitories where one lies forever beside hated or unknown beings. Museums; absurd abattoirs of painters and sculptors ferociously macerating each other with color-blows and line-blows, the length of the fought-over walls!

That one should make an annual pilgrimage, just as one goes to the graveyard on All Souls' Day—that I grant. That once a year one should leave a floral tribute beneath the *Gioconda*, I grant you that. . . . But I don't admit that our sorrows, our fragile courage, our morbid restlessness should be given a daily conducted tour through the museums. Why poison ourselves? Why rot?

And what is there to see in an old picture except the laborious contortions of an artist throwing himself against the barriers that thwart his desire to express his dream completely? . . . Admiring an old picture is the same as pouring our sensibility into a funerary urn instead of hurling it far off, in violent spasms of action and creation.

Do you, then, wish to waste all your best powers in this eternal and futile worship of the past, from which you emerge fatally exhausted, shrunken, beaten down?

In truth I tell you that daily visits to museums, libraries, and academies (cemeteries of empty exertion, calvaries of crucified dreams, registries of aborted beginnings!) is, for artists, as damaging as the prolonged supervision by parents of certain young people drunk with their talent and their ambitious wills. When the future is barred to them, the admirable past may be a solace for the ills of the moribund, the sickly, the prisoner. . . . But we want no part of it, the past, we the young and strong *Futurists!*

So let them come, the gay incendiaries with charred fingers! Here they are! Here they are! . . . Come on! set fire to the library shelves! Turn aside the canals to flood the museums! . . . Oh, the joy of seeing the glorious old canvases bobbing adrift on those waters, discolored and shredded! . . . Take up your pickaxes, your axes and hammers, and wreck, wreck the venerable cities, pitilessly!

*   *   *

The oldest of us is thirty: so we have at least a decade for finishing our work. When we are forty, other younger and stronger men will probably throw us in the wastebasket like useless manuscripts—we want it to happen!

They will come against us, our successors, will come from far away, from every quarter, dancing to the winged cadence of their first songs, flexing the hooked claws of predators, sniffing doglike at the academy doors the strong odor of our decaying minds, which already will have been promised to the literary catacombs.

But we won't be there. . . . At last they'll find us—one winter's night—in open country, beneath a sad roof drummed by a monotonous rain. They'll see us crouched beside our trembling airplanes in the act of warming our hands at the poor little blaze that our books of today will give out when they take fire from the flight of our images.

They'll storm around us, panting with scorn and anguish, and all of them, exasperated by our proud daring, will hurtle to kill us, driven by hatred: the more implacable it is, the more their hearts will be drunk with love and admiration for us.

Injustice, strong and sane, will break out radiantly in their eyes.

Art, in fact, can be nothing but violence, cruelty, and injustice.

The oldest of us is thirty: even so we have already scattered treasures, a thousand treasures of force, love, courage, astuteness, and raw will power; have thrown them impatiently away, with fury, carelessly, unhesitatingly, breathless and unresting. . . . Look at us! We are still untired! Our hearts know no weariness because they are fed with fire, hatred, and speed! . . . Does that amaze you? It should, because you can never remember having lived! Erect on the summit of the world, once again we hurl our defiance at the stars!

You have objections?—Enough! Enough! We know them . . . we've understood! . . . Our fine deceitful intelligence tells us that we are the revival and extension of our ancestors—perhaps! . . . If only it were so!—But who cares? We don't want to understand! . . . Woe to anyone who says those infamous words to us again!

Lift up your heads!

Erect on the summit of the world, once again we hurl defiance to the stars!

Chapter 27

Rosa Luxemburg (1870–1919)

"PEACE UTOPIAS" (1911)

A FERVENT ANTI-NATIONALIST AND AN ARDENT advocate of radical, revolutionary politics, Rosa Luxemburg considered the international working class to
be the sole hope of a democratic and socialist future. Hers was a rare voice against not
only the impending war but militarism generally, distinguishing herself from what she
called "the bourgeois apostles of peace" by maintaining that war would be abolished only
"with the destruction of the capitalist class state" and the establishment of a socialist
order. Her stirring pamphlet, *The Russian Revolution*, denounced the Bolshevik Revolution
as a danger to democracy. In the chaos and criminality of Berlin after Germany's defeat
in World War I, Rosa Luxemburg was assassinated by the illegal paramilitary organization that would later become Hitler's Brownshirts.

Rosa Luxemburg, "Peace Utopias," *Rosa Luxemburg Speaks* (May 6 and 8, 1911): 250–56. Also
published in *Labour Monthly* (July 1926).

I

What is our task in the question of peace? It does not consist merely in vigorously demonstrating at all times the love of peace of the social democrats; but first and foremost our task
is to make clear to the masses of people the nature of militarism and sharply and clearly to
bring out the differences in principle between the standpoint of the social democrats and that
of the bourgeois peace enthusiasts.

Wherein does this difference lie? Certainly not merely in the fact that the bourgeois
apostles of peace are relying on the influence of fine words, while we do not depend on words
alone. Our very points of departure are diametrically opposed: the friends of peace in bourgeois circles believe that world peace and disarmament can be realized within the framework
of the present social order, whereas we, who base ourselves on the materialistic conception
of history and on scientific socialism, are convinced that militarism can only be abolished
from the world with the destruction of the capitalist class state. From this follows the mutual
opposition of our tactics in propagating the idea of peace. The bourgeois friends of peace are

endeavoring—and from their point of view this is perfectly logical and explicable—to invent all sorts of "practical" projects for gradually restraining militarism, and are naturally inclined to consider every outward apparent sign of a tendency toward peace as the genuine article, to take every expression of the ruling diplomacy in this vein at its word, to exaggerate it into a basis for earnest activity. The social democrats, on the other hand, must consider it their duty in this matter, just as in all matters of social criticism, to expose the bourgeois attempts to restrain militarism as pitiful half measures, and the expressions of such sentiments on the part of the governing circles as diplomatic make-believe, and to oppose the bourgeois claims and pretences with the ruthless analysis of capitalist reality.

From this same standpoint the tasks of the social democrats with regard to the declarations of the kind made by the British government can only be to show up the idea of a partial limitation of armaments, in all its impracticability, as a half measure, and to endeavor to make it clear to the people that militarism is closely linked up with colonial politics, with tariff politics, and with international politics, and that therefore the present nations, if they really seriously and honestly wish to call a halt on competitive armaments, would have to begin by disarming in the commercial political field, give up colonial predatory campaigns and the international politics of spheres of influence in all parts of the world—in a word, in their foreign as well as in their domestic politics would have to do the exact contrary of everything which the nature of the present politics of a capitalist class state demands. And thus would be clearly explained what constitutes the kernel of the social democratic conception, that militarism in both its forms—as war and as armed peace—is a legitimate child, a logical result of capitalism, which can only be overcome with the destruction of capitalism, and that hence whoever honestly desires world peace and liberation from the tremendous burden of armaments must also desire socialism. Only in this way can real social democratic enlightenment and recruiting be carried on in connection with the armaments debate.

This work, however, will be rendered somewhat difficult and the attitude of the social democrats will become obscure and vacillating if, by some strange exchange of roles, our party tries on the contrary to convince the bourgeois state that it can quite well limit armaments and bring about peace and that it can do this from its own standpoint, from that of a capitalist class state.

It has until now been the pride and the firm scientific basis of our party that not only the general lines of our program but also the slogans of our practical everyday policy were not invented out of odds and ends as something desirable, but that in all things we relied on our knowledge of the tendencies of social development and made the objective lines of this development the basis of our attitude. For us the determining factor until now has not been the possibility from the standpoint of the relation of forces within the state, but the possibility from the standpoint of the tendencies of development of society. The limitation of armaments, the retrenchment of militarism does not coincide with the further development of international capitalism. Only those who believe in the mitigation and blunting of class antagonism, and in the checking of the economic anarchy of capitalism, can believe in the possibility of these international conflicts allowing themselves to be slackened, to be mitigated and wiped out. For the international antagonisms of the capitalist states are but the complement of class antagonisms, and the world political anarchy but the reverse side of the anarchic system of production of capitalism. Both can grow only together and be overcome only together. "A little order and peace" is, therefore, just as impossible, just as much a petty bourgeois utopia, with regard to the capitalist world market as to world politics, and with regard to the limitation of crises as to the limitation of armaments.

Let us cast a glance at the events of the last fifteen years of international development. Where do they show any tendency toward peace, toward disarmament, toward settlement of conflicts by arbitration?

During these fifteen years we had this: in 1895 the war between Japan and China, which is the prelude to the East Asiatic period of imperialism; in 1898 the war between Spain and the United States; in 1899–1902 the British Boer War in South Africa; in 1900 the campaign of the European powers in China; in 1904 the Russo-Japanese War; in 1904–7 the German Herero War in Africa; and then there was also the military intervention of Russia in 1908 in Persia; at the present moment the military intervention of France in Morocco, without mentioning the incessant colonial skirmishes in Asia and in Africa. Hence the bare facts alone show that for fifteen years hardly a year has gone by without some war activity.

But more important still is the aftereffect of these wars. The war with China was followed in Japan by a military reorganization which made it possible ten years later to undertake the war against Russia and which made Japan the predominant military power in the Pacific. The Boer War resulted in a military reorganization of England, the strengthening of her armed forces on land. The war with Spain inspired the United States to reorganize its navy and moved it to enter colonial politics with imperialist interests in Asia, and thus was created the germ of the antagonism of interests between the United States and Japan in the Pacific. The Chinese campaign was accompanied in Germany by a thorough military reorganization, the great Navy Law of 1900, which marks the beginning of the competition of Germany with England on the sea and the sharpening of the antagonisms between these two nations.

But there is another and extremely important factor besides: the social and political awakening of the hinterlands, of the colonies and the "spheres of interest," to independent life. The revolution in Turkey, in Persia, the revolutionary ferment in China, in India, in Egypt, in Arabia, in Morocco, in Mexico, all these are also starting points of world political antagonisms, tensions, military activities and armaments. It was just during the course of this fifteen years that the points of friction in international politics have increased to an unparalleled degree, a number of new states stepped into active struggle on the international stage, all the great powers underwent a thorough military reorganization. The antagonisms, in consequence of all these events, have reached an acuteness never known before, and the process is going further and further, since on the one hand the ferment in the Orient is increasing from day to day, and on the other every settlement between the military powers unavoidably becomes the starting point for fresh conflicts. The Reval Entente between Russia, Great Britain and France, which Jaures hailed as a guarantee for world peace, led to the sharpening of the crisis in the Balkans, accelerated the outbreak of the Turkish Revolution, encouraged Russia to military action in Persia and led to a rapprochement between Turkey and Germany which, in its turn, rendered the Anglo-German antagonisms more acute. The Potsdam agreement resulted in the sharpening of the crisis in China and the Russo-Japanese agreement had the same effect.

Therefore, on a mere reckoning with facts, to refuse to realize that these facts give rise to anything rather than a mitigation of the international conflicts, of any sort of disposition toward world peace, is willfully to close one's eyes.

In view of all this, how is it possible to speak of tendencies toward peace in bourgeois development which are supposed to neutralize and overcome its tendencies toward war? Wherein are they expressed?

In Sir Edward Grey's declaration and that of the French Parliament? In the "armament weariness" of the bourgeoisie? But the middle and petty bourgeois sections of the bourgeoisie have always been groaning at the burden of militarism, just as they groan at the devastation of free competition, at the economic crises, at the lack of conscience shown in stock exchange speculations, at the terrorism of the cartels and trusts. The tyranny of the trust magnates in America has even called forth a rebellion of broad masses of the people and a wearisome legal procedure against the trusts on the part of the state authorities. Do the social democrats interpret this as a symptom of the beginning of the limitation of trust development, or have they not rather a sympathetic shrug of the shoulders for that petty bourgeois rebellion and a scornful smile for that state campaign? The "dialectic" of the peace tendency of capitalist development, which was supposed to have cut across its war tendency and to have overcome it, simply confirms the old truth that the roses of capitalist profit-making and class domination also have thorns for the bourgeoisie, which it prefers to wear as long as possible round its suffering head, in spite of all pain and woe, rather than get rid of it along with the head on the advice of the social democrats.

To explain this to the masses, ruthlessly to scatter all illusions with regard to attempts made at peace on the part of the bourgeoisie and to declare the proletarian revolution as the first and only step toward world peace—that is the task of the social democrats with regard to all disarmament trickeries, whether they are invented in Petersburg, London or Berlin.

II

The utopianism of the standpoint which expects an era of peace and retrenchment of militarism in the present social order is plainly revealed in the fact that it is having recourse to project making. For it is typical of utopian strivings that, in order to demonstrate their practicability, they hatch "practical" recipes with the greatest possible details. To this also belongs the project of the "United States of Europe" as a basis for the limitation of international militarism.

"We support all efforts," said Comrade Ledebour in his speech in the Reichstag on April 3, "which aim at getting rid of the threadbare pretexts for the incessant war armaments. We demand the economic and political union of the European states. I am firmly convinced that, while it is certain to come during the period of socialism, it can also come to pass before that time, that we will live to see the United States of Europe, as confronted at present by the business competition of the United States of America. At least we demand that capitalist society, that capitalist statesmen, in the interests of capitalist development in Europe itself, in order that Europe will later not be completely submerged in world competition, prepare for this union of Europe into the United States of Europe."

And in the *Neue Zeit* of April 28, Comrade Kautsky writes: ". . . . For a lasting duration of peace, which banishes the ghost of war forever, there is only one way today: the union of the states of European civilization into a league with a common commercial policy, a league parliament, a league government and a league army—the formation of the United States of Europe. Were this to succeed, then a tremendous step would be achieved. Such a United States would possess such a superiority of forces that without any war they could compel all the other nations which do not voluntarily join them to liquidate their armies and give up their fleets. But in that case all necessity for armaments for the new United States themselves would disappear. They would be in a position not only to relinquish all further armaments, give up the standing army and all aggressive weapons on the sea, which we are demanding today, but even give up all means of defense, the militia system itself. Thus the era of permanent peace would surely begin."

Plausible as the idea of the United States of Europe as a peace arrangement may seem to some at first glance, it has on closer examination not the least thing in common with the method of thought and the standpoint of social democracy.

As adherents of the materialist conception of history, we have always adopted the standpoint that the modern states as political structures are not artificial products of a creative fantasy, like, for instance, the Duchy of Warsaw of Napoleonic memory, but historical products of economic development.

But what economic foundation lies at the bottom of the idea of a European State Federation? Europe, it is true, is a geographical and, within certain limits, a historical cultural conception. But the idea of Europe as an economic unit contradicts capitalist development in two ways. First of all there exist within Europe among the capitalist states—and will so long as these exist—the most violent struggles of competition and antagonisms, and secondly the European states can no longer get along economically without the non-European countries. As suppliers of foodstuffs, raw materials and wares, also as consumers of the same, the other parts of the world are linked in a thousand ways with Europe. At the present stage of development of the world market and of world economy, the conception of Europe as an isolated economic unit is a sterile concoction of the brain. Europe no more forms a special unit within world economy than does Asia or America.

And if the idea of a European union in the economic sense has long been outstripped, this is no less the case in the political sense.

The times when the center of gravity of political development and the crystallizing agent of capitalist contradictions lay on the European continent are long gone by. Today Europe is only a link in the tangled chain of international connections and contradictions. And what is of decisive significance—European antagonisms themselves no longer play their role on the European continent but in all parts of the world and on all the seas.

Only were one suddenly to lose sight of all these happenings and maneuvers, and to transfer oneself back to the blissful times of the European concert of powers, could one say, for instance, that for forty years we have had uninterrupted peace. This conception, which considers only events on the European continent, does not notice that the very reason why we have had no war in Europe for decades is the fact that international antagonisms have grown infinitely beyond the narrow confines of the European continent, and that European problems and interests are now fought out on the world seas and in the by-corners of Europe.

Hence the "United State of Europe" is an idea which runs directly counter both economically and politically to the course of development, and which takes absolutely no account of the events of the last quarter of a century.

That an idea so little in accord with the tendency of development can fundamentally offer no progressive solution in spite of all radical disguises is confirmed also by the fate of the slogan of the "United States of Europe." Every time that bourgeois politicians have championed the idea of Europeanism, of the union of European states, it has been with an open or concealed point directed against the "yellow peril," the "dark continent," against the "inferior races," in short, it has always been an imperialist abortion.

And now if we, as social democrats, were to try to fill this old skin with fresh and apparently revolutionary wine, then it must be said that the advantages would not be on our side but on that of the bourgeoisie. Things have their own objective logic. And the solution of the European union within the capitalist social order can objectively, in the economic sense, mean only a tariff war with America, and, in the political sense, only a colonial race war. The Chinese campaign of the united European regiments, with the World Field Marshal Waldersee at the head, and the gospel of the Hun as our standard—that is the actual and not the fantastic, the only possible expression of the "European State Federation" in the present social order.

Chapter 28

James Joyce (1882–1941)

"THE SHADE OF PARNELL" (1912)

I N THE YEARS LEADING UP to World War I, Britain faced three major social crises: the fight for women's rights, labor unrest, and the question of Irish Home Rule. All three were put on hold for the War's duration. Joyce, who had gone into self-exile on the Continent at the age of 22, remained obsessed with the Ireland he left behind and wrote of nothing else. He was especially bitter about Irish politics, supporting neither British imperialism nor the nationalist movement, but he identified strongly with Charles Stewart Parnell, the so-called "uncrowned king of Ireland," who, after being caught in an adulterous affair, was denounced from the pulpits of the Irish Catholic churches and, as Joyce viewed it, hounded to his death in 1891. Joyce wrote a number of essays on Irish politics, none more poignant than this piece denouncing his countrymen for turning against their leader and thereby betraying their own political cause. As the self-appointed "Parnell of art," Joyce deemed betrayal the central theme of his life and writing.

James Joyce, "The Shade of Parnell," *James Joyce: Occasional, Critical, and Political Writing*, ed. Kevin Barry. Oxford: Oxford UP, 2000. 191–96.

By voting for the bill on Irish autonomy on its second reading, the House of Commons has resolved the Irish question; a question which, like the hen of Mugello, is a hundred years of age but looks a month old.

The century that began with the buying and selling of the Dublin parliament is now closing with a triangular pact between England, Ireland and the United States. It was a century adorned by seven Irish revolutionary movements that, with dynamite, eloquence, boycotts, obstructionism, armed revolt and political assassination, managed to keep awake the slow, apprehensive conscience of English Liberalism.

The present law has been conceded in the full maturity of time under the double pressure of the Nationalist Party in Westminster which, for over half a century, has obstructed the operations of the British legislature, and the Irish Party across the Atlantic, which has blocked the much sought-after Anglo-American alliance. Devised and moulded with masterly cunning artistry, the bill fittingly crowns the tradition handed down to posterity by the pluterperfect Liberal statesman, William Gladstone. Suffice to say that, while reducing the strong ranks of the one hundred and three Irish constituencies, presently represented in Westminster by a handful of forty deputies, the bill automatically pushes these into the embrace of the small Labour Party so that from this incestuous embrace a coalition will probably arise and function as the far left. In other words, until it receives further orders, the coalition will work as an operational base for the Liberals in their campaign against Conservatism. There is no need to go into the intricacies of the financial clauses. At any rate, the future Irish government will have to cover the deficit skilfully created by the British treasury either by re-deploying local and imperial taxes, or by reducing public expenditure, or by increasing direct taxation. One way or the other, it will come up against the disillusioned hostility of the middle and lower classes.

The Irish separatist party would like to reject this Greek gift that makes the Dublin Chancellor of the Exchequer a titular minister who is fully responsible to the tax-payers yet still dependent upon the British cabinet. He may tax without having control over the proceeds of his ministry; he is like a vending-machine that cannot work unless the London energy source sends a current of the right voltage.

No matter: the appearance of autonomy is there. At the recent national assembly held in Dublin, the denunciations and protests of the nationalists belonging to the bitterly sceptical school of John Mitchel did not greatly disturb the popular jubilation. In their speeches, the deputies, grown old in their constitutional struggle, and worn out by years and years of disappointed hopes, hailed the end of a long period of misunderstandings. A young orator, Gladstone's nephew, amidst fervent applause from the crowd, called up the name of his uncle and saluted the prosperity of the new nation. In two years' time at the latest, with or without the assent of the House of Lords, the doors of the old parliament in Dublin will re-open, and Ireland, freed from her century-long imprisonmemt, will set out towards the palace like a new bride accompanied by music and nuptial torches. A grand-nephew of Gladstone (if there is one) will scatter flowers beneath the feet of the sovereign, but there will be a shade at the feast: the shade of Charles Parnell.

Recent criticism has attempted to minimize the greatness of this strange spirit by pointing to the different sources of his parliamentary tactics. Even if we concede to the historical critic that obstructionism was invented by Biggar and Ronayne, that the doctrine of independence of the Irish Party was launched by Gavan Duffy, and that the Land League was Michael Davitt's creation, these concessions evince all the more the extraordinary personality of a leader who, with no forensic gift or original political talent, forced the greatest English politicians to follow his orders. He, like another Moses, led a turbulent and volatile people out of the house of shame to the edge of the Promised Land. The influence that Parnell exercised over the Irish people defies the critic's analysis. Lisping, of delicate build, he was ignorant of the history of his country. His short, broken speeches lacked all eloquence, poetry or humour. His cold, polite behaviour divided him from his own colleagues. He was Protestant, a descendant of an aristocratic family, and (to complete the affliction) he spoke with a distinctly English accent. He would often come to committee meetings an hour or an hour and a half late and not excuse himself. He used to neglect his correspondence for whole weeks. Neither the applause nor the anger of the crowd, neither the invectives nor the praises of the press, neither the denunciations nor the defences of the British ministers ever perturbed the forlorn serenity of his character. It is even said that he did not know by sight many of those who sat with him in the Irish benches. When the Irish people presented him, in 1887, the national tribute of forty thousand pounds, he put the cheque in his wallet and, during the speech he addressed to the immense crowd, he made not the slightest mention of the gift that he had received. When he was shown the copy of *The Times* containing the famous autographed letter that was supposed to prove his complicity in the savage assassination in the Phoenix Park, he placed a finger on a letter in the signature, simply saying: 'I have not made an "S" that way since '78.' Later the investigations of the royal commission revealed the plot that had been ordered against him, and the perjurer and forger Pigott blew his brains out in a hotel in Madrid. The House of Commons, without regard to party, greeted Parnell's entrance with an ovation that has remained unprecedented in the annals of the British parliament. Is there any need to say that Parnell responded to the ovation with neither a smile, nor a bow, nor a nod? He walked over to his place across the aisle and sat down. Gladstone was probably thinking of this incident when he called the Irish leader an intellectual phenomenon.

Nothing more singular can be imagined than the appearance of this intellectual phenomenon in the midst of the stifling morals of Westminster. Now, looking back over the scenes of the drama and listening again to the speeches that caused his listeners' souls to tremble, it is useless to deny that all that eloquence and all those strategic triumphs begin to taste stale. But time is more merciful towards the 'uncrowned king' than towards the wag and the orator. The light of his mild, proud, silent and disconsolate sovereignty makes Disraeli look like an upstart diplomat dining whenever he can in rich people's houses, and Gladstone like a portly butler who has gone to night school. How little Disraeli's wit and Gladstone's culture weigh in the balance today! What trifles are Disraeli's studied witticisms, greasy hair and doltish novels, or Gladstone's high-sounding sentences, Homeric studies and speeches on Artemis or marmalade!

Although Parnell's tactic was to avail himself of any one of the English parties, Liberals or Conservatives, according to his pleasure, a set of circumstances involved him in the Liberal movement. Gladstonian Liberalism was an inconstant algebraic symbol whose coefficient was the political pressure of the moment and whose exponent was personal advantage. While, in internal politics, he temporized, retracted and justified himself in turn, he always, in the case of other nations, maintained (in so far as he could) a sincere admiration for liberty. This elastic quality of Gladstone's liberalism must be borne in mind if we are to appreciate the extent and degree of Parnell's task. Gladstone was, in a word, a politician. He shook with rage at the wickedness of O'Connell in 1835, yet he was the English legislator to proclaim the moral and material necessity of Irish autonomy. He thundered against the admission of Jews to public office, and yet he was the minister who, for the first time in English history, raised a Jew to the peerage. He used proud language towards the rebel Boers in 1881, and after the English defeat at Majuba, concluded a pact with Transvaal that the English themselves called a cowardly submission. In his first speech before parliament, he hotly rebutted Earl Grey's charges of cruelty against his father, a rich slave-owner in Demerara, who had earned two million francs by the sale of human flesh, while in his last letter to the Duke of Westminster, 'a childhood friend', he called down all possible curses upon the head of the great murderer of Constantinople.

Parnell, convinced that such a liberalism would only yield to force, united every element of national life behind him, and set out on a march along the borders of insurrection. Six years after entering Westminster, he already held the destiny of the government in his hands. He was imprisoned, but from his cell in Kilmainham he concluded a pact with the ministers who had jailed him. When the attempt at blackmail failed with the confession and suicide of Pigott, the Liberal government offered him a portfolio. Not only did Parnell turn it down, but he ordered all his followers likewise to refuse any ministerial post whatsoever, and forbade the municipalities and public corporations in Ireland from officially receiving any member of the British royal family until a British government restored autonomy to Ireland. The Liberals were forced to accept these humiliating conditions, and Gladstone, in 1886, read the first Home Rule Bill before parliament.

Parnell's fall came in the midst of these events like a bolt from the blue. He fell helplessly in love with a married woman, and when the husband Captain O'Shea requested a divorce, the ministers Gladstone and Morley openly refused to legislate in favour of Ireland if the felon stayed on as leader of the Nationalist Party. Parnell did not appear or defend himself at the trial. He denied the right of a minister to exercise a veto over the political affairs of Ireland, and refused to resign. He was deposed by the Nationalists obeying Gladstone's orders. Of the eighty-three deputies, only eight remained faithful to him. The Irish press poured the phials of their spitefulness over him and the woman he loved. The peasants of Castlecomer threw quicklime in his eyes. He went from county to county, from city to city, 'like a hunted hind', a spectral figure with the signs of death upon his brow. Within a year he died of a broken heart at the age of forty-five.

The shade of the 'uncrowned king' will weigh upon the hearts of those who remember him, when the new Ireland soon enters into the palace *fimbriis aureis circumamicta varietatibus*: but it will not be a vindictive shade. The sadness that devastated his soul was, perhaps, the profound conviction that, in his hour of need, one of the disciples who had dipped his hand into the bowl with him was about to betray him. To have fought until the very end with this desolating certainty in his soul is his first and greatest claim to nobility. In his last proud appeal to his people, he implored his fellow-countrymen not to throw him to the English wolves howling around him. It redounds to the honour of his fellow-countrymen that they did not fail that desperate appeal. They did not throw him to the English wolves: they tore him apart themselves.

Chapter 29

Henri Gaudier-Brzeska (1891–1915)

"VORTEX GAUDIER-BRZESKA" (1915)

GAUDIER-BRZESKA WAS A FRENCH SCULPTOR WHO developed a rough, primitive style of carving that left the tool marks visible on the finished work, thus emphasizing process as much as product. Influenced by Chinese calligraphy and cubism, Gaudier-Brzeska linked himself with the vorticism movement of Ezra Pound and Wyndham Lewis; in turn, he strongly impacted the modernist sculpture that followed him. He enlisted with the French army and was decorated for bravery before being killed in World War I. Writing "Vortex Gaudier-Brzeska" in the trenches, the sculptor extolled the action and violence of war as "a great remedy. In the individual it kills arrogance, self-esteem, pride." Ironically, Lewis' *Blast* published the piece alongside a notice of Gaudier-Brzeska's death in combat.

Henri Gaudier-Brzeska, "Vortex Gaudier-Brzeska," *Blast* (July 1915). 33–34.

Vortex Gaudier-Brzeska (written from the trenches)

Note.—The Sculptor writes from the French trenches, having been in the firing line since early in the war. In September he was one of a patrolling party of twelve, seven of his companions fell in the fight over a roadway. In November he was nominated for sergeancy and has been since slightly wounded, but expects to return to the trenches. He has been consistently employed in scouting and patrolling and in the construction of wire entanglements in close contact with the Boches.

I HAVE BEEN FIGHTING FOR TWO MONTHS and I can now gauge the intensity of life.

HUMAN MASSES teem and move, are destroyed and crop up again.

HORSES are worn out in three weeks, die by the roadside.

DOGS wander, are destroyed, and others come along.

WITH ALL THE DESTRUCTION that works around us NOTHING IS CHANGED, EVEN SUPERFICIALLY. *LIFE IS THE SAME STRENGTH*, THE MOVING AGENT THAT PERMITS THE SMALL INDIVIDUAL TO ASSERT HIMSELF.

THE BURSTING OF SHELLS, the volleys, wire entanglements, projectors, motors, the chaos of battle, DO NOT ALTER IN THE LEAST the outlines of the hill we are besieging. A company of PARTRIDGES scuttle along before our very trench.

IT WOULD BE FOLLY TO SEEK ARTISTIC EMOTIONS AMID THESE LITTLE WORKS OF OURS.

THIS PALTRY MECHANISM, WHICH SERVES AS A PURGE TO OVER-NUMEROUS HUMANITY.

THIS WAR IS A GREAT REMEDY.

IN THE INDIVIDUAL IT KILLS ARROGANCE, SELF-ESTEEM, PRIDE.

IT TAKES AWAY FROM THE MASSES NUMBERS OF UNIMPORTANT UNITS, WHOSE ECONOMIC ACTIVITIES BECOME NOXIOUS AS THE RECENT TRADES CRISES HAVE SHOWN US.

MY VIEWS ON SCULPTURE REMAIN ABSOLUTELY *THE SAME.*

IT IS THE *VORTEX* OF WILL, OF DECISION, THAT BEGINS.

I SHALL DERIVE MY EMOTIONS SOLELY FROM THE ARRANGEMENT OF SURFACES, I shall present my emotions by the *ARRANGEMENT OF MY SURFACES*, THE PLANES AND LINES BY WHICH THEY ARE DEFINED.

Just as this hill where the Germans are solidly entrenched, gives me a nasty feeling, simply because its gentle slopes are broken up by earthworks, which throw long shadows at sunset. Just so shall I get feeling, of whatsoever definition, from a statue, ACCORDING TO ITS SLOPES, varied to infinity.

I have made an experiment. Two days ago I pinched from an enemy a Mauser rifle. Its heavy unwieldy shape swamped me with a powerful image of brutality.

I was in doubt for a long time whether it pleased me or displeased me.

I found that I did not like it.

I broke the butt off and with my knife I carved in it a design, through which I tried to express a gentler order of things, which I preferred.

BUT I WILL EMPHASIZE that MY DESIGN *got its effect* (just as the gun had) from a very simple composition of lines and planes.

Mort pour la patrie

Henri Gaudier-Brzeska: after months of fighting and two promotions for gallantry Henri Gaudier-Brzeska was killed in a charge at Neuville St. Vaast, on June 5th, 1915.

Chapter 30

Siegfried Sassoon (1886–1967)

"FINISHED WITH THE WAR: A SOLDIER'S DECLARATION" (1917)

IN CONTRAST TO GAUDIER-BRZESKA, Siegfried Sassoon, who began as a gung-ho war supporter, was turned into a fierce pacifist by his experience at the front. His "Finished with the War: A Soldier's Declaration" denounced the War as one of "aggression and conquest" whose "evil and unjust" ends failed to validate the enormous suffering and destruction it was causing and which continued only because of "the callous complacency" of those at home. His declaration was published and read out in Parliament, but rather than being court-martialed, which would have given Sassoon the forum and publicity for his stance that he sought, he was marginalized as rabble-rousing and propagandistic, and his work deemed the result of cowardice or illness, earning him a reputation that carried over into the post-war years.

Siegfried Sassoon, "Finished with the War: A Soldier's Declaration." *The Times* (London), 31 July 1917; *Bradford Pioneer*, 27 July 1917. Read out in the British House of Commons, 30 July 1917.

I am making this statement as an act of wilful defiance of military authority because I believe that the war is being deliberately prolonged by those who have the power to end it. I am a soldier, convinced that I am acting on behalf of soldiers. I believe that the war upon which I entered as a war of defence and liberation has now become a war of aggression and conquest. I believe that the purposes for which I and my fellow soldiers entered upon this war should have been so clearly stated as to have made it impossible to change them and that had this been done the objects which actuated us would now be attainable by negotiation.

I have seen and endured the sufferings of the troops and I can no longer be a party to prolonging these sufferings for ends which I believe to be evil and unjust. I am not protesting against the conduct of the war, but against the political errors and insincerities for which the fighting men are being sacrificed.

On behalf of those who are suffering now, I make this protest against the deception which is being practised upon them; also I believe it may help to destroy the callous complacency with which the majority of those at home regard the continuance of agonies which they do not share and which they have not enough imagination to realise.

Chapter 31

THE KELLOGG–BRIAND PACT (1928)

A **TREATY TO OUTLAW WAR**, the Kellogg–Briand Pact (which was also known as "The General Treaty for the Renunciation of War" and "The World Peace Act") was signed by more than 50 nations, including the U.S., which, however, reserved the right of self-defense and stated that it was not obligated to act against those who violated it. The treaty did not, of course, prevent war, but it created the notion of war as a crime against peace, which was invoked at the Nuremberg Tribunal against a number of people who were judged responsible for the crime of starting World War II.

The interdiction of aggressive war was confirmed and broadened by the United Nations Charter, which states, "All Members shall refrain in their international relations from the threat or use of force against the territorial integrity or political independence of any state, or in any other manner inconsistent with the Purposes of the United Nations." As a consequence, nations taking military action since World War II have had to invoke the right of self-defense or collective defense and have also been prohibited from annexing territory by force.

Article I

The High Contracting Parties solemnly declare in the names of their respective peoples that they condemn recourse to war for the solution of international controversies, and renounce it, as an instrument of national policy in their relations with one another.

Article II

The High Contracting Parties agree that the settlement or solution of all disputes or conflicts of whatever nature or of whatever origin they may be, which may arise among them, shall never be sought except by pacific means.

Article III

The present Treaty shall be ratified by the High Contracting Parties named in the Preamble in accordance with their respective constitutional requirements, and shall take effect as between them as soon as all their several instruments of ratification shall have been deposited at Washington.

   This Treaty shall, when it has come into effect as prescribed in the preceding paragraph, remain open as long as may be necessary for adherence by all the other Powers of the world. Every instrument evidencing the adherence of a Power shall be deposited at Washington and the Treaty shall immediately upon such deposit become effective as between the Power thus adhering and the other Powers parties hereto.

   It shall be the duty of the Government of the United States to furnish each Government named in the Preamble and every Government subsequently adhering to this Treaty with a certified copy of the Treaty and of every instrument of ratification or adherence. It shall also be the duty of the Government of the United States telegraphically to notify such Governments immediately upon the deposit with it of each instrument of ratification or adherence.

   IN FAITH WHEREOF the respective Plenipotentiaries have signed this Treaty in the French and English languages both texts having equal force, and hereunto affix their seals.

   DONE at Paris, the twenty-seventh day of August in the year one thousand nine hundred and twenty-eight.

Chapter 32

Kenneth Burke (1897–1993)

"THE RHETORIC OF HITLER'S *BATTLE*" (1939)

B ETWEEN THEM, KENNETH BURKE'S "The Rhetoric of Hitler's *Battle*" and C.L.R. James's *My Friends: A Fireside Chat on the War* (see Chapter 33) provide a kind of coda for modernist statements on politics, race, and war. Taking as a given that Hitler represented an incomparable evil, Burke analyzes *Mein Kampf* in order to explain the process whereby Hitler developed his views, rose to power, and drove the world to the brink of World War II.

Kenneth Burke, "The Rhetoric of Hitler's *Battle*," *The Southern Review* 5 (1939): 191–220.

The appearance of *Mein Kampf* in unexpurgated translation has called forth far too many vandalistic comments. There are other ways of burning books than on the pyre—and the favorite method of the hasty reviewer is to deprive himself and his readers by inattention. I maintain that it is thoroughly vandalistic for the reviewer to content himself with the mere inflicting of a few symbolic wounds upon this book and its author, of an intensity varying with the resources of the reviewer and the time at his disposal. Hitler's "Battle" is exasperating, even nauseating; yet the fact remains: If the reviewer but knocks off a few adverse attitudiniz-ings and calls it a day, with a guaranty in advance that his article will have a favorable recep-tion among the decent members of our population, he is contributing more to our gratification than to our enlightenment.

Here is the testament of a man who swung a great people into his wake. Let us watch it carefully; and let us watch it, not merely to discover some grounds for prophesying what political move is to follow Munich, and what move to follow that move, etc.; let us try also to discover what kind of "medicine" this medicine-man has concocted, that we may know, with greater accuracy, exactly what to guard against, if we are to forestall the concocting of similar medicine in America.

Already, in many quarters of our country, we are "beyond" the stage where we are being saved from Nazism by our *virtues*. And fascist integration is being staved off, rather, by the *conflicts among our vices*. Our vices cannot get together in a grand united front of prejudices; and the result of this frustration, if or until they succeed in surmounting it, speaks, as the Bible might say, "in the name of" democracy. Hitler found a panacea, a "cure for what ails you," a "snakeoil," that made such sinister unifying possible within his own nation. And he was helpful enough to put his cards face up on the table, that we might examine his hands. Let us, then, for God's sake, examine them. This book is the well of Nazi magic; crude magic, but effective. A people trained in pragmatism should want to inspect this magic.

I

Every movement that would recruit its followers from among many discordant and divergent bands must have some spot towards which all roads lead. Each man may get there in his own way, but it must be the one unifying center of reference for all. Hitler considered this matter carefully, and decided that this center must be not merely a centralizing hub of *ideas*, but a mecca geographically located, towards which all eyes could turn at the appointed hours of prayer (or, in this case, the appointed hours of prayer-in-reverse, the hours of vituperation). So he selected Munich, as the *materialization* of his unifying panacea. As he puts it:

> The geo-political importance of a center of a movement cannot be overrated. Only the presence of such a center and of a place, bathed in the magic of a Mecca or a Rome, can at length give a movement that force which is rooted in the inner unity and in the recognition of a hand that represents this unity.

If a movement must have its Rome, it must also have its devil. For as Russell pointed out years ago, an important ingredient of unity in the Middle Ages (an ingredient that long did its unifying work despite the many factors driving towards disunity) was the symbol of a common enemy, the Prince of Evil himself. Men who can unite on nothing else can unite on the basis of a foe shared by all. Hitler himself states the case very succinctly:

> As a whole, and at all times, the efficiency of the truly national leader consists primarily in preventing the division of the attention of a people, and always in concentrating it on a single enemy. The more uniformly the fighting will of a people is put into action, the greater will be the magnetic force of the movement and the more powerful the impetus of the blow. It is part of the genius of a great leader to make adversaries of different fields appear as always belonging to one category only, because to weak and unstable characters the knowledge that there are various enemies will lead only too easily to incipient doubts as to their own cause.
>
> As soon as the wavering masses find themselves confronted with too many enemies, objectivity at once steps in, and the question is raised whether actually all the others are wrong and their own nation or their own movement alone is right.
>
> Also with this comes the first paralysis of their own strength. Therefore, a number of essentially different enemies must always be regarded as one in such a way that in the opinion of the mass of one's own adherents the war is being waged against one enemy alone. This strengthens the belief in one's own cause and increases one's bitterness against the attacker.

As everyone knows, this policy was exemplified in his selection of an "international" devil, the "international Jew" (the Prince was international, universal, "catholic"). This *materialization* of a religious pattern is, I think, one terrifically effective weapon of propaganda in a period where religion has been progressively weakened by many centuries of capitalist mate-rialism. You need but go back to the sermonizing of centuries to be reminded that religion had a powerful enemy long before organized atheism came upon the scene. Religion is based upon the "prosperity of poverty," upon the use of ways for converting our sufferings and handicaps into a good—but capitalism is based upon the prosperity of acquisitions, the only scheme of value, in fact, by which its proliferating store of gadgets could be sold, assuming for the moment that capitalism had not got so drastically in its own way that it can't sell its gadgets even after it has trained people to feel that human dignity, the "higher standard of living," could be attained only by their vast private accumulation.

So, we have, as unifying step No. 1, the international devil materialized, in the visible, point-to-able form of people with a certain kind of "blood," a burlesque of contemporary neo-positivism's ideal of meaning, which insists upon a *material* reference.

Once Hitler has thus essentialized his enemy, all "proof" henceforth is automatic. If you point out the enormous amount of evidence to show that the Jewish worker is at odds with the "international Jew stock exchange capitalist," Hitler replies with one hundred per cent regularity: That is one more indication of the cunning with which the "Jewish plot" is being engineered. Or would you point to "Aryans" who do the same as his conspiratorial Jews? Very well; that is proof that the "Aryan" has been "seduced" by the Jew.

The sexual symbolism that runs through Hitler's book, lying in wait to draw upon the responses of contemporary sexual values, is easily characterized: Germany in dispersion is the "dehorned Siegfried." The masses are "feminine." As such, they desire to be led by a dominating male. This male, as orator, woos them—and, when he has won them, he commands them. The rival male, the villainous Jew, would on the contrary "seduce" them. If he succeeds, he poisons their blood by intermingling with them. Whereupon, by purely associative connections of ideas, we are moved into attacks upon syphilis, prostitution, incest, and other similar misfortunes, which are introduced as a kind of "musical" argument when he is on the subject of "blood-poisoning" by intermarriage or, in its "spiritual" equiva-lent, by the infection of "Jewish" ideas, such as democracy.[1]

The "medicinal" appeal of the Jew as scapegoat operates from another angle. The middle class contains, within the mind of each member, a duality: its members simultaneously have a cult of money and a detestation of this cult. When capitalism is going well, this conflict is left more or less in abeyance. But when capitalism is balked, it comes to the fore. Hence, there is "medicine" for the "Aryan" members of the middle class in the projective device of the scapegoat, whereby the "bad" features can be allocated to the "devil," and one can "respect himself" by a distinction between "good" capitalism and "bad" capitalism, with those of a different lodge being the vessels of the "bad" capitalism. It is doubtless the "relief" of this solution that spared Hitler the necessity of explaining just how the "Jewish plot" was to work out. Nowhere does this book, which is so full of war plans, make the slightest attempt to explain the steps whereby the triumph of "Jewish Bolshevism," which destroys all finance, will be the triumph of "*Jewish*" finance. Hitler well knows the point at which his "elucidations" should rely upon the lurid alone.

The question arises, in those trying to gauge Hitler: Was his selection of the Jew, as his unifying devil-function, a purely calculating act? Despite the quotation I have already given, I believe that it was *not*. The vigor with which he utilized it, I think, derives from a much more complex state of affairs. It seems that, when Hitler went to Vienna, in a state close to total poverty, he genuinely suffered. He lived among the impoverished; and he describes his misery at the spectacle. He was *sensitive* to it; and his way of manifesting this sensitiveness impresses me that he is, at this point, wholly genuine, as with his wincing at the broken rela-tionships caused by alcoholism, which he in turn relates to impoverishment. During this time he began his attempts at political theorizing; and his disturbance was considerably increased by the skill with which Marxists tied him into knots. One passage in particular gives you reason, reading between the lines, to believe that the dialecticians of the class struggle, in their skill at blasting his muddled speculations, put him into a state of uncertainty that was finally "solved" by rage:

> The more I argued with them, the more I got to know their dialectics. First they counted on the ignorance of their adversary; then, when there was no way out, they themselves pretended stupidity. If all this was of no avail, they refused to understand or they changed the subject when driven into a corner; they brought up truisms, but they immediately transferred their acceptance to quite different subjects, and, if attacked again, they gave way and pretended to know nothing exactly. Wherever one attacked one of these prophets, one's hands seized slimy jelly; it slipped through one's fingers only to collect again in the next moment. If one smote one of them so thoroughly that, with the bystanders watching, he could but agree, and if one thus thought he had advanced at least one step, one was greatly astonished the following day. The Jew did not in the least remember the day before, he continued to talk in the same old strain as if nothing had happened, and if indignantly confronted, he pretended to be astonished and could not remember anything except that his assertions had already been proved true the day before.
>
> Often I was stunned.
>
> One did not know what to admire more: their glibness of tongue or their skill in lying.
>
> I gradually began to hate them.

At this point, I think, he is tracing the *spontaneous* rise of his anti-Semitism. He tells how, once he had discovered the "cause" of the misery about him, he could *confront it*. Where he had had to avert his eyes, he could now *positively welcome* the scene. Here his drastic structure of *acceptance* was being formed. He tells of the "internal happiness" that descended upon him.

> This was the time in which the greatest change I was ever to experience took place in me.
>
> From a feeble cosmopolite I turned into a fanatical anti-Semite,

and thence we move, by one of those associational tricks which he brings forth at all strategic moments, into a vision of the end of the world—out of which in turn he emerges with his slogan: "I am acting in the sense of the Almighty Creator: *By warding off Jews I am fighting for the Lord's work*" (italics his).

He talks of this transition as a period of "double life," a struggle of "reason" and "reality" against his "heart."[2] It was as "bitter" as it was "blissful." And finally, it was "reason" that won! Which prompts us to note that those who attack Hitlerism as a cult of the irrational should amend their statements to this extent: irrational it is, but it is carried on under the *slogan* of "Reason." Similarly, his cult of war is developed "in the name of" humility, love, and peace. Judged on a quantitative basis, Hitler's book certainly falls under the classification of hate. Its venom is everywhere, its charity is sparse. But the rationalized family tree for this hate situates it in "Aryan love." Some deep-probing German poets, whose work adumbrated the Nazi movement, did gravitate towards thinking *in the name of* war, irrationality, and hate. But Hitler was not among them. After all, when it is so easy to draw a doctrine of war out of a doctrine of peace, why should the astute politician do otherwise, particularly when Hitler has slung together his doctrines, without the slightest effort at logical symmetry? Furthermore,

Church thinking always got to its wars in Hitler's "sounder" manner; and the patterns of Hitler's thought are a bastardized or caricatured version of religious thought.

I spoke of Hitler's fury at the dialectics of those who opposed him when his structure was in the stage of scaffolding. From this we may move to another tremendously important aspect of his theory: his attack upon the parliamentary. For it is again, I submit, an important aspect of his medicine, in its function as medicine for him personally and as medicine for those who were later to identify themselves with him.

There is a "problem" in the parliament—and nowhere was this problem more acutely in evidence than in the pre-war Vienna that was to serve as Hitler's political schooling. For the parliament, at its best, is a "babel" of voices. There is the wrangle of men representing interests lying awkwardly on the bias across one another, sometimes opposing, sometimes vaguely divergent. Morton Prince's psychiatric study of "Miss Beauchamp," the case of a woman split into several sub-personalities at odds with one another, variously combining under hypnosis, and frequently in turmoil, is the allegory of a democracy fallen upon evil days. The parliament of the Habsburg Empire just prior to its collapse was an especially drastic instance of such disruption, such vocal diaspora, with movements that would reduce one to a disintegrated mass of fragments if he attempted to encompass the totality of its discordancies. So Hitler, suffering under the alienation of poverty and confusion, yearning for some integrative core, came to take this parliament as the basic symbol of all that he would move away from. He damned the tottering Habsburg Empire as a "State of Nationalities." The many conflicting voices of the spokesmen of the many political blocs arose from the fact that various separationist movements of a nationalistic sort had arisen within a Catholic imperial structure formed prior to the nationalistic emphasis and slowly breaking apart under its development. So, you had this Babel of voices; and, by the method of associative mergers, *using ideas as imagery*, it became tied up, in the Hitler rhetoric, with "Babylon," Vienna as the city of poverty, prostitution, immorality, coalitions, half-measures, incest, democracy (i. e., majority rule leading to "lack of personal responsibility"), death, internationalism, seduction, and anything else of thumbs-down sort the associative enterprise cared to add on this side of the balance.

Hitler's way of treating the parliamentary babel, I am sorry to say, was at one important point not much different from that of the customary editorial in our own newspapers. Every conflict among the parliamentary spokesmen represents a corresponding conflict among the material interests of the groups for whom they are speaking. But Hitler did not discuss the babel from this angle. He discussed it on a purely *symptomatic* basis. The strategy of our orthodox press, in thus ridiculing the cacophonous verbal output of Congress, is obvious: by thus centering attack upon the *symptoms* of business conflict, as they reveal themselves on the dial of political wrangling, and leaving the underlying cause, the business conflicts themselves, out of the case, they can gratify the very public they would otherwise alienate: namely, the businessmen who are the activating members of their reading public. Hitler, however, went them one better. For not only did he stress the purely *symptomatic* attack here. He proceeded to search for the "cause." And this "cause," of course, he derived from his medicine, his racial theory by which he could give a noneconomic interpretation of a phenomenon economically engendered.

Here again is where Hitler's corrupt use of religious patterns comes to the fore. Church thought, being primarily concerned with matters of the "personality," with problems of moral betterment, naturally, and I think rightly, stresses as a necessary feature, the act of will upon the part of the individual. Hence its resistance to a purely "environmental" account of human ills. Hence its emphasis upon the "person." Hence its proneness to seek a noneconomic explanation of economic phenomena. Hitler's proposal of a noneconomic "cause" for the disturbances thus had much to recommend it from this angle. And, as a matter of fact, it was Lueger's Christian-Social Party in Vienna that taught Hitler the tactics of tying up a program of social betterment with an anti-Semitic "unifier." The two parties that he carefully studied at that time were this Catholic faction and Schoenerer's Pan-German group. And his analysis of their attainments and shortcomings, from the standpoint of demagogic efficacy, is an extremely astute piece of work, revealing how carefully this man used the current situation in Vienna as an experimental laboratory for the maturing of his plans.

His unification device, we may summarize, had the following important features:

(1)   Inborn dignity. In both religious and humanistic patterns of thought, a "natural born" dignity of man is stressed. And this categorical dignity is considered to be an attribute of *all* men, if they will but avail themselves of it, by right thinking and right living. But Hitler gives this ennobling attitude an ominous twist by his theories of race and nation, whereby the "Aryan" is elevated above all others by the innate endowment of his blood, while other "races," in particular Jews and Negroes, are innately inferior. This sinister secularized revision of Christian theology thus puts the sense of dignity upon a fighting basis, requiring the conquest of "inferior races." After the defeat of Germany in the World War, there were especially strong emotional needs that this compensatory doctrine of an inborn superiority could gratify.

(2)   *Projection* device. The "curative" process that comes with the ability to hand over one's ills to a scapegoat, thereby getting purification by dissociation. This was especially medicinal, since the sense of frustration leads to a self-questioning. Hence if one can hand over his infirmities to a vessel, or "cause," outside the self, one can battle an external enemy instead of battling an enemy within. And the greater one's internal inadequacies, the greater the amount of evils one can load upon the back of "the enemy." This device is furthermore given a semblance of reason because the individual properly realizes that he is not alone responsible for his condition. There *are* inimical factors in the scene itself. And he wants to have them "placed," preferably in a way that would require a minimum change in the ways of thinking to which he had been accustomed. This was especially appealing to the middle class, who were encouraged to feel that they could conduct their businesses without any basic change whatever, once the businessmen of a different "race" were eliminated.

(3)   Symbolic rebirth. Another aspect of the two features already noted. The projective device of the scapegoat, coupled with the Hitlerite doctrine of inborn racial superiority, provides its followers with a "positive" view of life. They can again get the feel of *moving forward*, towards a *goal* (a promissory feature of which Hitler makes much). In Hitler, as the group's prophet, such rebirth involved a symbolic change of lineage. Here, above all, we see Hitler giving a malign twist to a benign aspect of Christian thought. For whereas the Pope, in the familistic pattern of thought basic to the Church, stated that the Hebrew prophets were the *spiritual ancestors* of Christianity, Hitler uses this same mode of thinking in reverse. He renounces this "ancestry" in a "materialistic" way by voting himself and the members of his lodge a different "blood stream" from that of the Jews.

(4)   Commercial use. Hitler obviously here had something to sell—and it was but a question of time until he sold it (i. e., got financial backers for his movement). For it provided a *noneconomic interpretation of economic ills*. As such, it served with maximum efficiency in deflecting the attention from the economic factors involved in modern conflict; hence by attacking "Jew finance" instead of *finance*, it could stimulate an enthusiastic movement that left "Aryan" finance in control.

Never once, throughout his book, does Hitler deviate from the above formula. Invariably, he ends his diatribes against contemporary economic ills by a shift into an insistence that we must get to the "true" cause, which is centered in "race." The "Aryan" is "constructive"; the Jew is "destructive"; and the "Aryan," to continue his *construction*, must *destroy* the Jewish *destruction*. The Aryan, as the vessel of *love*, must *hate* the Jewish *hate*.

Perhaps the most enterprising use of his method is in his chapter, "The Causes of the Collapse," where he refuses to consider Germany's plight as in any basic way connected with the consequences of war. Economic factors, he insists, are "only of second or even third importance," but "political, ethical-moral, as well as factors of blood and race, are of the first importance." His rhetorical steps are especially interesting here, in that he begins by seeming to flout the national susceptibilities: "The military defeat of the German people is not an undeserved catastrophe, but rather a deserved punishment by eternal retribution." He then proceeds to present the military collapse as but a "consequence of moral poisoning, visible to all, the consequence of a decrease in the instinct of self-preservation . . . which had already begun to undermine the foundations of the people and the Reich many years before." This moral decay derived from "a sin against the blood and the degradation of the race," so its innerness was an outerness after all: the Jew, who thereupon gets saddled with a vast amalgamation of evils, among them being capitalism, democracy, pacifism, journalism, poor housing, modernism, big cities, loss of religion, half measures, ill health, and weakness of the monarch.

2

Hitler had here another important psychological ingredient to play upon. If a State is in economic collapse (and his theories, tentatively taking shape in the pre-war Vienna, were but developed with greater efficiency in post-war Munich), you cannot possibly derive dignity from economic stability. Dignity must come first—and if you possess it, and implement it, from it may follow its economic counterpart. There is much justice to this line of reasoning, so far as it goes. A people in collapse, suffering under economic frustration and the defeat of nationalistic aspirations, with the very midrib of their integrative efforts (the army) in a state of dispersion, have little other than some "spiritual" basis to which they could refer their nationalistic dignity. Hence, the categorical dignity of superior race was a perfect recipe for the situation. It was "spiritual" in so far as it was "above" crude economic "interests," but it was "materialized" at the psychologically "right" spot in that "the enemy" was something you could *see*.

Furthermore, you had the desire for unity, such as a discussion of class conflict, on the basis of conflicting interests, could not satisfy. The yearning for unity is so great that people are always willing to meet you halfway if you will give it to them by fiat, by flat statement, regardless of the facts. Hence, Hitler consistently refused to consider internal political conflict on the basis of conflicting interests. Here again, he could draw upon a religious pattern, by insisting upon a *personal* statement of the relation between classes, the relation between leaders and followers, each group in its way fulfilling the same commonalty of interests, as the soldiers and captains of an army share a common interest in victory. People so dislike the idea of internal division that, where there is a real internal division, their dislike can easily be turned against the man or group who would so much as *name* it, let alone proposing to act upon it. Their natural and justified resentment against internal division itself, is turned against the diagnostician who states it as a *fact*. This diagnostician, it is felt, is the *cause* of the disunity he named.

Cutting in from another angle, therefore, we note how two sets of equations were built up, with Hitler combining or coalescing *ideas* the way a poet combines or coalesces *images*. On the one side, were the ideas, or images, of disunity, centering in the parliamentary wrangle of the Habsburg "State of Nationalities." This was offered as the antithesis of German nationality, which was presented in the curative imagery of unity, focused upon the glories of the Prussian Reich, with its mecca now moved to "folkish" Vienna. For though Hitler at first attacked the many "folkish" movements, with their hankerings after a kind of Wagnerian mythology of Germanic origins, he subsequently took "folkish" as a basic word by which to conjure. It was, after all, another noneconomic basis of reference. At first we find him objecting to "those who drift about with the word 'folkish' on their caps," and asserting that "such a Babel of opinions cannot serve as the basis of a political fighting movement." But later he seems to have realized, as he well should, that its vagueness was a major point in its favor. So it was incorporated in the grand coalition of his ideational imagery, or imagistic ideation; and Chapter XI ends with the vision of "a State which represents not a mechanism of economic considerations and interests, alien to the people, but a folkish organism."

So, as against the disunity equations, already listed briefly in our discussion of his attacks upon the parliamentary, we get a contrary purifying set; the wrangle of the parliamentary is to be stilled by the giving of *one* voice to the whole people, this to be the "inner voice" of Hitler, made uniform throughout the German boundaries, as leader and people were completely identified with each other. In sum: Hitler's inner voice, equals leader–people identification, equals unity, equals Reich, equals the mecca of Munich, equals plow, equals sword, equals work, equals war, equals army as midrib, equals responsibility (the personal responsibility of the absolute ruler), equals sacrifice, equals the theory of "German democracy" (the free popular choice of the leader, who then accepts the responsibility, and demands absolute obedience in exchange for his sacrifice), equals love (with the masses as feminine), equals idealism, equals obedience to nature, equals race, nation.[3]

And, of course, the two keystones of these opposite equations were Aryan "heroism" and "sacrifice" vs. Jewish "cunning" and "arrogance." Here again we get an astounding caricature of religious thought. For Hitler presents the concept of "Aryan" superiority, of all ways, in terms of "Aryan humility." This "humility" is extracted by a very delicate process that requires, I am afraid, considerable "good will" on the part of the reader who would follow it:

The Church, we may recall, had proclaimed an integral relationship between Divine Law and Natural Law. Natural Law was the expression of the Will of God. Thus, in the middle age, it was a result of natural law, working through tradition, that some people were serfs and other people nobles. And every good member of the Church was "obedient" to this law. Everybody resigned himself to it. Hence, the serf resigned himself to his poverty, and the noble resigned himself to his riches. The monarch resigned himself to his position as representative of the people. And at times the Churchmen resigned themselves to the need of trying to represent the people instead. And the pattern was made symmetrical by the consideration that each traditional "right" had its corresponding "obligations." Similarly, the Aryan doctrine is a doctrine of resignation, hence of humility. It is in accordance with the laws of nature that the "Aryan blood" is superior to all other bloods. Also, the "law of the survival of the fittest" is God's law, working through natural law. Hence, if the Aryan blood has been vested with the awful responsibility of its inborn superiority, the bearers of this "culture-creating" blood must resign themselves to struggle in behalf of its triumph. Otherwise, the laws of God have been disobeyed, with human decadence as a result. We must fight, he says, in order to "deserve to be alive." The Aryan "obeys" nature. It is only "Jewish arrogance" that thinks of "conquering nature by democratic ideals of equality."

This picture has some nice distinctions worth following. The major virtue of the Aryan race was its instinct for self-preservation (in obedience to natural law). But the major vice of the Jew was his instinct for self-preservation; for, if he did not have this instinct to a maximum degree, he would not be the "perfect" enemy—that is, he wouldn't be strong enough to account for the ubiquitousness and omnipotence of his conspiracy in destroying the world to become its master.

How, then, are we to distinguish between the benign instinct of self-preservation at the roots of Aryanism, and the malign instinct of self-preservation at the roots of Semitism? We shall distinguish thus: The Aryan self-preservation is based upon *sacrifice*, the sacrifice of the individual to the group, hence, militarism, army discipline, and one big company union. But Jewish self-preservation is based upon individualism, which attains its cunning ends by the exploitation of peace. How, then, can such arrant individualists concoct the world-wide plot? By the help of their "herd instinct." By their sheer "herd instinct" individualists can band together for a common end. They have no real solidarity, but unite opportunistically to seduce the Aryan. Still, that brings up another technical problem. For we have been hearing much about the importance of the person. We have been told how, by the "law of the survival of the fittest," there is a sifting of people on the basis of their individual capacities. We even have a special chapter of pure Aryanism: "The Strong Man is Mightiest Alone." Hence, another distinction is necessary: The Jew represents individualism; the Aryan represents "super-individualism."

I had thought, when coming upon the "Strong Man is Mightiest Alone" chapter, that I was going to find Hitler at his weakest. Instead, I found him at his strongest. (I am not refer-ring to *quality*, but to *demagogic effectiveness*.) For the chapter is not at all, as you might infer from the title, done in a "rise of Adolph Hitler" manner. Instead, it deals with the Nazis' gradual absorption of the many dis-related "folkish" groups. And it is managed throughout by means of a spontaneous identification between leader and people. Hence, the Strong Man's "aloneness" is presented as a *public* attribute, in terms of tactics for the struggle against the *Party's* dismemberment under the pressure of rival saviors. There is no explicit talk of Hitler at all. And it is simply taken for granted that his leadership is the norm, and all other leader-ships the abnorm. There is no "philosophy of the superman," in Nietzschean cast. Instead, Hitler's blandishments so integrate leader and people, commingling them so inextricably, that the politician does not even present himself as candidate. Somehow, the battle is over already, the decision has been made. "German democracy" has chosen. And the deployments of politics are, you might say, the chartings of Hitler's private mind translated into the vocab-ulary of nationalistic events. He says *what he thought* in terms of *what parties did*.

Here, I think, we see the distinguishing quality of Hitler's method as an instrument of persuasion, with reference to the question whether Hitler is sincere or deliberate, whether his vision of the omnipotent conspirator has the drastic honesty of paranoia or the sheer shrewdness of a demagogue trained in *Realpolitik* of the Machiavellian sort.[4] Must we choose? Or may we not, rather, replace the "either–or" with a "both–and"? Have we not by now offered grounds enough for our contention that Hitler's sinister powers of persuasion derive from the fact that he spontaneously evolved his "cure-all" in response to inner necessities?

3

So much, then, was "spontaneous." It was further channelized into the anti-Semitic pattern by the incentives he derived from the Catholic Christian-Social Party in Vienna itself. Add, now, the step into *criticism*. Not criticism in the "parliamentary" sense of doubt, of hearkening to the opposition and attempting to mature a policy in the light of counter-policies; but the "unified" kind of criticism that simply seeks for conscious ways of making one's position more "efficient," more thoroughly itself. This is the kind of criticism at which Hitler was an adept. As a result, he could *spontaneously* turn to a scapegoat mechanism, and he could, by conscious planning, perfect the symmetry of the solution towards which he had spontaneously turned.

This is the meaning of Hitler's diatribes against "objectivity." "Objectivity" is interference-criticism. What Hitler wanted was the kind of criticism that would be a pure and simple coefficient of power, enabling him to go most effectively in the direction he had chosen. And the "inner voice" of which he speaks would henceforth dictate to him the greatest amount of realism, as regards the tactics of efficiency. For instance, having decided that the masses required certainty, and simple certainty, quite as he did himself, he later worked out a 25-point program as the platform of his National Socialist German Workers Party. And he resolutely refused to change one single item in this program, even for purposes of "improvement." He felt that the *fixity* of the platform was more important for propagandistic purposes than any revision of his slogans could be, even though the revisions in themselves had much to be said in their favor. The astounding thing is that, although such an attitude gave good cause to doubt the Hitlerite promises, he could explicitly explain his tactics in his book and still employ them without loss of effectiveness.[5]

Hitler also tells of his technique in speaking, once the Nazi party had become effectively organized, and had its army of guards, or bouncers, to maltreat hecklers and throw them from the hall. He would, he recounts, fill his speech with *provocative* remarks, whereat his bouncers would promptly swoop down in flying formation, with swinging fists, upon anyone whom these provocative remarks provoked to answer. The efficiency of Hitlerism is the efficiency of the one voice, implemented throughout a total organization. The trinity of government which he finally offers is: *popularity* of the leader, *force* to back the popularity, and popularity and force maintained together long enough to become backed by a *tradition*. Is such thinking spontaneous or deliberate—or is it not rather both?[6]

Freud has given us a succinct paragraph that bears upon the spontaneous aspect of Hitler's persecution mania. (A persecution mania, I should add, different from the pure product in that it was constructed of *public* materials; all the ingredients Hitler stirred into his brew were already rife, with spokesmen and bands of followers, before Hitler "took them over." Both the pre-war and post-war periods were dotted with saviors, of nationalistic and "folkish" cast. This proliferation was analogous to the swarm of barter schemes and currency-tinkering that burst loose upon the United States after the crash of 1929. Also, the commercial availability of Hitler's politics was, in a low sense of the term, a *public* qualification, removing it from the realm of "pure" paranoia, where the sufferer develops a wholly *private* structure of interpretations.)

I cite from *Totem and Taboo*:

> Another trait in the attitude of primitive races towards their rulers recalls a mechanism which is universally present in mental disturbances, and is openly revealed in the so-called delusions of persecution. Here the importance of a particular person is extraordinarily heightened and his omnipotence is raised to the probable in order to make it easier to attribute to him responsibility for everything painful which happens to the patient. Savages really do not act differently towards their rulers when they ascribe to them power over rain and shine, wind and weather, and then de-throne them or kill them because nature has disappointed their expectation of a good hunt or a ripe harvest. The prototype which the paranoiac reconstructs in his persecution mania is found in the relation of the child to its father. Such omnipotence is regularly attributed to the father in the imagination of the son, and distrust of the father has been shown to be intimately connected with the heightened esteem for him. When a paranoiac names a person of his acquaintance as his "persecutor," he thereby elevates him to the paternal succession and brings him under conditions which enable him to make him responsible for all the misfortune which he experiences.

I have already proposed my modifications of this account when discussing the symbolic change of lineage connected with Hitler's project of a "new way of life." Hitler is symbolically changing from the "spiritual ancestry" of the Hebrew prophets to the "superior" ancestry of "Aryanism," and has given his story a kind of bastardized modernization, along the lines of naturalistic, materialistic "science," by his fiction of the special "blood-stream." He is voting himself a new identity (something contrary to the wrangles of the Habsburg Babylon, a soothing national unity); whereupon the vessels of the old identity become a "bad" father, i.e., the persecutor. It is not hard to see how, as his enmity becomes implemented by the backing of an organization, the rôle of "persecutor" is transformed into the rôle of persecuted, as he sets out with his like-minded band to "destroy the destroyer."

Were Hitler simply a poet, he might have written a work with an anti-Semitic turn, and let it go at that. But Hitler, who began as a student of painting, and later shifted to architecture, himself treats his political activities as an extension of his artistic ambitions. He remained, in his own eyes, an "architect," building a "folkish" State that was to match, in political materials, the "folkish" architecture of Munich.

We might consider the matter this way (still trying, that is, to make precise the relationship between the drastically sincere and the deliberately scheming): Do we not know of many authors who seem, as they turn from the rôle of citizen to the rôle of spokesman, to leave one room and enter another? Or who has not, on occasion, talked with a man in private conversation, and then been almost startled at the transformation this man undergoes when addressing a public audience? And I know persons today, who shift between the writing of items in the class of academic, philosophic speculation to items of political pamphleteering, and whose entire style and method changes with this change of rôle. In their academic manner, they are cautious, painstaking, eager to present all significant aspects of the case they are considering; but when they turn to political pamphleteering, they hammer forth with vituperation, they systematically misrepresent the position of their opponent, they go into a kind of political trance, in which, during its throes, they throb like a locomotive; and behold, a moment later, the mediumistic state is abandoned, and they are the most moderate of men.

Now, one will find few pages in Hitler that one could call "moderate." But there are many pages in which he gauges resistances and opportunities with the "rationality" of a skilled advertising man planning a new sales campaign. Politics, he says, must be sold like soap—and soap is not sold in a trance. But he did have the experience of his trance, in the "exaltation" of his anti-Semitism. And later, as he became a successful orator (he insists that revolutions are made solely by the power of the spoken word), he had this "poetic" rôle to draw upon, plus the great relief it provided as a way of slipping from the burden of logical analysis into the pure "spirituality" of vituperative prophecy. What more natural, therefore, than that a man so insistent upon unification would integrate this mood with less ecstatic moments, particularly when he had found the followers and the backers that put a price, both spiritual and material, upon such unification?

Once this happy "unity" is under way, one has a "logic" for the development of a method. One knows when to "spiritualize" a material issue, and when to "materialize" a spiritual one. Thus, when it is a matter of materialistic interests that cause a conflict between employer and employee, Hitler here disdainfully shifts to a high moral plane. He is "above" such low concerns. Everything becomes a matter of "sacrifices" and "personality." It becomes crass to treat employers and employees as different *classes* with a corresponding difference in the classification of their interests. Instead, relations between employer and employee must be on the "personal" basis of leader and follower, and "whatever may have a divisive effect in national life should be given a unifying effect through the army." When talking of national rivalries, however, he makes a very shrewd materialistic gauging of Britain and France with relation to Germany. France, he says, desires the "Balkanization of Germany" (i. e., its breakup into separationist movements—the "disunity" theme again) in order to maintain commercial hegemony on the continent. But Britain desires the "Balkanization of *Europe*," hence would favor a fairly strong and unified Germany, to use as a counter-weight against French hegemony. *German* nationality, however, is unified by the *spiritual* quality of Aryanism (that would produce the national organization via the Party) while this in turn is *materialized* in the myth of the blood-stream.

What are we to learn from Hitler's book? For one thing, I believe that he has shown, to a very disturbing degree, the power of endless repetition. Every circular advertising a Nazi meeting had, at the bottom, two slogans: "Jews not admitted" and "War victims free." And the substance of Nazi propaganda was built about these two "complementary" themes. He describes the power of spectacle; insists that mass meetings are the fundamental way of giving the individual the sense of being protectively surrounded by a movement, the sense of "community." He also drops one wise hint that I wish the American authorities would take in treating Nazi gatherings. He says that the presence of a special Nazi guard, in Nazi uniforms, was of great importance in building up, among the followers, a tendency to place the center of authority in the Nazi party. I believe that we should take him at his word here, but use the advice in reverse, by insisting that, where Nazi meetings are to be permitted, they be policed by the authorities alone, and that uniformed Nazi guards to enforce the law be prohibited.

And is it possible that an equally important feature of appeal was not so much in the repetitiousness per se, but in the fact that, by means of it, Hitler provided a "world view" for people who had previously seen the world but piecemeal? Did not much of his lure derive, once more, from the *bad* filling of a *good* need? Are not those who insist upon a purely *planless* working of the market asking people to accept far too slovenly a scheme of human purpose, a slovenly scheme that can be accepted so long as it operates with a fair degree of satisfaction, but becomes abhorrent to the victims of its disarray? Are they not then psychologically ready for a rationale, *any* rationale, if it but offer them some specious "universal" explanation? Hence, I doubt whether the appeal was in the sloganizing element alone (particularly as even slogans can only be hammered home, in speech after speech, and two or three hours at a stretch, by endless variations on the themes). And Hitler himself somewhat justifies my interpretation by laying so much stress upon the *half-measures* of the middle-class politicians, and the contrasting *certainty* of his own methods. He was not offering people a *rival* world view; rather, he was offering a world view to people who had no other to pit against it.

As for the basic Nazi trick: the "curative" unification by a fictitious devil-function, gradually made convincing by the sloganizing repetitiousness of standard advertising technique— the opposition must be as unwearying in the attack upon it. It may well be that people, in their human frailty, require an enemy as well as a goal. Very well: Hitlerism itself has provided us with such an enemy—and the clear example of its operation is guaranty that we have, in him and all he stands for, no purely fictitious "devil-function" made to look like a world menace by rhetorical blandishments, but a reality whose ominousness is clarified by the record of its conduct to date. In selecting his brand of doctrine as our "scapegoat," and in tracking down its equivalents in America, we shall be at the very center of accuracy. The Nazis themselves have made the task of clarification easier. Add to them Japan and Italy, and you have *case histories* of fascism for those who might find it more difficult to approach an understanding of its imperialistic drives by a vigorously economic explanation.

But above all, I believe, we must make it apparent that Hitler appeals by relying upon a bastardization of fundamentally religious patterns of thought. In this, if properly presented, there is no slight to religion. There is nothing in religion proper that requires a fascist state. There is much in religion, when misused, that does lead to a fascist state. There is a Latin proverb, *Corruptio optimi pessima*, "the corruption of the best is the worst." And it is the corruptors of religion who are a major menace to the world today, in giving the profound patterns of religious thought a crude and sinister distortion.

Our job, then, our anti-Hitler Battle, is to find all available ways of making the Hitlerite distortions of religion apparent, in order that politicians of his kind in America be unable to perform a similar swindle. The desire for unity is genuine and admirable. The desire for national unity, in the present state of the world, is genuine and admirable. But this unity, if attained on a deceptive basis, by emotional trickeries that shift our criticism from the accurate locus of our trouble, is no unity at all. For, even if we are among those who happen to be "Aryans," we solve no problems even for ourselves by such solutions, since the factors pressing towards calamity remain. Thus, in Germany, after all the upheaval, we see nothing beyond a drive for ever more and more upheaval, precisely because the "new way of life" was no new way, but the dismally oldest way of sheer deception—hence, after all the "change," the factors driving towards unrest are left intact, and even strengthened. True, the Germans had the resentment of a lost war to increase their susceptibility to Hitler's rhetoric. But in a wider sense, it has repeatedly been observed, the whole world lost the War—and the accumulating ills of the capitalist order were but accelerated in their movements towards confusion. Hence, here too there are the resentments that go with frustration of men's ability to work and earn. At that point a certain kind of industrial or financial monopolist may, annoyed by the contrary voices of our parliament, wish for the momentary peace of one voice, amplified by social organizations, with all the others not merely quieted, but given the quietus. So he might, under Nazi promptings, be tempted to back a group of gangsters who, on becoming the political rulers of the state, would protect him against the necessary demands of the workers. His gangsters, then, would be his insurance against his workers. But who would be his insurance against his gangsters?

Notes

1   Hitler also strongly insists upon the total identification between leader and people. Thus, in wooing the people, he would in a roundabout way be wooing himself. The thought might suggest how the Führer, dominating the feminine masses by his diction, would have an incentive to remain unmarried.

2   Other aspects of the career symbolism: Hitler's book begins: "Today I consider it my good fortune that Fate designated Braunau on the Inn as the place of my birth. For this small town is situated on the border between those two German States, the reunion of which seems, at least to us of the younger generation, a task to be furthered with every means our lives long," an indication of his "transitional" mind, what Wordsworth might have called the "borderer." He neglects to give the date of his birth, 1889, which is supplied by the editors. Again there is certain "correctness" here, as Hitler was not "born" until many years later—but he does give the exact date of his war wounds, which were indeed formative. During his early years in Vienna and Munich, he foregoes protest, on the grounds that he is "nameless." And when his party is finally organized and effective, he stresses the fact that his "nameless" period is over (i. e., he has shaped himself an identity). When reading in an earlier passage of his book some generalizations to the effect that one should not crystallize his political views until he is thirty, I made a note: "See what Hitler does at thirty." I felt sure that though such generalizations may be dubious as applied to people as a whole, they must, given the Hitler type of mind (with his complete identification between himself and his followers), be valid statements about himself. One *should* do what he *did*. The hunch was verified: about the age of thirty Hitler, in a group of seven, began working with the party that was to conquer Germany. I trace these steps particularly because I believe that the orator who has a strong sense of his own "rebirth" has this to draw upon when persuading his audiences that his is offering them the way to a "new life." However, I see no categorical objection to this attitude; its menace derives solely from the values in which it is exemplified. They may be wholesome or unwholesome. If they are unwholesome, but backed by conviction, the basic sincerity of the conviction acts as a sound virtue to reinforce a vice—and this combination is the most disastrous one that a people can encounter in a demagogue.

3   One could carry out the equations further, on both the disunity and unity side. In the aesthetic field, for instance, we have expressionism on the thumbs-down side, as against aesthetic hygiene on the thumbs-up side. This again is a particularly ironic moment in Hitler's strategy. For the expressionist movement was unquestionably a symptom of unhealthiness. It reflected the increasing alienation that went with the movement towards world war and the disorganization after the world war. It was "lost," vague in identity, a drastically accurate reflection of the response to material confusion, a pathetic attempt by sincere artists to make their wretchedness bearable at least to the extent that comes of giving it expression. And it attained its height during the period of wild inflation, when the capitalist world, which bases its morality of work and savings upon the soundness of its money structure, had this last prop of stability removed. The anguish, in short, reflected precisely the kind of disruption that made people *ripe* for a Hitler. It was the antecedent in a phrase of which Hitlerism was the consequent. But by thundering against this symptom he could gain persuasiveness, though attacking the very *foreshadowings of himself*.

4   I should not want to use the word "Machiavellian," however, without offering a kind of apology to Machiavelli. It seems to me that Machiavelli's *Prince* has more to be said in extenuation than is usually said of it. Machiavelli's strategy, as I see it, was something like this: He accepted the values of the Renaissance rule as a *fact*. That is: whether you like these values or not, they were there and operating, and it was useless to try persuading the ambitious ruler to adopt other values, such as those of the Church. These men believed in the cult of material power, and they had the power to implement their beliefs. With so much as "the given," could anything in the way of benefits for the people be salvaged? Machiavelli evolved a typical "Machiavellian" argument in favor of popular benefits, on the basis of the prince's own scheme of values. That is: the ruler, to attain the maximum strength, requires the backing of the populace. That this backing be as effective as possible, the populace should be made as strong as possible. And that the populace be as strong as possible, they should be well treated. Their gratitude would further repay itself in the form of increased loyalty.

It was Machiavelli's hope that, for this roundabout project, he would be rewarded with a well-paying office in the prince's administrative bureaucracy.

5   On this point Hitler reasons as follows: "Here, too, one can learn from the Catholic Church. Although its structure of doctrines in many instances collides, quite unnecessarily, with exact science and research, yet it is unwilling to sacrifice even one little syllable of its dogmas. It has rightly recognized that its resistibility does not lie in a more or less great adjustment to the scientific results of the moment, which in reality are always changing, but rather in a strict adherence to dogmas, once laid down, which alone give the entire structure the character of creed. Today, therefore, the Catholic Church stands firmer than ever. One can prophesy that in the same measure in which the appearances flee, the Church itself, as the resting pole in the flight of appearances, will gain more and more blind adherence."

6   Hitler also paid great attention to the conditions under which political oratory is most effective. He sums up thus:

> "All these cases involve encroachments upon man's freedom of will. This applies, of course, most of all to meetings to which people with a contrary orientation of will are coming, and who now have to be won for new intentions. It seems that in the morning and even during the day men's will power revolts with highest energy against an attempt at being forced under another's will and another's opinion. In the evening, however, they succumb more easily to the dominating force of a stronger will. For truly every such meeting presents a wrestling match between two opposed forces. The superior oratorical talent of a domineering apostolic nature will now succeed more easily in winning for the new will people who themselves have in turn experienced a weakening of their force of resistance in the most natural way, than people who still have full command of the energies of their minds and their will power.
>
> "The same purpose serves also the artificially created and yet mysterious dusk of the Catholic churches, the burning candles, incense, censers, etc."

Chapter 33

C.L.R. James ["Native Son"] (1901–89)

MY FRIENDS: A FIRESIDE CHAT ON THE WAR (1940)

U NLIKE KENNETH BURKE, C.L.R. JAMES, while granting that "Hitler is a vile criminal and should be driven off the face of the earth," saw no reason to fight for a racist and elitist country (the U.S.) that has, for far longer, treated Negroes and working-class people as badly as Hitler treats his victims: James's call is to "Unite and fight for our democracy here." The impending war that, along with the first, came to frame the modernist period proved as contentious as its predecessor in some fundamental ways.

C.L.R. James ["Native Son"], *My Friends: A Fireside Chat on the War*. New York: Workers Party, 1940. 3–12.

My Friends:

In this moment of crisis, it is proper that the voice of the working man should be heard. The President governs for all, the priests pray for all, the soldiers fight for all, (so, at any rate, we are told) but it is the working man who pays for all. In times of peace he pays in labor and in sweat. In war he pays in blood. It is always the working man and the farmers who are placed in the front line trenches. The sons of the rich stay behind the lines and direct. I have been to war and I know.

That is why I claim the privilege of a broadcast. I am a black working man, but I am a native son, as American as any white man in this country. My people were here as early as the family of President Roosevelt. We Negroes have labored and helped to make this country what it is. We have fought in all its wars, from the War of Independence to the first World War. In fact Crispus Attucks, a Negro, was the first American to die in the American Revolution. So that when the President talks about preparing America for war I demand my right to be heard. I know how to make a fireside chat. You are all sitting down listening to me and I am sitting down talking to you. You know it, I know it, everybody knows it. But in order to make you feel that you will be getting the real inside dope in a confidential manner, I shall begin by saying: "My friends, let us sit down, you and I, and talk this thing over together." That piece of baloney being out of the way, we can now get down to business.

Is America in danger?

The President says that Hitler seems to be winning the European war, and for that reason, this country is in danger of being invaded. Maybe the country is really in danger. But from the start this whole invasion business seemed phoney to me. I went to France in the last war, and I saw what it takes to carry a million men across the Atlantic and to keep them there. Germany is very near to England. Yet everybody says that Hitler had to capture Norway and the Channel ports and get within a few miles of England in order to attempt a successful invasion. Who is such a fool as to believe that Hitler can transport millions of men and all the arms and supplies needed to invade this country, across nearly 3,000 miles of sea? The Yankee Clipper takes only 20 passengers at a time. How many clippers will Hitler need to land a million men in America? Hitler would have to spend years in preparation before he could invade this country. Furthermore, the President knows that all this talk about invasion is just a lot of hooey. My wife Leonora, who is a Red, told me that the other day the generals of the army and navy made an official statement that this country was in no danger of invasion. And if they know that, and I know it, the President knows it too.

When I said to some of my friends, poor trembling Negroes, that they had many things to worry about but that invasion was not one of them, they asked me, "But do you think that the President is lying? Why should he lie? He only wants to protect the people." My friends, and particularly my young friends, let me show you how a President can lie. I went to hear President Wilson speak in 1916. He said that we must vote for him because he was the man who had kept us out of war. And as soon as he had won the elections he carried out the plan he had had in his pocket for almost a year before the elections, and we were in the war before you could wink. Since that time, my friends, I know how Presidents can lie. Wilson wanted to get us in and he used one jive. Roosevelt wants to get us in and he is using another one. He wants to frighten us with the fear of invasion, although his own generals and admirals tell us the exact opposite.

Defend what democracy?

My friends, why does the President want us to fight? He and all the writers in the papers say that it is to defend our democracy. Our democracy! My friends, when I heard that I laughed for ten minutes. Yes. Laughed. I'll tell you why. It was because I was so damned mad that if I didn't laugh I would have broken the radio. And that radio cost me $4 in the pawn shop and I didn't want to break it.

Tell me, Mr. President, what democracy do I defend by going to fight Hitler? Hitler is a vile criminal and should be driven off the face of the earth. But I have no democracy and the democracy I haven't got Hitler didn't take from me. I know all those who have been taking away democracy from me and my people. They are Cotton Ed Smith, Senator Bilbo, Vice-President Garner, all of them aided by you, President Roosevelt for all of you are in one Party together, the Democratic Party, and if you were any friend of the Negro, you couldn't be working so closely in the same Party with these Negro-hating, Negro-baiting little American Hitlers from the South. William Green, president of the American Federation of Labor, who discriminates against Negroes in his unions is another. There are thousands of others I could name. They have been lynching me and my people, giving us the dirtiest jobs, at the lowest pay, Jim Crowing us, taking the taxes we pay to teach white children, treating us worse than they treat their dogs. They were doing all this before Hitler was born, they do it now, they will do it long after Hitler is dead, unless we Negroes ourselves put a stop to it. I never heard any fireside chat from you, Mr. President, I never saw any campaign carried out by the Senate to give the American Negroes democracy, for instance, to pass the anti-lynching bill or abolish Jim Crow, and the poll tax which prevents Negroes in the South from voting. May I tell you Mr. President, politely as suits a fireside chat, that you and the hypocritical scoundrels who rule this country with you, should stop being so active in defense of democracy abroad and pay attention to the crimes against democracy at home. Instead, your newspapers spread a lot of lies about no lynchings having taken place during the past year. As if they don't know that nowadays the Southern lynchers get together in small bands and murder any Negro whom they want to get rid of, very quietly so as to keep it out of the papers.

The fifth column

My friends, the President warns us about the fifth column. I understand that this is the new name for the enemies of democracy. Where have the President's eyes been all this time? If he wants to find out who these fifth column people are, he just has to ask the Negroes. We know them. We spend our lives fighting against them. If the President sends a reporter to me, with a large notebook, I guarantee that between sunrise and sundown tomorrow I'll point out to him more fifth column enemies of democracy then he can find room for in all the jails of this country. No, Mr. President, we'll begin to listen to you about the fifth column when you begin to put in jail some of the really big enemies of democracy in this country, beginning with the United States Vice-President, Jack Garner, boss of the Jim Crow state of Texas.

My friends, the President and all the papers say that we must stop aggression. But when Mussolini made his aggression against Ethiopia, you, Mr. President, prevented us from sending arms to Ethiopia. Where was all your hatred of aggression then? But I notice that today you have the American fleet ready to fight Japan for the Dutch East Indies. My wife Leonora, who is a Red, tells me that America wants to fight Germany to prevent Hitler taking the colonies of the Allied countries, and to keep Germany as much as possible out of the fat trade with China and Spanish America. That makes sense to me. But what I know is this, that whatever President Roosevelt wants to fight about, it is not democracy. I have no interests in the Dutch East Indies. The natives there got no democracy from the Dutch. They will get no democracy from America. They will get none from Japan. They will get some democracy only when they drive out all these leeches and take charge of their country themselves.

Democracy begins at home

My friends, it is not only the poor Negroes who get no democracy. The other day I saw a picture, "The Grapes of Wrath." In it I saw whites, miserable and suffering almost as much as we Negroes suffer. Every week outside the relief station there are whites standing with me, no better off than I am. If these poor Okies and the Negroes and the white workers were to get together we could fight for some real democracy here. That is the fight I am willing to begin. I know who my enemies are. And when these same enemies come telling me about going to fight against Hitler, what I tell them in my mind is what would be very out of place in a fireside chat, so you will have to guess at it.

I know a Negro school teacher who says that we must fight with Roosevelt to defeat Hitler. I want to see Hitler defeated but why should I trust Roosevelt? How do I know that Roosevelt at some time or other wouldn't turn traitor? Look at the King of Belgium. He must have told the poor Belgians to come and fight with him for democracy. Now he has surrendered to Hitler and next thing he will be helping Hitler to impose fascism on the Belgian people. That is what you get when you listen to these Kings and Presidents and Generals all urging poor people to come and fight against Hitler. I have been watching that school teacher a long time. And I think that what he wants to defend is not democracy but the $35 a week he gets for teaching in the Jim Crow school. If he wants to die for democracy and his $35, that is his business. But he isn't going to lead me into that. When we have defeated the enemies of democracy here, then we can give Hitler a beating. I would be ready to fight against Hitler then.

Unite and fight!

My friends, Negroes are well known for their belief in God. And I notice that a good fireside chat always has something in it about God and prayers. But I notice too that Hitler in all his speeches talks about God and asks for his blessing. President Wilson, that smooth tongued rascal, was full of God too. But Roosevelt, Hitler and Wilson not only pray to God, but see to it that they have guns, battleships and planes. So tonight, my friends, my dear friends, I want to leave out the prayers and tell you plainly what is my policy for the American people and the Negroes in particular. It is this. Unite and fight for our democracy here. What I as a black man want is a steady job. I want good wages, $30 a week for 30 hours a week. I want a good relief check when I am out of work. I want my black children to go to any school in the neighborhood. I want a good house and I want it where I choose to have it. I want to travel where I want, go where I want, eat where I want, join any union or organization that I want. I want this for myself, I want it for all my black people, and if any white man is prepared to join with us to fight for that, I want it for him too. And it isn't Hitler who is keeping these things from me. It is those who are robbing, cheating and insulting my people.

My friends, to win those things I am prepared to fight. I may go to jail in that fight. I may get shot down by the police but I'll die contented. Death is death and I prefer to die fighting here for my rights and the rights of my people and those who will fight with us, than die so that President Roosevelt and his friends might get the Dutch East Indies or the British West Indies or any kind of Indies whatsoever. So, my friends, good night. I shall not quote scripture but I shall end with a piece of personal history. I went to the last war. I was treated like a dog before I went. I was treated like a dog while I was there. I was treated like a dog when I returned. I have been played for a sucker before, and I am not going to be played again.

PART V

Gender and sexuality

Gender and sexuality "questions" often intersected, in degree of interest and debate, with modernity's other "questions," for example, the Irish, Negro, Jewish, and Woman questions. As can be observed in the readings included in Part VI "Race and Ethnicity," the tensions beneath the social "questions" were often about civic rights, increased mobility and social acceptance for specific populations, expanded (often meaning equal) legal rights and protections, and social justice. Women's rights, homosexual rights, and a modern, complex and various understanding of sexuality and psychology were some of the goals of modern scientific and social research. Designations of abnormality could lead to incarceration, commitment in mental institutions, forced sterilization or other eugenic "public health" protections and practices. Great Britain's Labouchère Amendment of 1885 was one exhibit of the criminological response to sexual difference; Oscar Wilde would be sentenced to hard labor for his homosexual "crime" of "gross indecency" under the force of the Amendment's brutal and humiliating punishment. The Labouchère Amendment superseded Great Britain's death penalty for "buggery," which was abolished in 1861, but the draconian law was not abolished until 1967.[1]

Viennese Professor of Psychiatry and Neurology Richard von Krafft-Ebing's *Psychopathia Sexualis* (1886) predated Sigmund Freud's psychological and scientific study of human sexual behavior. Krafft-Ebing's subtitled "Medico-Forensic" research on sexual deviation relied heavily on Latinate legal and medical terminology to illustrate the seriousness of his scientific mode of inquiry and to discourage prurient readers who might sensationalize his investigations; his clinical examination of neurological and sexual pathologies was intended for scholarly use in the legal and medical professions.[2] In his "Foreword" to *Psychopathia Sexualis*, Dr. Daniel Blain describes the late nineteenth-century psychiatrist's attempts to fortify the technical language of psycho-sexual pathology in his subsequent editions of the work by representing the sexual acts in his case studies in Latin. But this scientific discursive framework for the clinical specificity of his sexual research was insufficiently coded for some of Krafft-Ebing's detractors. In 1893, the *British Medical Journal* remarked that *Psychopathia Sexualis* would have been "Better if it had been written entirely in Latin, and thus veiled in the decent obscurity of a dead language. . . ."[3] Krafft-Ebing's scholarship brought into late Victorian daylight topics including fetishism, incest, nymphomania, masturbation, homosexuality, and inversion, as well as the health benefits of women's clitoral orgasm.

Krafft-Ebing popularized the terms sadism and masochism, having derived them from the pornographic-philosophical writings of the Marquis de Sade (*120 Days of Sodom; Justine, Or The Misfortunes of Virtue; Juliette*) and Leopold von Sacher-Masoch's novella, *Venus in Furs* (1870), a sensual tale of a couple's experimentation with games of dominance and submission. Although many of his sexual theories are considered outmoded by today's psychiatric profession, Krafft-Ebing was central in legitimizing the study of sexuality and inspiring others to examine human sexual behavior in professional, modern, and rational terms. In the Preface to the first edition of his study, Krafft-Ebing described himself as an ethical guide and public servant; his stated intentions were the eradication of erroneous ideas, sexual biases, and prejudices, and the promotion of medical understanding and justice. Noting in his Preface that "the poet is the better psychologist," Krafft-Ebing credited artists for their sympathetic treatment of the strange "Physiology of Love." Ultimately, however, he believed that the scientist and "natural philosopher" could shed unsentimental scientific light on the mysteries of human sexuality. Quoting Tardieu, he asserted that "the sacred ministry of the physician, while obliging him to see everything, also permits him to say everything" (xiv). Krafft-Ebing's work paved the way for other modern scientists, theorists, and philosophers of human sexuality; he also crucially supported the professional advancement of a younger colleague at the University of Vienna who later revolutionized the study of human sexuality, Sigmund Freud.

Vienna and Germany were at the forefront of sexuality studies; in Germany in 1919, Magnus Hirschfeld and his colleagues Arthur Kronfeld and Friedrich Wertheim founded the Institute for Sexual Science, an organization whose missions were sex education, medical and psychological sexual research, sexual and criminal reform, and the modernization of public policies concerning sexual and social rights. The Institute advertised its facilities "for research, teaching, healing, and refuge"; its motto was *Per Scientiam ad Justitiam* (Justice through Science). Hirschfeld's Institute was part of Weimar culture's progressive ideological and cultural outlook, an ethos that was increasingly associated with urbanity, cosmopolitanism, and intellectual and artistic circles. Seized by the Nazis in 1933, the Institute was transformed into the Nazi Academy for Public Health Service, an institute for the development of "racial hygiene"—the Nazi's racist, sexist, and genocidal policies, which had deadly and definitive answers for the woman and homosexual questions, Jewish and Gypsy "problems," and the treatment of other "unruly" or "abnormal" bodies and "undesirable" types.

In Great Britain, Havelock Ellis, John Addington Symonds, and Edward Carpenter expanded upon and continued the study of inversion, the era's popular term for "homogenic" or homosexual sexuality. Ellis and Symonds' 1897 study, *Sexual Inversion*, attempted to locate the biological causes of sexual difference; for them, inversion was an abnormality, but not necessarily a pathological one. In *Sexual Inversion*, homosexual differences were compared to genetic and organic abnormalities like color blindness, criminality and genius, and "sports" of nature that one observes naturally occurring in plant and animal life. Ellis and Symonds' "invert" was pathological but they attempted, not altogether successfully, to use the term in a scientific and poetic rather than criminal way. In one of their study's footnotes, they cite their contemporary Rudolph Virchow's observation that "The pathological under some circumstances can be advantageous."[4] Ellis and Symonds reminded their readers of the etymological reasoning behind Virchow's conclusions: that in Greek "pathological" denotes an anomaly; that the word does not mean harmful and does not denote disease; and that "nosos" means disease. The linguistic rationale for a subtler and more sophisticated understanding of sexual behavior is indicative of Ellis and Symonds' equivocal discussion of homosexuality; for example, they noted that "Strictly speaking, the invert is degenerate: he has fallen away from the genus" (206). The invert is the carrier of a biological error; he is degenerate, not a degenerate. This is a fine and slightly ambivalent distinction that Edward Carpenter would appraise in a passionately unambivalent fashion in his study, *The Intermediate Sex* (1908).

Carpenter was deeply affected by Walt Whitman's *Leaves of Grass* (1868) and the American poet's utopian and democratic vision of society; his philosophical influence at Cambridge was appreciated by Bloomsbury Circle affiliates like E.M. Forster and Lytton Strachey. The early socialist, Pre-Raphaelite Brotherhood member, and central figure of the Arts and Crafts Movement William Morris was another inspiration for Carpenter, as were the feminist movement and Eastern religious philosophy, especially the Hindu epic *Mahabharata Bhagavad Gita*. Carpenter's sexual philosophy combined all of these influences; in his vision, the invert became a member of the "intermediate sex" or Uranist, a sensitive and refined, sexual-spiritual-artistic citizen of the future. As Carpenter wrote in the opening of *The Intermediate Sex*, "The Uranian people may be destined to form the advance guard of that great movement which will one day transform the common life by substituting the bond of personal affection and compassion for the monetary, legal and other external ties which now control and confine society." Carpenter's vision was of a classless, sexually liberated society in which socialists, New Women, and the Uranian tribes could together lead the way forward to a more egalitarian society. His Uranians have a "double nature," something akin to Virginia Woolf's ideal artist's androgynous mind (*A Room of One's Own*) or her gender-bending hero/ heroine in *Orlando*. Carpenter, like Woolf, considered Shakespeare to be a perfect embodiment of such a type; other artists who represented his ideal Uranian temperament were Michelangelo, Sweden's Queen Christina (played by Greta Garbo in the 1933 Rouben Mamoulian film), and the Greek poet Sappho. Carpenter's life-partner was George Merrill, a working-class man from Sheffield; the Merrill–Carpenter relationship was said to have influenced E.M. Forster's 1913 originated, but posthumously published, gay novel *Maurice* (1971). Merrill was the basis of the gamekeeper Scudder, as Carpenter was for the character Maurice Hall.[5] After the publication of *The Intermediate Sex*, Carpenter combined his Uranist studies with modernist ethnological primitivism; his *Intermediate Types among Primitive Folk: A Study in Social Evolution* (1914) examined non-Western cultures' indigenous traditions of Uranism in their priestly, prophetic, shamanistic, and artistic cultures.

A radical, ideological reading of sexuality like Carpenter's can also be seen in the work of feminist-anarchist Emma Goldman. A committed feminist, she fervently believed in the emancipation of women, but she wanted to maintain a delineation of sexual difference. For Goldman the modern challenge of sexual self-knowledge and expression was defined by a clear, but complex question: "The problem that confronts us today, and which the nearest future is to solve, is how to be one's self and yet be in oneness with others, to feel deeply with all human beings and still retain one's own characteristic qualities."[6] Goldman's feminism and anarchism were supported by a personal philosophy of self-expression; she was as alarmed by feminist and leftist orthodoxies as she was by political repression. As early as 1917, Goldman was examining the costs and paradoxes of gender equality. Emancipation might allow a woman to enter the professions but, she noted, "she is often compelled to exhaust all her energy, use up her vitality, and strain every nerve in order to reach the market value" (160). In Goldman's view, feminists broke free of external patriarchal fetters, only to succumb to their own "internal tyrannies," conflicted impulses of respectability and propriety, as well as anti-sex and biologi- cally unnatural, neo-puritanical barriers that damaged the "inner life of woman" (163). Woman's true and complete liberation would require her recognition of her inherent gifts of "naturalness, kindheartedness, and simplicity" (166); Goldman's vision of feminine freedom also included the celebration of free love. She was imprisoned for her anarchist speeches and actions and her distribution of birth control information.

Goldman openly supported the American birth control advocate Margaret Sanger after Sanger was arrested under the Comstock Law for publishing and distributing birth control information in the June 1914 edition of her monthly newsletter, *The Woman Rebel*. Goldman was arrested in February 1916 under the same law for championing her own pro-sex philosophies and Sanger's more practical family planning beliefs. Sanger's birth control advocacy had both feminist and nationalist concerns; control over her reproductive rights guaranteed the health of the woman and her family, and the health of the nation depended upon the reproduction of economically and eugenically "fit" families. Part of Sanger's inspiration for the formation of the American Birth Control League in 1921 was her Catholic mother's eighteen pregnancies and eleven live births; she was also inspired to birth control advocacy by her work with impoverished women on New York City's Lower East Side. Sanger knew personally several women who had died or become permanently injured after performing self-induced abortions; her activism was also inspired by socialism and her affiliations with American artists, intellectuals, and radicals, including Goldman, John Reed, Mabel Dodge, and Upton Sinclair. Sanger remains a controversial subject to date for her promotion of racial hygiene, open discussion of abortion practices, and scientific belief in family planning.

The British women's sexuality advocate and palaeobotanist Marie Stopes aimed to address the lack of interest among male scientists and philosophers in the serious study of female sexuality. In Stopes's view, women's alleged lack of interest in sexual activity was inappropriately and unjustly viewed as the result of their capricious and irrational nature, extreme prudishness, and lack of intellect. Stopes also recognized that a woman's economic dependency on men led her to shape her sexual self-image and understanding of her own drives to her husband's needs and demands. The chapter on "Woman's 'Contrariness'" from her bestselling marriage manual *Married Love: A New Contribution to the Solution of Sex Difficulties* (1931) celebrates a positive view of woman's distinctly feminine libidinal drives. Woman's alleged "contrariness" is but a "subtler ebb and flow" of sexual energy and psychology than the man's. Stopes's woman's mind and body are affected by love-tides, sex-tides, "wonderful tides" of physiological feeling, the knowledge of which can enormously benefit both partners in a marriage. Female consciousness and sexuality was not a "Dark Continent" as Freud once remarked; in Stopes's view, women's sexual instincts and bodies were uncharted seas holding as yet undiscovered treasures. In her conclusion to the chapter, Stopes referred to the modern study of light, sound, and particle waves, and the kinds of serious studies of physical matter conducted by late Victorian scientists like John Tyndall and modern ones like Albert Einstein. A comprehensive understanding of the tides of a woman's body would be, Stopes suggested, as culturally revolutionary and revealing as Einstein's discoveries. Stopes was also an advocate of eugenics and racial hygiene; in *Radiant Motherhood* (1920), she supported the compulsory sterilization of the unfit in order to prevent racial degeneration. The combination of progressive and disciplinary sexual beliefs simultaneously held by activists and reformers like Sanger and Stopes was not extraordinary; immigration anxieties, the mobility of racial and ethnic populations, and the prevalence of venereal diseases led visionary and reactionary thinkers to embrace eugenic policies that would in Nazi Germany characterize scientific zeal gone horrifically, murderously wrong.

Sigmund Freud's theories of sexuality, erotic drives, and the dynamic links between conscious and subconscious thoughts, memories and feelings, dreams and fantasies provided, arguably, the most powerful and broadly influential modern revolution in conscious thinking about human sexuality. Freud's work also liberated the arts from the discretion and propriety associated with artistic expression in the Victorian age. Using domestic tales from Greek classical mythology as the conceptual models for his psycho-sexual case studies, Freud popularized the language of neurotic sexual complexes and natural stages of sexual development. The Oedipal Complex, the Electra Complex (which he doubted and refuted) hysteria, penis envy, the castration complex – Freud's psychoanalytical studies blended Krafft-Ebing's science with poetic insight. Freud's use of stories and narratives gave the study of sexual normality and pathology a kind of social currency that his predecessor's deliberately remote language could not communicate. Freud's case studies were his own and his patients' stories and his theories were his interpretive devices; he published *The Interpretation of Dreams* (1900) after a long period of self-analysis. As some post-Freudian feminist scholars would argue, Freud's methodology was as artful as it was "scientific"; French feminists Hélène Cixous' *The Laugh of the Medusa* (1975) and Luce Irigaray's *The Speculum of the Other Women* (1985) would subject Freud's theories to case studies of their own. The woman's alleged "lack" that Freud discussed in "Female Sexuality" and elsewhere, woman's discovery of her absent phallus, was interpreted by the feminists as a conceptual "phallogocentric" bias, perhaps even a fear of the female body's power, fecundity, and productive plenitude, fears that were imported into philosophy and rooted in religion and myth. Those uncharted waves of the female body to which Marie Stopes referred in her marriage manual were, in the French feminists' view, women's bodies' uncontainable orgasmic capabilities and the female bodies' ability to lactate (Cixous' white writing). These kinds of feminine excesses prompted the post-Freudian feminists to use and supplement the modern psychoanalyst's work and theorize *l'écriture féminine*, a style of writing that can be related to modernists like Gertrude Stein and Virginia Woolf. Stein's word games can be understood in Freudian terms: "a rose is eros is eros"—her artful play heightens the suggestive and promiscuous nature of language.

Despite the limitations of Freud's science, his studies called new attention to the ways in which language usage in treatment could reveal a patient's repressed inner thoughts and fears; the notion of the Freudian slip is perhaps the most widely known of his offspring. The notion that language – symbols and signs – had unconscious power and could reveal supplementary and subtextual meanings inspired visual and narrative artists. Advances in the understanding of human sexuality and desire affected all of the modern arts: surrealist painting and film, Georgia O'Keefe's vaginal flora, Joyce's "continuous present" and Woolf's "stream-of-consciousness," dream, flashback, and malleability of time in narrative owe much to Freud's analysis of sexual desire and anxiety, memory, and emotion. In the arts, books like Joyce's *Ulysses* (1922), Radclyffe Hall's *The Well of Loneliness* (1928), D.H. Lawrence's *Lady Chatterley's Lover* (1928), and James Hanley's *Boy* (1931) were attacked as obscene and legally suppressed. Some believed that the reading public must be protected from works that artistically explored and represented homosexuality and open sexuality; Joyce's seaside masturbator, Leopold Bloom, and his orgasmic wife, Molly, were too much for even an experimental modernist like Virginia Woolf. *Ulysses'* "Nausicaa" episode manages to be simultaneously comical and deeply moving. As Joyce's lonely, cuckolded Odysseus, Leopold Bloom fantasizes about the nursemaid Gertie McDowell on Sandymount strand, he climaxes to a crescendo of fireworks, an over-the-top ejaculatory symbol that the reader "gets" thanks to Freudian symbology and its incorporation into popular media like film.

Freudian examination of myth also enabled understanding of some of the anxieties about actual women and their changing social status. While Edward Carpenter envisioned modernity's New Woman as the champion of a more egalitarian future, others were less certain that liberated and mobile women would be beneficial to society; the vamp, woman as vampire, emerges into the social imaginary alongside the suffragette. D.H. Lawrence's *Women in Love* (1920) uses a range of myths, from biblical to Teutonic, to explore modern sexuality and consciousness after World War I. The novel's Pussum is one embodiment of a modern woman; she is dependent on men and sexually debased. Gudrun, the modern artist, feminist, and willful "phallic" woman, is another, the devouring woman and man-killer. Lawrence's Ursula, the idealized essential female, is soft, lambent, and vascillating. Other modernist works like Luis Buñuel's surrealist film *Un chien andalou* (1929), Mulk Raj Anand's *Coolie* (1935), and Djuna Barnes' *Nightwood* (1936) represent sexual freedom and the exploration of gender as fundamental expressions of their protagonists' essential liberty and being. In modern times, sexuality itself had come out of the closet.

Notes

1   Edward Carpenter's first homo-philosophical publications, *Homogenic Love* and *Love's Coming-of-Age* (1896), coincided with Oscar Wilde's imprisonment.
2   Krafft-Ebing's psycho-sexual and medical-juridical terminology includes "anesthesia sexualis," the absence of sexual instinct; "hyperaesthesia," pathologically exaggerated sexual instinct; and "paraesthsia," the perversion of sexual instinct. *Psychopathia Sexualis* 46–52.
3   Daniel Blain, "Foreword," *Psychopathia Sexualis* xi.
4   Ellis and Symonds, *Sexual Inversion* 203–5. See also Chapter 34 of this volume, p. 306.
5   Forster was rumored to have shared *Maurice* with D.H. Lawrence, who wrote a heterosexual version of the cross-class sexual alliance in *Lady Chatterley's Lover* (1928), another infamous banned book of the early twentieth century.
6   Emma Goldman, "The Tragedy of Women's Emancipation" 158–59. See also Chapter 37 of this volume, p. 327.

Suggested further readings

Adkins, Lisa. *Revisions: Gender and Sexuality in Late Modernity*. Philadelphia: Open University Press, 2002.

Baldwin, James. *Giovanni's Room*. New York: Dial Press, 1956.

Barnes, Djuna. *Nightwood*. London: Faber and Faber, 1936.

Beckmann, Andrea. *The Social Construction of Sexuality and Perversion: Deconstructing Sadomasochism*. Basingstoke: Palgrave Macmillan, 2009.

Blain, Daniel. "Foreword." In Krafft-Ebing, *Psychopathia Sexualis*. New York: Scarborough Books, Stein and Day, 1978.

Boito, Camillo. *Senso and Other Stories*. New York: Hippocrene Books, 1999.

Buñuel, Luis. *Un chien andalou* (1929). Film.

Burton, Richard. *The Book of the Thousand Nights and a Night*. 17 vols. (1885–8). Whitefish, MT: Kessinger, 2003.

Carpenter, Edward. *Intermediate Types among Primitive Folk: A Study in Social Evolution*. London: G. Allen, 1914.

Cohen, Ed. *Talk on the Wilde Side: Towards a Genealogy of a Discourse on Male Sexualities*. New York: Routledge, 1992.

Collecott, Diana. *H.D. and Sapphic Modernism*. Cambridge: Cambridge UP, 2008.

Deren, Maya, and Alexander Hammid. *Meshes of the Afternoon* (1943). Film.

Doan, Laura, and Jane Garrity, eds. *Sapphic Modernities: Sexuality, Women and National Culture*. New York: Palgrave Macmillan, 2006.

Egan, Danielle R. *Theorizing the Sexual Child in Modernity*. Basingstoke: Palgrave Macmillan, 2010.

Foucault, Michel. *The History of Sexuality*. New York: Vintage, 1988–90.

Galvin, Mary E. *Queer Poetics: Five Modernist Women Writers*. New York: Praeger, 1998.

Hall, Radclyffe. *The Well of Loneliness*. London: Jonathan Cape, 1928.

Hirschfeld, Magnus. *The Sexual History of the World War*. New York: Falstaff Press, 1937.

Klein, Melanie. *The Psycho-Analysis of Children*. London: Hogarth Press, 1932.

Krafft-Ebing, Richard von. *Psychopathia Sexualis: With Especial Reference to the Antipathic Sexual Instinct, A Medico-Forensic Study* (1886). Ed. Daniel Blain. New York: Scarborough Books, 1978.

Lawrence, D.H. *Lady Chatterley's Lover* (1928). El Paso, TX: El Paso Norte Press, 2009.

Lowy, Dina. *The Japanese "New Woman": Images of Gender and Modernity*. New Brunswick, NJ: Rutgers UP, 2007.

Loy, Mina. "Love Songs." *The Lost Lunar Baedeker: The Poems of Mina Loy*. New York: Farrar, Straus and Giroux, 1996.

Luxemburg, Rosa. "The Proletarian Woman" (1914). *The Rosa Luxemburg Reader*. New York: Monthly Review Press, 2004.

McCormick, Richard W. *Gender and Sexuality in Weimar Modernity: Film, Literature, and "New Objectivity."* New York: Palgrave Macmillan, 2001.

Nair, Sashi. *Secrecy and Sapphic Modernism: Writing Romans à Clef between the Wars.* New York: Palgrave Macmillan, 2012.

Stein, Gertrude. *Tender Buttons: Objects, Food, Rooms.* New York: C. Marie, 1914.

Stopes, Marie. *Married Love: A New Contribution to the Solution of Sex Difficulties.* New York: Putnam, 1931.

Sturgis, Howard. *Tim: A Story of School Life.* London: Macmillan, 1891.

Symonds, John Addington. *A Problem in Greek Ethics.* London: privately printed, 1901.

Tova Linett, Maura. *Modernism, Feminism, and Jewishness.* Cambridge: Cambridge UP, 2011.

Woolf, Virginia. *A Room of One's Own* (1929). New York: Harcourt, Brace, 1991.

——. *Orlando: A Biography* (1928). New York: Mariner Books, 1973.

Chapter 34

Havelock Ellis (1859–1939) and
John Addington Symonds (1840–93)

"THE THEORY OF SEXUAL INVERSION"
(1897)

THIS MEDICAL TEXTBOOK ON HOMOSEXUALITY, the first in English, began as a collaboration between the sexologist Ellis and the poet and literary critic Symonds. Soon after the collaboration began, Symonds, best known for his studies of male love in ancient Greece, died, and Ellis went on to write the bulk of the text. Describing the genesis of the project in his preface, Ellis writes: "I realised that in England, more than in any other country, the law and public opinion combine to place a heavy penal burden and a severe social stigma on the manifestations of an instinct which to these persons who possess it frequently appears natural and normal." Written around the time of the Oscar Wilde trial, *Sexual Inversion* represents homosexuality not as a criminal practice, but, rather, as a congenital predisposition that occurs among various strata of society – criminals and geniuses alike.

Havelock Ellis and John Addington Symonds, "The Theory of Sexual Inversion," *Sexual Inversion: A Critical Edition*, ed. Ivan Crozier. London: Palgrave Macmillan, 2008. 201–9.

The rational way of regarding the normal sexual impulse is as an inborn organic impulse, developing about the time of puberty.[1] At this period suggestion and association may come in to play a part in defining the object of the emotion; the soil is now ready, but the variety of seeds likely to thrive in it is limited. That there is a greater indefiniteness in the aim of the sexual impulse at this period we may well believe. This is shown not only by occasional tentative signs of sexual emotion directed towards the same sex, but by the usually vague and non-sexual character of the normal passion at puberty. But the channel of sexual emotion is not thereby turned into an utterly abnormal path. Whenever this permanently happens we are, I think, bound to believe—and we have many grounds for believing—that we are dealing with an organism which from the beginning is abnormal.[2] The same seed of suggestion is sown in various soils; in the many it dies out, in the few it flourishes. The cause can only be a difference in the soil.

If, then, we must postulate a congenital abnormality in order to account satisfactorily for at least a large proportion of sexual inverts, wherein does that abnormality consist? Ulrichs explained the matter by saying that in sexual inverts a male body coexists with a female soul:

anima muliebris in corpore virili inclusa. Even writers with some pretension to scientific precision, like [Valentin] Magnan and [Eugene] Gley, have adopted this phrase in a modified form, considering that in inversion a female brain is combined with a male body or male glands. This is, however, not an explanation. It merely crystallises into an epigram the superficial impression of the matter. As an explanation it is to a scientific psychologist unthinkable. We only know soul as manifested through body; and, although if we say that a person seems to have the body of a man and the feelings of a woman we are saying what is often true enough, it is quite another matter to assert dogmatically that a female soul, or even a female brain, is expressing itself through a male body. That is simply unintelligible. I say nothing of the fact that in male inverts the feminine psychic tendencies may be little if at all marked, so that there is no 'feminine soul' in the question; nor of the further important fact that in a very large proportion of cases the body itself presents primary and secondary sexual characters that are distinctly modified.

We can probably grasp the nature of the abnormality better if we reflect on the development of the sexes and on the latent organic bi-sexuality in each sex. At an early stage of development the sexes are indistinguishable, and throughout life the traces of this early community of sex remain. The hen fowl retains in a rudimentary form the spurs which are so large and formidable in her lord, and sometimes she develops a capacity to crow, or puts on male plumage. Among mammals the male possesses useless nipples, which occasionally even develop into breasts, and the female possesses a clitoris, which is merely a rudimentary penis, and may also develop. The sexually inverted person does not usually possess any gross exaggeration of these signs of community with the opposite sex. But, as we have seen, there are a considerable number of more subtle approximations to the opposite sex in inverted persons, both on the physical and the psychic side. Putting the matter in a purely speculative shape, it may be said that at conception the organism is provided with about 50 per cent of male germs and about 50 per cent of female germs, and that as development proceeds either the male or the female germs assume the upper hand, killing out those of the other sex, until in the maturely developed individual only a few aborted germs of the opposite sex are left. In the homosexual person, however, and in the psychosexual hermaphrodite, we may imagine that the process has not proceeded normally, on account of some peculiarity in the number or character of either the original male germs or female germs, or both; the result being that we have a person who is organically twisted into a shape that is more fitted for the exercise of the inverted than of the normal sexual impulse, or else equally fitted for both.[3]

Thus in sexual inversion we have what may fairly be called a 'sport' or variation, one of those organic aberrations which we see throughout living nature, in plants and in animals.[4] It is not here asserted, as I would carefully point out, that an inverted sexual instinct, or organ for such instinct, is developed in early embryonic life; such a notion is rightly rejected as absurd. What we may reasonably regard as formed at an early stage of development is strictly a predisposition, that is to say, such a modification of the organism that it becomes more adapted than the normal or average organism to experience sexual attraction to the same sex. The sexual invert may thus be roughly compared to the congenital idiot, to the instinctive criminal, to the man of genius, who are all not strictly concordant with the usual biological variation (because this is of a less subtle character), but who become somewhat more intelligible to us if we bear in mind their affinity to variations. Symonds compared inversion to colour-blindness; and such a comparison is reasonable. Just as the ordinary colour-blind person is congenitally insensitive to those red-green rays which are precisely the most impressive to the normal eye, and gives an extended value to the other colours—finding that blood is the same colour as grass, and a florid complexion blue as the sky—so the invert fails to see emotional values patent to normal persons, transferring their values to emotional associations which for the rest of the world are utterly distinct. Or we may compare inversion to such a phenomenon as coloured-hearing in which there is not so much defect, as an abnormality of nervous tracks producing new and involuntary combinations.[5] Just as the colour-hearer instinctively associates colours with sounds, like the young Japanese lady who remarked when listening to singing, "That boy's voice is red!" so the invert has his sexual sensations brought into relationship with objects that are normally without sexual appeal. And inversion, like colour-hearing, is found more commonly in young subjects, tending to become less marked, or to die out, after puberty. Colour-hearing, while an abnormal phenomena, it must be added, cannot be called a diseased condition, and it is probably much less frequently associated with other abnormal or degenerative stigmata than is inversion. There is often a congenital element, shown by the tendency to hereditary transmission, while the associations are developed in very early life, and are too regular to be the simple result of suggestion.[6]

All these organic variations, which I have here mentioned to illustrate sexual inversion, are abnormalities. It is important that we should have a clear idea as to what an abnormality is. Many people imagine that what is abnormal is necessarily diseased. That is not the case, unless we give the word disease an inconveniently and illegitimately wide extension. It is both inconvenient and inexact to speak of colour-blindness, criminality and genius, as diseases, in the same sense as we speak of scarlet-fever or tuberculosis or general paralysis as diseases. Every congenital abnormality is doubtless due to a peculiarity in the sperm or oval elements or in their mingling or to some disturbance in their early development. But the same may doubtless be said of the normal dissimilarities between brothers and sisters. It is quite true that any of these aberrations may be due to antenatal disease, but to call them abnormal does not beg that question. If it is thought that any authority is needed to support this view, we can scarcely find a weightier than that of [Rudolph] Virchow, who has repeatedly insisted on the right use of the word "anomaly," and who teaches that, though an anomaly may constitute a predisposition to disease, the study of anomalies—pathology, as he would call it, teratology as we may perhaps prefer to call it—is not the study of disease, which, he would term nosology; the study of the abnormal is perfectly distinct from the study of the morbid.[7] Virchow considers that the region of the abnormal is the region of pathology, and that the study of disease must be regarded distinctly as nosology. Whether we adopt this terminology, or whether we consider the study of the abnormal as part of teratology, is a secondary matter, not affecting the right understanding of the term 'anomaly', and its due differentiation from the term 'disease'.

A word may be said as to the connection between sexual inversion and degeneration. In France especially, since the days of [Benedict-Augustin] Morel, the stigmata of degeneration are much spoken of and sexual inversion is frequently regarded as one of them, *i.e.*, as an episodic *syndrome* of an hereditary disease, taking its place beside other psychic stigmata, such as kleptomania and pyromania. Krafft-Ebing also so regards inversion. Strictly speaking, the invert is degenerate: he has fallen away from the genus. So is a colour-blind person. But Morel's conception of degenerescence has unfortunately been coarsened and vulgarised.[8] As it now stands we gain little or no information by being told that a person is a 'degenerate'. When we find a complexus [*sic*] of well-marked abnormalities, we are fairly justified in asserting that we have to deal with a condition of degeneration. Inversion is frequently found in such a condition. I have, indeed, already tried to suggest that a condition of diffused minor abnormality may be regarded as the basis of congenital inversion. In other words, inversion is bound up with a modification of the secondary sexual characters.[9] But little is gained by calling these modifications 'stigmata of degeneration', a term which threatens to disappear from scientific terminology, to become a mere term of literary and journalistic abuse. So much may be said concerning a conception or a phrase of which far too much has been made in popular literature. At the best it remains vague and little fitted for scientific use.[10]

Sexual inversion, therefore, remains a congenital abnormality to be classed with the other congenital abnormalities which have psychic concomitants. At the very least such congenital abnormality usually exists as a predisposition to inversion. It is probable that many persons go through the world with a congenital predisposition to inversion which always remains latent and unroused; in others the instinct is so strong that it forces its own way in spite of all obstacles; in others, again, the predisposition is weaker, and a powerful exciting cause plays the predominant part.

We are thus led to the consideration of the causes that excite the latent predisposition. A great variety of causes has been held to excite to sexual inversion. It is only necessary to mention those which I have found influential. The most important of these is undoubtedly our school system, with its segregation of boys and girls apart from each other during the important periods of puberty and adolescence. Many congenital inverts have not been to school at all, and many who have been, pass through school life without forming any passionate or sexual relationship; but there remain a large number who date the development of homosexuality from the influences and examples of school life. The impressions received at the time are not less potent because they are often purely sentimental and without any obvious sensual admixture. Whether they are sufficiently potent to generate permanent inversion alone may be doubtful, but if it is true that in early life the sexual instincts are less definitely determined than when adolescence is complete, it is conceivable, though unproved, that a very strong impression, acting even on a normal organism, may cause arrest of sexual development on the psychic side. It is a question I am not in a position to settle.

Another important exciting cause of inversion is seduction. By this I mean the initiation of the young boy or girl by some older and more experienced person in whom inversion is already developed, and who is seeking the gratification of the abnormal instinct. This appears to be a not uncommon incident in the early history of sexual inverts. That such seduction— sometimes an abrupt and inconsiderate act of mere sexual gratification—could by itself produce a taste for homosexuality is highly improbable; in individuals not already predis- posed it is far more likely to produce disgust, as it did in the case of the youthful Rousseau. "He only can be seduced", as Moll puts it, "who is capable of being seduced". No doubt it frequently happens in these, as so often in more normal 'seductions', that the victim has offered a voluntary or involuntary invitation.[11]

Another exciting cause of inversion, to which little importance is usually attached but which I find to have some weight, is disappointment in normal love. It happens that a man in whom the homosexual instinct is yet only latent, or at all events held in a state of repression, tries to form a relationship with a woman. This relationship may be ardent on one or both sides, but—often, doubtless, from the latent homosexuality of the lover—it comes to nothing. Such love-disappointments, in a more or less acute form, occur at some time or another to nearly everyone. But in these persons the disappointment with one woman consti- tutes motive strong enough to disgust the lover with the whole sex and to turn his attention towards his own sex. It is evident that the instinct which can thus be turned round can scarcely be strong, and it seems probable that in some of these cases the episode of normal love simply serves to bring home to the invert the fact that he is not made for normal love.[12] In other cases, doubtless—especially those that are somewhat feeble-minded and unbal- anced—a love-disappointment really does poison the normal instinct, and a more or less impotent love for women becomes an equally impotent love for men. The prevalence of homosexuality among prostitutes must certainly be in large extent explained by a similar and better-founded disgust with normal sexuality.

These three influences, therefore—example at school, seduction, disappointment in normal love—all of them drawing the subject away from the opposite sex and concen- trating him on his own sex, are powerful exciting causes of inversion; but they mostly require a favourable organic predisposition to act on, while there are a large number of cases in which no exciting cause at all can be found, but in which from the earliest childhood the subject's interest seems to be turned on his own sex, and continues to be so turned throughout life.

At this point I conclude the analysis of the psychology of sexual inversion as it presents itself to me. I have sought only to bring out the more salient points, neglecting minor points, neglecting also those groups of inverts who may be regarded as of secondary importance. The average invert, moving in ordinary society, so far as my evidence extends, is most usually a person of average general health, though very frequently with hereditary relationships that are markedly neurotic. He is usually the subject of a congenital predisposing abnormality, or complexus of minor abnormalities, making it difficult or impossible for him to feel sexual attraction to the opposite sex, and easy to feel sexual attraction to his own sex. This abnormality either appears spontaneously from the first, by development or arrest of development, or it is called into activity by some accidental circumstance.

Notes

1   It is denied by some ([Theodor] Meynert, [Paul] Näcke, etc.) that there is any sexual *instinct* at all. I may as well, therefore, explain in what sense I use the word. I mean an inherited aptitude the performance of which normally demands for its full satisfaction the presence of a person of the opposite sex. It might be asserted that there is no such thing as an instinct for food, that it is all imitation, etc. In a sense this is true, but the automatic basis remains. A chicken from an incubator needs no hen to teach it to eat. It seems to discover eating and drinking as it were by chance, at first eating awkwardly and eating everything, until it learns what will best satisfy its organic mechanism. There is no instinct for food, it may be, but there is an instinct which is only satisfied by food. It is the same with the 'sexual instinct'. The tentative and omnivorous habits of the newly-hatched chicken may be compared to the uncertainty of the sexual instinct at puberty; while the sexual pervert is like a chicken that should carry on into adult age an appetite for worsted and paper.

2   This remains true even when homosexuality is acquired in adult age. In the notorious case of Oscar Wilde it was apparently acquired late, but there can be no doubt whatever as to the existence of the congenital basis of abnormality. See Raffalovich's account of this case, *L'Uranisme*, pp. 241 *et seq.*

3   I do not present this view as more than a picture which helps us to realise the actual phenomena which we witness in homosexuality, although I may add that so able a teratologist as Dr. J.W. Ballantyne considers that "it seems a very possible theory". Lately (and independently) it has been somewhat more seriously and dogmatically set forth as an explanatory theory by Dr. G. de Letamendi, Dean of the Faculty of Medicine of Madrid, in a paper read before the International Medical Congress at Rome in 1894. Letamendi believes in a principle of panhermaphroditism—a hermaphroditic bipolarity—which involves the existence of latent female germs in the male, latent male germs in the female, which latent germs may strive for, and sometimes obtain, the mastery.

4   The idea that sexual inversion is a variation, perhaps due to imperfect sexual differentiation, or reversion of type, was suggested in America by [James] Kiernan ("Insanity: Sexual Perversion," *Detroit Lancet*, 7, 1884, p. 482; Kiernan, "Sexual Perversion and the Whitechapel Murders," *Medical Standard*, 4, 1888, pp. 556–70), and Lydston ("A Lecture on Sexual Perversion, Satyriasis and Nymphomania," in *Addresses and Essays*, 2nd ed., Louisville, Renz and Henry, 1892, pp. 243–64, orig. *Philadelphia Medical and Surgical Reporter*, September 7, 1889). In this work (p. 246) he remarks: "Just as we may have variations of physical form and of mental attributes, in general, so we may have variations and perversions of that intangible entity, sexual affinity" and (p. 246) he refers to failure of development and imperfect differentiation of generative centres, comparable to conditions like hypospadias and epispadias. In Germany a patient of Krafft-Ebing has worked out the same idea connecting inversion with fœtal bisexuality (8th ed. *Psychopathia Sexualis*, p. 117). Krafft-Ebing himself simply asserts that, whether congenital or acquired, there must be *Belastung* [taint]; inversion is a "degenerative phenomenon," a functional sign of degeneration (Krafft-Ebing, "Zur Erklärung [*sic;* Ellis meant Aetiologie] der conträren Sexualempfindung," *Jahrbuch für Psychiatrie und Neurologie*, 12, 1894, pp. 338–65).

5   Since this chapter was first published (as Ellis, "Die Theorie der conträren Sexualempfindung," *Seperatabdrück aus dem Centralblatt für Nervenheilkunde und Psychiatrie*, Februar-Heft, 1896, pp. 1–7),

[Charles] Féré has also compared congenital inversion to colour-blindness and similar anomalies (Féré, "La Descendance d'un Inverti," *Revue Génerale de Clinique et Therapie*, 1896), while [Theophile] Ribot has lately referred to the anomaly with coloured hearing (*Psychology of the Emotions*, Part ii., ch. 7).

6 See, *eg.*, [Theodore] Flournoy, *Des Phenomènes de Synopsie*, Geneva, Eggimann, 1893; and for a brief discussion of the general phenomena of synæsthesia, Edmund Parish, *Hallucinations and Illusions*, London, Walter Scott, 1897, ch. 7 and [Eugene] Bleuler, "Secondary Sensations" in Tuke's *Dictionary of Psychological Medicine*.

7 Thus at the Innsbruck meeting of the German Anthropological Society in 1894, Virchow thus expressed himself: "I am of opinion that a transformation, a metaplasia, a change from one species into another—whether in individual animals or plants, or individuals or their tissues—cannot take place without anomaly: for if no anomaly appears this new departure is impossible. *The physiological norm hitherto existing is changed*, and we cannot well call that anything else but an anomaly. But in old days an anomaly was called πάθος [pathos], and in this sense every departure from the norm is for me a pathological event. If we have ascertained such a pathological event we are further led to investigate what *pathos* was the special cause of it. . . . This cause may be, for example, an external force, or a chemical substance, or a physical agent, producing in the normal conditions of the body a change, an anomaly (πάθος). This can become hereditary under some circumstances, and then become the foundation for certain small hereditary characters which are propagated in a family; in themselves they belong to pathology, even although they produce no injury. For I must remark that pathological does not mean harmful: it does not indicate disease; disease in Greek is υόσος [nosos], and it is nosology that is concerned with disease. The pathological under some circumstances can be advantageous." (*Correspondenz-blatt der Deutsch Gesellschaft für Anthropologie,* 1894). Putting aside the question of terminology, these remarks are of interest when we are attempting to find the wider bearings of such an anomaly as sexual inversions.

8 It is this fact which has caused the Italians to be shy of using the word 'degeneration'; thus A. Marro, in his great work, *I Caratteri dei Delinquenti*, Torino, Bocca, 1887, has made a notable attempt to analyse the phenomena lumped together as degenerate into three groups. Atypical, Atavistic, and Morbid.

9 [Hans] Kurella goes so far as to regard the invert as a transitional form between the complete man or the complete woman and the genuine sexual hermaphrodite (Preface to the German edition of Émile Laurent's *Die Zwitterbildungen* [*Les Bisexués*], Leipzig, George Wigand, 1896; and Kurella in the *Centralblatt für Nervenheilkunde*, May, 1896). This view is supported by what we see in animals, but scarcely accounts for all the facts in the human subject.

10 The inverted impulse is sometimes (as by [Paul] Näcke) considered an obsession, developing on a neuræsthenic or neurotic basis. That there is an analogy and, indeed, a distinct relationship between obsessions and sexual perversions, I fully believe, but obsessions are so vague, capricious and ill-understood, that I am not inclined to press the analogy very far. We cannot explain the little known by the less known. I would rather explain obsessions by reference to the sexual impulse, than the sexual impulse by reference to obsessions.

11 Symonds knew an invert who, when staying at an hotel, heard a knock at his door after he had gone to bed; the boots entered with a light, locked the door behind him, and got into the bed. Another invert awoke to find the sentry posted at his door in the act of violating him. Both these inverts were of high social rank. "I feel dubious", remarks Symonds, "as to whether in each of these cues my informant did not draw on (by look, and appearance) the audacious inferior". It seems very probable, indeed; for such incidents very rarely happen to the normally constituted man.

12 See, for instance, an incident in the early life of Case XVIII.

Chapter 35

Sigmund Freud (1856–1939)

"FEMALE SEXUALITY" (1905)

FREUD'S THEORY OF THE OEDIPAL conflict had a powerful influence on modernism, appearing as a significant trope in works such as D.H. Lawrence's *Sons and Lovers*, James Joyce's *A Portrait of the Artist as a Young Man*, and Virginia Woolf's *To the Lighthouse*. As Freud concedes in "Female Sexuality," however, the basic theory did not account for female sexual development. In this late essay, influenced by a new generation of female psychoanalysts, Freud revisits the topic of female sexuality. Women did not experience a parallel "Electra Complex," a theory developed by Jung and often erroneously attributed to Freud, but rather underwent a complicated dissociation from their primary erotic attachment to the mother. He argues that in the pre-Oedipal phase of female development, girls experience sexual impulses that are initially connected to the clitoris (imagined as analogous to the penis), but that as the focus of their impulses shifts from the clitoris to the vagina and thus from masculine to feminine sexuality, their attachments undergo a parallel shift from the mother to the father. Cases where these transitions are incomplete or unsuccessful could, Freud argues, result in frigidity or homosexuality.

Sigmund Freud, "Female Sexuality," *The Standard Edition of the Complete Psychological Works of Sigmund Freud*, vol. 21 (1927–31), trans. James Strachey. London: Hogarth Press, 1961. 225–43.

I

During the phase of the normal Oedipus complex we find the child tenderly attached to the parent of the opposite sex, while its relation to the parent of its own sex is predominantly hostile. In the case of a boy there is no difficulty in explaining this. His first love-object was his mother. She remains so; and, with the strengthening of his erotic desires and his deeper insight into the relations between his father and mother, the former is bound to become his rival. With the small girl it is different. Her first object, too, was her mother. How does she find her way to her father? How, when and why does she detach herself from her mother? We have long understood that the development of female sexuality is complicated by the fact that the girl has the task of giving up what was originally her leading genital zone—the clitoris—in favour of a new zone—the vagina. But it now seems to us that there is a second change of the same sort which is no less characteristic and important for the development of the female: the exchange of her original object—her mother—for her father. The way in which the two tasks are connected with each other is not yet clear to us.

It is well known that there are many women who have a strong attachment to their father; nor need they be in any way neurotic. It is upon such women that I have made the observations which I propose to report here and which have led me to adopt a particular view of female sexuality. I was struck, above all, by two facts. The first was that where the woman's attachment to her father was particularly intense, analysis showed that it had been preceded by a phase of exclusive attachment to her mother which had been equally intense and passionate. Except for the change of her love-object, the second phase had scarcely added any new feature to her erotic life. Her primary relation to her mother had been built up in a very rich and many-sided manner. The second fact taught me that the *duration* of this attachment had also been greatly underestimated. In several cases it lasted until well into the fourth year—in one case into the fifth year—so that it covered by far the longer part of the period of early sexual efflorescence. Indeed, we had to reckon with the possibility that a number of women remain arrested in their original attachment to their mother and never achieve a true change-over towards men. This being so, the pre-Oedipus phase in women gains an importance which we have not attributed to it hitherto.

Since this phase allows room for all the fixations and repressions from which we trace the origin of the neuroses, it would seem as though we must retract the universality of the thesis that the Oedipus complex is the nucleus of the neuroses. But if anyone feels reluctant about making this correction, there is no need for him to do so. On the one hand, we can extend the content of the Oedipus complex to include all the child's relations to both parents; or, on the other, we can take due account of our new findings by saying that the female only reaches the normal positive Oedipus situation after she has surmounted a period before it that is governed by the negative complex. And indeed during that phase a little girl's father is not much else for her than a troublesome rival, although her hostility towards him never reaches the pitch which is characteristic of boys. We have, after all, long given up any expectation of a neat parallelism between male and female sexual development.

Our insight into this early, pre-Oedipus, phase in girls comes to us as a surprise, like the discovery, in another field, of the Minoan-Mycenean civilization behind the civilization of Greece.

Everything in the sphere of this first attachment to the mother seemed to me so difficult to grasp in analysis—so grey with age and shadowy and almost impossible to revivify—that it was as if it had succumbed to an especially inexorable repression. But perhaps I gained this impression because the women who were in analysis with me were able to cling to the very attachment to the father in which they had taken refuge from the early phase that was in question. It does indeed appear that women analysts—as, for instance, Jeanne Lampl-de Groot and Helene Deutsch—have been able to perceive these facts more easily and clearly because they were helped in dealing with those under their treatment by the transference to a suitable mother-substitute. Nor have I succeeded in seeing my way through any case completely, and I shall therefore confine myself to reporting the most general findings and shall give only a few examples of the new ideas which I have arrived at. Among these is a suspicion that this phase of attachment to the mother is especially intimately related to the aetiology of hysteria, which is not surprising when we reflect that both the phase and the neurosis are characteristically feminine, and further, that in this dependence on the mother we have the germ of later paranoia in women.[1] For this germ appears to be the surprising, yet regular, fear of being killed (? devoured) by the mother. It is plausible to assume that this fear corresponds to a hostility which develops in the child towards her mother in consequence of the manifold restrictions imposed by the latter in the course of training and bodily care and that the mechanism of projection is favoured by the early age of the child's psychical organization.

II

I began by stating the two facts which have struck me as new: that a woman's strong dependence on her father merely takes over the heritage of an equally strong attachment to her mother, and that this earlier phase has lasted for an unexpectedly long period of time. I shall now go back a little in order to insert these new findings into the picture of female sexual development with which we are familiar. In doing this, a certain amount of repetition will be inevitable. It will help our exposition if, as we go along, we compare the state of things in women with that in men.

First of all, there can be no doubt that the bisexuality, which is present, as we believe, in the innate disposition of human beings, comes to the fore much more clearly in women than in men. A man, after all, has only one leading sexual zone, one sexual organ, whereas a woman has two: the vagina—the female organ proper—and the clitoris, which is analogous to the male organ. We believe we are justified in assuming that for many years the vagina is virtually non-existent and possibly does not produce sensations until puberty. It is true that recently an increasing number of observers report that vaginal impulses are present even in these early years. In women, therefore, the main genital occurrences of childhood must take place in relation to the clitoris. Their sexual life is regularly divided into two phases, of which the first has a masculine character, while only the second is specifically feminine. Thus in female development there is a process of transition from the one phase to the other, to which there is nothing analogous in the male. A further complication arises from the fact that the clitoris, with its virile character, continues to function in later female sexual life in a manner which is very variable and which is certainly not yet satisfactorily understood. We do not, of course, know the biological basis of these peculiarities in women; and still less are we able to assign them any teleological purpose.

Parallel with this first great difference there is the other, concerned with the finding of the object. In the case of a male, his mother becomes his first love-object as a result of her feeding him and looking after him, and she remains so until she is replaced by someone who resembles her or is derived from her. A female's first object, too, must be her mother: the primary conditions for a choice of object are, of course, the same for all children. But at the end of her development, her father—a man—should have become her new love-object. In other words, to the change in her own sex there must correspond a change in the sex of her object. The new problems that now require investigating are in what way this change takes place, how radically or how incompletely it is carried out, and what the different possibilities are which present themselves in the course of this development.

We have already learned, too, that there is yet another difference between the sexes, which relates to the Oedipus complex. We have an impression here that what we have said about the Oedipus complex applies with complete strictness to the male child only and that we are right in rejecting the term 'Electra complex' which seeks to emphasize the analogy between the attitude of the two sexes. It is only in the male child that we find the fateful combination of love for the one parent and simultaneous hatred for the other as a rival. In his case it is the discovery of the possibility of castration, as proved by the sight of the female genitals, which forces on him the transformation of his Oedipus complex, and which leads to the creation of his super-ego and thus initiates all the processes that are designed to make the individual find a place in the cultural community. After the paternal agency has been internal-ized and become a super-ego, the next task is to detach the latter from the figures of whom it was originally the psychical representative. In this remarkable course of development it is precisely the boy's narcissistic interest in his genitals—his interest in preserving his penis—which is turned round into a curtailing of his infantile sexuality.

One thing that is left over in men from the influence of the Oedipus complex is a certain amount of disparagement in their attitude towards women, whom they regard as being castrated. In extreme cases this gives rise to an inhibition in their choice of object, and, if it is supported by organic factors, to exclusive homosexuality.

Quite different are the effects of the castration complex in the female. She acknowledges the fact of her castration, and with it, too, the superiority of the male and her own inferiority; but she rebels against this unwelcome state of affairs. From this divided attitude three lines of development open up. The first leads to a general revulsion from sexuality. The little girl, frightened by the comparison with boys, grows dissatisfied with her clitoris, and gives up her phallic activity and with it her sexuality in general as well as a good part of her masculinity in other fields. The second line leads her to cling with defiant self-assertiveness to her threat-ened masculinity. To an incredibly late age she clings to the hope of getting a penis some time. That hope becomes her life's aim; and the phantasy of being a man in spite of everything often persists as a formative factor over long periods. This 'masculinity complex' in women can also result in a manifest homosexual choice of object. Only if her development follows the third, very circuitous, path does she reach the final normal female attitude, in which she takes her father as her object and so finds her way to the feminine form of the Oedipus complex. Thus in women the Oedipus complex is the end-result of a fairly lengthy develop-ment. It is not destroyed, but created, by the influence of castration; it escapes the strongly hostile influences which, in the male, have a destructive effect on it, and indeed it is all too often not surmounted by the female at all. For this reason, too, the cultural consequences of its break-up are smaller and of less importance in her. We should probably not be wrong in saying that it is this difference in the reciprocal relation between the Oedipus and the castra-tion complex which gives its special stamp to the character of females as social beings.[2]

We see, then, that the phase of exclusive attachment to the mother, which may be called the *pre-Oedipus* phase, possesses a far greater importance in women than it can have in men. Many phenomena of female sexual life which were not properly understood before can be fully explained by reference to this phase. Long ago, for instance, we noticed that many women who have chosen their husband on the model of their father, or have put him in their father's place, nevertheless repeat towards him, in their married life, their bad relations with their mother. The husband of such a woman was meant to be the inheritor of her relation to her father, but in reality he became the inheritor of her relation to her mother. This is easily explained as an obvious case of regression. Her relation to her mother was the original one, and her attachment to her father was built up on it, and now, in marriage, the original rela-tion emerges from repression. For the main content of her development to womanhood lay in the carrying over of her affective object attachments from her mother to her father.

With many women we have the impression that their years of maturity are occupied by a struggle with their husband, just as their youth was spent in a struggle with their mother. In the light of the previous discussions we shall conclude that their hostile attitude to their mother is not a consequence of the rivalry implicit in the Oedipus complex, but originates from the preceding phase and has merely been reinforced and exploited in the Oedipus situ-ation. And actual analytic examination confirms this view. Our interest must be directed to the mechanisms that are at work in her turning away from the mother who was an object so intensely and exclusively loved. We are prepared to find, not a single factor, but a whole number of them operating together towards the same end.

Among these factors are some which are determined by the circumstances of infantile sexuality in general, and so hold good equally for the erotic life of boys. First and foremost we may mention jealousy of other people—of brothers and sisters, rivals, among whom the father too has a place. Childhood love is boundless; it demands exclusive possession, it is not content with less than all. But it has a second characteristic: it has, in point of fact, no aim and is incapable of obtaining complete satisfaction; and principally for that reason it is doomed to end in disappointment and to give place to a hostile attitude. Later on in life the lack of an ultimate satisfaction may favour a different result. This very factor may ensure the uninterrupted continuance of the libidinal cathexis, as happens with love-relations that are inhibited in their aim. But in the stress of the processes of development it regularly happens that the libido abandons its unsatisfying position in order to find a new one.

Another, much more specific motive for turning away from the mother arises from the effect of the castration complex on the creature who is without a penis. At some time or other the little girl makes the discovery of her organic inferiority—earlier and more easily, of course, if there are brothers or other boys about. We have already taken note of the three paths which diverge from this point: (*a*) the one which leads to a cessation of her whole sexual life, (*b*) the one which leads to a defiant over-emphasis of her masculinity, and (*c*) the first steps towards definitive femininity. It is not easy to determine the exact timing here or the typical course of events. Even the point of time when the discovery of castration is made varies, and a number of other factors seem to be inconstant and to depend on chance. The state of the girl's own phallic activity plays a part; and so too does the question whether this activity was found out or not, and how much interference with it she experienced afterwards.

Little girls usually discover for themselves their characteristic phallic activity—masturbation of the clitoris; and to begin with this is no doubt unaccompanied by phantasy. The part played in starting it by nursery hygiene is reflected in the very common phantasy which makes the mother or nurse into a seducer. Whether little girls masturbate less frequently and from the first less energetically than little boys is not certain; quite possibly it is so. Actual seduction, too, is common enough; it is initiated either by other children or by someone in charge of the child who wants to soothe it, or send it to sleep or make it dependent on them. Where seduction intervenes it invariably disturbs the natural course of the developmental processes, and it often leaves behind extensive and lasting consequences.

A prohibition of masturbation, as we have seen, becomes an incentive for giving it up; but it also becomes a motive for rebelling against the person who prohibits it—that is to say, the mother, or the mother-substitute who later regularly merges with her. A defiant persistence in masturbation appears to open the way to masculinity. Even where the girl has not succeeded in suppressing her masturbation, the effect of the apparently vain prohibition is seen in her later efforts to free herself at all costs from a satisfaction which has been spoilt for her. When she reaches maturity her object-choice may still be influenced by this persisting purpose. Her resentment at being prevented from free sexual activity plays a big part in her detachment from her mother. The same motive comes into operation again after puberty, when her mother takes up her duty of guarding her daughter's chastity. We shall, of course, not forget that the mother is similarly opposed to a boy's masturbating and thus provides him, too, with a strong motive for rebellion.

When the little girl discovers her own deficiency, from seeing a male genital, it is only with hesitation and reluctance that she accepts the unwelcome knowledge. As we have seen, she clings obstinately to the expectation of one day having a genital of the same kind too, and her wish for it survives long after her hope has expired. The child invariably regards castration in the first instance as a misfortune peculiar to herself; only later does she realize that it extends to certain other children and lastly to certain grown-ups. When she comes to understand the general nature of this characteristic, it follows that femaleness—and with it, of course, her mother—suffers a great depreciation in her eyes.

This account of how girls respond to the impression of castration and the prohibition against masturbation will very probably strike the reader as confused and contradictory. This is not entirely the author's fault. In truth, it is hardly possible to give a description which has general validity. We find the most different reactions in different individuals, and in the same individual the contrary attitudes exist side by side. With the first intervention of the prohibition, the conflict is there, and from now on it will accompany the development of the sexual function. Insight into what takes place is made particularly difficult by the fact of its being so hard to distinguish the mental processes of this first phase from later ones by which they are overlaid and are distorted in memory. Thus, for instance, a girl may later construe the fact of castration as a punishment for her masturbatory activity, and she will attribute the carrying out of this punishment to her father, but neither of these ideas can have been a primary one. Similarly, boys regularly fear castration from their father, although in their case, too, the threat most usually comes from their mother.

However this may be, at the end of this first phase of attachment to the mother, there emerges, as the girl's strongest motive for turning away from her, the reproach that her mother did not give her a proper penis—that is to say, brought her into the world as a female. A second reproach, which does not reach quite so far back, is rather a surprising one. It is that her mother did not give her enough milk, did not suckle her long enough. Under the conditions of modern civilization this may be true often enough, but certainly not so often as is asserted in analyses. It would seem rather that this accusation gives expression to the general dissatisfaction of children, who, in our monogamous civilization, are weaned from the breast after six or nine months, whereas the primitive mother devotes herself exclusively to her child for two or three years. It is as though our children had remained for ever unsated, as though they had never sucked long enough at their mother's breast. But I am not sure whether, if one analysed children who had been suckled as long as the children of primitive peoples, one would not come upon the same complaint. Such is the greed of a child's libido!

When we survey the whole range of motives for turning away from the mother which analysis brings to light—that she failed to provide the little girl with the only proper genital, that she did not feed her sufficiently, that she compelled her to share her mother's love with others, that she never fulfilled all the girl's expectations of love, and, finally, that she first aroused her sexual activity and then forbade it—all these motives seem nevertheless insufficient to justify the girl's final hostility. Some of them follow inevitably from the nature of infantile sexuality; others appear like rationalizations devised later to account for the uncomprehended change in feeling. Perhaps the real fact is that the attachment to the mother is bound to perish, precisely because it was the first and was so intense; just as one can often see happen in the first marriages of young women which they have entered into when they were most passionately in love. In both situations the attitude of love probably comes to grief from the disappointments that are unavoidable and from the accumulation of occasions for aggression. As a rule, second marriages turn out much better.

We cannot go so far as to assert that the ambivalence of emotional cathexes is a universally valid law, and that it is absolutely impossible to feel great love for a person without its being accompanied by a hatred that is perhaps equally great, or vice versa. Normal adults do undoubtedly succeed in separating those two attitudes from each other, and do not find themselves obliged to hate their love-objects and to love their enemy as well as hate him. But this seems to be the result of later developments. In the first phases of erotic life, ambivalence is evidently the rule. Many people retain this archaic trait all through their lives. It is characteristic of obsessional neurotics that in their object-relationships love and hate counterbalance each other. In primitive races, too, we may say that ambivalence predominates. We

shall conclude, then, that the little girl's intense attachment to her mother is strongly ambivalent, and that it is in consequence precisely of this ambivalence that (with the assistance of
the other factors we have adduced) her attachment is forced away from her mother—once
again, that is to say, in consequence of a general characteristic of infantile sexuality.

The explanation I have attempted to give is at once met by a question: 'How is it, then,
that boys are able to keep intact their attachment to their mother, which is certainly no less
strong than that of girls?' The answer comes equally promptly: 'Because boys are able to deal
with their ambivalent feelings towards their mother by directing all their hostility on to their
father.' But, in the first place, we ought not to make this reply until we have made a close
study of the pre-Oedipus phase in boys, and, in the second place, it is probably more prudent
in general to admit that we have as yet no clear understanding of these processes, with which
we have only just become acquainted.

III

A further question arises: 'What does the little girl require of her mother? What is the nature
of her sexual aims during the time of exclusive attachment to her mother?' The answer we
obtain from the analytic material is just what we should expect. The girl's sexual aims in
regard to her mother are active as well as passive and are determined by the libidinal phases
through which the child passes. Here the relation of activity to passivity is especially interesting. It can easily be observed that in every field of mental experience, not merely that of
sexuality, when a child receives a passive impression it has a tendency to produce an active
reaction. It tries to do itself what has just been done to it. This is part of the work imposed
on it of mastering the external world and can even lead to its endeavouring to repeat an
impression which it would have reason to avoid on account of its distressing content.
Children's play, too, is made to serve this purpose of supplementing a passive experience
with an active piece of behaviour and of thus, as it were, annulling it. When a doctor has
opened a child's mouth, in spite of his resistance, to look down his throat, the same child,
after the doctor has gone, will play at being the doctor himself, and will repeat the assault
upon some small brother or sister who is as helpless in his hands as he was in the doctor's.
Here we have an unmistakable revolt against passivity and a preference for the active role.
This swing-over from passivity to activity does not take place with the same regularity or
vigour in all children; in some it may not occur at all. A child's behaviour in this respect may
enable us to draw conclusions as to the relative strength of the masculinity and femininity that
it will exhibit in its sexuality.

The first sexual and sexually coloured experiences which a child has in relation to its
mother are naturally of a passive character. It is suckled, fed, cleaned, and dressed by her,
and taught to perform all its functions. A part of its libido goes on clinging to those experiences and enjoys the satisfactions bound up with them; but another part strives to turn them
into activity. In the first place, being suckled at the breast gives place to active sucking. As
regards the other experiences the child contents itself either with becoming self-sufficient—
that is, with itself successfully carrying out what had hitherto been done for it—or with
repeating its passive experiences in an active form in play; or else it actually makes its mother
into the object and behaves as the active subject towards her. For a long time I was unable to
credit this last behaviour, which takes place in the field of real action, until my observations
removed all doubts on the matter.

We seldom hear of a little girl's wanting to wash or dress her mother, or tell her to
perform her excretory functions. Sometimes, it is true, she says: 'Now let's play that I'm the
mother and you're the child'; but generally she fulfils these active wishes in an indirect way,

in her play with her doll, in which she represents the mother and the doll the child. The fondness girls have for playing with dolls, in contrast to boys, is commonly regarded as a sign of early awakened femininity. Not unjustly so; but we must not overlook the fact that what finds expression here is the *active* side of femininity, and that the little girl's preference for dolls is probably evidence of the exclusiveness of her attachment to her mother, with complete neglect of her father-object.

The very surprising sexual activity of little girls in relation to their mother is manifested chronologically in oral, sadistic, and finally even in phallic trends directed towards her. It is difficult to give a detailed account of these because they are often obscure instinctual impulses which it was impossible for the child to grasp psychically at the time of their occurrence, which were therefore only interpreted by her later, and which then appear in the analysis in forms of expression that were certainly not the original ones. Sometimes we come across them as transferences on to the later, father-object, where they do not belong and where they seriously interfere with our understanding of the situation. We find the little girl's aggressive oral and sadistic wishes in a form forced on them by early repression, as a fear of being killed by her mother—a fear which, in turn, justifies her death-wish against her mother, if that becomes conscious. It is impossible to say how often this fear of the mother is supported by an unconscious hostility on the mother's part which is sensed by the girl. (Hitherto, it is only in men that I have found the fear of being eaten up. This fear is referred to the father, but it is probably the product of a transformation of oral aggressivity directed to the mother. The child wants to eat up its mother from whom it has had its nourishment; in the case of the father there is no such obvious determinant for the wish.)

The women patients showing a strong attachment to their mother in whom I have been able to study the pre-Oedipus phase have all told me that when their mother gave them enemas or rectal douches they used to offer the greatest resistence and react with fear and screams of rage. This behaviour may be very frequent or even the habitual thing in children. I only came to understand the reason for such a specially violent opposition from a remark made by Ruth Mack Brunswick, who was studying these problems at the same time as I was, to the effect that she was inclined to compare the outbreak of anger after an enema to the orgasm following genital excitation. The accompanying anxiety should, she thought, be construed as a transformation of the desire for aggression which had been stirred up. I believe that this is really so and that, at the sadistic-anal level, the intense passive stimulation of the intestinal zone is responded to by an outbreak of desire for aggression which is manifested either directly as rage, or, in consequence of its suppression, as anxiety. In later years this reaction seems to die away.

In regard to the passive impulses of the phallic phase, it is noteworthy that girls regularly accuse their mother of seducing them. This is because they necessarily received their first, or at any rate their strongest, genital sensations when they were being cleaned and having their toilet attended to by their mother (or by someone such as a nurse who took her place). Mothers have often told me, as a matter of observation, that their little daughters of two and three years old enjoy these sensations and try to get their mothers to make them more intense by repeated touching and rubbing. The fact that the mother thus unavoidably initiates the child into the phallic phase is, I think, the reason why, in phantasies of later years, the father so regularly appears as the sexual seducer. When the girl turns away from her mother, she also makes over to her father her introduction into sexual life.

Lastly, intense *active* wishful impulses directed towards the mother also arise during the phallic phase. The sexual activity of this period culminates in clitoridal masturbation. This is probably accompanied by ideas of the mother, but whether the child attaches a sexual aim to the idea, and what that aim is, I have not been able to discover from my observations. It is only when all her interests have received a fresh impetus through the arrival of a baby brother or sister that we can clearly recognize such an aim. The little girl wants to believe that she has given her mother the new baby, just as the boy wants to; and her reaction to this event and her behaviour to the baby is exactly the same as his. No doubt this sounds quite absurd, but perhaps that is only because it sounds so unfamiliar.

The turning-away from her mother is an extremely important step in the course of a little girl's development. It is more than a mere change of object. We have already described what takes place in it and the many motives put forward for it; we may now add that hand in hand with it there is to be observed a marked lowering of the active sexual impulses and a rise of the passive ones. It is true that the active trends have been affected by frustration more strongly; they have proved totally unrealizable and are therefore abandoned by the libido more readily. But the passive trends have not escaped disappointment either. With the turning-away from the mother clitoridal masturbation frequently ceases as well; and often enough when the small girl represses her previous masculinity a considerable portion of her sexual trends in general is permanently injured too. The transition to the father-object is accomplished with the help of the passive trends in so far as they have escaped the catastrophe. The path to the development of femininity now lies open to the girl, to the extent to which it is not restricted by the remains of the pre-Oedipus attachment to her mother which she has surmounted.

If we now survey the stage of sexual development in the female which I have been describing, we cannot resist coming to a definite conclusion about female sexuality as a whole. We have found the same libidinal forces at work in it as in the male child and we have been able to convince ourselves that for a period of time these forces follow the same course and have the same outcome in each.

Biological factors subsequently deflect those libidinal forces [in the girl's case] from their original aims and conduct even active and in every sense masculine trends into feminine channels. Since we cannot dismiss the notion that sexual excitation is derived from the operation of certain chemical substances, it seems plausible at first to expect that biochemistry will one day disclose a substance to us whose presence produces a male sexual excitation and another substance which produces a female one. But this hope seems no less naïve than the other one—happily obsolete to-day—that it may be possible under the microscope to isolate the different exciting factors of hysteria, obsessional neurosis, melancholia, and so on.

Even in sexual chemistry things must be rather more complicated. For psychology, however, it is a matter of indifference whether there is a single sexually exciting substance in the body or two or countless numbers of them. Psycho-analysis teaches us to manage with a single libido, which, it is true, has both active and passive aims (that is, modes of satisfaction). This antithesis and, above all, the existence of libidinal trends with passive aims, contains within itself the remainder of our problem.

IV

An examination of the analytic literature on the subject shows that everything that has been said by me here is already to be found in it. It would have been superfluous to publish this paper if it were not that in a field of research which is so difficult of access every account of first-hand experiences or personal views may be of value. Moreover, there are a number of points which I have defined more sharply and isolated more carefully. In some of the other papers on the subject the description is obscured because they deal at the same time with the problems of the super-ego and the sense of guilt. This I have avoided doing. Also, in describing the various outcomes of this phase of development, I have refrained from discussing the complications which arise when a child, as a result of disappointment from her father, returns to the attachment to her mother which she had abandoned, or when, in the course of her life, she repeatedly changes over from one position to the other. But precisely because my paper is only one contribution among others, I may be spared an exhaustive survey of the literature, and I can confine myself to bringing out the more important points on which I agree or disagree with these other writings.

Abraham's (1921) description of the manifestations of the castration complex in the female is still unsurpassed; but one would be glad if it had included the factor of the girl's original exclusive attachment to her mother. I am in agreement with the principal points in Jeanne Lampl-de Groot's (1927) important paper. In this the complete identity of the pre-Oedipus phase in boys and girls is recognized, and the girl's sexual (phallic) activity towards her mother is affirmed and substantiated by observations. The turning-away from the mother is traced to the influence of the girl's recognition of castration, which obliges her to give up her sexual object, and often masturbation along with it. The whole development is summed up in the formula that the girl goes through a phase of the 'negative' Oedipus complex before she can enter the positive one. A point on which I find the writer's account inadequate is that it represents the turning-away from the mother as being merely a change of object and does not discuss the fact that it is accompanied by the plainest manifestations of hostility. To this hostility full justice is done in Helene Deutsch's latest paper, on feminine masochism and its relation to frigidity (1930), in which she also recognizes the girl's phallic activity and the intensity of her attachment to her mother. Helene Deutsch states further that the girl's turning towards her father takes place viâ her passive trends (which have already been awakened in relation to her mother). In her earlier book (1925) the author had not yet set herself free from the endeavour to apply the Oedipus pattern to the pre-Oedipus phase, and she therefore interpreted the little girl's phallic activity as an identification with her father.

Fenichel (1930) rightly emphasizes the difficulty of recognizing in the material produced in analysis what parts of it represent the unchanged content of the pre-Oedipus phase and what parts have been distorted by regression (or in other ways). He does not accept Jeanne Lampl-de Groot's assertion of the little girl's active attitude in the phallic phase. He also rejects the 'displacement backwards' of the Oedipus complex proposed by Melanie Klein (1928), who places its beginnings as early as the commencement of the second year of life. This dating of it, which would also necessarily imply a modification of our view of all the rest of the child's development, does not in fact correspond to what we learn from the analyses of adults, and it is especially incompatible with my findings as to the long duration of the girl's pre-Oedipus attachment to her mother. A means of softening this contradiction is afforded by the reflection that we are not as yet able to distinguish in this field between what is rigidly fixed by biological laws and what is open to movement and change under the influence of accidental experience. The effect of seduction has long been familiar to us and in just the same way other factors—such as the date at which the child's brothers and sisters are born or the time when it discovers the difference between the sexes, or again its direct observations of sexual intercourse or its parents' behaviour in encouraging or repelling it—may hasten the child's sexual development and bring it to maturity.

Some writers are inclined to reduce the importance of the child's first and most original libidinal impulses in favour of later developmental processes, so that—to put this view in its most extreme form—the only role left to the former is merely to indicate certain paths, while the [psychical] intensities which flow along those paths are supplied by later regressions and reaction-formations. Thus, for instance, Karin Horney (1926) is of the opinion that we greatly over-estimate the girl's primary penis-envy and that the strength of the masculine trend which she develops later is to be attributed to a *secondary* penis-envy which is used to fend off her feminine impulses and, in particular, her feminine attachment to her father. This does not tally with my impressions. Certain as is the occurrence of later reinforcements through regression and reaction-formation, and difficult as it is to estimate the relative strength of the confluent libidinal components, I nevertheless think that we should not over-look the fact that the first libidinal impulses have an intensity of their own which is superior to any that come later and which may indeed be termed incommensurable. It is undoubtedly true that there is an antithesis between the attachment to the father and the masculinity complex; it is the general antithesis that exists between activity and passivity, masculinity and femininity. But this gives us no right to assume that only one of them is primary and that the other owes its strength merely to the force of defence. And if the defence against femininity is so energetic, from what other source can it draw its strength than from the masculine trend which found its first expression in the child's penis-envy and therefore deserves to be named after it?

A similar objection applies to Ernest Jones's view (1927) that the phallic phase in girls is a secondary, protective reaction rather than a genuine developmental stage. This does not correspond either to the dynamic or the chronological position of things.

Notes

1   In the well-known case of delusional jealousy reported by Ruth Mack Brunswick (1928), the direct source of the disorder was the patient's pre-Oedipus fixation (to her sister).

2   It is to be anticipated that men analysts with feminist views, as well as our women analysts, will disa-gree with what I have said here. They will hardly fail to object that such notions spring from the 'masculinity complex' of the male and are designed to justify on theoretical grounds his innate incli-nation to disparage and suppress women. But this sort of psycho-analytic argumentation reminds us here, as it so often does, of Dostoevsky's famous 'knife that cuts both ways'. The opponents of those who argue in this way will on their side think it quite natural that the female sex should refuse to accept a view which appears to contradict their eagerly coveted equality with men. The use of analysis as a weapon of controversy can clearly lead to no decision.

Chapter 36

Edward Carpenter (1844–1929)

"THE INTERMEDIATE SEX" (1908)

CARPENTER, ANTICIPATING LATE TWENTIETH-CENTURY FEMINIST THEORY, argues that gender identity comprises not two types – the masculine and the feminine – but rather, a wide-ranging spectrum of gender identities. If the extremes of this spectrum |are the feminine and masculine "poles," then Carpenter situates the "intermediate types" somewhere in between. Citing statistics, psychological case studies, and historical examples, Carpenter describes a significant, and influential, portion of the population for whom biological sex differs from gender expression. He goes much further than Havelock Ellis in arguing not only that these "intermediate types" of men and women are not "morbid" or "degenerate," but that they represent an advancement in human evolution.

Edward Carpenter, "The Intermediate Sex," *The Intermediate Sex: A Study of Some Transitional Types of Men and Women.* London: George Allen and Unwin, 1908. 13–28.

> "Urning men and women, on whose book of life Nature has written her new word which sounds so strange to us, bear such storm and stress within them, such ferment and fluctuation, so much complex material having its outlet only towards the future; their individualities are so rich and many-sided, and withal so little understood, that, it is impossible to characterise them adequately in a few sentences."—*Otto de Joux.*

In late years (and since the arrival of the New Woman amongst us) many things in the relation of men and women to each other have altered, or at any rate become clearer. The growing sense of equality in habits and customs—university studies, art, music, politics, the bicycle, etc.—all these things have brought about a *rapprochement* between the sexes. If the modern woman is a little more masculine in some ways than her predecessor, the modern man (it is to be hoped), while by no means effeminate, is a little more sensitive in temperament and artistic in feeling than the original John Bull. It is beginning to be recognised that the sexes do not or should not normally form two groups hopelessly isolated in habit and feeling from each other, but that they rather represent the two poles of *one* group—which is the human race; so that while certainly the extreme specimens at either pole are vastly divergent, there are great numbers in the middle region who (though differing corporeally as men and women) are by emotion and temperament very near to each other. We all know women with a strong dash of the masculine temperament, and we all know men whose almost feminine sensibility and intuition seem to belie their bodily form. Nature, it might appear, in mixing the elements which go to compose each individual, does not always keep her two groups of ingredients—which represent the two sexes—properly apart, but often throws them crosswise in a somewhat baffling manner, now this way and now that; yet wisely, we must think—for if a severe distinction of elements were always maintained the two sexes would soon drift into far latitudes and absolutely cease to understand each other. As it is, there are some remarkable and (we think) indispensable types of character in whom there is such a union or balance of the feminine and masculine qualities that these people become to a great extent the interpreters of men and women to each other.

There is another point which has become clearer of late. For as people are beginning to see that the sexes form in a certain sense a continuous group, so they are beginning to see that Love and Friendship—which have been so often set apart from each other as things distinct—are in reality closely related and shade imperceptibly into each other. Women are beginning to demand that Marriage shall mean Friendship as well as Passion; that a comrade-like Equality shall be included in the word Love; and it is recognised that from the one extreme of a 'Platonic' friendship (generally between persons of the same sex) up to the other extreme of passionate love (generally between persons of opposite sex) no hard and fast line can at any point be drawn effectively separating the different kinds of attachment. We know, in fact, of Friendships so romantic in sentiment that they verge into love; we know of Loves so intellectual and spiritual that they hardly dwell in the sphere of Passion.

A moment's thought will show that the general conceptions indicated above—if anywhere near the truth—point to an immense diversity of human temperament and character in matters relating to sex and love; but though such diversity has probably always existed, it has only in comparatively recent times become a subject of study.

More than thirty years ago, however, an Austrian writer, K. H. Ulrichs, drew attention in a series of pamphlets (*Memnon*, *Ara Spei*, *Inclusa*, etc.) to the existence of a class of people who strongly illustrate the above remarks, and with whom specially this paper is concerned. He pointed out that there were people born in such a position—as it were on the dividing line between the sexes—that while belonging distinctly to one sex as far as their bodies are concerned they may be said to belong *mentally* and *emotionally* to the other; that there were men, for instance, who might be described as of feminine soul enclosed in a male body (*anima muliebris in corpore virili inclusa*), or in other cases, women whose definition would be just the reverse. And he maintained that this doubleness of nature was to a great extent proved by the special direction of their love-sentiment. For in such cases, as indeed might be expected, the (apparently) masculine person instead of forming a love-union with a female tended to contract romantic friendships with one of his own sex; while the apparently feminine would, instead of marrying in the usual way, devote herself to the love of another feminine.

People of this kind (*i. e.*, having this special variation of the love-sentiment) he called Urnings;[1] and though we are not obliged to accept his theory about the crosswise connexion between 'soul' and 'body,' since at best these words are somewhat vague and indefinite; yet his work was important because it was one of the first attempts, in modern times, to recognise the existence of what might be called an Intermediate sex, and to give at any rate *some* explanation of it.[2]

Since that time the subject has been widely studied and written about by scientific men and others, especially on the Continent (though in England it is still comparatively unknown), and by means of an extended observation of present-day cases, as well as the indirect testimony of the history and literature of past times, quite a body of general conclusions has been arrived at—of which I propose in the following pages to give some slight account.

Contrary to the general impression, one of the first points that emerges from this study is that 'Urnings,' or Uranians, are by no means so very rare; but that they form, beneath the surface of society, a large class. It remains difficult, however, to get an exact statement of their numbers; and this for more than one reason: partly because, owing to the want of any general understanding of their case, these folk tend to conceal their true feelings from all but their own kind, and indeed often deliberately act in such a manner as to lead the world astray—(whence it arises that a normal man living in a certain society will often refuse to believe that there is a single Urning in the circle of his acquaintance, while one of the latter, or one that understands the nature, living in the same society, can count perhaps a score or more)—and partly because it is indubitable that the numbers do vary very greatly, not only in different countries but even in different classes in the same country. The consequence of all this being that we have estimates differing very widely from each other. Dr. Grabowsky, a well-known writer in Germany, quotes figures (which we think must be exaggerated) as high as one man in every 22, while Dr. Albert Moll (*Die Conträre Sexualempfindung*, chap. 3) gives estimates varying from 1 to every 50 to as low as 1 in every 500.[3] These figures apply to such as are exclusively of the said nature, *i.e.*, to those whose deepest feelings of love and friendship go out only to persons of their own sex. Of course, if in addition are included those double-natured people (of whom there is a great number) who experience the normal attachment, with the homogenic tendency in less or greater degree superadded, the estimates must be greatly higher.

In the second place it emerges (also contrary to the general impression) that men and women of the exclusively Uranian type are by no means necessarily morbid in any way—unless, indeed, their peculiar temperament be pronounced in itself morbid. Formerly it was assumed as a matter of course, that the type was merely a result of disease and degeneration; but now with the examination of the actual facts it appears that, on the contrary, many are fine, healthy specimens of their sex, muscular and well-developed in body, of powerful brain, high standard of conduct, and with nothing abnormal or morbid of any kind observable in their physical structure or constitution. This is of course not true of all, and there still remain a certain number of cases of weakly type to support the neuropathic view. Yet it is very noticeable that this view is much less insisted on by the later writers than by the earlier. It is also worth noticing that it is now acknowledged that even in the most healthy cases the special affectional temperament of the 'Intermediate' is, as a rule, ineradicable; so much so that when (as in not a few instances) such men and women, from social or other considerations, have forced themselves to marry and even have children, they have still not been able to overcome their own bias, or the leaning after all of their life-attachment to some friend of their own sex.

This subject, though obviously one of considerable interest and importance, has been hitherto, as I have pointed out, but little discussed in this country, partly owing to a certain amount of doubt and distrust which has, not unnaturally perhaps, surrounded it. And certainly if the men and women born with the tendency in question were only exceedingly rare, though it would not be fair on that account to ignore them, yet it would hardly be necessary to dwell at great length on their case. But as the class is really, on any computation, numerous, it becomes a duty for society not only to understand them but to help them to understand themselves.

For there is no doubt that in many cases people of this kind suffer a great deal from their own temperament—and yet, after all, it is possible that they may have an important part to play in the evolution of the race. Anyone who realises what Love is, the dedication of the heart, so profound, so absorbing, so mysterious, so imperative, and always just in the noblest natures so strong, cannot fail to see how difficult, how tragic even, must often be the fate of those whose deepest feelings are destined from the earliest days to be a riddle and a stumbling-block, unexplained to themselves, passed over in silence by others. To call people of such temperament 'morbid,' and so forth, is of no use. Such a term is, in fact, absurdly inapplicable to many, who are among the most active, the most amiable and accepted members of society; besides, it forms no solution of the problem in question, and only amounts to marking down for disparagement a fellow-creature who has already considerable difficulties to contend with. Says Dr. Moll, "Anyone who has seen many Urnings will probably admit that they form a by no means enervated human group; on the contrary, one finds powerful, healthy-looking folk among them;" but in the very next sentence he says that they "suffer severely" from the way they are regarded; and in the manifesto of a considerable community of such people in Germany occur these words, "The rays of sunshine in the night of our existence are so rare, that we are responsive and deeply grateful for the least movement, for every single voice that speaks in our favour in the forum of mankind."[4]

In dealing with this class of folk, then, while I do not deny that they present a difficult problem, I think that just for that very reason their case needs discussion. It would be a great mistake to suppose that their attachments are necessarily sexual, or connected with sexual acts. On the contrary (as abundant evidence shows), they are often purely emotional in their character; and to confuse Uranians (as is so often done) with libertines having no law but curiosity in self-indulgence is to do them a great wrong. At the same time, it is evident that their special temperament may sometimes cause them difficulty in regard to their sexual relations. Into this subject we need not just now enter. But we may point out how hard it is, especially for the young among them, that a veil of complete silence should be drawn over the subject, leading to the most painful misunderstandings, and perversions and confusions of mind; and that there should be no hint of guidance; nor any recognition of the solitary and really serious inner struggles they may have to face! If the problem is a difficult one—as it undoubtedly is—the fate of those people is already hard who have to meet it in their own persons, without their suffering in addition from the refusal of society to give them any help. It is partly for these reasons, and to throw a little light where it may be needed, that I have thought it might be advisable in this paper simply to give a few general characteristics of the Intermediate types.

As indicated then already, in bodily structure there is, as a rule, nothing to distinguish the subjects of our discussion from ordinary men and women; but if we take the general mental characteristics it appears from almost universal testimony that the male tends to be of a rather gentle, emotional disposition—with defects, if such exist, in the direction of subtlety, evasiveness, timidity, vanity, etc.; while the female is just the opposite, fiery, active, bold and truthful, with defects running to brusqueness and coarseness. Moreover, the mind of the former is generally intuitive and instinctive in its perceptions, with more or less of artistic feeling; while the mind of the latter is more logical, scientific, and precise than usual with the normal woman. So marked indeed are these general characteristics that sometimes by means of them (though not an infallible guide) the nature of the boy or girl can be detected in childhood, before full development has taken place; and needless to say it may often be very important to be able to do this.

It was no doubt in consequence of the observation of these signs that K. H. Ulrichs proposed his theory; and though the theory, as we have said, does not by any means meet *all* the facts, still it is perhaps not without merit, and may be worth bearing in mind.

In the case, for instance, of a woman of this temperament (defined we suppose as "a male soul in a female body") the theory helps us to understand how it might be possible for her to fall *bonâ fide* in love with another woman. Krafft-Ebing gives[5] the case of a lady (A.), 28 years of age, who fell deeply in love with a younger one (B.). "I loved her divinely," she said. They lived together, and the union lasted four years, but was then broken by the marriage of B. A. suffered in consequence from frightful depression; but in the end—though without real love—got married herself. Her depression however only increased and deepened into illness. The doctors, when consulted, said that all would be well if she could only have a child. The husband, who loved his wife sincerely, could not understand her enigmatic behaviour. She was friendly to him, suffered his caresses, but for days afterwards remained "dull, exhausted, plagued; with irritation of the spine, and nervous." Presently a journey of the married pair led to another meeting with the female friend—who had now been wedded (but also unhappily) for three years. "Both ladies trembled with joy and excitement as they fell into each other's arms, and were thenceforth inseparable. The man found that this friendship relation was a singular one, and hastened the departure. When the opportunity occurred, he convinced himself from the correspondence between his wife and her 'friend' that their letters were exactly like those of two lovers."

It appears that the loves of such women are often very intense, and (as also in the case of male Urnings) life-long. Both classes feel themselves blessed when they love happily. Nevertheless, to many of them it is a painful fact that—in consequence of their peculiar temperament—they are, though fond of children, not in the position to found a family.

We have so far limited ourselves to some very general characteristics of the Intermediate race. It may help to clear and fix our ideas if we now describe more in detail, first, what may be called the extreme and exaggerated types of the race, and then the more normal and perfect types. By doing so we shall get a more definite and concrete view of our subject.

In the first place, then, the extreme specimens—as in most cases of extremes—are not particularly attractive, sometimes quite the reverse. In the male of this kind we have a distinctly effeminate type, sentimental, lackadaisical, mincing in gait and manners, something of a chatterbox, skilful at the needle and in woman's work, sometimes taking pleasure in dressing in woman's clothes; his figure not unfrequently betraying a tendency towards the feminine, large at the hips, supple, not muscular, the face wanting in hair, the voice inclining to be high-pitched, etc.; while his dwelling-room is orderly in the extreme, even natty, and choice of decoration and perfume. His affection, too, is often feminine in character, clinging, dependent and jealous, as of one desiring to be loved almost more than to love.[6]

On the other hand, as the extreme type of the homogenic female, we have a rather markedly aggressive person, of strong passions, masculine manners and movements, practical in the conduct of life, sensuous rather than sentimental in love, often untidy, and *outré* in attire;[7] her figure muscular, her voice rather low in pitch; her dwelling-room decorated with sporting-scenes, pistols, etc., and not without a suspicion of the fragrant weed in the atmosphere; while her love (generally to rather soft and feminine specimens of her own sex) is often a sort of furor, similar to the ordinary masculine love, and at times almost uncontrollable.

These are types which, on account of their salience, everyone will recognise more or less. Naturally, when they occur they excite a good deal of attention, and it is not an uncommon impression that most persons of the homogenic nature belong to either one or other of these classes. But in reality, of course, these extreme developments are rare, and for the most part the temperament in question is embodied in men and women of quite normal and unsensational exterior. Speaking of this subject and the connection between effeminateness and the homogenic nature in men, Dr. Moll says: "It is, however, as well to point out at the outset that effeminacy does not by any means show itself in all Urnings. Though one may find this or that indication in a great number of cases, yet it cannot be denied that a very large percentage, perhaps by far the majority of them do *not* exhibit pronounced Effeminacy." And it may be supposed that we may draw the same conclusion with regard to women of this class—namely, that the majority of them do not exhibit pronounced masculine habits. In fact, while these extreme cases are of the greatest value from a scientific point of view as marking tendencies and limits of development in certain directions, it would be a serious mistake to look upon them as representative cases of the whole phases of human evolution concerned.

If now we come to what may be called the more normal type of the Uranian man, we find a man who, while possessing thoroughly masculine powers of mind and body, combines with them the tenderer and more emotional soul-nature of the woman—and sometimes to a remarkable degree. Such men, as said, are often muscular and well-built, and not distinguishable in exterior structure and the carriage of body from others of their own sex; but emotionally they are extremely complex, tender, sensitive, pitiful and loving, "full of storm and stress, of ferment and fluctuation" of the heart; the logical faculty may or may not, in their case, be well-developed, but intuition is always strong; like women they read characters at a glance, and know, without knowing how, what is passing in the minds of others; for nursing and waiting on the needs of others they have often a peculiar gift; at the bottom lies the artist-nature, with the artist's sensibility and perception. Such an one is often a dreamer, of brooding, reserved habits, often a musician, or a man of culture, courted in society, which nevertheless does not understand him—though sometimes a child of the people, without any culture, but almost always with a peculiar inborn refinement. De Joux, who speaks on the whole favourably of Uranian men and women, says of the former: "They are enthusiastic for poetry and music, are often eminently skilful in the fine arts, and are overcome with emotion and sympathy at the least sad occurrence. Their sensitiveness, their endless tenderness for children, their love of flowers, their great pity for beggars and crippled folk are truly womanly." And in another passage he indicates the artist-nature, when he says: "The nerve-system of many an Urning is the finest and the most complicated musical instrument in the service of the interior personality that can be imagined."

It would seem probable that the attachment of such an one is of a tender and profound character; indeed, it is possible that in this class of men we have the love sentiment in one of its most perfect forms—a form in which from the necessities of the situation the sensuous element, though present, is exquisitely subordinated to the spiritual. Says one writer on this subject, a Swiss, "Happy indeed is that man who has won a real Urning for his friend—he walks on roses, without ever having to fear the thorns"; and he adds, "Can there ever be a more perfect sick-nurse than an Urning?" And though these are *ex parte* utterances, we may believe that there is an appreciable grain of truth in them. Another writer, quoted by De Joux, speaks to somewhat the same effect, and may perhaps be received in a similar spirit. "We form," he says, "a peculiar aristocracy of modest spirits, of good and refined habit, and in many masculine circles are representatives of the higher mental and artistic element. In us dreamers and enthusiasts lies the continual counterpoise to the sheer masculine portion of society—inclining, as it always does, to mere restless greed of gain and material sensual pleasures."

That men of this kind despise women, though a not uncommon belief, is one which hardly appears to be justified. Indeed, though naturally not inclined to "fall in love" in this direction, such men are by their nature drawn rather near to women, and it would seem that they often feel a singular appreciation and understanding of the emotional needs and destinies of the other sex, leading in many cases to a genuine though what is called 'Platonic' friendship. There is little doubt that they are often instinctively sought after by women, who, without suspecting the real cause, are conscious of a sympathetic chord in the homogenic which they miss in the normal man. To quote De Joux once more: "It would be a mistake to suppose that all Urnings must be woman-haters. Quite the contrary. They are not seldom their faithfulest friends, the truest allies, and most convinced defenders of women."

To come now to the more normal and perfect specimens of the homogenic *woman*, we find a type in which the body is thoroughly feminine and gracious, with the rondure and fulness of the female form, and the continence and aptness of its movements, but in which the inner nature is to a great extent masculine; a temperament active, brave, originative, somewhat decisive, not too emotional; fond of out-door life, of games and sports, of science, politics, or even business; good at organisation, and well-pleased with positions of responsibility, sometimes indeed making an excellent and generous leader. Such a woman, it is easily seen, from her special combination of qualities, is often fitted for remarkable work, in professional life, or as manageress of institutions, or even as ruler of a country. Her love goes out to younger and more feminine natures than her own; it is a powerful passion, almost of heroic type, and capable of inspiring to great deeds; and when held duly in leash may sometimes become an invaluable force in the teaching and training of girlhood, or in the creation of a school of thought or action among women. Many a Santa Clara, or abbess-founder of religious houses, has probably been a woman of this type; and in all times such women—not being bound to men by the ordinary ties—have been able to work the more freely for the interests of their sex, a cause to which their own temperament impels them to devote themselves *con amore*.

I have now sketched—very briefly and inadequately it is true—both the extreme types and the more healthy types of the 'Intermediate' man and woman: types which can be verified from history and literature, though more certainly and satisfactorily perhaps from actual life around us. And unfamiliar though the subject is, it begins to appear that it is one which modern thought and science will have to face. Of the latter and more normal types it may be said that they exist, and have always existed, in considerable abundance, and from that circumstance alone there is a strong probability that they have their place and purpose. As pointed out there is no particular indication of morbidity about them, unless the special nature of their love-sentiment be itself accounted morbid; and in the alienation of the sexes from each other, of which complaint is so often made to-day, it must be admitted that they do much to fill the gap.

The instinctive artistic nature of the male of this class, his sensitive spirit, his wavelike emotional temperament, combined with hardihood of intellect and body; and the frank, free nature of the female, her masculine independence and strength wedded to thoroughly feminine grace of form and manner; may be said to give them both, through their double nature, command of life in all its phases, and a certain freemasonry of the secrets of the two sexes which may well favour their function as reconcilers and interpreters. Certainly it is remarkable that some of the world's greatest leaders and artists have been dowered either wholly or in part with the Uranian temperament—as in the cases of Michel Angelo, Shakespeare, Marlowe, Alexander the Great, Julius Cæsar, or, among women, Christine of Sweden, Sappho the poetess, and others.

Notes

1   From *Uranos*, heaven; his idea being that the Uranian love was of a higher order than the ordinary attachment.
2   Charles G. Leland ("Hans Breitmann"), in his book "The Alternate Sex" (Funk, 1904), insists much on the frequent combination of the characteristics of both sexes in remarkable men and women, and has a chapter on "The Female Mind in Man," and another on "The Male Intellect in Woman."
3   Some late statistical inquiries (see "Statistische Untersuchungen," von Dr. M. Hirschfeld, Leipzig, 1904) yield 1.5 to 2.0 per cent, as a probable ratio.
4   See De Joux, "Die Enterliten dcs Liebesglückes" (Leipzig, 1893), p. 21.
5   "Psychopathia Sexualis," 7th ed., p. 276.

6   A good deal in this description may remind readers of history of the habits and character of Henry III of France.

7   Perhaps, like Queen Christine, of Sweden, who rode across Europe, on her visit to Italy, in jack-boots and sitting astride of her horse. It is said that she shook the Pope's hand, on seeing him, so heartily that the doctor had to attend to it afterwards!

Chapter 37

Emma Goldman (1869–1940)

"THE TRAGEDY OF WOMAN'S EMANCIPATION" (1917)

E MMA GOLDMAN'S WRITINGS AND SPEECHES were renowned for combining anarchist fervor with a passion for liberty, social justice, and radical humanist ideals. She summed up her worldview in her autobiography, *Living My Life* (1934), when she wrote, "I want freedom, the right to self expression, everybody's right to beautiful, radiant things" (56). Goldman would not disavow the use of violence in her political philosophy; she believed that violent revolutionary acts were often necessary in the fight for freedom and she defended those beliefs by combining the ideals of anti-capitalist ideology with American transcendentalist philosophy, libertarian democracy, and anarchist utopianism. Goldman's revolutionary vision was founded on the principles of freedom of speech, sexual liberty for all — including homosexuals — and the eradication of property relations in domestic and social life. Goldman was imprisoned numerous times for her birth control advocacy, anti-war activities, trade unionist organizing, and anarchist acts and speeches. The internationally famous Red Emma's public speeches attracted growing crowds of the committed and curious; she was deported to Russia in 1919 after the Russian Revolution and in the wake of a Red Scare in the United States. Goldman was an early critic of Leon Trostky and Vladimir Lenin's post-communist Soviet Union; her book *My Disillusionment in Russia* (1923) addressed the brutal repressiveness of Soviet life and the corruption of the Revolution's ideals.

Emma Goldman, "The Tragedy of Woman's Emancipation," *Red Emma Speaks: An Emma Goldman Reader*. New York: Humanity Books, 1996. 158–67. (Originally published in *Anarchism and Other Essays*, 1917.)

I begin with an admission: Regardless of all political and economic theories, treating of the fundamental differences between various groups within the human race, regardless of class and race distinctions, regardless of all artificial boundary lines between woman's rights and man's rights, I hold that there is a point where these differentiations may meet and grow into one perfect whole.

With this I do not mean to propose a peace treaty. The general social antagonism which has taken hold of our entire public life today, brought about through the force of opposing and contradictory interests, will crumble to pieces when the reorganization of our social life, based upon the principles of economic justice, shall have become a reality.

Peace or harmony between the sexes and individuals does not necessarily depend on a superficial equalization of human beings; nor does it call for the elimination of individual traits and peculiarities. The problem that confronts us today, and which the nearest future is to solve, is how to be one's self and yet in oneness with others, to feel deeply with all human beings and still retain one's own characteristic qualities. This seems to me to be the basis upon which the mass and the individual, the true democrat and the true individuality, man and woman, can meet without antagonism and opposition. The motto should not be: Forgive one another; rather, Understand one another. The oft-quoted sentence of Madame de Staël: "To understand everything means to forgive everything," has never particularly appealed to me; it has the odor of the confessional; to forgive one's fellow-being conveys the idea of pharisaical superiority. To understand one's fellow-being suffices. The admission partly represents the fundamental aspect of my views on the emancipation of woman and its effect upon the entire sex.

Emancipation should make it possible for woman to be human in the truest sense. Everything within her that craves assertion and activity should reach its fullest expression; all artificial barriers should be broken, and the road towards greater freedom cleared of every trace of centuries of submission and slavery.

This was the original aim of the movement for woman's emancipation. But the results so far achieved have isolated woman and have robbed her of the fountain springs of that happiness which is so essential to her. Merely external emancipation has made of the modern woman an artificial being, who reminds one of the products of French arboriculture with its arabesque trees and shrubs, pyramids, wheels, and wreaths; anything, except the forms which would be reached by the expression of her own inner qualities. Such artificially grown plants of the female sex are to be found in large numbers, especially in the so-called intellectual sphere of our life.

Liberty and equality for woman! What hopes and aspirations these words awakened when they were first uttered by some of the noblest and bravest souls of those days. The sun in all his light and glory was to rise upon a new world; in this world woman was to be free to direct her own destiny—an aim certainly worthy of the great enthusiasm, courage, perseverance, and ceaseless effort of the tremendous host of pioneer men and women, who staked everything against a world of prejudice and ignorance.

My hopes also move towards that goal, but I hold that the emancipation of woman, as interpreted and practically applied today, has failed to reach that great end. Now, woman is confronted with the necessity of emancipating herself from emancipation, if she really desires to be free. This may sound paradoxical, but is, nevertheless, only too true.

What has she achieved through her emancipation? Equal suffrage in a few States. Has that purified our political life, as many well-meaning advocates predicted? Certainly not. Incidentally, it is really time that persons with plain, sound judgment should cease to talk about corruption in politics in a boarding-school tone. Corruption of politics has nothing to do with the morals, or the laxity of morals, of various political personalities. Its cause is altogether a material one. Politics is the reflex of the business and industrial world, the mottos of which are: "To take is more blessed than to give"; "buy cheap and sell dear"; "one soiled hand washes the other." There is no hope even that woman, with her right to vote, will ever purify politics.

Emancipation has brought woman economic equality with man; that is, she can choose her own profession and trade; but as her past and present physical training has not equipped her with the necessary strength to compete with man, she is often compelled to exhaust all her energy, use up her vitality, and strain every nerve in order to reach the market value. Very few ever succeed, for it is a fact that women teachers, doctors, lawyers, architects, and engineers are neither met with the same confidence as their male colleagues, nor receive equal remuneration. And those that do reach that enticing equality generally do so at the expense of their physical and psychical well-being. As to the great mass of working girls and women, how much independence is gained if the narrowness and lack of freedom of the home is exchanged for the narrowness and lack of freedom of the factory, sweat-shop, department store, or office? In addition is the burden which is laid on many women of looking after a "home, sweet home"—cold, dreary, disorderly, uninviting—after a day's hard work. Glorious independence! No wonder that hundreds of girls are so willing to accept the first offer of marriage, sick and tired of their "independence" behind the counter, at the sewing or typewriting machine. They are just as ready to marry as girls of the middle class, who long to throw off the yoke of parental supremacy. A so-called independence which leads only to earning the merest subsistence is not so enticing, not so ideal, that one could expect woman to sacrifice everything for it. Our highly praised independence is, after all, but a slow process of dulling and stifling woman's nature, her love instinct and her mother instinct.

Nevertheless, the position of the working girl is far more natural and human than that of her seemingly more fortunate sister in the more cultured professional walks of life—teachers, physicians, lawyers, engineers, etc., who have to make a dignified, proper appearance, while the inner life is growing empty and dead.

The narrowness of the existing conception of woman's independence and emancipation; the dread of love for a man who is not her social equal; the fear that love will rob her of her freedom and independence; the horror that love or the joy of motherhood will only hinder her in the full exercise of her profession—all these together make of the emancipated modern woman a compulsory vestal, before whom life, with its great clarifying sorrows and its deep, entrancing joys, rolls on without touching or gripping her soul.

Emancipation, as understood by the majority of its adherents and exponents, is of too narrow a scope to permit the boundless love and ecstasy contained in the deep emotion of the true woman, sweetheart, mother, in freedom.

The tragedy of the self-supporting or economically free woman does not lie in too many, but in too few experiences. True, she surpasses her sister of past generations in knowledge of the world and human nature; it is just because of this that she feels deeply the lack of life's essence, which alone can enrich the human soul, and without which the majority of women have become mere professional automatons.

That such a state of affairs was bound to come was foreseen by those who realized that, in the domain of ethics, there still remained many decaying ruins of the time of the undisputed superiority of man; ruins that are still considered useful. And, what is more important, a goodly number of the emancipated are unable to get along without them. Every movement that aims at the destruction of existing institutions and the replacement thereof with something more advanced, more perfect, has followers who in theory stand for the most radical ideas, but who, nevertheless, in their every-day practice, are like the average Philistine, feigning respectability and clamoring for the good opinion of their opponents. There are, for example, Socialists, and even Anarchists, who stand for the idea that property is robbery, yet who will grow indignant if anyone owe them the value of a half-dozen pins.

The same Philistine can be found in the movement for woman's emancipation. Yellow journalists and milk-and-water littérateurs have painted pictures of the emancipated woman that make the hair of the good citizen and his dull companion stand up on end. Every member of the woman's rights movement was pictured as a George Sand in her absolute disregard of morality. Nothing was sacred to her. She had no respect for the ideal relation between man and woman. In short, emancipation stood only for a reckless life of lust and sin, regardless of society, religion, and morality. The exponents of woman's rights were highly indignant at such misrepresentation, and, lacking humor, they exerted all their energy to prove that they were not at all as bad as they were painted, but the very reverse. Of course, as long as woman was the slave of man, she could not be good and pure, but now that she was free and independent she would prove how good she could be and that her influence would have a purifying effect on all institutions in society. True, the movement for woman's rights has broken many old fetters, but it has also forged new ones. The great movement of *true* emancipation has not met with a great race of women who could look liberty in the face. Their narrow, puritanical vision banished man, as a disturber and doubtful character, out of their emotional life. Man was not to be tolerated at any price, except perhaps as the father of a child, since a child could not very well come to life without a father. Fortunately, the most rigid Puritans never will be strong enough to kill the innate craving for motherhood. But woman's freedom is closely allied with man's freedom, and many of my so-called emancipated sisters seem to overlook the fact that a child born in freedom needs the love and devotion of each human being about him, man as well as woman. Unfortunately, it is this narrow conception of human relations that has brought about a great tragedy in the lives of the modern man and woman.

About fifteen years ago appeared a work from the pen of the brilliant Norwegian Laura Marholm, called *Woman, a Character Study*. She was one of the first to call attention to the emptiness and narrowness of the existing conception of woman's emancipation, and its tragic effect upon the inner life of woman. In her work Laura Marholm speaks of the fate of several gifted women of international fame: the genius Eleonora Duse; the great mathematician and writer Sonya Kovalevskaia; the artist and poet-nature Marie Bashkirtzeff, who died so young. Through each description of the lives of these women of such extraordinary mentality runs a marked trail of unsatisfied craving for a full, rounded, complete, and beautiful life, and the unrest and loneliness resulting from the lack of it. Through these masterly psychological sketches one cannot help but see that the higher the mental development of woman, the less possible it is for her to meet a congenial mate who will see in her, not only sex, but also the human being, the friend, the comrade and strong individuality, who cannot and ought not lose a single trait of her character.

The average man with his self-sufficiency, his ridiculously superior airs of patronage towards the female sex, is an impossibility for woman as depicted in the *Character Study* by Laura Marholm. Equally impossible for her is the man who can see in her nothing more than her mentality and her genius, and who fails to awaken her woman nature.

A rich intellect and a fine soul are usually considered necessary attributes of a deep and beautiful personality. In the case of the modern woman, these attributes serve as a hindrance to the complete assertion of her being. For over a hundred years the old form of marriage, based on the Bible, "Till death doth part," has been denounced as an institution that stands for the sovereignty of the man over the woman, of her complete submission to his whims and commands, and absolute dependence on his name and support. Time and again it has been conclusively proved that the old matrimonial relation restricted woman to the function of man's servant and the bearer of his children. And yet we find many emancipated women who prefer marriage, with all its deficiencies, to the narrowness of an unmarried life: narrow and unendurable because of the chains of moral and social prejudice that cramp and bind her nature.

The explanation of such inconsistency on the part of many advanced women is to be found in the fact that they never truly understood the meaning of emancipation. They thought that all that was needed was independence from external tyrannies; the internal tyrants, far more harmful to life and growth—ethical and social conventions—were left to take care of themselves; and they have taken care of themselves. They seem to get along as beautifully in the heads and hearts of the most active exponents of woman's emancipation, as in the heads and hearts of our grandmothers.

These internal tyrants, whether they be in the form of public opinion or what will mother say, or brother, father, aunt, or relative of any sort; what will Mrs. Grundy, Mr. Comstock, the employer, the Board of Education say? All these busybodies, moral detectives, jailers of the human spirit, what will they say? Until woman has learned to defy them all, to stand firmly on her own ground and to insist upon her own unrestricted freedom, to listen to the voice of her nature, whether it call for life's greatest treasure, love for a man, or her most glorious privilege, the right to give birth to a child, she cannot call herself emancipated. How many emancipated women are brave enough to acknowledge that the voice of love is calling, wildly beating against their breasts, demanding to be heard, to be satisfied.

The French writer Jean Reibrach, in one of his novels, *New Beauty*, attempts to picture the ideal, beautiful, emancipated woman. This ideal is embodied in a young girl, a physician. She talks very cleverly and wisely of how to feed infants; she is kind, and administers medicines free to poor mothers. She converses with a young man of her acquaintance about the sanitary conditions of the future, and how various bacilli and germs shall be exterminated by the use of stone walls and floors, and by the doing away with rugs and hangings. She is, of course, very plainly and practically dressed, mostly in black. The young man, who at their first meeting, was overawed by the wisdom of his emancipated friend, gradually learns to understand her, and recognizes one fine day that he loves her. They are young, and she is kind and beautiful, and though always in rigid attire, her appearance is softened by a spotlessly clean white collar and cuffs. One would expect that he would tell her of his love, but he is not one to commit romantic absurdities. Poetry and the enthusiasm of love cover their blushing faces before the pure beauty of the lady. He silences the voice of his nature, and remains correct. She, too, is always exact, always rational, always well behaved. I fear if they had formed a union, the young man would have risked freezing to death. I must confess that I can see nothing beautiful in this new beauty, who is as cold as the stone walls and floors she dreams of. Rather would I have the love songs of romantic ages, rather Don Juan and Madame Venus, rather an elopement by ladder and rope on a moonlight night, followed by the father's curse, mother's moans, and the moral comments of neighbors, than correctness and propriety measured by yardsticks. If love does not know how to give and take without restrictions, it is not love, but a transaction that never fails to lay stress on a plus and a minus.

The greatest shortcoming of the emancipation of the present day lies in its artificial stiffness and its narrow respectabilities, which produce an emptiness in woman's soul that will not let her drink from the fountain of life. I once remarked that there seemed to be a deeper relationship between the old-fashioned mother and hostess, ever on the alert for the happiness of her little ones and the comfort of those she loves, and the truly new woman, than between the latter and her average emancipated sister. The disciples of emancipation pure and simple declared me a heathen, fit only for the stake. Their blind zeal did not let them see that my comparison between the old and the new was merely to prove that a goodly number of our grandmothers had more blood in their veins, far more humor and wit, and certainly a greater amount of naturalness, kind-heartedness, and simplicity, than the majority of our emancipated professional women who fill the colleges, halls of learning and various offices. This does not mean a wish to return to the past, nor does it condemn woman to her old sphere, the kitchen and the nursery.

Salvation lies in an energetic march onward towards a brighter and clearer future. We are in need of unhampered growth out of old traditions and habits. The movement for woman's emancipation has so far made but the first step in that direction. It is to be hoped that it will gather strength to make another. The right to vote, or equal civil rights, may be good demands, but true emancipation begins neither at the polls nor in courts. It begins in woman's soul. History tells us that every oppressed class gained true liberation from its masters through its own efforts. It is necessary that woman learn that lesson, that she realize that her freedom will reach as far as her power to achieve her freedom reaches. It is, therefore, far more important for her to begin with her inner regeneration, to cut loose from the weight of prejudices, traditions, and customs. The demand for equal rights in every vocation of life is just and fair; but, after all, the most vital right is the right to love and be loved. Indeed, if partial emancipation is to become a complete and true emancipation of woman, it will have to do away with the ridiculous notion that to be loved, to be sweetheart and mother, is synonymous with being slave or subordinate. It will have to do away with the absurd notion of the dualism of the sexes, or that man and woman represent two antagonistic worlds.

Pettiness separates; breadth unites. Let us be broad and big. Let us not overlook vital things because of the bulk of trifles confronting us. A true conception of the relation of the sexes will not admit of conqueror and conquered; it knows of but one great thing: to give of one's self boundlessly, in order to find one's self richer, deeper, better. That alone can fill the emptiness, and transform the tragedy of woman's emancipation into joy, limitless joy.

Chapter 38

Margaret Sanger (1879–1966)

"THE CASE FOR BIRTH CONTROL"
(1924)

ACCESS TO KNOWLEDGE ABOUT BIRTH control in the early twentieth century was unequally distributed between upper- and middle-class and working-class women. In making her "Case for Birth Control," Sanger highlights the roots of this inequality in obscenity laws, religious and political doctrines, and physician indifference, which combined to trap poor women in cycles of recurring unwanted pregnancies. By highlighting the plight of the poor, Sanger explains the structural inequalities at work in women's varying knowledge about birth control, thereby revealing her socialist commitments; addressing an audience that was likely to be middle or upper class and, no doubt, feeding into their fears about over-population among the poor, she thereby reveals her eugenicist views. The birth control movement, like many other movements of the twentieth-century, was both utopian – imagining a better future for women freed of the bondage of unwanted pregnancy – and dystopian – threatening degeneration and decline if population trends continued along their current path.

Margaret Sanger, "The Case for Birth Control," *The Woman Citizen* 8 (23 February 1924): 17–18.

Everywhere we look, we see poverty and large families going hand in hand. We see hordes of children whose parents cannot feed, clothe, or educate even one half of the number born to them. We see sick, harassed, broken mothers whose health and nerves cannot bear the strain of further child-bearing. We see fathers growing despondent and desperate, because their labor cannot bring the necessary wage to keep their growing families. We see that those parents who are least fit to reproduce the race are having the largest number of children; while people of wealth, leisure, and education are having small families.

It is generally conceded by sociologists and scientists that a nation cannot go on indefinitely multiplying without eventually reaching the point when population presses upon means of subsistence. While in this country there is perhaps no need for immediate alarm on this account, there are many other reasons for demanding birth control. At present, for the poor mother, there is only one alternative to the necessity of bearing children year after year, regardless of her health, of the welfare of the children she already has, and of the income of the family. This alternative is abortion, which is so common as to be almost universal, especially where there are rigid laws against imparting information for the prevention of conception. It has been estimated that there are about one million abortions in the United States each year.

To force poor mothers to resort to this dangerous and healthdestroying method of curtailing their families is cruel, wicked, and heartless, and it is often the mothers who care most about the welfare of their children who are willing to undergo any pain or risk to prevent the coming of infants for whom they cannot properly care.

There are definite reasons when and why parents should not have children, which will be conceded by most thoughtful people.

First – Children should not be born when either parent has an inheritable disease, such as insanity, feeble-mindedness, epilepsy, or syphilis.

Second – When the mother is suffering from tuberculosis, kidney disease, heart disease, or pelvic deformity.

Third – When either parent has gonorrhea. This disease in the mother is the cause of 90 percent of blindness in newborn babies.

Fourth – When children already born are not normal, even though both parents are in good physical and mental condition.

Fifth – Not until the woman is twenty-three years old and the man twenty-five.

Sixth – Not until the previous baby is at least three years old. This gives a year to recover from the physical ordeal of the birth of the baby, a year to rest, be normal and enjoy her motherhood, and another year to prepare for the coming of the next.

We want mothers to be fit. We want them to conceive in joy and gladness. We want them to carry their babies during the nine months in a sound and healthy body and with a happy, joyous, hopeful mind. It is almost impossible to imagine the suffering caused to women, the mental agony they endure, when their days and nights are haunted by the fear of undesired pregnancy.

Seventh – Children should not be born to parents whose economic circumstances do not guarantee enough to provide the children with the necessities of life.

A couple who can take care of two children and bring them up decently in health and comfort, give them an education and start them fairly in life, do more for their country and for mankind than the couple who recklessly reproduce ten or twelve children, some of them to die in infancy, others to survive but to enter the mill or factory at an early age, and all to sink to that level of degradation where charity, either state or private, is necessary to keep them alive. The man who cannot support three children should not have ten, notwithstanding all pleas of the militarists for numbers.

Eighth – A woman should not bear children when exhausted from labor. This especially applies to women who marry after spending several years in industrial or commercial life. Conception should not take place until she is in good health and has overcome her fatigue.

Ninth – Not for two years after marriage should a couple undertake the great responsibility of becoming parents. Thousands of young people enter marriage without the faintest idea of what marriage involves. They do not know its spiritual responsibilities. If children are born quickly and plentifully, people consider that the marriage is justified. I claim that this is barbaric and wrong. It is wrong for the wife, for the man, for the children.

It is impossible for two young people to really know each other until they have lived together in marriage. After the closeness and intimacy of that relation there often comes to the woman a rude awakening; the devoted lover becomes careless and dissatisfied. If she becomes pregnant immediately, she becomes physically disturbed, nervous, and irritable. The girl has changed, and the boy who knew her as a happy smiling sweetheart finds her disagreeable and disgruntled. Of course thousands of people learn to adjust themselves. Nevertheless, I maintain that young people should marry early and wait at least two years to adjust their own lives, to play and read together and to build up a cultural and spiritual friendship. Then will come the intense desire to call into being a little child to share their love and happiness. When children are conceived in love and born into an atmosphere of happiness, then will parenthood be a glorious privilege, and the children will grow to resemble gods. This can only be obtained through the knowledge and practice of Birth Control.

P.S. – The American Birth Control League desires that the instruction in birth control should be given by the medical profession. Only through individual care and treatment can a woman be given the best and safest means of controlling her offspring. We do not favor the indiscriminate diffusion of unreliable and unsafe birth control advice.

PART VI

Race and ethnicity

While Charles Darwin's scientific theories of evolutionary biological development fundamentally challenged spiritual explanations of life and creation, modern notions of racial and ethnic difference maintained some of their connections to earlier, pre-modern hierarchies of existence, like the Great Chain of Being. Modern science contributed new modes of analysis and energized innovative narratives and visions, but those novel ideas also clashed and mingled with ancient and atavistic ones. The divine account of Being placed non-spiritual life like rocks, the four elements, and plants at the bottom of the Chain; animals' place was in the middle of the Great Chain, while humans were near the top, beneath the angels and God the Divine maker. In St. Thomas Aquinas's demarcation of the Great Chain, "Gypsies" were placed between animals and "Thieves and Pirates"; the deep embeddedness of myths and fictions of race would be intellectually and creatively refuted and genocidally re-inscribed in modern times.

In *The Descent of Man* (1874), Darwin speculatively explores the issue of the "formation" of the different races and their shared, heterogeneous and distinct, homogeneous "stock." He appears to suggest that heterogeneity and mixture is a biological fact of human life; as humans move and come into contact with others, their branches cross. This "diffusion" of race can account for the "singular fact" that despite linguistic and cultural differences, "Europeans and Hindoos . . . belong to the same Aryan stock" and also share racial and ethnic characteristics with people of Semitic stock.[1] Darwin attempts to account for the superficial differences and genetic variations in the human species: what accounts for some Negroes' immunity from yellow fever? Why is the tropical climate so devastating to some racial and ethnic types? Why do dark-haired Europeans withstand hotter climates more easily than fair-haired Europeans? Why did the European settlers in America change in growth and stature so rapidly and dramatically? Darwin's focus on "external characteristic differences" could not combat long-held beliefs that racial and ethnic differences were eternal and essential. Early interpreters of his theories divided into two camps: one comprised the polygenists, who believed that human life was composed of many distinctly different and separate racial families, the other of the monogenists, who believed that human life evolved from one shared source. These differences of opinion are grounded in racial ideology and religious myth; the earliest versions of poly- and monogenetic thought were theological. Some believed that all of humankind descended from Adam and Eve; others believed that racial others were the product of post-lapserian sin, for example, dark-skinned people were the children of Ham or the product of Eve's coupling with an embodiment of the devil. As an ideological belief, polygenism supported the slave trade and legitimized the occupation and colonization of other lands and alleged lesser peoples; monogenism sometimes supported progressive campaigns, ranging from abolition to anti-imperialism to Pan-Indian nationalism.

Competing interpretations of Darwin's theories would affect politics, social and economic policies, and the biological and social sciences. Herbert Spencer, the "Father of Sociology," coined the term "the survival of the fittest" for his understanding of Darwin's theories of natural selection; evolution, as an idea, persuaded some people of the possibilities of reform and development; others saw it as evidence of insurmountable differences – lesser races might never "catch up" to advanced ones. Many modernist visual artists and writers were attracted to the "uncivilized" as a concept; perhaps, it was believed, "savage" peoples had a vital connectedness to the body and pre-modern states of consciousness and perception that had declined or become dulled in civilized peoples. Roger Fry's writings on African drawing and sculpture in *Vision and Design* (1920) display this kind of romantic primitivism, as do D.H. Lawrence's uses of Aztec mythology in *The Plumed Serpent* (1926), Jean Toomer's representation of Southern rural earth-consciousness and mysticism in *Cane* (1923), and Gertrude Stein's *Three Lives* (1909) story "Melanctha" and its exploration of modern angst and racial consciousness. Celebrations of the primitive would also be the cause of divisions among the Harlem Renaissance writers; Zora Neale Hurston's exuberant uses of Southern and rural vernacular speech appeared embarrassing minstrel throw-backs for a self-conscious cosmopolitan like Alain Locke.

The care with which Charles Darwin posits his questions about the nature and significance of what he described as "slight individual differences" and "external characteristic differences" reveals his fascination with the productive forces of evolution and awareness of the possible debates his theories will arouse. While his theory of natural selection was partially influenced by political economist Thomas Robert Malthus's notion of a natural system of population checks and balances, theorized in *An Essay on the Principle of Population, as it Affects the Future Improvement of Society* (1798), Darwin focuses on signs of health and the vibrancy of mobile life in transformation and mutation. Eugenics, the area of science most closely connected to racial and ethnic issues, was widely popular in the early decades of the twentieth century, but it fell into great disrepute because of its association with Nazism. Conceived of as "the self-direction of human evolution" (according to the Second International Eugenics Conference, 1921), eugenics sought to improve human genetic qualities. Drawing on the work of Darwin, the Victorian polymath Sir Francis Galton formulated the field and the term in 1883; its numerous supporters subsequently included John Maynard Keynes, Linus Pauling, Theodore Roosevelt, Margaret Sanger, George Bernard Shaw, Marie Stopes, H.G. Wells, Woodrow Wilson, W.B. Yeats, Julian Huxley, and Émile Zola. But after being taken up by Hitler as a means for advancing the creation of a master race by enforced racial hygiene, human experimentation, and the extermination of certain "degenerate" population groups, the practice of eugenics raised innumerable ethical and practical problems that alienated many initial supporters and have yet to be satisfactorily resolved; it remains a highly controversial and suspect field of inquiry.

Racial and ethnic issues weave a complex, often ugly, pattern through modernism, though antithetical visions and values also emerge. The Dreyfus Affair, which began in 1894 and lasted for a dozen years, sensationally revealed anti-Semitism in French politics and society, as well as the nation's cultural institutions, including the military, the press, and the Catholic Church. Captain Alfred Dreyfus, a young French military officer of Jewish descent, was falsely charged with treason for passing French military secrets to the German Embassy in Paris. Convicted and sentenced to life imprisonment, Dreyfus was sent to the penal colony at Devil's

Island, French Guiana, and placed in solitary confinement. When, two years later, evidence surfaced that Dreyfus was innocent, a cover-up began that included suppression of evidence by senior military officials, the quick trial and exoneration of the guilty officer, and further accusations against Dreyfus based on forged documents. As the truth began to emerge, Émile Zola published J'accuse (1898), an incandescent denunciation of the proceedings against Dreyfus that, despite fierce opposition from, among others, Edouard Drumont, the publisher of the anti-Semitic newspaper La Libre Parole, eventually led to Dreyfus being exonerated and reinstated in the military, which he served with distinction throughout World War I. Zola addresses the specificities of the false charges against Dreyfus; he also examines the "weak-minded" limitations of members of the liberal class and their social imagination, especially in regards to ethnic and racial myths. The bourgeois are "accomplices" in the Dreyfus Affair; they have unthinkingly consumed the narrative only a "cheap novel of the most outlandish sort" could offer. Zola describes the "stupid," "implausible," "childish" accusations against Dreyfus as being worthy of a medieval chronicle; he also touches upon the economic and cultural resentments that distinguish modern anti-Semitism: Jews are suspect for being both archaically other *and* urban and cosmopolitan. Zola caustically inquires, "So Dreyfus speaks several languages, does he? This is a crime. . . . He occasionally pays a visit to the region he hails from? A crime. He is a hard-working man, eager to know everything? A crime." Zola appeals to the French people to recognize the anti-Semitic and racist fictions that inflame their passions and redirects his fellow citizens to focus on and fight for truth, justice, and the ideals of the Republic.

For many European Jews, the Dreyfus Affair highlighted the vulnerability of Jewish peoples on the Continent; the humiliation and attempted destruction of Drefyus, a loyal French citizen and faithful national servant, led some to redefine Jewish identity and habits of affiliation. Theodor Herzl, a Viennese journalist who covered the Dreyfus trial, reoriented his views on the possibilities for thriving Jewish communal life after witnessing the trial; for Herzl, the Dreyfus Affair made the Jewish Question a national one. In The Jewish State: A Modern Solution to the Jewish Question (1896), Herzl reminded his audience,

> We have honestly attempted to assimilate everywhere into the societies surrounding us retaining nothing but the religion of our forefathers. But they will not let us assimilate. We are loyal, sometimes exaggerated, patriots – in vain. We bring the same sacrifices in life and in property as our fellow-citizens – in vain. We strive to increase the welfare of the countries we were born in – in vain. In the lands we have lived in for centuries we continue to be called strangers. It is useless to be a good patriot in order to be left in peace. I am afraid that we will never be left in peace.

Herzl saw "Jew baiting" as an ancient and still vibrant European tradition: "Old prejudice against us still lies deep in the hearts of the people," he warned.[2] That active prejudice was discernible in Europe's fairytales and proverbs, and in the "classic Berlin phrase 'Juden raus!' ' ("Out with the Jews!").[3] In March 1897, less than a year after the publication of The Jewish State, the First Zionist Congress was convened in Basle, Switzerland. Alain Locke, referencing ethnic people's fight for self-determination in the early twentieth century in his compendium The New Negro, envisions Harlem ("she is the home of the Negro's 'Zionism'") as the socially healthy and psychically protective homeland for American blacks, as Herzl envisioned the "State of Palestine" for European Jewry. In 1903, shortly after the end of the Dreyfus Affair a Russian newspaper serialized portions of The Protocols of the Elders of Zion, the most notorious and widely distributed anti-Semitic publication of the twentieth century. According to The Protocols a Jewish conspiracy, headed by the so-called "Elders of Zion," seeks to achieve world domination, though, as has repeatedly been demonstrated, neither the conspiracy nor the Elders ever existed. The document was, nonetheless, used throughout the modern period to spread lies about Jews, and it continues to be wielded today by those whose hatred of Jews causes them to blame Jews for whatever is deemed wrong with the world.

Anti-Semitism and racism made their way into the thinking and writing of many modernists. In *The Great Gatsby* (1925), for example, F. Scott Fitzgerald depicts Meyer Wolfshiem, the man Gatsby says fixed the 1919 baseball World Series, stereotypically: "A small, flat-nosed Jew . . . [with a] large head and . . . two fine growths of hair which luxuriated in either nostril. After a moment I discovered his tiny eyes in the half-darkness."[4] Supposedly Gatsby's close friend and a sentimentalist, Wolfshiem refuses to attend Gatsby's funeral because, he says, "I can't get mixed up in it." In *The Sun Also Rises* (1926), Ernest Hemingway makes the Jewish Robert Cohn an outsider from the book's opening lines – someone who overstays his welcome, never knows when he's not wanted, and almost invariably makes himself obnoxious, a figure of ridicule. Feeling insecure and shy as a Jew at Princeton, according to the narrator Jake Barnes, Cohn learned to box; he proved, surprisingly, so good at it that he was "promptly overmatched . . . and got his nose permanently flattened. This increased Cohn's distaste for boxing, but it gave him a certain satisfaction of some strange sort, and it certainly improved his nose."[5] Describing Jews as having prominent, ugly noses was long a staple of anti-Semitic writings.

Although he later denied the charge, T.S. Eliot, in such poems as "Burbank with a Baedeker: Bleistein with a Cigar" (1920) and "Gerontion" (1920), indulged in the growing anti-Semitism that followed from, among other things, the Dreyfus Affair and the forged *Protocols of the Elders of Zion*, while his crude, puerile King Bolo poems expressed racist fantasies of the sexual superiority (and therefore threat) of blacks. Eliot himself rejected political solutions, but many of his contemporaries – including Roy Campbell, D.H. Lawrence, Hugh MacDiarmid, F.T. Marinetti, and W.B. Yeats – at least flirted with fascism as the solution to the ills of the modernist era, while Wyndham Lewis in *Hitler* (1931) dismissed Nazi anti-Semitism as a "racial red-herring"[6] and Ezra Pound, who in Hugh Kenner's view gave his name to the era and was a great admirer of Eliot's King Bolo poems, most notoriously went all the way into virulent anti-Semitism, broadcasting on behalf of the fascists and ranting against President Roosevelt, Jews and usury during World War II. Pound was indicted by a U.S. grand jury for his treasonous broadcasts; he was arrested in Italy at the end of the war in May 1945. After suffering a breakdown during his Italian incarceration, Pound was hospitalized at St. Elizabeth's Hospital in Washington, DC for twelve years. The "Pisan Cantos," the poems he wrote while imprisoned in Italy, were awarded the Bollingen Prize in 1949, igniting debates about art and politics, and fascism and aesthetics, with which Pound continues to be associated.

Not all modernist writers fell for fascism or even flirted with it. Samuel Beckett fought as a member of the French resistance underground in German-occupied Paris until forced to flee; Bertolt Brecht and C.L.R. James were also outspoken anti-fascists and anti-imperialists (see Part IV "Politics and war" and Part VII "Global modernisms"). Joyce made the protagonist of *Ulysses* a wandering Jew (though not a practicing one) who at crucial moments proclaims his heritage and justice, risks physical harm to oppose anti-Semitism, and sings *Hatikvah*, the Jewish song of "Hope" that later became the Israeli national anthem. William Faulkner, in such novels as *The Sound and the Fury* (1929), *Light in August* (1932), *Absalom, Absalom!* (1936), *Go Down, Moses* (1942), and *Intruder in the Dust* (1948), represents African Americans, and sometimes Native Americans, as heroic figures and racism as enormously destructive – to its perpetrators as well as its intended targets. And Sinclair Lewis, who wrote numerous satires about aspects of capitalist society, depicted an American Hitler coming to power and eventually being overthrown in *It Can't Happen Here* (1935). Both Faulkner and Lewis, among America's fiercest cultural critics, concluded their Nobel Prize acceptance speeches with optimism and hope for an improved human species.

The Harlem Renaissance, which flourished from approximately 1917 to 1935 and was known for a time as "The New Negro Movement" (after Alain Locke's anthology, *The New Negro* [1925]), became a source of enormous racial pride. Centered in Harlem, the Negroes' promised land in the New York City neighborhood, the Harlem Renaissance directly influenced Parisian Francophone African and Caribbean writers such as Aimé Césaire, Léon Damas, and Leopold Senghor, who formed the Négritude Movement in the 1930s and '40s. Attracting both black and white patrons, the Harlem Renaissance had major African diasporic achievements in music (especially jazz), theatre, literature, art – and significant impact on white writers in such work as George Gershwin's opera *Porgy and Bess* and Virgil Thomson and Gertrude Stein's *Four Saints in Three Acts*. The new fiction of Langston Hughes, Zora Neale Hurston, James Weldon Johnson, Alain Locke, Claude McKay, and Jean Toomer became widely popular and influential; black American newspapers and magazines also highlighted the creative work and social commentary of a generation of new writers. Marita Bonner's radical, experimental, neo-Brechtian liberation "race play" *The Purple Flower* was first published in *The Crisis Magazine* in 1928, as was her essay "On Being Young – a Woman – and Colored" (1925). In the latter, Bonner articulates a longing for acceptance as a black American and as a modern woman; the essay details a double-entrapment and a desire for comfort and mobility "out, up, beyond things that have bodies and walls."[7] Bonner describes music and visual art as *potential* vehicles of transformation; the arts are contrasted by "old ideas" and "worm-eaten, out-grown, worthless, bitter" "old fundamentals," "fit for the scrap-heap of wisdom."[8] But Bonner also articulated a cryptic cautionary tale about culture that would be illustrated all too horrif-ically in Germany's Third Reich: cultures without "wisdom," the ability to reflect and discover actual truths (versus society's familiar and convenient fictions and material illusions), destroy and self-destruct:

> The Greeks had possessions, culture. They were lost because they did not under-stand.
> The Romans owned more than anyone else. Trampled under the heel of Vandals and Civilization, because they would not understand.
> Greeks. Did not understand.
> Romans. Would not understand.
> "They." Will not understand.

Bonner envisions herself, womanly, waiting for wisdom, and quiet like the Buddha, who is brown like her, "motionless and knowing."[9]

In America, the Ku Klux Klan was founded in 1865 by Tennessee veterans of the Confederate Army who were determined to restore white supremacy. Resisting Reconstruction, the Klan intimidated, assaulted, and murdered former slaves and white progressives, until it was finally suppressed by law enforcement, legislation, and judicial action. But the KKK had a second flowering during 1915–25, growing rapidly to about five million members in the postwar period due to social tensions that included industrialization in the North, waves of immigrants from southern and eastern Europe, and the Great Migration of Southern blacks (about five million moved north and west from 1915 to 1960). The second KKK preached anti-Catholicism and anti-communism, as well as racism, nativism, and anti-Semitism. Several factors, including the Depression and World War II, led to its equally rapid decline. Between 1926 and 1942 in the U.S., Father Charles Coughlin's radio broadcasts and his newspaper, *Social Justice*, were outspoken in support of the fascist policies of Mussolini and Hitler and increasingly virulent in denouncing the "international conspiracy of Jewish bankers" who supposedly caused the Russian Revolution and the Great Depression. His isolationism even after the Japanese attack on Pearl Harbor led to his being denounced as sympathetic to the enemy, and he was finally forced by his bishop to cease all political activity.

Racism was the driving force in the case of the so-called Scottsboro Boys, nine young black males (the youngest of whom was twelve) who, in 1931, were falsely accused of gang raping two young white women in Alabama. Throughout the 1930s and well into the 1940s they were repeatedly tried, found guilty, sentenced to death, held in prison, and retried after their convictions were overturned judicially. The NAACP, fearful of taking on such a controversial case and issue, left a vacuum that the Communist Party (in the guise of the International Labor Defense) rushed to fill – and turn into an international cause. Probably no case in U.S. history – especially one in which no crime was committed – produced as many trials, convictions, reversals, and retrials and became as infamous as this one. The defendants were all exonerated in the end, but only after their lives had been ruined by their treatment.

Among those who most loudly trumpeted the innocence of the Scottsboro Boys and raised money and international outrage for their defense was Nancy Cunard, a liberated 1920s flapper who became a writer, editor, publisher, outspoken political advocate of such causes as communism, anti-fascism, and racial justice – and the woman of her time who was probably most represented by writers, painters, and sculptors. A wealthy British heiress who had broken with her rich socialite mother, Emerald Cunard, after taking up with Henry Crowder, an African American jazz musician, Cunard wrote a polemical pamphlet, *Black Man and White Ladyship* (1931), which denounced her mother and her entire social class, and sent the tract to all of her mother's friends as a Christmas card. Cunard depicts "the Colour Question" as *the* modern question that presented her with the most disruptive "shocks" to her psyche and vision of social justice. She describes her mother and members of the British ruling class as hysterics and hypocrites; even George Moore, the Irish novelist whose *Esther Waters and A Drama in Muslin* exploded Victorian sexual mores and whom Cunard adored, is made to reveal his prejudices in her telling. Cunard recounts a conversation on the race question with Moore, who functions as the representative of the intelligentsia in the pamphlet. Cunard's "Self" asks Moore if he would "like to talk to an intelligent Indian or Negro?" G.M. "calmly" responds, "No. I do not think so. I do not think I should get on with a black man or a brown man. . . . I think the best I could do is a yellow man!"[10] Cunard's outraged tone is rhetorically forceful and satirical; she archly depicts the civilized language and affected diction of her class in its casual racist and homophobic brutality and violence. Blacks and homosexuals are tolerated in society only when they are artful or entertaining. At the same time that Cunard was championing the cause of the Scottsboro Boys, she was also compiling *Negro: An Anthology* (1934), a vast compendium of African and African diasporic literature and art depicting victimization and celebrating achievement; denouncing Mussolini's annexation of Ethiopia and Franco's forces in the Spanish Civil War (she presciently saw that the "events in Spain were a prelude to another world war"); and producing the anti-fascist pamphlet, *Authors Take Sides* (1937). During World War II she worked tirelessly on behalf of the French resistance.

More positive values and ideals than racism and anti-Semitism were also at work during this period. In the interwar period in particular, students, socialists, workers, and progressive activists supported international cooperation and opposed racism, colonial imperialism, and the exploitation of the world's poor and vulnerable. (See, for example, the entries by C.L.R. James, J.A. Hobson, Rosa Luxemburg, and Emma Goldman in this volume.) In the 1920s and '30s, a generation of European writers, artists, and intellectuals sought alternatives to the destructive forces of war and intolerance; the Spanish Civil War inspired international brigades from around the globe. Visionary former suffragists like Sylvia Pankhurst and Winifred Holtby strove to make comprehensible the intersections of racial, sexual, labor, and economic injustices; both were committed to the cause of African liberation: Holtby in South Africa and Pankhurst in Ethiopia. Jean Toomer's lifelong interest in questions of Being sought to transcend racial categories and binaries. Toomer, a devoted follower of the idealist philosopher George Ivanovitch Gurdjieff's Institute for Harmonious Development in France, also supported the values of the international community of Esperanto enthusiasts who believed that a new, transnational language could enable people to foster peace and transcend the fictions of racial, ethnic, cultural, and economic differences. His most long-term commitment was to Quakerism. The bi-racial Toomer, who at different times in his life passed as white and lived and identified as an African American, believed that spiritual self-development was the only possible answer to the world's increasing social problems. Modern life, in Toomer's view, would remain fluid and chaotic; business and enterprise would continue to foster competition and violence. Human life was a struggle for survival in Darwinian terms and spiritual ones. In "Race Problems and Modern Society" (1929), he observed that "the inner content of life is decreasing and rapidly losing significance."[11] Toomer viewed racial and national conflicts as symptoms of social and psychological maladjustment; he diagnoses increased race consciousness in the Negro, Zionism in the Jew, nationalism, the acquisitive impulse in dominant races as spiritual diseases. His solution lay in the embrace of diverse philosophical beliefs and biological wisdom: "it is thus everywhere where people meet. Let people meet – and they mingle. This is biology, the reproductive urge within man, acting with no thought of sociological differences."[12] At times as idealistic and short-sighted as Cunard, who suggested in *Black Man and White Ladyship* that "colour prejudice" was nonexistent in France and Germany,[13] Toomer proposed a kind of eugenic self-selection as the solution to the problem of race: "Stripped to its essentials, the positive aspect of the race problem can be expressed thus: how to bring about a selective fusion of the racial and cultural factors of America, in order that the best possible stock and culture may be produced."[14] The devastating complexity of race in modern times is evident in this shared solution of selectivity and selection; yet the solution envisioned as "idealistic" and utopian in Toomer's worldview was *final* and murderously genocidal in Hitler's.

In spite of the very dark realities of racism in modern times, the first half of the twentieth century was also a time when writers increasingly claimed authority over their own stories and lives. American Jewish writers and novels such as Abraham Cahan's *The Rise of David Levinsky* (1917), Michael Gold's *Jews without Money* (1930), and Henry Roth's *Call It Sleep* (1934) depict the harsh life of Jewish immigrants in New York's teeming Lower East Side and their success – for good and ill – in assimilating. Caribbean and Latin American writers expressed identity, possibility, and historical consciousness in Négritude poetry and verse; East and South Asian writers artistically challenged imposed colonial and indigenous cultural systems of oppression. Zora Neale Hurston's essay "How It Feels to Be Colored Me" (1928) exhibits the era's willful creative and political expression. Hurston's depiction of herself in the essay echoes W.E.B. DuBois' African American subject's "double consciousness," but the essay also exuberantly foreshadows what Frantz Fanon would, in a hopeful moment decades later, describe in *Black Skin, White Masks* (1952) as the necessity to transcend history and to add *invention* to existence. Hurston's essential self is "Zora of Orange County," a joyful, playful, entertaining, shameless, outgoing country girl. In Jacksonville, Florida she encountered the realities of the colored girl that is projected on to Zora's life-force, but she refuses to become that girl: "I am not tragically colored," she declares. "There is no great sorrow dammed up in my soul, nor lurking behind my eyes. . . . I do not belong to the sobbing school of Negrohood who hold that nature somehow has given them a lowdown dirty deal and whose feelings are all hurt about it." She is instead the "cosmic Zora" who is attached to the universe; she is, as

Langston Hughes describes in "The Negro Artist and the Great Racial Mountain" (see Part I "Culture and Aesthetics"), the spectacular accumulation of it *all* – pain and beauty, intolerance and comfort, oppression and opportunity, nature and culture: "How can any deny themselves the pleasure of my company? It's beyond me."[15] In addition to her sass and willful survival, the hard facts of history inspired Zora to keep her oyster knife sharp.

Notes

1   Darwin, *The Descent of Man* 218.
2   Herzl 15.
3   Herzl 21.
4   Fitzgerald, *The Great Gatsby* 69–70.
5   Hemingway, *The Sun Also Rises* 3.
6   It was, curiously given its title, in his book *The Jews, Are They Human?* (1939) that Lewis subsequently renounced anti-Semitism.
7   Bonner, "On Being Young – a Woman – and Colored" 4. (See also Chapter 41 of this volume, p. 360.)
8   Bonner 6.
9   Bonner 7.
10   Cunard, *Black Man and White Ladyship* 10.
11   Toomer, "Race Problems and Modern Society" 62. (See also Chapter 44 of this volume, p. 377.)
12   Toomer 69.
13   Cunard, *Black Man and White Ladyship* 9.
14   Toomer 74.
15   Hurston, "How It Feels to Be Colored Me" 153–55.

Suggested further readings

Anon. *The Protocols of the Elders of Zion* (1903; first published in English in 1919). Trans. Victor E. Marsden. London: Britons Publishing Society, 1933.

Arnold, James. *Modernism and Negritude: The Poetry and Poetics of Aimé Césaire*. Cambridge, MA: Harvard UP, 1982.

Bashford, Alison, and Philippa Levine, eds. *The Oxford Handbook of the History of Eugenics*. Oxford: Oxford UP, 2010.

Bonner, Marita. "On Being Young – a Woman – and Colored," *The Crisis Magazine* 31 (December 1925): 63–5. In *Frye Street and Environs: The Collected Works of Marita Bonner,* ed. Joyce Flynn and Joyce Occomy Stricklin. Boston: Beacon, 1987. 3–8.

Buber, Martin. *I and Thou* (1923). Eastford, CT: Martino Fine Books, 2010.

Campbell, Roy, and William Plomer, eds. *Vorslaag/Whiplash* (1926–27) (early South African anti-apartheid/modernist literary journal).

Carter, Mia, and Barbara Harlow, eds. "The Body Politic: Rationalizing Race." *Archives of Empire, vol. 2, The Scramble for Africa*. Durham: Duke UP, 2003: 83–90.

Casillo, Robert. *The Genealogy of Demons: Anti-Semitism, Fascism, and the Myths of Ezra Pound*. Chicago: Northwestern UP, 1988.

Chace, William M. *The Political Identities of Ezra Pound and T.S. Eliot* (1973). Stanford, CA: Stanford UP, 1973.

Childs, Donald J. *Modernism and Eugenics: Woolf, Eliot, Yeats, and the Culture of Degeneration*. Cambridge: Cambridge UP, 2001.

Cunard, Nancy. *Negro; An Anthology* (1934). New York: Ungar Publishing Company, 1970.

——. *Authors Take Sides on the Spanish War*. London: Left Review, 1937.

——. *Black Man and White Ladyship: An Anniversary*. London: Utopia Press, 1931.

Darwin, Charles. *The Descent of Man*. New York: A.L. Burt, 1874.

Doyle, Laura. *Bordering on the Body: The Racial Matrix of Modern Fiction and Culture*. Oxford: Oxford UP, 1994.

Doyle, Laura, and Laura Winkiel, eds. *Geomodernisms: Race, Modernism, Modernity*. Bloomington: Indiana UP, 2005.

Du Bois, W.E.B. *The Souls of Black Folk* (1903). New York: Modern Library, 2003.

Fanon, Frantz. *Black Skin, White Masks* (1952). Trans. Charles Lam Markmann. New York: Grove, 1968.

Fitzgerald, F. Scott. *The Great Gatsby* (1925). New York: Scribner's, 2004.

Francis, Jacqueline. *Making Race: Modernism and "Racial Art" in America*. Seattle: University of Washington Press, 2012.

Fry, Roger. "The Art of the Bushmen" (1910) and "Negro Sculpture" (1920). *Vision and Design* (1920). New York: Meridian, 1969.

Griffin, Roger. *Modernism and Fascism: The Sense of a Beginning under Mussolini and Hitler*. New York: Palgrave Macmillan, 2010.

Hedrick, Tace. *Mestizo Modernism: Race, Nation and Identity in Latin American Culture, 1900–1940*. New Brunswick, NJ: Rutgers UP, 2003.

Hemingway, Ernest. *The Sun Also Rises* (1926). New York: Scribner's, 1996.

Herzl, Theodor. *A Jewish State: Attempt at a Modern Solution of the Jewish Question*. New York: Maccabaen Publishing, 1904.

Hirschfeld, Magnus. *Racism* (1938). Port Washington, NY: Kennikat, 1973.

Hitler, Adolf. *Mein Kampf* (1925). Trans. Ralph Manheim. Boston: Houghton Mifflin, 1971.

Hurston, Zora Neale. "How It Feels to Be Colored Me." *I Love Myself When I Am Laughing: A Zora Neale Hurston Reader*. Ed. Alice Walker. New York: the Feminist Press, 1979.

Huxley, Julian. *The Stream of Life*. New York: Harper and Brothers, 1927.

Julius, Anthony. *T.S. Eliot, Anti-Semitism, and Literary Form* (1995). Cambridge and New York: Cambridge UP, 1995.

Lewis, Wyndham. *The Jews, Are They Human?* London: Allen and Unwin, 1939.

——. *Hitler*. London: Chatto and Windus, 1931.

Lovejoy, Arthur O. *The Great Chain of Being: A Study of the History of an Idea*. New Brunswick, NJ: Transaction Publishers, 2009.

Malthus, T.R. *An Essay on the Principle of Population* (1803). Cambridge and New York: Cambridge UP, 1992.

Marcus, Jane. *Hearts of Darkness: White Women Write Race*. New Brunswick, NJ: Rutgers UP, 2004.

Mendes-Flohr, Paul, and Jehuda Reinharz, eds. *The Jew in the Modern World: A Documentary History*. Oxford: Oxford UP, 2010.

Nietzsche, Friedrich. *The Antichrist* (1895); H.L. Mencken, "Introduction." New York: Knopf, 1920.

Platt, Len, ed. *Modernism and Race*. Cambridge: Cambridge UP, 2011.

Pound, Ezra. Broadcast (15 March 1942): http://www.stormfront.org/forum/sitemap/index.php/t-535973.html.

Renan, Ernest. *The Future of Science*. Boston: Roberts Brothers, 1893.

Seshagiri, Urmila. *Race and the Modernist Imagination*. Ithaca: Cornell UP, 2010.

Spencer, Herbert. *The Principles of Biology*. New York: Appleton, 1897.

Toomer, Jean. "Race Problems and Modern Society" (1929). *Jean Toomer: Selected Essays and Literary Criticism*, ed. Robert B. Jones. Knoxville: U of Tennessee P, 1996.

Wagner, Richard. "Judaism in Music" (1850). *Judaism in Music and Other Essays*. Trans. William Ashton Ellis. Lincoln, NE: U of Nebraska P, 1995.

Winkiel, Laura. *Modernism, Race and Manifestos*. Cambridge: Cambridge UP, 2008.

Chapter 39

Charles Darwin (1809–82)

"ON THE FORMATION OF THE RACES OF MAN," *THE DESCENT OF MAN* (1871)

BECAUSE DARWIN'S *On the Origin of Species* (1859) does not discuss human evolution, it led to immediate speculation about how the theory of natural selection applied to humans and, specifically, how it could explain the races of man. Twelve years later, Darwin's *The Descent of Man* addressed the debates stirred up by his earlier work and outlined the relation between his evolutionary theories and human development. In the section titled "On the Formation of the Races of Man," Darwin downplays the biological significance of racial characteristics and argues against natural selection as their cause: "The great variability of all the external differences between the races of man . . . indicates that they cannot be of much importance; for if important, they would long ago have been either fixed and preserved or eliminated" (226). Because humans are a single, protean species, Darwin speculates that such external differences as skin color, hair, and stature may be the work of sexual, rather than natural, selection. This was not the final word on race theory, however, and many of the ideas that Darwin rejected, such as the relation between climate and race, have continued to exercise a hold on the popular and scientific imagination.

Charles Darwin, "On the Formation of the Races of Man," *The Descent of Man*, vol. 2. New York: A.L. Burt, 1874. 218–27.

In some cases the crossing of distinct races has led to the formation of a new race. The singular fact that the Europeans and Hindoos, who belong to the same Aryan stock and speak a language fundamentally the same, differ widely in appearance, while Europeans differ but little from Jews, who belong to the Semitic stock and speak quite another language, has been accounted for by Broca,[1] through certain Aryan branches having been largely crossed by indigenous tribes during their wide diffusion. When two races in close contact cross the first result is a heterogeneous mixture; thus Mr. Hunter, in describing the Santali or hill-tribes of India, says hundreds of imperceptible gradations may be traced "from the black, squat tribes of the mountains to the tall olive-colored Brahman, with his intellectual brow, calm eyes, and high but narrow head;" so that it is necessary in courts of justice to ask the witnesses whether they are Santalis or Hindoos.[2] Whether a heterogeneous people, such as the inhabitants of some of the Polynesian islands, formed by the crossing of two distinct races, with few or no pure members left, would ever become homogeneous, is not known from direct evidence. But as with our domesticated animals, a crossbreed can certainly be fixed and made uniform by careful selection[3] in the course of a few generations, we may infer that the free intercrossing of a heterogeneous mixture during a long descent would supply the place of selection and overcome any tendency to reversion; so that the crossed race would ultimately become homogeneous, though it might not partake in an equal degree of the characters of the two parent-races.

Of all the differences between the races of man, the color of the skin is the most conspicuous and one of the best marked. It was formerly thought that differences of this kind could be accounted for by long exposure to different climates; but Pallas first showed that this is not tenable and he has since been followed by almost all anthropologists.[4] This view has been rejected chiefly because the distribution of the variously colored races, most of whom must have long inhabited their present homes, does not coincide with corresponding differences of climate. Some little weight may be given to such cases as that of the Dutch families, who, as we hear on excellent authority,[5] have not undergone the least change of color after residing for three centuries in S. Africa. An argument on the same side may likewise be drawn from the uniform appearance in various parts of the world of gypsies and Jews, though the uniformity of the latter has been somewhat exaggerated.[6] A very damp or a very dry atmosphere has been supposed to be more influential in modifying the color of the skin than mere heat; but as D'Orbigny in South America, and Livingstone in Africa, arrived at diametrically opposite conclusions with respect to dampness and dryness, any conclusion on this head must be considered as very doubtful.[7]

Various facts, which I have given elsewhere, prove that the color of the skin and hair is sometimes correlated in a surprising manner with a complete immunity from the action of certain vegetable poisons, and from the attacks of certain parasites. Hence it occurred to me, that negroes and other dark races might have acquired their dark tints by the darker individuals escaping from the deadly influence of the miasma of their native countries, during a long series of generations.

I afterward found that this same idea had long ago occurred to Dr. Wells.[8] It has long been known that negroes, and even mulattoes are almost completely exempt from the yellow fever, so destructive in tropical America.[9] They likewise escape to a large extent the fatal intermittent fevers that prevail along at least 2,600 miles of the shores of Africa, and which annually cause one-fifth of the white settlers to die and another fifth to return home invalided.[10] This immunity in the negro seems to be partly inherent, depending on some unknown peculiarity of constitution and partly the result of acclimatization. Pouchet[11] states that the negro regiments recruited near the Soudan and borrowed from the Viceroy of Egypt for the Mexican war escaped the yellow fever almost equally with the negroes originally brought from various parts of Africa and accustomed to the climate of the West Indies. That acclimatization plays a part is shown by the many cases in which negroes have become somewhat liable to tropical fevers, after having resided for some time in a colder climate.[12] The nature of the climate under which the white races have long resided, likewise has some influence on them; for during the fearful epidemic of yellow fever in Demerara during 1837 Dr. Blair found that the death-rate of the immigrants was proportional to the latitude of the country whence they had come. With the negro the immunity, as far as it is the result of acclimatization, implies exposure during a prodigious length of time; for the aborigines of tropical America who have resided there from time immemorial are not exempt from yellow fever; and the Rev. H. B. Tristram states that there are districts in Northern Africa which the native inhabitants are compelled annually to leave, though the negroes can remain with safety.

That the immunity of the negro is in any degree correlated with the color of his skin is a mere conjecture; it may be correlated with some difference in his blood, nervous system or other tissues. Nevertheless, from the facts above alluded to and from some connection apparently existing between complexion and a tendency to consumption, the conjecture seemed to me not improbable. Consequently I endeavored, with but little success,[13] to ascertain how far it holds good. The late Dr. Daniell, who had long lived on the west coast of Africa, told me that he did not believe in any such relation. He was himself unusually fair and had withstood the climate in a wonderful manner. When he first arrived as a boy on the coast an old and experienced negro chief predicted from his appearance that this would prove the case. Dr. Nicholson, of Antigua, after having attended to this subject, writes to me that dark-colored Europeans escape the yellow fever more than those that are light colored. Mr. J. M. Harris altogether denies that Europeans with dark hair withstand a hot climate better than other men; on the contrary, experience has taught him in making a selection of men for service on the coast of Africa to choose those with red hair.[14] As far, therefore, as these slight indications go, there seems no foundation for the hypothesis that blackness has resulted from the darker and darker individuals having survived better during long exposure to fever-generating miasma.

Dr. Sharpe remarks,[15] that a tropical sun, which burns and blisters a white skin, does not injure a black one at all; and, as he adds, this is not due to habit in the individual, for children only six or eight months old are often carried about naked, and are not affected. I have been assured by a medical man that some years ago during each summer, but not during the winter, his hands became marked with light brown patches, like, although larger than freckles, and that these patches were never affected by sun-burning, while the white parts of his skin have on several occasions been much inflamed and blistered. With the lower animals there is, also, a constitutional difference in liability to the action of the sun between those parts of the skin clothed with white hair and other parts.[16] Whether the saving of the skin from being thus burned is of sufficient importance to account for a dark tint having been gradually acquired by man through natural selection I am unable to judge. If it be so, we should have to assume that the natives of tropical America have lived there for a much shorter time than the negroes in Africa, or the Papuans in the southern parts of the Malay Archipelago, just as the lighter-colored Hindoos have resided in India for a shorter time than the darker aborigines of the central and southern parts of the peninsula.

Although with our present knowledge we cannot account for the differences of color in the races of man, through any advantage thus gained, or from the direct action of climate; yet we must not quite ignore the latter agency, for there is good reason to believe that some inherited effect is thus produced.[17]

We have seen in the second chapter that the conditions of life affect the development of the bodily frame in a direct manner, and that the effects are transmitted. Thus, as is generally admitted, the European settlers in the United States undergo a slight but extraordinary rapid change of appearance. Their bodies and limbs become elongated; and I hear from Col. Bernys that during the late war in the United States, good evidence was afforded of this fact by the ridiculous appearance presented by the German regiments when dressed in ready-made clothes manufactured for the American market, and which were much too long for the men in every way. There is, also, a considerable body of evidence showing that in the Southern States the house slaves of the third generation present a markedly different appearance from the field slaves.[18]

If, however, we look to the races of man as distributed over the world we must infer that their characteristic differences cannot be accounted for by the direct action of different conditions of life, even after exposure to them for an enormous period of time. The Esquimaux live exclusively on animal food; they are clothed in thick fur, and are exposed to intense cold and to prolonged darkness; yet they do not differ in any extreme degree from the inhabitants of Southern China, who live entirely on vegetable food and are exposed almost naked to a hot, glaring climate. The unclothed Fuegians live on the marine productions of their inhospitable shores; the Botocudos of Brazil wander about the hot forests of the interior and live chiefly on vegetable productions; yet these tribes resemble each other so closely that the Fuegians on board the "Beagle" were mistaken by some Brazilians for Botocudos. The Botocudos again, as well as the other inhabitants of tropical America, are wholly different from the negroes who inhabit the opposite shores of the Atlantic, are exposed to a nearly similar climate and follow nearly the same habits of life.

Nor can the differences between the races of man be accounted for by the inherited effects of the increased or decreased use of parts except to a quite insignificant degree. Men who habitually live in canoes may have their legs somewhat stunted; those who inhabit lofty regions may have their chests enlarged; and those who constantly use certain sense organs may have the cavities in which they are lodged somewhat increased in size, and their features consequently a little modified. With civilized nations the reduced size of the jaws from lessened use—the habitual play of different muscles serving to express different emotions—and the increased size of the brain from greater intellectual activity have together produced a considerable effect on their general appearance when compared with savages.[19] Increased bodily stature, without any corresponding increase in the size of the brain, may (judging from the previously adduced case of rabbits), have given to some races an elongated skull of the dolichocephalic type.

Lastly, the little understood principle of correlated development has sometimes come into action, as in the case of great muscular development and strongly projecting supra-orbital ridges. The color of the skin and hair are plainly correlated, as is the texture of the hair with its color in the Mandans of North America.[20] The color also of the skin and the odor emitted by it are likewise in some manner connected. With the breeds of sheep the number of hairs within a given space and the number of the excretory pores are related.[21] If we may judge from the analogy of our domesticated animals, many modifications of structure in man probably come under this principle of correlated development.

We have now seen that the external characteristic differences between the races of man cannot be accounted for in a satisfactory manner by the direct action of the conditions of life, nor by the effects of the continued use of parts, nor through the principle of correlation. We are therefore led to inquire whether slight individual differences, to which man is eminently liable, may not have been preserved and augmented during a long series of generations through natural selection. But here we are at once met by the objection that beneficial variations alone can be thus preserved; and as far as we are enabled to judge, although always liable to err on this head, none of the differences between the races of man are of any direct or special service to him. The intellectual and moral or social faculties must of course be excepted from this remark. The great variability of all the external differences between the races of man, likewise indicates that they cannot be of much importance; for if important, they would long ago have been either fixed and preserved or eliminated. In this respect man resembles those forms, called by naturalists protean or polymorphic, which have remained extremely variable, owing, as it seems, to such variations being of an indifferent nature, and to their having thus escaped the action of natural selection.

We have thus far been baffled in all our attempts to account for the differences between the races of man; but there remains one important agency, namely Sexual Selection, which appears to have acted powerfully on man, as on many other animals. I do not intend to assert that sexual selection will account for all the differences between the races. An unexplained residuum is left, about which we can only say, in our ignorance, that as individuals are continually born with, for instance, heads a little rounder or narrower, and with noses a little longer or shorter, such slight differences might become fixed and uniform, if the unknown agencies which induced them were to act in a more constant manner, aided by long-continued intercrossing. Such variations come under the provisional class, alluded to in our second chapter, which for the want of a better term are often called spontaneous. Nor do I pretend that the effects of sexual selection can be indicated with scientific precision; but it can be shown that it would be an inexplicable fact if man had not been modified by this agency, which appears to have acted powerfully on innumerable animals. It can further be shown that the differences between the races of man, as in color, hairiness, form of features, etc., are of a kind which might have been expected to come under the influence of sexual selection. But in order to treat this subject properly, I have found it necessary to pass the whole animal kingdom in review.

Notes

1   "On Anthropology," translation "Anthropolog. Review," Jan., 1868, p.38.
2   "The Annals of Rural Bengal," 1868, p.134.
3   "The Variation of Animals and Plants under Domestication," vol. 2, p.95.
4   Pallas, "Act. Acad. St. Petersburg," 1780, part 2, p.69. He was followed by Rudolphi, in his "Beyträge zur Anthropologic," 1812. An excellent summary of the evidence is given by Godron, "De l'Espèce," 1859, vol. 2, p.246, etc.
5   Sir Andrew Smith, as quoted by Knox, "Races of Man," 1850, p.473.
6   See De Quatrefages on this head, "Revue des Cours Scientifiques," Oct. 17, 1868, p.731.
7   Livingstone's "Travels and Researches in S. Africa," 1857, pp.338, 339. D'Orbigny, as quoted by Godron, "De l'Espèce," vol. 2, p.266.
8   See a paper read before the Royal Soc. in 1813 and published in his Essays in 1818. I have given an account of Dr. Wells' views in the Historical Sketch (p.16) to my "Origin of Species." Various cases of color correlated with constitutional peculiarities are given in my "Variation of Animals under Domestication," vol. 2, pp.227, 335.
9   See, for instance, Nott and Gliddon, "Types of Mankind," p.68.
10   Maj. Tulloch, in a paper read before the Statistical Society, April [?], 1840, and given in the "Athenaeum," 1840, p.353.
11   "The Plurality of the Human Race" (translat.), 1864, p.60.
12   Quatrefages, "Unité de l'Espèce Humaine," 1861, p.205. Waitz, "Intro. to Anthropology," trans., vol. 1, 1863, p.124. Livingstone gives analogous cases in his "Travels."
13   In the spring of 1862 I obtained permission from the Director-General of the Medical Department of the Army to transmit to the surgeons of the various regiments on foreign service a blank table, with the following appended remarks, but I have received no returns: "As several well-marked cases have been recorded with our domestic animals of a relation between the color of the dermal appendages and the constitution; and it being notorious that there is some limited degree of relation between the color of the races of man and the climate inhabited by them; the following investigation seems worth consideration. Namely, whether there is any relation in Europeans between the color of their hair and their liability to the diseases of tropical countries. If the surgeons of the several regiments, when stationed in unhealthy tropical districts, would be so good as first to count, as a standard of comparison, how many men, in the force whence the sick are drawn, have dark and light-colored hair and hair of intermediate or doubtful tints; and if a similar account were kept by the same medical gentlemen of all the men who suffered from malarious and yellow fevers, or from dysentery, it would soon be apparent, after some thousand cases had been tabulated, whether there exists any relation between the color of the hair and constitutional liability to tropical diseases. Perhaps no such relation would be discovered, but the investigation is well worth making. In case any positive result were obtained it might be of some practical use in selecting men for any particular service. Theoretically the result would be of high interest, as indicating one means by which a race of men inhabiting from a remote period an unhealthy tropical climate, might have become dark-colored by the better preservation of dark-haired or dark-complexioned individuals during a long succession of generations."
14   "Anthropological Review," Jan., 1866, p.21. Dr. Sharpe also says, with respect to India ("Man a Special Creation," 1873, p.118), "that it has been noticed by some medical officers that Europeans

with light hair and florid complexions suffer less from diseases of tropical countries than persons with dark hair and sallow complexions; and, so far as I know, there appear to be good grounds for this remark." On the other hand, Mr. Heddle, of Sierra Leone. "who has had more clerks killed under him than any other man," by the climate of the West African Coast (W. Reade, "African Sketch Book," vol. 2, p.522), holds a directly opposite view, as does Capt. Burton.

15   "Man a Special Creation" 1873, p.119.

16   "Variation of Animals and Plants under Domestication," vol. 2, pp.336, 337.

17   See, for instance, Quatrefages ("Revue des Cours Scientifiques," Oct. 10, 1868, p. 724) on the effects of residence in Abyssinia and Arabia, and other analogous cases. Dr. Rolle ("Der Mensch, seine Abstammung," etc., 1865, s. 99) states, on the authority of Khanikof, that the greater number of German families settled in Georgia have acquired in the course of two generations dark hair and eyes. Mr. D. Forbes informs me that the Quichuas in the Andes vary greatly in color, according to the position of the valleys inhabited by them.

18   Harlan, "Medical Researches," p. 532. Quatrefages ("Unité de l'Espèce Humaine," 1861, p. 128) has collected much evidence on this head.

19   See Prof. Schaaffhausen, translat., in "Anthropological Review," Oct., 1868, p.429.

20   Mr. Catlin states ("North American Indians," 3d ed., 1842, vol. 1, p.49) that in the whole tribe of the Mandans, about one in ten or twelve of the members, of all ages and both sexes, have bright silvery gray hair, which is hereditary. Now this hair is as coarse and harsh as that of a horse's mane, while the hair of other colors is fine and soft.

21   On the odor of the skin, Godron, "Sur l'Espèce," tom 2, p.217. On the pores in the skin, Dr. Wilckens, "Die Aufgaben der Landwirth. Zootechnik," 1869, s. 7.

Chapter 40

Émile Zola (1840–1902)

"J'ACCUSE" (1898)

IN HIS OPEN LETTER TO the President of France, the novelist Émile Zola boldly accuses officers of the French War Office of falsely condemning Alfred Dreyfus, a Jewish military captain, of treason and imprisoning him in solitary confinement on Devil's Island (French Guiana) long after his innocence was known within the War Office. This hugely publicized case divided French public opinion and exposed the anti-Semitic and xenophobic tensions that would continue to escalate, reaching their apotheosis during World War II. The Dreyfus Affair, like the Spanish Civil War four decades later, was a galvanizing event for the intellectual left in Europe with writers such as Zola and Anatole France leading the charge against the military establishment, the conservative press, and the Catholic Church.

Émile Zola, "J'accuse," *The Dreyfus Affair: "J'accuse" and Other Writings,* ed. Alain Pagès; trans. Eleanor Levieux. New Haven and London: Yale UP, 1996.

Letter to M. Félix Faure, President of the Republic ('J'accuse')

Monsieur le Président,

Will you allow me, out of my gratitude for the gracious manner in which you once granted me an audience, to express my concern for your well-deserved glory? Will you allow me to tell you that although your star has been in the ascendant hitherto, it is now in danger of being dimmed by the most shameful and indelible of stains?

You have emerged unscathed from libellous slurs, you have won the people's hearts. You are the radiant centre of our apotheosis, for the Russian alliance has been indeed, for France, a patriotic celebration. And now you are about to preside over our World Fair. What a solemn triumph it will be, the crowning touch on our grand century of diligent labour, truth and liberty. But what a blot on your name (I was about to say, on your reign) this abominable Dreyfus Affair is! A court martial, acting on orders, has just dared to acquit such a man as Esterhazy. Truth itself and justice itself have been slapped in the face. And now it is too late, France's cheek has been sullied by that supreme insult, and History will record that it was during your Presidency that such a crime against society was committed.

They have dared to do this. Very well, then, I shall dare too. I shall tell the truth, for I pledged that I would tell it, if our judicial system, once the matter was brought before it through the normal channels, did not tell the truth, the whole truth. It is my duty to speak up; I will not be an accessory to the fact. If I were, my nights would be haunted by the spectre of that innocent man so far away, suffering the worst kind of torture as he pays for a crime he did not commit.

And it is to you, M. le Président, that I will shout out the truth with all the revulsion of a decent man. To your credit, I am convinced that you are unaware of the truth. And to whom should I denounce the evil machinations of those who are truly guilty if not to you, the First Magistrate in the land?

*   *   *

First of all, the truth about the trial and the verdict against Dreyfus.

One wicked man has led it all, done it all: Lt-Col du Paty de Clam. At the time he was only a Major. He *is* the entire Dreyfus Affair. Not until a fair inquiry has clearly established his actions and his responsibilities will we understand the Dreyfus Affair. He appears to have an unbelievably fuzzy and complicated mind, haunted by implausible plots and indulging in the methods that litter cheap novels – stolen papers, anonymous letters, rendez-vous in deserted places, mysterious women who flit about at night to peddle damaging proof. It was his idea to dictate the bordereau to Dreyfus; it was his idea to examine it in a room entirely lined with mirrors; it was du Paty de Clam, Major Forzinetti tells us, who went out with a dark lantern intending to slip into the cell where the accused man was sleeping and flash the light on his face all of a sudden so that he would be taken by surprise and blurt out a confession. And there is more to reveal, but it is not up to me to reveal it all; let them look, let them find what there is to be found. I shall simply say that Major du Paty de Clam, in charge of investigating the Dreyfus Affair, in his capacity as a criminal police officer, bears the greatest burden of guilt – in terms of chronological order and rank – in the appalling miscarriage of justice that has been committed.

For some time already, the bordereau had been in the possession of Colonel Sandherr, head of the Intelligence Bureau, who has since died of total paralysis. There were 'leaks', papers disappeared, just as papers continue to disappear today; and efforts were being made to find out who had written the bordereau when a conviction slowly grew up that that person could only be an officer from the General Staff, and an artillery officer at that. This was a glaring double error, which shows how superficially the bordereau had been examined, since a close and rational scrutiny of it proves that it could only have been written by an infantry officer.

Accordingly, they searched throughout the premises; they examined handwriting samples as if it were a family matter; a traitor was to be caught by surprise in the offices themselves and expelled from them. Now, the story is partly familiar to us and I do not wish to repeat it all over again; but this is where Major du Paty de Clam comes into it, as soon as the first suspicion falls on Dreyfus. From that moment on, it was du Paty de Clam who invented Dreyfus. The Affair became *his* affair. He was sure that he could confound the traitor and wring a complete confession from him. Of course, there is the War Minister, General Mercier, whose intelligence seems to be on a mediocre level; and of course, there is the Chief of the General Staff, General de Boisdeffre, who appears to have been swayed by his intense clericalism, and there is the Deputy Chief, General Gonse, whose conscience managed to make room for a good many things. But to begin with, there was really only Major du Paty de Clam. He led those men by the nose. He hypnotized them. Yes indeed, he also dabbles in spiritism and occultism; he converses with spirits. The experiments to which he subjected the unfortunate Dreyfus and the whole demented system of torture – the traps he attempted to make him fall into, the foolish investigations, the monstrous fabrications – are beyond belief.

Ah, for anyone who knows the true details of the first affair, what a nightmare it is! Major du Paty de Clam arrests Dreyfus and has him placed in solitary confinement. He rushes to the home of Madame Dreyfus and terrifies her, saying that if she speaks up, her husband is lost. Meanwhile the unfortunate man is tearing out his hair, clamouring his innocence. And that is how the investigation proceeded, as in some fifteenth-century chronicle, shrouded in mystery and a wealth of the wildest expedients, and all on the basis of a single, childish accusation, that idiotic bordereau, which was not only a very ordinary kind of treason but also the most impudent kind of swindle, since almost all of the so-called secrets that had supposedly been turned over to the enemy were of no value. I dwell on this point because this is the egg from which the real crime – the dreadful denial of justice which has laid France low – was later to hatch. I would like to make it perfectly clear how the miscarriage of justice came about, how it is the product of Major du Paty de Clam's machinations, how General Mercier and Generals de Boisdeffre and Gonse came to be taken in by it and gradually became responsible for this error and how it is that later they felt they had a duty to impose it as the sacred truth, a truth that will not admit of even the slightest discussion. At the beginning, all they contributed was negligence and lack of intelligence. The worst we can say is that they gave in to the religious passions of the circles they move in and the prejudices wrought by esprit de corps. They let stupidity have its way.

But now, here is Dreyfus summoned before the court martial. The most utter secrecy is demanded. They could not have imposed stricter silence and been more rigorous and mysterious if a traitor had actually opened our borders to the enemy and led the German Emperor straight to Notre Dame. The entire nation is flabbergasted. Terrible deeds are whispered about, monstrous betrayals that scandalize History itself, and of course the nation bows to these rumours. No punishment can be too severe; the nation will applaud the traitor's public humiliation; the nation is adamant: the guilty man shall remain on the remote rock where infamy has placed him and he shall be devoured by remorse. But then, those unspeakable accusations, those dangerous accusations that might inflame all of Europe and had to be so carefully concealed behind the closed doors of a secret session – are they true? No, they are not! There is nothing behind all that but the extravagant, demented flights of fancy of Major du Paty de Clam. It's all a smokescreen with just one purpose: to conceal a cheap novel of the most outlandish sort. And to be convinced of this, one need only examine the formal indictment that was read before the court martial.

How hollow that indictment is! Is it possible a man has been found guilty on the strength of it? Such iniquity is staggering. I challenge decent people to read it: their hearts will leap with indignation and rebellion when they think of the disproportionate price Dreyfus is paying so far away on Devil's Island. So Dreyfus speaks several languages, does he? This is a crime. Not one compromising paper was found in his home? A crime. He occasionally pays a visit to the region he hails from? A crime. He is a hard-working man, eager to know everything? A crime. He does not get flustered? A crime. He does get flustered? A crime. And how naively it is worded! How baseless its claims are! They told us he was indicted on fourteen different counts but in the end there is actually only one: that famous bordereau; and we even find out that the experts did not all agree, that one of them, M. Gobert, was subjected to some military pressure because he dared to come to a different conclusion from the one they wanted him to reach. We were also told that twenty-three officers had come and testified against Dreyfus. We still do not know how they were questioned, but what is certain is that not all of their testimony was negative. Besides, all of them, you will notice, came from the offices of the War Department. This trial is a family conclave; they all *belong*. We must not forget that. It is the General Staff who wanted this trial; it is they who judged Dreyfus; and they have just judged him for the second time.

So all that was left was the bordereau, on which the experts had not agreed. They say that in the council chambers, the judges were naturally leaning towards acquittal. And if that is the case then you can understand why, on the General Staff, they are so desperately insistent today on proclaiming, in order to justify the judgement, that there was a damning but secret document; they cannot reveal it but it makes everything legitimate and we must bow before it, as before an invisible and unknowable God! I deny the existence of any such document, I deny it with all my strength! Some ridiculous piece of paper, possibly; perhaps the one that talks about easy women and mentions a man named D . . . who is becoming too demanding; no doubt some husband or other who feels they're not paying him enough for the use of his wife. But a document that concerns the national defence, a document that would cause war to be declared immediately if ever it was produced? No! No! It's a lie! And what makes the whole business all the more odious and cynical is that they are lying with impunity and there is no way to convict them. They turn France inside out, they shelter behind the legitimate uproar they have caused, they seal mouths by making hearts quake and perverting minds. I know of no greater crime against society.

These, M. le Président, are the facts that explain how a miscarriage of justice has come to be committed. And the evidence as to Dreyfus's character, his financial situation, his lack of motives, the fact that he has never ceased to clamour his innocence – all these demonstrate that he has been a victim of Major du Paty de Clam's overheated imagination, and of the clericalism that prevails in the military circles in which he moves, and of the hysterical hunt for 'dirty Jews' that disgraces our times.

*   *   *

Now we come to the Esterhazy affair. Three years have passed. Many people's consciences are still profoundly uneasy; worried, they look further, and ultimately they become convinced that Dreyfus is innocent.

I will not retrace the story of M. Scheurer-Kestner's doubts and then of the certainty he came to feel. But while he was conducting his investigation, very serious events were taking place within the General Staff itself. Colonel Sandherr had died and Lt-Col Picquart had succeeded him at the head of the Intelligence Bureau. And it is in that capacity and in the exercise of his functions that Picquart one day held in his hands a special delivery letter addressed to Major Esterhazy by an agent of a foreign power. It was Picquart's strictest duty to launch an investigation. It is clear that he never acted otherwise than with the consent of his superior officers. So he outlined his suspicions to his hierarchical superiors – General Gonse, then General de Boisdeffre, then General Billot, who had succeeded General Mercier as Minister of War. The famous Picquart file that has been talked about so much was never anything more nor less than the Billot file, by which I mean the file that a subaltern prepared for his Minister, the file that they must still have in the War Ministry. The inquiry lasted from May to September 1896, and two things must be stated in no uncertain terms: General Gonse was convinced that Esterhazy was guilty, and neither General de Boisdeffre nor General Billot questioned the fact that the bordereau was in Esterhazy's handwriting. Lt-Col Picquart's investigation had led to that indubitable conclusion. But feeling ran very high, for if Esterhazy was found guilty, then inevitably the Dreyfus verdict would have to be revised, and that was what the General Staff was determined to avoid at all costs.

At that point there must have been an instant of the most intense psychological anguish. Note that General Billot was not compromised in any way; he had just come on stage; it was within his power to reveal the truth. But he dared not do it – terrified of public opinion, no doubt, and certainly afraid as well of handing over the entire General Staff, including General de Boisdeffre and General Gonse, not to mention the subalterns. Then there was but one minute of struggle between his conscience and what he thought was in the best interests of the army. Once that minute was over, it was already too late. He had made his choice; he was compromised. And ever since then his share of responsibility has grown and grown; he has taken the others' crime upon himself; he is as guilty as the others; he is guiltier than the others, for he had the power to see that justice was done and he did nothing. Understand that if you can! For a year now, General Billot, General de Boisdeffre and General Gonse have known that Dreyfus is innocent, and they have kept this appalling knowledge to themselves! And people like that sleep soundly! And they have wives and children, and love them dearly!

Lt-Col Picquart had done his duty as a decent man. In the name of justice, he insisted to his superior officers. He even begged them; he told them how impolitic their dithering was, what a terrible storm was building up, how it was going to burst once the truth became known. Later on, M. Scheurer-Kestner used the same words to General Billot; out of patriotism, he implored him to get a grip on the Affair instead of letting it go from bad to worse until it became a public disaster. But no, the crime had been committed and the General Staff could no longer confess to it. And Lt-Col Picquart was sent away on mission; they sent him farther and farther away, all the way to Tunisia where one day they even tried to do his bravery the honour of assigning him to a mission that would assuredly have got him slaughtered, in the same region where the Marquis de Morès had been killed. Mind you, Picquart was not in disgrace; General Gonse had a friendly exchange of letters with him. Only, there are some secrets it is not wise to have discovered.

In Paris, the all-conquering truth was on the march, and we know how the predictable storm eventually burst. M. Mathieu Dreyfus denounced Major Esterhazy as the real author of the bordereau just as M. Scheurer-Kestner was about to place in the hands of the Minister of Justice a request for a revision of the Dreyfus trial. And this is where Major Esterhazy appears. Witnesses state that at first he panicked; he was on the verge of suicide or about to flee. Then suddenly he became boldness itself and grew so violent that all Paris was astonished. The reason is that help had suddenly materialized in the form of an anonymous letter warning him of his enemies' doings; a mysterious lady had even gone to the trouble one night of bringing him a document that had been stolen from the General Staff and was supposed to save him. And I cannot help suspecting Lt-Col du Paty de Clam, for I recognize the type of expedients in which his fertile imagination delights. His achievement – the decision that Dreyfus was guilty – was in danger, and no doubt he wished to defend his achievement. A revision of the verdict? Why, that would put an end to the far-fetched, tragic work of cheap fiction whose abominable last chapter is being written on Devil's Island! He could not allow that to happen, Henceforth, a duel was bound to take place between Lt-Col Picquart and Lt-Col du Paty de Clam. The one shows his face for all to see; the other is masked. Soon we will see them both in the civil courts. Behind it all is the General Staff, still defending itself, refusing to admit to its crime, which becomes more of an abomination with every passing hour.

In a daze, people wondered who Major Esterhazy's protectors could be. Behind the scenes there was Lt-Col du Paty de Clam, first of all; he cobbled it all together, led the whole thing. The means used were so preposterous that they give him away. Then, there are General de Boisdeffre and General Gonse and General Billot himself, who are obliged to get Esterhazy acquitted since they dare not let Dreyfus's innocence be acknowledged lest the War Office collapse as the public heaps scorn on it. It's a prodigious situation and the impressive result is that Lt-Col Picquart, the one decent man involved, the only one who has done his duty, is going to be the victim, the person they will ride rough-shod over and punish. Ah justice! what dreadful despair grips my heart! They are even claiming that Picquart is the forger, that he forged the letter-telegram purposely to cause Esterhazy's downfall. But in heaven's name, why? To what end? State one motive. Is he too paid by the Jews? The funniest thing about the whole story is that in fact he was anti-Semitic. Yes, we are witnessing an infamous sight: men heavily in debt and guilty of evil deeds but whose innocence is being proclaimed while the very honour of a man whose record is spotless is being dragged in the mud! When a society comes to that, it begins to rot away.

This, M. le Président, is the Esterhazy affair: a guilty man who had to be proved innocent. For almost two months now, we have been following every single episode of this pitiful business. I am simplifying, for by and large this is only a summary of the story, but one day every one of its turbulent pages will be written in full. So it is that we saw General de Pellieux, first of all, then Major Ravary, conduct a villainous investigation from which the scoundrels emerged transfigured while decent people were besmirched. Then, the court martial was convened.

* * *

Did anyone really hope that one court martial would undo what another court martial had done in the first place?

I am not even talking about the judges, who could have been chosen differently. Since these soldiers have a lofty idea of discipline in their blood, isn't that enough to disqualify them from arriving at an equitable judgement? Discipline means obedience. Once the Minister of War, the supreme commander, has publicly established the authority of the original verdict, and has done so to the acclamations of the nation's representatives, how can you expect a court martial to override his judgement officially? In hierarchical terms, that is impossible. General Billot, in his statement, planted certain ideas in the judges' minds, and they proceeded to judge the case in the same way as they would proceed to go into battle, that is, without stopping to think. The preconceived idea that they brought with them to the judges' bench was of course as follows: 'Dreyfus was sentenced for treason by a court martial, therefore he is guilty; and we, as a court martial, cannot find him innocent. Now, we know that if we recognize Esterhazy's guilt we will be proclaiming Dreyfus's innocence.' And nothing could make them budge from that line.

They reached an iniquitous verdict which will forever weigh heavy on all our future courts martial and forever make their future decisions suspect. There may be room for doubt as to whether the first court martial was intelligent but there is no doubt that the second has been criminal. Its excuse, I repeat, is that the commander in chief had spoken and declared the previous verdict unattackable, holy and superior to mere mortals – and how could his subordinates dare to contradict him? They talk to us about the honour of the army; they want us to love the army, respect the army. Oh yes, indeed, if you mean an army that would rise up at the very first hint of danger, that would defend French soil; that army is the French people themselves, and we have nothing but affection and respect for it. But the army that is involved here is not the dignified army that our need for justice calls out for. What we are faced with here is the sabre, the master that may be imposed on us tomorrow. Should we kiss the hilt of that sabre, that god, with pious devotion? No, we should not!

As I have already shown, the Dreyfus Affair was the affair of the War Office: an officer from the General Staff denounced by his fellow officers on the General Staff, sentenced under pressure from the Chiefs of the General Staff. And I repeat, he cannot emerge from his trial innocent without all of the General Staff being guilty. Which is why the War Office employed every means imaginable – campaigns in the press, statements and innuendoes, every type of influence – to cover Esterhazy, in order to convict Dreyfus a second time. The republican government should take a broom to that nest of Jesuits (General Billot calls them that himself) and make a clean sweep! Where, oh where is a strong and wisely patriotic ministry that will be bold enough to overhaul the whole system and make a fresh start? I know many people who tremble with alarm at the thought of a possible war, knowing what hands our national defence is in! and what a den of sneaking intrigue, rumour-mongering and back-biting that sacred chapel has become – yet that is where the fate of our country is decided! People take fright at the appalling light that has just been shed on it all by the Dreyfus Affair, that tale of human sacrifice! Yes, an unfortunate, a 'dirty Jew' has been sacrificed. Yes, what an accumulation of madness, stupidity, unbridled imagination, low police tactics, inquisitorial and tyrannical methods this handful of officers have got away with! They have crushed the nation under their boots, stuffing its calls for truth and justice down its throat on fallacious and sacrilegious pretext that they are acting for the good of the country!

And they have committed other crimes. They have based their action on the foul press and let themselves be defended by all the rogues in Paris – and now the rogues are triumphant and insolent while law and integrity go down in defeat. It is a crime to have accused individuals of rending France apart when all those individuals ask for is a generous nation at the head of the procession of free, just nations – and all the while the people who committed that crime were hatching an insolent plot to make the entire world swallow a fabrication. It is a crime to lead public opinion astray, to manipulate it for a death-dealing purpose and pervert it to the point of delirium. It is a crime to poison the minds of the humble, ordinary people, to whip reactionary and intolerant passions into a frenzy while sheltering behind the odious bastion of anti-Semitism. France, the great and liberal cradle of the rights of man, will die of anti-Semitism if it is not cured of it. It is a crime to play on patriotism to further the aims of hatred. And it is a crime to worship the sabre as a modern god when all of human science is labouring to hasten the triumph of truth and justice.

Truth and justice – how ardently we have striven for them! And how distressing it is to see them slapped in the face, overlooked, forced to retreat! I can easily imagine the harrowing dismay that must be filling M. Scheurer-Kestner's soul, and one day, no doubt, he will wish that when he was questioned before the Senate he had taken the revolutionary step of revealing everything he knew, ripping away all pretence. He was your true good man, a man who could look back on an honest life. He assumed that truth alone would be enough – could not help but be enough, since it was plain as day to him. What was the point of upsetting everything, since the sun would soon be shining? He was serene and confident, and how cruelly he is being punished for that now! The same is true of Lt-Col Picquart: out of a lofty sense of dignity, he refrained from publishing General Gonse's letters. His scruples do him honour, particularly since while he was being respectful of discipline, his superior officers were busy slinging mud at him, conducting the investigation prior to his trial themselves, in the most outrageous and unbelievable way. There are two victims, two decent, stout-hearted men, who stood back to let God have His way – and all the while the devil was doing his work. And where Lt-Col Picquart is concerned, we have even seen this ignoble thing: a French court first allowed the rapporteur to bring charges against a witness publicly, accuse him publicly of every wrong in the book, and then, when that witness was called to give an account of himself and speak in his own defence, that same court held its session behind closed doors. I say that that is still another crime, and I say that it will arouse the conscience of all mankind. Our military tribunals certainly do have a peculiar idea of justice.

That, M. le Président, is the plain truth. It is appalling. It will remain an indelible blot on your term as President. Oh, I know that you are powerless to deal with it, that you are the prisoner of the Constitution and of the people nearest to you. But as a man, your duty is clear, and you will not overlook it, and you will do your duty. Not for one minute do I despair that truth will triumph. I am confident and I repeat, more vehemently even than before, the truth is on the march and nothing shall stop it. The Affair is only just beginning, because only now have the positions become crystal clear: on the one hand, the guilty parties, who do not want the truth to be revealed; on the other, the defenders of justice, who will give their lives to see that justice is done. I have said it elsewhere and I repeat it here: if the truth is buried underground, it swells and grows and becomes so explosive that the day it bursts, it blows everything wide open along with it. Time will tell; we shall see whether we have not prepared, for some later date, the most resounding disaster.

*   *   *

But this letter has been a long one, M. le Président, and it is time to bring it to a close.

I accuse Lt-Col du Paty de Clam of having been the diabolical agent of a miscarriage of justice (though unwittingly, I am willing to believe) and then of having defended his evil deed for the past three years through the most preposterous and most blameworthy machinations.

I accuse General Mercier of having been an accomplice, at least by weak-mindedness, to one of the most iniquitous acts of this century.

I accuse General Billot of having had in his hands undeniable proof that Dreyfus was innocent and of having suppressed it, of having committed this crime against justice and against humanity for political purposes, so that the General Staff, which had been compromised, would not lose face.

I accuse Generals de Boisdeffre and Gonse of having been accomplices to this same crime, one out of intense clerical conviction, no doubt, and the other perhaps because of the esprit de corps which makes the War Office the Holy of Holies and hence unattackable.

I accuse General de Pellieux and Major Ravary of having led a villainous inquiry, by which I mean a most monstrously one-sided inquiry, the report on which, by Ravary, constitutes an imperishable monument of naive audacity.

I accuse the three handwriting experts, Messrs Belhomme, Varinard and Couard, of having submitted fraudulent and deceitful reports – unless a medical examination concludes that their eyesight and their judgement were impaired.

I accuse the War Office of having conducted an abominable campaign in the press (especially in *L'Eclair* and *L'Echo de Paris*) in order to cover up its misdeeds and lead public opinion astray.

Finally, I accuse the first court martial of having violated the law by sentencing a defendant on the basis of a document which remained secret, and I accuse the second court martial of having covered up that illegal action, on orders, by having, in its own turn, committed the judicial crime of knowingly acquitting a guilty man.

In making these accusations, I am fully aware that my action comes under Articles 30 and 31 of the law of 29 July 1881 on the press, which makes libel a punishable offence. I deliberately expose myself to that law.

As for the persons I have accused, I do not know them; I have never seen them; I feel no rancour or hatred towards them. To me, they are mere entities, mere embodiments of social malfeasance. And the action I am taking here is merely a revolutionary means to hasten the revelation of truth and justice.

I have but one goal: that light be shed, in the name of mankind which has suffered so much and has the right to happiness. My ardent protest is merely a cry from my very soul. Let them dare to summon me before a court of law! Let the inquiry be held in broad daylight!

I am waiting.

M. le Président, I beg you to accept the assurance of my most profound respect.

L'Aurore, 13 January 1898

Chapter 41

Marita Bonner (1899–1971)

"ON BEING YOUNG – A WOMAN – AND COLORED" (1925)

MARITA ODETTE BONNER was one of the female writers in the Harlem Renaissance circle, along with Jesse Fauset, Zora Neale Hurston, and Nella Larsen. Bonner began her literary apprenticeship writing for *The Sagamore*, the newspaper at Brookline High School in Massachusetts; she then attended Harvard University's Radcliffe College, graduating in 1922. The educator, poet, playwright, and essayist published her work in *Opportunity*, the journal of the National Urban League, which was founded in 1923, and in *The Crisis Magazine*, the official publication of the NAACP founded by W.E.B. Du Bois fifteen years earlier. The African American independent journals provided a venue for a range of aspiring race-conscious and cosmopolitan writers. Bonner's first professional publication was "On Being Young – a Woman – and Colored." A member of the African American educated class that DuBois referred to as "the talented tenth," Bonner addresses the realities of racism; but as an artist and activist, she chose the immense calm of a Buddha, a calm that is not passivity but a storing of wisdom and experience before action. The essay is both an indictment of a discriminatory society and a statement of belief in the individual's ability to transcend racism and sexism and attain a "true discrimination" between souls.

Marita Bonner, "On Being Young – a Woman – and Colored." *The Crisis Magazine* 131 (December 1925): 63 –5. In *Frye Street and Environs: The Collected Works of Marita Bonner*, ed. Joyce Flynn and Joyce Occomy Stricklin. Boston: Beacon, 1987. 3–8.

You start out after you have gone from kindergarten to sheepskin covered with sundry Latin phrases.

At least you know what you want life to give you. A career as fixed and as calmly brilliant as the North Star. The one real thing that money buys. Time. Time to do things. A house that can be as delectably out of order and as easily put in order as the doll-house of "playing-house" days. And of course, a husband you can look up to without looking down on yourself.

Somehow you feel like a kitten in a sunny catnip field that sees sleek, plump brown field mice and yellow baby chicks sitting coyly, side by side, under each leaf. A desire to dash three or four ways seizes you.

That's Youth.

But you know that things learned need testing—acid testing—to see if they are really after all, an interwoven part of you. All your life you have heard of the debt you owe "Your People" because you have managed to have the things they have not largely had.

So you find a spot where there are hordes of them—of course below the Line—to be your catnip field while you close your eyes to mice and chickens alike.

If you have never lived among your own, you feel prodigal. Some warm untouched current flows through them—through you—and drags you out into the deep waters of a new sea of human foibles and mannerisms; of a peculiar psychology and prejudices. And one day you find yourself entangled—enmeshed—pinioned in the seaweed of a Black Ghetto.

Not a Ghetto, placid like the Strasse that flows, outwardly unperturbed and calm in a stream of religious belief, but a peculiar group. Cut off, flung together, shoved aside in a bundle because of color and with no more in common.

Unless color is, after all, the real bond.

Milling around like live fish in a basket. Those at the bottom crushed into a sort of stupid apathy by the weight of those on top. Those on top leaping, leaping; leaping to scale the sides; to get out.

There are two "colored" movies, innumerable parties—and cards. Cards played so intensely that it fascinates and repulses at once.

Movies.

Movies worthy and worthless—but not even a low-caste spoken stage.

Parties, plentiful. Music and dancing and much that is wit and color and gaiety. But they are like the richest chocolate; stuffed costly chocolates that make the taste go stale if you have too many of them. That make plain whole bread taste like ashes.

There are all the earmarks of a group within a group. Cut off all around from ingress from or egress to other groups. A sameness of type. The smug self-satisfaction of an inner measurement; a measurement by standards known within a limited group and not those of an unlimited, seeing, world. . . . Like the blind, blind mice. Mice whose eyes have been blinded.

Strange longing seizes hold of you, You wish yourself back where you can lay your dollar down and sit in a dollar seat to hear voices, strings, reeds that have lifted the World out, up, beyond things that have bodies and walls. Where you can marvel at new marbles and bronzes and flat colors that will make men forget that things exist in a flesh more often than in spirit. Where you can sink your body in a cushioned seat and sink your soul at the same time into a section of life set before you on the boards for a few hours.

You hear that up at New York this is to be seen; that, to be heard.

You decide the next train will take you there.

You decide the next second that that train will not take you, nor the next—nor the next for some time to come.

For you know that—being a woman—you cannot twice a month or twice a year, for that matter, break away to see or hear anything in a city that is supposed to see and hear too much.

That's being a woman. A woman of any color.

You decide that something is wrong with a world that stifles and chokes; that cuts off and stunts; hedging in, pressing down on eyes, ears and throat. Somehow all wrong.

You wonder how it happens there that—say five hundred miles from the Bay State—Anglo Saxon intelligence is so warped and stunted.

How judgment and discernment are bred out of the race. And what has become of discrimination? Discrimination of the right sort. Discrimination that the best minds have told you weighs shadows and nuances and spiritual differences before it catalogues. The kind they have taught you all of your life was best: that looks clearly past generalization and past appearance to dissect, to dig down to the real heart of matters. That casts aside rapid summary conclusions, drawn from primary inference, as Daniel did the spiced meats.

Why can't they then perceive that there is a difference in the glance from a pair of eyes that look, mildly docile, at "white ladies" and those that, impersonally and perceptively—aware of distinctions—see only women who happen to be white?

Why do they see a colored woman only as a gross collection of desires, all uncontrolled, reaching out for their Apollos and the Quasimodos with avid indiscrimination?

Why unless you talk in staccato squawks—brittle as sea-shells—unless you "champ" gum—unless you cover two yards square when you laugh—unless your taste runs to violent colors—impossible perfumes and more impossible clothes—are you a feminine Caliban craving to pass for Ariel?

An empty imitation of an empty invitation. A mime; a sham; a copy-cat. A hollow re-echo. A froth, a foam. A fleck of the ashes of superficiality?

Everything you touch or taste now is like the flesh of an unripe persimmon.

. . . Do you need to be told what that is being . . .?

Old ideas, old fundamentals seem worm-eaten, out-grown, worthless, bitter; fit for the scrap-heap of Wisdom.

What you had thought tangible and practical has turned out to be a collection of "blue-flower" theories.

If they have not discovered how to use their accumulation of facts, they are useless to you in Their world.

Every part of you becomes bitter.

But—"In Heaven's name, do not grow bitter. Be bigger than they are"—exhort white friends who have never had to draw breath in a Jim-Crow train. Who have never had petty putrid insult dragged over them—drawing blood—like pebbled sand on your body where the skin is tenderest. On your body where the skin is thinnest and tenderest.

You long to explode and hurt everything white; friendly; unfriendly. But you know that you cannot live with a chip on your shoulder even if you can manage a smile around your eyes—without getting steely and brittle and losing the softness that makes you a woman.

For chips make you bend your body to balance them. And once you bend, you lose your poise, your balance, and the chip gets into you. The real you. You get hard.

. . . And many things in you can ossify . . .

And you know, being a woman, you have to go about it gently and quietly, to find out and to discover just what is wrong. Just what can be done.

You see clearly that they have acquired things.

Money; money. Money to build with, money to destroy. Money to swim in. Money to drown in. Money.

An ascendancy of wisdom. An incalculable hoard of wisdom in all fields, in all things collected from all quarters of humanity.

A stupendous mass of things.

Things.

So, too, the Greeks . . . Things.

And the Romans . . . .

And you wonder and wonder why they have not discovered how to handle deftly and skillfully, Wisdom, stored up for them—like the honey for the Gods on Olympus—since time unknown.

You wonder and you wonder until you wander out into Infinity, where—if it is to be found anywhere—Truth really exists.

The Greeks had possessions, culture. They were lost because they did not understand.

The Romans owned more than anyone else. Trampled under the heel of Vandals and Civilization, because they would not understand.

Greeks. Did not understand.

Romans. Would not understand.

"They." Will not understand.

So you find they have shut Wisdom up and have forgotten to find the key that will let her out. They have trapped, trammeled, lashed her to themselves with thews and thongs and theories. They have ransacked sea and earth and air to bring every treasure to her. But she sulks and will not work for a world with a whitish hue because it has snubbed her twin sister, Understanding.

You see clearly—off there in Infinity—Understanding. Standing alone, waiting for someone to really want her.

But she is so far out there is no way to snatch at her and really drag her in.

So—being a woman—you can wait.

You must sit quietly without a chip. Not sodden—and weighted as if your feet were cast in the iron of your soul. Not wasting strength in enervating gestures as if two hundred years of bonds and whips had really tricked you into nervous uncertainty.

But quiet; quiet. Like Buddha—who brown like I am—sat entirely at ease, entirely sure of himself; motionless and knowing, a thousand years before the white man knew there was so very much difference between feet and hands.

Motionless on the outside. But on the inside?

Silent.

Still . . . "Perhaps Buddha is a woman."

So you too. Still; quiet; with a smile, ever so slight, at the eyes so that Life will flow into and not by you. And you can gather, as it passes, the essences, the overtones, the tints, the shadows; draw understanding to yourself.

And then you can, when Time is ripe, swoop to your feet—at your full height—at a single gesture.

Ready to go where?

Why . . . Wherever God motions.

Chapter 42

Alain Locke (1886–1954)

"INTRODUCTION," *THE NEW NEGRO* (1925)

H OWARD UNIVERSITY PROFESSOR OF PHILOSOPHY Alaine Locke intro- duces his ground-breaking anthology of African American writing by situating it in the context of the the "Great Migration," the mass exodus of African Americans from the American South fleeing discrimination, violence, and economic depression to northern cities such as New York, Boston, Philadelphia, Detroit, and Chicago. According to Locke this migration led to the development of the "New Negro," who was urban rather than rural, northern rather than southern, and an active participant in cultural life rather than the subject of white hostility or paternalism. The epicenter of this change was Harlem, where many of the writers collected in *The New Negro* lived and worked. Locke compares Harlem to Dublin and Prague, where other artistic movements emerged outside the estab- lished literary metropolises of Manhattan, London, and Paris. Locke's anthology includes essays, fiction, poetry, plays, and music by such prominent Harlem Renaissance writers as Claude McKay, Countee Cullen, and Langston Hughes. This anthology provided many readers their first contact with these writers and their works, and so, like Nancy Cunard's later anthology *Negro* (1934), it served both to catalyze and to canonize a literary movement.

Alain Locke, "Introduction," *The New Negro*. New York: Atheneum, 1970. 3–16.

Introduction

In the last decade something beyond the watch and guard of statistics has happened in the life of the American Negro and the three norns who have traditionally presided over the Negro problem have a changeling in their laps. The Sociologist, the Philanthropist, the Race-leader are not unaware of the New Negro, but they are at a loss to account for him. He simply cannot be swathed in their formulæ. For the younger generation is vibrant with a new psychology; the new spirit is awake in the masses, and under the very eyes of the professional observers is transforming what has been a perennial problem into the progressive phases of contemporary Negro life.

Could such a metamorphosis have taken place as suddenly as it has appeared to? The answer is no; not because the New Negro is not here, but because the Old Negro had long become more of a myth than a man. The Old Negro, we must remember, was a creature of moral debate and historical controversy. His has been a stock figure perpetuated as an historical fiction partly in innocent sentimentalism, partly in deliberate reactionism. The Negro himself has contributed his share to this through a sort of protective social mimicry forced upon him by the adverse circumstances of dependence. So for generations in the mind of America, the Negro has been more of a formula than a human being—a something to be argued about, condemned or defended, to be "kept down," or "in his place," or "helped up," to be worried with or worried over, harassed or patronized, a social bogey or a social burden. The thinking Negro even has been induced to share this same general attitude, to focus his attention on controversial issues, to see himself in the distorted perspective of a social problem. His shadow, so to speak, has been more real to him than his personality. Through having had to appeal from the unjust stereotypes of his oppressors and traducers to those of his liberators, friends and benefactors he has had to subscribe to the traditional positions from which his case has been viewed. Little true social or self-understanding has or could come from such a situation.

But while the minds of most of us, black and white, have thus burrowed in the trenches of the Civil War and Reconstruction, the actual march of development has simply flanked these positions, necessitating a sudden reorientation of view. We have not been watching in the right direction; set North and South on a sectional axis, we have not noticed the East till the sun has us blinking.

Recall how suddenly the Negro spirituals revealed themselves; suppressed for generations under the stereotypes of Wesleyan hymn harmony, secretive, half-ashamed, until the courage of being natural brought them out—and behold, there was folk-music. Similarly the mind of the Negro seems suddenly to have slipped from under the tyranny of social intimidation and to be shaking off the psychology of imitation and implied inferiority. By shedding the old chrysalis of the Negro problem we are achieving something like a spiritual emancipation. Until recently, lacking self-understanding, we have been almost as much of a problem to ourselves as we still are to others. But the decade that found us with a problem has left us with only a task. The multitude perhaps feels as yet only a strange relief and a new vague urge, but the thinking few know that in the reaction the vital inner grip of prejudice has been broken.

With this renewed self-respect and self-dependence, the life of the Negro community is bound to enter a new dynamic phase, the buoyancy from within compensating for whatever pressure there may be of conditions from without. The migrant masses, shifting from countryside to city, hurdle several generations of experience at a leap, but more important, the same thing happens spiritually in the life-attitudes and self-expression of the Young Negro, in his poetry, his art, his education and his new outlook, with the additional advantage, of course, of the poise and greater certainty of knowing what it is all about. From this comes the promise and warrant of a new leadership. As one of them has discerningly put it:

> We have tomorrow
> Bright before us
> Like a flame.
>
> Yesterday, a night-gone thing
> A sun-down name.
>
> And dawn today
> Broad arch above the road we came.
> We march!

This is what, even more than any "most creditable record of fifty years of freedom," requires that the Negro of to-day be seen through other than the dusty spectacles of past controversy. The day of "aunties," "uncles" and "mammies" is equally gone. Uncle Tom and Sambo have passed on, and even the "Colonel" and "George" play barnstorm rôles from which they escape with relief when the public spotlight is off. The popular melodrama has about played itself out, and it is time to scrap the fictions, garret the bogeys and settle down to a realistic facing of facts.

First we must observe some of the changes which since the traditional lines of opinion were drawn have rendered these quite obsolete. A main change has been, of course, that shifting of the Negro population which has made the Negro problem no longer exclusively or even predominantly Southern. Why should our minds remain sectionalized, when the problem itself no longer is? Then the trend of migration has not only been toward the North and the Central Midwest, but city-ward and to the great centers of industry—the problems of adjustment are new, practical, local and not peculiarly racial. Rather they are an integral part of the large industrial and social problems of our present-day democracy. And finally, with the Negro rapidly in process of class differentiation, if it ever was warrantable to regard and treat the Negro *en masse* it is becoming with every day less possible, more unjust and more ridiculous.

In the very process of being transplanted, the Negro is becoming transformed.

The tide of Negro migration, northward and city-ward, is not to be fully explained as a blind flood started by the demands of war industry coupled with the shutting off of foreign migration, or by the pressure of poor crops coupled with increased social terrorism in certain sections of the South and Southwest. Neither labor demand, the boll-weevil nor the Ku Klux Klan is a basic factor, however contributory any or all of them may have been. The wash and rush of this human tide on the beach line of the northern city centers is to be explained primarily in terms of a new vision of opportunity, of social and economic freedom, of a spirit to seize, even in the face of an extortionate and heavy toll, a chance for the improvement of conditions. With each successive wave of it, the movement of the Negro becomes more and more a mass movement toward the larger and the more democratic chance—in the Negro's case a deliberate flight not only from countryside to city, but from medieval America to modern.

Take Harlem as an instance of this. Here in Manhattan is not merely the largest Negro community in the world, but the first concentration in history of so many diverse elements of Negro life. It has attracted the African, the West Indian, the Negro American; has brought together the Negro of the North and the Negro of the South; the man from the city and the man from the town and village; the peasant, the student, the business man, the professional man, artist, poet, musician, adventurer and worker, preacher and criminal, exploiter and social outcast. Each group has come with its own separate motives and for its own special ends, but their greatest experience has been the finding of one another. Proscription and prejudice have thrown these dissimilar elements into a common area of contact and interaction. Within this area, race sympathy and unity have determined a further fusing of sentiment and experience. So what began in terms of segregation becomes more and more, as its elements mix and react, the laboratory of a great race-welding. Hitherto, it must be admitted that American Negroes have been a race more in name than in fact, or to be exact, more in sentiment than in experience. The chief bond between them has been that of a common condition rather than a common consciousness; a problem in common rather than a life in common. In Harlem, Negro life is seizing upon its first chances for group expression and self-determination. It is—or promises at least to be—a race capital. That is why our comparison is taken with those nascent centers of folk-expression and self-determination which are playing a creative part in the world to-day. Without pretense to their political significance,

Harlem has the same rôle to play for the New Negro as Dublin has had for the New Ireland or Prague for the New Czechoslovakia.

Harlem, I grant you, isn't typical—but it is significant, it is prophetic. No sane observer, however sympathetic to the new trend, would contend that the great masses are articulate as yet, but they stir, they move, they are more than physically restless. The challenge of the new intellectuals among them is clear enough—the "race radicals" and realists who have broken with the old epoch of philanthropic guidance, sentimental appeal and protest. But are we after all only reading into the stirrings of a sleeping giant the dreams of an agitator? The answer is in the migrating peasant. It is the "man farthest down" who is most active in getting up. One of the most characteristic symptoms of this is the professional man, himself migrating to recapture his constituency after a vain effort to maintain in some Southern corner what for years back seemed an established living and clientele. The clergyman following his errant flock, the physician or lawyer trailing his clients, supply the true clues. In a real sense it is the rank and file who are leading, and the leaders who are following. A transformed and transforming psychology permeates the masses.

When the racial leaders of twenty years ago spoke of developing race-pride and stimulating race-consciousness, and of the desirability of race solidarity, they could not in any accurate degree have anticipated the abrupt feeling that has surged up and now pervades the awakened centers. Some of the recognized Negro leaders and a powerful section of white opinion identified with "race work" of the older order have indeed attempted to discount this feeling as a "passing phase," an attack of "race nerves" so to speak, an "aftermath of the war," and the like. It has not abated, however, if we are to gauge by the present tone and temper of the Negro press, or by the shift in popular support from the officially recognized and orthodox spokesmen to those of the independent, popular, and often radical type who are unmistakable symptoms of a new order. It is a social disservice to blunt the fact that the Negro of the Northern centers has reached a stage where tutelage, even of the most interested and well-intentioned sort, must give place to new relationships, where positive self-direction must be reckoned with in ever increasing measure. The American mind must reckon with a fundamentally changed Negro.

The Negro too, for his part, has idols of the tribe to smash. If on the one hand the white man has erred in making the Negro appear to be that which would excuse or extenuate his treatment of him, the Negro, in turn, has too often unnecessarily excused himself because of the way he has been treated. The intelligent Negro of to-day is resolved not to make discrimination an extenuation for his shortcomings in performance, individual or collective; he is trying to hold himself at par, neither inflated by sentimental allowances nor depreciated by current social discounts. For this he must know himself and be known for precisely what he is, and for that reason he welcomes the new scientific rather than the old sentimental interest. Sentimental interest in the Negro has ebbed. We used to lament this as the falling off of our friends; now we rejoice and pray to be delivered both from self-pity and condescension. The mind of each racial group has had a bitter weaning, apathy or hatred on one side matching disillusionment or resentment on the other; but they face each other to-day with the possibility at least of entirely new mutual attitudes.

It does not follow that if the Negro were better known, he would be better liked or better treated. But mutual understanding is basic for any subsequent coöperation and adjustment. The effort toward this will at least have the effect of remedying in large part what has been the most unsatisfactory feature of our present stage of race relationships in America, namely the fact that the more intelligent and representative elements of the two race groups have at so many points got quite out of vital touch with one another.

The fiction is that the life of the races is separate, and increasingly so. The fact is that they have touched too closely at the unfavorable and too lightly at the favorable levels.

While inter-racial councils have sprung up in the South, drawing on forward elements of both races, in the Northern cities manual laborers may brush elbows in their everyday work, but the community and business leaders have experienced no such interplay or far too little of it. These segments must achieve contact or the race situation in America becomes desperate. Fortunately this is happening. There is a growing realization that in social effort the co-operative basis must supplant long-distance philanthropy, and that the only safeguard for mass relations in the future must be provided in the carefully maintained contacts of the enlightened minorities of both race groups. In the intellectual realm a renewed and keen curiosity is replacing the recent apathy; the Negro is being carefully studied, not just talked about and discussed. In art and letters, instead of being wholly caricatured, he is being seriously portrayed and painted.

To all of this the New Negro is keenly responsive as an augury of a new democracy in American culture. He is contributing his share to the new social understanding. But the desire to be understood would never in itself have been sufficient to have opened so completely the protectively closed portals of the thinking Negro's mind. There is still too much possibility of being snubbed or patronized for that. It was rather the necessity for fuller, truer self-expression, the realization of the unwisdom of allowing social discrimination to segregate him mentally, and a counter-attitude to cramp and fetter his own living—and so the "spite-wall" that the intellectuals built over the "color-line" has happily been taken down. Much of this reopening of intellectual contacts has centered in New York and has been richly fruitful not merely in the enlarging of personal experience, but in the definite enrichment of American art and letters and in the clarifying of our common vision of the social tasks ahead.

The particular significance in the re-establishment of contact between the more advanced and representative classes is that it promises to offset some of the unfavorable reactions of the past, or at least to re-surface race contacts somewhat for the future. Subtly the conditions that are molding a New Negro are molding a new American attitude.

However, this new phase of things is delicate; it will call for less charity but more justice; less help, but infinitely closer understanding. This is indeed a critical stage of race relationships because of the likelihood, if the new temper is not understood, of engendering sharp group antagonism and a second crop of more calculated prejudice. In some quarters, it has already done so. Having weaned the Negro, public opinion cannot continue to paternalize. The Negro to-day is inevitably moving forward under the control largely of his own objectives. What are these objectives? Those of his outer life are happily already well and finally formulated, for they are none other than the ideals of American institutions and democracy. Those of his inner life are yet in process of formation, for the new psychology at present is more of a consensus of feeling than of opinion, of attitude rather than of program. Still some points seem to have crystallized.

Up to the present one may adequately describe the Negro's "inner objectives" as an attempt to repair a damaged group psychology and reshape a warped social perspective. Their realization has required a new mentality for the American Negro. And as it matures we begin to see its effects; at first, negative, iconoclastic, and then positive and constructive. In this new group psychology we note the lapse of sentimental appeal, then the development of a more positive self-respect and self-reliance; the repudiation of social dependence, and then the gradual recovery from hyper-sensitiveness and "touchy" nerves, the repudiation of the double standard of judgment with its special philanthropic allowances and then the sturdier desire for objective and scientific appraisal; and finally the rise from social disillusionment to race pride, from the sense of social debt to the responsibilities of social contribution, and offsetting the necessary working and commonsense acceptance of restricted conditions, the belief in ultimate esteem and recognition. Therefore the Negro to-day wishes to be known for what he is, even in his faults and shortcomings, and scorns a craven and precarious survival at the price of seeming to be what he is not. He resents being spoken of as a social ward or minor, even by his own, and to being regarded a chronic patient for the sociological clinic, the sick man of American Democracy. For the same reasons, he himself is through with those social nostrums and panaceas, the so-called "solutions" of his "problem," with which he and the country have been so liberally dosed in the past. Religion, freedom, education, money— in turn, he has ardently hoped for and peculiarly trusted these things; he still believes in them, but not in blind trust that they alone will solve his life-problem.

Each generation, however, will have its creed, and that of the present is the belief in the efficacy of collective effort, in race co-operation. This deep feeling of race is at present the mainspring of Negro life. It seems to be the outcome of the reaction to proscription and prejudice; an attempt, fairly successful on the whole, to convert a defensive into an offensive position, a handicap into an incentive. It is radical in tone, but not in purpose and only the most stupid forms of opposition, misunderstanding or persecution could make it otherwise. Of course, the thinking Negro has shifted a little toward the left with the world-trend, and there is an increasing group who affiliate with radical and liberal movements. But fundamentally for the present the Negro is radical on race matters, conservative on others, in other words, a "forced radical," a social protestant rather than a genuine radical. Yet under further pressure and injustice iconoclastic thought and motives will inevitably increase. Harlem's quixotic radicalisms call for their ounce of democracy to-day lest to-morrow they be beyond cure.

The Negro mind reaches out as yet to nothing but American wants, American ideas. But this forced attempt to build his Americanism on race values is a unique social experiment, and its ultimate success is impossible except through the fullest sharing of American culture and institutions. There should be no delusion about this. American nerves in sections unstrung with race hysteria are often fed the opiate that the trend of Negro advance is wholly separatist, and that the effect of its operation will be to encyst the Negro as a benign foreign body in the body politic. This cannot be—even if it were desirable. The racialism of the Negro is no limitation or reservation with respect to American life; it is only a constructive effort to build the obstructions in the stream of his progress into an efficient dam of social energy and power. Democracy itself is obstructed and stagnated to the extent that any of its channels are closed. Indeed they cannot be selectively closed. So the choice is not between one way for the Negro and another way for the rest, but between American institutions frustrated on the one hand and American ideals progressively fulfilled and realized on the other.

There is, of course, a warrantably comfortable feeling in being on the right side of the country's professed ideals. We realize that we cannot be undone without America's undoing. It is within the gamut of this attitude that the thinking Negro faces America, but with varia-tions of mood that are if anything more significant than the attitude itself. Sometimes we have it taken with the defiant ironic challenge of McKay:

> Mine is the future grinding down to-day
> Like a great landslip moving to the sea,
> Bearing its freight of débris far away
> Where the green hungry waters restlessly
> Heave mammoth pyramids, and break and roar
> Their eerie challenge to the crumbling shore.

Sometimes, perhaps more frequently as yet, it is taken in the fervent and almost filial appeal and counsel of Weldon Johnson's:

O Southland, dear Southland!
Then why do you still cling
To an idle age and a musty page,
To a dead and useless thing?

But between defiance and appeal, midway almost between cynicism and hope, the prevailing mind stands in the mood of the same author's *To America*, an attitude of sober query and stoical challenge:

How would you have us, as we are?
    Or sinking 'neath the load we bear,
Our eyes fixed forward on a star,
    Or gazing empty at despair?

Rising or falling? Men or things?
    With dragging pace or footsteps fleet?
Strong, willing sinews in your wings,
    Or tightening chains about your feet?

More and more, however, an intelligent realization of the great discrepancy between the American social creed and the American social practice forces upon the Negro the taking of the moral advantage that is his. Only the steadying and sobering effect of a truly characteristic gentleness of spirit prevents the rapid rise of a definite cynicism and counter-hate and a defiant superiority feeling. Human as this reaction would be, the majority still deprecate its advent, and would gladly see it forestalled by the speedy amelioration of its causes. We wish our race pride to be a healthier, more positive achievement than a feeling based upon a realization of the shortcomings of others. But all paths toward the attainment of a sound social attitude have been difficult; only a relatively few enlightened minds have been able as the phrase puts it "to rise above" prejudice. The ordinary man has had until recently only a hard choice between the alternatives of supine and humiliating submission and stimulating but hurtful counter-prejudice. Fortunately from some inner, desperate resourcefulness has recently sprung up the simple expedient of fighting prejudice by mental passive resistance, in other words by trying to ignore it. For the few, this manna may perhaps be effective, but the masses cannot thrive upon it.

Fortunately there are constructive channels opening out into which the balked social feelings of the American Negro can flow freely.

Without them there would be much more pressure and danger than there is. These compensating interests are racial but in a new and enlarged way. One is the consciousness of acting as the advance-guard of the African peoples in their contact with Twentieth Century civilization; the other, the sense of a mission of rehabilitating the race in world esteem from that loss of prestige for which the fate and conditions of slavery have so largely been responsible. Harlem, as we shall see, is the center of both these movements; she is the home of the Negro's "Zionism." The pulse of the Negro world has begun to beat in Harlem. A Negro newspaper carrying news material in English, French and Spanish, gathered from all quarters of America, the West Indies and Africa has maintained itself in Harlem for over five years. Two important magazines, both edited from New York, maintain their news and circulation consistently on a cosmopolitan scale. Under American auspices and backing, three pan-African congresses have been held abroad for the discussion of common interests, colonial questions and the future co-operative development of Africa. In terms of the race question as a world problem, the Negro mind has leapt, so to speak, upon the parapets of prejudice and extended its cramped horizons. In so doing it has linked up with the growing group con-sciousness of the dark-peoples and is gradually learning their common interests. As one of our writers has recently put it: "It is imperative that we understand the white world in its relations to the non-white world." As with the Jew, persecution is making the Negro international.

As a world phenomenon this wider race consciousness is a different thing from the much asserted rising tide of color. Its inevitable causes are not of our making. The consequences are not necessarily damaging to the best interests of civilization. Whether it actually brings into being new Armadas of conflict or argosies of cultural exchange and enlightenment can only be decided by the attitude of the dominant races in an era of critical change. With the American Negro, his new internationalism is primarily an effort to recapture contact with the scattered peoples of African derivation. Garveyism may be a transient, if spectacular, phenomenon, but the possible rôle of the American Negro in the future development of Africa is one of the most constructive and universally helpful missions that any modern people can lay claim to.

Constructive participation in such causes cannot help giving the Negro valuable group incentives, as well as increased prestigé at home and abroad. Our greatest rehabilitation may possibly come through such channels, but for the present, more immediate hope rests in the revaluation by white and black alike of the Negro in terms of his artistic endowments and cultural contributions, past and prospective. It must be increasingly recognized that the Negro has already made very substantial contributions, not only in his folk-art, music espe-cially, which has always found appreciation, but in larger, though humbler and less acknowl-edged ways. For generations the Negro has been the peasant matrix of that section of America which has most undervalued him, and here he has contributed not only materially in labor and in social patience, but spiritually as well. The South has unconsciously absorbed the gift of his folk-temperament. In less than half a generation it will be easier to recognize this, but the fact remains that a leaven of humor, sentiment, imagination and tropic nonchalance has gone into the making of the South from a humble, unacknowledged source. A second crop of the Negro's gifts promises still more largely. He now becomes a conscious contributor and lays aside the status of a beneficiary and ward for that of a collaborator and participant in American civilization. The great social gain in this is the releasing of our talented group from the arid fields of controversy and debate to the productive fields of creative expression. The especially cultural recognition they win should in turn prove the key to that revaluation of the Negro which must precede or accompany any considerable further betterment of race relationships. But whatever the general effect, the present generation will have added the motives of self-expression and spiritual development to the old and still unfinished task of making material headway and progress. No one who understandingly faces the situation with its substantial accomplishment or views the new scene with its still more abundant promise can be entirely without hope. And certainly, if in our lifetime the Negro should not be able to celebrate his full initiation into American democracy, he can at least, on the warrant of these things, celebrate the attainment of a significant and satisfying new phase of group development, and with it a spiritual Coming of Age.

Chapter 43

Zora Neale Hurston (1903–60)

"HOW IT FEELS TO BE COLORED ME" (1928)

AS A TODDLER, THE ALABAMA-BORN Zora Neale Hurston moved to Eatonville, Florida, the first black incorporated community in the United States. Eatonville's proud African American community and Hurston's family status enabled her to be raised in a social atmosphere that was relatively untroubled by the virulent and often violent racism that many black people experienced in the deep South. Hurston's father, John, a Baptist minister, served as the Mayor of Eatonville; her mother, Lucy Potts Hurston, was a Christian educator who energetically inspired her children's dreams and aspirations. When her mother died, the thirteen-year-old Hurston and her siblings were largely left to fend for themselves. After hitting the road as a singer with a Gilbert and Sullivan review, Hurston eventually made her way to New York City where she studied under the acclaimed anthropologist Franz Boas and received a BA in anthropology from Columbia University's Barnard College in 1928. Her interest in folklore and narrative led her to embrace rural and vernacular speech in her literary works – a cause of dissension with some of the Harlem Renaissance's more self-conscious and cosmopolitan writers. The colorfully exuberant Hurston was a playwright, essayist, anthropologist, and folklorist; her best-known works include *Mules and Men* (1935; folklore) and *Their Eyes Were Watching God* (1937; novel). Her autobiography, *Dust Tracks on a Road*, was published in 1942. The American writer Alice Walker, who was inspired by Hurston's work, reclaimed the independent-minded Hurston from obscurity in the 1970s and provided the marker for her previously unmarked grave.

Zora Neale Hurston, "How It Feels to Be Colored Me," *The World Tomorrow* 11.5 (May 1928): 215–16. Reprinted in *I Love Myself When I Am Laughing . . . And Then Again When I Am Looking Mean and Impressive: A Zora Neale Hurston Reader*, ed. Alice Walker. New York: the Feminist Press, 1979. 152–55.

I am colored but I offer nothing in the way of extenuating circumstances except the fact that I am the only Negro in the United States whose grandfather on the mother's side was *not* an Indian chief.

I remember the very day that I became colored. Up to my thirteenth year I lived in the little Negro town of Eatonville, Florida. It is exclusively a colored town. The only white people I knew passed through the town going to or coming from Orlando. The native whites rode dusty horses, the Northern tourists chugged down the sandy village road in automobiles. The town knew the Southerners and never stopped cane chewing when they passed. But the Northerners were something else again. They were peered at cautiously from behind curtains by the timid. The more venturesome would come out on the porch to watch them go past and got just as much pleasure out of the tourists as the tourists got out of the village.

The front porch might seem a daring place for the rest of the town, but it was a gallery seat to me. My favorite place was atop the gate-post. Proscenium box for a born first-nighter. Not only did I enjoy the show, but I didn't mind the actors knowing that I liked it. I usually spoke to them in passing. I'd wave at them and when they returned my salute, I would say something like this: "Howdy-do-well-I-thank-you-where-you-goin'?" Usually automobile or the horse paused at this, and after a queer exchange of compliments, I would probably "go a piece of the way" with them, as we say in farthest Florida. If one of my family happened to come to the front in time to see me, of course negotiations would be rudely broken off. But even so, it is clear that I was the first "welcome-to-our-state" Floridian, and I hope the Miami Chamber of Commerce will please take notice.

During this period, white people differed from colored to me only in that they rode through town and never lived there. They liked to hear me "speak pieces" and sing and wanted to see me dance the parse-me-la, and gave me generously of their small silver for doing these things, which seemed strange to me for I wanted to do them so much that I needed bribing to stop. Only they didn't know it. The colored people gave no dimes. They deplored any joyful tendencies in me, but I was their Zora nevertheless. I belonged to them, to the nearby hotels, to the county—everybody's Zora.

But changes came in the family when I was thirteen, and I was sent to school in Jacksonville. I left Eatonville, the town of the oleanders, as Zora. When I disembarked from the river-boat at Jacksonville, she was no more. It seemed that I had suffered a sea change. I was not Zora of Orange County any more. I was now a little colored girl. I found it out in certain ways. In my heart as well as in the mirror, I became a fast brown—warranted not to rub nor run.

But I am not tragically colored. There is no great sorrow dammed up in my soul, nor lurking behind my eyes. I do not mind at all. I do not belong to the sobbing school of Negrohood who hold that nature somehow has given them a lowdown dirty deal and whose feelings are all hurt about it. Even in the helter-skelter skirmish that is my life, I have seen that the world is to the strong regardless of a little pigmentation more or less. No, I do not weep at the world—I am too busy sharpening my oyster knife.

Someone is always at my elbow reminding me that I am the grand-daughter of slaves. It fails to register depression with me. Slavery is sixty years in the past. The operation was successful and the patient is doing well, thank you. The terrible struggle that made me an American out of a potential slave said "On the line!" The Reconstruction said "Get set!"; and the generation before said "Go!" I am off to a flying start and I must not halt in the stretch to look behind and weep. Slavery is the price I paid for civilization, and the choice was not with me. It is a bully adventure and worth all that I have paid through my ancestors for it. No one on earth ever had a greater chance for glory. The world to be won and nothing to be lost. It is thrilling to think—to know that for any act of mine, I shall get twice as much praise or twice as much blame. It is quite exciting to hold the center of the national stage, with the spectators not knowing whether to laugh or to weep.

The position of my white neighbor is much more difficult. No brown specter pulls up a chair beside me when I sit down to eat. No dark ghost thrusts its leg against mine in bed. The game of keeping what one has is never so exciting as the game of getting.

I do not always feel colored. Even now I often achieve the unconscious Zora of Eatonville before the Hegira. I feel most colored when I am thrown against a sharp white background.

For instance at Barnard. "Beside the waters of the Hudson" I feel my race. Among the thousand white persons, I am a dark rock surged upon, overswept by a creamy sea. I am surged upon and overswept, but through it all, I remain myself. When covered by the waters, I am; and the ebb but reveals me again.

Sometimes it is the other way around. A white person is set down in our midst, but the contrast is just as sharp for me. For instance, when I sit in the drafty basement that is The New World Cabaret with a white person, my color comes. We enter chatting about any little nothing that we have in common and are seated by the jazz waiters. In the abrupt way that jazz orchestras have, this one plunges into a number. It loses no time in circumlocutions, but gets right down to business. It constricts the thorax and splits the heart with its tempo and narcotic harmonies. This orchestra grows rambunctious, rears on its hind legs and attacks the tonal veil with primitive fury, rending it, clawing it until it breaks through to the jungle beyond. I follow those heathen—follow them exultingly. I dance wildly inside myself; I yell within, I whoop; I shake my assegai above my head, I hurl it true to the mark *yeeeeooww!* I am in the jungle and living in the jungle way. My face is painted red and yellow and my body is painted blue. My pulse is throbbing like a war drum. I want to slaughter something—give pain, give death to what, I do not know. But the piece ends. The men of the orchestra wipe their lips and rest their fingers. I creep back slowly to the veneer we call civilization with the last tone and find the white friend sitting motionless in his seat, smoking calmly.

"Good music they have here," he remarks, drumming the table with his fingertips.

Music! The great blobs of purple and red emotion have not touched him. He has only heard what I felt. He is far away and I see him but dimly across the ocean and the continent that have fallen between us. He is so pale with his whiteness then and I am *so* colored.

At certain times I have no race, I am *me*. When I set my hat at a certain angle and saunter down Seventh Avenue, Harlem City, feeling as snooty as the lions in front of the Forty-Second Street Library, for instance. So far as my feelings are concerned, Peggy Hopkins Joyce on the Boule Mich with her gorgeous raiment, stately carriage, knees knocking together in a most aristocratic manner, has nothing on me. The cosmic Zora emerges. I belong to no race nor time. I am the eternal feminine with its string of beads.

I have no separate feeling about being an American citizen and colored. I am merely a fragment of the Great Soul that surges within the boundaries. My country, right or wrong.

Sometimes, I feel discriminated against, but it does not make me angry. It merely astonishes me. How *can* any deny themselves the pleasure of my company! It's beyond me.

But in the main, I feel like a brown bag of miscellany propped against a wall. Against a wall in company with other bags, white, red and yellow. Pour out the contents, and there is discovered a jumble of small things priceless and worthless. A first-water diamond, an empty spool, bits of broken glass, lengths of string, a key to a door long since crumbled away, a rusty knife-blade, old shoes saved for a road that never was and never will be, a nail bent under the weight of things too heavy for any nail, a dried flower or two, still a little fragrant.

In your hand is the brown bag. On the ground before you is the jumble it held—so much like the jumble in the bags, could they be emptied, that all might be dumped in a single heap and the bags refilled without altering the content of any greatly. A bit of colored glass more or less would not matter. Perhaps that is how the Great Stuffer of Bags filled them in the first place—who knows?

Chapter 44

Jean Toomer (1894–1967)

"RACE PROBLEMS AND MODERN SOCIETY" (1929)

NATHAN EUGENE PINCHBACK TOOMER WAS born into a distinguished multi-racial family. One of his grandfathers, Pinckney Benton Steward Pinchback, was a Union officer during the Civil War. His maternal grandfather was the first African American to serve as Governor in the United States (Louisiana). Both of Jean Toomer's parents were bi-racial; throughout his life Toomer observed the racial dynamics of the northern and southern United States and continually negotiated his cultural and racial-ethnic identity. Inspired and mentored by the writer Waldo Frank (*Our America*, 1919), Toomer most consistently identified himself as an American. His modernist masterpiece *Cane* (1923) represents, in poems and stories, post-World War I's Great Migration of rural African Americans to northern industrial cities. Toomer maintained spiritual ties to both Georgia, in the south, and Washington, DC and New York City in the north. After following the spiritual leader George Ivanovitch Gurdjieff in the 1930s, Toomer sought haven from U.S. social and racial politics in the Quaker religious community. His collected papers are housed at Yale University's Beinecke Library.

Jean Toomer, "Race Problems and Modern Society," *Jean Toomer: Selected Essays and Literary Criticism*, ed. Robert B. Jones. Knoxville: U of Tennessee P, 1996. 60–76. Originally published in *Problems of Civilization*, ed. Baker Brownell. New York: Van Nostrand, 1929.

From whatever angle one views modern society and the various forms of contemporary life, the records of flux and swift changes are everywhere evident. Even the attitude which holds that man's fundamental nature has not altered during the past ten thousand years must admit the changes of forms and of modes which have occurred perhaps without precedent and certainly with an ever increasing rapidity during the life period of the now living generations. If the world is viewed through one or more of the various formulated interpretations of this period, or if one's estimate rests upon the comparatively inarticulate records of day to day experience, the results have the common factor of change. Let it be Spengler's *Decline of the West*, or Keyserling's *The World in the Making*, or Waldo Frank's survey of Western culture,[1] or Joseph Wood Krutch's analysis of the modern temper,[2] and there is found testimony to the effect that the principles of cohesion and crystallization are being rapidly withdrawn from the materials of old forms, with a consequent break up of these forms, a setting free of these materials, with the possibility that the principles of cohesion and crystallization will recombine the stuff of life and make new forms.

Bertrand Russell[3] has indicated the revisions of mental outlook made necessary by recent scientific and philosophic thinking. James Harvey Robinson has shown why we *must* create new forms of thinking and bring about a transformation of attitude.[4] From a different angle, the social science of the world-wide struggle between the owning and the laboring classes, clearly summarized by Scott Nearing,[5] comes to much the same conclusion, in so far as the factor of change is concerned. Again, the records of psychology bear striking witness of this factor. For though, on the one hand, there are in vogue a number of dogmas and pat formulas which assume a constant set of simple factors, and allow, say, Leonardo da Vinci to be seen at a glance, and which offer ready explanations of why, say, George Santayana writes, on the other hand, the practice of psychology discloses a surprising and bewildering flux and chaos, both in the individual and in the collective psyche. And in general, what is taking place in most fields of life is sufficiently radical for Baker Brownell to see it resulting in a new human universe.[6]

*   *   *

And at the same time—paradoxical[ly] enough—it is also evident that there are certain forms of modern society which, at least for the time being, are not only not changing in the above sense, but are growing and strengthening as they now exist. I refer to the established economic and political systems—and their immediate by products—of Western nations, especially of the English speaking nations. For despite the disorganized aspect of the economic situation as a consequence of the War, and as described by Keynes, it is, I think, the agreed opinion of students of Western economic and political institutions, particularly of those which obtain in the United States, that these systems, and especially the philosophy[7] which has grown up about them, have become stronger and more organized within the past thirty years. Their development during this period in the United States, for example, is suggested by these general facts: that this country now turns out, and is increasingly turning out, a surplus of both money and products; that it is sending in larger quantities of this surplus into foreign fields; that since 1900 it has become a lending, instead of a borrowing nation; that Henry Ford has become a philosopher. One student of economic conditions states that within ten years all the main European boards of directors will be dominated and controlled by Americans. Thus, irrespective of all the changes suggested at the beginning of this article, irrespective of the example and influence of the Soviet Union from without, and within, the World War notwithstanding, and despite the protests and revolts of foreign peoples, the business, political, legal, and military organizations and expansion of Western nations have advanced. At the present time they at least appear to be more solid and crystallized than ever. And they are growing stronger. So true is this, and so dominant an influence do these systems exercise on all the other forms of life, that, should one view the modern Western nations from within the business and political worlds—and their outgrowths—one might well conclude that there were no radical changes occurring anywhere, or that at most these changes were taking place only in minor social forms and concerned only an uninfluential minority.

For the growth of business and of business-technique, and the increased support that the political and legal systems give to the dominant economic practices, this growth and this increase have parallels in all the forms of life that are at all connected with these systems. Thus, wealth, and such power as wealth gives, are increasingly considered valuable: more and more men are devoting themselves to their attainment, seeing in them the end of life, and the highest goal that life offers. The big business man is the modern hero. The average man, that is, the average business man, is already the ideal, even the idol, of millions of people; and there is a growing tendency for institutions of higher education, physicians, and psychologists to accept and affirm the average business man as the ideal at which all people of sound sense should aim. The notions of prosperity and of necessary progress go hand in hand, and both are being elevated in the public mind. To have a larger bank-account, to live in a socially better located house, to drive a better car, to be able to discuss the stock-exchange and the servant problem—these are items which have an ever stronger appeal to an ever larger number of people. And not a bit of so-called religion is used as an aid to such fulfillment. The fact that most of us are just one step ahead of the sheriff is a thing that one mentions less and less. As our need to keep ahead of him increases, so does our optimism. Yes, crime does increase, but we are thousands of years in advance of backward peoples, and each day sees us further outdistance them. Social position is a matter of spending-power and possession of the items of prosperity. Never has aristocracy been taken so seriously. Results are looked for, and measured in terms of, silver dollars. Even sermons and poems must pass the success test before anyone considers them of merit. And all the while, the inner content of life is decreasing and rapidly losing significance. The inclination to prosperity and the inclination to suicide are somehow compatible. At any rate, both are increasing.

* * *

Thus, while it is a fact that modern society is in flux, it is also a fact that modern society is crystallized and formed about the solid structure of big business; and while modern psychology is the psychology of a transitional period, it is also the psychology of a stabilized big business period. It is desirable to keep both of these general facts in mind when we now turn to consider the particular matter of race problems and their relation to the other forms of the modern social order.

But now, in order to give this article focus and points of concrete reference, I shall take America—that is, the United States—as a sufficiently representative modern society, and as a social scheme that contains a sufficiently representative class of race problems. For here in America there are changing forms and established forms; and, with the possible exception of the Soviet Union, the main features of our economic and political systems and their social outgrowths have points in common with those that obtain in other modern nations. And—again with the exception of the Soviet Union, in which, I am told, the economic and political causes of race problems either no longer exist or are being removed, the minority races and peoples being guaranteed similar rights, the children of all peoples being taught, that all races are similar—American race problems have points in common with the race problems of other countries (the British and Hindu, the Eurasian, the gentile and Jew on the Continent, the whites and blacks in South Africa) and with the large number of problems everywhere—such as nationality problems—which are psychologically similar to race problems.

It will be well to note here that no serious student of race claims to know what race really is; nor do we know. Therefore the term "race problem" is a loose sociological term, which contains a variety of vague meanings; it is subject to being used with whatever meaning one happens to give it.

Scientific opinion is in doubt as to what race is. Authorities such as Roland Dixon, Franz Boas, A. L. Kroeber, Ellsworth Huntington, and Flinders Petrie agree that from the point of view of exact knowledge, the whole subject of race is uncertain and somewhat confused. It is clear that the human race is something different from the other orders of life of the natural kingdom. It is noticeable that there are differences within the human group. But it is not admissible to define and understand race solely on the basis of an obvious variation of a single physical feature, such as color of skin; and when one seeks for a fundamental knowledge of it, then, despite the exact biological ideas of the germ-plasm and genes, and despite the exact anthropological ideas associated with measurements of physical features, the difficulties encountered tend to mount faster than one's understanding.

One may, with Professor Kroeber,[8] try to understand and use the term "race" in its strict biological sense, and hold it to mean an hereditary subdivision of a species. I personally think that this is a much needed practice, because, among other things, it calls attention to the strictly biological aspect of race, it points to race as an organic phenomenon, and it allows the purely sociological aspects of racial matters to be distinguished and seen for what they are. Surely, there cannot be much advance in the understanding of race problems until we do clearly distinguish between their organic and social factors. But from the point of exact definition and real knowledge, the term "hereditary subdivision of a species" is hardly better understood than the term "race." For again we are brought up to the questions: What is a subdivision? Upon what criteria should our ideas of a subdivision rest? Can these criteria be used to adequately define and understand race? Does anyone really know what a subdivision is? The fact is that the difficulties involved in the present ideas of, and approach to, race are causing thoughtful men to recast their data and take new directions.

* * *

This being the case with the main term, how then am I to give any real clarity to the term "race problem"? What is it that distinguishes race problems from all the other problems with which man is belabored? In what real way do racial maladjustments differ from the scores of maladjustments that burden men's psyche? Just how are sociological debates about race different from the endless series of debates on all possible subjects that men are continually engaging in? In another place[9] I have pursued an investigation of race problems that gives these questions a more detailed treatment than is possible here. And in the same work I have indicated, among other things, that the answer which is often given, namely, that biological race-differences explain the nature of race problems—that this answer is incorrect. For this answer is involved in the confusion between organic and social factors. Professor Kroeber has pointed out the error of such practice. It assumes that biological race-phenomena give rise to sociological race problems. But the strictly racial history of man, with its repeated crossings and recrossings of all the sub-groups of the human stock, with its great number of intermixtures of all kinds, shows clearly that as organisms we are noticeably free from concern with the issues that we sociologically contend with—that so-called race problems are not due to biological causes, but to the superimposed forms and controversies of our social *milieu*.

The same conclusion is reached by both social and personal psychology. For herein it is seen that it is first necessary that we be conditioned by the factors of our social environment, before we do and can respond in terms of racial similarities and differences. If we were never taught and never acquired ideas, opinions, beliefs, and superstitions about race, if we were never conditioned to have feelings, and so-called instincts about these notions and beliefs, we would never have any responses or behavior in terms of race: we would not experience race prejudice and animosity. To an unconditioned child—that is, to a child that has not acquired racial notions and feelings from its environment, let the child be of what ever race you will—differences of skin color are no more and no less than differences of color of its toys or dresses. No child has prejudice against a toy because its color is white or black. No racially unconditioned child has prejudice against a person because his color is white or black. Differences of texture of hair are similarly no more and no less than differences of texture between the hair of different animals—a shaggy dog, and a sleek cat. And so it is with all the other physical characteristics that are commonly supposed to provoke supposedly innate racial prejudices and preferences. There are no such things as innate racial antipathies. We are not born with them. Either we acquire them from our environment, or else we do not have them at all. So that, paradoxical as it may sound, the fact is that race, as such, does not give rise to race problems. The physical aspects of race do not cause the problems that center around what are called racial hatreds and prejudices. This is the conclusion of experimental psychology.[10] And biologists, those who hold no brief in favor of environment as a dominant factor in the making of adult man, are inclined to agree with this position as to the origin of race problems. "It is only just to admit at once," says Professor East, a geneticist, "that many cases of racial antagonism have no biological warrant."[11]

The meaning and the importance of the above conclusion consists in this: since race problems are social and psychological in origin, they can be fundamentally dealt with— they can be radically changed and even eliminated—by use of the proper social and psychological instruments. It is possible for man and society to constructively handle the racial situation.

*   *   *

In considering race problems, we may, I think, for the present purpose divide them into three classes. First, there is the class of race problems which falls in the domain of scientific investigation. These consist of the racial matters dealt with in biology, anthropology, and psychology. They have to do with man's biological and cultural make up and behavior. They involve the attempt to ascertain the facts and understand the principles of human organic, social, and psychological existence—in so far as these are particularly concerned with matters of race. They include the aim of applying the knowledge thus gained for the best possible regulation of human affairs.

Second, there are race problems that take the form of discussion and debate. There are serious discussions of the race question. These discussions often draw upon the data of science, and, pressing beyond prejudice and petty issues, they also aim to arrive at a theoretically sound understanding of racial matters, and at practical conclusions that can be relied upon to guide men in the developing of intelligence, character, and ability. These discussions are frequently reducible to the question of interbreeding—of intermarriage. Sometimes they get entangled in arguments about heredity and environment, about superiority and inferiority. Too often they get lost in a maze of unconscious assumptions in favor of one's own type of life, one's own standards. As often as not they tend to lose sense of genuine values. The race-theme can compel the partial or total eclipse of all else. They are sometimes too solemn, too serious; too seldom does a good laugh relieve the tenseness. And now and again, I am afraid, the people who engage in these discussions are taken in by the humbug of education and civilization. In these cases the serious discussions of race fall far below the intelligence displayed by creative thinking in other fields. At their best, however, they do lead to clarification, and to the taking of measures for increasing constructive racial life and interracial relationships.

Then there are all manner of absurd and sometimes explosive remarks and debates over racial issues. These range all the way from parlor and backyard gossip about "niggers," "crackers," "kikes," "wops," etc., through naive verbal releases for hurt emotions, to propagandist and pathological speeches, articles and books. Debates of this type are particularly notable in that they usually repeat what has already been said to no profit thousands of times, and in that they take place in shameless ignorance of new and constructive ideas and attitudes.

Then, third, there is the class of race problems which arise from, or, better, which are the actual day to day experiences of maladjustments due to factors of a racial character. These include experiences caused by the drawing of the color line; by fights—physical, legal, and otherwise—between the races; by all manner of racial aggressions, resistances, oppositions, oppressions, fears, prejudices, hatreds; and by the occasional stoning and burning of houses, riots, lynchings.

*   *   *

Recalling what was said as to the existence in modern society of two classes of forms, one of which was undergoing radical changes, one of which was becoming more crystallized, we may now ask: Into which class of forms do race problems fall? It is probable, and I think it is accurate to say, that race problems of the scientific and of the serious discussion type belong to the changing category. They are among the forms that are undergoing radical changes. For not only are they in touch with the forces and factors that are in general producing new intellectual and conscious outlooks, but they are also being strongly influenced by the particular discovery of new racial data and of new methods of dealing with race. Though the science of man shows less striking revolutions than the science of physics, it is nevertheless certain that its progress has caused the forming of new attitudes and of new approaches to racial phenomena. From the scientific point of view, the whole matter of race is something different—perhaps quite different—from what it was twenty or thirty years ago. But race problems of this type comprise only a small fraction of the racial situation.

The bulk of racial behavior belongs to the established crystallizing category. Most race problems, in their given forms, are tending, not to radically change, but to crystallize. By far the larger part of our racial situation, with its already given patterns and tendencies, is rapidly growing more acute. These facts, if such they be, will be brought out if we note with what other social forms race problems are most closely associated, and if we see some of the main patterns and tendencies.

*   *   *

In America, the "acquisitive urge" for land, natural resources, and cheap labor variously gave rise to the problems of the whites and the Indians, the whites and the Negroes, the whites and the Asiatics, the old stock and the immigrants. The Indian problem began over land deals, and, in so far as it still exists, it is still a matter of white men desiring Indian territory for economic profit. Political and legal devices have all tended to be in the service of this interest. The Asiatic problem is obviously economic, and its "solution" is always seen with an eye to the economic situation. Immigrant problems are the direct outgrowth of demands for cheap labor, and of the circumstances attending the immigrant's economic condition after he arrives in this country. While the way in which the Negro problem has been and still is tied up with our economic and political systems, and their social outgrowths, is even more evident. This is not to say that economic causes and factors are the only ones giving rise to race problems; there are certainly other causes and factors, while the basic cause of all of man's negative problems must be sought, I think, in some abnormal feature of man's fundamental make up. Here I am simply indicating the relationship between the organized expressions of man's acquisitive urge, namely, between our economic and political systems, and race problems. In addition to the various historical and social science studies that show this relationship, it can be clearly seen if one has the patience to go over the *Congressional Records* that bear on this subject. And there recently appeared in *Harper's Magazine* an article[12] dealing with the future of America, written by an eminent biologist, wherein much that is relevant to the present point, and indeed to the general trend of this paper, is considered.

Just as race problems are closely associated with our economic and political systems, so are they with one of the main outgrowths of these systems—our social scheme of caste distinctions. No small measure of racial animosity is due to this scheme. This scheme of racial animosity is due to this scheme. This scheme is crystallizing. The economic and political systems are increasing. And so are race problems. How could it be otherwise than that the things which are causing an increased anti-Americanism abroad, and an increase of crime and degeneracy, and a decrease of intelligence at home, also cause more and more race antagonism.

Certain factors of American race problems, particularly certain of the factors involved in the race problems of the whites and Negroes, were modified by the Civil War. Many more factors were added then, and have been added since then. But the main forms of these problems, namely, the sharp sociological divisions between the white and colored people, have persisted from the beginning of American history, and they have steadily become more and more fixed and crystallized. They have grown up, so to speak, with the growth of our economic, political, and social systems. And the probability is that they will continue to increase with the increase of these systems. Scientific and liberal opinion, and intelligent humanism, will tend to have as much, and no more, influence on the character of race problems as they have on the character of big business and on the characters of Republican and Democratic party politics.

* * *

The South—that is, the Southern section of the United States—is particularly open to strange descriptions. Reports of the South would have it that white Southerners are always indefatigably engaged on the one hand, in keeping the Negro in his place, and on the other, in prying into the family closets of their white economic, political, and social enemies, with the intent of discovering there some trace of dark blood with which to stigmatize and break these enemies. Doubtless such things do happen. I am told that occasionally it is somehow discovered that some white family of hitherto high repute has indeed a drop of Negro blood—whereon this family is likely to fall below the social level of prosperous Negroes. And there are reports of ingenious tests devised and used for detecting the presence of dark blood in those who otherwise would pass for pure white. This is similar to the assertion that some people in Vienna wish to make a blood test compulsory for every schoolchild, in order that any trace of Semitic blood may be detected. Doubtless there are such tests, or wishes for such tests, in both places. And, of course, in our South there are lynchings, peonage, false legal trials, and no court procedure at all, political disfranchisement, segregation, and, on the social level, a rigid maintenance of caste distinctions. And, among Negroes, there is a sizable amount of discontent, fear, hatred, and an effort to get better conditions. Certainly both races are enslaved by the situation. But there are, on the other hand, intelligent attempts on the part of both white and colored men to constructively deal with the existing factors.[13] And there are thousands of both whites and blacks who from day to day experience no active form of race problem, but who are, like masses of people everywhere, sufficiently content to go their way and live their life, counting their day lucky if, without working them too hard, it has given them the means to eat and sleep and reproduce their kind.

There is no doubt, however, that the race problem is at least a latent problem with almost everyone, not only in the South, but everywhere within the United States. For America is a nation in name only. In point of fact, she is a social form containing racial, national, and cultural groups which the existing economic, political, and social systems tend to keep divided and repellent. Moreover, each group is left to feel, and often taught and urged to feel, that some other group is the cause of its misfortune. Against the actual and potential antagonisms thus caused, many of our churches and other orders of so-called brotherhood and good will do no more than make feeble, and, often enough, hypocritical gestures.

Below the sociological level, all the races and stocks present in America—and almost all of the main peoples in some numbers are assembled here—have met and mingled their bloods. Biologically, what has taken place here somewhat justifies the name "melting pot." But it is thus everywhere where people meet. Let people meet—and they mingle. This is biology, the productive urge within man, acting with no thought of sociological differences, acting even in the face of social prohibitions and restraints of all sorts. The organic acts are fundamental in human biology. This mingling of bloods has been recognized and formulated as a maxim by anthropology.[14] Subject to the influence of the American environment, the different peoples and stocks have so intermixed here, that—among others, and notably—Dr. Ales Hrdlicka sees the forming of a distinct racial type, which he calls the American type. But the consciousness of most so-called Americans lags far behind the organic process.

When we view the scene sociologically, then, as I have said, we everywhere see strong tendencies to form separatist and repellent groups. On the social level, the term "melting pot" is somewhat of a misnomer. Of so-called racial divisions and antagonisms, there is the nation wide separation of the white and colored groups. Jews and gentiles tend to remain apart. The bewildering number of nationalistic groups—English, German, French, Italians, Greeks, Russians, etc.—tend to do likewise. And it sometimes happens that those of Northern and Southern European descent are as prejudiced against each other, or against newly arrived technical citizens, as they are against Negroes. Negroes do not care too much for foreigners. There are a number of fairly defined prejudices within each of the several groups; while the lines drawn, and the animosities aroused, by differences of sectional, fraternal, business, political, social, artistic, religious, and scientific allegiance are quite considerable. So that, all in all, it is rare indeed to find anyone who is genuinely conscious of being an American. We have slogans: one hundred percent American; America first; etc. But they do not mean much. The character of perhaps the greatest American—Walt Whitman—is as antipathetic to the conduct of the majority of those who dwell here as the ideals of liberty and union, and the high values that have ever been and still are antipathetic to this same conduct.

Just as separatism has everywhere increased since the War, so the above mentioned separatistic tendencies have here increased since then.

The World War and its consequences gave a decided turn to the racial situation within the Negro group. But this turn was not, and is not, in a radically new direction. Rather, it has resulted in a strengthening of certain of the forces and factors implicit in the form that has existed since the Civil War, and indeed ever since the introduction of Negroes into America—the form, namely, which in its main outline divides white from black. And thus this form itself has become further strengthened and crystallized. A number of factors, among which are greater pressure from without, increased organization and articulateness within the group, and, as a result of the World War, a deeper seated disillusion as regards the promises of the dominant white American—these, together with other factors, have caused an intensification of Negro race consciousness. And with this there has come an increased aggressiveness—more fight. It is no small factor in favor of this fighting attitude that it is being recognized and affirmed by other American minority groups. It is remarked, for instance, that whereas the Indians are hopeless because they do not try to fight for and help themselves, the Negroes demand and therefore deserve better conditions. There is more bitterness, an ever increasing absorption and concern with race issues; very few intelligent Negroes are permitted to be interested in anything else. Within the Negro world there has come about a parallel growth and organization of economic and professional activities, and consequently, an increased group independence and the emergence of a fairly well defined middle class, a tendency to deliberately withdraw from attempts to participate as Americans in the general life of the United States, a greater attempt to participate as Negroes in the general life, a stronger demand, from some, for social equality, and from others, for economic and educational opportunity, some spread of proletarian class consciousness, some activity in art and literature.

From the point of view of deliberate intention, it would seem that the new Negro is much more Negro and much less American than was the old Negro of fifty years ago. From the point of view of sociological types, the types which are arising among Negroes, such as the business man, the politician, the educator, the professional person, the college student, the writer, the propagandist, the movie enthusiast, the bootlegger, the taxi driver, etc.—these types among Negroes are more and more approaching the corresponding white types. But, just as certain as it is that this increasing correspondence of types makes the drawing of distinctions supposedly based on skin color or blood composition appear more and more ridiculous, so it is true that the lines are being drawn with more force between the colored and white groups. Negroes are themselves now drawing these lines. Interbreeding and intermarriage, for instance, are becoming as taboo among Negroes as among whites.

A similar increase of separatism is to be seen among Nordics. There are those who, with greater urgency than ever, are aiming toward an inviolate white aristocracy. Their already fixed inclination toward a Western modification of the caste systems is stimulated, and sometimes over stimulated, by the threat that the rising, tide of Southern and darker peoples may cause them to lose control. They tend to see all virtue menaced by this rising tide. They increasingly tend to feel and think that not only their own souls, but also the very spirit of America, and even in the world, would be violated, should any save those of their own stock exercise decisive influence. And there are some whites who would like to see the darker peoples, particularly the Negroes, either deported, or sterilized, or swept off by a pestilence.

There are Jews who are more and more emphasizing the actuality and distinction of the Jewish race. They would have the Jews remain strictly as they are, preserving and transmitting their character and culture in more or less isolation from the other peoples of America.

While the Indian, still being pressed off his land and increasingly compelled to attend United States schools, holds aloof so far as possible from the white man, and sometimes indicates the white man's presence in America by a symbolic pile of tin cans.

The main tendencies toward separatism are observed and given a brilliant record in André Siegfried's *America Comes of Age*. And therein will also be found an excellent summary, from one point of view, of the deadlock existing in the American racial situation. For despite the movement above suggested, the situation is indeed in deadlock. The races cannot draw nearer together; nor can they draw much farther apart—and still remain races in America. But they will undoubtedly push away from one another, until they have completely occupied what small room for withdrawal is still left. For, as I have indicated, the strongest forces now active are tending to intensify and crystallize the very patterns, tendencies, and conditions that brought about the present situation.

Thus, from a racial point of view, and, to my mind, from several other points of view, America, which set out to be a land of the free, has become instead a social trap. The dominant forms of her social life—her economic, political, educational, social, and racial forms—compel her people to exist and meet in just the ways most conducive to the maintenance of this trap. All Americans are in it—the white no less than the black, the black no more than the red, the Jew no more than the gentile. It is sometimes thought, both by themselves and by others, that the dominant white Protestant holds the keys to the situation, and could, by a simple turn of the hand, unlock it if he wished to. But this is not fact—it is fiction. The dominant white is just as much a victim of his form as is the Negro of his; while both are equally held by the major American customs and institutions. This is sound social science and it is sound psychology. And until all parties recognize it to be so, and stop berating one another, and get down to work to bring about basic constructive changes, it is romance to talk about solving race problems. As it is, both white and colored people share the same stupidity; for both see no other way out than by intensifying the very attitudes which entrapped them. And so, Americans of all colors and of most descriptions are crawling about their social prison, which is still called Democracy. They are unable to see, and indeed they do not suspect, what it is that holds them; perhaps they do not realize that they are held, so busy are they with their by now habitual rivalries, fears, egotisms, hatreds, and illusions.

But perhaps it is premature to call the prevalent racial tendencies stupid and short sighted. It may be that a solution does lie in the direction which calls for an increase to bursting point of the existing conditions. Circumstances have been known to change as a result of the accentuation of their negative factors. But as often as not, the change, when summed up, is seen to have consisted of no more than a complete disappearance of all positive factors. However this may be, there is no doubt that race prejudice, and all associated with it, is tending to carry the entire body of America toward some such climax. Much of the writing about Nordics and Negroes, and much of the talk as to who is superior and who is inferior and who is equal, and all the other nonsense about race, is just so much verbal fanfare accompanying the actual march.

Too often the very agencies and instruments that might turn its course, or even change its character, are themselves either no more than adjuncts of the prevalent economic, social, and racial forms, or else the force of these forms tends to render them helpless. Thus our churches, our schools, colleges, universities, newspapers, large lecture platforms, are frequently just so many systematized parts of the machine itself; while even the science of anthropology is sometimes constrained to use the language of popular opinion and prejudice. And, as I have said before, liberal opinion and intelligent humanism affect the race question just about as much as they affect the practice of big business and the politics of the Republican and Democratic parties.

But no description of the situation in America is faithful to the entire scene, which fails to notice and consider the positive possibilities contained in the emergence of a large number of the type of people who cannot be classified as separatist and racial. These people are truly synthetic and human. They exist all over America. And though they may not be so defined and articulate as the separatist type, and though they are less in numbers, it is quite possible that their qualitative significance will exercise the greater influence in shaping the future of this country. Siegfried and others failed either to note this type or to give due weight to it, with the consequence that their pictures of the American situation are, to say the least, incomplete.

There are present here individuals, and even groups, drawn from all fields of life—business, the crafts, the professions, the arts and sciences—who, in the first place, and in general affirm truly human values, and sincerely strive that life may contain the greatest possible positive meaning, and who, in the second place, actually do something towards bringing about a worth-while day to day existence. When people of this type face the racial situation, they either have no prejudices or antagonisms, or else they press beyond them, in order to apply the standards of intelligence, character, and ability to this aspect of life also. And it is generally agreed that both individual growth and the development of America as a whole are intimately concerned with achieving a creative synthesis of the best elements here present.

*   *   *

Stripped to its essentials, the positive aspect of the race problem can be expressed thus: how to bring about a selective fusion of the racial and cultural factors of America, in order that the best possible stock and culture may be produced. This implies the need and desirability of breeding on the basis of biological fitness. It implies the need and desirability of existing and exchanging on the basis of intelligence, character, and ability. It means that the process of racial and cultural amalgamation should be guided by these standards.

We have, as I have said, enough knowledge to start solving this problem. Why don't we do something? Why do we, instead, let the negative features of the racial situation run on and intensify? How comes it that in this age of increasing general scientific knowledge, these and other undesirable aspects of life also increase? Why is it that in the midst of such radical changes as we noted at the beginning of this article, race problems, in their established forms, are becoming more crystallized?

There is the obvious answer that all of this is so because race problems are closely associated with the other main forms of our social order, which are also increasing, namely, with our economic, political, and social systems. These systems express and stimulate acquisitive passion for money, power, antisocial urges, and (since it is their nature to arouse and maintain all kinds of antagonisms, it is only natural that they also stimulate and feed) racial animosities. Socially constructive forms of activity, being less powerful and in the minority, can make but little impression upon and headway against them. Put differently, the most influential men and women of our age and nation are so committed to practices that are against intelligence and hostile to well being, that they either consciously or unconsciously do not favor and are often opposed to the use of those agencies and instruments that could bring about constructive changes. These men and women are sufficiently powerful in their hostility to good measures to prevent their being tried. Men and women of sound sense and good conscience are comparatively helpless. Essentialized, this means that man, the destructive being, still is stronger than man, the intelligent being. The destructive part of us is increasing, even while our intelligence expands. These parts are in vital contest. It is a critical struggle for supremacy in its most fundamental aspect. Thus far, the negative has proven stronger than the positive. This is the explanation that is given, not only to tell why race problems are unsolved, but also to explain the presence among us of war, degeneracy, and most of the other ills of man.

As regards racial animosities, I should like to add two other brief considerations. For one: all that has to do with race prejudice and beliefs about race, falls into the class of opinions and feelings which James Harvey Robinson has shown to stubbornly resist and resent questioning and change under any conditions. Prejudices and superstitions of all kinds are among the stubborn decorations of man's psyche. It is regrettable—more, it is shameful, but it is no cause for wonder—that they throw us, far more often than we successfully contend with them.

For another: our psychological posture is prostrate. With much activity outside, our spirit is strangely inactive. We are so habituated to living miserably, that it is hard for most of us to realize that we contain within us the possibility of living otherwise. It is difficult for people born and reared in prison to envisage and wish for a free life. We have lied and cheated so much and so long, that we have become cynical as to the existence of real virtue. Too much routine and cheap pleasure, and perhaps an overdose of book learning, have dulled our sense of potentialities. Too little meaning too long in life has led us to doubt that life has any real significance. When men are in psychological states of these kinds, it is difficult for positive appeals to energize them. They are inclined not to see or recognize good means when these are offered them. They are inclined to let the best of tools lie useless. And thus we face the possibility that we, who have almost enough knowledge to separate the atom, may fail to separate men from their antagonisms.

Notes

1   A series of articles by Waldo Frank, in *The New Republic*, 1927–28.
2   Articles by Joseph Wood Krutch, in *The Atlantic Monthly*, 1927–28.
3   *Philosophy*, by Bertrand Russell.
4   *The Mind in the Making*, by James Harvey Robinson. New York and London: Harper and Brothers, 1921.
5   *Where is Civilization Going?* by Scott Nearing.
6   *The New Universe*, by Baker Brownell.
7   See Chapter VII, "The Sickness of an Acquisitive Society", *The Mind in the Making*.
8   See *Anthropology*, by A. L. Kroeber, particularly the first five chapters.
9   "The Crock of Problems," by Jean Toomer.
10   General psychological facts bearing on this conclusion will be found in *Behaviorism*, by John B. Watson.
11   *Heredity and Human Affairs*, by Edward M. East.
12   "The Future of America, A Biological Forecast," anonymous, in *Harper's Magazine*, April 1928.
13   In this connection, see *The Advancing South*, by Edwin Mims.
14   For a concise statement of this maxim, together with data to this effect drawn from a study of racial crossing in America, see *The American Negro*, by Melville J. Herskovits.

Chapter 45

Nancy Cunard (1896–1965)

"HER LADYSHIP," *BLACK MAN AND WHITE LADYSHIP: AN ANNIVERSARY* (1931)

NANCY CUNARD WAS THE MODERNIST New Woman par excellence: a society debutante turned flapper, she was sexually liberated, politically radical, and tirelessly provocative. While she has often been dismissed as a dilettante, her anti-racist activism led to disinheritance by her family and, when she traveled through America with the African American actor Paul Robeson, anonymous death threats. *Black Man and White Ladyship* is a direct attack aimed at Cunard's mother, Lady Maud Alice Burke Cunard, who was born in America and married into the Cunard family, whose immense shipping lines notably included the *Titanic*, and who was a patroness and muse of artists such as the Irish novelist George Moore and the British composer Thomas Beecham, both of whom Cunard also satirizes in the piece. Cunard's portrait of "Her Ladyship" is a scathing indictment of race, class, and sexual prejudices within British "society." Though deeply personal, the essay's polemic extends well beyond family grievances and includes a comprehensive dismantling of racist assumptions as well as a political invective against contemporary cases of racial injustice such as the Scottsboro Boys trial. The Francophilia that Cunard wields against American and British racism would later be refuted by writers such as Frantz Fanon, who exposed the racism within French *fraternité*; however, it was also highly typical of a time when Paris was the adopted homeland of African American artists such as Josephine Baker and Louis Armstrong.

Nancy Cunard, "Her Ladyship," *Black Man and White Ladyship: An Anniversary*. London: Utopia Press, 1931. 1–11.

Her Ladyship

An anniversary is coming and that is why this is printed now, and the reason for its having been written will, I imagine, be clear to those who read it.

By anniversary I am not, indeed, referring to Christmas, but to the calendric moment of last year when the Colour Question first presented me personally with its CLASH or SHOCK aspect.

I have a Negro friend, a very close friend (and a great many other Negro friends in France, England and America). Nothing extraordinary in that. I have also a mother—whom we will at once call: Her Ladyship. We are extremely different but I had remained on fairly good (fairly distant) terms with her for a number of years. The english channel and a good deal of determination on my part made this possible. I sedulously avoid her social circle both in France and in England. My Negro friend has been in London with me five or six times. So far so good. But, a few days before our going to London last year, what follows had just taken place, and I was unaware of it until our arrival. At a large lunch party in Her Ladyship's house things are set rocking by one of those bombs that throughout her 'career' Margot Asquith, Lady Oxford, has been wont to hurl. No-one could fail to wish he had been at that lunch to see the effect of Lady Oxford's entry: "Hello Maud, what is it now—drink, drugs or niggers?" (A variant is that by some remark Her Ladyship had annoyed the other Ladyship, who thus triumphantly retaliated.) The house is a seemly one in Grosvenor Square and what take place in it is far from 'drink, drugs or niggers.' There is confusion. A dreadful confusion between Her Ladyship and myself! For I am known to have a great Negro friend—the drink and the drugs do not apply. Half of social London is immediately telephoned to: "Is it *true* my daughter knows a Negro?" etc., etc.

It appears that Sir Thomas Beecham, in the light of 'the family friend' was then moved sufficiently to pen me a letter, in the best Trollope style, in which he pointed out that, as the only one qualified to advise, it would, at that juncture, be a grave mistake to come to England with a gentleman of american-african extraction whose career, he believed, it was my desire to advance, as, while friendships between races were viewed with tolerance on the continent, by some, it was . . . in other words it was a very different pair of shoes in England especially as viewed by the Popular Press!. This letter (which was sent to the wrong address and not received till a month later on my return to Paris) was announced by a telegram "strongly advising" me not to come to London until I got it adding that the subject was unmentionable by wire! I was packing my trunk and laid the telegram on top – time will show. . . . We took the four o'clock train.

What happened in London?

Some detectives called, the police looked in, the telephone rang incessantly at our hotel. The *patron* (so he said) received a *mysterious message* that he himself would be imprisoned "undt de other vil be kilt." Madame wept: "Not even a *black* man, why he's only *brown*." Her Ladyship did not go so far as to step round herself. The Popular Press was unmoved. This lasted about a month and I used to get news of it daily, enough to fill a dossier on the hysteria caused by a difference of pigmentation.

The question that interested a good many people for two and a quarter years (does Her Ladyship know or not?) was thus brilliantly settled.

But, your Ladyship, you cannot kill or deport a person from England for being a Negro and mixing with white people. You may take a ticket to the cracker southern States of U.S.A. and assist at some of the choice lynchings which are often announced in advance. You may add your purified-of-that-horrible-american-twang voice to the yankee outbursts: America for white folks—segregation for the 12 million blacks we can't put up with—or do without . . . .

No, with you it is the other old trouble—class.

Negroes, besides being black (that is, from jet to as white as yourself but not so pink) have not yet 'penetrated into London Society's consciousness.' You exclaim: they are not 'received.' (You would be surprised to know just how much they are 'received'.) They are not found in the Royal Red Book. Some big hostess give a lead and the trick is done!

For as yet only the hefty shadow of the Negro falls across the white assembly of High Society and spreads itself, it would seem, quite particularly and agonisingly over you.

And what has happened since this little dust-up of December last, 1930? We have not met, I trust we shall never meet again. You have cut off, first a quarter (on plea of your high income tax) than half of my allowance. You have stated that I am out of your will. Excellent—for at last we have a little truth between us. The black man is a well-known factor in the changing of testaments (at least in America), and parents, as we all know, are not to be held responsible for the existence of children.

Concerning this last I have often heard Her Ladyship say that it is the children who owe their parents nothing. But I am grateful to her for the little crop of trivalia that has flowered this year:

Mr. George Moore—(at one time her best friend and thence my first friend) whose opinion I was interested to have on the whole matter which I obtained by the silence that followed my frank letter to him—was said to have decided not to leave me his two Manets as he intended, but has subsequently contradicted this . . . .

Her Ladyship's hysteria has produced the following remarks:

that—no hotel would accommodate my black friend.

that—he was put out of England (exquisitely untrue, for we came, stayed and left together after a month.)

that—she would not feel *chic* in Paris any longer as she had heard that all the chic Parisians nowadays consorted with Negroes.

that—I now wrote for the Negro Press. (One poem and one article have appeared in the Crisis, New-York.)

that—where would I be in a few years' time.

that she does not mind the Negroes now artistically or in an *abstract* sense but . . . oh, that terrible colour (I invite Her Ladyship to send in writing a short definition of a Negro in the *abstract sense*.)

that—she knew *nothing at all of the whole thing* till Mr. Moore read her my letter. Now, to be exact: my letter to Mr. Moore was written Jan. 24 whereas Her Ladyship severely put through it several friends of mine in the preceding December, and had her bank signify to me on Jan. 21, 1931, that owing to the exigencies of her Income Tax. . . . I suspect Her Ladyship of having conveniently forgotten that what seems indeed to have struck her as a bomb exploded before many witnesses in her own house. (This is very interesting and I don't doubt the psychologists have many such cases on their books—the washing of hands, let us add, by the main party.)

I am told that Her Ladyship was invited to a night-club, saw some coloured singers, turned faint and left . . . yet at least one paid coloured entertainer has been to her house.

I am told that she believes all the servants in a London house gave notice because a coloured gentleman came to dinner.

AND I AM TOLD

that Sir Thomas Beecham says I ought to be tarred and feathered!

It is now necessary to see Her Ladyship in her own fort, to perceive her a little more visually.

I will ring up the curtain on a typical scene. *Petite* and desirable as per all attributes of the Nattier court lady she is in militant mood over the contents of a Book on Beauty which is just out. She figures in it, pleasantly enough—a few words endow her with the brightness of the canary and the charm of the Dresden shepherdess. Other beauties, more or less descriptively, have been compared to Madonnas, Bacchantes, Robot women and nippy, flat-chested messenger boys. Her Ladyship has just thrown this 25/- worth of modern history into the fire and with a poker holds it down. A beautiful, but roman-catholic lady is present. This alarms her greatly, for there is a photograph of her in the book too, and for oneself to be burned if only on paper . . . a malaise comes at the thought of the little wax effigies. Her Ladyship swears such things ought to be put down—she is *not* going to be a Dresden shepherdess—at least not in that copy.

But the memory of it cannot be put in the fire. What is the matter with people these days? Bolshevism is going on too, England breaking up. As for that rich young couple in the Labour party . . . she really doesn't want them in her house though she does invite them. And why *does* Mr. S, when she asks him point blank what he thinks of the British Aristocracy, answer "I really know nothing about it"—what does he *mean*? The die-hards come and tell her they alone can 'save the country.' Meanwhile, she is worried enough saving her skin—from the authors, for they have discovered her and come to meet. And after due gestation. . . . Well, she will never speak to *them* again, says she—to the sly edification of the next lot. Boiling point is often reached. Her Ladyship may be as buoyant as a dreadnought but one touch of ridicule goes straight to her heart. And she is so alone—between these little lunches of sixteen, a few callers at ten, and two or three invitations per night.

Some of the afternoons are for the Art game or Picture racket. This consists of being *done*. Done by dealers and galleries in the peculiar ramifications of interchange. A good or a valuable paining is traded for a questionable one—then two doubtfuls against a decidedly bad one. After receiving the hesitating criticism of the habitués this last passes quickly into the wedding-present zone. A Marie Laurencin costs three hundred pounds, but Her Ladyship's walls, besides six or seven real ones, show two excellent 'in the manner of' executed expressly at thirty pounds each. Meanwhile a Braque, a Masson, a Picasso drawing have gone their way. "And nobody ever tells me." It is impossible to tell her ladyship anything. A variant of the Art game is the Jewel racket. (Same system, same result.)

In the Sunday Express of Nov. 22, 1931, can be read in detail of how Her Ladyship spends a fortune on clothes she never wears. "I have not the faintest idea of how much I spend on clothes every year—it may run into thousands. I have never bothered to think about it. But that is because I do not have to bother about money." (Which tallies interestingly with her bank's statement concerning the exigencies of her Income Tax—see previously.) . . . "I want to tell you candidly why it is that so-called 'Society' women spend so much on their clothes. It is not that the cost of each garment is so very large; it is simply that we won't be bothered."

The Market may be going on at any time, and generally is. Others play it but Her Ladyship plays it best. Rich Mrs. XYZ will be "taken out" if she guesses or takes the hint that she is to do her duty by . . . (the object varies). No sign of the hint ever being administered! But the participants are well-trained, each is looking for what the other can supply, and each felicitously finds. Many results have been come by in this excellent manner. Snobbery opens purses, starvation fails.

Her Ladyship's own snobbery is quite simple. If a thing is *done* she will, with a few negligible exceptions, do it too. And the last person she has talked to is generally right, providing he is *someone*. The British Museum seems to guarantee that African art is art? some dealers, too, are taking it up, so the thick old Congo ivories that she thinks are slave bangles are perhaps not so hideous after all though still very *strange*; one little diamond one would be better. . . . though of course that is different.

Her Ladyship likes to give—and to control. It is unbearable for her not to be able to give someone something. But suppose they don't want it—what does this *mean*? Her reaction to being given something herself generally produces the phrase that people shouldn't do such things! Yet the house is full of noble gifts.

Her ladyship has a definite fear of certain words. Some days she will even shy at the word "lover." But as for the tabooed subject of pederasty it is frequently introduced and worried like a fox in death-throes by a whole pack of . . . allusions. An unsafe enough topic in this milieu but made positively, imminently hot by the hostess' concern to hear about something she still can't quite believe. . . . "You know, those dreadful people who . . . well, you know those horrid . . ." and in a whisper "I'm told he got a loathsome disease, *an old man's disease*, like that." The homo-sexuals present grin. " Just her way." One or two, a touch uneasy, confides to her privately his unrequited passion for some woman. The blind does its work.[1] And the subject goes on merrily—sometimes unwittingly. "We all say now —— is a fairy, he is so . . . unreal, so . . . inhuman—yes-he-is-like-a-fairy, he-is-a-fairy-don't-you-think?" Wilde's case is really too *on*pleasant to be discussed. Of course the classics . . . it is different— what didn't they do in those days? But oh dear me, no-one who may ever have had any trouble that way will ever be spoken to by her again. He will be spoken *of*. And how.

Another time it is Communism. "You don't mean to say those people you talk of are communists? they couldn't be, no-one as intelligent, as intellectual as they are. . . . You can't *know* people like that," etc. . . . And away with the troubling thought. Her Ladyship is the most conscientious of ostriches and when she comes up again she hopes the *on*pleasant thing has disappeared. Perhaps it doesn't really exist. She is also a great cross-questioner and all her ingenuous ingenuity is seen at work on the picking of brains. As those she puts through it are generally less quick in defence than she is in attack, and as she has a fantastic imagination she generally arrives at some result. Look out! as in the farce, evidence will be taken down, altered and used against you. It will make quite a farce in itself. She is a great worker for she is never content to leave things as they are. In digging away she may turn up some startling facts. She is shocked. She is suspicious. All is not as it should be. She does not recognise . . . there may be no precedent—why it may even be scandalous. . . . it *is* scandalous! it is unheard of!! WHAT is to be done? Why, talk about it! What do people say? A mountain is thrown up by this irreducible mole. There—of course it is *monstrous!* It cannot be true . . . and, though it is she who has informed the world, she is astounded presently when it all gets out of hand and falls back on her in anything but gentle rain.

Her Ladyship is american and this is all part of that great american joke: *l'inconscience*. Here she is, ex-cathedra at the lunch table, here she is telling some specimen A1 illiterate of the greatness of the last great book, here—wistfully puzzled by some little matter everyone knows, here—praising rightly, praising wrongly, making and missing the point all in one breath. Generous to the rich, trying always to do the right thing (serve only the best champagne, the food is always perfect). One day the footmen have frayed trousers. The butler has taken a leaf from Her Ladyship's book and explains that *no good enough* ready-made trousers are procurable in London, and that the tailor being dear, and slow . . . he falters. There is a scene. The interior economy is impeccable.

All this is the lighter side and to one who can stomach its somewhat suspect 57 varieties it may prove an acceptable entertainment not lacking in style. But let him look to his possible enemies that also frequent the house—should one of these, how easily, impress Her Ladyship that for any reason he is undesirable he will find the door shut. He may get through it again if someone considerable enough puts in a good word—then, like to like, he may do the same to his detractor. The wheel turns. Is it an amusing atmosphere? *It is a stultifying hypocrisy.* Yet, away from it it has no importance; it is, yes *it is unreal.* There is no contact, the memories of it are so many lantern-slides. They move and shift together in a crazy blur of dixhuitième, gold-plate and boiserie, topped with the great capital C, Conversation, rounded off with snobbery and gossip. The company has got mixed up with the background and the *savonnerie* it all makes waves for a moment in the wind of this distant and real place where I find myself suddenly wondering if it all still goes on . . . .

Then—Her voice went cold on the telephone—"You mean to say my daughter does know a Negro and that you know him too? Well, don't speak of it to anyone—nobody knows anything about it. *Good Bye.*"

The black man

Consider the following extract of what happened. From 1619 to after the middle of the 19th century hundreds of thousands of Negroes, men, women and children, were sold, stolen and torn out of Africa. They were herded into boats at one time specially built for their transport. The trade prospered; more profits were made at it, and more quickly, than at any other trade in history. Its apex, in number of slaves shipped from Africa to the New World, was the last two decades of the 18th and the first two of the 19th centuries—about the time there was most agitation for its abolition. An estimate puts the figure at over 100,000 slaves a year. On the special boats the slaves were manacled to each other two by two and to the ship itself; a space of 6ft. by 1ft. 4 was allotted each on deck for the many weeks of the voyage. At night they were stuffed into the hold. Many would be found dead in the morning. Those that looked for death from starvation were forcibly fed—many hanged themselves, leapt overboard, died of the flux and of despair. They were made to jump up and down in their irons after eating; this was called 'dancing,' to obtain exercise. They were flogged, tortured and maimed. After three or four such passages the slave ships had to be abandoned—having become unusable from filth. The stench of them spread some four miles out at sea. Once landed the slaves were sold by auction. Everyone knows how thing went for them till 1863. 244 years of slavery in America, and Charles Lynch existed—a Virginian *Quaker*. From the World Almanac figures — *admitted official* figures,—3,226 Negroes have been lynched in U.S.A. between 1885 and 1927, an average of over 6 a month.

For the first six months of this year, 1931, 30 cases of Negro lynching are reported. Nine young coloured labourers are now in jail in Alabama (the Scottsboro case) pending electrocution (for eight of them, and life-imprisonment for the ninth, a boy of 14) on a false charge of attempted 'intimacy' with two white prostitutes who later stated they did *not* recognise the accused. After a first trial and condemnation the case has been postponed for re-trial in Jan. next, but the possibilities are that the verdict will hold good and come into effect, unless the mob take the law into its own hands and treats itself to a sight of "the quickest way"—lynching. The authorities take part in, often encourage the lynching. In the name of white american womanhood! Yet the fathers and mothers and ancestors of this superlative womanhood (as well as of the manhood that so superlatively 'protects' it) were in a very great number of cases suckled at the black breast. I asked a Virginian how these two things can be accorded. He replied promptly "Oh d'black women 'r allright separately—but yu *caun'* go raoun' 'n tawk 'n all that with the colored folks, yu just *caun'*—there's *tu many*. Yu caun' explain these things to 'n english person." I think one can explain the Virginian in two words: Fear and jealousy. But d'black women 'r awlright, were very much alright for breeding bastards as new hands on the master's plantation. These were invariably treated worse than the rest. It is now legally laid down in some states that one-sixteenth of black blood constitutes a Negro. No wonder there are so many! The 100 per cent. white americans (and they are all 100 per cent. he-males and 100 per cent. supreme examples of white womanhood) go so far as to profess quite friendly if distant feeling towards their long-suffering ex-slaves—only the damned niggers must be kept in their place and 'yu *caun* go raoun' 'n talk with them an' all that because there's *tu many*. Why not send them all back to Africa? A little matter of between 12 and 13 million. Let us also scrap machinery and have the next war fought by representatives with stone cannon-balls.

Now how does it seem to you put this way: several hundreds of thousands of whites have been torn from their country, chained in pairs to boats, flogged across the Atlantic, flayed at work by a nigger overseer's whip, hunted and shot for trying to get away, insulted, injured, thrown out, emprisoned, threatened with lynching if they dare ride in the black man's part of the train, their houses burned down, if, despite everything, they seem to get too prosperous, their women spoken of as 'dirty white sluts' and raped at every corner by a big Negro buck, told there's no job in the office for anyone with a bleedin white mug and that their stinkin white bitches needn't go on trying to 'pass' nor hope to send their white vermin to any decent school—Over 300 years of it in all its different phases, substituting white for black all along the line. . . . You would say Justice was strangely absent. You would say the hell of a lot more than that. Had this happened also to the white race as it has to the black one may well wonder which would have come out of it best.

I suppose if the Esquimaux had been more accessible the same as with the Negroes might have taken place. Only a less frightening miscegenation would have ensued—the white could have swallowed them quicker. Nothing to be alarmed about. But the Devil is a Black Man. Do you fear the Devil? Of course you do still — though God has gone by the board. You have the whimpering nursery mind in the age of fact. Or if the black man is Paul Robeson . . . ah then it is quite different, he becomes 'the noble Moor.' Yet you may think yourself too good to sit with him at supper after the play.

For Louis XIV on the other hand it was an honour to entertain and make presents to a royal black man. Negroes were invited, fêted, sought after in the salons of 17th and 18th century France. In the realm of war black Haitian Christopher was Napoleon's successful and unsubdued antagonist. From even the briefest study of colour-prejudice it would seem that this is based on economic reasons, it can be traced back to these.[2] Many people of different classes have no race or colour prejudice whatsoever. In France it is non-existent. It is not a problem but a glory to have so many black subjects. When in Montmartre some Negroes shot in self-defence a bunch of drunken yankee sailors who had attacked them the french took the Negroes' side. A french person experiences no difficulty in shaking hands with a black man; the Negro is not excluded from commercial enterprise and competition, from social contacts, from social functions. Segregation *as a word* would have to be explained. The same with Germany to an even greater extent.

Not so with America. Its inconsistencies, too, are flaming.

When the american gold star mothers were sent over at government expense to visit the war graves the Negro gold star mothers were segregated in a special ship (many refused this highly questionable honour). But this year General Pershing, and other american notables including the ambassador, presided at a banquet given in a very smart Parisian restaurant at government expense to these same Negro mothers who had every right to consider themselves particularly insulted by the differentiation made in their transport and during their tour, the more so as they were no longer in white America. To have the Negro killed in war for 'his' country is of course perfectly laudable—as well as indicated—but later to put the black mothers on a par with the white . . . an official banquet no doubt obviates the difference.

I believe that no fallacy about the Negroes is too gross for the Anglo Saxon to fall into. You are told they are coarse, lascivious, lazy, ignorant, undisciplined, unthrifty, undependable, drunkards, jealous, envious, violent, that their lips, noses and hair are ugly, that they have a physical odour—In the name of earth itself what peoples, individually, can disclaim any of these? The knave and the fool will out, the dirty will stink. But *all* Negroes are said to be thus, and all of it. The nigger Christy Minstrel conception prevails—to be fair, mainly with the older generation—as does the Pip and Squeak Daily Mirror children's page idea of the Bolshevik, all beard and bombs. So perhaps in London's high social circles of supposedly well educated arts-and-letters-appreciating aristocrats and hostesses it is a thing of age. It is certainly a thing of ignorance. These people simply do not *know* (and may be incapable of believing) that very great changes have taken place amongst the Negroes in America. (As the 12 million there are anglo-saxon by civilisation, education and speech, the greatest mass all together, as such, where it can be examined in the most advanced world-development

conditions the American Negro is always taken as the case in point, the example, the leader.)
Academies, colleges, schools, newspaper association, business of most sorts, science, medicine, sociology, philosophy, research work of every kind, societies, art, music, drama, and a
definite, definable intellectual and literary movement which has a great deal to show in as
brief a time as the first thirty years of this century—all these entirely Negro—are the
proof. The days of Rastus and Sambo are long gone and will not return. The english prejudice
gets a hard knock by the revelation that the pore ole down-trodden canticle-singing
nigger daddy who used to be let out to clown for the whites has turned into the very much
up to date, well educated, keen, determined man of action (in all and any of these different
fields) who is making it his business, for himself and his race, not to be put upon any more.
In fact the *real* freeing. Though the lynchings and other abuses go on and on he will certainly
achieve it.

Are intellectuals generally the least biassed in race questions? Here are two
reactionaries:—

A little conversation with Mr. George Moore in Ebury St.

Self Yes, people certainly feel very differently about race. I cannot understand colour
    prejudice. Do you think you have it?
G.M. No, I don't think so.
Self Have you ever known any people of colour?
G.M. No.
Self What, not even an Indian?
G.M. No—though my books are translated into Chinese.
Self Not even an Indian . . . such as might have happened had you met, shall we say, an Indian
    student. Don't you think you'd like to talk to an intelligent Indian or Negro?
G.M. calmly No. I do not think so. I do not think I should get on with a black man or a brown
    man. (*then warmly, opening the stops*) I think the best I could do is a yel-low man!

Thus Mr. Moore—after a whole long life of 'free' thought, 'free' writing, anti-bigotry
of all kinds, with his engrossment in human nature, after the *injustice* of the Boer war, as he
says himself, had driven him out of England. . . . There is no consistency; there *is* race or
colour prejudice.

Sir Thomas Beecham's remark about the Negro making his own music left me puzzled,
and I don't doubt, puzzled for ever. Her Ladyship was evincing a very querulous astonishment at the Negro (in general) having any achievements (in particular). I was informing her
that, for one, everybody knows the Negroes have a particular genius for music. At which
Sir Thomas condescendingly remarked "They make their own music too." The tone of this
pronouncement was so superior that I remained too dumb to ask whether at that moment he
meant tribal or jazz. And Her Ladyship, far from being quieted became as uneasy as an animal
scenting a danger on the wind.

This is all what's aptly enough called '*Old* stuff.' What's actual since some twenty years
is a direct African influence in sculpture and painting. None but fools separate Africa from the
living Negro. But the american press is constantly confusing their civic nationality with their
blood nationality; (the 12 million blacks are the loyalest, best *americans*; a Negro in the States
has written a good book, therefore he is a good *american* writer; the same of the coloured
musician, the coloured artist, etc.).

'In Africa,' you say, 'the Negro is a savage, he has produced nothing, he has no history.'
It is certainly true he has not got himself mixed up with machinery and science to fly the
Atlantic, turn out engines, run up skyscrapers and contrive holocausts. There are no tribal
Presses emitting the day's lies and millions of useless volumes. There remain no written

records; the wars, the kingdoms and the changes have sufficed unto themselves. It is not one country but many; well over 400 separate languages and their dialects are known to exist. Who tells you you are the better off for being 'civilised' when you live in the shadow of the next war or revolution in constant terror of being ruined or killed? Things in Africa are on a different scale—but the european empire-builders have seen, are seeing to this hand over fist. And what, against this triumph of organised villainy had the black man to show? His own example of Homo Sepiens on better terms with life than are the conquering whites. Anthropology gives him priority in human descent. He had his life, highly organised, his logic, his customs, his laws rigidly adhered to. He made music and unparalleled rhythm and some of the finest sculpture in the world. Nature gave him the best body amongst all the races. Yet he is a 'miserable savage' because there are no written records, no super-cities, no machines—but to prove the lack of these an insuperable loss, a sign of racial inferiority, you must attack the root of all things and see where—if anywhere—lies truth. There are many truths. How come, white man, is the rest of the world to be re-formed in your dreary and decadent image?

Notes

1   I have even been *proposed* to in Her L's house by a noted member of the cult—pretty half-heartedly—
     still it was part of the shield.
2   Walter White's admirably clear book *Rope and Faggot* and Professor Scott Nearing's equally fine *Black
     America* are the best approach to this immense subject.

PART VII

Global modernisms

"All literature becomes propaganda once you show it to someone else."

Lu Xun (1928)

"Poetry has an aim: absolute human freedom."

Malcolm de Chazal (1947)

In his essay " 'Simultaneous Uncontemporaneities': Theorising Modernism and Empire," Patrick Williams examines the "mutual impact" of modernism and imperialism as cultural and political forces. He notes that modernism and "high imperialism" appeared simultaneously at the end of the nineteenth century (the Berlin Conference, the Scramble for Africa) and that both collapsed concurrently around 1945. In Williams' view, modernism can be understood, in part, as a "marker of crisis within European colonialism" (17). Following Edward Said's argument in *Culture and Imperialism* (1994) that the narrative representation of empire links realism and modernism, Williams reads modernist crises (epistemological uncertainty, shock, instability) and ambivalence as aesthetic and historical and, perhaps, as having as much to do with imperial exhaustion and collapse as with metropolitan culture's technological and scientific changes and advances.

In a New Modernist Studies analytical remapping, a dynamic and transcultural understanding would dislodge modernism from a strictly metropolitan location and focus instead on the transmission of aesthetics and ideologies, and the mobility of subjects, both metropolitan and colonial. These intersecting and colliding circuits of bodies, artistic and philosophical movements, politics and aesthetics are what Said refers to as cultural voyages out and voyages in – overlapping and distinct processes, polyphonous and diverse articulations of modernity in modernism's various forms. To address modernity's spatial and temporal peculiarities and specificities, Williams borrows the term "simultaneous uncontemporaneities" from the Frankfurt School critic and theorist of utopia, Ernst Bloch. Williams notes that,

> In this perspective, the related and different temporalities and trajectories of modernism and modernity (and imperialism) would be "combined and uneven" within the same social formation, but there would also be simultaneous

uncontemporaneities, in that while at a particular moment modernism might be
fully developed in Europe, it might not exist at all in Africa, for example.[1]

Anthropologist Anna Tsing describes these distinct manifestations of modern change as
friction, "the awkward, unequal, unstable, and creative quality of interconnection across
difference."[2]

An illustration of such friction in narrative form can be found in Mulk Raj Anand's " 'How
Unpleasant to Meet Mr. Eliot': A Talk in the Etoile with T.S. Eliot and Bonamy Dobrée," a
remembered and recreated conversation in his *Conversations in Bloomsbury* (1981). In the
memoir, Anand casts himself as a "naive poet of the earth" who is unnerved by the meeting's
formal setting and by Eliot's austere manner and businessman's attire. The two converse at
cross-purposes on the subjects of poetry, Indian mysticism, and politics. Eliot disparages the
Indian uprising: "Look how Indians throw bombs. . . . Look at you people running riot in spite
of Gandhi's talk of nonviolence" (43–44), while Anand tries to explain why his generation of
Indian artists and activists are uninterested in Karma and Indian religions' maintenance
of communalist and sectarian divisions. The young poet speaks of independence and the
possibilities of India's pan-nationalist rebirth; Eliot, of disenchantment, doomsday, and his
opposition to defiance of British law. Anand silently observes, "I felt that there was no way
for anyone to suggest to the divided self of Eliot that millions of people survived through
sheer instinct" (*Conversations in Bloomsbury* 49). One of the most prominent differences
in these discrepant modernities is Western artists' and intellectuals' cynicism about or distrust
of nationalist passions, an exhaustion related to global and civil wars (for example, World
War I and the Spanish Civil War) and the fervor for independence and nationhood in colonized
African, Caribbean, Latin American, and Asian countries. This impasse in political sympathy,
respect, and understanding is dramatized in the final section of E.M. Forster's *A Passage to
India* (1924), when their words, horses, and the earth itself rise up between the formerly
hopeful friends, the romantic Dr. Aziz and the English liberal idealist, Cyril Fielding. In the
final section of the novel in particular, Forster's narrator displays what seems the author's own
uncertainty and ambivalence about Indian and Islamic nationalism. The aesthetic implications
of these geopolitical continental shifts are also evident in some of the global modernists'
investments in realist and revolutionary aesthetics; communism and socialism appealed to
many of the colonized subjects, as did an embrace of culture as a productive disseminator of
ideology, a view echoed in the epigraph from the Chinese poet Lu Xun above.

Another historically flexible and particularized vision of the modern can be found
in Marshall Berman's *All That Is Solid Melts into Air: The Experience of Modernity* (1982).
For Berman, "Modernism is realism," is dependent, in definition and conceptualization, upon
analyses of the ways in which people live and move in and through the world. Modernism, he
notes,

> cuts across physical and social space, and reveals solidarities between great
> artists and ordinary people, and between residents of what we clumsily call the
> Old, the New and the Third Worlds. It unites people across the bounds of ethnicity
> and nationality, of sex and class and race. . . . If we think of modernism as a
> struggle to make ourselves home in a constantly changing world, we will realize
> that no mode of modernism can ever be definitive.[3]

Berman's views of modernism as an aesthetic and modernity as a historical experience
of change are historically and geographically expansive; modernity is associated with the
technological-industrial, political, philosophical, and scientific developments that have typically distinguished the Western-European modern world, but modern forces of change manifest

differently in cultural and geographical spaces (those "simultaneous uncontemporaneities" to which Patrick Williams refers). Berman uses his 1987 visit to Brasília, one of the most ultra-modern, planned cities of the 1950s and '60s, to exemplify modernity's efflorescence in Latin America and its unpredictable and complex utopian and dystopian double nature: the Brazilian city designed by the Le Corbusier-inspired "disciples," Lucio Costa and Oscar Niermeyer, concretely realizes "the new" and simultaneously destroys the city's vibrant communal public space. However "late" Brasília's modern emergence was temporally, the social, economic, cultural, political, and environmental dynamics of modernization that Berman's example illuminates remain relevant today, for example with the twenty-first-century modernization of China and that nation's enterprising expansion across the globe on the African continent and beyond.

Marxist cultural critic Raymond Williams similarly questions modernism's parameters by challenging its academic and institutional definitions with what he refers to as "real truths" and material evidence at "the first historical level."[4] Williams' critique of literary high modernism is underscored by his Marxist view of history and (base-superstructure) notions of cultural production; the economic structure of a society affects, in a diverse range of ways, all of its institutions and traditions. Williams eschews disciplinarily created markers of distinct periods to focus instead on the dynamics of change; in his view, all literary productions contain and can articulate social facts. His engaged artist is an observer and documenter of processes of historical transformation and socio-economic tensions and contradictions; the artist uses imaginative culture to express in form what he or she is witnessing or experiencing. A poem or novel is read as a "structure of feeling," a form which contains concrete evidence of material conditions on the ground; culture, in Williams' view, does not necessarily represent the "best that has been known and thought in the world," as Matthew Arnold proclaimed. Rather, expressive culture is historical evidence of conflict and change; it reflects crises of perspectives. Culture reflects the state of things and searchingly maps out possibilities for new ways of being, seeing, and knowing. Some of the questions that Williams asked about institutionalized high modernism remain cogent and relevant. Why, for example, are social realists who are contemporary with the period of modernity typically excluded from the modernist canon? In his view, Charles Dickens is as inventive and modern an observer of the transforming world as James Joyce; both of their bodies of work express, in different aesthetic modes, the development of modern consciousness. Why did the symbolist poets became canonically "superannuated" by the imagists, surrealists, and formalists? How has the modernist myth of detachment, rootlessness, exile, and national disengagement overshadowed more nationally and ideologically invested modernist artists and works, for example the Harlem Renaissance writers, Négritude poets, and Indian fiction writers like Anand and Munshi Premchand, who simultaneously maintained cosmopolitan aesthetics, realist traditions, and connections to specifically local commitments?

Raymond Williams' modernist critiques also reject modernism's linear historiography, the trajectory from the modern to the postmodern: "If we are to break out of the non-historical fixity of post-modernism, then we must search out and counterpose an alternative tradition taken from the neglected works left in the wide margin of the century . . ."[5] These questions about the mapping of modernity and modernist temporalities – modernity's wheres, hows, and whens – have been further explored in recent modernist studies. Laura Doyle and Laura Winkiel's anthology, *Geomodernisms: Race, Modernism, Modernity* (2005), grew out of two seminars at the Modernist Studies Association's annual conference in 2000. The essays in *Geomodernisms* focus on the plural— *modernisms* —and the colliding and merging significance of perspectives and places. Jahan Ramazani's *A Transnational Poetics* (2009), which examines the fecund and unbounded aspects of the poetic imagination, calls attention to language's dialogical and hybrid nature, to genres' promiscuity, and the cross-pollinating influences of poets' mobility, migration, as well as their diasporic and multiple habits of affiliation and attachment. The specificity of locally inflected modernist representations is also worth noting here: for example, William Faulkner's Mississippi, Jean Toomer's Georgia, Woolf's London, and Joyce's Dublin. The intersections between and across local and global spaces map modernism in ways that scholars are still processing. Toomer's *Cane* (1923) traverses spaces both rural and urban: his rural modern characters are haunted by Georgia's fecund soil and its bloody past; their lives are juxtaposed against the lives of DC urbanites and the city's glaring uncertainties of class and sexual politics. In challenging Harlem Renaissance cosmopolitan expressions and ideals with their insistence on the contemporary significance of agrarian subjects and communities, both Toomer and Zora Neale Hurston were marginalized.

The term "efflorescing modernism," which was coined by Elleke Boehmer,[6] describes the emergence of the modern in different and connected and, often, colliding spaces and times. Paul Gilroy's black Atlantic modernism and Mary Louise Pratt's notion of transcultural contact zones trace patterns of movement – the mobility of people, information, science, art, ideals and ideologies, laws and policies, consumer goods – those material realities to which Berman and Williams refer.[7] Was aesthetic modernism a European continental invention? Were European modern arts responding or relating to traditions from the non-European world, for example, primitivism and orientalism? Did colonial elites embrace and appropriate modernisms for visionary projects and purposes – what Susan Stanford Friedman refers to as indigenized modernism?[8] Pratt's theory of contact zones potentially defuses debates over the directionality of modernism as an import, export, imposition, or appropriation; languages and styles proliferate and mutate heterogeneously, and in ways that reveal social relations as processes of combat and negotiation, selection and interpretation, and reinvention, as well. Aimé Césaire's Afro-Caribbean engagement with symbolist and surrealist poets exhibits this kind of combination of transnational aesthetics and culturally specific interests. Boehmer's recent work examines more closely some of the geographical, political, and cultural relationships that developed in and across metropolitan and colonial boundaries; modern artistic exchanges between colonized elites and metropolitan avant-garde artists, like Irish poet W.B. Yeats and Bengali poet Rabindranath Tagore, are another aspect of the still-emerging history of global modernisms. Patricia Ondek Laurence's *Lily Briscoe's Chinese Eyes: Bloomsbury, Modernism and China* (2003) depicts the intersecting paths of Tagore and the modern Chinese poets, and the Chinese fiction writer Shuhua Ling's desired mentorship and correspondence with Virginia Woolf. Robin D.G. Kelley's edited collection, *Black, Brown, and Beige: Surrealist Writings from the African Diaspora* (2009), contains a vibrant and fecund archive of international Afro-Caribbean efflorescing modernisms.

The works of the writers in this part on "Global modernisms" reveal some of these cultural dynamics and the cross-pollination of traditions, politics, aesthetics, and philosophies. At the turn of the century, Cuban revolutionary thinker and anti-colonial journalist, political theorist, poet, professor, and translator José Martí (1853–95) extolled the virtues of organic intellectuals, against what he considered unnatural European-identified Latin American cosmopolitans. For Martí, Latin America and the Caribbean had their own indigenous cultural resources, which could combat the "artificial" influences of Spanish and French colonizers and provide the foundation for a "natural," dignified, free, and formidable post-colonial regional identity, the "Our America" to which he refers in his legendary essay. A poem from Martí's *Versos sencillos* (*Simple Verses*) would provide the lyrics to Cuba's patriotic anthem, "Guantanamera": "*Yo soy un hombre sincero/De donde crece la palma/Y antes de morirme quiero/Echar mis versos del alma*" ("I am a sincere man/From where the palm tree grows/And before dying I want/To share the verses of my soul").

While for many, the European-started world wars confirmed the most destructive tendencies of nationalism and patriotism, beyond and within the West, present and former colonized subjects were embracing new national and communal possibilities. Cosmopolitan and local colonial modernists selectively used cultural traditions like realistic, oral, and mythic story-telling, vernacular poetics, modern philosophies, aesthetics, and ideas, to articulate post-independence identities, national communities, and international affiliations. In London, the Marxist, communist, and socialist oriented All-India Progressive Writers Association (PWA) embraced the vision of a caste, class, and sect that would obliterate Pan-Indian nationalism and ensure a distinctly modern collective identity and challenge while demystifying local archa-isms and potentially explosive communal divisions. In India, writers like Premchand used realistic and direct storytelling to challenge local superstitions and protest the debasement of women. In *In Another Country: Colonialism, Culture, and the English Novel in India*, a study of the modern Indian novel's literary influences, Priya Joshi depicts a heritage of surprising cross-pollination. Her archival research of Indian publishing patterns, library purchasing, and Indian readers' habits of consumption reveals the influence of "lowbrow" popular English novels, family romances, and social realism and utilitarian problem novels (the conventional novels that Woolf deemed outmoded in "Mr. Bennett and Mrs. Brown") on the formation of modern and contemporary Indian literature. Mulk Raj Anand appreciated the writings of Charles Dickens, Arnold Bennett, and H.G. Wells for their sympathetic concern with the human condition, particularly those "in lower depths" (*Conversations in Bloomsbury* ix). He also claimed Iqbal and James Joyce as major influences; his novels *Untouchable* and *Coolie* use the *Bildungsroman* tradition and modernist existentialism to document the lives of the low-caste central protagonists. Anand, who would leave London to return permanently to India in 1947, became known as the Father of Dalit (untouchables) literature and was referred to as "India's Charles Dickens." In 1946, he started the modernist, Indian, and international art journal, *Marg* (Modernist Art and Architecture Research Group), a publication and a publishing house that still exist. "Marg," the Sanskrit word for "pathways," aptly reflects Anand's hopeful cultural and artistic ideals.

The Russian Revolution, nineteenth-century Russian realists like Ivan Turgenev and Nikolai Gogol, and early modern Russian writers Anton Chekov and Fyodor Dostoyevsky were primary cultural influences on the Chinese modern poet, essayist, and fiction writer, Lu Xun, whose Chinese "imperial" education coincided with early English translations of those writers' works. In his essay "The Ties between Chinese and Russian Literatures" (1932), Xun confesses, "Of course we knew that tsarist Russia was invading China, but that literature taught us the important lesson that there are two sorts of men in the world: the oppressors and the oppressed! From the vantage point of today, this is common knowledge . . . But in those days it was a great discovery." For the Chinese revolutionary poet, Russian literature became "our guide and friend" (Xun, "The Ties" 210). The titles of the literary magazines Xun edited reflect the traces of his artistic and political hopes: *New Youth* and *Sprouts*. Like Jean Toomer, Xun was interested in Esperanto as a politically neutral, stateless, and pacifist language of the future.

The aspiring Indo-Pakistani poet Muhammad Iqbal (1877–1938) blended his family's religious Islamic Sufism with Persian and Urdu poetic traditions. At university in Lahore, he studied law as well as orientalism and English literature with Sir Thomas Walker Arnold. William Cowper, Alfred Tennyson, Henry Wadsworth Longfellow, and other English poets influenced Iqbal's desire to bridge East and West. In 1904, Iqbal, while studying European philosophy at Cambridge University, incorporated into his worldview the works of Friedrich Nietzsche, Henri Bergson, Ralph Waldo Emerson, Johann Wolfgang von Goethe, and George Wilhelm Hegel. (Iqbal wrote tribute poems to many of the German philosophers.) After earning a PhD from Munich University, Iqbal returned to Lahore; he was disaffected with Western materialism, individualism, and decadence, but he maintained selective connections to his immersion in Western tradition. The Nietzschean notion of the will to power, for example, partially informed his anti-imperialist and nationalist politics. Although he died before the creation of Pakistan, Iqbal is considered one of the most influential modern Islamic philosophers for his vision of a global, transnational Islamic revival – the subject of his book *The Reconstruction of Religious Thought in Islam* (1930). Iqbal's "Sare Jahan Se Achcha/ Tarana-e-Hind/Song of India" remains a beloved patriotic song today. The aforementioned Indian poet Rabindranath Tagore authored the national anthems of both India and Bangladesh.

In Paris, symbolism and surrealism, existentialism and cubism,[9] and communist trade unionism, Third World nationalism, and Pan-Africanism influenced the Négritude poets. In 1935 Aimé Césaire, Léopold Senghor, and Léon Damas started the literary review *L'Étudiant Noir* (*The Black Student*), the journal that gave birth to Négritude poetry. Senghor, the first President of post-independence Senegal and author of his country's national anthem, expanded his poetic skills while he was a French army officer imprisoned in a German military camp in 1940; he would later use his rhythmically inflected Négritude poetry to bridge sub-Saharan Africa, northern Africa, and Europe and celebrate African nationalism. Senghor was the first African writer to be elected as a member of l'Académie Française (in June 1983). The writers of the "*Légitime Défense Manifesto*" pungently combined the ideology of Leninist communism with the aesthetics and politics of surrealism; their 1932 manifesto aggressively assails the assimilative or integrative cultural politics of the educated French black middle class. The manifesto's signatories declared international affiliation with all treasonous dreamers who shared their radical rejection of capitalism, imperialism, and the bourgeois status quo; their mission was the liberation of both bodies and the individual and collective minds' unconscious powers.

Mary Louise Pratt notes that, "While subordinate peoples do not usually control what emanates from the dominant culture, they do determine to varying extents what gets absorbed into their own and what it gets used for."[10] In other words, metropolitan culture's power is not wholly hegemonic; global modernists who had access to books and education wrote works that reflect these cultural negotiations, ones that were productive and, sometimes, painfully felt, as well. The stories of the modern Japanese writer Ryunosuke Akutagawa are filled with the conversations of Japanese educated gentlemen, men who are privileged but not rich, cosmopolitan but alienated. They exchange witty repartee in French, German, and English, discuss Marx and Darwin, Strindberg, Wilde, and Shaw, wear treasured *chanpas* (sweaters/ jumpers) from abroad, trade literary and topical riffs, and smoke and philosophize. Yet the traces of subjective displacement and alienation haunt the stories as pungently as do the ghosts and Samurai warriors of the past. In his fiction, Akutagawa, "the father of the Japanese short story," reveals the landscape of changing times; Japan's urbanizing landscape causes feelings of instability and unease. And some of Akutagawa's stories reveal the limitations of his cosmopolitan characters' worldliness and the author's gender anxieties, as well. In "An Enlightened Husband," the aforementioned modern gentleman is cuckolded and betrayed by his wife, who falls under what is depicted as the corrupting influence of a feminist. The Japanese student of German, French, and English literature, admirer of Yeats, Schopenhauer, and Baudelaire who wrote his thesis on William Morris, could not withstand the tumult in the social world and his own mind. The author, whom cultural critic Frederic Jameson identifies as a victim of the colliding forces of late capitalism, committed suicide in July 1927.[11] Perhaps Akutagawa's best-known work is *Rashomon* (1950), Akira Kurosawa's cinematic translation of his short story "In a Grove" (1922) – a story about the uncertain nature of knowledge, truth, and experience.

A central line that runs through many of the global modernists' works is the ethical and rhetorical focus on communal identity. Individualism is identified as a Western affliction; art and beauty are valued for reflection and a range of aesthetics is embraced, but contemplation divorced from action, collective inspiration, and struggle is viewed as decadent. Many global modernist writers produced their works during a period that is often described as late modernist, in and after the late 1930s and '40s; strict temporal markers might, however, be particularly inadequate for understanding the dynamics of international and transnational modernism. Dilip Parameshwar Gaonkar argues that any periodization of modernity and description of cultural modernism that fails to take into account global and political changes would be blind to some of the monumental realities of modernity: "to announce the general end of modernity even as an epoch . . . seems premature, if not patently ethnocentric, at a time when non-Western people everywhere began to engage critically their own hybrid modernities."[12] Even our knowledge of a literary high modernist press like the Woolfs' Hogarth Press may be only partial in formation: the press that first published the works of Sigmund Freud in English and T.S. Eliot's *The Waste Land* also published the works of Caribbean and African nationalists and extensive, explicitly anti-imperialist works, along with the Auden–Spender circle of young radical poets that emerged in the 1930s.[13] A conceptual image of global modernity could be envisioned as a kind of palimpsest or pointillist map, with areas of density, intersecting traces, blurred lines of demarcation, and connections yet to be made – an appropriately modernist mapping.

Notes

1   Patrick Williams 31.
2   Tsing 3.
3   Berman 5–6.
4   Raymond Williams, "When was Modernism?" 33.
5   Raymond Williams, "When was Modernism?" 35.
6   Boehmer, *Colonial and Postcolonial Literature* 130.
7   Pratt 33–40.
8   See Stanford Friedman 425–43.
9   Jean-Paul Sartre wrote, "Orphée noir" ("Black Orpheus"), the introduction to Senghor's anthology of African Francophone poetry, *Anthologie de la nouvelle poésie nègre et malgache* (1948). Pablo Picasso provided the illustrations for Aimé Césaire's collection of poems, *Lost Body* (1950).
10   Pratt 2.
11   See Jameson, "Third World Literature in the Era of Multinational Capitalism."
12   Gaonkar, "On Alternative Modernities" (2001): 14.
13   For example, Edward Thompson's *The Other Side of the Medal* (1925), a critical history of the Indian uprising; J. A Hobson's *Notes on Law and Order* (1926); Alice Ritchie's *Occupied Territory* (1930); K.M. Panikkar, *Caste and Democracy* (1933); and Parmenas Githendu Mockerie, *An African Speaks for His People* (1934). Hogarth also published *The Merttens Lectures on War and Peace, 1927–36*. Their Day-to-Day Pamphlet series (1930–39) addressed world politics, peace, and social justice issues.

Suggested further readings

Akutagawa, Ryunosuke. *Mandarins: Stories by Ryunosuke Akutagawa*. Trans. Charles De Wolf. New York: Archipelago Books, 2007.
——. *Rashomon and Other Stories*. New York: Liveright, 1952.
All-India Progressive Writers Movement (PWA). "London Manifesto." *Left Review* (February 1935). Indian version (October 1935).
Anand, Mulk Raj. *Conversations in Bloomsbury*. Delhi: Oxford UP, 1981, 1995.
——. *Untouchable* (1935). "Introduction" by E.M. Forster. London: Penguin, 1940.
——. *Coolie*. London: Lawrence and Wishart, 1936.
Ardis, Ann L. *Modernism and Cultural Conflict, 1880–1920*. Cambridge: Cambridge UP, 2002.

Barkan, Elazar, and Ronald Bush, eds. *Prehistories of the Future: The Primitivist Project and the Culture of Modernism*. Stanford: Stanford UP, 1995.

Bate, David. *Photography and Surrealism: Sexuality, Colonialism and Social Dissent*. London: I.B. Tauris, 2004.

Begam, Richard, and Michael Valdez Moses, ed. *Modernism and Colonialism: British and Irish Literature, 1899–1939*. Durham, NC: Duke UP, 2007.

Berman, Marshall. *All That Is Solid Melts into Air: The Experience of Modernity*. New York: Penguin, 1988.

Blakeney Williams, Louise. *Modernism and the Ideology of History: Literature, Politics, and the Past*. Cambridge: Cambridge UP, 2002.

Bloch, Ernst. *The Heritage of Our Times* (1935). Hoboken, NJ: Polity, 2009.

Bluemel, Kristin. *George Orwell and the Radical Eccentrics: Intermodernism in Literary London*. London: Palgrave Macmillan, 2004.

——, ed. *Intermodernism: Literary Culture in Mid-Twentieth Century Britain*. Edinburgh: Edinburgh UP, 2009.

Boehmer, Elleke. " 'Immeasurable Strangeness' between Empire and Modernism: W.B. Yeats, Rabindranath Tagore, and Leonard Woolf." *Empire, the National, and the Postcolonial, 1890–1920: Resistance in Interaction*. Oxford: Oxford UP, 2002.

——. *Colonial and Postcolonial Literature: Migrant Metaphors*. Oxford: Oxford UP, 1995.

Booth, Donald J., and Nigel Rigby, ed. *Modernism and Empire*. Manchester: Manchester UP, 2000.

Brooker, Peter, and Andrew Thacker, eds. *Geographies of Modernism*. London: Routledge, 2005.

Bunn, O. "A Plea for the Historical Novel" and Roy Campbell's response to O. Bunn. *Voorslag* 1.5 (October 1926).

Campbell, Roy. "The Significance of Turbott Wolfe." *Voorslag* 1.1 (June 1926): 122–27.

Casement, Roger. *The Diaries of Roger Casement*. Ed. Roger Sawyer. London: Pimlico, 1997.

Césaire, Aimé. *Cahier d'un retour au pays natal (Notebook of a Return to My Native Land)*. Paris: Volontés, 1939.

Chazal, Malcolm de. *Sens-plastique* (1947). Los Angeles: Green Integer, 2007.

Childs, Donald. *Modernism and Eugenics: Woolf, Eliot, Yeats, and the Culture of Degeneration*. Cambridge: Cambridge UP, 2001.

Conisbee Baer, Ben. "Shit Writing: Mulk Raj Anand's *Untouchable*, the Image of Gandhi, and the Progressive Writers' Association." *Modernism/Modernity* 16.3 (September 2009): 575–95.

Conrad Joseph. *Heart of Darkness* (1898). New York: Norton, 2005.

Däumer, Elisabeth, and Shyamal Bagchee, eds. *The International Reception of T.S. Eliot*. New York and London: Continuum, 2007.

Doyle, Laura, and Laura Winkiel, eds. *Geomodernisms: Race, Modernism, Modernity*. Bloomington: Indiana UP, 2005.

Eisenstein, Sergei. "A Dialectical Approach to Film Form" (1929). *Film Form: Essays in Film Theory*. Orlando, FL: Houghton Mifflin Harcourt, 1949.

Forster, E.M. *A Passage to India* (1924). San Diego: Harcourt, 1984.

——. *Alexandria: A History and a Guide* (1922). Garden City, NY: Doubleday Anchor, 1961.

Gaonkar, Dilip Parameshwar, ed. *Alternative Modernities*. Durham: Duke UP, 2001.

Hart, Matthew. *Nations of Nothing But Poetry: Modernism, Transnationalism, and Synthetic Vernacular Writing*. New York: Oxford UP, 2010.

Holtby, Winifred. *Mandoa, Mandoa!: A Comedy of Irrelevance* (1933). New York: Macmillan, 1933.

James, C.L.R. *The Case for West-Indian Self Government*. London: Hogarth Press, Day-to-Day Pamphlet Series, 1933.

Jameson, Frederic. "Third World Literature in the Era of Multinational Capitalism." *Social Text* 15 (Autumn 1986): 65–88.

Jay, Paul. *Global Matters: The Transnational Turn in Literary Studies*. Ithaca: Cornell UP, 2010.

Joshi, Priya. *In Another Country: Colonialism, Culture, and the English Novel in India*. New York: Columbia UP, 2002.

Lawrence, Karen, ed. *Decolonizing Tradition: New Views of Twentieth-Century "British" Literary Canons*. Urbana: U of Illinois P, 1992.

Laye, Camara. *The Dark Child (L'enfant noir)*. London: Collins, 1955.

Marks, Robert B. *The Origins of the Modern World: A Global and Ecological Narrative from the Fifteenth to the Twenty-First Century*. New York: Rowman and Littlefield, 2006.

Miller, Tyrus. *Late Modernism: Politics, Fiction, and the Arts between the World Wars*. Berkeley: U of California P, 1999.

Moore, G.E. *Principia ethica*. New York: Cambridge UP, 1993.

Nichols, Peter. *Modernisms: A Literary Guide*. New York: Palgrave Macmillan, 2009.

Orwell, George. *Burmese Days* (1934). Orlando: Harcourt, 1962.

Panikkar, K.M. *Caste and Democracy*. London: Hogarth Press, 1933.

Plomer, William. *Turbott Wolfe* (1925). New York: Modern Library, 2003.

——. "Johannesburg I & II" and "Ula Mandoa's Dream." *Selected Poems*. Hogarth Press, 1940.

Pratt, Mary Louise. "Arts of the Contact Zone." *Profession* 91 (1991): 33–40.

Premchand, Munshi. "The Aim of Literature." *The Oxford India Premchand*. New Delhi: Oxford UP, 2004.

Racevskis, Karlis. *Modernity's Pretenses: Making Reality Fit Reason from Candide to the Gulag*. Albany: State UP of New York, 1998.

Ramazani, Jahan. *A Transnational Poetics*. Chicago: U of Chicago P, 2009.

Reinhold, Natalia, ed. *Woolf across Cultures*. New York: Pace UP, 2004.

Rosemont, Franklin, and Robin D.G. Kelley, eds. *Black, Brown, and Beige: Surrealist Writings from Africa and the Diaspora*. Austin: U of Texas P, 2009.

Sackville West, Vita. "To Iraq" and "Round Teheran." *Passenger to Teheran* (1926). New York: Tauris Parke, 2007.

Said, Edward. *Culture and Imperialism*. New York: Vintage, 1994.

Senghor, Léopold Sédar. *Anthologie de la nouvelle poésie nègre et malgache de langue française* (1948). Introduction, "Orphée noir," by Jean-Paul Sartre. Paris: Presses Universitaires de France, 1972.

Shuhua, Ling. *Ancient Melodies*. Introduction by Vita Sackville West. New York: Universe Books, 1988.

Spivak, Gayatri Chakravorty. *An Aesthetic Education in the Era of Globalization*. Cambridge, MA: Harvard UP, 2012.

Stanford Friedman, Susan. "Periodizing Modernism: Postcolonial Modernities and the Space/Time Borders of Modernist Studies." *Modernism/Modernity* 13.3 (September 2006): 425–43.

Tsing, Anna. *Friction: An Ethnography of Global Connection*. Princeton: Princeton UP, 2005.

Walkowitz, Rebecca L. *Cosmopolitan Style: Modernism beyond the Nation*. New York: Columbia UP, 2007.

Williams, Patrick. " 'Simultaneous Uncontemporaneities': Theorising Modernism and Empire." *Modernism and Empire*, ed. Howard J. Booth and Nigel Rigby. Manchester: Manchester UP, 2000: 13–38.

Williams, Raymond. "When was Modernism?" *The Politics of Modernism: Against the New Conformists*. London: Verso, 1989.

——. "The Bloomsbury Fraction." *Culture and Materialism*. London: Verso, 1980. 148–69.

——. *The Country and the City*. Oxford: Oxford UP, 1973.

Winkiel, Laura. *Modernism, Race, and Manifestos*. Cambridge: Cambridge UP, 2008.

Woolf, Virginia. "Mr. Bennett and Mrs. Brown" (1924). *The Captain's Death Bed and Other Essays*. New York: Harcourt, Brace, 1950.

Yeats, W.B. "Introduction." In Rabindranath Tagore, *Gitanjali* (1912). New York: Macmillan, 1971.

Xun, Lu. *The Real Story of Ah-Q and Other Tales of China: The Complete Fiction of Lu Xun*. Trans. Julia Lovell. London: Penguin Books, 2009.

——. "The Ties between Chinese and Russian Literatures." *Lu Xun: Selected Works*, vol. 3. Beijing: Foreign Languages Press, 1980.

Chapter 46

José Martí (1853–95)

"OUR AMERICA" (1891)

LATIN AMERICA HAS ITS OWN distinctive tradition of literary modernism, beginning earlier than European modernism and eventually leading to the postmodernism of Borges and Gabriel García Márquez. José Martí's impassioned plea to Latin Americans to develop ideas from the native soil would shape this rich continental canon. Like writers of the Harlem Renaissance and the Irish Literary Revival, Martí renounces works that imitate foreign cultures, particularly those of Europe and the United States, and instead, tells his readers to look to their own national traditions, indigenous histories, and natural environments. While much of the article focuses on the creation of native governments, Martí both implicitly and explicitly includes artists in this task.

José Martí, "Our America," *La Revista Illustrada* (January 1, 1891). 1–6.

The conceited villager believes the entire world to be his village. Provided that he can be mayor, humiliate the rival who stole his sweetheart, or add to the savings in his strongbox, he considers the universal order good, unaware of those giants with seven-league boots who can crush him underfoot, or of the strife in the heavens between comets that go through the air asleep, gulping down worlds. What remains of the village in America must rouse itself. These are not the times for sleeping in a nightcap, but with weapons for a pillow, like the warriors of Juan de Castellanos: weapons of the mind, which conquer all others. Barricades of ideas are worth more than barricades of stones.

There is no prow that can cut through a cloudbank of ideas. A powerful idea, waved before the world at the proper time, can stop a squadron of iron-clad ships, like the mystical flag of the Last Judgement. Nations that do not know one another should quickly become acquainted, as men who are to fight a common enemy. Those who shake their fists, like jealous brothers coveting the same tract of land, or like the modest cottager who envies the esquire his mansion, should clasp hands and become one. Those who use the authority of a criminal tradition to lop off the hands of their defeated brother with a sword stained with his own blood, ought to return the lands to the brother already punished sufficiently, if they do not want the people to call them robbers. The honest man does not absolve himself of debts of honor with money, at so much a slap. We can no longer be a people of leaves, living in the air, our foliage heavy with blooms and crackling or humming at the whim of the sun's caress, or buffeted and tossed by the storms. The trees must form ranks to keep the giant with seven-league boots from passing! It is the time of mobilization, of marching together, and we must go forward in close ranks, like silver in the veins of the Andes.

Only those born prematurely are lacking in courage. Those without faith in their country are seven-month weaklings. Because they have no courage, they deny it to the others. Their puny arms – arms with bracelets and hands with painted nails, arms of Paris or Madrid – can hardly reach the bottom limb, and they claim the tall tree to be unclimbable. The ships should be loaded with those harmful insects that gnaw at the bone of the country that nourishes them. If they are Parisians or from Madrid, let them go to the Prado, to boast around, or to Tortoni's, in high hats. Those carpenters' sons who are ashamed that their fathers are carpenters! Those born in America who are ashamed of the mother that reared them, because she wears an Indian apron, and who disown their sick mothers, the scoundrels, abandoning her on her sickbed! Then who is a real man? He who stays with his mother and nurses her in her illness, or he who puts her to work out of sight, and lives at her expense on decadent lands, sporting fancy neckties, cursing the womb that carried him, displaying the sign of the traitor on the back of his paper frockcoat? These sons of our America, which will be saved by its Indians in blood and is growing better; these deserters who take up arms in the army of a North America that drowns its Indians in blood and is growing worse! These delicate creatures who are men but are unwilling to do men's work! The Washington who made this land for them, did he go to live with the English at a time when he saw them fighting against his own country. These unbelievable of honor who drag the honor over foreign soil like their counterparts in the French Revolution with their dancing, their affections [sic], their drawling speech!

For in what lands can men take more pride than in our long-suffering American republics, raised up among the silent Indian masses by the bleeding arms of a hundred apostles, to the sound of battle between the book and processional candle? Never in history have such advanced and united nations been forged in so short a time from such disorganized elements. The presumptuous man feels that the earth was made to serve as his pedestal, because he happens to have a facile pen or colourful speech, and he accuses his native land of being worthless and beyond redemption because its virgin jungles fail to provide him with a constant means of travelling over the world, driving Persian ponies and lavishing champagne like a tycoon. The incapacity does not lie with the emerging country in quest of suitable forms and utilitarian greatness; it lies rather with those who attempt to rule nations of a unique and violent character by means of laws inherited from four centuries of freedom in the United States and nineteen centuries of monarchy in France. A decree by Hamilton does not halt the charge of the plainsman's horse. A phrase by Sieyes does nothing to quicken the stagnant blood of the Indian race. To govern well, one must see things as they are. And the able governor in America is not the one who knows how to govern the Germans or the French; he must know the elements that make up his own country, and how to bring them together, using methods and institutions originating within the country, to reach that desirable state where each man can attain self-realization and all may enjoy the abundance that Nature has bestowed in everyone in the nation to enrich with their toil and defend with their lives. Government must originate in the country. The spirit of government must be that of the country. Its structure must conform to rules appropriate to the country. Good government is nothing more than the balance of the country's natural elements.

That is why in America the imported book has been conquered by the natural man. Natural men have conquered learned and artificial men. The native half-breed has conquered the exotic Creole. The struggle is not between civilization and barbarity, but between false erudition and Nature. The natural man is good, and he respects and rewards superior intelligence as long as his humility is not turned against him, or he is not offended by being disregarded – something the natural man never forgives, prepared as he is to forcibly regain the respect of whoever has wounded his pride or threatened his interests. It is by conforming with these disdained native elements that the tyrants of America have climbed to power, and have fallen as soon as they betrayed them. Republics have paid with oppression for their inability to recognize the true elements of their countries, to derive from them the right kind of government, and to govern accordingly. In a new nation a government means a creator.

In nations composed of both cultured and uncultured elements, the uncultured will govern because it is their habit to attack and resolve doubts with their fists in cases where the cultured have failed in the art of governing. The uncultured masses are lazy and timid in the realm of intelligence, and they want to be governed well. But if the government hurts them, they shake it off and govern themselves. How can the universities produce governors if not a single university in America teaches the rudiments of the art of government, the analysis of elements peculiar to the peoples of America? The young go out into the world wearing Yankee or French spectacles, hoping to govern a people they do not know. In the political race entrance should not go for the best ode, but for the best study of the political factors of one's country. Newspapers, universities and schools should encourage the study of the country's pertinent components. To know them is sufficient, without mincing words; for whoever brushes aside even a part of the truth, whether through intention or oversight, is doomed to fall. The truth is built without it. It is easy to resolve our problem knowing its components than resolve them without knowing them. Along comes the natural man, strong and indignant, and he topples all the justice accumulated from books because he has not been governed in accordance with the obvious needs of the country. Knowing is what counts. To know one's country and govern it with that knowledge is the only way to free it from tyranny. The European university must bow to the American university. The history of America, from the Incas to the present, must be taught in clear detail and to the letter, even if the archons of Greece are overlooked. Our Greece must take priority over the Greece which is not ours. We need it more. Nationalist statement must replace foreign statement. Let the world be grafted onto our republics, but the trunk must be our own. And let the vanquished pedant hold his tongue, for there are no lands in which a man may take greater pride than in our long-suffering American republics.

With the rosary as our guide, our heads white and our bodies mottled, both Indians and Creoles, we fearlessly entered the world of nations. We set out to conquer freedom under the banner of the virgin. A priest, a few lieutenants, and a woman raised the Republic of Mexico onto the shoulders of the Indians. A few heroic students, instructed in French liberty by a Spanish cleric, made Central America rise in revolt against Spain under a Spanish general. In monarchic garb emblazoned with the sun, the Venezuelans to the north and the Argentineans to the south began building nations. When the heroes clashed and the continent was about to rock, one of them, and not the lesser, handed the reins to the other. And since heroism in times of peace is rare because it is not as glorious as in times of war, it is easier to govern when feelings are exalted and united than after a battle, when divisive, arrogant, exotic, or ambitious thinking emerges. The forces routed in the epic struggle – with the feline cunning of the species, and using the weight of realities – were undermining the new structure which comprised both the rough-and-ready, unique regions of our half-breed America and the silk-stockinged and frockcoated people of Paris beneath the flag of freedom and reason borrowed from nations skilled in the arts of government. The hierarchical constitution of the colonies resisted the democratic organization of the republics. The cravatted capitals left their country boots in the vestibule. The bookworm redeemers failed to realize that the revolution succeeded because it came from the soul of the nation; they had to govern with that soul and not without or against it. America began to suffer, and still suffers, from the tiresome task of reconciling the hostile and discordant elements it inherited from the despotic and perverse

colonizer, and the imported methods and ideas which have been retarding logical government because they are lacking in local realities. Thrown out of gear for three centuries by a
power which denied men the right to use their reason, the continent disregarded or closed its
ears to the unlettered throngs that helped bring it to redemption, and embarked on a government based on reason – a reason belonging to all for the common good, not the university
brand of reason over the peasant brand. The problem is independence did not lie in a change
of forms but in change of spirit.

It was imperative to make common cause with the oppressed, in order to secure a new
system opposed to the ambitions and governing habits of the oppressors. The tiger, frightened by gunfire, returns at night to his prey. He dies with his eyes shooting flames and his
claws unsheathed. He cannot be heard coming because he approaches with velvet tread.
When the prey awakens, the tiger is already upon it. The colony lives on the republic, and
our America is saving itself from its enormous mistakes – the pride of its capital cities, the
blind triumph of a scorned peasantry, the excessive influx of foreign ideas and formulas, the
wicked and unpolitical disdain for the aboriginal race – because of the higher virtue, enriched
with necessary blood, of a republic struggling against a colony. The tiger lurks behind every
tree, lying in wait at every turn. He will die with his claws unsheathed and his eyes shooting
flames.

But "these countries will be saved", as was announced by the Argentinean Rivadivia,
whose only sin was being a gentleman in these rough-and-ready times. A man does not
sheathe a machete in a silken scabbard, nor can he lay aside the short lance merely because he
is angered and stands at the door of Iturbide's Congress, "demanding that the fair-haired one
be named emperor". These countries will be saved because a genius for moderation, found in
the serene harmony of Nature, seems to prevail in the continent of light, where there emerges
a new real man schooled for these real times in the critical philosophy of guesswork and
phalanstery that saturated the previous generation.

We were a phenomenon with the chest of an athlete, the hands of a dandy, and the brain
of a child. We were a masquerader in English breeches, Parisian vest, North America jacket,
and Spanish cap. The Indian hovered near us in silence, and went off to the hills to baptize his
children. The Negro was seen pouring out the songs of his heart at night, alone and unrecog-
nised among the rivers and wild animals. The peasant, the creator, turned in blind indignation against the disdainful city, against his own child. As for us, we were nothing but epaulets
and professors' gowns in countries that came into the world wearing hemp sandals and head-
bands. It would have been the mark of genius to couple the headband and the professors'
gown with the founding fathers' generosity and courage, to rescue the Indian, to make a place
for the competent Negro, to fit liberty to the body of those who rebelled and conquered for
it. We were left with the hearer, the general, the scholar, and the sinecured. The angelic
young, as if caught in the tentacles of an octopus, lunged heavenward, only to fall back,
crowned with clouds in sterile glory. The native, driven by instinct, swept away the golden
staffs of office in blind triumph. Neither the Europeans nor the Yankee could provide the key
to the Spanish American riddle. Hate was attempted, and every year the countries amounted
to less. Exhausted by the senseless struggle between the book and the lance, between reason
and the processional candle, between the city and the country, weary of the impossible rule
by rival urban cliques over the natural nation tempestuous or inert by turns, we are beginning
almost unconsciously to try love. Nations stand up and greet one another. "What are we?" is
the mutual question, and little by little they furnish answers. When a problem arises in
Cojímar, they do not seek its solution in Danzig. The frockcoats are still French, but thought
begins to be American. The youth of America are rolling up their sleeves, digging their hands
in the dough, and making it rise with the sweat of their brows. They realize that there is too
much imitation, and that creation holds the key to salvation. "Create" is the password of this

generation. The wine is made from plantain, but even if it turns sour, it is our own wine! That a country's form of government must be in keeping with its natural elements is a foregone conclusion. Absolute ideas must take relative forms if they are not to fail because of an error in form. Freedom, to be viable, has to be sincere and complete. If a republic refuses to open its arms to all, and move ahead with all, it dies. The tiger within sneaks in through the crack; so does the tiger from without. The general holds back his cavalry to a pace that suits his infantry, for if its infantry is left behind, the cavalry will be surrounded by the enemy. Politics and strategy are one. Nations should live in an atmosphere of self-criticism because it is healthy, but always with one heart and one mind. Stoop to the unhappy, and lift them up in your arms! Thaw out frozen America with the fire of your hearts! Make the natural blood of the nations course vigorously through their veins! The new Americans are on their feet, saluting each other from nation to nation, the eyes of the laborers shining with joy. The natural statesman arises, schooled in the direct study of Nature. He reads to apply his knowledge, not to imitate. Economists study the problems at their point of origin. Speakers begin a policy of moderation. Playwrights bring native characters to the stage. Academies discuss practical subjects. Poetry shears off its Zorrilla-like locks and hangs its red vest on the glorious tree. Selective and sparkling prose is filled with ideas. In the Indian republics, the governors are learning Indian.

America is escaping all its dangers. Some of the republics are still beneath the sleeping octopus, but others, under the law of averages, are draining their land with sublime and furious haste, as if to make up for centuries lost. Still others, forgetting that Juarez went about in a carriage drawn by mules, hitch their carriages to the wind, their coachmen soap bubbles. Poisonous luxury, the enemy of freedom, corrupts the frivolous and opens the door to the foreigner. In others, where independence is threatened, an epic spirit heightens their manhood. Still others spawn an army capable of devouring them in voracious wars. But perhaps our America is running another risk that does not come from itself but from the difference in origins, methods, and interests between the two halves of the continent, and the time is near at hand when an enterprising and vigorous people who scorn and ignore our America will even so approach it and demand a close relationship. And since strong nations, self-made by law and shotgun, love strong nations and them alone; since the time of madness and ambition – from which North America may be freed by the predominance of the purest elements in its blood, or on which it may be launched by its vindictive and sordid masses, its tradition of expansion, or the ambition of some powerful leader – is not so near at hand, even to the most timorous eye, that there is no time for the test of discreet and unwavering pride that could confront and dissuade it; since its good name as a republic in the eyes of the world's perceptive nations puts upon North America a restraint that cannot be taken away by childish provocations or pompous arrogance or parricidal discords among our American nations – the pressing need of our America is to show itself as it is, one in spirit and intent, swift conquerors of a suffocating past, stained only by the enriching blood drawn from the scars left upon us by our masters. The scorn of our formidable neighbor who does not know us is our America's greatest danger. And since the day of the visit is near, it is imperative that our neighbor know us, and soon, so that it will not scorn us. Through ignorance it might even come to lay hands on us. Once it does know us, it will remove its hands out of respect. One must have faith in the best in men and distrust the worst. One must allow the best to be shown so that it reveals and prevails over the worst. Nations should have a pillory for whoever stirs up useless hate, and another for whoever fails to tell them the truth in time.

There can be no racial animosity, because there are no races. The theorist and feeble thinkers string together and warm over the bookshelf races which the well-disposed observer and the fair-minded traveller vainly seek in the justice of Nature where man's universal identity springs forth from triumphant love and the turbulent hunger for life. The soul, equal and eternal, emanates from bodies of different shapes and colors. Whoever foments and spreads antagonism and hate between the races sins against humanity. But as nations take shape among other different nations, there is condensation of vital and individual characteristics of thought and habit, expansion and conquest, vanity and greed which could – from the latent state of national concern, and in the period of internal disorder, or the rapidity with which the country's character has been accumulating – be turned into a serious threat for the weak and isolated neighbouring countries, declared by the strong country to be inferior and perishable. The thought is father to the deed. And one must not attribute, through a provincial antipathy, a fatal and inborn wickedness to the continent's fair-skinned nation simply because it does not speak our language, nor see the world as we see it, nor resemble us in its political defects, so different from ours, nor favourably regard the excitable, dark-skinned people, or look charitably, from its still uncertain eminence, upon those less favored by history, who climb the road of republicanism by heroic stages. The self-evident facts of the problem should not be obscured, because the problem can be resolved, for peace of centuries to come, by appropriate study, and by tacit and immediate union in the continental spirit. With a single voice the hymn is already being sung; the present generation is carrying industrious America along the road enriched by their sublime fathers; from Rio Grande to the Straits of Magellan, the Great Semi, astride its condor, spread the seed of the new America over the romantic nations of the continent and the sorrowful islands of the sea!

Chapter 47

Ryosuke Akutagawa (1892–1927)

"A FOOL'S LIFE" (1927)

AKUTAGAWA, KNOWN AS THE "father of the short story" in Japan, narrates a fragmented, autobiographical portrait of the modern artist through a series of short aphorisms. Ranging in topics from literature to marriage, these aphorisms focus on the conflict between the desires of the individual and the demands of the community. The first aphorism establishes this underlying tension as the protagonist leans upon a ladder in a bookstore reading works by European writers of the *fin de siècle*, while below him he views the "shabby" crowd of clerks and customers. In contrast to Martí, Akutagawa does not represent his European reading as "imitation," but rather, finds sustenance in native Japanese traditions like the haiku and the works of writers such as Baudelaire and Nietzsche, whose own aphorisms may have inspired the unique structure of this work (see Chapter 24 above).

Ryosuke Akutagawa, "A Fool's Life," *The Essential Akutagawa*, ed. Seiji M. Lippit; trans. Will Petersen. Aphorisms #1–2, 4–8, 10–11, 13–16, 17–20, 22, 26–29, 33–35, 40–42, 45, 49.

1. The age

It was the second level of a bookshop. Twenty years old, he was climbing a Western style ladder leaning against the shelves, looking for new books. De Maupassant, Baudelaire, Strindberg, Ibsen, Shaw, Tolstoy. . . .

The twilight was beginning to press in. But feverishly he continued poring over the letters on the books' backs. Gathered before him, rather than books, was the *fin de siècle* itself. Nietzsche, Verlaine, the brothers Goncourt, Dostoevski, Hauptmann, Flaubert, . . .

Resisting the darkness, he tried to make out names. But the books themselves were sinking into shadow. His nerves strained, he was ready to go down. Just then a bare bulb, directly over his head, burst on. Perched at the ladder's top, he looked down. Among the books the moving clerks and customers. Odd, how very small they seemed. How shabby.

"The sum of human life adds-up to less than a line of Baudelaire."

For a time, from the ladder's top, he had been watching them.

2. Mother

The mad people were all made to dress alike in grey kimono. It made the enormous room even more depressing. One of them was facing an organ, fervently playing hymns. Another, standing in the very middle of the room, no, you couldn't call it dancing, was capering.

With a hale and hearty doctor he stood looking on. His mother, ten years ago, hadn't been a bit different. Not a bit,—their odor was his mother's odor.

. . .

4. Tokyo

The Sumida river heavy under cloud. Looking out of the moving steam launch window at the Mukojima cherry trees. In full bloom the blossoms in his eyes a line of rags, sad. In the trees,—dating from Edo times. In the cherry trees of Mukojima, seeing himself.

5. Self

With an older graduate, sitting at a café table, puffing at one cigarette after another. He hardly opened his mouth. But listened intently to the graduate's words.

"Today I spent half a day riding in a car."

"On business, I suppose?"

His senior, cheek reclining on palm, replied extremely casually.

"Huh?—just felt like it."

The words opened for him an unknown realm,—close to the gods, a realm of *Self*. It was painful. And ecstatic.

The café was cramped. Under a painting of the god Pan, in a red pot, a gum tree. Its fleshly leaves. Limp.

6. Sickness

In a salt breeze without let, the big English dictionary open wide, his finger searching for words.

Talaria: *Winged boots, sandals.*
Tale: *Narrative.*
Talipot: *East Indian palm. Height 50 to 100 ft. Leaves made into umbrellas, fans, hats. Blossoms once in 70 years.*

His imagination vividly projected the palm's blossom. As he did he became aware of an itch in his throat. In spite of himself, phlegm dribbled onto the page. Phlegm?—but it wasn't phlegm. Thinking of life's brevity, once more he conjured up the blossom of the palm. Over the remote sea, aloft, soaring higher, the blossom.

7. Painting

All at once he was struck. Standing in front of a bookshop looking at a collection of paintings by Van Gogh, it hit him. *This* was painting. Of course, these Van Goghs were merely photo reproductions. But even so, he could feel in them a self rising intensely to the surface.

The passion of these paintings renewed his vision. He saw now the undulations of a tree's branching, the curve of a woman's cheek.

One overcast autumn dusk outside the city he had walked through an underpass. There at the far side of the embankment stood a cart. As he walked by he had the feeling that somebody had passed this way before him. Who?—There was for him no longer need to question. In his twenty-three year old mind, an ear lopped off, a Dutchman, in his mouth a long stemmed pipe, on the sullen landscape set piercing eyes.

8. Sparks

Drenched by the rain, he walked on the asphalt. The rain was ferocious. In the downpour he breathed in the rubber coat odor.

Before his eyes an aerial power line released sparks of violet. Strangely he was moved. Tucked away in his jacket pocket, meant for publication in the group magazine, was his manuscript. Walking on in the rain, once more he looked back at the line.

Unremittingly it emitted its prickly sparks. Though he considered all of human existence, there was nothing special worth having. But those violet blossoms of fire,—those awesome fireworks in the sky, to hold them, he would give his life.

  . . .

10. Mentor

Under a large oak tree he was reading his mentor's book. In the autumn sunlight the oak stirring not a slightest twig's leaf. Somewhere off in the far sky a pair of glass pans hung from a balance, in perfect equilibrium.—Reading his mentor's book, he imagined the scene. . . .

11. Night's end

Dawn slowly breaking. He found himself on a corner somewhere looking out over a wide marketplace. Converging on the market place people, wagons, all gently suffused with rose.

Lighting a cigarette, he quietly approached the market's center. As he advanced, a lean black dog barked. But he felt no fear. Even for the dog there was love.

In the market's center, a plane tree, its branches spreading wide in each direction. Standing at the root he looked up through the weave of branches into the high sky. In the sky exactly overhead glittered a star.

His twenty-fifth year,—three months since he had met his mentor.

  . . .

13. Mentor's death

In the wind dragging after the rain he was pacing the newly constructed railway platform. The sky was bleak. Beyond the platform chanting at high pitch three or four railworkers lifted and let hammers fall.

The after rain wind ripped the workers' chant and his sentiment to shreds. His cigarette unlit, his anguish was close to exaltation. *Mentor's condition critical*, the telegram was crushed into his overcoat pocket. . . .

From behind the pine mountain in the long six a.m. Tokyo-bound, pale smoke laid low, meandering, approached.

14. Marriage

The very day after his marriage, "Right off, you start wasting money," already he was carping at his bride. Though actually it was not so much his as his aunt's complaint. To him, of course, but to his aunt as well, his bride bowed apologetically. A bowl of yellow narcissus, her gift to him, in front of her.

15. They

They lived in peace. In the expansive shade of a great *basho* tree's leaves.—Even by train, over an hour away from Tokyo, in a house in a town on the seacoast. That's why.

16. Pillow

Pillowed on rose leaf scented skepticism, he was reading a book by Anatole France. That even such a pillow might house a centaur, he didn't seem to realize.

17. Butterfly

In wind reeking of duckweed, a butterfly flashed. Only for an instant, on his dry lips he felt the touch of the butterfly's wings. But years afterward, on his lips, the wings' imprinted dust still glittered.

18. Moon

In a certain hotel, halfway up the stairs, he happened to pass her. In the afternoon her face seemed moonlit. Following her with his eyes (they hadn't even a nodding acquaintance) he felt a loneliness such as he'd never known. . . .

19. Man-made wings

From Anatole France he shifted to the 18th century philosophers. But he avoided Rousseau. One side of his nature,—a side easily swayed by passion, was perhaps already too near Rousseau. The other,—the side endowed with icy intellect, brought him nearer the author of *Candide*.

Twenty nine years of human existence had offered him little illumination. But Voltaire at least equipped him with artificial wings.

Unfolding these man-made wings, easily he glided up into the sky. Bathed with reason's light, human joy and sorrow sank away beneath his eyes. Over squalid towns, letting irony and mockery fall, he soared into unobstructed space, heading straight for the sun. That with just such man-made wings, scorched by the sun's radiance an ancient Greek had hurtled into the sea, dead, he'd seemed to have forgotten . . . .

20. Shackles

It was settled that he and his wife would share the same roof with his foster parents. That was due to his being hired by a certain publisher. He had depended wholly on the contract's words, written out on a single sheet of yellow paper. But later, looking at the contract, it was plain the publisher was under no obligation. All the obligations were his.

. . .

22. A painter

It was a magazine illustration. But, a cock in black and white expressing an unmistakable individuality. He asked a friend about the painter.

About a week later the painter paid him a visit. This was one of the events of his life. He discovered in the painter a poetry unknown to anyone. And more, he discovered a soul even the painter himself was unaware of.

One chill autumn dusk, in a solitary stalk of corn suddenly he saw the painter. Tall, armed with aggressive leaf, from the sod its roots like fine nerves, exposed. This was, of course, also a portrait of his own vulnerable self. But the discovery led only to despair.

"Too late. But when the time comes . . ."

. . .

25. Strindberg

Standing in the doorway, in the pomegranate blossoming moonlight looking out on drab Chinamen playing mah-jong. He went back to his room. Under a low lamp he began reading *Le Plaidoyer d'un Fou*. But before he read even two pages he found himself smiling sardonically.— Strindberg was not so different. In letters to his lover, the Countess, he too wrote lies . . . .

26. Antiquity

Discolored Buddhas, celestial beings, horses, lotus blossoms nearly overcame him. Gazing up at them everything was forgotten. Even his own fortune in escaping from the hands of the madwoman.

27. Spartan discipline

With a friend, walking up a backstreet. Moving directly toward them, a hooded rickshaw approaching. Totally unexpected, riding it, she of last night. In the daytime too, her face seemed lit by the moon. His friend present, naturally there couldn't be any sign of recognition.

"A beauty."

His friend noted. He, looking off to where the street banged up against the spring hills, not able to hold back.

"Yes, a real beauty."

. . .

29. Form

An iron wine bottle. Some time or other this finely incised wine bottle had taught him the beauty of *form*.

. . .

33. Hero

How long had he been gazing out of the window of Voltaire's house, up at the towering mountain? Up on the icy summit not even the shadow of a condor could be seen. Only the stumpy Russian stubbornly continuing up the slope.

After darkness had closed Voltaire's house, under a bright lamp he began composing a poem. In his head the figure of the mountain-climbing Russian emerging . . . .

> Above all others you
>   Kept the Decalogue,
> Above all others you
>   Broke the Decalogue,
>   Above all others you
>   Loved the people,
>   Above all others you
>   Despised the people.
>
> Above all others you
>   Burned with ideals,
> Above all others you
>   Knew the real.
>   You, born of our Orient
>   Weed scented
>   Electro-
>   loco motive.

34. Color

Thirty years old, he had for some time been in love with a vacant lot. A ground of moss, on it broken bricks, fragments of roof tile. But in his eyes a landscape by Cézanne.

He remembered his passions of seven or eight years ago. That seven or eight years ago he hadn't understood color, he realized now.

35. Manikin

Not to care when he died, to live a life of intensity was his desire. But actually his life was one of constant deference to foster parents and aunt. This submissiveness formed both the light and shadow of his being. He studied the manikin standing in the tailor's shop window, curious as to how much he resembled it. Yet his other self lying beyond his consciousness—his second self—had already settled the question. In a short story.

. . .

40. Catechism

You attack the present social system, why?

Because I see the evils born of capitalism.

Evils? I didn't think you discriminated between good and evil. In that case, how about your own life?

—The discussion was with an angel. Impeccable. In a silk hat . . .

41. Sickness

He began suffering from insomnia. His strength was beginning to fail. A number of doctors diagnosed his sickness.—Acid dyspepsia, gastric atony, dry pleurisy, nervous prostration, chronic conjunctivitus, brain fatigue . . . .

But he knew the cause of his malady. It was his sense of shame before himself, mingled with his dread of them. *Them*,—the public he despised.

On a snow cloud clouded over afternoon in a corner of a café, a lighted cigar in his mouth, his ears inclined toward music flowing toward him from the gramophone. Strangely penetrating music. He waited for its end, then went over to the machine, to examine the label on the record:

Magic Flute—Mozart

All at once he understood. The Decalogue-breaking Mozart, after all, also suffered. But, Mozart never, . . . His head lowered, silently. He returned to his table.

42. Laughter of the gods

Thirty five years old, strolling through a grove of pines struck by the spring sun. "The gods, pity them, unlike us cannot kill themselves." These words of two, three years ago returned . . .

. . .

45. The Divan

The Divan was going to give him a new life. Till now he had been unaware of the "Oriental Goethe." With an envy almost approaching despair he saw Goethe standing on the far shore beyond good and evil, immense. In his eyes the poet Goethe was larger than the poet Christ. The poet's soul holds not only the Acropolis or Golgotha. In it the Arabian rose also blooms. If only he had strength enough to grope in the poet's footsteps,—*The Divan* finished, the awful excitement abating, there was only contempt for himself. Born a eunuch.

. . .

49. Stuffed swan

Draining what strength remained, he attempted an autobiography. It was harder than he had imagined. Self-importance and skepticism and calculation of advantages or disadvantages were all in him. He despised this self of his. At the same time he couldn't help thinking, "Remove a layer of skin and everybody is alike." *Dichtung und Wahrheit*—the title of that book would be a fitting title for all autobiography. But he also was well aware that works of literature did not move many. His own work would only appeal to those whose lives were close to his; outside of those readers there would be none.—Such was the feeling working inside of him. He would try, concisely, to write down his own *Dichtung und Wahrheit*.

After completing *A Fool's Life* he happened to see in a junk shop a stuffed swan. It stood with its neck held erect, its wings yellowed, motheaten. Recalling his whole life, he felt a sudden onrush of tears and cold laughter. In front of him was either madness or suicide. In the twilight he walked the street alone, determined, patiently, to wait for his fate, for slowly approaching destruction.

Chapter 48

Lu Xun (Zhou Shuren) (1881–1936)

"LITERATURE AND REVOLUTION" (1928)

LIKE RAINER MARIA RILKE'S "Letters to a Young Poet" (1902–08) and Virginia Woolf's "A Letter to a Young Poet" (1932), Lu Xun's letter to a Beijing University student named Dong Qiufen details his opinions on the current state of litera-ture. Writing in China during a period of revolutionary fervor – the Republic of China had been officially founded in 1912, replacing the Manchu dynasty and ushering in a period of struggle between warlords, nationalists, and communists – Xun argues that literature can and should serve as a political tool. Mao Tse-tung, who would later endorse the revolu-tionary spirit of Xun's work, was just beginning to come into power and communism was finding supporters among the peasantry and intelligentsia alike. Against this backdrop, Xun argues that all art is propaganda but not all propaganda is art. He cites Upton Sinclair, whose novels, such as *The Jungle*, exposed the sordid effects of capitalism in America, as an example of a politically engaged writer.

Lu Xun (Zhou Shuren), "Literature and Revolution," *Lu Xun: Selected Works*, vol. 3, trans. Yang Xianyi and Gladys Yang. Beijing: Foreign Languages Press, 1973. 25–28.

April 4, 1928
Dear Mr. Dongfen,[1]

Not being a critic I am no artist either, for nowadays, to be any sort of specialist you have to be a critic too, or have a friend who is one. Without backing you are helpless, on the Shanghai Bund today at any rate. And not being an artist I have no special veneration for art, just as none but a quack doctor will give a boxing exhibition to cry up his wares. I regard art as merely a social phenomenon, a record of the life of the times. And if mankind advances, then whether you write on externals or on the inner life your works are bound to grow out-of-date or to perish. But recently the critics seem terrified of this prospect—they are set on immortality in the world of letters.

The outcrop of different "isms" is an unavoidable phenomenon too. Since revolutions are constantly taking place, naturally there is revolutionary literature. Quite a number of the world's peoples are awakening and, though many of them are still suffering, some already hold power. Naturally this gives rise to popular literature or, to put it more bluntly, litera-ture of the fourth class.

I am not too clear, not too interested, either, regarding current trends in China's literary criticism. But from all I hear and see, different authorities seem to use a great variety of criteria: Anglo-American, German, Russian, Japanese and of course Chinese, or a combina-tion of these. Some demand truth, others struggle. Some say literature should transcend its age, others pass sarcastic remarks behind people's backs. Yet others, who set themselves up as authoritative literary critics, are disgusted when anyone else encourages writing. What are they up to? This is most incomprehensible to me, for without writing what is there to criticize?

Let us leave aside other questions for the moment. The so-called revolutionary writers today profess themselves militants or transcendentalists. Actually, transcending the present is a form of escapism. And this is the path they are bound to take, consciously or otherwise, if they lack the courage to look reality in the face yet insist on styling themselves revolution-aries. If you live in this world, how can you get away from it? This is as much of a fraud as claiming that you can hoist yourself off this earth by pulling on your ear. If society remains static, literature cannot fly ahead on its own. If it flourishes in such a static society, this means it is tolerated by that society and has turned its back on revolution, the only result being a slightly larger magazine circulation or the chance for publication in the journals put out by big commercial firms.

To struggle is right, I believe. If people are oppressed, why shouldn't they struggle? But since this is what respectable gentlemen[2] dread, they condemn it as "radical," alleging that men the world over are meant to love each other and would do so were they not now corrupted by a gang of bad characters. The well-fed may quite likely love the starving, but the starving never love the well-fed. In the days of Huang Chao[3] when men ate each other, the starving did not even love the starving; however, this was not due to trouble stirred up by the literature of struggle. I have never believed that literature has the power to move heaven and earth, but if people want to put it to other uses that is all right with me. It can be used for "propaganda" for example.

Upton Sinclair of America has said: All literature is propaganda. Our revolutionary writers treasure this saying and have printed it in large type, whereas the serious critics call Upton Sinclair a "shallow socialist." But I, being shallow myself, agree with him. All litera-ture becomes propaganda once you show it to someone else. This applies to individualist works, too, as soon as you write them down. Indeed, the only way to avoid propaganda is by never writing, never opening your mouth. This being so, literature can naturally be used as a tool of revolution.

But I think we should first try to achieve rich content and skilful technique, and not be in a hurry to set ourselves up as writers. The old trade-marks Dao Xiang Cun and Lu Gao Jian[4] have already lost their appeal, and I doubt whether a firm calling itself "The Dowager Empress Shoe Shop" could attract more customers than "The Empress Shoe Shop." Revolutionary writers bridle at the mere mention of "technique." To my mind, however, though all literature is propaganda, not all propaganda is literature; just as all flowers have colour (I count white as a colour), but not all coloured things are flowers. In addition to slogans, posters, proclamations, telegrams, textbooks and so forth, the revolution needs literature—just because it is literature.

But China's so-called revolutionary literature seems to be an exception again. The sign-board has been hung up and our writers are busy patting each other on the back, but they dare not look unflinchingly at today's tyranny and darkness. Some works have been published, true, but often more clumsily written than journalese. Or it is left to the actors in a play to supply the stage-directions, such writing being regarded as "out-of-date." Surely, then, the ideological content left must be most revolutionary? Let me quote you the two superb last lines of a play by Feng Naichao![5]

Prostitute: I no longer dread the darkness.
Thief: Let us revolt!

Lu Xun

Notes

1   Reply to a letter from Dong Qiufen, then a student of Beijing University.
2   This refers to members of the Crescent Moon Society, a cultural and political association representing the compradore bourgeoisie.
3   Leader of a peasant revolt at the end of the Tang Dynasty.
4   Well-known delicatessens in Shanghai.
5   Member of the Creation Society.

Chapter 49

Mulk Raj Anand (1905–2004)

"MUHAMMAD IQBAL" (1933)

MULK RAJ ANAND HAS BEEN referred to as the Zola and Dickens of India; his revolutionary realist literature also had modernist roots. Anand's *Untouchable* (1935) sought to expose the irrationality and brutality of the Indian caste system; its representation of one day in the life of Bakha the low caste sweeper was partially inspired by Joyce's *Ulysses*. Anand's literary influences included writers like Joyce, D.H. Lawrence, and E.M. Forster, who championed the work and introduced Anand to Leonard and Virginia Woolf and T.S. Eliot. Anand briefly copy-edited for the Woolfs at the Hogarth Press and for Eliot at *The Criterion*; his *Conversations in Bloomsbury* (1981) is a collection of remembered conversations with the London luminaries. Anand later befriended George Orwell whom he met while working for the BBC in London. Politically, Anand became involved with the Indian national movement and Mohandas Gandhi's satyagraha movement while he was an adolescent; he crossed paths with political figures, including the Fabian suffragist and Irish and Indian nationalist Annie Besant and the poet and Islamic philosopher Muhammad Iqbal. Educated at Cambridge University, Anand volunteered for military service during the Spanish Civil War; his novel of World War I, *Across the Black Waters* (1940), was conceived in 1937 while Anand was in Spain with the International Brigades. Depicting the tragic experiences of a troop of Indian sepoys fighting in the trenches in Flanders, the novel was adapted for the stage by London's Mán Melá Theatre Company and directed by Domenic Rai in fall 1998, to commemorate the 80th anniversary of the war's end.

Mulk Raj Anand, "Muhammad Iqbal," *The Golden Breath: Studies in Five Poets of the New India*. New York: Dutton, 1933. 61–74, 83–85.

Muhammad Iqbal is by far the most imposing Musalman literary figure of modern times. A great poet, and a profound philosopher, he has been indirectly responsible not only for a prodigious share in strengthening the backbone of the Indian literary and national revival, but also for supplying to Turkey, Persia, Egypt, Afghanistan, Arabia, and almost all Muslim societies, the inspiration of a poetic-philosophic consciousness during the process of their regeneration.

Iqbal was born in 1876 at Sialkot, Punjab, into a middle-class Muslim family of strong sufi-istic tendencies, a fact which is significant in view of the influence on him of Maulana Jalal-ud-Din Rumi and other mystical poets of Persia. As a child he attended a local Government school at Sialkot, and had the good fortune to sit at the feet of an old refined Persian and Arabic scholar, Shams-ul-Ulema (the Sun of the Learned), Maulana Sayyid Mir Hasan, who, like a few other old-world people, was carrying on the traditions of Mughal culture in the India of the Victorian age; and it was under the tutorship of this kindly sage that there was kindled in the poet the love of Persian literature which is the conspicuous feature of his mature writing.

Like most Indian youths of his day, Iqbal also read voraciously in Ghalib, Zok, Mir, Hali, and other Urdu poets, who had already built up a vast body of poetical literature on the debris of the new language which had grown up in the mixed camps of Mughal civil and military life. It seems that it was his study of these poets that first inspired him into writing poetry himself, for he is known as a boy to have sent some of his verses for correction to Nawab Mirza Khan Dag Dihlawi, the greatest Hindustani poet of his day, and sometime tutor to the Nizam of Hyderabad, which that illustrious poet laureate returned with the remark that there was not much room for correction.

The fine efflorescence of Iqbal's genius did not appear, however, till he came as an undergraduate to the university town of Lahore; for here in the seething atmosphere of student life he had increased facilities for social intercourse and wider experience of things, and the bud bloomed forth into a full flower at the magic touch of knowledge. From the very beginning of his career, probably on account of the sufi-istic atmosphere which surrounded the home of his parents, Iqbal had been acutely interested in philosophical speculation. On coming to Lahore, he sought naturally the guidance of the late Sir Thomas Arnold, the celebrated Orientalist who had come to teach at the University of North India with the reputation of a scholar deeply interested in Islam, and as one who had already stimulated many an Indian intellect to the study of Eastern thought and culture at the Muslim University of Aligarh. That guidance was unstintedly placed at his disposal, and Iqbal's poem to Arnold is an eloquent record of his indebtedness to this learned and lovable teacher.

It was at this time, about the beginning of the twentieth century, that Iqbal's poetic activity really began, for it was on coming to Lahore that he uttered those exquisite lines—

Divine grace the dew of remorse has gathered,
Thinking them pearls, as they studded my forehead,

which attracted the attention of the cultured world towards him. Nawab Sir Zulfiqar Ali Khan of Malerkotta has paid a glowing tribute to the poet in his comment on these lines:

"In one sublime verse the poet depicts the angelic sanctity of a soul after its resurrection. How the divine love rejoices to see the ennobling virtue of remorse. Supremely exquisite is the analogy of drops of perspiration to pearls whose purity resembles the chastity of awakened conscience. The poetic euphony which embellishes the dignity of the human soul with incomparable vesture lays claim to be enjoyed as a free work of art."

It is said that many a poet and critic thought of laying down their pens in defeat when they heard that the author of this verse was a young man newly arrived at Lahore, and they unanimously proclaimed the coming into the field of Hindustani poetry of the greatest force since Ghalib.

From now onwards Iqbal frequently began to be dragged by his college friends to *mushairas* (poetical festivals that are held every now and then all over Northern India), and he began to write more consistently than he had done during his schooldays at Sialkot. At one of these *mushairas* he read his well-known poem on the Himalayas, written partly under English and partly under Persian influences, and his reputation emerged from its first stronghold in the hearts of the student community to become a national name. The strong flavour of patriotism that distinguished it had struck a new note in Indian poetry. Added to this was Iqbal's powerful lyric gift. The Himalayas captured the tongue of the nation, so that, like many of his later songs, notably the one about India which has become the Indian national anthem, it spread throughout the length and breadth of Hindustan with the rapidity and intensity of a cyclone, and the lanes and alleys of village, town, and city resounded with the echoes of little boys and girls, who ran about wildly singing it in deafening choruses. Iqbal was at once greeted as the foremost prophet of the national awakening.

Looking at the first authentic period of Iqbal's poetic activity, which begins about 1901 when he came to Lahore, and lasts till 1905 when he sailed for England to prosecute higher studies there, one finds that although the English and Persian influences so peculiarly noticeable in the poem on the Himalayas are not perfectly assimilated, the poet has already achieved that mastery of conception and expression which is the seal of finality in art. Already there is a throbbing, palpitating rhythm in his song, already he marches with a majestic dignity, with his power of thought beautifully in tune with his silver speech, so that this, his first utterance, is, I think, also his noblest; nowhere else, except in his later Persian verse, does he rise quite so high. No doubt many of these poems are expressly stated to be written on English models—for instance, *Hamdardi* (Sympathy) is fashioned on Cowper, *Piam-i-Subha* (The Message of the Morning) on Longfellow, *Ishk aur Mot* (Love and Death) on Tennyson, *Rukhsat-i Bazm-Jahan* (Farewell, O World), and *Ek Pahaaur Ek Gulehri* (The Squirrel and the Mountain) on Emerson; but such is the charm, the loveliness, of that extravagant metaphor and imagery which in the true Oriental manner breaks, as it were, the limits of space and time in its fantastic flights, that one sits caught and imprisoned in the meshes of his harmony, careless as to the sources of his complicated rhythm.

In one of his Urdu poems (a prayer of the poet uttered at the pious moments of dawn, to breathe the secret of his newly awakened consciousness) the words of the song are so finely woven on the chain of music that it has become a sort of rosary to many of his admirers, in telling which they lose themselves in the realms of a boundless joy. Who would not lose himself by saying such a prayer as this:

> When the world-illumining Sun
> Rushed upon night, like a brigand,
> My weeping bedewed the face of the rose,
> My tears washed sleep away from the eyes of the narcissus,
> My passion waked the grass and made it grow . . .
> My being was an unfinished statue,
> Uncomely, worthless, and good for nothing.
> Love chiselled me; I became a man
> And gained knowledge of the nature of the Universe,
> I have seen the movement of the sinews of the sky,
> And the blood coursing in the veins of the moon.

Iqbal's early success depended, however, not only on the delicacy and refinement of his musical sentiments, but on his attempting to perform another remarkable feat. He is trying to enrich the poor vocabulary of Urdu by introducing into it the touching metaphors and the tender images of Persian as well as of Punjabi and other Indian dialects. He is seeking to mould Urdu into shape, to modernise it, because he dreams of a national India possessing a national language. In one of his verses he draws a true picture of the state of Urdu of his day:

The comb seeks still the locks of Urdu to tame,
This wild-hearted moth still burns on the flame;

and in his homage to the spirits of Ghalib and Dag, the last two greatest names in Urdu poetry, he consciously proclaims himself their true successor, imposing on himself the task of reforming the language which they before him had striven to perfect.

The hardships involved in achieving this ideal which Iqbal placed before himself are clearly reflected throughout the verses of his first period. But he is a born fighter, a vigorous propagandist, and he never swerves an inch from his course in the face of obstacles and impediments. Whenever he feels he is in difficulties, he raises his pen to relate himself to his forerunners in the same cause. His poem to Sir Sayyid Ahmad, the great educationist who united the ideals of Western universities and the spirit of the ancient *madrassas* (schools) and *ashrams* (hermitages) of the East in founding the University of Aligarh, and who himself fixed the conventions of Hindustani prose, is, for instance, written in such a state of mind, and it is Iqbal's noblest Indian dedicatory poem, because it suited the poet to write it.

There is one other thing Iqbal wants to do. He wants to express his vehement support of the belief then generally held in India that the blending of the East and West would produce a better world. Whatever contribution the Western nations might make to further this ideal, Iqbal believed he would answer for India, where the ideal was already beginning to be fulfilled, and seemed most possible of realisation. India must, however, be adequately prepared for this formidable task by being rid of its social evils, and its diverse elements must be united. Hoping to weld its heterogeneous forces into a solid whole, Iqbal sings of "our India which lives while Greece and Rome and Egypt lie dead." Indians begin to feel proud of themselves on hearing this, and the strong suggestion issuing from the poet's virile pen transmutes them into a self-conscious nation. Seeking to remove racial and communal hatred, he sings of the *Nia-Shiwala* (the New Temple) of universal worship, where—

Our pilgrimage will be higher than all the pilgrimages of this world,
We will raise the pinnacles of our temple to meet the very edge of the sky,
We will rise every morning to sing sweet hymns,
We will dispense to all worshippers the wine of love.

For—

Power and peace is in the songs of the devoted,
The true end of the men of earth is to love each other.

II

In 1905 the poet booked a passage to England. It was a fortunate circumstance that, immediately on arriving, he came into contact with such outstanding men as McTaggart, the Hegelian, then at the height of his fame as a philosopher; E. G. Browne, the brilliant historian of Persian literature; and Professor R. A. Nicholson, the translator of his long philosophical poem, the *Asrar-i-Khudi* (The Secrets of the Self). The two important preoccupations of his soul in his younger days, philosophy and Persian literature, which had been clouded by the dust of nationalism that his pen had raised, emerged into a new life, and matured under the influence of these friends. The lectures of McTaggart taught him the scientific mode of philosophising, which he, like most other students from the Indian soil, lacked; and the friendship of Browne and Nicholson moulded into final shape the vast knowledge of Persian he had already amassed by his discursive studies at home.

The outcome of his researches in England was an essay on the "Development of Persian Thought," later accepted by the University of Munich for the degree of Doctor of Philosophy, an illuminating little treatise, soundly written, and important, not only because it is still the only book on the history of Persian philosophy, but also in view of Iqbal's philosophical Persian poems, to the writing of which he was soon to dedicate all his fiery genius.

During the period of his stay in Europe, Iqbal wrote very little poetry. Most of what he wrote, however, betrays the intense influence on him of Persian romanticism. The poet seems to have been at that critical period of life when the beauty of the child's dream-world of fancy becomes the beauty of the heart's passionate desire, crying for expression and fulfilment by union with concrete objects. Love dominates this phase of Iqbal's poetry. He is seeking at first to analyse all its implications in the traditional young poet's way. What is love? he asks himself. What is the truth in beauty? What is the relation of beauty and love? What is fulfillment? All the incidental situations that arise in the everyday thoughts of lovers claim his attention. He bursts into a rhapsody, *on seeing a cat in her lap*; he celebrates *the splendour of her beauty*; he writes *messages of love*, and weeps on the irony of *separation,* idolises the moon and the stars, wakes up at dawn to see his earthly beloved enshrined in every particle of nature, and sings to the tune of his palpitating heart tossed and buffeted by the angry waves of passion in the stormy sea of love. When, however, the futile attempt has been made to fathom the depths of that sea and to battle with its waves, the path is clear for the poet to soar up from earth to heaven.

The Oriental poet does not regard earthly love as real. For him it is an illusion which has only enough of the real in it to lead him to God, Whose love alone is true and desirable. Iqbal has a glimpse of the secret. So he writes in memory of that God-intoxicated genius of the India of the nineteenth century, Swami Ram Tirath, still connected in the minds of America as one of the greatest Hindus who brought the spiritual message of the East to them; and the poet has sheltered himself under the wings of the phœnix, who is going to bring him immortality. In poems like *Kali* (Bud), *Salimi, Tanhai* (Solitude), and *An Evening on River Neckar near Heidelberg*, Iqbal seems already to have emancipated himself from the love bound by the circumstances of space and time, and to have reached the realms of divine love.

But as soon as the ecstasy of love's youthful fire had burnt itself out, and as soon as the phœnix of divine love arose from the ashes, he found the atmosphere of Europe uncongenial to him. The outcome of his revolt was the poem in which he sounded a prophetic warning to Western nations of the dangers inherent in their blind devotion to matter and the enjoyment of the senses. In the following translation of this poem one can perceive a prologue to his own proclamation of the new Muslim religious and political theocracy in his later writings:

> The veil shall soon be lifted, the One Beloved to disclose,
> The secret hidden behind love's nature to expose.
> No longer shall Saqi to secret drinkers wine dispense,
> The world shall soon a tavern be, openly shall wine be served hence.
> In towns shall rest those who wildly wandered,
> Their naked feet in meadows fresh shall be comfortable rendered.
> Hejaz in silence has to anxious ears proclaimed
> That God's old compact with desert dwellers shall be re-ordained.
> The lion which sprang from the wilds and shattered Rome,
> The angels say, shall be reborn in its old home.
> O ye who in Western lands reside, learn, God's home is not a business concern,
> The gold you think is pure, soon shall impure turn.
> A suicide's death awaits your civilisation,

A slender bough to rest a nest is no safe position.
In angry seas, where storms and furies rage, the ant shall ride,
Contemptible, but safe, in a frail rose-leaf caravan it shall stride.
For when one day to the dove I breathed, "The freemen here are slaves to earth,"
Suddenly the buds cried out, "He has discovered the secret of our birth."

It was the last poem that Iqbal wrote in Europe, and may fitly be considered his parting word to the West; and, though not very complimentary, it seeks to diagnose its disease with precision. "You have made of God's home a shop," he says to the Western people. "You have corrupted your civilisation; you will soon commit suicide with the very weapons with which you have forged your destinies." And if there is hardly a word of doubt in his casting the horoscope of Europe, his message of hope to the Orient, too, is extended with an almost baffling sureness and certainty of the promise of that greatness which it was soon to achieve. He had felt the inner rhythm of the rising Eastern tide, and he could talk about its future with authority. "A new era is about to begin," he says to Asia. He heralds a new awakening. The world shall soon become a tavern where everyone will come to drink the wine of ideas, for all men are equal before God. Then there will no longer be an intellectual aristocracy usurping all rights to knowledge. The culture of the East, he explains—the little, but redoubtable ant—shall dominate history once more.

The centre of this cultural renaissance will, of course, be Hejaz, for it was there that the prophet's faith first flourished in its pure simplicity; and its motive force will be the compact God made with the people of Arabia in the holy Koran: "God has promised to those of you who believe and do the things that are right that He will cause them to be the rulers of the earth, as He made those who were before them, and that He will establish for them that religion which He has chosen for them, and that after their fears He will give them security in exchange." This divine promise, Iqbal believed, made the Arabs the masters of the world in the seventh century; this and other precepts kept their star in ascendance so long as they followed them. But they forgot themselves, he thinks, when their religious zeal gave place to the evils which luxury and wealth brought to the courts of the Caliphs; they forgot the exhortation in the Koran which enjoins the faithful "to be virtuous, and God commands you to be scrupulously just, and act in a manner that people may be grateful to you." Now Iqbal announces that the believers would rediscover the meaning of those old ideals and rise to form an ideal Muslim Empire—a Utopia with its pivot at Mecca, to which all Muslims will look up as brothers belonging to a common faith, in love with Allah, and devoted to the prophets.

This was the Muezzin's call, the call of the Muezzin of the new Ka'aba. He would go home to the East and stand on the highest pinnacle of the mosque of glory, and day and night call the forgetful men and women of the old faith to prayer with his new message of love and life. The full implication of Iqbal's call was not yet worked out. As soon, however, as he reached India in 1908 he set to work to elaborate his plan, and since then each successive volume of verse that has come from him has been concerned in some way or other with the furtherance of the ideal he conceived in Europe.

. . .

There is an echo of the old, old theme of the *Asrar* and *Ramuz* in the *Pyam*, which the poet drives home with ever new power:

Knowest thou life's secret? Neither seek nor take
A heart unwounded by the thorn, Desire.
Live as the mountain, self-secure and strong,
Not as the sticks and straws that dance along;
   For fierce is the wind and merciless is the fire.

Life and Action, a poem in reply to Heine's *Fragen*, also recalls the *Asrar* doctrine:

> "I have lived a long, long while," said the fallen shore.
> "What I am I know as ill as I knew of yore."
> Then swiftly advanced a wave, from the sea upshot;
> "If I roll, I am," it said; "if I rest, I am not."

Time, which in the *Asrar* was declared to be everlasting, is the subject of a melodious song from which I shall quote two stanzas:

> Sun and stars in my bosom I hold;
> By me, who am nothing, thou art ensouled.
>   In light and in darkness, in city and wold,
> I am pain, I am balm, I am life manifold.
>   Destroyer, quickener, I from of old.
>
>   Chengiz, Timur, specks of my dust they came,
> And Europe's turmoil is a spark of my flame,
>   Blood of his heart my spring flowers claim,
> Hell fire and Paradise I, be it told.

Iqbal's criticism of Western life and thought is both amusing and instructive. His general complaint against it is that—

> Amassing lore, thou hast lost thy heart to-day.
> Ah, what a precious boon thou hast given away!

The League of Nations is described with peculiar irony:

> To the end that wars may cease on this old planet, the suffering
> Peoples of the world have founded a new institution.
> So far as I can see, it amounts to this: a number of undertakers have
> Formed a company to allot the graves!

"Hegel," writes Iqbal, "is a hen that by a dint of enthusiasm lays eggs without association with the cock." Nietzsche, with "whose will to power," meaning "the fullest possible realisation of a complete self-reliant personality," Iqbal has much sympathy, is nevertheless attacked as the "madman of the European china-shop" because he is an atheist:

> If song thou crave, flee from him! Thunder roars in the reed of his pen.
> He plunged a lancet into Europe's heart;
> His hand is red with the blood of the cross.
> He reared a pagoda on the ruins of the Temple.
> His heart is a true-believer, but his brain is an infidel.
> Burn thyself in the fire of Nimrod,
> For the garden of Abraham is produced from fire.

Iqbal renders Bergson's message thus:

> If thou wouldst read life as an open book,
>   Be not a spark divided from the brand,

Bring the familiar eye, the friendly look,
    Nor visit stranger-like thy native land.
O thou by vain imaginings befooled,
Get thee a reason which the heart hath schooled.

Einstein is styled "the hierophant of light, the descendant of Moses and Aaron, who has revived the religion of Zoroaster." Lenin, proclaiming the triumph of Communism to Kaiser Wilhelm, gets the retort that the people have only exchanged one master for another: "Shirin never lacks a lover; if it be not Khusrau, then it is Farhad."

Iqbal's leanings towards Socialism are suggested by the dialogue between *Comte and the Workman*, and the *Workman's Song*; from which last I quote a stanza:

Clad in cotton rags I toil as a slave for hire
To earn for an idle master his silk attire.
The Governor's ruby seal 'tis my sweat that buys,
His horse is gemmed with tears from my children's eyes.

Severe as are his judgments of the West, he is, however, no ungrateful wretch, as is evident from this poem to England:

An Eastern tasted once the wine in Europe's glass,
No wonder if he broke old vows in reckless glee.
The blood came surging up in the veins of his new-born thought.
Predestination's bond slave, he learnt that man is free.
Let not thy soul be vexed with the drunkard's noise and rout!
O Saqi, tell me fairly who 'twas that broached this jar.
The scent of the rose showed first the way into the garden,
Else how should the nightingale have known that roses are?

Chapter 50

Munshi Premchand (Dhanpat Rai) (1880–1936)

"THE AIM OF LITERATURE" (1936)

MUNSHI PREMCHAND IS RENOWNED FOR being the father of the Urdu short story (the *afsana*); however, he wrote in both Urdu and Hindi. Premchand's style of Hindi was distinguished for its commonness and authenticity; the author, like the American author Zora Neale Hurston, celebrated the vernacular poetry heard in everyday speech. Premchand's Hindi novels, stories, and plays reflected the spoken dialects of people of both high and low caste origins. His social realist stories examine the politics of everyday relations between rich and poor, landlords and peasants, and women and society; corruption, colonialism, and the psychological effects of power are themes in Premchand's frequently darkly comic-tragic stories. Premchand's progressivism inspired his anti-communalist vision of Hindu and Muslim unity; he argued in "The Aim of Literature" that, "It is the duty of a writer to support and defend those who are in some way oppressed, suffering or deprived. . . . He pleads justice on their behalf. . . ." Premchand's career as a writer coincided with the Indian anti-colonial and independence movements; his first collection of stories written under the pen name Nawabrai, *Soz-e-Watan* (*Dirge of the Nation*, 1910), was labeled seditious by the British colonial administration, confiscated, and destroyed. In 1921, Premchand quit his job as a teacher in support of Mohandas Gandhi's non-cooperation movement. Impoverished but undeterred, he continued to write and produced more than three hundred short stories, twelve novels, and two plays over the course of his life. The Indian movie director Satyajit Ray adapted two of Premchand's literary works, *Sadgati* (*Salvation*, 1984; television) and *The Chess Players* (1977).

Munshi Premchand, "The Aim of Literature," trans. Francesca Orsini. Delivered at the first All-India Progressive Writers' Conference, Lucknow, India (9 April 1936). *The Oxford India Premchand*. Oxford: Oxford UP, 2004. 2–9.

Gentlemen, this conference is a landmark in our literary history. To date, our conferences and associations have usually only discussed language and language propaganda. So much so that the first [modern] literature available in Hindi and Urdu was written not with the aim of moulding ideas and feelings but only in order to create the language. That, too, was an important task. Until it acquires a stable, fixed form, where will a language find the capacity to express thoughts and feelings? We would be ungrateful if we did not feel thankful towards those language 'pioneers' who cleared our path by creating the Hindustani language. They have done a great thing for our national community.

Language is a means, not an end. Now that our language has acquired a stable form we should move on and turn our attention to the content and the aim for which that foundational work was started in the first place. The language in which works like *Bagh-o bahar* and *Baital pacchisi* initially marked the peak of service to literature has now become a suitable medium for enquiry into scholarly and scientific matters. This conference marks the clear recognition of this fact.

Language is both for ordinary conversation and for writing. The language of ordinary conversation existed also at the time of Mir Amman and Lallujilal, but the language in which they took their first, tentative steps was the written language, and that is literature. Ordinary conversation serves to impress our ideas upon our friends and close ones, to draw out our feelings of joy and sadness. Writers do the same thing with their pens. True, their audience is much wider, and if their words contain some truth their works continue to influence the hearts for centuries.

I do not mean to say, however, that anything that is written is literature. We call literature a work which expresses some truth, whose language is mature, polished and beautiful, and which has the ability to leave an impression on the heart and mind. In literature, this power emerges in full when it is the truths and experiences of life that find expression. Although we once used to be impressed by stories of magical adventures, ghost tales and romances of parted lovers, now they hardly hold any interest for us. Undoubtedly a writer who knows human nature can describe the truths of life even in tales of magic and in love stories about princes and princesses, but this confirms the dictum that in order for literature to exert any influence it necessarily has to mirror the truths of life. Then you can turn it any way you want—even the tale of a cock-sparrow or the rose and the nightingale can come handy.

There have been many definitions of literature, but in my opinion the best definition for it is—'the criticism of life'. Whether in the form of an essay or a poem, literature should criticize and explain life.

The age that we have just crossed had no concern for life. Our literary people would use their imagination to conjure magical worlds, whether it was *Fasana e-'Ajaib*, *Bostan-e Khyal* or *Chandrakanta Santati*.[1] The aim of those tales was simply to entertain and satisfy our taste for the wondrous. That literature should have anything to do with life was beyond imagination. A story is a story, life is life—the two were considered opposites. Similarly, poets were tainted by individualism. The satisfaction of desire was their ideal of love, the satisfaction of the eyes, their ideal of beauty. Poetry circles would display their fireworks and talents in order to express these erotic feelings. A new wordplay, a new fancy was enough to earn praises, however distant they might have been from objective reality. Fanciful images involving *ashiyana* (nest) and *qafas* (cage), *barq* (lightning) and *khirman* (heapstack) were used with such skill to illustrate the various states of despair and suffering of the lover separated from his beloved that the listeners would have to clasp their bosoms. And just how popular this kind of poetry is still today, is something you and I know very well.

There is no doubt that the aim of poetry and of literature is to sharpen our perceptions, but human life is not just confined to love between man and woman. Can a literature whose themes are confined to the emotional states of love and the pain of separation and despair that spring from it, a literature which believes that escaping from the problems of the world is the meaning of life, answer our needs for thoughts and feelings? The mental and emotional states of love are only a part of human life, and if literature remains largely confined to them it brings little honour to the community and the age it belongs to, and their taste.

Whether in Hindi or Urdu, poetry was pretty much in the same condition. It is not easy to remain uninfluenced by the popular literary and poetic taste of one's age. And everybody longs for praise and appreciation. For poets, poetry was their means of livelihood, and who but the wealthy elites could appreciate poetry? Our poets never had the chance to confront ordinary life nor could they be influenced by its truths, and they were all, rich and poor, victims of a general intellectual crisis, which meant that no mental and intellectual life was left.

We cannot blame the literary people of that period for this. Literature is but a mirror of its age. The same feelings and thoughts which animate people's hearts also come to dominate literature. In that decadent age, people either made love or became engrossed in spiritual matters and asceticism. And when literature comes to be seen through the filter of the world's transience, when each and every word is coloured with despair and filled with moanings about the iniquity of the times or reflects erotic feeling, you can rest assured that the national community will be trapped in inertia and decadence and will have no strength of purpose and struggle left. It will have blinded itself to high ideals and will lose its ability to see and understand the world.

However, our literary tastes are changing rapidly. Nowadays literature is not just meant for relaxation, it has a further aim apart from entertainment. It no longer only tells stories of happy and unhappy lovers, but it ponders on the problems of life and solves them too. It no longer seeks inspiration and vigour from wondrous and stupefying tales, or allure in alliteration, but concerns itself with issues affecting society and individuals. Currently, good literature is judged by the sharpness of its perception, which stirs our feelings and thoughts into motion.

The aims of ethics and of literature are the same—the difference is only in their manner of teaching. Ethics tries to mould intelligence and character through arguments and preaching, while the chosen field of literature are mental and emotional states. Whatever we see in our lives and whatever experiences and blows we encounter, once they reach the imagination they inspire literary creativity. The sharper a poet or a writer is, the more attractive and of high order the literary work will be. A literature which brings no challenge to our tastes, which does not provide us with mental and spiritual satisfaction, which does not awaken strength and dynamism within us, which fails to raise from slumber our sense of beauty, and which does not produce in us true determination and true resolve to overcome difficulties— such a literature is of no use to us today and it is not even worthy of the name.

In earlier times, religion kept society in check. Religious imperatives were the basis for the spiritual and ethical civility of man, and religion used either fear or reward—virtue or sin as its instrument. Now literature has taken this task upon itself, and its instrument is the love of beauty. Literature tries to awaken in man this love for beauty. There is no human being who does not have a perception of beauty. And the more developed and active this tendency is in a writer, the more influential his or her work will be. By contemplating nature and sharpening perception, the writer's sense of beauty becomes so acute that anything ugly, uncivilized and lacking in humanness becomes unbearable to him and he will attack it with words and feelings. In other words, one could say that the writer weaves a cloak of humanness, divineness and civility. It is the duty of a writer to support and defend those who are in some way oppressed, suffering or deprived, whether they be individuals or groups. He pleads justice on their behalf and considers himself successful when through his efforts the court's sense of justice and beauty is awakened.

However, unlike an ordinary lawyer, a writer cannot plead for the innocence of his clients using just any kinds of arguments, fair or unfair. A writer cannot employ exaggeration, nor can he spin tales. In the courtroom of society, the writer knows, such methods fail to make any impression. Society can change its heart only when he does not shy an inch from the truth, otherwise the jury will form a bad opinion and will decide against him. A writer writes stories, but keeping in mind reality. A writer shapes images, but so that they may be alive and expressive. A writer surveys human nature with sharp eyes, studies psychology and tries to have characters who behave in every situation as if they were made of flesh and blood. Thanks to natural empathy and love of beauty, a writer can reach even the most subtle areas which human beings are usually unable to reach because of their humanity.

The tendency towards depicting reality is growing so much in modern literature that stories nowadays try not to go beyond the limits of direct experience. We are not content to think that characters resemble real human beings in their psychological makeup, but we want to be sure that they really are human beings and that the writer has succeeded, as much as possible, in writing their life story. Because we no longer believe in characters created from fantasy, their acts and thoughts fail to impress us. We want to rest assured that what the writer has created is based on actual experiences and that he himself is speaking through his characters. That is why some critics call literature the psychological history of a writer.

The same event or situation does not leave the same impression on everyone. Every person has a different mentality and point of view. A writer's ability lies in having the reader agree with his own mentality or way of looking at things. Herein lies an author's success. At the same time, we also expect every writer to awaken our senses and broaden our mental horizon thanks to his wide knowledge and breadth of ideas—his vision should be subtle, deep and wide enough so as to give us spiritual pleasure and strength.

In every individual, whatever stage of self-reform he or she may be at, lies the potential to reach a better state. But we are affected by our weaknesses as by diseases. Just as physical health is our natural state and sickness is its opposite, in the same way mental and moral health are also our natural states, and we are unhappy about our mental and moral deficiencies in the same way as a sick person is unhappy about his sickness. And just as a patient keeps searching for a cure, we, too, strive to get rid of our weaknesses in order to become better human beings. We go in search of holy men and *faqirs*, perform religious rituals, sit at the feet of our elders, listen to the sermons of wise men, or study literature. It is our lowly tastes and our lack of love that are responsible for all our weaknesses. How can weaknesses persist where there is true love for beauty and wide-ranging love? Love is the real spiritual food, and all weaknesses stem from not getting this food or from getting it in a polluted form. The writer or artist produces within us this experience of beauty and the warm spirit of love. One sentence, one word, one hint and we feel lit up inside. But until the artist himself is drunk with love for beauty and his own soul is lit up by this light, how can he bestow it upon us?

The question is: what is beauty? This seems like a meaningless question at first sight, because we have no doubt in our minds as to what beauty is. We have seen the sun rise and set, we have seen the glow of dawn and sunset, we have seen fragrant flowers, birds chirping sweetly, brooks gurgling gently, springs dancing—this is beauty.

Why do we feel happy inside when we see these things? Because of the harmony of colour and sound. Music bewitches us because of the harmony between musical instruments. We ourselves have been created by different elements coming together in equal measure, and therefore our soul is constantly yearning for that harmony and balance. Literature expresses an artist's spiritual harmony in a visible form. And harmony creates beauty, it does not destroy it. It strengthens within us feelings of loyalty, truthfulness, sympathy, love for justice and equality. And wherever these feelings exist we find strength and life; wherever they are absent we find division, opposition, self-interest, hatred, enmity and death. This alienation and conflict are signs of a life contrary to nature, just as sickness is a sign of an unnatural way of life. How can narrow-mindedness and self-interest possibly exist where affinity with life and equality exist? When our soul is nurtured in the free atmosphere of nature, the germs of baseness and wickedness die of their own accord, exposed to the light and the air. It is by setting oneself apart from life that all these mental and emotional diseases are created. Literature makes our lives natural and free. In other words, it is thanks to literature that our minds are refined. This is the main aim of literature.

The 'Progressive Writers' Association'—this name sounds wrong to me. A writer or artist is naturally progressive. Were this not his nature, he would probably not be an artist. A writer is someone who feels something lacking, both within and also outside himself. It is to remedy this lack that his soul is restless. A writer feels that the individual and society are not in the happy and carefree state he or she would like to see them in. This is why he chafes under the present mental and social conditions. He wants to put an end to these unpleasant conditions so that the world can become a better place to live and to die. This pain, this feeling keeps his brain and heart active. His heart, laden with pain, cannot bear to see any group suffering under the constraint of rules and conventions. Why cannot we find the needful to free that group from slavery and poverty? The more acutely a writer feels this pain, the greater the force and truth his work will produce. How a writer manages to control the intensity with which his perceptions are expressed is the secret of his craft. It is perhaps necessary to emphasize this special quality here because not every writer or author has the same understanding of progress (*unnati*). What one community considers to be progress, another may well consider decadence, and for this reason the writer does not want to subject his art to any objective. To the writer, art means the expression of mental dispositions, whatever good or bad effect they may have on an individual or society.

What I mean by progress, is the condition which produces in us the resolve and energy to act, that which makes us realize the unhappy state we are in, the internal and external causes which have brought us to this wretched and lifeless state, and that which makes us strive to remove them.

To me, poetic ideas have no meaning if they make the impermanence of the world have a stronger hold over our hearts (our monthly journals are filled with these ideas) and if they do not arouse within us dynamism and zeal. If we tell the story of two young lovers in a way that makes no impact on our love of beauty and only makes us weep for them because they are apart, what movement have we brought to the mind and taste? Perhaps once people did get sentimental about them, but nowadays these stories are useless. The time for this sentimental art is gone. Nowadays we need an art which carries a message of action. Now, I also say with Mister Iqbal:

> Ramz-e hayat joi juz dar tapish nayabi
> radakuljum armidan nang ast ab-e ju ra.
> Ba ashiyan na nashinam ze lazzat-e parvaz
> gahe bashakh-e gulam gahe bar lab-e juyam.

[If you are searching for the water of life you will not find it but amid struggle. For a river, to go and rest in the ocean is shameful. I never sit in the nest to enjoy flying, I am sometimes on a rose branch, sometimes on the bank of a river.]

In other words, egotism, giving prominence to our individual point of view, is what pulls us down towards inertia, decadence and indifference, and this kind of art is useless for us, both as individuals and as a community.

I have no hesitation in saying that I weigh art on the same scales of usefulness as I do with other things. Undoubtedly, the aim of art is to strengthen our sense of beauty, and art is the key to our spiritual happiness, but there is no mental and spiritual happiness one can achieve through taste which does not also have a useful aspect. Happiness is naturally allied with usefulness, and a useful thing can give us both pleasure and pain.

A glowing sky at sunset is undoubtedly the most beautiful spectacle, but the same glow in the sky, if seen during the monsoon, will not give us any pleasure. During the monsoon we want to see black rainclouds. When we see flowers we feel happy, because we look forward to their fruit. We get spiritual pleasure from tuning our life in accordance with nature because our life is enhanced and developed by it. It is nature's course to grow and develop, and the feelings, perceptions and ideas that give us pleasure enhance this growth and development. An artist is someone who prepares the condition for development by creating beauty through art.

But beauty, too, like any other element, is not neutral and objective, it is relative. A thing which will give pleasure to a wealthy man may be a source of displeasure to somebody else. Whereas a rich man enjoys perfect bliss by sitting in a garden full of fragrant flowers and listening to the birds chirping, a sensible man may be repulsed by the same display of opulence.

Since the beginning of life, fraternity, equality, civility and love have been a golden dream for idealists. Religious prophets have always tried, albeit unsuccessfully, to make this dream come true by means of religious, moral and spiritual rules. Buddha, Jesus, Muhammad and all the other prophets and religious founders have tried to build equality on ethical foundations, but no one has been successful, and perhaps the difference between rich and poor is more cruelly evident now than ever before.

'It is stupid to try what has been tried before'; according to this saying, if we try now to reach the high goal of equality by holding on to religion and ethics we will not be successful. Should we therefore forget this dream as if it were the product of an excitable mind? But then there will be no ideal left to guide man towards progress and fulfilment. In that case it would be better for humankind to stop living. We must consider that the ideal which mankind has pursued and cultivated from the beginning of civilization and for which it has made so many sacrifices, the ideal thanks to which religions came into being, is an imperishable truth and we must step onto the path of progress. We need to create a new association that will be comprehensive and in which equality, no longer based only on moral obligations, will acquire a concrete shape. This is the ideal that our literature must set for itself.

Note

1   *Fasana-e 'Ajaib* (1824), by Mirza Rajab 'Ali Beg Surur (1787–1867), *Bostan-e khyal* (1882–91) and *Chandrakanta Santati*, the multi-volume sequel by Devkinandan Khatri and his son Durgaprasad Khatri of *Chandrakanta* (1892), were all popular examples of narratives of wonder and adventure.

Chapter 51

LÉGITIME DÉFENSE MANIFESTO
(1932)

T HE *LÉGITIME DÉFENSE* (SELF-DEFENSE) GROUP was formed in Paris and comprised young, aspiring poets from Martinique: Etienne Léro (a philosophy student and leader of the group), Thélus Léro, Réné Ménil, Jules-Marcel Monnerot, Michel Pilotin, Maurice-Sabas Quitman, Auguste Thésée, and Pierre Yoyotte, whose sister Simone was also centrally involved with the group. The students were between the ages of twenty and twenty-four when they collectively wrote their manifesto; their impatience with their petit bourgeois French Antillean compatriots and elders is captured in the unapologetically zealous language of the Far Left. They formed the short-lived *Légitime Défense* revue as an alternative to the more moderate *La Revue du Monde Noir* (1931–32). In addition to proclaiming allegiance to European surrealists like André Breton, Leautréamont, Tristan Tzara, and Salvador Dali, they also recognized a kinship with the Harlem Renaissance writers Langston Hughes, Zora Neale Hurston, and Claude McKay, and with Race Men, including Marcus Garvey, W.E.B. Du Bois, and C.L.R. James. The *Légitime Défense* group made a point of calling attention to international crimes of oppression; they were galvanized by Pan-Afro-Caribbean independence movements and injustices like the 1931 trial of the Scottsboro Boys, nine boys ranging in age from twelve to nineteen who had been falsely accused of rape and condemned to death in Scottsboro, Alabama. For a comprehensive discussion of the group see Franklin Rosemont and Robin G. Kelley's "Introduction: Invisible Surrealists" and chapter 1, "The First Black Surrealists" in *Black, Brown, and Beige: Surrealist Writings from Africa and the Diaspora.*

"*Légitime Défense Manifesto*," trans. Alex Wilder. *Black, Brown, and Beige: Surrealist Writings from Africa and the Diaspora*, ed. Franklin Rosemont and Robin D.G. Kelley. Austin: U of Texas P, 2009. 36–38.

This is only a preliminary warning. We consider ourselves totally committed. We are sure that there are other young people like us who could add their signatures to ours and who—to the extent that it is compatible with remaining alive—refuse to adjust to the surrounding dishonor. And we are against all those who attempt, consciously or not, by their smiles, work, exactitude, propriety, speech, writings, actions and their very persons, to pretend that everything can continue as it is. We rise up here against all those who are not suffocated by this capitalist, Christian, bourgeois world to which, involuntarily, our protesting bodies belong.

In every country the Communist Party (Third International) is in the process of playing the decisive card of the Spirit—in the Hegelian sense of the word. Its defeat, impossible as we think it to be, would be for us the definitive *Je ne peux plus*. We believe unreservedly in its triumph because we accept the dialectical materialism of Marx, freed of all misleading interpretation and victoriously put to the test of experience by Lenin. We are ready, on this plane, to submit to the discipline that such convictions demand.

On the concrete plane of modes of human expression, we equally and unreservedly accept surrealism to which, in 1932, we relate our becoming. We refer our readers to the two *Manifestoes* of André Breton, to the complete works of Aragon, André Breton, René Crevel, Salvador Dali, Paul Éluard, Benjamin Péret and Tristan Tzara. It must be said that it is one of the disgraces of our time that these works are not better known everywhere that French is read. And in the works of Sade, Hegel, Lautréamont, Rimbaud—to mention only a few—we seek everything surrealism has taught us to find. As for Freud, we are ready to utilize the immense machine that he set in motion to dissolve the bourgeois family. We are moving with sincerity at a furious pace. We want to see clearly into our dreams and we listen to their voices. And our dreams permit us to see clearly into the life that has been imposed on us for so long.

Among the filthy bourgeois conventions, we despise above all the humanitarian hypocrisy, this stinking emanation of Christian decay. We loathe pity. We don't give a damn about sentiment. We intend to shed light on human psychic concretions—a light related to that which illuminates Salvador Dali's splendid, convulsive, plastic works, where it seems sometimes, suddenly, that love-birds could be ink-bottles or shoes or little bits of bread, taking wing from assassinated conventions.

If this little journal, a temporary instrument, breaks down, we shall find other instruments. We accept with indifference the conditions of time and space which, by defining us in 1932 as people of the French West Indies, have thus settled our boundaries without at all limiting our field of action. This first collection of texts is particularly devoted to the West Indian question as it appears to us. (The following issues, without abandoning this matter, will take up many others.) And if, by its content, this collection is addressed primarily to *young* French West Indians, it is because we think it is a good idea that our first effort finds its way to people whose capacity for revolt we are far from underestimating. And if it is aimed especially at young *blacks*, this is because we believe that they especially have had to suffer from capitalism (outside Africa, witness Scottsboro) and that they seem to offer, in that they have a materially determined ethnic personality, a generally higher potential for revolt and for joy. For want of a black proletariat, to whom international capitalism has not given the means to understand us, we speak to the children of the black bourgeoisie; we speak to those who are not already killed established fucked-up academic successful decorated decayed endowed decorative prudish decided opportunist; we speak to those who can still accept life with some appearance of truthfulness.

Having decided to be as objective as possible, we know nothing of each other's personal lives. We want to go a long way, and if we expect much from psychoanalytic investigation, we do not underestimate (from those acquainted with psychoanalytic theory) pure and simple psychological confessions which, provided that the obstacles of social conventions are removed, can tell us a great deal. We do not admit that one can be ashamed of what he suffers. The Useful—social convention—constitutes the backbone of the bourgeois "reality" that we want to break. In the realm of intellectual investigation, we pit against this "reality" the sincerity that allows man to disclose in his love, for example, the ambivalence which permits the elimination of the contradiction decreed by logic. According to logic, once an object with an affective value appears, we must respond to it either with the feeling called love or with the feeling called hate. Contradiction is a function of the Useful. It does not exist in love. It does not exist in the dream. And it is only by horribly gritting our teeth that we are able to endure the abominable system of constraints and restrictions, the extermination of love and the limitation of the dream, generally known by the name of western civilization.

Emerging from the French black bourgeoisie, which is one of the saddest things on this earth, we declare—and we shall not go back on this declaration—that we are opposed to all the corpses: administrative, governmental, parliamentary, industrial, commercial and all the others. We intend, as traitors to this class, to take the path of treason as far as it will go. We spit on everything that they love and venerate, especially those things that give them sustenance and joy.

And all those who adopt the same attitude as we, no matter where they come from, will be welcome among us.[1]

Etienne LÉRO, Thélus LÉRO, René MÉNIL, Jules-Marcel MONNEROT, Michel PILOTIN, Maurice-Sabas QUITMAN, Auguste THÉSÉE, Pierre YOYOTTE. 1932

Note

1   If our critique is purely negative here, if we do not propose any positive efforts in place of that which we mercilessly condemn, we excuse ourselves on the grounds that it was necessary to begin—a necessity which did not enable us to await the full development of our ideas. In our next issue, we hope to develop our ideology of revolt.

READINGS IN LITERARY CRITICISM BY MODERNIST WRITERS

The extraordinary scientific breakthroughs made during the latter part of the nineteenth century and the beginning of the twentieth – the theory of evolution, radio waves, X-rays, radioactivity, relativity, among many others – challenged traditional beliefs in a supreme being and a universe created and ordered on a specific, knowable date. The results of these advances in knowledge and understanding were, ironically, disorienting and destabilizing for many – and they made the universe more rather than less mysterious. Although often labeled "user unfriendly," so-called high modernist literature was, for the most part, rarely willfully obscure and difficult – though it was, more or less overtly, self-reflexive, aware of being made of language, as well as of other literature. Certain modernists – painters like Marcel Duchamp, the dadaist poet Tristan Tzara, Gertrude Stein in *Tender Buttons*, Joyce in *Finnegans Wake* – transcended realist boundaries, yet many others (perhaps most) did not consider themselves anti-realists. Rather, having come to understand reality to be different from the way their predecessors viewed it, they considered it the task of artists to become their own contemporaries by representing the new reality – as they perceived it – as honestly and faithfully as they could. Conrad and Ford adopted the missionary zeal of many of their contemporaries, though they framed their task in secular terms. Conrad assured his readers that his "task . . . is . . . to make you hear, to make you feel – it is, before all, to make you see."[1] Ford, like Woolf and D.H. Lawrence, sought to align fiction with life as he understood it: "it became very early evident to us that what was the matter with the Novel . . . was that it went straight forward, whereas in your gradual making acquaintanceship with your fellows you never do go straight forward." Even if the effect was disorienting to readers, doing justice to a character meant that "you must first get him in with a strong impression and then work backwards and forwards over his past,"[2] for this is what happens when one meets and then gets to know someone. "The general effect of a novel," Ford insists, "must be the general effect that life makes on mankind. A novel must therefore not be a narration, a report."[3] Woolf, who agreed that the task of the writer who would keep faith with reality had changed, assailed the popular Edwardian novelists – Arnold Bennett, H.G. Wells, and John Galsworthy – as "materialists" who were indifferent to actual lives that people lived, their inner realities: these writers, Woolf maintains, meticulously constructed superb fictional houses, but their characters fail to inhabit them. They write, she says, "of unimportant things; . . . they spend immense skill and immense industry making the trivial and the transitory appear the true and the enduring."[4] But, she adds, "Life escapes; and perhaps without life nothing else is worth while." In contrast, she viewed Georgian novelists like Joyce (for all his lower-class crudities) and herself as "spiritualists" concerned with the inner life, and she charged them "to record the atoms as they fall upon the mind in the order in which they fall, let us trace the pattern, however disconnected and incoherent in appearance, which each sight or incident scores upon the consciousness."[5] So fully and accurately representing character, she prophesied, would bring into being the great age of literature on whose verge they were trembling.[6]

Even as they treat everyday affairs, modernist novels such as *The Good Soldier*, *Women in Love*, *Mrs. Dalloway*, and *As I Lay Dying*, as if bent on fulfilling Woolf's prescription and exhortation, provide associational and allusive narratives and little in the way of physical description (of buildings or characters) other than what happens to appear in someone's consciousness. For example, the remarkable, but undetailed representation of the house in the "Time Passes" section of Woolf's *To the Lighthouse* bears little resemblance to those in Arnold Bennett's novels. Instead, the section tracks the house's falling into decay – "Not only was furniture confounded,"[7] but so too are all other traces of human presence – and then the resuscitation, or "some rusty laborious birth,"[8] of something animate that somehow becomes, once again, a site for human habitation. Of *Ulysses*, Joyce (perhaps misleadingly) said, "I want to give a picture of Dublin so complete that if the city one day suddenly disappeared from the earth it could be reconstructed out of my book,"[9] but while *Ulysses* depicts the texture and impression of 1904 Dublin, it provides far less physical description of its places (and people) than Joyce promises, or that it seems at first to offer. One of Pound's prescriptions for the poet was "Don't be descriptive; remember that the painter can describe a landscape much better than you can."[10] The result of taking such advice was imagism and *The Waste Land* and Pound's *Cantos*, disorientingly modern poems comprising "fragments" of a civilization that Pound, in *Hugh Selwyn Mauberley*, calls "an old bitch gone in the teeth."

Modernist writings, like the age that produced them, were obsessed with perspective, human psychology, and ways of knowing that fostered an epistemological literature, verging on detective fiction,[11] that often challenges its readers to tease out what the texts only imply (as in Henry James's *What Maisie Knew* and *The Turn of the Screw*; Conrad's *Heart of Darkness*[12] and *Lord Jim*; and Ford's *The Good Soldier*), or to follow the allusive workings of human consciousness (Dorothy Richardson, Proust, Joyce). Modernist narrators came to seem increasingly unreliable and partial (in both senses), often making a virtue of fore-grounding – making overt, proclaiming, *flaunting* – their constructed nature, which most earlier narratives had sought to conceal. Determined to represent as precisely as they could what had come to seem increasingly complex, mysterious, and nuanced, modernists sought or created imagery and language – out of the raw materials of their culture's and their personal pasts, of other cultures, and of the depths of the human psyche – that reprise Flaubert's notion of *le mot juste*.

A fragmented age produced a fragmented, cubistic art and sculpture that was often made from found objects, broken up and reassembled in ostensibly random ways that represented multiple viewpoints simultaneously. Influencing movements in music and architecture, cubism also stimulated or paralleled the creation of fragmented novels (Joyce's *Dubliners*, Sherwood Anderson's *Winesburg, Ohio*, Hemingway's *In Our Time*, Faulkner's *Go Down, Moses*) and narratives (Eliot, *The Waste Land*; Pound, *The Cantos*; Faulkner, *The Sound and the Fury* and *As I Lay Dying*) made, as Eliot has it, of fragments shorn against a culture's ruins. The form of the well-made novel was broken, just as dramatists like Ibsen, Chekhov, Shaw, Pirandello, and Brecht were breaking the form of the well-made play, and writers like Amy Lowell, Wallace Stevens, Pound, H.D., Eliot, and Hart Crane subverted and inverted traditional forms and notions of poetry. In addition, an anti-heroic age (rendered mundane in many ways by the disastrous World War I and the subsequent flu pandemic) produced an anti-heroic literature that often flaunted bodily functions like sex and excretion, and yet was largely peopled by the cuckolded (*The Good Soldier, Ulysses*), impotent (*The Sun Also Rises*, Aldington's *Death of a Hero*), shell-shocked and amnesiac (West's *The Return of a Soldier*, Faulkner's *Soldier's Pay*), paralyzed (*Parade's End, Lady Chatterley's Lover*), emasculated (*The Sound and the Fury, Light in August*), or those reduced to a shell (*Johnny Got His Gun*). As if attempting to cure the era of its sense of deracination, cultural dislocation, and purposeless drift, high modernist literature became allusive, intertextual, mythic, encyclopedic, precise if often obscure, grounded in little-known history and myth (*The Waste Land, The Cantos, Ulysses, Absalom, Absalom!, Finnegans Wake*).

Yet there was, as there always is, a counter-narrative to that of the predominant paradigm. Woolf's critiques of those she denounced as Edwardian materialists were objected to by, for example, Rosa Luxemburg, and further complicated by Munshi Premchand's locally invested realism, Richard Wright's urgent and socio-politically invested narratives, and Mulk Raj Anand's hybrid modernist-realist influences. Antonio Gramsci, like George Lukacs after him, also presents a useful counter-narrative to formalist high modernists' appreciations of density, difficulty, irony, ambiguity, irresolution, and the like as the ideal modern literary narrative and poetic aesthetics. A little magazine like *Others* and a writer like Mina Loy, who at times aggressively and satirically challenged canonical high modernism in its very formation and process of self-reverent institutionalization, also illustrate the debates that were contemporary with modernism and remain central to the broad field of modernist studies. For little magazines such as *Others, The Little Review, The English Review, The Crisis, Poetry*, and *Blast* that addressed minority, highly literary, and politically radical audiences espoused and generated experimental writing, critical exegisis, and manifestos. Robert Scholes and Clifford Wulfman claim that "modernism began in the magazines,"[13] as these small-circulation publications allowed writers not only to publish avant-garde poetry and prose that would have baffled or threatened editors of popular magazines and presses, but also gave writers and critics a platform to define, explicate, and debate new literary movements. As an alternative forum for writing and literary criticism outside the university or the popular press, the little magazines enabled writers to stake bold, provocative claims for their work.

The audience for English literature in its many variants – experimental, popular, classical, and highbrow – expanded dramatically in the twentieth century with growing literary audiences of women and the lower classes, the global spread of English, and the proliferation of cheaper and more widely accessible published material. Many modernists reached out to this growing readership, giving lectures and, with the expansion of broadcast media, on-air talks on literary topics for a general audience. Others viewed it with suspicion as a "lowering" of the reading public. Paul Fussell writes that in England during World War I, "the appeal of popular education and 'self-improvement' was at its peak, and such education was still conceived largely in humanistic terms."[14] Readers from all classes believed that intimate knowledge of Shakespeare's plays, John Bunyan's *Pilgrim's Progress*, and John Milton's *Paradise Lost* led to social and moral betterment. In England, democratic schemes such as the Workmen's Institutes and the National Home Reading Union sought to educate working-class readers, and cheaper editions of canonical texts provided by World's Classics and the Everyman's Library created further opportunities for self-education. In the late nineteenth and early twentieth centuries, women began to be admitted to universities from which they had previously been excluded, and since they were not taught Greek or Latin like their male counterparts in the British public schools, many gravitated to studying literature in English. Among poorer women, literary aspirations and those that they passed on to their children came to represent a path out of poverty. Aggressively literary female characters in works such as

Theodore Dreiser's *Sister Carrie* (1900), D.H. Lawrence's *Sons and Lovers* (1913), and Willa Cather's *A Lost Lady* (1923) represent the enormous expectations and disappointments brought on by cultivating literariness in otherwise desperate circumstances. For readers throughout the British Empire the study of English literature was deeply enmeshed in the experience of imperialism. In the nineteenth-century, colonial administrators like Thomas Babington Macaulay, whose "A Minute on Indian Education" (1835) denigrated native literary traditions, urged imperial states to establish educational programs focused on the English canon. For readers in India, the West Indies, and Africa, learning English and studying English literature became prerequisites for breaking into the middle class and carried the heavy burden of imperial authority.

Modernism's first readers included the inner circle of little magazine subscribers as well as a more popular imagined audience that Woolf calls the "common reader" and that Joyce describes in *Ulysses* as an "ordinary man on an ordinary day." Acknowledging the need to explain, explicate, and critique their own writings and those of their contemporaries, they became the first great generation of literary critics, thereby spawning the discipline that became Literary Criticism and that entered the academy in the form of English Studies. Joyce, for one, did so intentionally, saying that "I've put in so many enigmas and puzzles that it will keep the professors busy for centuries arguing over what I meant, and that's the only way of insuring one's immortality,"[15] though he subsequently admitted that "I may have oversystema-tized *Ulysses*."[16] Great literary critics had certainly appeared prior to the modernist period – Philip Sidney (1554–86), John Dryden (1631–1700), Samuel Johnson (1709–84), Samuel Taylor Coleridge (1772–1834), Matthew Arnold (1822–88), among others – but no age before the modernist gave rise to literary criticism on such a scale and extent, and so self-consciously, and perhaps cannily, seemed to mandate that its practitioners critique themselves and their contemporaries, thereby birthing an academic enterprise of its own. The idea of a poetics of fiction, for example, antedates the twentieth century hardly at all: in 1884 James refers to such a notion in the somewhat defensive tone we might expect from an attempt to define a poetics of TV soap opera. James refers to his "temerity" in affixing "so comprehen-sive a title [as 'The Art of Fiction'] to these few remarks. . . . Only a short time ago it might have been supposed that the English novel was not what the French call *discutable*. It had no air of having a theory, a conviction, a consciousness of itself behind it – of being the expression of an artistic faith, the result of choice and comparison. . . . there was a comfortable, good-humoured feeling abroad that a novel is a novel, as a pudding is a pudding, and that our only business with it could be to swallow it."[17] Self-conscious concerning the obscurity and allusive-ness of their enterprise, the modernists became their own initial critics, producing a great deal of explanatory literature about what they and their contemporaries were all about: Henry James's prefaces to his novels and Shaw's to his plays; Joyce's charts for *Ulysses*; Eliot's notes for *The Waste Land*; Woolf's diaries and letters; critical essays and books by Eliot, Ford, Forster, Lawrence, Pound, Woolf, among many others.

Terry Eagleton suggests that contemporary literary studies were an unintended consequence of the Great War: "we owe the University study of English, in part at least, to a meaningless massacre. The Great War, with its carnage of ruling-class rhetoric, put paid to some of the more strident forms of chauvinism on which English had previously thrived."[18] But to simplify Eagleton's argument somewhat, he maintains that they also resulted from both the difficulty of modernist texts and the equally complex and problematic explanations of them proffered by the modernists themselves: "the definition of an academic subject was what could be examined, and since English was no more than idle gossip about literary taste it was difficult to know how to make it unpleasant enough to qualify as a proper academic pursuit. This, it might be said, is one of the few problems associated with the study of English which have since been effectively resolved."[19] Of course, whether the study of English is viewed as "unpleasant" is a matter of individual taste, but the high modernists certainly went a long way to establish the basis for such consideration when they created both the literary and critical foundational texts of their era. The question of whether such commentary and criticism is more elucidating than obscuring has itself been much debated. In any event, we provide a representative sample of modernist criticism – of self and others – in the Foundational Readings of this section.

Notes

1   Conrad, "Preface" to "The Nigger of the *Narcissus*."
2   Ford, *Joseph Conrad* 129–30.
3   Ford, *Joseph Conrad* 129–30.
4   Woolf, "Modern Fiction" 153. (See also Chapter 58 of this volume, p. 474.)
5   Woolf, "Modern Fiction" 155. (See also Chapter 58 of this volume, p. 477.)
6   Woolf, "Mr. Bennett and Mrs. Brown," 119.
7   Woolf, *To the Lighthouse* 126.
8   Woolf, *To the Lighthouse* 139.
9   Joyce, in Budgen 67; also quoted in Norris 1.
10   Pound, "A Few Don'ts by an Imagiste" 203. (See also Chapter 56 of this volume, p. 468.)
11   Poe, Dickens, Wilkie Collins, Conan Doyle, among others, laid the groundwork for detective fiction. Modernists who put epistemological questions and doubts at the center of their conception and representation of reality raise detective-like questions in their writings. Postmodernism's focus on ontology and multiple realities, on the other hand, seems grounded in science fiction, whose origins are also in the nineteenth century: Mary Shelley's *Frankenstein* and *The Last Man*, Jules Verne, H.G. Wells, among others.
12   Ford praises *Heart of Darkness* for its use of "detective story" technique (*March of Literature* 771).
13   Scholes and Wulfman 73–74.
14   Fussell 157.
15   Quoted in Ellmann 521.
16   Quoted in Ellmann 702.
17   James, "The Art of Fiction" 165. (See also Chapter 52 of this volume, p. 452.)
18   Eagleton 30. Fussell also considers what he calls the "system of 'high' diction" to be one "of the ultimate casualties of the war" 22.
19   Eagleton 29.

Suggested further readings

Modernist writers on themselves

Ford, Ford Madox. *The March of Literature: From Confucius to Modern Times* (1938). Champaign, London, Dublin: Dalkey Archive Press, 1994.
——. *The English Novel*. London: Constable, 1930.
——. *Joseph Conrad: A Personal Remembrance*. London: Duckworth, 1924.
Forster, E.M. *Aspects of the Novel* (1927). Harmondsworth: Penguin, 1962.
——. "Art for Art's Sake" (1949). *Two Cheers for Democracy*. New York: Harcourt, Brace, 1951. 88–95.
Gide, André. "Journal of *The Counterfeiters*" (1927). *The Counterfeiters*. New York: Vintage, 1973.
James, Henry. Preface, *The Turn of the Screw* (1898). New York: Penguin, 2011.
——. Preface, *The Princess Casamassima* (1908). New York: Harper and Row, 1968.
——. "Future of the Novel: An Analysis and a Forecast" (1900). *The Future of the Novel: Essays on the Art of Fiction*. Ed. Leon Edel. New York: Vintage, 1956.

Lewis, Wyndham. *Time and Western Man* (1927). Santa Rosa: Black Sparrow Press, 1993.
Lubbock, Percy. *The Craft of Fiction* (1921). New York: Viking, 1957.
Pound, Ezra. *ABC of Reading* (1934). New York: New Directions, 1960.
——. *How to Read*. London: D. Harmsworth, 1931.
Strachey, Lytton. *Eminent Victorians* (1918). New York: Penguin, 1990.

Modernist writers on their contemporaries

Anand, Mulk Raj. " 'How Unpleasant to Meet Mr Eliot': A Talk in the Etoile with T.S. Eliot and Bonamy Dobrée"; "Under the Chestnut Tree in Tavistock Square with E.M. Forster and Leonard Woolf"; "White Gods and Dark Gods – A Talk with T.S. Eliot in the *Criterion* Office"; "Reason and Romanticism – A Talk with T.S. Eliot in Schmidt's Restaurant in Charlotte Street." *Conversations in Bloomsbury*. London: Wildwood House, 1981. 43–52, 68–77, 118–24, 144–51.
Forster, E.M. "Our Second Greatest Novel?" (1943); "Two Books by T.S. Eliot" (1949, 1950). *Two Cheers for Democracy*. New York: Harcourt, Brace, 1951. 223–27, 259–62.
——. *Abinger Harvest* (1936). London: Edward Arnold, 1936.
Joyce, James. "Ibsen's New Drama" (1900); "James Clarence Mangan" (1907). *James Joyce: Occasional, Critical, and Political Writing*. Ed. Kevin Barry. Oxford: Oxford UP, 2000. 30–49, 127–36.
Lehmann, John, *et al.* "The Leaning Tower: Replies." *Folios of New Writing*. London: Hogarth, 1941. 24–46.
Morgan, Emmanuel (Witter Bynner), and Anne Knish (Arthur Davison Ficke). "The Spectric School of Poetry." *Others: A Magazine of the New Verse* 3.5 (January 1917).
Riding, Laura, and Robert Graves. *A Survey of Modernist Poetry* (1927). Garden City, NY: Doubleday, Doran, 1928.
Stanford Friedman, Susan. *Psyche Reborn: The Emergence of H.D.* Bloomington: Indiana UP, 1981.
Woolf, Virginia. "The Novels of E.M. Forster" (1927). *The Death of the Moth and Other Essays* (1942). New York: Harcourt, Brace, 1970. 162–75.
——. "Joseph Conrad" (1924). *The Common Reader: First Series* (1925). New York: Harcourt, Brace, 1953. 228–35.
——. "Mr. Bennett and Mrs. Brown" (1924). *The Captain's Death Bed and Other Essays*. New York: Harcourt, Brace, 1950. 94–119.

Further reading

Anand, Mulk Raj. *Conversations in Bloomsbury* (1981). New York: Oxford UP, 1995.
Budgen, Frank. *James Joyce and the Making of* Ulysses. Bloomington: Indiana UP 1960.
Eagleton, Terry. *Literary Theory: An Introduction*. Minneapolis: U of Minnesota P, 1983.
Ellison, Ralph. *Living with Music: Ralph Ellison's Jazz Writings*. Ed. Robert O'Meally. New York: Modern Library, 2002.
Ellmann, Richard. *James Joyce* (1959). Rev. edn. Oxford: Oxford UP, 1982.
Ford, Ford Madox. *Joseph Conrad: A Personal Remembrance*. London: Duckworth, 1924.
——. *English Literature of Today* (1909–10).
Forster, E.M. *Aspects of the Novel, and Related Writings* (1927). London: E. Arnold, 1974.
——. *Two Cheers for Democracy* (1938). New York: Harcourt, Brace, 1951.
Fussell, Paul. *The Great War and Modern Memory*. London, Oxford, and New York: Oxford UP, 1975.
Gide, André. *The Counterfeiters, with Journal of The Counterfeiters* (1927). New York: Knopf, 1962.
James, Henry. *The Turn of the Screw: Authoritative Text, Contexts, Criticism*, 2nd edn. Ed. Deborah Esch and Jonathan Warren (1898). New York: Norton, 1999.
——. *What Maisie Knew*. Harmondsworth: Penguin, 1985.

——. *The Princess Casamassima* (1886). New York: Harper and Row, 1968.

Lawrence, D.H. *The Collected Letters of D.H. Lawrence.* 8 vols. Ed. James T. Boulton *et al.* Cambridge: Cambridge UP, 1979–2001.

——. *Phoenix: The Posthumous Papers of D.H. Lawrence* (1936). New York: Viking, 1972.

Lewis, Wyndham. *Time and Western Man* (1927). Santa Rosa: Black Sparrow, 1993.

Loy, Mina. "Modern Poetry." *The Lost Lunar Baedeker.* Ed. Roger L. Conover. New York: Farrar, Straus and Giroux, 1996.

Lubbock, Percy. *The Craft of Fiction.* New York: Viking, 1921.

Norris, Margot. *A Companion to James Joyce's* Ulysses. New York: Bedford Books, 1998.

Pound, Ezra. *How to Read.* London: Harmsworth, 1931.

Scholes, Robert, and Clifford Wulfman. *Modernism in the Magazines: An Introduction.* New Haven: Yale UP, 2000.

Shaw, George Bernard. *The Quintessence of Ibsenism; Now Completed to the Death of Ibsen* (1891). New York: Hill and Wang, 1963.

Strindberg, August. *Miss Julie and Other Plays* (1888). Oxford and New York: Oxford UP, 1998.

Wilde, Oscar. *The Picture of Dorian Gray* (1891). New York: Viking, 2001.

Woolf, Virginia. *The Death of the Moth and Other Essays* (1942). New York: Harcourt, Brace, 1970.

——. *The Common Reader: First Series* (1925). New York: Harcourt, Brace, 1953.

——. *The Captain's Death Bed and Other Essays.* New York: Harcourt, Brace, 1950.

Yeats, W.B. *Per Amica Silentia Lunae.* London and New York: Macmillan, 1918.

PART VIII

Modernist writers on themselves

Chapter 52

Henry James (1843–1916)

"THE ART OF FICTION" (1884)

AMERICAN-BORN AND BRITISH-RESIDENT, Henry James was a prolific novelist, short story writer, critic, and playwright who was regarded as a leader of nineteenth-century literary realism. His father, Henry James, Sr., was a wealthy intellectual as well as a clergyman; his friends included Ralph Waldo Emerson, Henry David Thoreau, Nathaniel Hawthorne, Thomas Carlyle, and Henry Wadsworth Longfellow, all of whom had a profound effect on the young James. Henry Jr.'s brother was the philosopher and psychologist William James and his sister the diarist Alice James. Henry James's fiction explores themes of personal morality, individual freedom, and feminism, within highly constrained social milieus, as well as clashes between Old and New World customs and values. Having lived most of his adult life in Europe (mainly Paris and England), James became a British citizen in 1915 (in least in part due to America's reluctance to join World War I); in 1916 he was awarded the Order of Merit by King George V. His writings are commonly divided into three main periods: to 1890, romances narrated using a conventional omniscient point of view; 1890–7, mostly short stories and plays; 1897 on, large works with complex, even convoluted, indirect sentences and paragraphs, relying increasingly on interior monologue and character perspective, and containing deferred verbs and laden with adjectives, adverbs, pronouns, and prepositional phrases. His major works include *Daisy Miller* (1878), *The Portrait of a Lady* (1881), *The Princess Casamassima* (1886), *The Aspern Papers* (1888), *What Maisie Knew* (1897), *The Turn of the Screw* (1898), *The Wings of the Dove* (1902), *The Ambassadors* (1903), *The Beast in the Jungle* (1903), and *The Golden Bowl* (1904).

Henry James, "The Art of Fiction," *The Art of Criticism: Henry James on the Theory and the Practice of Fiction*, ed. William Veeder and Susan M. Griffin. Chicago: U of Chicago P, 1986. 165, 166–67, 168–69, 170, 171–73, 174–75, 182, 183.

I should not have affixed so comprehensive a title to these few remarks, necessarily wanting in any completeness upon a subject the full consideration of which would carry us far, did I not seem to discover a pretext for my temerity in the interesting pamphlet lately published under this name by Mr. Walter Besant. Mr. Besant's lecture at the Royal Institution—the original form of his pamphlet—appears to indicate that many persons are interested in the art of fiction, and are not indifferent to such remarks, as those who practise it may attempt to make about it. I am therefore anxious not to lose the benefit of this favourable association, and to edge in a few words under cover of the attention which Mr. Besant is sure to have excited. There is something very encouraging in his having put into form certain of his ideas on the mystery of story-telling.

It is a proof of life and curiosity—curiosity on the part of the brotherhood of novelists as well as on the part of their readers. Only a short time ago it might have been supposed that the English novel was not what the French call *discutable*. It had no air of having a theory, a conviction, a consciousness of itself behind it—of being the expression of an artistic faith, the result of choice and comparison. I do not say it was necessarily the worse for that: it would take much more courage than I possess to intimate that the form of the novel as Dickens and Thackeray (for instance) saw it had any taint of incompleteness. It was, however, *naif* (if I may help myself out with another French word); and evidently if it be destined to suffer in any way for having lost its *naïveté* it has now an idea of making sure of the corresponding advantages. During the period I have alluded to there was a comfortable, good-humoured feeling abroad that a novel is a novel, as a pudding is a pudding, and that our only business with it could be to swallow it. But within a year or two, for some reason or other, there have been signs of returning animation—the era of discussion would appear to have been to a certain extent opened. . . .

The old superstition about fiction being "wicked" has doubtless died out in England; but the spirit of it lingers in a certain oblique regard directed toward any story which does not more or less admit that it is only a joke. Even the most jocular novel feels in some degree the weight of the proscription that was formerly directed against literary levity: the jocularity does not always succeed in passing for orthodoxy. It is still expected, though perhaps people are ashamed to say it, that a production which is after all only a "make-believe" (for what else is a "story"?) shall be in some degree apologetic—shall renounce the pretension of attempting really to represent life. This, of course, any sensible, wide-awake story declines to do, for it quickly perceives that the tolerance granted to it on such a condition is only an attempt to stifle it disguised in the form of generosity. The old evangelical hostility to the novel, which was as explicit as it was narrow, and which regarded it as little less favourable to our immortal part than a stage-play, was in reality far less insulting. The only reason for the existence of a novel is that it does attempt to represent life. When it relinquishes this attempt, the same attempt that we see on the canvas of the painter, it will have arrived at a very strange pass. It is not expected of the picture that it will make itself humble in order to be forgiven; and the analogy between the art of the painter and the art of the novelist is, so far as I am able to see, complete. Their inspiration is the same, their process (allowing for the different quality of the vehicle) is the same, their success is the same. They may learn from each other, they may explain and sustain each other. Their cause is the same, and the honour of one is the honour of another. . . . as the picture is reality, so the novel is history. That is the only general description (which does it justice) that we may give of the novel. But history also is allowed to represent life; it is not, any more than painting, expected to apologise. The subject-matter of fiction is stored up likewise in documents and records, and if it will not give itself away, as they say in California, it must speak with assurance, with the tone of the historian. Certain accomplished novelists have a habit of giving themselves away which must often bring tears to the eyes of people who take their fiction seriously. I was lately struck, in reading over many pages of Anthony Trollope, with his want of discretion in this particular. In a digression, a parenthesis or an aside, he concedes to the reader that he and this trusting friend are only "making believe." He admits that the events he narrates have not really happened, and that he can give his narrative any turn the reader may like best. Such a betrayal of a sacred office seems to me, I confess, a terrible crime; it is what I mean by the attitude of apology, and it shocks me every whit as much in Trollope as it would have shocked me in Gibbon or Macaulay. It implies that the novelist is less occupied in looking for the truth (the truth, of course I mean, that he assumes, the premises that we must grant him, whatever they may be), than the historian, and in doing so it deprives him at a stroke of all his standing-room. To represent and illustrate the past, the actions of men, is the task of either writer, and the only difference that I can see is, in proportion as he succeeds, to the honour of the novelist, consisting as it does in his having more difficulty in collecting his evidence, which is so far from being purely literary. It seems to me to give him a great character, the fact that he has at once so much in common with the philosopher and the painter; this double analogy is a magnificent heritage. . . .

"Art," in our Protestant communities, where so many things have got so strangely twisted about, is supposed in certain circles to have some vaguely injurious effect upon those who make it an important consideration, who let it weigh in the balance. It is assumed to be opposed in some mysterious manner to morality, to amusement, to instruction. When it is embodied in the work of the painter (the sculptor is another affair!) you know what it is: it stands there before you, in the honesty of pink and green and a gilt frame; you can see the worst of it at a glance, and you can be on your guard. But when it is introduced into literature it becomes more insidious—there is danger of its hurting you before you know it. Literature should be either instructive or amusing, and there is in many minds an impression that these artistic preoccupations, the search for form, contribute to neither end, interfere indeed with both. They are too frivolous to be edifying, and too serious to be diverting; and they are moreover priggish and paradoxical and superfluous. That, I think, represents the manner in which the latent thought of many people who read novels as an exercise in skipping would explain itself if it were to become articulate. They would argue, of course, that a novel ought to be "good," but they would interpret this term in a fashion of their own, which indeed would vary considerably from one critic to another. One would say that being good means representing virtuous and aspiring characters, placed in prominent positions; another would say that it depends on a "happy ending," on a distribution at the last of prizes, pensions, husbands, wives, babies, millions, appended paragraphs, and cheerful remarks. Another still would say that it means being full of incident and movement, so that we shall wish to jump ahead, to see who was the mysterious stranger, and if the stolen will was ever found, and shall not be distracted from this pleasure by any tiresome analysis or "description." But they would all agree that the "artistic" idea would spoil some of their fun. One would hold it accountable for all the description, another would see it revealed in the absence of sympathy. Its hostility to a happy ending would be evident, and it might even in some cases render any ending at all impossible. The "ending" of a novel is, for many persons, like that of a good dinner, a course of dessert and ices, and the artist in fiction is regarded as a sort of meddlesome doctor who forbids agreeable aftertastes. It is therefore true that this conception of Mr. Besant's of the novel as a superior form encounters not only a negative but a positive indifference. It matters little that as a work of art it should really be as little or as much of its essence to supply happy endings, sympathetic characters, and an objective tone, as if it were a work of mechanics: the association of ideas, however incongruous, might easily be too much for it if an eloquent voice were not sometimes raised to call attention to the fact that it is at once as free and as serious a branch of literature as any other.

Certainly this might sometimes be doubted in presence of the enormous number of works of fiction that appeal to the credulity of our generation, for it might easily seem that there could be no great character in a commodity so quickly and easily produced. . . . The only obligation to which in advance we may hold a novel, without incurring the accusation of being arbitrary, is that it be interesting. That general responsibility rests upon it, but it is the only one I can think of. The ways in which it is at liberty to accomplish this result (of interesting us) strike me as innumerable, and such as can only suffer from being marked out or fenced in by prescription. They are as various as the temperament of man, and they are successful in proportion as they reveal a particular mind, different from others. A novel is in its broadest definition a personal, a direct impression of life: that, to begin with, constitutes its value, which is greater or less according to the intensity of the impression. But there will be no intensity at all, and therefore no value, unless there is freedom to feel and say. The tracing of a line to be followed, of a tone to be taken, of a form to be filled out, is a limitation of that freedom and a suppression of the very thing that we are most curious about. The form, it seems to me, is to be appreciated after the fact: then the author's choice has been made; his standard has been indicated; then we can follow lines and directions and compare tones and resemblances. Then in a word we can enjoy one of the most charming of pleasures, we can estimate quality, we can apply the test of execution. The execution belongs to the author alone; it is what is most personal to him, and we measure him by that. The advantage, the luxury, as well as the torment and responsibility of the novelist, is that there is no limit to what he may attempt as an executant—no limit to his possible experiments, efforts, discoveries, successes. . . .

The characters, the situation, which strike one as real will be those that touch and interest one most, but the measure of reality is very difficult to fix. The reality of Don Quixote or of Mr. Micawber is a very delicate shade; it is a reality so coloured by the author's vision that, vivid as it may be, one would hesitate to propose it as a model: one would expose one's self to some very embarrassing questions on the part of a pupil. It goes without saying that you will not write a good novel unless you possess the sense of reality; but it will be difficult to give you a recipe for calling that sense into being. Humanity is immense, and reality has a myriad forms; the most one can affirm is that some of the flowers of fiction have the odour of it, and others have not; as for telling you in advance how your nosegay should be composed, that is another affair. It is equally excellent and inconclusive to say that one must write from experience; to our supposititious aspirant such a declaration might savour of mockery. What kind of experience is intended, and where does it begin and end? Experience is never limited, and it is never complete; it is an immense sensibility, a kind of huge spiderweb of the finest silken threads suspended in the chamber of consciousness, and catching every airborne particle in its tissue. It is the very atmosphere of the mind; and when the mind is imaginative—much more when it happens to be that of a man of genius—it takes to itself the faintest hints of life, it converts the very pulses of the air into revelations. The young lady living in a village has only to be a damsel upon whom nothing is lost to make it quite unfair (as it seems to me) to declare to her that she shall have nothing to say about the military. Greater miracles have been seen than that, imagination assisting, she should speak the truth about some of these gentlemen. I remember an English novelist, a woman of genius, telling me that she was much commended for the impression she had managed to give in one of her tales of the nature and way of life of the French Protestant youth. She had been asked where she learned so much about this recondite being, she had been congratulated on her peculiar opportunities. These opportunities consisted in her having once, in Paris, as she ascended a staircase, passed an open door where, in the household of a *pasteur*, some of the young Protestants were seated at table round a finished meal. The glimpse made a picture; it lasted only a moment, but that moment was experience. She had got her direct personal impression, and she turned out her type. She knew what youth was, and what Protestantism; she also had the advantage of having seen what it was to be French, so that she converted these ideas into a concrete image and produced a reality. Above all, however, she was blessed with the faculty which when you give it an inch takes an ell, and which for the artist is a much greater source of strength than any accident of residence or of place in the social scale. The power to guess the unseen from the seen, to trace the implication of things, to judge the whole piece by the pattern, the condition of feeling life in general so completely that you are well on your way to knowing any particular corner of it—this cluster of gifts may almost be said to constitute experience, and they occur in country and in town, and in the most differing stages of education. If experience consists of impressions, it may be said that impressions *are* experience, just as (have we not seen it?) they are the very air we breathe. Therefore, if I should certainly say to a novice, "Write from experience and experience only," I should feel that this was rather a tantalising monition if I were not careful immediately to add, "Try to be one of the people on whom nothing is lost!"

I am far from intending by this to minimise the importance of exactness—of truth of detail. One can speak best from one's own taste, and I may therefore venture to say that the air of reality (solidity of specification) seems to me to be the supreme virtue of a novel – the merits on which all its other merits . . . helplessly and submissively depend. If it be not there they are all as nothing, and if these be there they owe their effect to the success with which the author has produced the illusion of life. The cultivation of this success, the study of this exquisite process, form, to my taste, the beginning and the end of the art of the novelist. They are his inspiration, his despair, his reward, his torment, his delight. . . . A novel is a living thing, all one and continuous, like any other organism, and in proportion as it lives will it be found, I think, that in each of the parts there is something of each of the other parts. . . . [T]he only classification of the novel that I can understand is into that which has life and that which has it not. . . .

[T]he only condition that I can think of attaching to the composition of the novel is . . . that it be sincere. This freedom is a splendid privilege, and the first lesson of the young novelist is to learn to be worthy of it. "Enjoy it as it deserves," I should say to him; "take possession of it, explore it to its utmost extent, publish it, rejoice in it. All life belongs to you, and do not listen either to those who would shut you up into corners of it and tell you that it is only here and there that art inhabits, or to those who would persuade you that this heavenly messenger wings her way outside of life altogether, breathing a superfine air, and turning away her head from the truth of things. There is no impression of life, no manner of seeing it and feeling it, to which the plan of the novelist may not offer a place; you have only to remember that talents so dissimilar as those of Alexandre Dumas and Jane Austen, Charles Dickens and Gustave Flaubert have worked in this field with equal glory. Do not think too much about optimism and pessimism; try and catch the colour of life itself. . . . If you must indulge in conclusions, let them have the taste of a wide knowledge. Remember that your first duty is to be as complete as possible—to make as perfect a work. Be generous and delicate and pursue the prize."

Chapter 53

Oscar Wilde (1854–1900)

"PREFACE," *THE PICTURE OF DORIAN GRAY* (1891)

THE PICTURE OF DORIAN GRAY, a gothic tale of unpunished immorality set in contemporary London, shocked elements of the reading public and prompted vitriolic attacks by critics and moralists. In reply to these attacks, Wilde published a polemic Preface composed of twenty-two epigrams for his second edition of the novel. The "Preface" stands alongside Walter Pater's "Conclusion" to *The Renaissance* (see Chapter 2) as a critical manifesto for the aesthetic movement of the late nineteenth century.

Oscar Wilde, "Preface," *The Picture of Dorian Gray.* New York and London: Norton, 1988. 3–4.

The artist is the creator of beautiful things.
To reveal art and conceal the artist is art's aim.
The critic is he who can translate into another manner or a new material his impression of beautiful things.
The highest as the lowest form of criticism is a mode of autobiography.
Those who find ugly meanings in beautiful things are corrupt without being charming. This is a fault.
Those who find beautiful meanings in beautiful things are the cultivated. For these there is hope.
They are the elect to whom beautiful things mean only Beauty.
There is no such thing as a moral or an immoral book. Books are well written, or badly written. That is all.
The nineteenth century dislike of Realism is the rage of Caliban seeing his own face in a glass.
The nineteenth century dislike of Romanticism is the rage of Caliban not seeing his own face in a glass.
The moral life of man forms part of the subject-matter of the artist, but the morality of art consists in the perfect use of an imperfect medium.
No artist desires to prove anything. Even things that are true can be proved.
No artist has ethical sympathies. An ethical sympathy in an artist is an unpardonable mannerism of style.

No artist is ever morbid. The artist can express everything.

Thought and language are to the artist instruments of an art.

Vice and virtue are to the artist materials for an art.

From the point of view of form, the type of all the arts is the art of the musician.

From the point of view of feeling, the actor's craft is the type.

All art is at once surface and symbol.

Those who go beneath the surface do so at their peril.

Those who read the symbol do so at their peril.

It is the spectator, and not life, that art really mirrors.

Diversity of opinion about a work of art shows that the work is new, complex, and vital.

When critics disagree the artist is in accord with himself.

We can forgive a man for making a useful thing as long as he does not admire it.

The only excuse for making a useless thing is that one admires it intensely.

All art is quite useless.

Chapter 54

Joseph Conrad (1857–1924)

"PREFACE," *THE NIGGER OF THE* *"NARCISSUS"* (1897)

A POLISH-BORN ENGLISH NOVELIST, CONRAD wrote in what was probably his fourth language: in addition to Polish, he would have studied Russian in school and learned French when he sailed with the French merchant navy. Resisting imperial Russian authority, Conrad's parents were arrested, sent into exile, and died young, leaving Conrad an orphan at age eleven. At sixteen he went to sea, where he had various adventures including gunrunning and political conspiracy, retiring to England in 1894. In the early 1900s he honed his English language and literary skills by collaborating with Ford Madox Ford on three novels, becoming one of the great English stylists even though the collaborative novels are generally considered unsuccessful. He gained popular and financial success with *Chance* (1913), which is now viewed as one of his weaker novels. His major works include *The Nigger of the "Narcissus"* (1897), *Heart of Darkness* (1899), *Lord Jim* (1900), *Nostromo* (1904), *The Secret Agent* (1907), and *Under Western Eyes* (1911). Conrad is viewed as a romantic writer (for his depictions of exotic settings, the challenges faced by men confronting nature, and moral conflict), a conservative (he actively disliked democracy and socialism), and a precursor of modernism in his treatment of perspectivism, symbolism, and impressionism.

Joseph Conrad, "Preface," *The Nigger of the "Narcissus"*. Ed. Robert Kimbrough. New York: Norton, 1979. 145–48.

Preface

A work that aspires, however humbly, to the condition of art should carry its justification in every line. And art itself may be defined as a single-minded attempt to render the highest kind of justice to the visible universe, by bringing to light the truth, manifold and one, underlying its every aspect. It is an attempt to find in its forms, in its colours, in its light, in its shadows, in the aspects of matter and in the facts of life, what of each is fundamental, what is enduring and essential—their one illuminating and convincing quality—the very truth of their existence. The artist, then, like the thinker or the scientist, seeks the truth and makes his appeal.

Impressed by the aspect of the world the thinker plunges into ideas, the scientist into facts—whence, presently emerging, they make their appeal to those qualities of our being that fit us best for the hazardous enterprise of living. They speak authoritatively to our common sense, to our intelligence, to our desire of peace, or to our desire of unrest; not seldom to our prejudices, sometimes to our fears, often to our egoism—but always to our credulity. And their words are heard with reverence; for their concern is with weighty matters; with the cultivation of our minds and the proper care of our bodies; with the attainment of our ambitions; with the perfection of the means and the glorification of our precious aims.

It is otherwise with the artist.

Confronted by the same enigmatical spectacle the artist descends within himself, and in that lonely region of stress and strife, if he be deserving and fortunate, he finds the terms of his appeal. His appeal is made to our less obvious capacities; to that part of our nature which, because of the warlike conditions of existence, is necessarily kept out of sight within the more resisting and hard qualities—like the vulnerable body within a steel armour. His appeal is less loud, more profound, less distinct, more stirring—and sooner forgotten. Yet its effect endures for ever. The changing wisdom of successive generations discards ideas, questions facts, demolishes theories. But the artist appeals to that part of our being which is not dependent on wisdom; to that in us which is a gift and not an acquisition—and, therefore, more permanently enduring. He speaks to our capacity for delight and wonder, to the sense of mystery surrounding our lives; to our sense of pity, and beauty, and pain; to the latent feeling of fellowship with all creation; and to the subtle but invincible conviction of solidarity that knits together the loneliness of innumerable hearts: to that solidarity in dreams, in joy, in sorrow, in aspirations, in illusions, in hope, in fear, which binds men to each other, which binds together all humanity—the dead to the living, and the living to the unborn.

It is only some such train of thought, or rather of feeling, that can in a measure explain the aim of the attempt made in the tale which follows, to present an unrestful episode in the obscure lives of a few individuals out of all the disregarded multitude of the bewildered, the simple, and the voiceless. For, if there is any part of truth in the belief confessed above, it becomes evident that there is not a place of splendour or a dark corner of the earth that does not deserve, if only a passing glance of wonder and pity. The motive, then, may be held to justify the matter of the work; but this preface, which is simply an avowal of endeavour, cannot end here—for the avowal is not yet complete.

Fiction—if it at all aspires to be art—appeals to temperament. And in truth it must be, like painting, like music, like all art, the appeal of one temperament to all the other innumerable temperaments whose subtle and resistless power endows passing events with their true meaning, and creates the moral, the emotional atmosphere of the place and time. Such an appeal, to be effective, must be an impression conveyed through the senses; and, in fact, it cannot be made in any other way, because temperament, whether individual or collective, is not amenable to persuasion. All art, therefore, appeals primarily to the senses, and the artistic aim when expressing itself in written words must also make its appeal through the senses, if its high desire is to reach the secret spring of responsive emotions. It must strenuously aspire to the plasticity of sculpture, to the colour of painting, and to the magic suggestiveness of music—which is the art of arts. And it is only through complete, unswerving devotion to the perfect blending of form and substance; it is only through an unremitting, never-discouraged care for the shape and ring of sentences, that an approach can be made to plasticity, to colour; and the light of magic suggestiveness may be brought to play for an evanescent instant over the commonplace surface of words: of the old, old words, worn thin, defaced by ages of careless usage.

The sincere endeavour to accomplish that creative task, to go as far on that road as his strength will carry him, to go undeterred by faltering, weariness, or reproach, is the only valid justification for the worker in prose. And if his conscience is clear, his answer to those who in the fulness of a wisdom which looks for immediate profit, demand specifically to be edified, consoled, amused; who demand to be promptly improved, or encouraged, or frightened; or shocked, or charmed, must run thus: My task which I am trying to achieve is, by the power of the written word, to make you hear, to make you feel—it is, before all, to make you *see*! That—and no more: and it is everything! If I succceed, you shall find there according to your deserts: encouragement, consolation, fear, charm—all you demand; and, perhaps, also that glimpse of truth for which you have forgotten to ask.

To snatch in a moment of courage, from the remorseless rush of time, a passing phase of life, is only the beginning of the task. The task approached in tenderness and faith is to hold up unquestioningly, without choice and without fear, the rescued fragment before all eyes and in the light of a sincere mood. It is to show its vibration, its colour, its form; and through its movement, its form, and its colour, reveal the substance of its truth—disclose its inspiring secret: the stress and passion within the core of each convincing moment. In a single-minded attempt of that kind, if one be deserving and fortunate, one may perchance attain to such clearness of sincerity that at last the presented vision of regret or pity, of terror or mirth, shall awaken in the hearts of the beholders that feeling of unavoidable solidarity; of the solidarity in mysterious origin, in toil, in joy, in hope, in uncertain fate—which binds men to each other and all mankind to the visible world.

It is evident that he who, rightly or wrongly, holds by the convictions expressed above cannot be faithful to any one of the temporary formulas of his craft. The enduring part of them—the truth which each only imperfectly veils—should abide with him as the most precious of his possessions, but they all: Realism, Romanticism, Naturalism, even the unofficial sentimentalism (which, like the poor, is exceedingly difficult to get rid of); all these gods must, after a short period of fellowship, abandon him—even on the very threshold of the temple—to the stammerings of his conscience and to the outspoken consciousness of the difficulties of his work. In that uneasy solitude the cry of Art for Art itself, loses the exciting ring of its apparent immorality. It sounds far off. It has ceased to be a cry, and is heard only as a whisper, often incomprehensible, but at times, and faintly, encouraging.

Sometimes, stretched at ease in the shade of a roadside tree, we watch the motions of a labourer in a distant field, and, after a time, begin to wonder languidly as to what the fellow may be at. We watch the movements of his body, the waving of his arms; we see him bend down, stand up, hesitate, begin again. It may add to the charm of an idle hour to be told the purpose of his exertions. If we know he is trying to lift a stone, to dig a ditch, to uproot a stump, we look with a more real interest at his efforts; we are disposed to condone the jar of his agitation upon the restfulness of the landscape; and even, if in a brotherly frame of mind, we may bring ourselves to forgive his failure. We understood his object, and, after all, the fellow has tried, and perhaps he had not the strength—and perhaps he had not the knowledge. We forgive, go on our way—and forget.

And so it is with the workman of art. Art is long and life is short, and success is very far off. And thus, doubtful of strength to travel so far, we talk a little about the aim—the aim of art, which, like life itself, is inspiring, difficult—obscured by mists. It is not in the clear logic of a triumphant conclusion; it is not in the unveiling of one of those heartless secrets which are called the Laws of Nature. It is not less great, but only more difficult!

To arrest, for the space of a breath, the hands busy about the work of the earth, and compel men entranced by the sight of distant goals to glance for a moment at the surrounding vision of form and colour, of sunshine and shadows; to make them pause for a look, for a sigh, for a smile—such is the aim, difficult and evanescent, and reserved only for a very few to achieve. But sometimes, by the deserving and the fortunate, even that task is accomplished. And when it is accomplished—behold!—all the truth of life is there: a moment of vision, a sigh, a smile—and the return to an eternal rest.

Chapter 55

W.B. Yeats (1865–1939)

"THE SYMBOLISM OF POETRY" (1900)

A N ANGLO-IRISH POET, PLAYWRIGHT (who was deeply influenced by Pound's version of Japanese Noh plays), essayist, autobiographer, spiritualist, and politician, Yeats was a leader of the Irish Literary Revival and co-founder of the Abbey Theatre, Dublin. With his life-long interest in mysticism, spiritualism, occultism, and astrology, Yeats joined such groups as the Dublin Hermetic Order, the Theosophical Society in London, and Rosicrucianism of the Golden Dawn, and engaged in paranormal research, including séances, hermeticism, and automatic writing. Pursuing this last, Yeats and his wife encountered spirits they called "Instructors" who communicated a complex and esoteric system of characters and history, which Yeats captured in A Vision (1925). After the Irish Free State was established in 1922, Yeats served as a Senator, championing free speech and the legalization of divorce, and helping to select the design for the state's first currency. In 1923 he received the Nobel Prize for Literature, the first Irishman so honoured, for what the awards committee described as "inspired poetry, which in a highly artistic form gives expression to the spirit of a whole nation." He flirted with fascism, aligning himself with Pound and praising Benito Mussolini. Known to a large extent as a symbolist poet, Yeats in the work excerpted here speaks of the moving force of poetry that derives from "philosophical or critical power" beautifully combined with the "musical relation" of "sound, and colour, and form."

W.B. Yeats, "The Symbolism of Poetry," Yeats's Poetry, Drama, and Prose, ed. James Pethica. New York and London: Norton, 2000. 271–75.

All writers, all artists of any kind, in so far as they have had any philosophical or critical power, perhaps just in so far as they have been deliberate artists at all, have had some philosophy, some criticism of their art; and it has often been this philosophy, or this criticism, that has evoked their most startling inspiration, calling into outer life some portion of the divine life, or of the buried reality, which could alone extinguish in the emotions what their philosophy or their criticism would extinguish in the intellect. They have sought for no new thing, it may be, but only to understand and to copy the pure inspiration of early times, but because the divine life wars upon our outer life, and must needs change its weapons and its movements as we change ours, inspiration has come to them in beautiful startling shapes. The scientific movements [*sic*] brought with it a literature which was always tending to lose itself in externalities of all kinds, in opinion, in declamation, in picturesque writing, in word-painting, or in what Mr. Symons has called an attempt 'to build in brick and mortar inside the covers of a book'; and now writers have begun to dwell upon the element of evocation, of suggestion, upon what we call the symbolism in great writers.

II

In 'Symbolism in Painting' I tried to describe the element of symbolism that is in pictures and sculpture, and described a little the symbolism in poetry, but did not describe at all the continuous indefinable symbolism which is the substance of all style.

There are no lines with more melancholy beauty than these by Burns—

'The white moon is setting behind the white wave,
And Time is setting with me, O!'

and these lines are perfectly symbolical. Take from them the whiteness of the moon and of the wave, whose relation to the setting of Time is too subtle for the intellect, and you take from them their beauty. But, when all are together, moon and wave and whiteness and setting Time and the last melancholy cry, they evoke an emotion which cannot be evoked by any other arrangement of colours and sounds and forms. We may call this metaphorical writing, but it is better to call it symbolical writing, because metaphors are not profound enough to be moving, when they are not symbols, and when they are symbols they are the most perfect, because the most subtle, outside of pure sound, and through them one can best find out what symbols are. If one begins the reverie with any beautiful lines that one can remember, one finds they are like those by Burns. Begin with this line by Blake—

'The gay fishes on the wave when the moon sucks up the dew;'

or these lines by Nash—

'Brightness falls from the air,
Queens have died young and fair,
Dust hath closed Helen's eye;'

or these lines by Shakespeare—

'Timon hath made his everlasting mansion
Upon the beached verge of the salt flood;
Who once a day with his embossed froth
The turbulent surge shall cover;'

or take some line that is quite simple, that gets its beauty from its place in a story, and see how it flickers with the light of the many symbols that have given the story its beauty, as a sword-blade may flicker with the light of burning towers.

All sounds, all colours, all forms, either because of their preordained energies or because of long association, evoke indefinable and yet precise emotions, or, as I prefer to think, call down among us certain disembodied powers, whose footsteps over our hearts we call

emotions; and when sound, and colour, and form are in a musical relation, a beautiful relation to one another, they become, as it were, one sound, one colour, one form, and evoke
an emotion that is made out of their distinct evocations and yet is one emotion. The same
relation exists between all portions of every work of art, whether it be an epic or a song, and
the more perfect it is, and the more various and numerous the elements that have flowed into
its perfection, the more powerful will be the emotion, the power, the god it calls among us.
Because an emotion does not exist, or does not become perceptible and active among us, till
it has found its expression, in colour or in sound or in form, or in all of these, and because no
two modulations or arrangements of these evoke the same emotion, poets and painters and
musicians, and in a less degree because their effects are momentary, day and night and cloud
and shadow, are continually making and unmaking mankind. It is indeed only those things
which seem useless or very feeble that have any power, and all those things that seem useful
or strong, armies moving wheels, modes of architecture, modes of government, speculations
of the reason, would have been a little different if some mind long ago had not given itself to
some emotion, as a woman gives herself to her lover, and shaped sounds or colours or forms,
or all of these, into a musical relation, that their emotion might live in other minds. A little
lyric evokes an emotion, and this emotion gathers others about it and melts into their being
in the making of some great epic; and at last, needing an always less delicate body, or symbol,
as it grows more powerful, it flows out, with all it has gathered, among the blind instincts of
daily life, where it moves a power within powers, as one sees ring within ring in the stem of
an old tree. . . .

III

The purpose of rhythm, it has always seemed to me, is to prolong the moment of contemplation, the moment when we are both asleep and awake, which is the one moment of creation,
by hushing us with an alluring monotony, while it holds us waking by variety, to keep us in
that state of perhaps real trance, in which the mind liberated from the pressure of the will is
unfolded in symbols. If certain sensitive persons listen persistently to the ticking of a watch,
or gaze persistently on the monotonous flashing of a light, they fall into the hypnotic trance;
and rhythm is but the ticking of a watch made softer, that one must needs listen, and various,
that one may not be swept beyond memory or grow weary of listening; while the patterns of
the artist are but the monotonous flash woven to take the eyes in a subtler enchantment. I
have heard in meditation voices that were forgotten the moment they had spoken; and I have
been swept, when in more profound meditation, beyond all memory but of those things that
came from beyond the threshold of waking life. . . . So I think that in the making and in the
understanding of a work of art, and the more easily if it is full of patterns and symbols and
music, we are lured to the threshold of sleep, and it may be far beyond it, without knowing
that we have ever set our feet upon the steps of horn or of ivory.

IV

Besides emotional symbols, symbols that evoke emotions alone,—and in this sense all
alluring or hateful things are symbols, although their relations with one another are too subtle
to delight us fully, away from rhythm and pattern,—there are intellectual symbols, symbols
that evoke ideas alone, or ideas mingled with emotions; and outside the very definite traditions of mysticism and the less definite criticism of certain modern poets, these alone are
called symbols. Most things belong to one or another kind, according to the way we speak of

them and the companions we give them, for symbols, associated with ideas that are more than fragments of the shadows thrown upon the intellect by the emotions they evoke, are the playthings of the allegorist or the pedant, and soon pass away. If I say 'white' or 'purple' in an ordinary line of poetry, they evoke emotions so exclusively that I cannot say why they move me; but if I say them in the same mood, in the same breath with such obvious intellectual symbols as a cross or a crown of thorns, I think of purity and sovereignty; while in numerable meanings, which are held to one another by the bondage of subtle suggestion, and alike in the emotions and in the intellect, move visibly through my mind, and move invisibly beyond the threshold of sleep casting lights and shadows of an indefinable wisdom on what had seemed before, it may be, but sterility and noisy violence. It is the intellect that decides where the reader shall ponder over the procession of the symbols, and if the symbols are merely emotional, he gazes from amid the accidents and destinies of the world; but if the symbols are intellectual too, he becomes himself a part of pure intellect, and he is himself mingled with the procession. If I watch a rushy pool in the moonlight, my emotion at its beauty is mixed with memories of the man that I have seen ploughing by its margin, or of the lovers I saw there a night ago; but if I look at the moon herself and remember any of her ancient names and meanings, I move among divine people, and things that have shaken off our mortality, the tower of ivory, the queen of waters, the shining stag among enchanted woods, the white hare sitting upon the hilltop, the fool of faery with his shining cup full of dreams, and it may be 'make a friend of one of these images of wonder,' and 'meet the Lord in the air.' So, too, if one is moved by Shakespeare, who is content with emotional symbols that he may come the nearer to our sympathy, one is mixed with the whole spectacle of the world; while if one is moved by Dante, or by the myth of Demeter, one is mixed into the shadow of God or of a goddess. So, too, one is furthest from symbols when one is busy doing this or that, but the soul moves among symbols and unfolds in symbols when trance, or madness, or deep meditation has withdrawn it from every impulse but its own. . . . [the arts] cannot overcome the slow dying of men's hearts that we call the progress of the world, and lay their hands upon men's heart-strings again, without becoming the garment of religion as in old times.

V

If people were to accept the theory that poetry moves us because of its symbolism, what change should one look for in the manner of our poetry? A return to the way of our fathers, a casting out of descriptions of nature for the sake of nature, of the moral law for the sake of the moral law, a casting out of all anecdotes and of that brooding over scientific opinion that so often extinguished the central flame in Tennyson, and of that vehemence that would make us do or not do certain things; or, in other words, we should come to understand that the beryl stone was enchanted by our fathers that it might unfold the pictures in its heart, and not to mirror our own excited faces, or the boughs waving outside the window. With this change of substance, this return to imagination, this understanding that the laws of art, which are the hidden laws of the world, can alone bind the imagination, would come a change of style, and we would cast out of serious poetry those energetic rhythms, as of a man running, which are the invention of the will with its eyes always on something to be done or undone; and we would seek out those wavering, meditative, organic rhythms, which are the embodiment of the imagination, that neither desires nor hates, because it has done with time, and only wishes to gaze upon some reality, some beauty; nor would it be any longer possible for anybody to deny the importance of form, in all its kinds, for although you can expound an opinion, or describe a thing when your words are not quite well chosen, you cannot give a body to something that moves beyond the senses, unless your words are as subtle, as complex, as full of mysterious life, as the body of a flower or of a woman. The form of sincere poetry, unlike the form of the popular poetry, may indeed be sometimes obscure, or ungrammatical as in some of the best of the Songs of Innocence and Experience, but it must have the perfections that escape analysis, the subtleties that have a new meaning every day, and it must have all this whether it be but a little song made out of a moment of dreamy indolence, or some great epic made out of the dreams of one poet and of a hundred generations whose hands were never weary of the sword.

Chapter 56

Ezra Pound (1885–1972)

"A FEW DON'TS BY AN IMAGISTE"
(1912–13)

A N AMERICAN EXPATRIATE POET AND critic, Pound fled what he considered American puritanism and lived in London 1908–20, where he met Yeats, whom he considered the greatest living poet, wrote prolifically, edited little magazines, discovered and promoted such writers as Eliot, Frost, Joyce, and Hemingway, and was a driving force behind both imagism and vorticism. After World War I he denounced Jewish financiers, usury, and international capitalism; moving to Italy in 1924, he embraced Mussolini's fascism, and later expressed support for Hitler and wrote for publications owned by the British fascist Oswald Mosley. During World War II he made hundreds of radio broadcasts denouncing the United States, Franklin Roosevelt, and Jews. Arrested for treason after the war, he was deemed unfit to stand trial and was incarcerated in a psychiatric hospital in Washington, DC; released in 1958 after a campaign led by writers and literary critics, Pound lived out his last years in Italy. His major works include *Hugh Selwyn Mauberley* (1920), *Personæ: The Collected Poems of Ezra Pound* (1926), *How to Read* (1931), *ABC of Economics* (1933), *Homage to Sextus Propertius* (1934), *ABC of Reading* (1934), *Make It New* (1935), and his unfinished epic, *The Cantos* (1917–69). "A Few Don'ts by an Imagiste" lays out Pound's basic precepts for writing imagist poetry.

Ezra Pound, "A Few Don'ts by an Imagiste," *Poetry: A Magazine of Verse* 1 (October 1912– March 1913): 200–6. Reprinted in *Manifesto: A Century of Isms*, ed. Mary Ann Caws. Lincoln, NE: U of Nebraska P, 2001. 356–59.

An "Image" is that which presents an intellectual and emotional complex in an instant of time. I use the term "complex" rather in the technical sense employed by the newer psychologists, such as Hart, though we might not agree absolutely in our application.

It is the presentation of such a "complex" instantaneously which gives that sense of sudden liberation; that sense of freedom from time limits and space limits; that sense of sudden growth, which we experience in the presence of the greatest works of art.

It is better to present one Image in a lifetime than to produce voluminous works.

All this, however, some may consider open to debate. The immediate necessity is to tabulate a LIST OF DONT'S for those beginning to write verses. But I can not put all of them into Mosaic negative.

To begin with, consider the three rules recorded by Mr. Flint, not as dogma—never consider anything as dogma—but as the result of long contemplation, which, even if it is some one else's contemplation, may be worth consideration.

Pay no attention to the criticism of men who have never themselves written a notable work. Consider the discrepancies between the actual writing of the Greek poets and dramatists, and the theories of the Graeco-Roman grammarians, concocted to explain their metres.

Language

Use no superfluous word, no adjective, which does not reveal something.

Don't use such an expression as "dim lands *of peace*." It dulls the image. It mixes an abstraction with the concrete. It comes from the writer's not realizing that the natural object is always the *adequate* symbol.

Go in fear of abstractions. Don't retell in mediocre verse what has already been done in good prose. Don't think any intelligent person is going to be deceived when you try to shirk all the difficulties of the unspeakably difficult art of good prose by chopping your composition into line lengths.

What the expert is tired of today the public will be tired of tomorrow.

Don't imagine that the art of poetry is any simpler than the art of music, or that you can please the expert before you have spent at least as much effort on the art of verse as the average piano teacher spends on the art of music.

Be influenced by as many great artists as you can, but have the decency either to acknowledge the debt outright, or to try to conceal it.

Don't allow "influence" to mean merely that you mop up the particular decorative vocabulary of some one or two poets whom you happen to admire. A Turkish war correspondent was recently caught red-handed babbling in his dispatches of "dove-gray" hills, or else it was "pearl-pale," I can not remember.

Use either no ornament or good ornament.

Rhythm and rhyme

Let the candidate fill his mind with the finest cadences he can discover, preferably in a foreign language so that the meaning of the words may be less likely to divert his attention from the movement; e. g., Saxon charms, Hebridean Folk Songs, the verse of Dante, and the lyrics of Shakespeare—if he can dissociate the vocabulary from the cadence. Let him dissect the lyrics of Goethe coldly into their component sound values, syllables long and short, stressed and unstressed, into vowels and consonants.

It is not necessary that a poem should rely on its music, but if it does rely on its music that music must be such as will delight the expert.

Let the neophyte know assonance and alliteration, rhyme immediate and delayed, simple and polyphonic, as a musician would expect to know harmony and counterpoint and all the minutiae of his craft. No time is too great to give to these matters or to any one of them, even if the artist seldom have need of them.

Don't imagine that a thing will "go" in verse just because it's too dull to go in prose.

Don't be "viewy"—leave that to the writers of pretty little philosophic essays. Don't be descriptive; remember that the painter can describe a landscape much better than you can, and that he has to know a deal more about it.

When Shakespeare talks of the "Dawn in russet mantle clad" he presents something which the painter does not present. There is in this line of his nothing that one can call description; he presents.

Consider the way of the scientists rather than the way of an advertising agent for a new soap.

The scientist does not expect to be acclaimed as a great scientist until he has *discovered* something. He begins by learning what has been discovered already. He goes from that point onward. He does not bank on being a charming fellow personally. He does not expect his friends to applaud the results of his freshman class work. Freshmen in poetry are unfortunately not confined to a definite and recognizable class room. They are "all over the shop." Is it any wonder "the public is indifferent to poetry?"

Don't chop your stuff into separate *iambs*. Don't make each line stop dead at the end, and then begin every next line with a heave. Let the beginning of the next line catch the rise of the rhythm wave, unless you want a definite longish pause.

In short, behave as a musician, a good musician, when dealing with that phase of your art which has exact parallels in music. The same laws govern, and you are bound by no others.

Naturally, your rhythmic structure should not destroy the shape of your words, or their natural sound, or their meaning. It is improbable that, at the start, you will be able to get a rhythm-structure strong enough to affect them very much, though you may fall a victim to all sorts of false stopping due to line ends and caesurae.

The musician can rely on pitch and the volume of the orchestra. You can not. The term harmony is misapplied to poetry; it refers to simultaneous sounds of different pitch. There is, however, in the best verse a sort of residue of sound which remains in the ear of the hearer and acts more or less as an organ-base. A rhyme must have in it some slight element of surprise if it is to give pleasure; it need not be bizarre or curious, but it must be well used if used at all.

Vide further Vildrac and Duhamel's notes on rhyme in "*Technique Poetique.*"

That part of your poetry which strikes upon the imaginative *eye* of the reader will lose nothing by translation into a foreign tongue; that which appeals to the ear can reach only those who take it in the original.

Consider the definiteness of Dante's presentation, as compared with Milton's rhetoric. Read as much of Wordsworth as does not seem too unutterably dull.

If you want the gist of the matter go to Sappho, Catullus, Villon, Heine when he is in the vein, Gautier when he is not too frigid; or, if you have not the tongues, seek out the leisurely Chaucer. Good prose will do you no harm, and there is good discipline to be had by trying to write it.

Translation is likewise good training, if you find that your original matter "wobbles" when you try to rewrite it. The meaning of the poem to be translated can not "wobble."

If you are using a symmetrical form, don't put in what you want to say and then fill up the remaining vacuums with slush.

Don't mess up the perception of one sense by trying to define it in terms of another. This is usually only the result of being too lazy to find the exact word. To this clause there are possibly exceptions.

The first three simple proscriptions will throw out nine-tenths of all the bad poetry now accepted as standard and classic; and will prevent you from many a crime of production.

". . . *Mais d'abord il faut etre un poete*," as MM. Duhamel and Vildrac have said at the end of their little book, "*Notes sur la Technique Poetique*"; but in an American one takes that at least for granted, otherwise why does one get born upon that august continent!

Chapter 57

T.S. Eliot (1888–1965)

"TRADITION AND THE INDIVIDUAL TALENT" (1919)

AN AMERICAN-BORN POET, PLAYWRIGHT, and literary critic, Eliot moved to England in 1914 and became a British citizen in 1927 when he famously proclaimed himself "classicist in literature, royalist in politics, and anglo-catholic in religion"; three decades later he said that he combined "a Catholic cast of mind, a Calvinist heritage, and a Puritanical temperament." Yet he continued to champion many modernist authors, including Djuna Barnes, David Jones, Gide, Pound, the early Auden. Many of Eliot's greatest poems, which include "The Love Song of J. Alfred Prufrock" (1915), "Gerontion" (1920), *The Waste Land* (1922), and "The Hollow Men" (1925), are dramatic or interior monologues compounded of startling imagery, fragments of contemporary civilization, obscure allusions to other cultures, languages, and literature, and were often written in what, writing about Joyce, he called the mythic method. *Four Quartets* (1945), his longest and most complex poem, is an extended meditation on time, human existence, and theological meaning. Eliot, who also wrote seven plays, including *Murder in the Cathedral* (1935) and *The Cocktail Party* (1949), and a good deal of criticism, won the Nobel Prize for Literature in 1948. In "Tradition and the Individual Talent" he maintains that, while every artist inherits a tradition that is already complete and achieved, every significant new work both derives from and reshapes the tradition, so that it comes to seem inevitable as well as new, unanticipated and yet a culmination of all that has preceded it.

T.S. Eliot, "Tradition and the Individual Talent," *The Sacred Wood: Essays on Poetry and Criticism*. London: Metheun; New York: Barnes and Noble, 1960. 47–52.

In English writing we seldom speak of tradition, though we occasionally apply its name in deploring its absence. We cannot refer to "the tradition" or to "a tradition"; at most, we employ the adjective in saying that the poetry of So-and-so is "traditional" or even "too traditional." Seldom, perhaps, does the word appear except in a phrase of censure. If otherwise, it is vaguely approbative, with the implication, as to the work approved, of some pleasing archaeological reconstruction. You can hardly make the word agreeable to English ears without this comfortable reference to the reassuring science of archaeology.

Certainly the word is not likely to appear in our appreciations of living or dead writers. Every nation, every race, has not only its own creative, but its own critical turn of mind; and is even more oblivious of the shortcomings and limitations of its critical habits than of those of its creative genius. We know, or think we know, from the enormous mass of critical writing that has appeared in the French language the critical method or habit of the French; we only conclude (we are such unconscious people) that the French are "more critical" than we, and sometimes even plume ourselves a little with the fact, as if the French were the less spontaneous. Perhaps they are; but we might remind ourselves that criticism is as inevitable as breathing, and that we should be none the worse for articulating what passes in our minds when we read a book and feel an emotion about it, for criticizing our own minds in their work of criticism. One of the facts that might come to light in this process is our tendency to insist, when we praise a poet, upon those aspects of his work in which he least resembles anyone else. In these aspects or parts of his work we pretend to find what is individual, what is the peculiar essence of the man. We dwell with satisfaction upon the poet's difference from his predecessors, especially his immediate predecessors; we endeavour to find something that can be isolated in order to be enjoyed. Whereas if we approach a poet without his prejudice we shall often find that not only the best, but the most individual parts of his work may be those in which the dead poets, his ancestors, assert their immortality most vigorously. And I do not mean the impressionable period of adolescence, but the period of full maturity.

Yet if the only form of tradition, of handing down, consisted in following the ways of the immediate generation before us in a blind or timid adherence to its successes, "tradition" should positively be discouraged. We have seen many such simple currents soon lost in the sand; and novelty is better than repetition. Tradition is a matter of much wider significance. It cannot be inherited, and if you want it you must obtain it by great labour. It involves, in the first place, the historical sense, which we may call nearly indispensable to anyone who would continue to be a poet beyond his twenty-fifth year; and the historical sense involves a perception, not only of the pastness of the past, but of its presence; the historical sense compels a man to write not merely with his own generation in his bones, but with a feeling that the whole of the literature of Europe from Homer and within it the whole of the litera-ture of his own country has a simultaneous existence and composes a simultaneous order. This historical sense, which is a sense of the timeless as well as of the temporal and of the timeless and of the temporal together, is what makes a writer traditional. And it is at the same time what makes a writer most acutely conscious of his place in time, of his contemporaneity.

No poet, no artist of any art, has his complete meaning alone. His significance, his appre-ciation is the appreciation of his relation to the dead poets and artists. You cannot value him alone; you must set him, for contrast and comparison, among the dead. I mean this as a prin-ciple of aesthetic, not merely historical, criticism. The necessity that he shall conform, that he shall cohere, is not one-sided; what happens when a new work of art is created is some-thing that happens simultaneously to all the works of art which preceded it. The existing monuments form an ideal order among themselves, which is modified by the introduction of the new (the really new) work of art among them. The existing order is complete before the new work arrives; for order to persist after the supervention of novelty, the *whole* existing order must be, if ever so slightly, altered; and so the relations, proportions, values of each work of art toward the whole are readjusted; and this is conformity between the old and the new. Whoever has approved this idea of order, of the form of European, of English litera-ture, will not find it preposterous that the past should be altered by the present as much as the present is directed by the past. And the poet who is aware of this will be aware of great difficulties and responsibilities.

In a peculiar sense he will be aware also that he must inevitably be judged by the stan-dards of the past. I say judged, not amputated, by them; not judged to be as good as, or worse or better than, the dead; and certainly not judged by the canons of dead critics. It is a judgment, a comparison, in which two things are measured by each other. To conform merely would be for the new work not really to conform at all; it would not be new, and would therefore not be a work of art. And we do not quite say that the new is more valuable because it fits in; but its fitting in is a test of its value—a test, it is true, which can only be slowly and cautiously applied, for we are none of us infallible judges of conformity. We say: it appears to conform, and is perhaps individual, or it appears individual, and may conform; but we are hardly likely to find that it is one and not the other.

To proceed to a more intelligible exposition of the relation of the poet to the past: he can neither take the past as a lump, an indiscriminate bolus, nor can he form himself wholly on one or two private admirations, nor can he form himself wholly upon one preferred period. The first course is inadmissible, the second is an important experience of youth, and the third is a pleasant and highly desirable supplement. The poet must be very conscious of the main current, which does not at all flow invariably through the most distinguished reputations. He must be quite aware of the obvious fact that art never improves, but that the material of art is never quite the same. He must be aware that the mind of Europe—the mind of his own country—a mind which he learns in time to be much more important than his own private mind—is a mind which changes; and that this change is a development which abandons nothing *en route,* which does not superannuate either Shakespeare, or Homer, or the rock drawing of the Magdalenian draughtsmen. That this development, refinement perhaps, complication certainly, is not, from the point of view of the artist, any improvement. Perhaps not even an improvement from the point of view of the psychologist or not to the extent which we imagine; perhaps only in the end based upon a complication in economics and machinery. But the difference between the present and the past is that the conscious present is an awareness of the past in a way and to an extent which the past's awareness of itself cannot show. Some one said: "The dead writers are remote from us because we *know* so much more than they did." Precisely, and they are that which we know.

Chapter 58

Virginia Woolf (1882–1941)

"MODERN FICTION" (1919)

ADELINE VIRGINIA STEPHEN, THE WRITER who would become known as Virginia Woolf, was born into a family with distinguished literary and artistic roots. Her father, Sir Leslie Stephen, was a prominent historian, biographer, ethical philosopher, and the editor of *The Cornhill Magazine* and *The Dictionary of National Biography*; his associates included George Eliot, Henry James, Thomas Hardy, and Matthew Arnold. Her mother, Julia Prinsep Stephen, was a renowned beauty with ties to the Pre-Raphaelite Brotherhood painters and the niece of the Victorian portrait photographer, Julia Margaret Cameron. Woolf was an aspiring writer as a young child; her first submitted publication was to the Victorian children's magazine *Tit Bits*. Like many young women of her class, she was educated at home – a cause of great disappointment throughout her life; however, Woolf's intellectual and scholarly prowess was recognized by her father who granted her access to his library and afforded her a classical education; her Latin tutor was Dr. George Warr and her Greek tutors were Clara Pater and Janet Case. Upon her father's death she and her siblings moved from staid Kensington to 46 Gordon Square in Bloomsbury. The group of artists and intellectuals who would come to be known as the Bloomsbury Circle included her brothers Thoby and Adrian Stephen and their Cambridge University friends and associates (Clive Bell, Duncan Grant, Lytton Strachey, John Maynard Keynes, T.S. Eliot, Roger Fry, and others). In 1912, Virginia Stephen married Leonard Woolf, one of the Cambridge set. The two Woolfs founded the Hogarth Press in 1917; the cutting-edge publishing house published many emerging modernist writers and visual artists, including Gertrude Stein, Eliot, Katherine Mansfield, Robert Graves, William Plomer, and Christopher Isherwood. The press gave Woolf remarkable creative freedom; one of its first commercial successes was her collection of stories, *Kew Gardens* (1919). With the exception of her earliest novels, *The Voyage Out* (1915) and *Night and Day* (1919), all of Woolf's experimental novels were published by Hogarth. Woolf's literary corpus of essays, short stories, and novels is renowned for the author's experiments with genre, narration, and form, and her fascination with interiority, consciousness, and temporality. Her best-known works include *Mrs. Dalloway* (1925, novel), *To the Lighthouse* (1927, novel), the feminist classic *A Room of One's Own* (1929, essay), *The Waves* (1931, novel), and *Three Guineas* (1938, essay).

Virginia Woolf, "Modern Fiction." *The Common Reader: First Series* (1925). New York: Harcourt, Brace, 1953. 150–58.

In making any survey, even the freest and loosest, of modern fiction it is difficult not to take it for granted that the modern practice of the art is somehow an improvement upon the old. With their simple tools and primitive materials, it might be said, Fielding did well and Jane Austen even better, but compare their opportunities with ours! Their masterpieces certainly have a strange air of simplicity. And yet the analogy between literature and the process, to choose an example, of making motor cars scarcely holds good beyond the first glance. It is doubtful whether in the course of the centuries, though we have learnt much about making machines, we have learnt anything about making literature. We do not come to write better; all that we can be said to do is to keep moving, now a little in this direction, now in that, but with a circular tendency should the whole course of the track be viewed from a sufficiently lofty pinnacle. It need scarcely be said that we make no claim to stand, even momentarily, upon that vantage ground. On the flat, in the crowd, half blind with dust, we look back with envy to those happier warriors, whose battle is won and whose achievements wear so serene an air of accomplishment that we can scarcely refrain from whispering that the fight was not so fierce for them as for us. It is for the historian of literature to decide; for him to say if we are now beginning or ending or standing in the middle of a great period of prose fiction, for down in the plain little is visible. We only know that certain gratitudes and hostilities inspire us; that certain paths seem to lead to fertile land, others to the dust and the desert; and of this perhaps it may be worth while to attempt some account.

Our quarrel, then, is not with the classics, and if we speak of quarrelling with Mr. Wells, Mr. Bennett, and Mr. Galsworthy it is partly that by the mere fact of their existence in the flesh their work has a living, breathing, every-day imperfection which bids us take what liberties with it we choose. But it is also true that, while we thank them for a thousand gifts, we reserve our unconditional gratitude for Mr. Hardy, for Mr. Conrad, and in a much lesser degree for the Mr. Hudson, of *The Purple Land*, *Green Mansions*, and *Far Away and Long Ago*. Mr. Wells, Mr. Bennett, and Mr. Galsworthy have excited so many hopes and disappointed them so persistently that our gratitude largely takes the form of thanking them for having shown us what they might have done but have not done; what we certainly could not do, but as certainly, perhaps, do not wish to do. No single phrase will sum up the charge or grievance which we have to bring against a mass of work so large in its volume and embodying so many qualities, both admirable and the reverse. If we tried to formulate our meaning in one word we should say that these three writers are materialists. It is because they are concerned not with the spirit but with the body that they have disappointed us, and left us with the feeling that the sooner English fiction turns its back upon them, as politely as may be, and marches, if only into the desert, the better for its soul. Naturally, no single word reaches the centre of three separate targets. In the case of Mr. Wells it falls notably wide of the mark. And yet even with him it indicates to our thinking the fatal alloy in his genius, the great clod of clay that has got itself mixed up with the purity of his inspiration. But Mr. Bennett is perhaps the worst culprit of the three, inasmuch as he is by far the best workman. He can make a book so well constructed and solid in its craftsmanship that it is difficult for the most exacting of critics to see through what chink or crevice decay can creep in. There is not so much as a draught between the frames of the windows, or a crack in the boards. And yet—if life should refuse to live there? That is a risk which the creator of *The Old Wives' Tale*, George Cannon, Edwin Clayhanger, and hosts of other figures, may well claim to have surmounted. His characters live abundantly, even unexpectedly, but it remains to ask how do they live, and what do they live for? More and more they seem to us, deserting even the well-built villa in the Five Towns, to spend their time in some softly padded first-class railway carriage, pressing bells and buttons innumerable; and the destiny to which they travel so luxuriously becomes more and more unquestionably an eternity of bliss spent in the very best hotel in Brighton. It can scarcely be said of Mr. Wells that he is a materialist in the sense that he takes too much delight in the solidity of his fabric. His mind is too generous in its sympathies to allow him to spend much time in making things shipshape and substantial. He is a materialist from sheer goodness of heart, taking upon his shoulders the work that ought to have been discharged by Government officials, and in the plethora of his ideas and facts scarcely having leisure to realise, or forgetting to think important, the crudity and coarseness of his human beings. Yet what more damaging criticism can there be both of his earth and of his Heaven than that they are to be inhabited here and hereafter by his Joans and his Peters? Does not the inferiority of their natures tarnish whatever institutions and ideals may be provided for them by the generosity of their creator? Nor, profoundly though we respect the integrity and humanity of Mr. Galsworthy, shall we find what we seek in his pages.

If we fasten, then, one label on all these books, on which is one word, materialists, we mean by it that they write of unimportant things; that they spend immense skill and immense industry making the trivial and the transitory appear the true and the enduring.

We have to admit that we are exacting, and, further, that we find it difficult to justify our discontent by explaining what it is that we exact. We frame our question differently at different times. But it reappears most persistently as we drop the finished novel on the crest of a sigh—Is it worth while? What is the point of it all? Can it be that owing to one of those little deviations which the human spirit seems to make from time to time Mr. Bennett has come down with his magnificent apparatus for catching life just an inch or two on the wrong side? Life escapes; and perhaps without life nothing else is worth while. It is a confession of vagueness to have to make use of such a figure as this, but we scarcely better the matter by speaking, as critics are prone to do, of reality. Admitting the vagueness which afflicts all criticism of novels, let us hazard the opinion that for us at this moment the form of fiction most in vogue more often misses than secures the thing we seek. Whether we call it life or spirit, truth or reality, this, the essential thing, has moved off, or on, and refuses to be contained any longer in such ill-fitting vestments as we provide. Nevertheless, we go on perseveringly, conscientiously, constructing our two and thirty chapters after a design which more and more ceases to resemble the vision in our minds. So much of the enormous labour of proving the solidity, the likeness to life, of the story is not merely labour thrown away but labour misplaced to the extent of obscuring and blotting out the light of the conception. The writer seems constrained, not by his own free will but by some powerful and unscrupulous tyrant who has him in thrall to provide a plot, to provide comedy, tragedy, love, interest, and an air of probability embalming the whole so impeccable that if all his figures were to come to life they would find themselves dressed down to the last button of their coats in the fashion of the hour. The tyrant is obeyed; the novel is done to a turn. But sometimes, more and more often as time goes by, we suspect a momentary doubt, a spasm of rebellion, as the pages fill themselves in the customary way. Is life like this? Must novels be like this?

Look within and life, it seems, is very far from being "like this." Examine for a moment an ordinary mind on an ordinary day. The mind receives a myriad impressions—trivial, fantastic, evanescent, or engraved with the sharpness of steel. From all sides they come, an incessant shower of innumerable atoms; and as they fall, as they shape themselves into the life of Monday or Tuesday, the accent falls differently from of old; the moment of importance came not here but there; so that if a writer were a free man and not a slave, if he could write what he chose, not what he must, if he could base his work upon his own feeling and not upon convention, there would be no plot, no comedy, no tragedy, no love interest or catastrophe in the accepted style, and perhaps not a single button sewn on as the Bond Street tailors would have it. Life is not a series of gig lamps symmetrically arranged; but a luminous halo, a semi-transparent envelope surrounding us from the beginning of consciousness to the end. Is it not the task of the novelist to convey this varying, this unknown and uncircumscribed spirit, whatever aberration or complexity it may display, with as little mixture of the alien and external as possible? We are not pleading merely for courage and sincerity; we are suggesting that the proper stuff of fiction is a little other than custom would have us believe it.

It is, at any rate, in some such fashion as this that we seek to define the quality which distinguishes the work of several young writers, among whom Mr. James Joyce is the most notable, from that of their predecessors. They attempt to come closer to life, and to preserve more sincerely and exactly what interests and moves them, even if to do so they must discard most of the conventions which are commonly observed by the novelist. Let us record the atoms as they fall upon the mind in the order in which they fall, let us trace the pattern, however disconnected and incoherent in appearance, which each sight or incident scores upon the consciousness. Let us not take it for granted that life exists more fully in what is commonly thought big than in what is commonly thought small. Any one who has read *A Portrait of the Artist as a Young Man* or, what promises to be a far more interesting work, *Ulysses*, now appearing in the *Little Review*, will have hazarded some theory of this nature as to Mr. Joyce's intention. On our part, with such a fragment before us, it is hazarded rather than affirmed; but whatever the intention of the whole there can be no question but that it is of the utmost sincerity and that the result, difficult or unpleasant as we may judge it, is undeniably important. In contrast with those whom we have called materialists Mr. Joyce is spiritual; he is concerned at all costs to reveal the flickerings of that innermost flame which flashes its messages through the brain, and in order to preserve it he disregards with complete courage whatever seems to him adventitious, whether it be probability, or coherence or any other of these signposts which for generations have served to support the imagination of a reader when called upon to imagine what he can neither touch nor see. The scene in the cemetery, for instance, with its brilliancy, its sordidity, its incoherence, its sudden lightning flashes of significance, does undoubtedly come so close to the quick of the mind that, on a first reading at any rate, it is difficult not to acclaim a masterpiece. If we want life itself here, surely we have it. Indeed, we find ourselves fumbling rather awkwardly if we try to say what else we wish, and for what reason a work of such originality yet fails to compare, for we must take high examples, with *Youth* or *The Mayor of Casterbridge*. It fails because of the comparative poverty of the writer's mind, we might say simply and have done with it. But it is possible to press a little further and wonder whether we may not refer our sense of being in a bright yet narrow room, confined and shut in, rather than enlarged and set free, to some limitation imposed by the method as well as by the mind. Is it the method that inhibits the creative power? Is it due to the method that we feel neither jovial nor magnanimous, but centred in a self which, in spite of its tremor of susceptibility, never embraces or creates what is outside itself and beyond? Does the emphasis laid, perhaps didactically, upon indecency, contribute to the effect of something angular and isolated? Or is it merely that in any effort of such originality it is much easier, for contemporaries especially, to feel what it lacks than to name what it gives? In any case it is a mistake to stand outside examining "methods." Any method is right, every method is right, that expresses what we wish to express, if we are writers; that brings us closer to the novelist's intention if we are readers. This method has the merit of bringing us closer to what we were prepared to call life itself; did not the reading of *Ulysses* suggest how much of life is excluded or ignored, and did it not come with a shock to open *Tristram Shandy* or even *Pendennis* and be by them convinced that there are not only other aspects of life, but more important ones into the bargain.

However this may be, the problem before the novelist at present, as we suppose it to have been in the past, is to contrive means of being free to set down what he chooses. He has to have the courage to say that what interests him is no longer "this" but "that": out of "that" alone must he construct his work. For the moderns "that," the point of interest, lies very likely in the dark places of psychology. At once, therefore, the accent falls a little differently; the emphasis is upon something hitherto ignored; at once a different outline of form becomes necessary, difficult for us to grasp, incomprehensible to our predecessors. No one but a modern, perhaps no one but a Russian, would have felt the interest of the situation which Tchekov has made into the short story which he calls "Gusev." Some Russian soldiers lie ill on board a ship which is taking them back to Russia. We are given a few scraps of their talk and some of their thoughts; then one of them dies, and is carried away; the talk goes on among the others for a time, until Gusev himself dies, and looking "like a carrot or a radish" is thrown overboard. The emphasis is laid upon such unexpected places that at first it seems as if there were no emphasis at all; and then, as the eyes accustom themselves to twilight and discern the shapes of things in a room we see how complete the story is, how profound, and how truly in obedience to his vision Tchekov has chosen this, that, and the other, and placed them together to compose something new. But it is impossible to say "this is comic," or "that is tragic," nor are we certain, since short stories, we have been taught, should be brief and conclusive, whether this, which is vague and inconclusive, should be called a short story at all.

The most elementary remarks upon modern English fiction can hardly avoid some mention of the Russian influence, and if the Russians are mentioned one runs the risk of feeling that to write of any fiction save theirs is waste of time. If we want understanding of the soul and heart where else shall we find it of comparable profundity? If we are sick of our own materialism the least considerable of their novelists has by right of birth a natural reverence for the human spirit. "Learn to make yourself akin to people. . . . But let this sympathy be not with the mind—for it is easy with the mind—but with the heart, with love towards them." In every great Russian writer we seem to discern the features of a saint, if sympathy for the sufferings of others, love towards them, endeavour to reach some goal worthy of the most exacting demands of the spirit constitute saintliness. It is the saint in them which confounds us with a feeling of our own irreligious triviality, and turns so many of our famous novels to tinsel and trickery. The conclusions of the Russian mind, thus comprehensive and compassionate, are inevitably, perhaps, of the utmost sadness. More accurately indeed we might speak of the inconclusiveness of the Russian mind. It is the sense that there is no answer, that if honestly examined life presents question after question which must be left to sound on and on after the story is over in hopeless interrogation that fills us with a deep, and finally it may be with a resentful, despair. They are right perhaps; unquestionably they see further than we do and without our gross impediments of vision. But perhaps we see something that escapes them, or why should this voice of protest mix itself with our gloom? The voice of protest is the voice of another and an ancient civilisation which seems to have bred in us the instinct to enjoy and fight rather than to suffer and understand. English fiction from Sterne to Meredith bears witness to our natural delight in humour and comedy, in the beauty of earth, in the activities of the intellect, and in the splendour of the body. But any deductions that we may draw from the comparison of two fictions so immeasurably far apart are futile save indeed as they flood us with a view of the infinite possibilities of the art and remind us that there is no limit to the horizon, and that nothing—no "method," no experiment, even of the wildest—is forbidden, but only falsity and pretence. "The proper stuff of fiction" does not exist; everything is the proper stuff of fiction, every feeling, every thought; every quality of brain and spirit is drawn upon; no perception comes amiss. And if we can imagine the art of fiction come alive and standing in our midst, she would undoubtedly bid us break her and bully her, as well as honour and love her, for so her youth is renewed and her sovereignty assured.

Chapter 59

Luigi Pirandello (1867–1936)

"PREFACE," *SIX CHARACTERS IN SEARCH OF AN AUTHOR* (1925)

ITALIAN WRITER OF A HALF dozen novels, hundreds of short stories, plus about 40 plays, Pirandello was controversial for both his writings and his politics. He was, for example, hooted from the theatre on opening night of his most famous work, *Six Characters in Search of an Author* (1921), but a revival shortly thereafter was acclaimed; his *Henry IV* (1922) was universally acclaimed from the first. In 1925, when Pirandello, with the help of Mussolini, became artistic director and owner of the Teatro d'Arte di Roma, he publicly stated: "I am a Fascist because I am Italian." Yet some saw his relationship with Mussolini as a calculated career move since he also said, "I'm apolitical, I'm only a man in the world." After numerous conflicts with fascist leaders, he destroyed his party membership card in front of the secretary-general of the Fascist Party in 1927 and for the rest of his life was watched by the secret police. Yet, and against his wishes, he received a state funeral upon his death.

Pirandello was part of a movement in the early twentieth century called theatricalism or anti-illusionism. The theatricalists rejected realist drama – which they thought could not depict the inner life since it had abandoned poetry, interaction between actors and audience, soliloquies, asides, and bare stages – and relied on the dreamlike, the expressive, and the symbolic. Pirandello's tragic farces, which are considered forerunners of Theatre of the Absurd, won him the Nobel Prize for Literature in 1934 for his "bold and brilliant renovation of the drama and the stage."

Six Characters, he suggests in his "Preface," not only concerns "the mystery of artistic creation," but depicts it in process as the family of characters plead – even demand – to have their tragic story realized by the Manager, whose rehearsal of another Pirandello play (*Tonight We Improvise*) they interrupt. They thereby produce "a mixture of tragic and comic, fantastic and realistic, in a humorous situation that was quite new and infinitely complex . . . an obscure, ambiguous drama . . . [comprising] the inherent tragic conflict between life (which is always moving and changing) and form (which fixes it, immutable)."

Luigi Pirandello, "Preface," *Six Characters in Search of an Author*. In *Naked Masks: Five Plays by Luigi Pirandello*, ed. and trans. Eric Bentley. New York: Dutton, 1951. 363–75.

It seems like yesterday but is actually many years ago that a nimble little maidservant entered the service of my art. However, she always comes fresh to the job.

She is called Fantasy.

A little puckish and malicious, if she likes to dress in black no one will wish to deny that she is often positively bizarre and no one will wish to believe that she always does everything in the same way and in earnest. She sticks her hand in her pocket, pulls out a cap and bells, sets it on her head, red as a cock's comb, and dashes away. Here today, there tomorrow. And she amuses herself by bringing to my house – since I derive stories and novels and plays from them – the most disgruntled tribe in the world, men, women, children, involved in strange adventures which they can find no way out of; thwarted in their plans; cheated in their hopes; with whom, in short, it is often torture to deal.

Well, this little maidservant of mine, Fantasy, several years ago, had the bad inspiration or ill-omened caprice to bring a family into my house. I wouldn't know where she fished them up or how, but, according to her, I could find in them the subject for a magnificent novel.

I found before me a man about fifty years old, in a dark jacket and light trousers, with a frowning air and ill-natured mortified eyes; a poor woman in widow's weeds leading by one hand a little girl of four and by the other a boy of rather more than ten; a cheeky and "sexy" girl, also clad in black but with an equivocal and brazen pomp, all atremble with a lively, biting contempt for the mortified old man and for a young fellow of twenty who stood on one side closed in on himself as if he despised them all. In short, the six characters who are seen coming on stage at the beginning of the play. Now one of them and now another – often beating down one another – embarked on the sad story of their adventures, each shouting his own reasons, and projecting in my face his disordered passions, more or less as they do in the play to the unhappy Manager.

What author will be able to say how and why a character was born in his fantasy? The mystery of artistic creation is the same as that of birth. A woman who loves may desire to become a mother; but the desire by itself, however intense, cannot suffice. One fine day she will find herself a mother without having any precise intimation when it began. In the same way an artist imbibes very many germs of life and can never say how and why, at a certain moment, one of these vital germs inserts itself into his fantasy, there to become a living creature on a plane of life superior to the changeable existence of every day.

I can only say that, without having made any effort to seek them out, I found before me, alive – you could touch them and even hear them breathe – the six characters now seen on the stage. And they stayed there in my presence, each with his secret torment and all bound together by the one common origin and mutual entanglement of their affairs, while I had them enter the world of art, constructing from their persons, their passions, and their adventures a novel, a drama, or at least a story.

Born alive, they wished to live.

To me it was never enough to present a man or a woman and what is special and characteristic about them simply for the pleasure of presenting them; to narrate a particular affair, lively or sad, simply for the pleasure of narrating it; to describe a landscape simply for the pleasure of describing it.

There are some writers (and not a few) who do feel this pleasure and, satisfied, ask no more. They are, to speak more precisely, historical writers.

But there are others who, beyond such pleasure, feel a more profound spiritual need on whose account they admit only figures, affairs, landscapes which have been soaked, so to speak, in a particular sense of life and acquire from it a universal value. These are, more precisely, philosophical writers.

I have the misfortune to belong to these last.

I hate symbolic art in which the presentation loses all spontaneous movement in order to become a machine, an allegory – a vain and misconceived effort because the very fact of giving an allegorical sense to a presentation clearly shows that we have to do with a fable which by itself has no truth either fantastic or direct; it was made for the demonstration of some moral truth. The spiritual need I speak of cannot be satisfied – or seldom, and that to the end of a superior irony, as for example in Ariosto – by such allegorical symbolism. This latter starts from a concept, and from a concept which creates or tries to create for itself an image. The former on the other hand seeks in the image – which must remain alive and free throughout – a meaning to give it value.

Now, however much I sought, I did not succeed in uncovering this meaning in the six characters. And I concluded therefore that it was no use making them live.

I thought to myself: "I have already afflicted my readers with hundreds and hundreds of stories. Why should I afflict them now by narrating the sad entanglements of these six unfortunates?"

And, thinking thus, I put them away from me. Or rather I did all I could to put them away.

But one doesn't give life to a character for nothing.

Creatures of my spirit, these six were already living a life which was their own and not mine any more, a life which it was not in my power any more to deny them.

Thus it is that while I persisted in desiring to drive them out of my spirit, they, as if completely detached from every narrative support, characters from a novel miraculously emerging from the pages of the book that contained them, went on living on their own, choosing certain moments of the day to reappear before me in the solitude of my study and coming – now one, now the other, now two together – to tempt me, to propose that I present or describe this scene or that, to explain the effects that could be secured with them, the new interest which a certain unusual situation could provide, and so forth.

For a moment I let myself be won over. And this condescension of mine, thus letting myself go for a while, was enough, because they drew from it a new increment of life, a greater degree of clarity and addition, consequently a greater degree of persuasive power over me. And thus as it became gradually harder and harder for me to go back and free myself from them, it became easier and easier for them to come back and tempt me. At a certain point I actually became obsessed with them. Until, all of a sudden, a way out of the difficulty flashed upon me.

"Why not," I said to myself, "present this highly strange fact of an author who refuses to let some of his characters live though they have been born in his fantasy, and the fact that these characters, having by now life in their veins, do not resign themselves to remaining excluded from the world of art? They are detached from me; live on their own; have acquired voice and movement; have by themselves – in this struggle for existence that they have had to wage with me – become dramatic characters, characters that can move and talk on their own initiative; already see themselves as such; have learned to defend themselves against me; will even know how to defend themselves against others. And so let them go where dramatic characters do go to have life: on a stage. And let us see what will happen."

That's what I did. And, naturally, the result was what it had to be: a mixture of tragic and comic, fantastic and realistic, in a humorous situation that was quite new and infinitely complex, a drama which is conveyed by means of the characters, who carry it within them and suffer it, a drama, breathing, speaking, self-propelled, which seeks at all costs to find the means of its own presentation; and the comedy of the vain attempt at an improvised realization of the drama on stage. First, the surprise of the poor actors in a theatrical company rehearsing a play by day on a bare stage (no scenery, no flats). Surprise and incredulity at the sight of the six characters announcing themselves as such in search of an author. Then, immediately afterwards, through that sudden fainting fit of the Mother veiled in black, their instinctive interest in the drama of which they catch a glimpse in her and in the other members of the strange family, an obscure, ambiguous drama, coming about so unexpectedly on a stage that is empty and unprepared to receive it. And gradually the growth of this interest to the bursting forth of the contrasting passions of Father, of Step-Daughter, of Son, of that poor Mother, passions seeking, as I said, to overwhelm each other with a tragic, lacerating fury.

And here is the universal meaning at first vainly sought in the six characters, now that, going on stage of their own accord, they succeed in finding it within themselves in the excitement of the desperate struggle which each wages against the other and all wage against the Manager and the actors, who do not understand them.

Without wanting to, without knowing it, in the strife of their bedevilled souls, each of them, defending himself against the accusations of the others, expresses as his own living passion and torment the passion and torment which for so many years have been the pangs of my spirit: the deceit of mutual understanding irremediably founded on the empty abstraction of the words, the multiple personality of everyone corresponding to the possibilities of being to be found in each of us, and finally the inherent tragic conflict between life (which is always moving and changing) and form (which fixes it, immutable).

Two above all among the six characters, the Father and the Step-Daughter, speak of that outrageous unalterable fixity of their form in which he and she see their essential nature expressed permanently and immutably, a nature that for one means punishment and for the other revenge; and they defend it against the factitious affectations and unaware volatility of the actors, and they try to impose it on the vulgar Manager who would like to change it and adapt it to the so-called exigencies of the theatre.

If the six characters don't all seem to exist on the same plane, it is not because some are figures of first rank and others of the second, that is, some are main characters and others minor ones – the elementary perspective necessary to all scenic or narrative art – nor is it that any are not completely created – for their purpose. They are all six at the same point of artistic realization and on the same level of reality, which is the fantastic level of the whole play. Except that the Father, the Step-Daughter, and also the Son are realized as mind; the Mother as nature; the Boy as a presence watching and performing a gesture and the Baby unaware of it all. This fact creates among them a perspective of a new sort. Unconsciously I had had the impression that some of them needed to be fully realized (artistically speaking), others less so, and others merely sketched in as elements in a narrative or presentational sequence: the most alive, the most completely created, are the Father and the Step-Daughter who naturally stand out more and lead the way, dragging themselves along beside the almost dead weight of the others – first, the Son, holding back; second, the Mother, like a victim resigned to her fate, between the two children who have hardly any substance beyond their appearance and who need to be led by the hand.

And actually! actually they had each to appear in that stage of creation which they had attained in the author's fantasy at the moment when he wished to drive them away.

If I now think about these things, about having intuited that necessity, having unconsciously found the way to resolve it by means of a new perspective, and about the way in which I actually obtained it, they seem like miracles. The fact is that the play was really conceived in one of those spontaneous illuminations of the fantasy when by a miracle all the elements of the mind answer to each other's call and work in divine accord. No human brain, working "in the cold," however stirred up it might be, could ever have succeeded in penetrating far enough, could ever have been in a position to satisfy all the exigencies of the play's form. Therefore the reasons which I will give to clarify the values of the play must not be thought of as intentions that I conceived beforehand when I prepared myself for the job and which I now undertake to defend, but only as discoveries which I have been able to make afterwards in tranquillity.

I wanted to present six characters seeking an author. Their play does not manage to get presented – precisely because the author whom they seek is missing. Instead is presented the comedy of their vain attempt with all that it contains of tragedy by virtue of the fact that the six characters have been rejected.

But can one present a character while rejecting him? Obviously, to present him one needs, on the contrary, to receive him into one's fantasy before one can express him. And I have actually accepted and realized the six characters: I have, however, accepted and realized them as rejected: in search of *another* author.

What have I rejected of them? Not themselves, obviously, but their drama, which doubtless is what interests them above all but which did not interest me – for the reasons already indicated.

And what is it, for a character – his drama?

Every creature of fantasy and art, in order to exist, must have his drama, that is, a drama in which he may be a character and for which he is a character. This drama is the character's *raison d'être*, his vital function, necessary for his existence.

In these six, then, I have accepted the "being" without the reason for being. I have taken the organism and entrusted to it, not its own proper function, but another more complex function into which its own function entered, if at all, only as a datum. A terrible and desperate situation especially for the two – Father and Step-Daughter – who more than the others crave life and more than the others feel themselves to be characters, that is, absolutely need a drama and therefore their own drama – the only one which they can envisage for themselves yet which meantime they see rejected: an "impossible" situation from which they feel they must escape at whatever cost; it is a matter of life and death. True, I have given them another *raison d'être*, another function: precisely that "impossible" situation, the drama of being in search of an author and rejected. But that this should be a *raison d'être*, that it should have become their real function, that it should be necessary, that it should suffice, they can hardly suppose; for they have a life of their own. If someone were to tell them, they wouldn't believe him. It is not possible to believe that the sole reason for our living should lie in a torment that seems to us unjust and inexplicable.

I cannot imagine, therefore, why the charge was brought against me that the character of the Father was not what it should have been because it stepped out of its quality and position as a character and invaded at times the author's province and took it over. I who understand those who don't quite understand me see that the charge derives from the fact that the character expresses and makes his own a torment of spirit which is recognized as mine. Which is entirely natural and of absolutely no significance. Aside from the fact that this torment of spirit in the character of the Father derives from causes, and is suffered and lived for reasons, that have nothing to do with the drama of my personal experience, a fact which alone removes all substance from the criticism, I want to make it clear that the inherent torment of my spirit is one thing, a torment which I can legitimately – provided that it be organic – reflect in a character, and that the activity of my spirit as revealed in the realized work, the activity that succeeds in forming a drama out of the six characters in search of an author is another thing. If the Father participated in this latter activity, if he competed in forming the drama of the six characters without an author, then and only then would it by all means be justified to say that he was at times the author himself and therefore not the man he should be. But the Father suffers and does not create his existence as a character in search of an author. He suffers it as an inexplicable fatality and as a situation which he tries with all his powers to rebel against, which he tries to remedy: hence it is that he is a character in search of an author and nothing more, even if he expresses as his own the torment of my spirit. If he, so to speak, assumed some of the author's responsibilities, the fatality would be completely explained. He would, that is to say, see himself accepted, if only as a rejected character, accepted in the poet's heart of hearts, and he would no longer have any reason to suffer the despair of not finding someone to construct and affirm his life as a character. I mean that he would quite willingly accept the *raison d'être* which the author gives him and without regrets would forego his own, throwing over the Manager and the actors to whom in fact he runs as his only recourse.

There is one character, that of the Mother, who on the other hand does not care about being alive (considering being alive as an end in itself). She hasn't the least suspicion that she is not alive. It has never occurred to her to ask how and why and in what manner she lives. In short, she is not aware of being a character, inasmuch as she is never, even for a moment, detached from her role. She doesn't know she has a role.

This makes her perfectly organic. Indeed, her role of Mother does not of itself, in its natural essence, embrace mental activity. And she does not exist as a mind. She lives in an endless continuum of feeling, and therefore she cannot acquire awareness of her life – that is, of her existence as a character. But with all this, even she, in her own way and for her own ends, seeks an author, and at a certain stage seems happy to have been brought before the Manager. Because she hopes to take life from him, perhaps? No: because she hopes the Manager will have her present a scene with the Son in which she would put so much of her own life. But it is a scene which does not exist, which never has and never could take place. So unaware is she of being a character, that is, of the life that is possible to her, all fixed and determined, moment by moment, in every action, every phrase.

She appears on stage with the other characters but without understanding what the others make her do. Obviously, she imagines that the itch for life with which the husband and the daughter are afflicted and for which she herself is to be found on stage is no more than one of the usual incomprehensible extravagances of this man who is both tortured and torturer and – horrible, most horrible – a new equivocal rebellion on the part of that poor erring girl. The Mother is completely passive. The events of her own life and the values they assume in her eyes, her very character, are all things which are "said" by the others and which she only once contradicts, and that because the maternal instinct rises up and rebels within her to make it clear that she didn't at all wish to abandon either the son or the husband: the Son was taken from her and the husband forced her to abandon him. She is only correcting data; she explains and knows nothing. In short, she is nature. Nature fixed in the figure of a mother. This character gave me a satisfaction of a new sort, not to be ignored. Nearly all my critics, instead of defining her, after their habit, as "unhuman" – which seems to be the peculiar and incorrigible characteristic of all my creatures without exception – had the goodness to note "with real pleasure" that at last a very human figure had emerged from my fantasy. I explain this praise to myself in the following way: since my poor Mother is entirely limited to the natural attitude of a Mother with no possibility of free mental activity, being, that is, little more than a lump of flesh completely alive in all its functions – procreation, lactation, caring for and loving its young – without any need therefore of exercising her brain, she realizes in her person the true and complete "human type." That must be how it is, since in a human organism nothing seems more superfluous than the mind.

But the critics have tried to get rid of the Mother with this praise without bothering to penetrate the nucleus of poetic values which the character in the play represents. A *very human* figure, certainly, because mindless, that is, unaware of being what she is or not caring to explain it to herself. But not knowing that she is a character doesn't prevent her from being one. That is her drama in my play. And the most living expression of it comes spurting out in her cry to the Manager who wants her to think all these things have happened already and therefore cannot now be a reason for renewed lamentations: "No, it's happening now, it's happening always! My torture is not a pretence, signore! I am alive and present, always, in every moment of my torture: it is renewed, alive and present, always!" This she *feels,* without being conscious of it, and feels it therefore as something inexplicable: but she feels it so terribly that she doesn't think it can be something to explain either to herself or to others. She feels it and that is that. She feels it as pain, and this pain is immediate; she cries it out. Thus she reflects the growing fixity of life in a form – the same thing, which in another way, tortures the Father and the Step-Daughter. In them, mind. In her, nature. The mind rebels and, as best it may, seeks an advantage; nature, if not aroused by sensory stimuli, weeps.

Conflict between life-in-movement and form is the inexorable condition not only of the mental but also of the physical order. The life which in order to exist has become fixed in our corporeal form little by little kills that form. The tears of a nature thus fixed lament the irreparable, continuous aging of our bodies. Hence the tears of the Mother are passive and perpetual. Revealed in three faces, made significant in three distinct and simultaneous dramas, this inherent conflict finds in the play its most complete expression. More: the Mother declares also the particular value of artistic form – a form which does not delimit or destroy its own life and which life does not consume – in her cry to the Manager. If the Father and Step-Daughter began their scene a hundred thousand times in succession, always, at the appointed moment, at the instant when the life of the work of art must be expressed with that cry, it would always be heard, unaltered and unalterable in its form, not as a mechanical repetition, not as a return determined by external necessities, but on the contrary, alive every time and as new, suddenly born *thus forever!* embalmed alive in its incorruptible form. Hence, always, as we open the book, we shall find Francesca alive and confessing to Dante her sweet sin, and if we turn to the passage a hundred thousand times in succession, a hundred thousand times in succession Francesca will speak her words, never repeating them mechanically, but saying them as though each time were the first time with such living and sudden passion that Dante every time will turn faint. All that lives, by the fact of living, has a form, and by the same token must die – except the work of art which lives forever in so far as it is form.

The birth of a creature of human fantasy, a birth which is a step across the threshold between nothing and eternity, can also happen suddenly, occasioned by some necessity. An imagined drama needs a character who does or says a certain necessary thing; accordingly this character is born and is precisely what he had to be. In this way Madame Pace is born among the six characters and seems a miracle, even a trick, realistically portrayed on the stage. It is no trick. The birth is real. The new character is alive not because she was alive already but because she is now happily born as is required by the fact of her being a character – she is obliged to be as she is. There is a break here, a sudden change in the level of reality of the scene, because a character can be born in this way only in the poet's fancy and not on the boards of a stage. Without anyone's noticing it, I have all of a sudden changed the scene: I have gathered it up again into my own fantasy without removing it from the spectator's eyes. That is, I have shown them, instead of the stage, my own fantasy in the act of creating – my own fantasy in the form of this same stage. The sudden and uncontrollable changing of a visual phenomenon from one level of reality to another is a miracle comparable to those of the saint who sets his own statue in motion: it is neither wood nor stone at such a moment. But the miracle is not arbitrary. The stage – a stage which accepts the fantastic reality of the six characters – is no fixed, immutable datum. Nothing in this play exists as given and preconceived. Everything is in the making, is in motion, is a sudden experiment: even the place in which this unformed life, reaching after its own form, changes and changes again contrives to shift position organically. The level of reality changes. When I had the idea of bringing Madame Pace to birth right there on the stage, I felt I could do it and I did it. Had I noticed that this birth was unhinging and silently, unnoticed, in a second, giving another shape, another reality to my scene, I certainly wouldn't have brought it about. I would have been afraid of the apparent lack of logic. And I would have committed an ill-omened assault on the beauty of my work. The fervor of my mind saved me from doing so. For, despite appearances, with their specious logic, this fantastic birth is sustained by a real necessity in mysterious, organic relation with the whole life of the work.

That someone now tells me it hasn't all the value it could have because its expression is not constructed but chaotic, because it smacks of romanticism, makes me smile.

I understand why this observation was made to me: because in this work of mine the presentation of the drama in which the six characters are involved appears tumultuous and never proceeds in an orderly manner. There is no logical development, no concatenation of the events. Very true. Had I hunted it with a lamp I couldn't have found a more disordered, crazy, arbitrary, complicated, in short, romantic way of presenting "the drama in which the six characters are involved." Very true. But I have not presented that drama. I have presented another – and I won't undertake to say again what! – in which, among the many fine things that everyone, according to his tastes, can find, there is a discreet satire on romantic procedures: in the six characters thus excited to the point where they stifle themselves in the roles which each of them plays in a certain drama while I present them as characters in another play which they don't know and don't suspect the existence of, so that this inflammation of their passions – which belongs to the realm of romantic procedures – is humorously "placed," located in the void. And the drama of the six characters presented not as it would have been organized by my fantasy had it been accepted but in this way, as a rejected drama, could not exist in the work except as a "situation," with some little development, and could not come out except in indications, stormily, disorderedly, in violent foreshortenings, in a chaotic interrupted, manner: continually sidetracked, contradicted (by one of its characters), denied, and (by two others) not even seen.

There is a character indeed – he who denies the drama which makes him a character, the Son – who draws all his importance and value from being a character not of the comedy in the making – which as such hardly appears – but from the presentation that I made of it. In short, he is the only one who lives solely as "a character in search of an author" – inasmuch as the author he seeks is not a dramatic author. Even this could not be otherwise. The character's attitude is an organic product of my conception, and it is logical that in the situation it should produce greater confusion and disorder and another element of romantic contrast.

But I had precisely to *present* this organic and natural chaos. And to present a chaos is not at all to present chaotically, that is, romantically. That my presentation is the reverse of confused, that it is quite simple, clear, and orderly, is proved by the clarity which the intrigue, the characters, the fantastic and realistic, dramatic and comic levels of the work have had for every public in the world and by the way in which, for those with more searching vision, the unusual values enclosed within it come out.

Great is the confusion of tongues among men if criticisms thus made find words for their expression. No less great than this confusion is the intimate law of order which, obeyed in all points, makes this work of mine classical and typical and at its catastrophic close forbids the use of words. Though the audience eventually understands that one does not create life by artifice and that the drama of the six characters cannot be presented without an author to give them value with his spirit, the Manager remains vulgarly anxious to know how the thing turned out, and the "ending" is remembered by the Son in its sequence of actual moments, but without any sense and therefore not needing a human voice for its expression. It happens stupidly, uselessly, with the going-off of a mechanical weapon on stage. It breaks up and disperses the sterile experiment of the characters and the actors, which has apparently been made without the assistance of the poet.

The poet, unknown to them, as if looking on at a distance during the whole period of the experiment, was at the same time busy creating – with it and of it – his own play.

Chapter 60

D.H. Lawrence (1885–1930)

"WHY THE NOVEL MATTERS" (1925)

DAVID HERBERT LAWRENCE, THE SON of a largely illiterate miner and pridefully intellectual, former schoolteacher, was born in Eastwood, Nottinghamshire, where the coal industry's ravaged wastelands existed side-by-side with the region's fabled bucolic countryside and the forests of the legendary Robin Hood. Lawrence was a working-class "scholarship boy" and of the first generation of beneficiaries of educational reform in Great Britain. He attended the prestigious Nottingham High School and Nottingham University. Lawrence's northern and working-class roots made him a singular figure in early twentieth-century literary England. While an aspiring writer, he worked as a factory clerk and grammar school teacher; Lawrence's radical anti-materialism and anti-industrialism, continental interests (Friedrich Neitzsche, German philosophy), identification with northern renegades and rebels like the Luddites, and fascination with primitive cultures further distinguished him as an outsider in London's more genteel literary circles. While he sought and was afforded the patronage of Lady Ottoline Morrell (whom he would viciously parody as Hermoine Roddice in *Women in Love,* 1920) and had collegial relations with other writers, including Ford Madox Ford, Aldous Huxley, E.M. Forster, David ("Bunny") Garnett, Bertrand Russell, and Katherine Mansfield, Lawrence's political and cultural inclinations led him far beyond England's borders. Like Richard Somers, the protagonist of his Australian-set novel *Kangaroo* (1923), he willfully became a man without a country: Lawrence left England in 1919 and lived in Italy for several years. His travels would take him to Ceylon/Sri Lanka, Australia, and Mexico – where Lawrence became fascinated with the primitivism of Aztec culture, the subject of his novel *The Plumed Serpent* (1926). While he was living in the United States, the heiress and arts patron Mabel Dodge attempted to conscript Lawrence and his wife, Frieda, into her planned utopian artists' commune in Taos, New Mexico. Lawrence was plagued by censorship battles and severe respiratory problems throughout his career; undaunted by both, his visionary and rebellious artistic corpus comprises a wealth of materials, including paintings, poetry, short stories, plays, essays, literary criticism – including the groundbreaking *Studies in Classic American Literature* (1923) – poems, and novels. Lawrence's major works include *Sons and Lovers* (1913, novel), *The Prussian Officer and Other*

Stories (1914), *The Rainbow* (1915, novel), *Birds, Beasts and Flowers* (1923, poetry), and *Lady Chatterley's Lover* (1928, novel).

D.H. Lawrence, "Why the Novel Matters," *Phoenix: The Posthumous Papers of D.H. Lawrence*. New York: Viking, 1936. 533–38.

We have curious ideas of ourselves. We think of ourselves as a body with a spirit in it, or a body with a soul in it, or a body with a mind in it. *Mens sana in corpore sano*. The years drink up the wine, and at last throw the bottle away, the body, of course, being the bottle.

It is a funny sort of superstition. Why should I look at my hand, as it so cleverly writes these words, and decide that it is a mere nothing compared to the mind that directs it? Is there really any huge difference between my hand and my brain? Or my mind? My hand is alive, it flickers with a life of its own. It meets all the strange universe in touch, and learns a vast number of things, and knows a vast number of things. My hand, as it writes these words, slips gaily along, jumps like a grasshopper to dot an *i*, feels the table rather cold, gets a little bored if I write too long, has its own rudiments of thought, and is just as much *me* as is my brain, my mind, or my soul. Why should I imagine that there is a *me* which is more a *me* than my hand is? Since my hand is absolutely alive, me alive.

Whereas, of course, as far as I am concerned, my pen isn't alive at all. My pen *isn't me* alive. Me alive ends at my finger-tips.

Whatever is me alive is me. Every tiny bit of my hands is alive, every little freckle and hair and fold of skin. And whatever is me alive is me. Only my finger-nails, those ten little weapons between me and an inanimate universe, they cross the mysterious Rubicon between me alive and things like my pen, which are not alive, in my own sense.

So, seeing my hand is all alive, and me alive, wherein is it just a bottle, or a jug, or a tin can, or a vessel of clay, or any of the rest of that nonsense? True, if I cut it it will bleed, like a can of cherries. But then the skin that is cut, and the veins that bleed, and the bones that should never be seen, they are all just as alive as the blood that flows. So the tin can business, or vessel of clay, is just bunk.

And that's what you learn, when you're a novelist. And that's what you are very liable *not* to know, if you're a parson, or a philosopher, or a scientist, or a stupid person. If you're a parson, you talk about souls in heaven. If you're a novelist, you know that paradise is in the palm of your hand, and on the end of your nose, because both are alive; and alive, and man alive, which is more than you can say for certain, of paradise. Paradise is after life, and I for one am not keen on anything that is *after* life. If you are a philosopher, you talk about infinity, and the pure spirit which knows all things. But if you pick up a novel, you realize how immediately that infinity is just a handle to this self-same jug of a body of mine; while as for knowing, if I find my finger in the fire, I know that fire burns, with a knowledge so emphatic and vital, it leaves Nirvana merely a conjecture. Oh, yes, my body, me alive, *knows*, and knows intensely. And as for the sum of all knowledge, it can't be anything more than an accumulation of all the things I know in the body, and you, dear reader, know in the body.

These damned philosophers, they talk as if they suddenly went off in steam, and were then much more important than they are when they're in their shirts. It is nonsense. Every man, philosopher included, ends in his own finger-tips. That's the end of his man alive. As for the words and thoughts and sighs and aspirations that fly from him, they are so many tremulations in the ether, and not alive at all. But if the tremulations reach another man alive, he may receive them into his life, and his life may take on a new colour, like a chameleon creeping from a brown rock on to a green leaf. All very well and good. It still doesn't alter the fact that the so-called spirit, the message or teaching of the philosopher or the saint, isn't alive at all, but just a tremulation upon the ether, like a radio message. All this spirit stuff is just tremulations upon the ether. If you, as man alive, quiver from the tremulation of the ether into new life, that is because you are man alive, and you take sustenance and stimulation into your alive man in a myriad ways. But to say that the message, or the spirit which is communicated to you, is more important than your living body, is nonsense. You might as well say that the potato at dinner was more important.

Nothing is important but life. And for myself, I can absolutely see life nowhere but in the living. Life with a capital L is only man alive. Even a cabbage in the rain is cabbage alive. All things that are alive are amazing. And all things that are dead are subsidiary to the living. Better a live dog than a dead lion. But better a live lion than a live dog. *C'est la vie!*

It seems impossible to get a saint, or a philosopher, or a scientist, to stick to this simple truth. They are all, in a sense, renegades. The saint wishes to offer himself up as spiritual food for the multitude. Even Francis of Assisi turns himself into a sort of angel-cake, of which anyone may take a slice. But an angel-cake is rather less than man alive. And poor St. Francis might well apologize to his body, when he is dying: "Oh, pardon me, my body, the wrong I did you through the years!" It was no wafer, for others to eat.

The philosopher, on the other hand, because he can think, decides that nothing but thoughts matter. It is a if a rabbit, because he can make little pills, should decide that nothing but little pills matter. As for the scientist, he has absolutely no use for me so long as I am man alive. To the scientist, I am dead. He puts under the microscope a bit of dead me, and calls it me. He takes me to pieces, and says first one piece, and then another piece, is me. My heart, my liver, my stomach have all been scientifically me, according to the scientist; and nowadays I am either a brain, or nerves, or glands, or something more up-to-date in the tissue line.

Now I absolutely flatly deny that I am a soul, or a body, or a mind, or an intelligence, or a brain, or a nervous system, or a bunch of glands, or any of the rest of these bits of me. The whole is greater than the part. And therefore, I, who am man alive, am greater than my soul, or spirit, or body, or mind, or consciousness, or anything else that is merely a part of me. I am a man, and alive. I am man alive, and as long as I can, I intend to go on being man alive.

For this reason I am a novelist. And being a novelist, I consider myself superior to the saint, the scientist, the philosopher, and the poet, who are all great masters of different bits of man alive, but never get the whole hog.

The novel is the one bright book of life. Books are not life. They are only tremulations on the ether. But the novel as a tremulation can make the whole man alive tremble. Which is more than poetry, philosophy, science, or any other book-tremulation can do.

The novel is the book of life. In this sense, the Bible is a great confused novel. You may say, it is about God. But it is really about man alive. Adam, Eve, Sarai, Abraham, Isaac, Jacob, Samuel, David, Bath-Sheba, Ruth, Esther, Solomon, Job, Isaiah, Jesus, Mark, Judas, Paul, Peter: what is it but man alive, from start to finish? Man alive, not mere bits. Even the Lord is another man alive, in a burning bush, throwing the tablets of stone at Moses's head.

I do hope you begin to get my idea, why the novel is supremely important, as a tremulation on the ether. Plato makes the perfect ideal being tremble in me. But that's only a bit of me. Perfection is only a bit, in the strange make-up of man alive. The Sermon on the Mount makes the selfless spirit of me quiver. But that, too, is only a bit of me. The Ten Commandments set the old Adam shivering in me, warning me that I am a thief and a murderer, unless I watch it. But even the old Adam is only a bit of me.

I very much like all these bits of me to be set trembling with life and the wisdom of life. But I do ask that the whole of me shall tremble in its wholeness, some time or other.

And this, of course, must happen in me, living.

But as far as it can happen from a communication, it can only happen when a whole novel communicates itself to me. The Bible—but *all* the Bible—and Homer, and Shakespeare; these are the supreme old novels. These are all things to all men. Which means that in their wholeness they affect the whole man alive, which is the man himself, beyond any part of him. They set the whole tree trembling with a new access of life, they do not just stimulate growth in one direction.

I don't want to grow in any one direction any more. And, if I can help it, I don't want to stimulate anybody else into some particular direction. A particular direction ends in a *cul-de-sac*. We're in a *cul-de-sac* at present.

I don't believe in any dazzling revelation, or in any supreme Word. "The grass withereth, the flower fadeth, but the Word of the Lord shall stand for ever." That's the kind of stuff we've drugged ourselves with. As a matter of fact, the grass withereth, but comes up all the greener for that reason, after the rains. The flower fadeth, and therefore the bud opens. But the Word of the Lord, being man-uttered and a mere vibration on the ether, becomes staler and staler, more and more boring, till at last we turn a deaf ear and it ceases to exist, far more finally than any withered grass. It is grass that renews its youth like the eagle, not any Word.

We should ask for no absolutes, or absolute. Once and for all and for ever, let us have done with the ugly imperialism of any absolute. There is no absolute good, there is nothing absolutely right. All things flow and change, and even change is not absolute. The whole is a strange assembly of apparently incongruous parts, slipping past one another.

Me, man alive, I am a very curious assembly of incongruous parts. My yea! of today is oddly different from my yea! of yesterday. My tears of tomorrow will have nothing to do with my tears of a year ago. If the one I love remains unchanged and unchanging, I shall cease to love her. It is only because she changes and startles me into change and defies my inertia, and is herself staggered in her inertia by my changing, that I can continue to love her. If she stayed put, I might as well love the pepper-pot.

In all this change, I maintain a certain integrity. But woe betide me if I try to put my finger on it. If I say of myself, I am this, I am that!—then, if I stick to it, I turn into a stupid fixed thing like a lamp-post. I shall never know wherein lies my integrity, my individuality, my me. I *can* never know it. It is useless to talk about my ego. That only means that I have made up an *idea* of myself, and that I am trying to cut myself out to pattern. Which is no good. You can cut your cloth to fit your coat, but you can't clip bits off your living body, to trim it down to your idea. True, you can put yourself into ideal corsets. But even in ideal corsets, fashions change.

Let us learn from the novel. In the novel, the characters can do nothing but *live*. If they keep on being good, according to pattern, or bad, according to pattern, or even volatile, according to pattern, they cease to live, and the novel falls dead. A character in a novel has got to live, or it is nothing.

We, likewise, in life have got to live, or we are nothing.

What we mean by living is, of course, just as indescribable as what we mean by *being*. Men get ideas into their heads, of what they mean by Life, and they proceed to cut life out to pattern. Sometimes they go into the desert to seek God, sometimes they go into the desert to seek cash, sometimes it is wine, woman, and song, and again it is water, political reform, and votes. You never know what it will be next: from killing your neighbour with hideous bombs and gas that tears the lungs, to supporting a Foundlings Home and preaching infinite Love, and being co-respondent in a divorce.

In all this wild welter, we need some sort of guide. It's no good inventing Thou Shalt Nots!

What then? Turn truly, honourably to the novel, and see wherein you are man alive, and wherein you are dead man in life. You may love a woman as man alive, and you may be making love to a woman as sheer dead man in life. You may eat your dinner as man alive, or as a mere masticating corpse. As man alive you may have a shot at your enemy. But as a ghastly simulacrum of life you may be firing bombs into men who are neither your enemies nor your friends, but just things you are dead to. Which is criminal, when the things happen to be alive.

To be alive, to be man alive, to be whole man alive: that is the point. And at its best, the novel, and the novel supremely, can help you. It can help you not to be dead man in life. So much of a man walks about dead and a carcass in the street and house, today: so much of women is merely dead. Like a pianoforte with half the notes mute.

But in the novel you can see, plainly, when the man goes dead, the woman goes inert. You can develop an instinct for life, if you will, instead of a theory of right and wrong, good and bad.

In life, there is right and wrong, good and bad, all the time. But what is right in one case is wrong in another. And in the novel you see one man becoming a corpse, because of his so-called goodness, another going dead because of his so-called wickedness. Right and wrong is an instinct: but an instinct of the whole consciousness in a man, bodily, mental, spiritual at once. And only in the novel are *all* things given full play, or at least, they may be given full play, when we realize that life itself, and not inert safety, is the reason for living. For out of the full play of all things emerges the only thing that is anything, the wholeness of a man, the wholeness of a woman, man alive, and live woman.

PART IX

Modernist writers on their contemporaries

Chapter 61

George Bernard Shaw (1856–1950)

"THE TECHNICAL NOVELTY IN IBSEN'S PLAYS" (1913)

S HAW CHIDES CONTEMPORARY DRAMA CRITICS for failing to hail what he calls "a new technical factor in the art of popular stage-play making" – "the discussion." Beginning with Ibsen's *A Doll's House* (1879) – specifically the moment in the last act when Nora says "We must sit down and discuss all this that has been happening between us" – the "discussion" made European drama serious and interesting again, creating plays "in which problems of conduct and character of personal importance to the audience are raised and suggestively discussed." Worthwhile drama that follows Ibsen often begins with discussion and ends with action or has the discussion and action interpenetrated throughout, is written by women, depicts conflicts of unsettled ideals, and may have neither hero nor villain. In fact, it is not catastrophe or strangeness that compels a theatre audience or catches its conscience, for, as Ibsen saw, "the more familiar the situation, the more interesting the play."

George Bernard Shaw, "The Technical Novelty in Ibsen's Plays," *Major Critical Essays*. London: Constable, 1948. 135–46.

It is a striking and melancholy example of the preoccupation of critics with phrases and formulas to which they have given life by taking them into the tissue of their own living minds, and which therefore seem and feel vital and important to them whilst they are to everybody else the deadest and dreariest rubbish (this is the great secret of academic dryasdust), that to this day they remain blind to a new technical factor in the art of popular stage-play making which every considerable playwright has been thrusting under their noses night after night for a whole generation. This technical factor in the play is the discussion. Formerly you had in what was called a well made play an exposition in the first act, a situation in the second, and unravelling in the third. Now you have exposition, situation, and discussion; and the discussion is the test of the playwright. The critics protest in vain. They declare that discussions are not dramatic, and that art should not be didactic. Neither the playwrights nor the public take the smallest notice of them. The discussion conquered Europe in Ibsen's *Doll's House*; and now the serious playwright recognizes in the discussion not only the main test of his highest powers, but also the real centre of his play's interest. Sometimes he even takes every possible step to assure the public beforehand that his play will be fitted with that newest improvement.

This was inevitable if the drama was ever again to be raised above the childish demand for fables without morals. Children have a settled arbitrary morality: therefore to them moralizing is nothing but an intolerable platitudinizing. The morality of the grown-up is also very largely a settled morality, either purely conventional and of no ethical significance, like the rule of the road or the rule that when you ask for a yard of ribbon the shopkeeper shall give you thirty-six inches and not interpret the word yard as he pleases, or else too obvious in its ethics to leave any room for discussion: for instance, that if the boots keeps you waiting too long for your shaving water you must not plunge your razor into his throat in your irritation, no matter how great an effort of self-control your forbearance may cost you.

Now when a play is only a story of how a villain tries to separate an honest young pair of betrothed lovers; to gain the hand of the woman by calumny; and to ruin the man by forgery, murder, false witness, and other commonplaces of the Newgate Calendar, the introduction of a discussion would clearly be ridiculous. There is nothing for sane people to discuss; and any attempt to Chadbandize on the wickedness of such crimes is at once resented as, in Milton's phrase, "moral babble."

But this sort of drama is soon exhausted by people who go often to the theatre. In twenty visits one can see every possible change rung on all the available plots and incidents out of which plays of this kind can be manufactured. The illusion of reality is soon lost: in fact it may be doubted whether any adult ever entertains it; it is only to very young children that the fairy queen is anything but an actress. But at the age when we cease to mistake the figures on the stage for *dramatis personae*, and know that they are actors and actresses, the charm of the performer begins to assert itself; and the child who would have been cruelly hurt by being told that the Fairy Queen was only Miss Smith dressed up to look like one, becomes the man who goes to the theatre expressly to see Miss Smith, and is fascinated by her skill or beauty to the point of delighting in plays which would be unendurable to him without her. Thus we get plays "written round" popular performers, and popular performers who give value to otherwise useless plays by investing them with their own attractiveness. But all these enterprises are, commercially speaking, desperately precarious. To begin with, the supply of performers whose attraction is so far independent of the play that their inclusion in the cast sometimes makes the difference between success and failure is too small to enable all our theatres, or even many of them, to depend on their actors rather than on their plays. And to finish with, no actor can make bricks entirely without straw. From Grimaldi to Sothern, Jefferson, and Henry Irving (not to mention living actors) we have had players succeeding once in a lifetime in grafting on to a play which would have perished without them some figure imagined wholly by themselves; but none of them has been able to repeat the feat nor to save many of the plays in which he has appeared from failure. In the long run nothing can retain the interest of the playgoer after the theatre has lost its illusion for his childhood, and its glamor for his adolescence, but a constant supply of interesting plays; and this is specially true in London, where the expense and trouble of theatre going have been raised to a point at which it is surprising that sensible people of middle age go to the theatre at all. As a matter of fact, they mostly stay at home.

Now an interesting play cannot in the nature of things mean anything but a play in which problems of conduct and character of personal importance to the audience are raised and suggestively discussed. People have a thrifty sense of taking away something from such plays: they not only have had something for their money but they retain that something as a permanent possession. Consequently none of the commonplaces of the box office hold good of such plays. In vain does the experienced acting manager declare that people want to be amused and not preached at in the theatre; that they will not stand long speeches; that a play must not contain more than 18,000 words; that it must not begin before nine nor last beyond eleven; that there must be no politics and no religion in it; that breach of these golden rules will drive people to the variety theatres; that there must be a woman of bad character, played by a very attractive actress, in the piece; and so on and so forth. All these counsels are valid for plays in which there is nothing to discuss. They may be disregarded by the playwright who is a moralist and a debater as well as a dramatist. From him, within the inevitable limits set by the clock and by the physical endurance of the human frame, people will stand anything as soon as they are matured enough and cultivated enough to be susceptible to the appeal of his particular form of art. The difficulty at present is that mature and cultivated people do not go to the theatre, just as they do not read penny novelets; and when an attempt is made to cater for them they do not respond to it in time, partly because they have not the habit of play-going, and partly because it takes too long for them to find out that the new theatre is not like all the other theatres. But when they do at last find their way there, the attraction is not the firing of blank cartridges at one another by actors, nor the pretence of falling down dead that ends the stage combat, nor the simulation of erotic thrills by a pair of stage lovers, nor any of the other tomfooleries called action, but the exhibition and discussion of the character and conduct of stage figures who are made to appear real by the art of the playwright and the performers.

This, then, is the extension of the old dramatic form effected by Ibsen. Up to a certain point in the last act, *A Doll's House* is a play that might be turned into a very ordinary French drama by the excision of a few lines, and the substitution of a sentimental happy ending for the famous last scene: indeed the very first thing the theatrical wiseacres did with it was to effect exactly this transformation, with the result that the play thus pithed had no success and attracted no notice worth mentioning. But at just that point in the last act, the heroine very unexpectedly (by the wiseacres) stops her emotional acting and says: "We must sit down and discuss all this that has been happening between us." And it was by this new technical feature: this addition of a new movement, as musicians would say, to the dramatic form, that *A Doll's House* conquered Europe and founded a new school of dramatic art.

Since that time the discussion has expanded far beyond the limits of the last ten minutes of an otherwise "well made" play. The disadvantage of putting the discussion at the end was not only that it came when the audience was fatigued, but that it was necessary to see the play over again, so as to follow the earlier acts in the light of the final discussion, before it became fully intelligible. The practical utility of this book is due to the fact that unless the spectator at an Ibsen play has read the pages referring to it beforehand, it is hardly possible for him to get its bearings at a first hearing if he approaches it, as most spectators still do, with conventional idealist prepossessions. Accordingly, we now have plays, including some of my own, which begin with discussion and end with action, and others in which the discussion interpenetrates the action from beginning to end. When Ibsen invaded England discussion had vanished from the stage; and women could not write plays. Within twenty years women were writing better plays than men; and these plays were passionate arguments from beginning to end. The action of such plays consists of a case to be argued. If the case is uninteresting or stale or badly conducted or obviously trumped up, the play is a bad one. If it is important and novel and convincing, or at least disturbing, the play is a good one. But anyhow the play in which there is no argument and no case no longer counts as serious drama. It may still please the child in us as Punch and Judy does; but nobody nowadays pretends to regard the well made play as anything more than a commercial product which is not in question when modern schools of serious drama are under discussion. Indeed within ten years of the production of *A Doll's House* in London, audiences had become so derisive of the more obvious and hackneyed features of the methods of Sardou that it became dangerous to resort to them; and playwrights who persisted in "constructing" plays in the old French manner lost ground not for lack of ideas, but because their technique was unbearably out of fashion.

In the new plays, the drama arises through a conflict of unsettled ideals rather than through vulgar attachments, rapacities, generosities, resentments, ambitions, misunderstandings, oddities and so forth as to which no moral question is raised. The conflict is not between clear right and wrong: the villain is as conscientious as the hero, if not more so: in fact, the question which makes the play interesting (when it *is* interesting) is which is the villain and which the hero. Or, to put it another way, there are no villains and no heroes. This strikes the critics mainly as a departure from dramatic art; but it is really the inevitable return to nature which ends all the merely technical fashions. Now the natural is mainly the everyday; and its climaxes must be, if not everyday, at least every life, if they are to have any importance for the spectator. Crimes, fights, big legacies, fires, shipwrecks, battles, and thunderbolts are mistakes in a play, even when they can be effectively simulated. No doubt they may acquire dramatic interest by putting a character through the test of an emergency; but the test is likely to be too obviously theatrical, because, as the playwright cannot in the nature of things have much experience of such catastrophes, he is forced to substitute a set of conventions or conjectures for the feelings they really produce.

In short, pure accidents are not dramatic: they are only anecdotic. They may be sensational, impressive, provocative, ruinous, curious, or a dozen other things; but they have no specifically dramatic interest. There is no drama in being knocked down or run over. The catastrophe in *Hamlet* would not be in the least dramatic had Polonius fallen downstairs and broken his neck, Claudius succumbed to delirium tremens, Hamlet forgotten to breathe in the intensity of his philosophic speculation, Ophelia died of Danish measles, Laertes been shot by the palace sentry, and Rosencrantz and Guildenstern drowned in the North Sea. Even as it is, the Queen, who poisons herself by accident, has an air of being polished off to get her out of the way: her death is the one dramatic failure of the piece. Bushels of good paper have been inked in vain by writers who imagined they could produce a tragedy by killing everyone in the last act accidentally. As a matter of fact no accident, however sanguinary, can produce a moment of real drama, though a difference of opinion between husband and wife as to living in town or country might be the beginning of an appalling tragedy or a capital comedy.

It may be said that everything is an accident: that Othello's character is an accident, Iago's character another accident, and the fact that they happened to come together in the Venetian service an even more accidental accident. Also that Torvald Helmer might just as likely have married Mrs Nickleby as Nora. Granting this trifling for what it is worth, the fact remains that marriage is no more an accident than birth or death: that is, it is expected to happen to everybody. And if every man has a good deal of Torvald Helmer in him, and every woman a good deal of Nora, neither their characters nor their meeting and marrying are accidents. *Othello*, though entertaining, pitiful, and resonant with the thrills a master of language can produce by mere artistic sonority is certainly much more accidental than *A Doll's House*; but it is correspondingly less important and interesting to us. It has been kept alive not by its manufactured misunderstandings and stolen handkerchiefs and the like, nor even by its orchestral verse, but by its exhibition and discussion of human nature, marriage, and jealousy; and it would be a prodigiously better play if it were a serious discussion of the highly interesting problem of how a simple Moorish soldier would get on with a "supersubtle" Venetian lady of fashion if he married her. As it is, the play turns on a mistake; and though a mistake can produce a murder, which is the vulgar substitute for a tragedy, it cannot produce a real tragedy in the modern sense. Reflective people are not more interested in the Chamber of Horrors than in their own homes, nor in murderers, victims, and villains than in themselves; and the moment a man has acquired sufficient reflective power to cease gaping at waxworks, he is on his way to losing interest in Othello, Desdemona, and Iago exactly to the extent to which they become interesting to the police. Cassio's weakness for drink comes much nearer home to most of us than Othello's strangling and throat cutting, or Iago's theatrical confidence trick. The proof is that Shakespear's professional colleagues, who exploited all his sensational devices, and piled up torture on murder and incest on adultery until they had far out Heroded Herod, are now unmemorable and unplayable. Shakespear survives because he coolly treated the sensational horrors of his borrowed plots as inorganic theatrical accessories, using them simply as pretexts for dramatizing human character as it exists in the normal world. In enjoying and discussing his plays we unconsciously discount the combats and murders: commentators are never so astray (and consequently so ingenious) as when they take Hamlet seriously as a madman, Macbeth as a homicidal Highlander, and impish humorists like Richard and Iago as lurid villains of the Renascence. The plays in which these figures appear could be changed into comedies without altering a hair of their beards. Shakespear, had anyone been intelligent enough to tax him with this, would perhaps have said that most crimes are accidents that happen to people exactly like ourselves, and that Macbeth, under propitious circumstances, would have made an exemplary rector of Stratford, a real criminal being a defective monster, a human accident, useful on the stage only for minor parts such as Don Johns, second murderers, and the like. Anyhow, the fact remains that Shakespear survives by what he has in common with Ibsen, and not by what he has in common with Webster and the rest. Hamlet's surprise at finding that he "lacks gall" to behave in the idealistically conventional manner, and that no extremity of rhetoric about the duty of revenging "a dear father slain" and exterminating the "bloody bawdy villain" who murdered him seems to make any difference in their domestic relations in the palace in Elsinore, still keeps us talking about him and going to the theatre to listen to him, whilst the older Hamlets, who never had any Ibsenist hesitations, and shammed madness, and entangled the courtiers in the arras and burnt them, and stuck hard to the theatrical school of the fat boy in Pickwick ("I wants to make your flesh creep"), are as dead as John Shakespear's mutton.

We have progressed so rapidly on this point under the impulse given to the drama by Ibsen that it seems strange now to contrast him favorably with Shakespear on the ground that he avoided the old catastrophes which left the stage strewn with the dead at the end of an Elizabethan tragedy. For perhaps the most plausible reproach levelled at Ibsen by modern critics of his own school is just that survival of the old school in him which makes the death rate so high in his last acts. Do Oswald Alving, Hedvig Ekdal, Rosmer and Rebecca, Hedda Gabler, Solness, Eyolf, Borkman, Rubeck and Irene die dramatically natural deaths, or are they slaughtered in the classic and Shakespearean manner, partly because the audience expects blood for its money, partly because it is difficult to make people attend seriously to anything except by startling them with some violent calamity? It is so easy to make out a case for either view that I shall not argue the point. The post-Ibsen playwrights apparently think that Ibsen's homicides and suicides were forced. In Tchekov's *Cherry Orchard*, for example, where the sentimental ideals of our amiable, cultured, Schumann playing propertied class are reduced to dust and ashes by a hand not less deadly than Ibsen's because it is so much more caressing, nothing more violent happens than that the family cannot afford to keep up its old house. In Granville-Barker's plays, the campaign against our society is carried on with all Ibsen's implacability; but the one suicide (in *Waste*) is unhistorical; for neither Parnell nor Dilke, who were the actual cases in point of the waste which was the subject of the play, killed himself. I myself have been reproached because the characters in my plays "talk but do nothing", meaning that they do not commit felonies. As a matter of fact we have come to see that it is no true *dénouement* to cut the Gordian knot as Alexander did with a stroke of the sword. If people's souls are tied up by law and public opinion it is much more tragic to leave them to wither in these bonds than to end their misery and relieve the salutary compunction of the audience by outbreaks of violence. Judge Brack was, on the whole, right when he said that people don't do such things. If they did, the idealists would be brought to their senses very quickly indeed.

But in Ibsen's plays the catastrophe, even when it seems forced, and when the ending of the play would be more tragic without it, is never an accident; and the play never exists for its sake. His nearest to an accident is the death of little Eyolf, who falls off a pier and is drowned. But this instance only reminds us that there is one good dramatic use for an accident: it can awaken people. When England wept over the deaths of little Nell and Paul Dombey, the strong soul of Ruskin was moved to scorn: to novelists who were at a loss to make their books sell he offered the formula: When at a loss, kill a child. But Ibsen did not kill little Eyolf to manufacture pathos. The surest way to achieve a thoroughly bad performance of *Little Eyolf* is to conceive it as a sentimental tale of a drowned darling. Its drama lies in the awakening of Allmers and his wife to the despicable quality and detestable rancors of the life they have been idealizing as blissful and poetic. They are so sunk in their dream that the awakening can be effected only by a violent shock. And that is just the one dramatically useful thing an accident can do. It can shock. Hence the accident that befalls Eyolf.

As to the deaths in Ibsen's last acts, they are a sweeping up of the remains of dramatically finished people. Solness's fall from the tower is as obviously symbolic as Phaeton's fall from the chariot of the sun. Ibsen's dead bodies are those of the exhausted or destroyed: he does not kill Hilda, for instance, as Shakespear killed Juliet. He is ruthless enough with Hedvig and Eyolf because he wants to use their deaths to expose their parents; but if he had written *Hamlet* nobody would have been killed in the last act except perhaps Horatio, whose correct nullity might have provoked Fortinbras to let some of the moral sawdust out of him with his sword. For Shakespearean deaths in Ibsen you must go back to Lady Inger and the plays of his nonage, with which this book is not concerned.

The drama was born of old from the union of two desires: the desire to have a dance and the desire to hear a story. The dance became a rant: the story became a situation. When Ibsen began to make plays, the art of the dramatist had shrunk into the art of contriving a situation. And it was held that the stranger the situation, the better the play. Ibsen saw that, on the contrary, the more familiar the situation, the more interesting the play. Shakespear had put ourselves on the stage but not our situations. Our uncles seldom murder our fathers, and cannot legally marry our mothers; we do not meet witches; our kings are not as a rule stabbed and succeeded by their stabbers; and when we raise money by bills we do not promise to pay pounds of our flesh. Ibsen supplies the want left by Shakespear. He gives us not only ourselves, but our selves in our own situations. The things that happen to his stage figures are things that happen to us. One consequence is that his plays are much more important to us than Shakespear's. Another is that they are capable both of hurting us cruelly and of filling us with excited hopes of escape from idealistic tyrannies, and with visions of intenser life in the future.

Changes in technique follow inevitably from these changes in the subject matter of the play. When a dramatic poet can give you hopes and visions, such old maxims as that stage-craft is the art of preparation become boyish, and may be left to those unfortunate playwrights who, being unable to make anything really interesting happen on the stage, have to acquire the art of continually persuading the audience that it is going to happen presently. When he can stab people to the heart by shewing them the meanness or cruelty of something they did yesterday and intend to do tomorrow, all the old tricks to catch and hold their attention become the silliest of superfluities. The play called *The Murder of Gonzago*, which Hamlet makes the players act before his uncle, is artlessly constructed; but it produces a greater effect on Claudius than the *Oedipus* of Sophocles, because it is about himself. The writer who practises the art of Ibsen therefore discards all the old tricks of preparation, catastrophe, *dénouement,* and so forth without thinking about it, just as a modern rifleman never dreams of providing himself with powder horns, percussion caps, and wads: indeed he does not know the use of them. Ibsen substituted a terrible art of sharpshooting at the audience, trapping them, fencing with them, aiming always at the sorest spot in their consciences. Never mislead an audience, was an old rule. But the new school will trick the spectator into forming a meanly false judgment, and then convict him of it in the next act, often to his grievous mortification. When you despise something you ought to take off your hat to, or admire and imitate something you ought to loathe, you cannot resist the dramatist who knows how to touch these morbid spots in you and make you see that they are morbid. The dramatist knows that as long as he is teaching and saving his audience, he is as sure of their strained attention as a dentist is, or the Angel of the Annunciation. And though he may use all the magic of art to make you forget the pain he causes you or to enhance the joy of the hope and courage he awakens, he is never occupied in the old work of manufacturing interest and expectation with materials that have neither novelty, significance, nor relevance to the experience or prospects of the spectators.

Hence a cry has arisen that the post-Ibsen play is not a play, and that its technique, not being the technique described by Aristotle, is not a technique at all. I will not enlarge on this: the fun poked at my friend Mr A. B. Walkley in the prologue of *Fanny's First Play* need not be repeated here. But I may remind him that the new technique is new only on the modern stage. It has been used by preachers and orators ever since speech was invented. It is the technique of playing upon the human conscience; and it has been practised by the playwright whenever the playwright has been capable of it. Rhetoric, irony, argument, paradox, epigram, parable, the rearrangement of haphazard facts into orderly and intelligent situations: these are both the oldest and the newest arts of the drama; and your plot construction and art of preparation are only the tricks of theatrical talent and the shifts of moral sterility, not the weapons of dramatic genius. In the theatre of Ibsen we are not flattered spectators killing an idle hour with an ingenious and amusing entertainment: we are "guilty creatures sitting at a play"; and the technique of pastime is no more applicable than at a murder trial.

The technical novelties of the Ibsen and post-Ibsen plays are, then: first, the introduction of the discussion and its development until it so overspreads and interpenetrates the action that it finally assimilates it, making play and discussion practically identical; and, second, as a consequence of making the spectators themselves the persons of the drama, and the incidents of their own lives its incidents, the disuse of the old stage tricks by which audiences had to be induced to take an interest in unreal people and improbable circumstances, and the substitution of a forensic technique of recrimination, disillusion, and penetration through ideals to the truth, with a free use of all the rhetorical and lyrical arts of the orator, the preacher, the pleader, and the rhapsodist.

Ezra Pound (1885–1972)

"DUBLINERS AND MR. JAMES JOYCE" (1914)

A MONG THE FIRST TO RECOGNIZE JOYCE'S GENIUS, Pound, echoing Pater's "Conclusion" to *The Renaissance* (see Chapter 2), hailed *Dubliners* as the work of an impressionist writing in "a clear hard prose" – an impressionist descended from "Flaubert's definitiveness" rather than "Monet's softness," and therefore a realist who "gives us Dublin as it presumably is." Joyce's classicism lies in his depicting "common emotions. . . . he deals with normal things and with normal people" by means of "rigorous selection of the presented detail" – a style that Joyce himself called "scrupulous meanness."

Ezra Pound, "Dubliners and Mr. James Joyce," *The Egoist* 1.14 (June 15, 1914); 267–68. Reprinted in *Critical Essays on James Joyce*, ed. Bernard Benstock. Boston: G.K. Hall, 1985. 19–21.

Freedom from sloppiness is so rare in contemporary English prose that one might well say simply, 'Mr Joyce's book of short stories is prose free from sloppiness,' and leave the intelligent reader ready to run from his study, immediately to spend three and sixpence on the volume [*Dubliners*].

Unfortunately one's credit as a critic is insufficient to produce this result.

The readers of *The Egoist*, having had Mr Joyce under their eyes for some months, will scarcely need to have his qualities pointed out to them. Both they and the paper have been very fortunate in his collaboration.

Mr Joyce writes a clear hard prose. He deals with subjective things, but he presents them with such clarity of outline that he might be dealing with locomotives or with builders' specifications. For that reason one can read Mr Joyce without feeling that one is conferring a favour. I must put this thing my own way. I know about 168 authors. About once a year I read something contemporary without feeling that I am softening the path for poor Jones or poor Fulano de Tal.

I can lay down a good piece of French writing and pick up a piece of writing by Mr Joyce without feeling as if my head were being stuffed through a cushion. There are still impressionists about and I dare say they claim Mr Joyce. I admire impressionist writers. English prose writers who haven't got as far as impressionism (that is to say, 95 per cent of English writers of prose and verse) are a bore.

Impressionism has, however, two meanings, or perhaps I had better say, the word "impressionism" gives two different "impressions."

There is a school of prose writers, and of verse writers for that matter, whose forerunner was Stendhal and whose founder was Flaubert. The followers of Flaubert deal in exact presentation. They are often so intent on exact presentation that they neglect intensity, selection, and concentration. They are perhaps the most clarifying and they have been perhaps the most beneficial force in modern writing.

There is another set, mostly of verse writers, who founded themselves not upon anybody's writing but upon the pictures of Monet. Every movement in painting picks up a few writers who try to imitate in words what someone has done in paint. Thus one writer saw a picture by Monet and talked of "pink pigs blossoming on a hillside," and a later writer talked of 'slate-blue' hair and "raspberry-coloured flanks."

These "impressionists" who write in imitation of Monet's softness instead of writing in imitation of Flaubert's definiteness, are a bore, a grimy, or perhaps I should say, a rosy, floribund bore.

The spirit of a decade strikes properly upon all of the arts. There are "parallel movements." Their causes and their effects may not seem, superficially, similar.

This mimicking of painting ten or twenty years late, is not in the least the same as the "literary movement" parallel to the painting movement imitated.

The force that leads a poet to leave out a moral reflection may lead a painter to leave out representation. The resultant poem may not suggest the resultant painting.

Mr Joyce's merit, I will not say his chief merit but his most engaging merit, is that he carefully avoids telling you a lot that you don't want to know. He presents his people swiftly and vividly, he does not sentimentalize over them, he does not weave convolutions. He is a realist. He does not believe "life" would be all right if we stopped vivisection or if we instituted a new sort of "economics." He gives the thing as it is. He is not bound by the tiresome convention that any part of life, to be interesting, must be shaped into the conventional form of a "story." Since De Maupassant we have had so many people trying to write "stories" and so few people presenting life. Life for the most part does not happen in neat little diagrams and nothing is more tiresome than the continual pretence that it does.

Mr Joyce's *Araby*, for instance, is much better than a "story," it is a vivid waiting.

It is surprising that Mr Joyce is Irish. One is so tired of the Irish or "Celtic" imagination (or "phantasy" as I think they now call it) flopping about. Mr Joyce does not flop about. He defines. He is not an institution for the promotion of Irish peasant industries. He accepts an international standard of prose writing and lives up to it.

He gives us Dublin as it presumably is. He does not descend to farce. He does not rely upon Dickensian caricature. He gives us things as they are, not only for Dublin, but for every city. Erase the local names and a few specifically local allusions, and a few historic events of the past, and substitute a few different local names, allusions and events, and these stories could be retold of any town.

That is to say, the author is quite capable of dealing with things about him, and dealing directly, yet these details do not engross him, he is capable of getting at the universal element beneath them.

The main situations of *Madame Bovary* or of *Doña Perfecta* do not depend on local colour or upon local detail, that is their strength. Good writing, good presentation can be specifically local, but it must not depend on locality. Mr Joyce does not present "types" but individuals. I mean he deals with common emotions which run through all races. He does not bank on "Irish character." Roughly speaking, Irish literature has gone through three phases in our time, the shamrock period, the dove-grey period, and the Kiltartan period. I think there is a new phase in the works of Mr Joyce. He writes as a contemporary of continental writers. I do not mean that he writes as a faddist, mad for the last note, he does not imitate Strindberg, for instance, or Bang. He is not ploughing the underworld for horror. He is not presenting a macabre subjectivity. He is classic in that he deals with normal things and with normal people. A committee room, Little Chandler, a nonentity, a boarding house full of clerks—these are his subjects and he treats them all in such a manner that they are worthy subjects of art.

Francis Jammes, Charles Vildrac and D. H. Lawrence have written short narratives in verse, trying, it would seem, to present situations as clearly as prose writers have done, yet more briefly. Mr Joyce is engaged in a similar condensation. He has kept to prose, not needing the privilege supposedly accorded to verse to justify his method.

I think that he excels most of the impressionist writers because of his more rigorous selection, because of his exclusion of all unnecessary detail.

There is a very clear demarcation between unnecessary detail and irrelevant detail. An impressionist friend of mine talks to me a good deal about "preparing effects," and on that score he justifies much unnecessary detail, which is not "irrelevant," but which ends by being wearisome and by putting one out of conceit with his narrative.

Mr Joyce's more rigorous selection of the presented detail marks him, I think, as belonging to my own generation, that is, to the "nineteen-tens," not to the decade between "the nineties" and to-day.

At any rate these stories and the novel now appearing in serial form [*A Portrait of the Artist as a Young Man*] are such as to win for Mr Joyce a very definite place among English contemporary prose writers, not merely a place in the "Novels of the Week" column, and our writers of good clear prose are so few that we cannot afford to confuse or to overlook them.

Chapter 63

T.S. Eliot (1888–1965)

"*ULYSSES*, ORDER, AND MYTH" (1923)

AN EARLY APPRECIATOR OF JOYCE'S *Ulysses* (published in February 1922), Eliot praised it as "the most important expression which the present age has found; it is a book to which we are all indebted, and from which none of us can escape." Although he initially hailed and championed Joyce's "superb new novel" while it was being serialized, Eliot came to view *Ulysses* more as epic than novel. He was particularly taken with its replacement of narrative with what he called "the mythical method," which he considered a major artistic advance (one that he had previously found only in Yeats) and crucial for modernist representation. And as Eliot's letters reveal, *Ulysses* was deeply influential both on the text of *The Waste Land* (published in February 1922) and on Eliot himself. Both this essay and "Tradition and the Individual Talent" can be read as a primer for the work that soon followed: *The Waste Land*. In many ways, these essays outline a philosophical and aesthetic stance that sets the stage for and preemptively defend Eliot's future poem.

T.S. Eliot, "*Ulysses*, Order, and Myth," *The Dial* 75 (November 1923). Reprinted in *Critical Essays on James Joyce*, ed. Bernard Benstock. Boston: G.K. Hall, 1985. 25–27.

Mr Joyce's book has been out long enough for no more general expression of praise, or expostulation with its detractors, to be necessary; and it has not been out long enough for any attempt at a complete measurement of its place and significance to be possible. All that one can usefully do at this time, and it is a great deal to do, for such a book, is to elucidate any aspect of the book—and the number of aspects is indefinite—which has not yet been fixed. I hold this book to be the most important expression which the present age has found; it is a book to which we are all indebted, and from which none of us can escape. These are postulates for anything that I have to say about it, and I have no wish to waste the reader's time by elaborating my eulogies; it has given me all the surprise, delight, and terror that I can require, and I will leave it at that.

Amongst all the criticisms I have seen of the book, I have seen nothing—unless we except, in its way, M Valery Larbaud's valuable paper which is rather an Introduction than a criticism—which seemed to me to appreciate the significance of the method employed—the parallel to the *Odyssey*, and the use of appropriate styles and symbols to each division. Yet one might expect this to be the first peculiarity to attract attention; but it has been treated as an amusing dodge, or scaffolding erected by the author for the purpose of disposing his realistic tale, of no interest in the completed structure. The criticism which Mr Aldington directed upon *Ulysses* several years ago seems to me to fail by this oversight—but, as Mr Aldington wrote before the complete work had appeared, fails more honourably than the attempts of those who had the whole book before them. Mr Aldington treated Mr Joyce as a prophet of chaos; and wailed at the flood of Dadaism which his prescient eye saw bursting forth at the tap of the magician's rod. Of course, the influence which Mr Joyce's book may have is from my point of view an irrelevance. A very great book may have a very bad influence indeed; and a mediocre book may be in the event most salutary. The next generation is responsible for its own soul; a man of genius is responsible to his peers, not to a studio-full of uneducated and undisciplined coxcombs. Still, Mr Aldington's pathetic solicitude for the half-witted seems to me to carry certain implications about the nature of the book itself to which I cannot assent; and this is the important issue. He finds the book, if I understand him, to be an invitation to chaos, and an expression of feelings which are perverse, partial, and a distortion of reality. But unless I quote Mr Aldington's words I am likely to falsify. "I say, moreover," he says,[1] "that when Mr Joyce, with his marvellous gifts, uses them to disgust us with mankind, he is doing something which is false and a libel on humanity." It is somewhat similar to the opinion of the urbane Thackeray upon Swift. "As for the moral, I think it horrible, shameful, unmanly, blasphemous: and giant and great as this Dean is, I say we should hoot him." (This, of the conclusion of the Voyage to the Houyhnhnms—which seems to me one of the greatest triumphs that the human soul has ever achieved.—It is true that Thackeray later pays Swift one of the finest tributes that a man has ever given or received: "So great a man he seems to me that thinking of him is like thinking of an empire falling." And Mr Aldington, in his time, is almost equally generous.)

Whether it is possible to libel humanity (in distinction to libel in the usual sense, which is libelling an individual or a group in contrast with the rest of humanity) is a question for philosophical societies to discuss; but of course if *Ulysses* were a "libel" it would simply be a forged document, a powerless fraud, which would never have extracted from Mr Aldington a moment's attention. I do not wish to linger over this point: the interesting question is that begged by Mr Aldington when he refers to Mr Joyce's "great *undisciplined* talent."

I think that Mr Aldington and I are more or less agreed as to what we want in principle, and agreed to call it classicism. It is because of this agreement that I have chosen Mr Aldington to attack on the present issue. We are agreed as to what we want, but not as to how to get it, or as to what contemporary writing exhibits a tendency in that direction. We agree, I hope, that "classicism" is not an alternative to "romanticism," as of political parties, Conservative and Liberal, Republican and Democrat, on a "turn-the-rascals-out" platform. It is a goal toward which all good literature strives, so far as it is good, according to the possibilities of its place and time. One can be "classical," in a sense, by turning away from nine-tenths of the material which lies at hand, and selecting only mummified stuff from a museum—like some contemporary writers, about whom one could say some nasty things in this connexion, if it were worth while (Mr Aldington is not one of them). Or one can be classical in tendency by doing the best one can with the material at hand. The confusion springs from the fact that the term is applied to literature and to the whole complex of interests and modes of behaviour and society of which literature is a part; and it has not the same bearing in both applications. It is much easier to be a classicist in literary criticism than in creative art—because in criticism you are responsible only for what you want, and in creation you are responsible for what you can do with material which you must simply accept. And in this material I include the emotions and feelings of the writer himself, which, for that writer, are simply material which he must accept—not virtues to be enlarged or vices to be diminished. The question, then, about Mr Joyce, is: how much living material does he deal with, and how does he deal with it: deal with, not as a legislator or exhorter, but as an artist?

It is here that Mr Joyce's parallel use of the *Odyssey* has a great importance. It has the importance of a scientific discovery. No one else has built a novel upon such a foundation before: it has never before been necessary. I am not begging the question in calling *Ulysses* a "novel"; and if you call it an epic it will not matter. If it is not a novel, that is simply because the novel is a form which will no longer serve; it is because the novel, instead of being a form, was simply the expression of an age which had not sufficiently lost all form to feel the need of something stricter. Mr Joyce has written one novel—the *Portrait*; Mr Wyndham Lewis has written one novel—*Tarr*. I do not suppose that either of them will ever write another "novel." The novel ended with Flaubert and with James. It is, I think, because Mr Joyce and Mr Lewis, being "in advance" of their time, felt a conscious or probably unconscious dissatisfaction with the form, that their novels are more formless than those of a dozen clever writers who are unaware of its obsolescence.

In using the myth, in manipulating a continuous parallel between contemporaneity and antiquity, Mr Joyce is pursuing a method which others must pursue after him. They will not be imitators, any more than the scientist who uses the discoveries of an Einstein in pursuing his own, independent, further investigations. It is simply a way of controlling, of ordering, of giving a shape and a significance to the immense panorama of futility and anarchy which is contemporary history. It is a method already adumbrated by Mr Yeats, and of the need for which I believe Mr Yeats to have been the first contemporary to be conscious. It is a method for which the horoscope is auspicious. Psychology (such as it is, and whether our reaction to it be comic or serious), ethnology, and *The Golden Bough* have concurred to make possible what was impossible even a few years ago. Instead of narrative method, we may now use the mythical method. It is, I seriously believe, a step toward making the modern world possible for art, toward that order and form which Mr Aldington so earnestly desires. And only those who have won their own discipline in secret and without aid, in a world which offers very little assistance to that end, can be of any use in furthering this advance.

Note

1   *English Review*, April 1921.

Chapter 64

D.H. Lawrence (1885–1930)

"SURGERY FOR THE NOVEL – OR A BOMB?" (1923)

L AWRENCE'S MUSCULAR AND PUGNACIOUS CRITIQUE of the conventional bourgeois novel and its recent modernist and experimental manifestations attacks the staid and exhausted traditions of the former and the absorbed self-consciousness of the latter. James Joyce is Lawrence's main target in the essay, and the recently published novel *Ulysses* (1922) serves as the bull's eye for what the renegade Lawrence considers the modernist novel's mistaken, insufficiently dynamic insular turn.

D.H. Lawrence, "Surgery for the Novel – Or a Bomb?" *International Book Review* (April 1923). Reprinted in *D.H. Lawrence: Selected Literary Criticism*, ed. Anthony Beal. Melbourne, London, and Toronto: Heinemann, 1955. 517–20.

You talk about the future of the baby, little cherub, when he's in the cradle cooing; and it's a romantic, glamorous subject. You also talk, with the parson, about the future of the wicked old grandfather who is at last lying on his death-bed. And there again you have a subject for much vague emotion, chiefly of fear this time.

How do we feel about the novel? Do we bounce with joy thinking of the wonderful novelistic days ahead? Or do we grimly shake our heads and hope the wicked creature will be spared a little longer? Is the novel on his death-bed, old sinner? Or is he just toddling round his cradle, sweet little thing? Let us have another look at him before we decide this rather serious case.

There he is, the monster with many faces, many branches to him, like a tree: the modern novel. And he is almost dual, like Siamese twins. On the one hand, the pale-faced, high-browed, earnest novel, which you have to take seriously; on the other, that smirking, rather plausible hussy, the popular novel.

Let us just for the moment feel the pulses of *Ulysses* and of Miss Dorothy Richardson and M. Marcel Proust, on the earnest side, of Briareus; on the other, the throb of *The Sheik* and Mr. Zane Grey, and, if you will, Mr. Robert Chambers and the rest. Is *Ulysses* in his cradle? Oh, dear! What a grey face! And *Pointed Roofs*, are they a gay little toy for nice little girls? And M. Proust? Alas! You can hear the death-rattle in their throats. They can hear it themselves.

They are listening to it with acute interest, trying to discover whether the intervals are minor thirds or major fourths. Which is rather infantile, really.

So there you have the "serious" novel, dying in a very long-drawn-out fourteen-volume death-agony, and absorbedly, childishly interested in the phenomenon. "Did I feel a twinge in my little toe, or didn't I?" asks every character of Mr. Joyce or of Miss Richardson or M. Proust. Is my aura a blend of frankincense and orange pekoe and boot-blacking, or is it myrrh and bacon-fat and Shetland tweed? The audience round the death-bed gapes for the answer. And when, in a sepulchral tone, the answer comes at length, after hundreds of pages: "It is none of these, it is abysmal chloro-coryambasis," the audience quivers all over, and murmurs: "That's just how I feel myself."

Which is the dismal, long-drawn-out comedy of the death-bed of the serious novel. It is self-consciousness picked into such fine bits that the bits are most of them invisible, and you have to go by smell. Through thousands and thousands of pages Mr. Joyce and Miss Richardson tear themselves to pieces, strip their smallest emotions to the finest threads, till you feel you are sewed inside a wool mattress that is being slowly shaken up, and you are turning to wool along with the rest of the woolliness.

It's awful. And it's childish. It really is childish, after a certain age, to be absorbedly self-conscious. One has to be self-conscious at seventeen: still a little self-conscious at twenty-seven; but if we are going it strong at thirty-seven, then it is a sign of arrested development, nothing else. And if it is still continuing at forty-seven, it is obvious senile precocity.

And there's the serious novel: senile-precocious. Absorbedly, childishly concerned with *what I am*. "I am this, I am that, I am the other. My reactions are such, and such, and such. And, oh, Lord, if I liked to watch myself closely enough, if I liked to analyse my feelings minutely, as I unbutton my gloves, instead of saying crudely I unbuttoned them, then I could go on to a million pages instead of a thousand. In fact, the more I come to think of it, it is gross, it is uncivilised bluntly to say: I unbuttoned my gloves. After all, the absorbing adventure of it! Which button did I begin with?" etc.

The people in the serious novels are so absorbedly concerned with themselves and what they feel and don't feel, and how they react to every mortal button; and their audience as frenziedly absorbed in the application of the author's discoveries to their own reactions: "That's me! That's exactly it! I'm just finding myself in this book!" Why, this is more than death-bed, it is almost post-mortem behaviour.

Some convulsion or cataclysm will have to get this serious novel out of its self-consciousness. The last great war made it worse. What's to be done? Because, poor thing, it's really young yet. The novel has never become fully adult. It has never quite grown to years of discretion. It has always youthfully hoped for the best, and felt rather sorry for itself on the last page. Which is just childish. The childishness has become very long-drawn-out. So very many adolescents who drag their adolescence on into their forties and their fifties and their sixties! There needs some sort of surgical operation, somewhere.

Then the popular novels—the *Sheiks* and *Babbitts* and Zane Grey novels. They are just as self-conscious, only they do have more illusions about themselves. The heroines do think they are lovelier, and more fascinating, and purer. The heroes do see themselves more heroic, braver, more chivalrous, more fetching. The mass of the populace "find themselves" in the popular novels. But nowadays it's a funny sort of self they find. A sheik with a whip up his sleeve, and a heroine with weals on her back, but adored in the end, adored, the whip out of sight, but the weals still faintly visible.

It's a funny sort of self they discover in the popular novels. And the essential moral of *If Winter Comes*, for example, is so shaky. "The gooder you are, the worse it is for you, poor you, oh, poor you. Don't you be so blimey good, it's not good enough." Or *Babbitt*: "Go on, you make your pile, and then pretend you're too good for it. Put it over the rest of the grabbers that way. They're only pleased with themselves when they've made their pile. You go one better."

Always the same sort of baking-powder gas to make you rise: the soda counteracting the cream of tartar, and the tartar counteracted by the soda. Sheik heroines, duly whipped, wildly adored. Babbitts with solid fortunes, weeping from self-pity. Winter-Comes heroes as good as pie, hauled off to jail, *Moral:* Don't be too good, because you'll go to jail for it. *Moral:* Don't feel sorry for yourself till you've made your pile and don't need to feel sorry for yourself. *Moral:* Don't let him adore you till he's whipped you into it. Then you'll be partners in mild crime as well as in holy matrimony.

Which again is childish. Adolescence which *can't* grow up. Got into the self-conscious rut and going crazy, quite crazy in it. Carrying on their adolescence into middle age and old age, like the looney Cleopatra in *Dombey and Son*, murmuring "Rose-coloured curtains" with her dying breath.

The future of the novel? Poor old novel, it's in a rather dirty, messy tight corner. And it's either got to get over the wall or knock a hole through it. In other words, it's got to grow up. Put away childish things like: "Do I love the girl, or don't I?"—"Am I pure and sweet, or am I not?"—"Do I unbutton my right glove first, or my left?"—"Did my mother ruin my life by refusing to drink the cocoa which my bride had boiled for her?" These questions and their answers don't really interest me any more, though the world still goes sawing them over. I simply don't care for any of these things now, though I used to. The purely emotional and self-analytical stunts are played out in me. I'm finished. I'm deaf to the whole band. But I'm neither *blasé* nor cynical, for all that. I'm just interested in something else.

Supposing a bomb were put under the whole scheme of things, what would we be after? What feelings do we want to carry through into the next epoch? What feelings will carry us through? What is the underlying impulse in us that will provide the motive power for a new state of things, when this democratic-industrial-lovey-dovey-darling-take-me-to-mamma state of things is bust?

What next? That's what interests me. "What now?" is no fun any more.

If you wish to look into the past for what-next books, you can go back to the Greek philosophers. Plato's Dialogues are queer little novels. It seems to me it was the greatest pity in the world, when philosophy and fiction got split. They used to be one, right from the days of myth. Then they went and parted, like a nagging married couple, with Aristotle and Thomas Aquinas and that beastly Kant. So the novel went sloppy, and philosophy went abstract-dry. The two should come together again—in the novel.

You've got to find a new impulse for new things in mankind, and it's really fatal to find it through abstraction. No, no; philosophy and religion, they've both gone too far on the algebraical tack: Let X stand for sheep and Y for goats: then X minus Y equals Heaven, and X plus Y equals Earth, and Y minus X equals Hell. Thank you! But what coloured shirt does X have on?

The novel has a future. It's got to have the courage to tackle new propositions without using abstractions; it's got to present us with new, really new feelings, a whole line of new emotion, which will get us out of the emotional rut. Instead of snivelling about what is and has been, or inventing new sensations in the old line, it's got to break a way through, like a hole in the wall. And the public will scream and say it is sacrilege: because, of course, when you've been jammed for a long time in a tight corner, and you get really used to its stuffiness and its tightness, till you find it suffocatingly cosy; then, of course, you're horrified when you see a new glaring hole in what was your cosy wall. You're horrified. You back away from the cold stream of fresh air as if it were killing you. But gradually, first one and then another of the sheep filters through the gap and finds a new world outside.

Chapter 65

Mina Loy (1882–1966)

"MODERN POETRY" (1923)

THE BRITISH-BORN LOY WAS TRAINED AS A PAINTER in London, Munich, and Paris; several of her works were included in Paris's Salon d'Automne in 1905. After living in Paris for several years and becoming familiar with Gertrude and Leo Stein and that city's bohemian and avant-garde circles (including Apollinaire and Picasso), Loy moved to Greenwich Village, New York in 1916. Loy was a New Woman and feminist, poet, playwright, craftswoman, and conceptual artist; she was also affiliated for a time – romantically and intellectually – with Marinetti and the futurists. Her "Aphorisms on Futurism" (1914) were published in Alfred Steiglitz's *Camera Work*. Loy's 1918 "Feminist Manifesto" notes her break with Marinetti and with the futurists' misogyny and fascism. In New York, Loy became affiliated with Arthur Kreymbourg, Man Ray, William Carlos Williams, and the renegade poets of the little magazine, *Others*. Her frankly irreverent, erotic, and uninhibited "Love Songs" (1915) helped to initiate *Others* and scandalized some of her contemporaries with their images of "laughing honey/And spermatozoa," "lunar lusts," saliva, and vivid flesh "tumbling together." Loy was embraced by Williams, Gertrude Stein, Ezra Pound, Djuna Barnes, and Marcel Duchamp; she also became a favorite of the New York dadaists. Her poems were published in several little magazines, including *Trend, Rogue,* and *The Dial*. In her *Autobiography of Alice B. Toklas* (1933), Stein describes the incomparable Loy as the "Curie/of the laboratory/of vocabulary." Loy's collected papers are at Yale University's Beinecke Library.

Mina Loy, "Modern Poetry," *The Lost Lunar Baedeker: Poems of Mina Loy*, ed. Roger L. Conover. New York: Farrar, Straus and Giroux, 1996. 157–61.

Poetry is prose bewitched, a music made of visual thoughts, the sound of an idea.

The new poetry of the English language has proceeded out of America. Of things American it attains the aristocratic situation of vitality. This unexpectedly realized valuation of American jazz and American poetry is endorsed by two publics; the one universal, the other infinitesimal in comparison.

And why has the collective spirit of the modern world, of which both are the reflection, recognized itself unanimously in the new music of unprecedented instruments, and so rarely in the new poetry of unprecedented verse? It is because the sound of music capturing our involuntary attention is so easy to get in touch with, while the silent sound of poetry requires our voluntary attention to obliterate the cold barrier of print with the whole "intelligence of our senses." And many of us who have no habit of reading not alone with the eye but also with the ear, have—especially at a superficial first reading—overlooked the beauty of it.

More than to read poetry we must listen to poetry. All reading is the evocation of speech; the difference in our approach, then, in reading a poem or a newspaper is that our attitude in reading a poem must be rather that of listening to and looking at a pictured song. Modern poetry, like music, has received a fresh impetus from contemporary life; they have both gained in precipitance of movement. The structure of all poetry is the movement that an active individuality makes in expressing itself. Poetic rhythm, of which we have all spoken so much, is the chart of a temperament.

The variety and felicity of these structural movements in modern verse has more than vindicated the rebellion against tradition. It will be found that one can recognize each of the modern poets' work by the gait of their mentality. Or rather that the formation of their verses is determined by the spontaneous tempo of their response to life. And if at first it appears irksome to adjust pleasure to unaccustomed meters, let us reflect in time that hexameters and alexandrines, before they became poetic laws, originated as the spontaneous structure of a poet's inspiration.

Imagine a tennis champion who became inspired to write poetry, would not his verse be likely to embody the rhythmic transit of skimming balls? Would not his meter depend on his way of life, would it not form itself, without having recourse to traditional, remembered, or accepted forms? This, then, is the secret of the new poetry. It is the direct response of the poet's mind to the modern world of varieties in which he finds himself. In each one we can discover his particular inheritance of that world's beauty.

Close as this relationship of poetry to music is, I think only once has the logical transition from verse to music, on which I had so often speculated, been made, and that by the American, Ezra Pound. To speak of the modern movement is to speak of him; the masterly impresario of modern poets, for without the discoveries he made with his poet's instinct for poetry, this modern movement would still be rather a nebula than the constellation it has become. Not only a famous poet, but a man of action, he gave the public the required push on to modern poetry at the psychological moment. Pound, the purveyor of geniuses to such journals as the "Little Review," on which he conferred immortality by procuring for its pages the manuscripts of Joyce's "Ulysses." Almost together with the publication of his magnificent Cantos, his music was played in Paris; it utters the communings of a poet's mind with itself making decisions on harmony.

It was inevitable that the renaissance of poetry should proceed out of America, where latterly a thousand languages have been born, and each one, for purposes of communication at least, English—English enriched and variegated with the grammatical structure and voice-inflection of many races, in novel alloy with the fundamental time-is-money idiom of the United States, discovered by the newspaper cartoonists.

This composite language is a very living language, it grows as you speak. For the true American appears to be ashamed to say anything in the way it has been said before. Every moment he ingeniously coins new words for old ideas, to keep good humor warm. And on the baser avenues of Manhattan every voice swings to the triple rhythm of its race, its citizenship and its personality.

Out of the welter of this unclassifiable speech, while professors of Harvard and Oxford labored to preserve "God's English," the muse of modern literature arose, and her tongue had been loosened in the melting-pot.

You may think it impossible to conjure up the relationship of expression between the high browest modern poets and an adolescent Slav who has speculated in a wholesale job-lot of mandarines and is trying to sell them in a retail market on First Avenue. But it lies simply in this: both have had to become adapted to a country where the mind has to put on its verbal clothes at terrific speed if it would speak in time; where no one will listen if you attack him twice with the same missile of argument. And, that the ear that has listened to the greatest number of sounds will have the most to choose from when it comes to self-expression, each has been liberally educated in the flexibility of phrases.

So in the American poet wherever he may wander, however he may engage himself with an older culture, there has occurred no Europeanization of his fundamental advantage, the acuter shock of the New World consciousness upon life. His is still poetry that has proceeded out of America.

The harvest from this recent fertiliser is the poetry of E. E. Cummings. Where other poets have failed for being too modern he is more modern still, and altogether successful; where others were entirely anti-human in their fear of sentimentality, he keeps that rich compassion that poets having for common things leads them to deck them [sic] with their own conception; for surely if there were a heaven it would be where this horrible ugliness of human life would arise self-consciously as that which the poet has made of it.

Cummings has united free verse and rhyme which so urgently needed to be married. His rhymes are quite fresh—"radish-red" and "hazarded," and the freeness of his verse gives them a totally new metric relationship.

But fundamentally he is a great poet because his verse wells up abundantly from the foundations of his soul; a sonorous dynamo. And as I believe that the quality of genius must be largely unconscious, I can understand how Cummings can turn out such gabble when he is not being sublime. He is very often sublime.

In reading modern poetry one should beware of allowing mere technical eccentricities or grammatical disturbances to turn us from the main issue which is to get at the poem's reality. We should remember that this seeming strangeness is inevitable when any writer has come into an independent contact with nature: to each she must show herself in a new manner, for each has a different organic personality for perceiving her.

When the little controversies over what is permissible in art evaporate, we will always find that the seeming strangeness has disappeared with them in the larger aspect of the work which has the eternal quality that is common to all true art.

Out of the past most poets, after all, call to us with one or two perfect poems. And we have not complained of being too poor. You will find that the moderns have already done as much.

H. D., who is an interesting example of my claims for the American poet who engages with an older culture, has written at least two perfect poems: one about a swan.

Marianne Moore, whose writing so often amusingly suggests the soliloquies of a library clock, has written at least one perfect poem, "The Fish."

Lawrence Vail has written one perfect poem, the second "Cannibalistic Love Song," a snatch of primitive ideation with a rhythm as essential as daylight. Maxwell Bodenheim, I think, had one among his early work, and perfect also is a poem of Carlos Williams about the wind on a window-pane.

Williams brings me to a distinction that it is necessary to make in speaking of modern poets. Those I have spoken of are poets according to the old as well as the new reckoning; there are others who are poets only according to the new reckoning. They are headed by the doctor, Carlos Williams. Here is the poet whose expression derives from his life. He is a doctor. He loves bare facts. He is also a poet, he must recreate everything to suit himself. How can he reconcile these two selves?

Williams will make a poem of a bare fact—just show you something he noticed. The doctor wishes you to know just how uncompromisingly itself that fact is. But the poet would like you to realize all that it means to him, and he throws that bare fact onto paper in such a way that it becomes a part of Williams' own nature as well as the thing itself. That is the new rhythm.

Chapter 66

Ford Madox Ford (1873–1939)

JOSEPH CONRAD: A PERSONAL REMEMBRANCE (1924)

FORD MADOX HUEFFER (Ford's original name, which he changed during World War I because of its Germanic resonance) was a prolific English novelist, poet, memoirist, and literary critic best known for *The Fifth Queen* trilogy (1906–08), *The Good Soldier* (1915), and the *Parade's End* tetralogy (1924–28). In the early 1900s he collaborated with Joseph Conrad on three novels generally considered important to their creative development though not successful in their own right. During the war he worked for the War Propaganda Bureau and then served on the Western Front, where much of *Parade's End* is set. Despite his Tory demeanor, he was, like Pound, a great supporter of literary innovation and a generous editor, first of *The English Review* (which published Conrad, Norman Douglas, John Galsworthy, Hardy, James, D.H. Lawrence, Wyndham Lewis, H.G. Wells, and Yeats) and then *The Transatlantic Review* (whose writers included Hemingway, Joyce, Pound, Jean Rhys, and Gertrude Stein). His criticism includes *The English Novel: From the Earliest Days to the Death of Joseph Conrad* (1929), an accessible overview of the development of the English novel, and memoirs and reviews of many of his contemporaries, especially Conrad. His *Personal Remembrance* practices the impressionism in which he and Conrad believed: "here . . . you have a projection of Joseph Conrad as, little by little, he revealed himself to a human being during many years of close intimacy. . . . It is the writer's impression of a writer who avowed himself impressionist. Where the writer's memory has proved to be at fault over a detail afterwards out of curiosity looked up, the writer has allowed the fault to remain on the page; but as to the truth of the impression as a whole the writer believes that no man would care – or dare – to impugn it."

Ford Madox Ford, *Joseph Conrad: A Personal Remembrance*. London: Duckworth, 1924. 5–6, 129–30, 171–73, 174, 180–85.

Nine years ago the writer had occasion to make a hasty will. Since one of the provisions of this document appointed Conrad the writer's literary executor we fell to discussing the question of literary biographies in general and our own in particular. We hit, as we generally did, very quickly upon a formula, both having a very great aversion from the usual official biography for men of letters whose

514   FORD MADOX FORD

lives are generally uneventful. But we agreed that should a writer's life have interests beyond the mere writing upon which he had employed himself this life might well be the subject of a monograph. It should then be written by an artist and be a work of art. To write: "Joseph Conrad Kurzeniowski was born on such a day of such a year in the town of 'So and So' in the Government of Kieff" *and so to continue would not conduce to such a rendering as this great man desired. So, here, to the measure of the ability vouchsafed, you have a projection of Joseph Conrad as, little by little, he revealed himself to a human being during many years of close intimacy. It is so that, by degrees, Lord Jim appeared to Marlowe, or that every human soul by degrees appears to every other human soul. For, according to our view of the thing, a novel should be the biography of a man or of an affair, and a biography whether of a man or of an affair should be a novel, both being, if they are efficiently performed, renderings of such affairs as are our human lives.*

This then is a novel, not a monograph; a portrait, not a narration: for what it shall prove to be worth, a work of art, not a compilation. It is conducted exactly along the lines laid down by us, both for the novel which is biography and for the biography which is a novel. It is the rendering of an affair intended first of all to make you see the subject in his scenery. It contains no documentation at all; for it no dates have been looked up, even all the quotations but two have been left unverified, coming from the writer's memory. It is the writer's impression of a writer who avowed himself impressionist. Where the writer's memory has proved to be at fault over a detail afterwards out of curiosity looked up, the writer has allowed the fault to remain on the page; but as to the truth of the impression as a whole the writer believes that no man would care—or dare—to impugn it. It was that that Joseph Conrad asked for: the task has been accomplished with the most pious scrupulosity. For something human was to him dearer than the wealth of the Indies.

It will be as well to attempt here some sort of chronology. This is a novel exactly on the lines of the formula that Conrad and the writer evolved. For it became very early evident to us that what was the matter with the Novel, and the British novel in particular, was that it went straight forward, whereas in your gradual making acquaintanceship with your fellows you never do go straight forward. You meet an English gentleman at your golf club. He is beefy, full of health, the moral of the boy from an English Public School of the finest type. You discover, gradually, that he is hopelessly neurasthenic, dishonest in matters of small change, but unexpectedly self-sacrificing, a dreadful liar but a most painfully careful student of lepidoptera and, finally, from the public prints, a bigamist who was once, under another name, hammered on the Stock Exchange. . . . Still, there he is, the beefy, full-fed fellow, moral of an English Public School product. To get such a man in fiction you could not begin at his beginning and work his life chronologically to the end. You must first get him in with a strong impression, and then work backwards and forwards over his past. . . . That theory at least we gradually evolved . . . .

Openings for us, as for most writers, were matters of great importance, but probably we more than most writers realised of what primary importance they are. A real short story must open with a breathless sentence; a long-short story may begin with an 'as' or a 'since' and some leisurely phrases. At any rate the opening paragraph of book or story should be of the tempo of the whole performance. That is the *règle generale.* Moreover, the reader's attention must be gripped by that first paragraph. So our ideal novel must begin either with a dramatic scene or with a note that should suggest the whole book. The *Nigger* begins:

> "Mr. Baker, chief mate of the *Narcissus*, stepped in one stride out of his lighted cabin into the darkness of the quarter-deck . . . ."

The Secret Agent:

"Mr. Verloc, going out in the morning, left his shop nominally in charge of his brother-in-law . . . ."

The End of the Tether:

"For a long time after the course of the steamer *Sophala* had been altered . . . ."

this last being the most fitting beginning for the long-short story that the *End of the Tether* is.

Romance, on the other hand begins:

"To yesterday and to-day I say my polite *vaya usted con dios*. What are those days to me? But that far-off day of my romance, when from between the blue and white bales in Don Ramon's darkened store-room in Kingston . . . ."

an opening for a long novel in which the dominant interest lies far back in the story and the note must be struck at once.

The Inheritors' – first lines are, as has been already quoted:

"'Ideas,' she said. 'Oh, as for ideas . . . '"

an opening for a short novel.

Conrad's tendency and desire made for the dramatic opening: the writer's as a rule for the more pensive approach, but we each, as a book would go on were apt to find that we must modify our openings. This was more often the case with Conrad than with the writer since Conrad's books depended much more on the working out of an intrigue which he would develop as the book was in writing: the writer has seldom begun on a book without having, at least, the intrigue, the 'affair,' completely settled in his mind.

The disadvantage of the dramatic opening is that after the dramatic passage is done you have to go back to getting your characters in, a proceeding that the reader is apt to dislike. The danger with the reflective opening is that the reader is apt to miss being gripped at once by the story. Openings are therefore of necessity always affairs of compromise.

The note should here be struck that in all the conspiracies that went on at the Pent or round the shores of the Channel there was absolutely no mystery. We thought just simply of the reader: Would this passage grip him? If not it must go. Will this word make him pause and so slow down the story? If there is any danger of that, away with it. That is all that is meant by the dangerous word *technique* . . . .

[. . .]

General effect

We agreed that the general effect of a novel must be the general effect that life makes on mankind. A novel must therefore not be a narration, a report. Life does not say to you: In 1914 my next door neighbour, Mr. Slack, erected a greenhouse and painted it with Cox's green aluminium paint. . . . If you think about the matter you will remember, in various unordered pictures, how one day Mr. Slack appeared in his garden and contemplated the wall of his house. You will then try to remember the year of that occurrence and you will fix it as August 1914 because having had the foresight to bear the municipal stock of the city of Liège you were able to afford a first-class season ticket for the first time in your life. You will remember

Mr. Slack—then much thinner because it was before he found out where to buy that cheap Burgundy of which he has since drunk an inordinate quantity though whisky you think would be much better for him! Mr. Slack again came into his garden, this time with a pale, weasely-faced fellow, who touched his cap from time to time. Mr. Slack will point to his house-wall several times at different points, the weasely fellow touching his cap at each pointing. Some days after, coming back from business you will have observed against Mr. Slack's wall. . . . At this point you will remember that you were then the manager of the fresh-fish branch of Messrs. Catlin and Clovis in Fenchurch Street. . . . What a change since then! Millicent had not yet put her hair up. . . . You will remember how Millicent's hair looked, rather pale and burnished in plaits. You will remember how it now looks, henna'd: and you will see in one corner of your mind's eye a little picture of Mr. Mills the vicar talking—oh, very kindly—to Millicent after she has come back from Brighton. . . . But perhaps you had better not risk that. You remember some of the things said by means of which Millicent has made you cringe—and her expression! . . . Cox's Aluminium Paint! . . . You remember the half empty tin that Mr. Slack showed you—he had a most undignified cold—with the name in a horse-shoe over a blue circle that contained a red lion asleep in front of a real-gold sun . . . .

And, if that is how the building of your neighbour's greenhouse comes back to you, just imagine how it will be with your love-affairs that are so much more complicated . . . .

Impressionism

We accepted without much protest the stigma: "Impressionists" that was thrown at us. In those days Impressionists were still considered to be bad people: Atheists, Reds, wearing red ties with which to frighten householders. But we accepted the name because Life appearing to us much as the building of Mr. Slack's greenhouse comes back to you, we saw that Life did not narrate, but made impressions on our brains. We in turn, if we wished to produce on you an effect of life, must not narrate but render . . . impressions.

Selection

We agreed that the whole of Art consists in selection. To render your remembrance of your career as a fish-salesman might enhance the story of Mr. Slack's greenhouse, or it might *not*. A little image of iridescent, blue-striped, black-striped, white fish on a white marble slab with water trickling down to them round a huge mass of orange salmon-roe; a vivid description of a horrible smell caused by a cat having stolen and hidden in the thick of your pelargoniums a cod's head that you had brought back as a perquisite, you having subsequently killed the cat with a hammer, but long, long before you had rediscovered her fishy booty. . . . Such little impressions might be useful as contributing to illustrate your character—one should not kill a cat with a hammer! They might illustrate your sense of the beautiful—or your fortitude under affliction—or the disagreeableness of Mr. Slack, who had a delicate sense of smell—or the point of view of your only daughter Millicent.

We should then have to consider whether your sense of the beautiful or your fortitude could in our rendering carry the story forward or interest the reader. If it did we should include it; if in our opinion it was not likely to, we should leave it out. Or the story of the cat might in itself seem sufficiently amusing to be inserted as a purposed *longueur*, so as to give the idea of the passage of time. . . . It may be more amusing to read the story of a cat with your missing dinner than to read: "A fortnight elapsed. . . . " Or it might be better after all to write boldly: "Mr. Slack, after a fortnight had elapsed, remarked, one day very querulously: 'That smell seems to get worse instead of better.'"

Selection (speeches)

That last would be compromise, for it would be narration instead of rendering: it would be far *better* to give an idea of the passage of time by picturing a cat with a cod's head, but the length of the story must be considered. Sometimes to render anything at all in a given space will take up too much room—even to render the effect and delivery of a speech. Then just boldly and remorselessly you must relate and *risk* the introduction of yourself as author, with the danger that you may destroy all the illusion of the story.

Conrad and the writer would have agreed that the ideal rendering of Mr. Slack's emotions would be as follows:

> "A scrawny, dark-brown neck, with an immense Adam's apple quivering over the blue stripes of a collar erected itself between the sunflower stems above the thin oaken flats of the dividing fence. An unbelievably long, thin gap of a mouth opened itself beneath a black-spotted handkerchief, to say that the unspeakable odour was sufficient to slay all the porters in Covent Garden. Last week it was only bad enough to drive a regiment of dragoons into a faint. The night before the people whom he had had to supper—I wondered who could eat any supper with any appetite under the gaze of those yellow eyes—people, mind you, to whom he had hoped to sell a little bit of property in the neighbourhood. Good people. With more than a little bit in the bank. People whose residence would give the whole neighbourhood a lift. They had asked if he liked going out alone at night with so many undiscovered murders about . . . . 'Undiscovered murders!' he went on repeating as if the words gave him an intimate sense of relief. He concluded with the phrase: 'I *don't* think!'"

That would be a very fair *rendering* of part of an episode: it would have the use of getting quite a lot of Mr. Slack in; but you might want to get on towards recounting how you had the lucky idea of purchasing shares in a newspaper against which Mr. Slack had counselled you . . . . And you might have got Mr. Slack in already!

Chapter 67

Virginia Woolf

"HOW IT STRIKES A CONTEMPORARY" (1925) AND "THE LEANING TOWER" (1941)

WOOLF'S EXPERIMENTAL MODERNIST NOVELS frequently contain a story alongside a metanarrative, a running conversation with past literary traditions and forms. For example, in *To the Lighthouse* (1927) the artistic quest of the modernist painter Lily Briscoe is inseparable from her emotional and aesthetic attachments to and desire to escape from the influences of the Victorian Mr. and Mrs. Ramsay. Woolf's intertexts in the novel include a distant relative's as yet unpublished contemporary poem (Charles Elton's "Luriana Lurilee"), Elizabethan sonnets (by Shakespeare and William Browne), Tennyson's high Victorian poem "The Charge of the Light Brigade," a fable by the Brothers Grimm, and the Romantic poet Willam Cowper's "The Castaway." Woolf professionally supported younger contemporaries even while criticizing what she viewed as their rash departures from their cultural heritage and class. Like Woolf's "Phases of Fiction" (1929) and "A Letter to a Young Poet" (1932), these essays represent her deep engagement with notions of necessary rupture and continuity, and spontaneous and gradual creative evolution.

Virginia Woolf, "How It Strikes a Contemporary," *The Common Reader*. New York: Harcourt, Brace, 1953. 236–46.
——. "The Leaning Tower" (1941). *The Moment and Other Essays*. New York and London: Harcourt, Brace, 1974. 128–54.

"How It Strikes a Contemporary"

In the first place a contemporary can scarcely fail to be struck by the fact that two critics at the same table at the same moment will pronounce completely different opinions about the same book. Here, on the right, it is declared a masterpiece of English prose; on the left, simultaneously, a mere mass of wastepaper which, if the fire could survive it, should be thrown upon the flames. Yet both critics are in agreement about Milton and about Keats. They display an exquisite sensibility and have undoubtedly a genuine enthusiasm. It is only when they discuss the work of contemporary writers that they inevitably come to blows. The book in question, which is at once a lasting contribution to English literature and a mere farrago of pretentious mediocrity, was published about two months ago. That is the explanation; that is why they differ.

The explanation is a strange one. It is equally disconcerting to the reader who wishes to take his bearings in the chaos of contemporary literature and to the writer who had a natural desire to know whether his own work, produced with infinite pains and in almost utter darkness, is likely to burn for ever among the fixed luminaries of English letters or, on the contrary, to put out the fire. But if we identify ourselves with the reader and explore his dilemma first, our bewilderment is short-lived enough. The same thing has happened so often before. We have heard the doctors disagreeing about the new and agreeing about the old twice a year on the average, in spring and autumn, ever since Robert Elsmere, or was it Stephen Phillips, somehow pervaded the atmosphere, and there was the same disagreement among grown-up people about them. It would be much more marvellous, and indeed much more upsetting, if, for a wonder, both gentlemen agreed, pronounced Blank's book an undoubted masterpiece, and thus faced us with the necessity of deciding whether we should back their judgement to the extent of ten and sixpence. Both are critics of reputation; the opinions tumbled out so spontaneously here will be starched and stiffened into columns of sober prose which will uphold the dignity of letters in England and America.

It must be some innate cynicism, then, some ungenerous distrust of contemporary genius, which determines us automatically as the talk goes on that, were they to agree—which they show no signs of doing—half a guinea is altogether too large a sum to squander upon contemporary enthusiasms, and the case will be met quite adequately by a card to the library. Still the question remains, and let us put it boldly to the critics themselves. Is there no guidance nowadays for a reader who yields to none in reverence for the dead, but is tormented by the suspicion that reverence for the dead is vitally connected with understanding of the living? After rapid survey both critics are agreed that there is unfortunately no such person. For what is their own judgement worth where new books are concerned? Certainly not ten and sixpence. And from the stores of their experience they proceed to bring forth terrible examples of past blunders; crimes of criticism which, if they had been committed against the dead and not against the living, would have lost them their jobs and imperilled their reputations. The only advice they can offer is to respect one's own instincts, to follow them fearlessly and, rather than submit them to the control of any critic or reviewer alive, to check them by reading and reading again the masterpieces of the past.

Thanking them humbly, we cannot help reflecting that it was not always so. Once upon a time, we must believe, there was a rule, a discipline, which controlled the great republic of readers in a way which is now unknown. That is not to say that the great critic—the Dryden, the Johnson, the Coleridge, the Arnold—was an impeccable judge of contemporary work, whose verdicts stamped the book indelibly and saved the reader the trouble of reckoning the value for himself. The mistakes of these great men about their own contemporaries are too notorious to be worth recording. But the mere fact of their existence had a centralising influence. That alone, it is not fantastic to suppose, would have controlled the disagreements of the dinner-table and given to random chatter about some book just out an authority now entirely to seek. The diverse schools would have debated as hotly as ever, but at the back of every reader's mind would have been the consciousness that there was at least one man who kept the main principles of literature closely in view; who, if you had taken to him some eccentricity of the moment, would have brought it into touch with permanence and tethered it by his own authority in the contrary blasts of praise and blame.[1] But when it comes to the making of a critic, nature must be generous and society ripe. The scattered dinner-tables of the modern world, the chase and eddy of the various currents which compose the society of our time, could only be dominated by a giant of fabulous dimensions. And where is even the very tall man whom we have the right to expect? Reviewers we have but no critic; a million competent and incorruptible policemen but no judge. Men of taste and learning and ability are for ever lecturing the young and celebrating the dead. But the too frequent result of their able and industrious pens is a desiccation of the living tissues of literature into a network of little bones. Nowhere shall we find the downright vigour of a Dryden, or Keats with his fine and natural bearing, his profound insight and sanity, or Flaubert and the tremendous power of his fanaticism, or Coleridge, above all, brewing in his head the whole of poetry and letting issue now and then one of those profound general statements which are caught up by the mind when hot with the friction of reading as if they were of the soul of the book itself.

And to all this, too, the critics generously agree. A great critic, they say, is the rarest of beings. But should one miraculously appear, how should we maintain him, on what should we feed him? Great critics, if they are not themselves great poets, are bred from the profusion of the age. There is some great man to be vindicated, some school to be founded or destroyed. But our age is meagre to the verge of destitution. There is no name which dominates the rest. There is no master in whose workshop the young are proud to serve apprenticeship. Mr. Hardy has long since withdrawn from the arena, and there is something exotic about the genius of Mr. Conrad which makes him not so much an influence as an idol, honoured and admired, but aloof and apart. As for the rest, though they are many and vigorous and in the full flood of creative activity, there is none whose influence can seriously affect his contemporaries, or penetrate beyond our day to that not very distant future which it pleases us to call immortality. If we make a century our test, and ask how much of the work produced in these days in England will be in existence then, we shall have to answer not merely that we cannot agree upon the same book, but that we are more than doubtful whether such a book there is. It is an age of fragments. A few stanzas, a few pages, a chapter here and there, the beginning of this novel, the end of that, are equal to the best of any age or author. But can we go to posterity with a sheaf of loose pages, or ask the readers of those days, with the whole of literature before them, to sift our enormous rubbish heaps for our tiny pearls? Such are the questions which the critics might lawfully put to their companions at table, the novelists and poets.

At first the weight of pessimism seems sufficient to bear down all opposition. Yes, it is a lean age, we repeat, with much to justify its poverty; but, frankly, if we pit one century against another the comparison seems overwhelmingly against us. *Waverley, The Excursion, Kubla Khan, Don Juan, Hazlitt's Essays, Pride and Prejudice, Hyperion,* and *Prometheus Unbound* were all published between 1800 and 1821. Our century has not lacked industry; but if we ask for masterpieces it appears on the face of it that the pessimists are right. It seems as if an age of genius must be succeeded by an age of endeavour; riot and extravagance by cleanliness and hard work. All honour, of course, to those who have sacrificed their immortality to set the house in order. But if we ask for masterpieces, where are we to look? A little poetry, we may feel sure, will survive; a few poems by Mr. Yeats, by Mr. Davies, by Mr. De la Mare. Mr. Lawrence, of course, has moments of greatness, but hours of something very different. Mr. Beerbohm, in his way, is perfect, but it is not a big way. Passages in *Far Away and Long Ago* will undoubtedly go to posterity entire. *Ulysses* was a memorable catastrophe—immense in daring, terrific in disaster. And so, picking and choosing, we select now this, now that, hold it up for display, hear it defended or derided, and finally have to meet the objection that even so we are only agreeing with the critics that it is an age incapable of sustained effort, littered with fragments, and not seriously to be compared with the age that went before.

But it is just when opinions universally prevail and we have added lip service to their authority that we become sometimes most keenly conscious that we do not believe a word that we are saying. It is a barren and exhausted age, we repeat; we must look back with envy to the past. Meanwhile it is one of the first fine days of spring. Life is not altogether lacking in colour. The telephone, which interrupts the most serious conversations and cuts short the most weighty observations, has a romance of its own. And the random talk of people who have no chance of immortality and thus can speak their minds out has a setting, often, of lights, streets, houses, human beings, beautiful or grotesque, which will weave itself into the moment for ever. But this is life; the talk is about literature. We must try to disentangle the two, and justify the rash revolt of optimism against the superior plausibility, the finer distinction, of pessimism.

Our optimism, then, is largely instinctive. It springs from the fine day and the wine and the talk; it springs from the fact that when life throws up such treasures daily, daily suggests more than the most voluble can express, much though we admire the dead, we prefer life as it is. There is something about the present which we would not exchange, though we were offered a choice of all past ages to live in. And modern literature, with all its imperfections, has the same hold on us and the same fascination. It is like a relation whom we snub and scarify daily, but, after all, cannot do without. It has the same endearing quality of being that which we are, that which we have made, that in which we live, instead of being something, however august, alien to ourselves and beheld from the outside. Nor has any generation more need than ours to cherish its contemporaries. We are sharply cut off from our predecessors. A shift in the scale—the war, the sudden slip of masses held in position for ages—has shaken the fabric from top to bottom, alienated us from the past and made us perhaps too vividly conscious of the present. Every day we find ourselves doing, saying, or thinking things that would have been impossible to our fathers. And we feel the differences which have not been noted far more keenly than the resemblances which have been very perfectly expressed. New books lure us to read them partly in the hope that they will reflect this re-arrangement of our attitude—these scenes, thoughts, and apparently fortuitous groupings of incongruous things which impinge upon us with so keen a sense of novelty—and, as literature does, give it back into our keeping, whole and comprehended. Here indeed there is every reason for optimism. No age can have been more rich than ours in writers determined to give expression to the differences which separate them from the past and not to the resemblances which connect them with it. It would be invidious to mention names, but the most casual reader dipping into poetry, into fiction, into biography can hardly fail to be impressed by the courage, the sincerity, in a word, by the widespread originality of our time. But our exhilaration is strangely curtailed. Book after book leaves us with the same sense of promise unachieved, of intellectual poverty, of brilliance which has been snatched from life but not transmuted into literature. Much of what is best in contemporary work has the appearance of being noted under pressure, taken down in a bleak shorthand which preserves with astonishing brilliance the movements and expressions of the figures as they pass across the screen. But the flash is soon over, and there remains with us a profound dissatisfaction. The irritation is as acute as the pleasure was intense.

After all, then, we are back at the beginning, vacillating from extreme to extreme, at one moment enthusiastic, at the next pessimistic, unable to come to any conclusion about our contemporaries. We have asked the critics to help us, but they have deprecated the task. Now, then, is the time to accept their advice and correct these extremes by consulting the masterpieces of the past. We feel ourselves indeed driven to them, impelled not by calm judgment but by some imperious need to anchor our instability upon their security. But, honestly, the shock of the comparison between past and present is at first disconcerting. Undoubtedly there is a dullness in great books. There is an unabashed tranquillity in page after page of Wordsworth and Scott and Miss Austen which is sedative to the verge of somnolence. Opportunities occur and they neglect them. Shades and subtleties accumulate and they ignore them. They seem deliberately to refuse to gratify those senses which are stimulated so briskly by the moderns; the senses of sight, of sound, of touch—above all, the sense of the human being, his depth and the variety of his perceptions, his complexity, his confusion, his self, in short. There is little of all this in the works of Wordsworth and Scott and Jane Austen. From what, then, arises that sense of security which gradually, delightfully, and completely overcomes us? It is the power of their belief—their conviction, that imposes itself upon us. In Wordsworth, the philosophic poet, this is obvious enough. But it is equally true of the careless Scott, who scribbled masterpieces to build castles before breakfast, and of the modest maiden lady who wrote furtively and quietly simply to give pleasure. In both there is the same natural conviction that life is of a certain quality. They have their judgment of conduct. They know the relations of human beings towards each other and towards the universe. Neither of them probably has a word to say about the matter outright, but everything depends on it. Only believe, we find ourselves saying, and all the rest will come of itself. Only believe, to take a very simple instance which the recent publication of *The Watsons* brings to mind, that a nice girl will instinctively try to soothe the feelings of a boy who has been snubbed at a dance, and then, if you believe it implicitly and unquestioningly, you will not only make people a hundred years later feel the same thing, but you will make them feel it as literature. For certainty of that kind is the condition which makes it possible to write. To believe that your impressions hold good for others is to be released from the cramp and confinement of personality. It is to be free, as Scott was free, to explore with a vigour which still holds us spell-bound the whole world of adventure and romance. It is also the first step in that myste-rious process in which Jane Austen was so great an adept. The little grain of experience once selected, believed in, and set outside herself, could be put precisely in its place, and she was then free to make of it, by a process which never yields its secrets to the analyst, into that complete statement which is literature.

So then our contemporaries afflict us because they have ceased to believe. The most sincere of them will only tell us what it is that happens to himself. They cannot make a world, because they are not free of other human beings. They cannot tell stories because they do not believe the stories are true. They cannot generalise. They depend on their sense and emotions, whose testimony is trustworthy, rather than on their intellects whose message is obscure. And they have perforce to deny themselves the use of some of the most powerful and some of the most exquisite of the weapons of their craft. With the whole wealth of the English language at the back of them, they timidly pass about from hand to hand and book to book only the meanest copper coins. Set down at a fresh angle of the eternal prospect they can only whip out their notebooks and record with agonised intensity the flying gleams, which light on what? and the transitory splendours, which may, perhaps, compose nothing whatever. But here the critics interpose, and with some show of justice.

If this description holds good, they say, and is not, as it may well be, entirely dependent upon our position at the table and certain purely personal relationships to mustard pots and flower vases, then the risks of judging contemporary work are greater than ever before. There is every excuse for them if they are wide of the mark; and no doubt it would be better to retreat, as Matthew Arnold advised, from the burning ground of the present to the safe tranquillity of the past. "We enter on burning ground," wrote Matthew Arnold, "as we approach the poetry of times so near to us, poetry like that of Byron, Shelley, and Wordsworth, of which the estimates are so often not only personal, but personal with passion," and this, they remind us, was written in the year 1880. Beware, they say, of putting under the micro-scope one inch of a ribbon which runs many miles; things sort themselves out if you wait; moderation and a study of the classics are to be recommended. Moreover, life is short; the Byron centenary is at hand; and the burning question of the moment is, did he, or did he not, marry his sister? To sum up, then—if indeed any conclusion is possible when everybody is talking at once and it is time to be going—it seems that it would be wise for the writers of the present to renounce for themselves the hope of creating masterpieces. Their poems, plays, biographies, novels are not books but notebooks, and Time, like a good schoolmaster, will take them in his hands, point to their blots and erasions, and tear them across; but he will not throw them into the waste-paper basket. He will keep them because other students will find them very useful. It is from notebooks of the present that the masterpieces of the future are made. Literature, as the critics were saying just now, has lasted long, has undergone many changes, and it is only a short sight and a parochial mind that will exaggerate the importance of these squalls, however they may agitate the little boats now tossing out at sea. The storm and the drenching are on the surface; and continuity and calm are in the depths.

As for the critics whose task it is to pass judgement upon the books of the moment, whose work, let us admit, is difficult, dangerous, and often distasteful, let us ask them to be generous of encouragement, but sparing of those wreaths and coronets which are so apt to get awry, and fade, and make the wearers, in six months time, look a little ridiculous. Let them take a wider, a less personal view of modern literature, and look indeed upon the writers as if they were engaged upon some vast building, which being built by common effort, the separate workmen may well remain anonymous. Let them slam the door upon the cosy company where sugar is cheap and butter plentiful, give over, for a time at least, the discussion of that fascinating topic—whether Byron married his sister—and, withdrawing, perhaps, a hands-breadth from the table where we sit chattering, say something interesting about literature. Let us buttonhole them as they leave, and recall to their memory that gaunt aristocrat, Lady Hester Stanhope, who kept a milk-white horse in her stable in readiness for the Messiah and was for ever scanning the mountain tops, impatiently but with confidence, for signs of his approach, and ask them to follow her example; scan the horizon; see the past in relation to the future; and so prepare the way for masterpieces to come.

Note

1   How violent these are two quotations will show. "It [*Told by an Idiot*] should be read as *The Tempest* should be read, and as *Gulliver's Travels* should be read, for if Miss Macaulay's poetic gift happens to be less sublime than those of the author of the *Tempest,* and if her irony happens to be less tremendous than that of the author of *Gulliver's Travels*, her justice and wisdom are no less noble than theirs."—*The Daily News.*
     The next day we read: "For the rest one can only say that if Mr. Eliot had been pleased to write in demotic English *The Waste Land* might not have been, as it just is to all but anthropologists, and literati, so much waste-paper."—*The Manchester Guardian.*
     . . .

"The Leaning Tower"[1]

A writer is a person who sits at a desk and keeps his eye fixed, as intently as he can, upon a certain object – that figure of speech may help to keep us steady on our path if we look at it for a moment. He is an artist who sits with a sheet of paper in front of him trying to copy what he sees. What is his object—his model? Nothing so simple as a painter's model; it is not a bowl of flowers, a naked figure, or a dish of apples and onions. Even the simplest story deals with more than one person, with more than one time. Characters begin young; they grow old; they move from scene to scene, from place to place. A writer has to keep his eye upon a model that moves, that changes, upon an object that is not one object but innumerable objects. Two words alone cover all that a writer looks at—they are, human life.

Let us look at the writer next. What do we see—only a person who sits with a pen in his hand in front of a sheet of paper? That tells us little or nothing. And we know very little.

Considering how much we talk about writers, how much they talk about themselves, it is odd how little we know about them. Why are they so common sometimes; then so rare? Why do they sometimes write nothing but masterpieces, then nothing but trash? And why should a family, like the Shelleys, like the Keatses, like the Brontës, suddenly burst into flame and bring to birth Shelley, Keats, and the Brontës? What are the conditions that bring about that explosion? There is no answer—naturally. Since we have not yet discovered the germ of influenza, how should we yet have discovered the germ of genius? We know even less about the mind than about the body. We have less evidence. It is less than two hundred years since people took an interest in themselves; Boswell was almost the first writer who thought that a man's life was worth writing a book about. Until we have more facts, more biographies, more autobiographies, we cannot know much about ordinary people, let alone about extraordinary people. Thus at present we have only theories about writers—a great many theories, but they all differ. The politician says that a writer is the product of the society in which he lives, as a screw is the product of a screw machine; the artist, that a writer is a heavenly apparition that slides across the sky, grazes the earth, and vanishes. To the psychologists a writer is an oyster; feed him on gritty facts, irritate him with ugliness, and by way of compensation, as they call it, he will produce a pearl. The genealogists say that certain stocks, certain families, breed writers as fig trees breed figs—Dryden, Swift, and Pope they tell us were all cousins. This proves that we are in the dark about writers; anybody can make a theory; the germ of a theory is almost always the wish to prove what the theorist wishes to believe.

Theories then are dangerous things. All the same we must risk making one this afternoon since we are going to discuss modern tendencies. Directly we speak of tendencies or movements we commit ourselves to the belief that there is some force, influence, outer pressure which is strong enough to stamp itself upon a whole group of different writers so that all their writing has a certain common likeness. We must then have a theory as to what this influence is. But let us always remember—influences are infinitely numerous; writers are infinitely sensitive; each writer has a different sensibility. That is why literature is always changing, like the weather, like the clouds in the sky. Read a page of Scott; then of Henry James; try to work out the influences that have transformed the one page into the other. It is beyond our skill. We can only hope therefore to single out the most obvious influences that have formed writers into groups. Yet there are groups. Books descend from books as families descend from families. Some descend from Jane Austen; others from Dickens. They resemble their parents, as human children resemble their parents; yet they differ as children differ, and revolt as children revolt. Perhaps it will be easier to understand living writers as we take a quick look at some of their forebears. We have not time to go far back—certainly we have not time to look closely. But let us glance at English writers as they were a hundred years ago—that may help us to see what we ourselves look like.

In 1815 England was at war, as England is now. And it is natural to ask, how did their war—the Napoleonic war—affect them? Was that one of the influences that formed them into groups? The answer is a very strange one. The Napoleonic wars did not affect the great majority of those writers at all. The proof of that is to be found in the work of two great novelists—Jane Austen and Walter Scott. Each lived through the Napoleonic wars; each wrote through them. But, though novelists live very close to the life of their time, neither of them in all their novels mentioned the Napoleonic wars. This shows that their model, their vision of human life, was not disturbed or agitated or changed by war. Nor were they themselves. It is easy to see why that was so. Wars were then remote; wars were carried on by soldiers and sailors, not by private people. The rumour of battles took a long time to reach England. It was only when the mail coaches clattered along the country roads hung with laurels that the people in villages like Brighton knew that a victory had been won and lit their candles and stuck them in their windows. Compare that with our state today. Today we hear the gunfire in the Channel. We turn on the wireless; we hear an airman telling us how this very afternoon he shot down a raider; his machine caught fire; he plunged into the sea; the light turned green and then black; he rose to the top and was rescued by a trawler. Scott never saw the sailors drowning at Trafalgar; Jane Austen never heard the cannon roar at Waterloo. Neither of them heard Napoleon's voice as we hear Hitler's voice as we sit at home of an evening.

That immunity from war lasted all through the nineteenth century. England, of course, was often at war – there was the Crimean War; the Indian Mutiny; all the little Indian frontier wars, and at the end of the century the Boer War. Keats, Shelley, Byron, Dickens, Thackeray, Carlyle, Ruskin, the Brontës, George Eliot, Trollope, the Brownings—all lived through all those wars. But did they ever mention them? Only Thackeray, I think; in *Vanity Fair* he described the Battle of Waterloo long after it was fought; but only as an illustration, as a scene. It did not change his characters' lives; it merely killed one of his heroes. Of the poets, only Byron and Shelley felt the influence of the nineteenth-century wars profoundly.

War then we can say, speaking roughly, did not affect either the writer or his vision of human life in the nineteenth century. But peace—let us consider the influence of peace. Were the nineteenth-century writers affected by the settled, the peaceful and prosperous state of England? Let us collect a few facts before we launch out into the dangers and delights of theory. We know for a fact, from their lives, that the nineteenth-century writers were all of them fairly well-to-do middle-class people. Most had been educated either at Oxford or at Cambridge. Some were civil servants like Trollope and Matthew Arnold. Others, like Ruskin, were professors. It is a fact that their work brought them considerable fortunes. There is visible proof of that in the houses they built. Look at Abbotsford, bought out of the proceeds of Scott's novels; or at Farringford, built by Tennyson from his poetry. Look at Dickens's great house in Marylebone; and at his great house at Gadshill. All these are houses needing many butlers, maids, gardeners, grooms to keep the tables spread, the cans carried, and the gardens neat and fruitful. Not only did they leave behind them large houses; they left too an immense body of literature—poems, plays, novels, essays, histories, criticism. It was a very prolific, creative, rich century—the nineteenth century. Now let us ask—is there any connection between that material prosperity and that intellectual creativeness? Did one lead to the other? How difficult it is to say—for we know so little about writers, and what conditions help them, what hinder them. It is only a guess, and a rough guess; yet I think that there is a connection. "I think"—perhaps it would be nearer the truth to say "I see." Thinking should be based on facts; and here we have intuitions rather than facts—the lights and shades that come after books are read, the general shifting surface of a large expanse of print. What I see, glancing over that shifting surface, is the picture I have already shown you; the writer seated in front of human life in the nineteenth century; and, looking at it through their eyes, I see that life divided up, herded together, into many different classes. There is the aristocracy; the landed gentry; the professional class; the commercial class; the working class; and there, in one dark blot, is that great class which is called simply and comprehensively "The Poor." To the nineteenth-century writer human life must have looked like a landscape cut up into separate fields. In each field was gathered a different group of people. Each to some extent had its own traditions; its own manners; its own speech; its own dress; its own occupation. But owing to that peace, to that prosperity, each group was tethered, stationary—a herd grazing within its own hedges. And the nineteenth-century writer did not seek to change those divisions; he accepted them. He accepted them so completely that he became unconscious of them. Does that serve to explain why it is that the nineteenth-century writers are able to create so many characters who are not types but individuals? Is it because he did not see the hedges that divide classes; he saw only the human beings that live within those hedges? Is that why he could get beneath the surface and create many-sided characters—Pecksniff,

Becky Sharp, Mr. Woodhouse—who change with the years, as the living change? To us now the hedges are visible. We can see now that each of those writers only dealt with a very small section of human life—all Thackeray's characters are upper middle-class people; all Dickens's characters come from the lower or middle class. We can see that now; but the writer himself seems unconscious that he is only dealing with one type; with the type formed by the class into which the writer was born himself, with which he is most familiar. And that unconsciousness was an immense advantage to him.

Unconsciousness, which means presumably that the under-mind works at top speed while the upper-mind drowses, is a state we all know. We all have experience of the work done by unconsciousness in our own daily lives. You have had a crowded day, let us suppose, sightseeing in London. Could you say what you had seen and done when you came back? Was it not all a blur, a confusion? But after what seemed a rest, a chance to turn aside and look at something different, the sights and sounds and sayings that had been of most interest to you swam to the surface, apparently of their own accord; and remained in memory; what was unimportant sank into forgetfulness. So it is with the writer. After a hard day's work, trudging round, seeing all he can, feeling all he can, taking in the book of his mind innumerable notes, the writer becomes—if he can—unconscious. In fact, his under-mind works at top speed while his upper-mind drowses. Then, after a pause the veil lifts; and there is the thing—the thing he wants to write about—simplified, composed. Do we strain Wordsworth's famous saying about emotion recollected in tranquillity when we infer that by tranquillity he meant that the writer needs to become unconscious before he can create?

If we want to risk a theory, then, we can say that peace and prosperity were influences that gave the nineteenth-century writers a family likeness. They had leisure; they had security; life was not going to change; they themselves were not going to change. They could look; and look away. They could forget; and then—in their books – remember. Those then are some of the conditions that brought about a certain family likeness, in spite of the great individual differences, among the nineteenth-century writers. The nineteenth century ended; but the same conditions went on. They lasted, roughly speaking, till the year 1914. Even in 1914 we can still see the writer sitting as he sat all through the nineteenth century looking at human life; and that human life is still divided into classes; he still looks most intently at the class from which he himself springs; the classes are still so settled that he has almost forgotten that there are classes; and he is still so secure himself that he is almost unconscious of his own position and of its security. He believes that he is looking at the whole of life; and will always so look at it. That is not altogether a fancy picture. Many of those writers are still alive. Sometimes they describe their own position as young men, beginning to write, just before August 1914. How did you learn your art? one can ask them. At College they say—by reading; by listening; by talking. What did they talk about? Here is Mr. Desmond MacCarthy's answer, as he gave it, a week or two ago, in the *Sunday Times*. He was at Cambridge just before the war began and he says: "We were not very much interested in politics. Abstract speculation was much more absorbing; philosophy was more interesting to us than public causes. . . . What we chiefly discussed were those 'goods' which were ends in themselves . . . the search for truth, esthetic emotions and personal relations." In addition they read an immense amount; Latin and Greek, and of course French and English. They wrote too—but they were in no hurry to publish. They travelled;—some of them went far afield—to India, to the South Seas. But for the most part they rambled happily in the long summer holidays through England, through France, through Italy. And now and then they published books— books like Rupert Brooke's poems; novels like E. M. Forster's *Room with a View*; essays like G. K. Chesterton's essays, and reviews. It seemed to them that they were to go on living like that, and writing like that, for ever and ever. Then suddenly, like a chasm in a smooth road, the war came.

But before we go on with the story of what happened after 1914, let us look more closely for a moment, not at the writer himself, nor at his model; but at his chair. A chair is a very important part of a writer's outfit. It is the chair that gives him his attitude towards his model; that decides what he sees of human life; that profoundly affects his power of telling us what he sees. By his chair we mean his upbringing, his education. It is a fact, not a theory, that all writers from Chaucer to the present day, with so few exceptions that one hand can count them, have sat upon the same kind of chair—a raised chair. They have all come from the middle class; they have had good, at least expensive, educations. They have all been raised above the mass of people upon a tower of stucco—that is their middle-class birth; and of gold—that is their expensive education. That was true of all the nineteenth-century writers, save Dickens; it was true of all the 1914 writers, save D. H. Lawrence. Let us run through what are called "representative names": G. K. Chesterton; T. S. Eliot; Belloc; Lytton Strachey; Somerset Maugham; Hugh Walpole; Wilfred Owen; Rupert Brooke; J. E. Flecker; E. M. Forster; Aldous Huxley; G. M. Trevelyan; O. and S. Sitwell; Middleton Murry. Those are some of them; and all, with the exception of D. H. Lawrence, came of the middle class, and were educated at public schools and universities. There is another fact, equally indisputable: the books that they wrote were among the best books written between 1910 and 1925. Now let us ask, is there any connection between those facts? Is there a connection between the excellence of their work and the fact that they came of families rich enough to send them to public schools and universities?

Must we not decide, greatly though those writers differ, and shallow as we admit our knowledge of influences to be, that there must be a connection between their education and their work? It cannot be a mere chance that this minute class of educated people has produced so much that is good as writing; and that the vast mass of people without education has produced so little that is good. It is a fact, however. Take away all that the working class has given to English literature and that literature would scarcely suffer; take away all that the educated class has given, and English literature would scarcely exist. Education must then play a very important part in a writer's work.

That seems so obvious that it is astonishing how little stress has been laid upon the writer's education. It is perhaps because a writer's education is so much less definite than other educations. Reading, listening, talking, travel, leisure—many different things it seems are mixed together. Life and books must be shaken and taken in the right proportions. A boy brought up alone in a library turns into a book worm; brought up alone in the fields he turns into an earth worm. To breed the kind of butterfly a writer is you must let him sun himself for three or four years at Oxford or Cambridge—so it seems. However it is done, it is there that it is done—there that he is taught his art. And he has to be taught his art. Again, is that strange? Nobody thinks it strange if you say that a painter has to be taught his art; or a musician; or an architect. Equally a writer has to be taught. For the art of writing is at least as difficult as the other arts. And though, perhaps because the education is indefinite, people ignore this education; if you look closely you will see that almost every writer who has practised his art successfully had been taught it. He had been taught it by about eleven years of education—at private schools, public schools, and universities. He sits upon a tower raised above the rest of us; a tower built first on his parents' station, then on his parents' gold. It is a tower of the utmost importance; it decides his angle of vision; it affects his power of communication.

All through the nineteenth century, down to August 1914, that tower was a steady tower. The writer was scarcely conscious either of his high station or of his limited vision. Many of them had sympathy, great sympathy, with other classes; they wished to help the working class to enjoy the advantages of the tower class; but they did not wish to destroy the tower, or to descend from it—rather to make it accessible to all. Nor had the model, human life, changed essentially since Trollope looked at it, since Hardy looked at it: and Henry James, in 1914, was still looking at it. Further, the tower itself held firm beneath the writer during all the most impressionable years, when he was learning his art, and receiving all those complex influences and instructions that are summed up by the word education. These were conditions that influenced their work profoundly. For when the crash came in 1914 all those young men, who were to be the representative writers of their time, had their past, their education, safe behind them, safe within them. They had known security; they had the memory of a peaceful boyhood, the knowledge of a settled civilisation. Even though the war cut into their lives, and ended some of them, they wrote, and still write, as if the tower were firm beneath them. In one word, they are aristocrats; the unconscious inheritors of a great tradition. Put a page of their writing under the magnifying-glass and you will see, far away in the distance, the Greeks, the Romans; coming nearer, the Elizabethans; coming nearer still, Dryden, Swift, Voltaire, Jane Austen, Dickens, Henry James. Each, however much he differs individually from the others, is a man of education; a man who has learnt his art.

From that group let us pass to the next—to the group which began to write about 1925 and, it may be, came to an end as a group in 1939. If you read current literary journalism you will be able to rattle off a string of names – Day Lewis, Auden, Spender, Isherwood, Louis MacNeice and so on. They adhere much more closely than the names of their predecessors. But at first sight there seems little difference, in station, in education. Mr. Auden in a poem written to Mr. Isherwood says: Behind us we have stucco suburbs and expensive educations. They are tower dwellers like their predecessors, the sons of well-to-do parents, who could afford to send them to public schools and universities. But what a difference in the tower itself, in what they saw from the tower! When they looked at human life what did they see? Everywhere change; everywhere revolution. In Germany, in Russia, in Italy, in Spain, all the old hedges were being rooted up; all the old towers were being thrown to the ground. Other hedges were being planted; other towers were being raised. There was communism in one country; in another fascism. The whole of civilisation, of society, was changing. There was, it is true, neither war nor revolution in England itself. All those writers had time to write many books before 1939. But even in England towers that were built of gold and stucco were no longer steady towers. They were leaning towers. The books were written under the influence of change, under the threat of war. That perhaps is why the names adhere so closely; there was one influence that affected them all and made them, more than their predecessors, into groups. And that influence, let us remember, may well have excluded from that string of names the poets whom posterity will value most highly, either because they could not fall into step, as leaders or as followers, or because the influence was adverse to poetry, and until that influence relaxed, they could not write. But the tendency that makes it possible for us to group the names of these writers together, and gives their work a common likeness, was the tendency of the tower they sat on—the tower of middle-class birth and expensive education—to lean.

Let us imagine, to bring this home to us, that we are actually upon a leaning tower and note our sensations. Let us see whether they correspond to the tendencies we observe in those poems, plays, and novels. Directly we feel that a tower leans we become acutely conscious that we are upon a tower. All those writers too are acutely tower conscious; conscious of their middle-class birth; of their expensive educations. Then when we come to the top of the tower how strange the view looks—not altogether upside down, but slanting, sidelong. That too is characteristic of the leaning-tower writers; they do not look any class straight in the face; they look either up, or down, or sidelong. There is no class so settled that they can explore it unconsciously. That perhaps is why they create no characters. Then what do we feel next, raised in imagination on top of the tower? First discomfort; next self-pity for that discomfort; which pity soon turns to anger—to anger against the builder, against society, for making us uncomfortable. Those too seem to be tendencies of the leaning-tower writers. Discomfort; pity for themselves; anger against society. And yet—here is another tendency—how can you altogether abuse a society that is giving you, after all, a very fine view and some sort of security? You cannot abuse that society whole-heartedly while you continue to profit by that society. And so very naturally you abuse society in the person of some retired admiral or spinster or armament manufacturer; and by abusing them hope to escape whipping yourself. The bleat of the scapegoat sounds loud in their work, and the whimper of the schoolboy crying "Please, Sir, it was the other fellow, not me." Anger; pity; scapegoat beating; excuse finding—these are all very natural tendencies; if we were in their position we should tend to do the same. But we are not in their position; we have not had eleven years of expensive education. We have only been climbing an imaginary tower. We can cease to imagine. We can come down.

But they cannot. They cannot throw away their education; they cannot throw away their upbringing. Eleven years at school and college have been stamped upon them indelibly. And then, to their credit but to their confusion, the leaning tower not only leant in the thirties, but it leant more and more to the left. Do you remember what Mr. MacCarthy said about his own group at the university in 1914? "We were not very much interested in politics . . . philosophy was more interesting to us than public causes"? That shows that his tower leant neither to the right nor to the left. But in 1930 it was impossible—if you were young, sensitive, imaginative—not to be interested in politics; not to find public causes of much more pressing interest than philosophy. In 1930 young men at college were forced to be aware of what was happening in Russia; in Germany; in Italy; in Spain. They could not go on discussing esthetic emotions and personal relations. They could not confine their reading to the poets; they had to read the politicians. They read Marx. They became communists; they became antifascists. The tower they realised was founded upon injustice and tyranny; it was wrong for a small class to possess an education that other people paid for; wrong to stand upon the gold that a bourgeois father had made from his bourgeois profession. It was wrong; yet how could they make it right? Their education could not be thrown away; as for their capital—did Dickens, did Tolstoy ever throw away their capital? Did D. H. Lawrence, a miner's son, continue to live like a miner? No; for it is death for a writer to throw away his capital; to be forced to earn his living in a mine or a factory. And thus, trapped by their education, pinned down by their capital, they remained on top of their leaning tower, and their state of mind as we see it reflected in their poems and plays and novels is full of discord and bitterness, full of confusion and of compromise.

These tendencies are better illustrated by quotation than by analysis. There is a poem by one of those writers, Louis MacNeice, called *Autumn Journal*. It is dated March 1939. It is feeble as poetry, but interesting as autobiography. He begins of course with a snipe at the scapegoat—the bourgeois, middle-class family from which he sprang. The retired admirals, the retired generals, and the spinster lady have breakfasted off bacon and eggs served on a silver dish, he tells us. He sketches that family as if it were already a little remote and more than a little ridiculous. But they could afford to send him to Marlborough and then to Merton, Oxford. This is what he learnt at Oxford:

> We learned that a gentleman never misplaces his accents,
> That nobody knows how to speak, much less how to write
> English who has not hob-nobbed with the great-grandparents of English.

Besides that he learnt at Oxford Latin and Greek; and philosophy, logic, and metaphysics:

> Oxford, *he says*, crowded the mantelpiece with gods—
> Scaliger, Heinsius, Dindorf, Bentley, Wilamowitz.

It was at Oxford that the tower began to lean. He felt that he was living under a system—

> That gives the few at fancy prices their fancy lives
> While ninety-nine in the hundred who never attend the banquet
> Must wash the grease of ages off the knives.

But at the same time, an Oxford education had made him fastidious:

> It is so hard to imagine
> A world where the many would have their chance without
> A fall in the standard of intellectual living
> And nothing left that the highbrow cares about.

At Oxford he got his honours degree; and that degree – in humane letters—put him in the way of a "cushy job"—seven hundred a year, to be precise, and several rooms of his own.

> If it were not for Lit. Hum. I might be climbing
> A ladder with a hod,
> And seven hundred a year
> Will pay the rent and the gas and the phone and the grocer—

And yet, again, doubts break in; the "cushy job" of teaching more Latin and Greek to more undergraduates does not satisfy him—

> . . . the so-called humane studies
> May lead to cushy jobs
> But leave the men who land them spiritually bankrupt,
> Intellectual snobs.

And what is worse, that education and that cushy job cut one off, he complains, from the common life of one's kind.

> All that I would like to be is human, having a share
> In a civilised, articulate and well-adjusted
> Community where the mind is given its due
> But the body is not distrusted.

Therefore in order to bring about that well-adjusted community he must turn from literature to politics, remembering, he says,

> Remembering that those who by their habit
> Hate politics, can no longer keep their private
> Values unless they open the public gate
> To a better political system.

So, in one way or another, he takes part in politics, and finally he ends:

> What is it we want really?
> For what end and how?
> If it is something feasible, obtainable,

Let us dream it now,
And pray for a possible land
Not of sleep-walkers, not of angry puppets,
But where both heart and brain can understand
The movements of our fellows,
Where life is a choice of instruments and none
Is debarred his natural music . . .
Where the individual, no longer squandered
In self-assertion, works with the rest . . .

Those quotations give a fair description of the influences that have told upon the leaning-tower group. Others could easily be discovered. The influence of the films explains the lack of transitions in their work and the violently opposed contrasts. The influence of poets like Mr. Yeats and Mr. Eliot explains the obscurity. They took over from the elder poets a technique which, after many years of experiment, those poets used skilfully, and used it clumsily and often inappropriately. But we have time only to point to the most obvious influences; and these can be summed up as Leaning Tower Influences. If you think of them, that is, as people trapped on a leaning tower from which they cannot descend, much that is puzzling in their work is easier to understand. It explains the violence of their attack upon bourgeois society and also its half-heartedness. They are profiting by a society which they abuse. They are flogging a dead or dying horse because a living horse, if flogged, would kick them off its back. It explains the destructiveness of their work; and also its emptiness. They can destroy bourgeois society, in part at least; but what have they put in its place? How can a writer who has no first-hand experience of a towerless, of a classless society create that society? Yet as Mr. MacNeice bears witness, they feel compelled to preach, if not by their living, at least by their writing, the creation of a society in which every one is equal and every one is free. It explains the pedagogic, the didactic, the loud speaker strain that dominates their poetry. They must teach; they must preach. Everything is a duty—even love. Listen to Mr. Day Lewis ingeminating love. "Mr. Spender," he says, "speaking from the living unit of himself and his friends appeals for the contraction of the social group to a size at which human contact may again be established and demands the destruction of all impediments to love. Listen." And we listen to this:

We have come at last to a country
Where light, like shine from snow, strikes all faces.
Here you may wonder
How it was that works, money, interest, building could ever
Hide the palpable and obvious love of man for man.

We listen to oratory, not poetry. It is necessary, in order to feel the emotion of those lines, that other people should be listening too. We are in a group, in a class-room as we listen.

Listen now to Wordsworth:

Lover had he known in huts where poor men dwell,
His daily teachers had been woods and rills,
The silence that is in the starry sky,
The sleep that is among the lonely hills.

We listen to that when we are alone. We remember that in solitude. Is that the difference between politician's poetry and poet's poetry? We listen to the one in company; to the other when we are alone? But the poet in the thirties was forced to be a politician. That explains why the artist in the thirties was forced to be a scapegoat. If politics were "real," the ivory tower was an escape from "reality." That explains the curious, bastard language in which so much of this leaning-tower prose and poetry is written. It is not the rich speech of the aristocrat: it is not the racy speech of the peasant. It is betwixt and between. The poet is a dweller in two worlds, one dying, the other struggling to be born. And so we come to what is perhaps the most marked tendency of leaning-tower literature—the desire to be whole; to be human. "All that I would like to be is human"—that cry rings through their books—the longing to be closer to their kind, to write the common speech of their kind, to share the emotions of their kind, no longer to be isolated and exalted in solitary state upon their tower, but to be down on the ground with the mass of human kind.

These then, briefly and from a certain angle, are some of the tendencies of the modern writer who is seated upon a leaning tower. No other generation has been exposed to them. It may be that none has had such an appallingly difficult task. Who can wonder if they have been incapable of giving us great poems, great plays, great novels? They had nothing settled to look at; nothing peaceful to remember; nothing certain to come. During all the most impressionable years of their lives they were stung into consciousness—into self-consciousness, into class-consciousness, into the consciousness of things changing, of things falling, of death perhaps about to come. There was no tranquillity in which they could recollect. The inner mind was paralysed because the surface mind was always hard at work.

Yet if they have lacked the creative power of the poet and the novelist, the power—does it come from a fusion of the two minds, the upper and the under?—that creates characters that live, poems that we all remember, they have had a power which, if literature continues, may prove to be of great value in the future. They have been great egotists. That too was forced upon them by their circumstances. When everything is rocking round one, the only person who remains comparatively stable is oneself. When all faces are changing and obscured, the only face one can see clearly is one's own. So they wrote about themselves—in their plays, in their poems, in their novels. No other ten years can have produced so much autobiography as the ten years between 1930 and 1940. No one, whatever his class or his obscurity, seems to have reached the age of thirty without writing his autobiography. But the leaning-tower writers wrote about themselves honestly, therefore creatively. They told the unpleasant truths, not only the flattering truths. That is why their autobiography is so much better than their fiction or their poetry. Consider how difficult it is to tell the truth about oneself—the unpleasant truth; to admit that one is petty, vain, mean, frustrated, tortured, unfaithful, and unsuccessful. The nineteenth-century writers never told that kind of truth, and that is why so much of the nineteenth-century writing is worthless; why, for all their genius, Dickens and Thackeray seem so often to write about dolls and puppets, not about full-grown men and women; why they are forced to evade the main themes and make do with diversions instead. If you do not tell the truth about yourself you cannot tell it about other people. As the nineteenth century wore on, the writers knew that they were crippling themselves, diminishing their material, falsifying their object. "We are condemned," Stevenson wrote, "to avoid half the life that passes us by. What books Dickens could have written had he been permitted! Think of Thackeray as unfettered as Flaubert or Balzac! What books I might have written myself? But they give us a little box of toys and say to us 'You mustn't play with anything but these!'" Stevenson blamed society—bourgeois society was his scapegoat too. Why did he not blame himself? Why did he consent to go on playing with his little box of toys?

The leaning-tower writer has had the courage, at any rate, to throw that little box of toys out of the window. He has had the courage to tell the truth, the unpleasant truth, about himself. That is the first step towards telling the truth about other people. By analysing themselves honestly, with help from Dr. Freud, these writers have done a great deal to free us from nineteenth-century suppressions. The writers of the next generation may inherit from them a whole state of mind, a mind no longer crippled, evasive, divided. They may inherit that unconsciousness which, as we guessed—it is only a guess—at the beginning of this paper, is necessary if writers are to get beneath the surface, and to write something that people remember when they are alone. For that great gift of unconsciousness the next generation will have to thank the creative and honest egotism of the leaning-tower group.

The next generation—there will be a next generation, in spite of this war and whatever it brings. Have we time then for a rapid glance, for a hurried guess at the next generation? The next generation will be, when peace comes, a post-war generation too. Must it too be a leaning-tower generation—an oblique, sidelong, squinting, self-conscious generation with a foot in two worlds? Or will there be no more towers and no more classes and shall we stand, without hedges between us, on the common ground?

There are two reasons which lead us to think, perhaps to hope, that the world after the war will be a world without classes or towers. Every politician who has made a speech since September 1939 has ended with a peroration in which he has said that we are not fighting this war for conquest; but to bring about a new order in Europe. In that order, they tell us, we are all to have equal opportunities, equal chances of developing whatever gifts we may possess. That is one reason why, if they mean what they say, and can effect it, classes and towers will disappear. The other reason is given by the income tax. The income tax is already doing in its own way what the politicians are hoping to do in theirs. The income tax is saying to middle-class parents: You cannot afford to send your sons to public schools any longer; you must send them to the elementary schools. One of these parents wrote to the *New Statesman* a week or two ago. Her little boy, who was to have gone to Winchester, had been taken away from his elementary school and sent to the village school. "He has never been happier in his life," she wrote. "The question of class does not arise; he is merely interested to find how many different kinds of people there are in the world . . . ." And she is only paying twopence-halfpenny a week for that happiness and instruction instead of 35 guineas a term and extras. If the pressure of the income tax continues, classes will disappear. There will be no more upper classes; middle classes; lower classes. All classes will be merged in one class. How will that change affect the writer who sits at his desk looking at human life? It will not be divided by hedges any more. Very likely that will be the end of the novel, as we know it. Literature, as we know it, is always ending, and beginning again. Remove the hedges from Jane Austen's world, from Trollope's world, and how much of their comedy and tragedy would remain? We shall regret our Jane Austens and our Trollopes; they gave us comedy, tragedy, and beauty. But much of that old-class literature was very petty; very false; very dull. Much is already unreadable. The novel of a classless and towerless world should be a better novel than the old novel. The novelist will have more interesting people to describe— people who have had a chance to develop their humour, their gifts, their tastes; real people, not people cramped and squashed into featureless masses by hedges. The poet's gain is less obvious; for he has been less under the dominion of hedges. But he should gain words; when we have pooled all the different dialects, the clipped and cabined vocabulary which is all that he uses now should be enriched. Further, there might then be a common belief which he could accept, and thus shift from his shoulders the burden of didacticism, of propaganda. These then are a few reasons, hastily snatched, why we can look forward hopefully to a stronger, a more varied literature in the classless and towerless society of the future.

But it is in the future; and there is a deep gulf to be bridged between the dying world and the world that is struggling to be born. For there are still two worlds, two separate worlds. "I want," said the mother who wrote to the paper the other day about her boy, "the best of both worlds for my son." She wanted, that is, the village school, where he learnt to mix with the living; and the other school—Winchester it was—where he mixed with the dead. "Is he to continue," she asked, "under the system of free national education, or shall he go on—or should I say back – to the old public-school system which really is so very, very private?" She wanted the new world and the old world to unite, the world of the present and the world of the past.

But there is still a gulf between them, a dangerous gulf, in which, possibly, literature may crash and come to grief. It is easy to see that gulf; it is easy to lay the blame for it upon England. England has crammed a small aristocratic class with Latin and Greek and logic and metaphysics and mathematics until they cry out like the young men on the leaning tower, "All that I would like to be is human." She has left the other class, the immense class to which almost all of us must belong, to pick up what we can in village schools; in factories; in work-shops; behind counters; and at home. When one thinks of that criminal injustice one is tempted to say England deserves to have no literature. She deserves to have nothing but detective stories, patriotic songs, and leading articles for generals, admirals, and business men to read themselves to sleep with when they are tired of winning battles and making money. But let us not be unfair; let us avoid if we can joining the embittered and futile tribe of scapegoat hunters. For some years now England has been making an effort—at last—to bridge the gulf between the two worlds. Here is one proof of that effort—this book. This book was not bought; it was not hired. It was borrowed from a public library. England lent it to a common reader, saying "It is time that even you, whom I have shut out from all my universities for centuries, should learn to read your mother tongue. I will help you." If England is going to help us, we must help her. But how? Look at what is written in the book she has lent us. "Readers are requested to point out any defects that they may observe to the local librarian." That is England's way of saying: "If I lend you books, I expect you to make yourselves critics."

We can help England very greatly to bridge the gulf between the two worlds if we borrow the books she lends us and if we read them critically. We have got to teach ourselves to understand literature. Money is no longer going to do our thinking for us. Wealth will no longer decide who shall be taught and who not. In future it is we who shall decide whom to send to public schools and universities; how they shall be taught; and whether what they write justifies their exemption from other work. In order to do that we must teach ourselves to distinguish—which is the book that is going to pay dividends of pleasure for ever; which is the book that will pay not a penny in two years' time? Try it for yourselves on new books as they come out; decide which are the lasting, which are the perishing. That is very difficult. Also we must become critics because in future we are not going to leave writing to be done for us by a small class of well-to-do young men who have only a pinch, a thimbleful of experience to give us. We are going to add our own experience, to make our own contribution. That is even more difficult. For that too we need to be critics. A writer, more than any other artist, needs to be a critic because words are so common, so familiar, that he must sieve them and sift them if they are to become enduring. Write daily; write freely; but let us always compare what we have written with what the great writers have written. It is humiliating, but it is essential. If we are going to preserve and to create, that is the only way. And we are going to do both. We need not wait till the end of the war. We can begin now. We can begin, practically and prosaically, by borrowing books from public libraries, by reading omnivo-rously, simultaneously, poems, plays, novels, histories, biographies, the old and the new. We must sample before we can select. It never does to be a nice feeder; each of us has an appetite that must find for itself the food that nourishes it. Nor let us shy away from the kings because we are commoners. That is a fatal crime in the eyes of Aeschylus, Shakespeare, Virgil, and Dante, who, if they could speak—and after all they can—would say, "Don't leave me to the wigged and gowned. Read me, read me for yourselves." They do not mind if we get our accents wrong, or have to read with a crib in front of us. Of course—are we not commoners, outsiders?—we shall trample many flowers and bruise much ancient grass. But let us bear in mind a piece of advice that an eminent Victorian who was also an eminent pedestrian once gave to walkers: "Whenever you see a board up with 'Trespassers will be prosecuted,' trespass at once."

Let us trespass at once. Literature is no one's private ground; literature is common ground. It is not cut up into nations; there are no wars there. Let us trespass freely and fearlessly and find our own way for ourselves. It is thus that English literature will survive this war and cross the gulf—if commoners and outsiders like ourselves make that country our own country, if we teach ourselves how to read and to write, how to preserve, and how to create.

Note

1 A paper read to the Workers' Educational Association, Brighton, May 1940.

Chapter 68

E.M. Forster (1879–1970)

"VIRGINIA WOOLF" (1941)

FORSTER, A CLOSE FRIEND OF Woolf's, appraised her writing career and achievements in the novel form shortly after her death. He levels some of the same critiques of Woolf's work that Arnold Bennett did; namely, that she did not create memorable characters and that her works were sometimes too preoccupied with form and design. While praising her creative daring and the sensual vividness of her work, Forster describes Woolf as a poet at heart, one who wanted "to write something as near to the novel as possible" (251). Woolf's feminist works, such as her "cantankerous" *Three Guineas* (1938), greatly discomfited Forster; having little interest in his friend's critiques of patriarchy, he failed to appreciate what subsequent readers praise: the essay's subversive wit and feminist historiography. Forster's view of Woolf as a product of a refined, upper-middle class world can also be heard echoing in his voice; his more resonant tribute to Woolf is as a passionate and committed writer who "pushed the light of the English language a little further against darkness" (258).

E.M. Forster, "Virginia Woolf," *Two Cheers for Democracy.* New York: Harcourt, Brace, 1951. 242–58.

When I was appointed to this lectureship the work of Virginia Woolf was much in my mind, and I asked to be allowed to speak on it. To speak on it, rather than to sum it up. There are two obstacles to a summing up. The first is the work's richness and complexity. As soon as we dismiss the legend of the Invalid Lady of Bloomsbury, so guilelessly accepted by Arnold Bennett, we find ourselves in a bewildering world where there are few headlines. We think of *The Waves* and say "Yes—that is Virginia Woolf"; then we think of *The Common Reader*, where she is different, of *A Room of One's Own* or of the preface to *Life as we have known it*: different again. She is like a plant which is supposed to grow in a well-prepared garden bed—the bed of esoteric literature—and then pushes up suckers all over the place, through the gravel of the front drive, and even through the flagstones of the kitchen yard. She was full of interests, and their number increased as she grew older, she was curious about life, and she was tough, sensitive but tough. How can her achievement be summed up in an hour? A headline sometimes serves a lecturer as a life-line on these occasions, and brings him safely into the haven where he would be. Shall I find one today? The second obstacle is that 1941 is not a good year in which to sum up anything. Our judgments, to put it mildly, are not at their prime. We are all of us upon the Leaning Tower, as she called it, even those of us who date from the nineteenth century, when the earth was still horizontal and the buildings perpendicular. We cannot judge the landscape properly as we look down, for everything is tilted. Isolated objects are not so puzzling; a tree, a wave, a hat, a jewel, an old gentleman's bald head look much as they always did. But the relation between objects—that we cannot estimate, and that is why the verdict must be left to another generation. I have not the least faith that anything which we now value will survive historically (something which we should have valued may evolve, but that is a different proposition); and maybe another generation will dismiss Virginia Woolf as worthless and tiresome. However, this is not my opinion, nor I think yours; we still have the word, and I wonder whether I cannot transmit some honour to her from the university she so admired, and from the central building of that university. She would receive the homage a little mockingly, for she was somewhat astringent over the academic position of women. "What? I in the Senate House?" she might say. "Are you sure that is quite proper? And why, if you want to discuss my books, need you first disguise yourselves in caps and gowns?" But I think she would be pleased. She loved Cambridge. Indeed, I cherish a private fancy that she once took her degree here. She, who could disguise herself as a member of the suite of the Sultan of Zanzibar, or black her face to go aboard a Dreadnought as an Ethiopian[1]—she could surely have hoaxed our innocent praelectors, and, kneeling in this very spot, have presented to the Vice-Chancellor the exquisite but dubious head of Orlando.

There is, after all, one little life-line to catch hold of: she liked writing.

These words, which usually mean so little, must be applied to her with all possible intensity. She liked receiving sensations—sights, sounds, tastes—passing them through her mind, where they encountered theories and memories, and then bringing them out again, through a pen, on to a bit of paper. Now began the higher delights of authorship. For these pen-marks on paper were only the prelude to writing, little more than marks on a wall. They had to be combined, arranged, emphasised here, eliminated there, new relationships had to be generated, new pen-marks born, until out of the interactions, something, one thing, one, arose. This one thing, whether it was a novel or an essay or a short story or a biography or a private paper to be read to her friends, was, if it was successful, itself analogous to a sensation. Although it was so complex and intellectual, although it might be large and heavy with facts, it was akin to the very simple things which had started it off, to the sights, sounds, tastes. It could be best described as we describe them. For it was not about something. It was something. This is obvious in "esthetic" works, like *Kew Gardens* and *Mrs. Dalloway*; it is less obvious in a work of learning, like the *Roger Fry*, yet here too the analogy holds. We know, from an article by R. C. Trevelyan, that she had, when writing it, a notion corresponding to the notion of a musical composition. In the first chapter she stated the themes, in the subsequent chapters she developed them separately, and she tried to bring them all in again at the end. The biography is duly about Fry. But it is something else too; it is one thing, one.

She liked writing with an intensity which few writers have attained, or even desired. Most of them write with half an eye on their royalties, half an eye on their critics, and a third half eye on improving the world, which leaves them with only half an eye for the task on which she concentrated her entire vision. She would not look elsewhere, and her circumstances combined with her temperament to focus her. Money she had not to consider, because she possessed a private income, and though financial independence is not always a safeguard against commercialism, it was in her case. Critics she never considered while she was writing, although she could be attentive to them and even humble afterwards. Improving the world she would not consider, on the ground that the world is man-made, and that she, a woman, had no responsibility for the mess. This last opinion is a curious one, and I shall be returning to it; still, she held it, it completed the circle of her defences, and neither the desire for money nor the desire for reputation nor philanthropy could influence her. She had a singleness of purpose which will not recur in this country for many years, and writers who have liked writing as she liked it have not indeed been common in any age.

Now the pitfall for such an author is obvious. It is the Palace of Art, it is that bottomless chasm of dullness which pretends to be a palace, all glorious with corridors and domes, but which is really a dreadful hole into which the unwary esthete may tumble, to be seen no more. She has all the esthete's characteristics: selects and manipulates her impressions; is not a great creator of character; enforces patterns on her books; has no great cause at heart. So how did she avoid her appropriate pitfall and remain up in the fresh air, where we can hear the sound of the stable boy's boots, or boats bumping, or Big Ben; where we can taste really new bread, and touch real dahlias?

She had a sense of humour, no doubt, but our answer must go a little deeper than that hoary nostrum. She escaped, I think, because she liked writing for fun. Her pen amused her, and in the midst of writing seriously this other delight would spurt through. A little essay, called *On being Ill*, exemplifies this. It starts with the thesis that illness in literature is seldom handled properly (de Quincey and Proust were exceptional), that the body is treated by novelists as if it were a sheet of glass through which the soul gazes, and that this is contrary to experience. There are possibilities in the thesis, but she soon wearies of exploring them. Off she goes amusing herself, and after half a dozen pages she is writing entirely for fun, caricaturing the type of people who visit sick-rooms, insisting that Augustus Hare's *Two Noble Lives* is the book an invalid most demands, and so on. She could describe illness if she chose—for instance, in *The Voyage Out*—but she gaily forgets it in *On being Ill*. The essay is slight, still it does neatly illustrate the habit of her mind. Literature was her merry-go-round as well as her study. This makes her amusing to read, and it also saves her from the Palace of Art. For you cannot enter the Palace of Art, therein to dwell, if you are tempted from time to time to play the fool. Lord Tennyson did not consider that. His remedy, you remember, was that the Palace would be purified when it was inhabited by all mankind, all behaving seriously at once. Virginia Woolf found a simpler and a sounder solution.

No doubt there is a danger here—there is danger everywhere. She might have become a glorified diseuse, who frittered away her broader effects by mischievousness, and she did give that impression to some who met her in the flesh; there were moments when she could scarcely see the busts for the moustaches she pencilled on them, and when the bust was a modern one, whether of a gentleman in a top hat or of a youth on a pylon, it had no chance of remaining sublime. But in her writing, even in her light writing, central control entered. She was master of her complicated equipment, and though most of us like to write sometimes seriously and sometimes in fun, few of us can so manage the two impulses that they speed each other up, as hers did.

The above remarks are more or less introductory. It seems convenient now to recall what she did write, and to say a little about her development. She began back in 1915 with *The Voyage Out*—a strange, tragic, inspired novel about English tourists in an impossible South American hotel; her passion for truth is here already, mainly in the form of atheism, and her passion for wisdom is here in the form of music. The book made a deep impression upon the few people who read it. Its successor, *Night and Day*, disappointed them. This is an exercise in classical realism, and contains all that has characterised English fiction, for good and evil, during the last two hundred years: faith in personal relations, recourse to humorous side-shows, geographical exactitude, insistence on petty social differences: indeed most of the devices she so gaily derides in *Mr. Bennett and Mrs. Brown*. The style has been normalised and dulled. But at the same time she published two short stories, *Kew Gardens*, and *The Mark on the Wall.* These are neither dull nor normal; lovely little things; her style trails after her as she walks and talks, catching up dust and grass in its folds, and instead of the precision of the earlier writing we have something more elusive than had yet been achieved in English. Lovely little things, but they seemed to lead nowhere, they were all tiny dots and coloured blobs, they were an inspired breathlessness, they were a beautiful droning or gasping which trusted to luck. They were perfect as far as they went, but that was not far, and none of us guessed that out of the pollen of those flowers would come the trees of the future. Consequently when *Jacob's Room* appeared in 1922 we were tremendously surprised. The style and sensitiveness of *Kew Gardens* remained, but they were applied to human relationships, and to the structure of society. The blobs of colour continue to drift past, but in their midst, interrupting their course like a closely sealed jar, stands the solid figure of a young man. The improbable has occurred; a method essentially poetic and apparently trifling has been applied to fiction. She was still uncertain of the possibilities of the new technique, and *Jacob's Room* is an uneven little book, but it represents her great departure, and her abandonment of the false start of *Night and Day*. It leads on to her genius in its fullness; to *Mrs. Dalloway* (1925), *To the Lighthouse* (1927), and *The Waves* (1931). These successful works are all suffused with poetry and enclosed in it. *Mrs. Dalloway* has the framework of a London summer's day, down which go spiralling two fates: the fate of the sensitive worldly hostess, and the fate of the sensitive obscure maniac; though they never touch they are closely connected, and at the same moment we lose sight of them both. It is a civilised book, and it was written from personal experience. In her work, as in her private problems, she was always civilised and sane on the subject of madness. She pared the edges off this particular malady, she tied it down to being a malady, and robbed it of the evil magic it has acquired through timid or careless thinking; here is one of the gifts we have to thank her for. *To the Lighthouse* is, however, a much greater achievement, partly because the chief characters in it, Mr. and Mrs. Ramsay, are so interesting. They hold us, we think of them away from their surroundings, and yet they are in accord with those surroundings, with the poetic scheme. *To the Lighthouse* is in three movements. It has been called a novel in sonata form, and certainly the slow central section, conveying the passing of time, does demand a musical analogy. We have, when reading it, the rare pleasure of inhabiting two worlds at once, a pleasure only art can give: the world where a little boy wants to go to a lighthouse but never manages it until, with changed emotions, he goes there as a young man; and the world where there is pattern, and this world is emphasised by passing much of the observation through the mind of Lily Briscoe, who is a painter. Then comes *The Waves*. Pattern here is supreme—indeed it is italicised. And between the motions of the sun and the waters, which preface each section, stretch, without interruption, conversation, words in inverted commas. It is a strange conversation, for the six characters, Bernard, Neville, Louis, Susan, Jinny, Rhoda, seldom address one another, and it is even possible to regard them (like Mrs. Dalloway and Septimus) as different facets of one single person. Yet they do not conduct internal monologues, they are in touch amongst themselves, and they all touch the character who never speaks, Percival. At the end, most perfectly balancing their scheme, Bernard, the would-be novelist, sums up, and the pattern fades out. *The Waves* is an extraordinary achievement, an immense extension of the possibilities of *Kew Gardens* and *Jacob's Room*. It is trembling on the edge. A little less—and it would lose its poetry. A little more—and it would be over into the abyss, and be dull and arty. It is her greatest book, though *To the Lighthouse* is my favourite.

It was followed by *The Years*. This is another experiment in the realistic tradition. It chronicles the fortunes of a family through a documented period. As in *Night and Day*, she deserts poetry, and again she fails. But in her posthumous novel *Between the Acts* she returns to the method she understood. Its theme is a village pageant, which presents the entire history of England, and into which, at the close, the audience is itself drawn, to continue that history;

"The curtain rose" is its concluding phrase. The conception is poetic, and the text of the pageant is mostly written in verse. She loved her country—the country that is the country-side, and emerges from the unfathomable past. She takes us back in this exquisite final tribute, and she points us on, and she shows us through her poetic vagueness something more solid than patriotic history, and something better worth dying for.

Amongst all this fiction, nourishing it and nourished by it, grow other works. Two volumes of *The Common Reader* show the breadth of her knowledge and the depth of her literary sympathy; let anyone who thinks her an exquisite recluse read what she says on Jack Mytton the foxhunter. As a critic she could enter into anything—anything lodged in the past, that is to say; with her contemporaries she sometimes had difficulties. Then there are the biographies, fanciful and actual. *Orlando* is, I need hardly say, an original book, and the first part of it is splendidly written: the description of the Great Frost is already received as a "passage" in English literature, whatever a passage may be. After the transformation of sex things do not go so well; the authoress seems unconvinced by her own magic and somewhat fatigued by it, and the biography finishes competently rather than brilliantly; it has been a fancy on too large a scale, and we can see her getting bored. But *Flush* is a complete success, and exactly what it sets out to be; the material, the method, the length, accord perfectly, it is doggie without being silly, and it does give us, from the altitude of the carpet or the sofa-foot, a peep at high poetic personages, and a new angle on their ways. The biography of Roger Fry—one should not proceed direct from a spaniel to a Slade Professor, but Fry would not have minded and spaniels mind nothing—reveals a new aspect of her powers, the power to suppress herself. She indulges in a pattern, but she never intrudes her personality or over-handles her English; respect for her subject dominates her, and only occasionally—as in her description of the divinely ordered chaos of Fry's studio with its still-life of apples and eggs labelled "please do not touch"—does she allow her fancy to play. Biographies are too often described as "labours of love," but the *Roger Fry* really is in this class; one artist is writing with affection of another, so that he may be remembered and may be justified.

Finally, there are the feminist books—*A Room of One's Own* and *Three Guineas*—and several short essays, etc., some of them significant. It is as a novelist that she will be judged. But the rest of her work must be remembered, partly on its merits, partly because (as William Plomer has pointed out) she is sometimes more of a novelist in it than in her novels.

After this survey, we can state her problem. Like most novelists worth reading, she strays from the fictional norm. She dreams, designs, jokes, invokes, observes details, but she does not tell a story or weave a plot, and—can she create character? That is her problem's centre. That is the point where she felt herself open to criticism—to the criticisms, for instance, of her friend Hugh Walpole. Plot and story could be set aside in favour of some other unity, but if one is writing about human beings, one does want them to seem alive. Did she get her people to live?

Now there seem to be two sorts of life in fiction, life on the page, and life eternal. Life on the page she could give; her characters never seem unreal, however slight or fantastic their lineaments, and they can be trusted to behave appropriately. Life eternal she could seldom give; she could seldom so portray a character that it was remembered afterwards on its own account, as Emma is remembered, for instance, or Dorothea Casaubon, or Sophia and Constance in *The Old Wives' Tale*. What wraiths, apart from their context, are the wind-sextet from *The Waves*, or Jacob away from *Jacob's Room*! They speak no more to us or to one another as soon as the page is turned. And this is her great difficulty. Holding on with one hand to poetry, she stretches and stretches to grasp things which are best gained by letting go of poetry. She would not let go, and I think she was quite right, though critics who like a novel to be a novel will disagree. She was quite right to cling to her specific gift, even if this entailed sacrificing something else vital to her art. And she did not always have to sacrifice; Mr. and

Mrs. Ramsay do remain with the reader afterwards, and so perhaps do Rachel from *The Voyage Out*, and Clarissa Dalloway. For the rest—it is impossible to maintain that here is an immortal portrait gallery. Socially she is limited to the upper-middle professional classes, and she does not even employ many types. There is the bleakly honest intellectual (St. John Hirst, Charles Tansley, Louis, William Dodge), the monumental majestic hero (Jacob, Percival), the pompous amorous pillar of society (Richard Dalloway as he appears in *The Voyage Out*, Hugh Whitbread), the scholar who cares only for young men (Bonamy, Neville), the pernickety independent (Mr. Pepper, Mr. Banks); even the Ramsays are tried out first as the Ambroses. As soon as we understand the nature of her equipment, we shall see that as regards human beings she did as well as she could. Belonging to the world of poetry, but fascinated by another world, she is always stretching out from her enchanted tree and snatching bits from the flux of daily life as they float past, and out of these bits she builds novels. She would not plunge. And she should not have plunged. She might have stayed folded up in her tree singing little songs like *Blue-Green* in the *Monday or Tuesday* volume, but fortunately for English literature she did not do this either.

So that is her problem. She is a poet, who wants to write something as near to a novel as possible.

I must pass on to say a little—it ought to be much—about her interests. I have emphasised her fondness for writing both seriously and in fun, and have tried to indicate how she wrote: how she gathered up her material and digested it without damaging its freshness, how she rearranged it to form unities, how she was a poet who wanted to write novels, how these novels bear upon them the marks of their strange gestation—some might say the scars. What concerns me now is the material itself, her interests, her opinions. And not to be too vague I will begin with food.

It is always helpful, when reading her, to look out for the passages which describe eating. They are invariably good. They are a sharp reminder that here is a woman who is alert sensuously. She had an enlightened greediness which gentlemen themselves might envy, and which few masculine writers have expressed. There is a little too much lamp oil in George Meredith's wine, a little too much paper crackling on Charles Lamb's pork, and no savour whatever in any dish of Henry James', but when Virginia Woolf mentions nice things they get right into our mouths, so far as the edibility of print permits. We taste their deliciousness. And when they are not nice, we taste them equally, our mouths awry now with laughter. I will not torture this great university of Oxbridge by reminding it of the exquisite lunch which she ate in a don's room here in the year 1929; such memories are now too painful. Nor will I insult the noble college of women in this same university—Fernham is its name—by reminding it of the deplorable dinner which she ate that same evening in its Hall—a dinner so lowering that she had to go to a cupboard afterwards and drink something out of a bottle; such memories may still be all too true to fact. But I may without offence refer to the great dish of Bœuf en Daube which forms the centre of the dinner of union in *To the Lighthouse*, the dinner round which all that section of the book coheres, the dinner which exhales affection and poetry and loveliness, so that all the characters see the best in one another at last and for a moment, and one of them, Lily Briscoe, carries away a recollection of reality. Such a dinner cannot be built on a statement beneath a dish-cover which the novelist is too indifferent or incompetent to remove. Real food is necessary, and this, in fiction as in her home, she knew how to provide. The Bœuf en Daube, which had taken the cook three days to make and had worried Mrs. Ramsay as she did her hair, stands before us "with its confusion of savoury brown and yellow meats and its bay leaves and its wine"; we peer down the shiny walls of the great casserole and get one of the best bits, and like William Banks, generally so hard to please, we are satisfied. Food with her was not a literary device put in to make the book seem real. She put it in because she tasted it, because she saw pictures, because she smelt flowers, because she heard Bach, because her senses were both exquisite and catholic, and were always bringing her first-hand news of the outside world. Our debt to her is in part this: she reminds us of the importance of sensation in an age which practises brutality and recommends ideals. I could have illustrated sensation more reputably by quoting the charming passage about the florists' shop in *Mrs. Dalloway*, or the passage where Rachel plays upon the cabin piano. Flowers and music are conventional literary adjuncts. A good feed isn't, and that is why I preferred it and chose it to represent her reactions. Let me add that she smokes, and now let the Bœuf en Daube be carried away. It will never come back in our lifetime. It is not for us. But the power to appreciate it remains, and the power to appreciate all distinction.

After the senses, the intellect. She respected knowledge, she believed in wisdom. Though she could not be called an optimist, she had, very profoundly, the conviction that mind is in action against matter, and is winning new footholds in the void. That anything would be accomplished by her or in her generation, she did not suppose, but the noble blood from which she sprang encouraged her to hope. Mr. Ramsay, standing by the geraniums and trying to think, is not a figure of fun. Nor is this university, despite its customs and costumes: she speaks of "the light shining there—the light of Cambridge."

No light shines now from Cambridge visibly, and this prompts the comment that her books were conditioned by her period. She could not assimilate this latest threat to our civilisation. The submarine perhaps. But not the flying fortress or the land mine. The idea that all stone is like grass, and like all flesh may vanish in a twinkling, did not enter into her consciousness, and indeed it will be some time before it can be assimilated by literature. She belonged to an age which distinguished sharply between the impermanency of man and the durability of his monuments, and for whom the dome of the British Museum Reading Room was almost eternal. Decay she admitted: the delicate grey churches in the Strand would not stand for ever; but she supposed, as we all did, that decay would be gradual. The younger generation—the Auden-Isherwood generation, as it is convenient to call it—saw more clearly here than could she, and she did not quite do justice to its vision, any more than she did justice to its experiments in technique—she who had been in her time such an experimenter. Still, to belong to one's period is a common failing, and she made the most of hers. She respected and acquired knowledge, she believed in wisdom. Intellectually, no one can do more; and since she was a poet, not a philosopher or a historian or a prophetess, she had not to consider whether wisdom will prevail and whether the square upon the oblong, which Rhoda built out of the music of Mozart, will ever stand firm upon this distracted earth. The square upon the oblong. Order. Justice. Truth. She cared for these abstractions, and tried to express them through symbols, as an artist must, though she realised the inadequacy of symbols.

> They come with their violins, said Rhoda; they wait; count; nod; down come their bows. And there is ripples and laughter like the dance of olive trees . . . .
> "Like" and "like" and "like"—but what is the tiling that lies, beneath the semblance of the thing? Now that lightning has gashed the tree and the flowering branch has fallen . . . let me see the thing. There is a square. There is an oblong. The players take the square and place it upon the oblong. They place it very accurately; they make a perfect dwelling-place. Very little is left outside. The structure is now visible; what is inchoate is here stated; we are not so various or so mean; we have made oblongs and stood them upon squares. This is our triumph; this is our consolation.

The consolation, that is to say, of catching sight of abstractions. They have to be symbolised, and "the square upon the oblong" is as much a symbol as the dancing olive trees, but because of its starkness it comes nearer to conveying what she seeks. Seeking it, "we are not so various or so mean"; we have added to the human heritage and reaffirmed wisdom.

The next of her interests which has to be considered is society. She was not confined to sensations and intellectualism. She was a social creature, with an outlook both warm and shrewd. But it was a peculiar outlook, and we can best get at it by looking at a very peculiar side of her: her feminism.

Feminism inspired one of the most brilliant of her books—the charming and persuasive *A Room of One's Own*; it contains the Oxbridge lunch and the Fernham dinner, also the immortal encounter with the beadle when she tried to walk on the college grass, and the touching reconstruction of Shakespeare's sister—Shakespeare's equal in genius, but she perished because she had no position or money, and that has been the fate of women through the ages. But feminism is also responsible for the worst of her books—the cantankerous *Three Guineas*—and for the less successful streaks in *Orlando*. There are spots of it all over her work, and it was constantly in her mind. She was convinced that society is man-made, that the chief occupations of men are the shedding of blood, the making of money, the giving of orders, and the wearing of uniforms, and that none of these occupations is admirable. Women dress up for fun or prettiness, men for pomposity, and she had no mercy on the judge in his wig, the general in his bits and bobs of ribbon, the bishop in his robes, or even on the harmless don in his gown. She felt that all these mummers were putting something across over which women had never been consulted, and which she at any rate disliked. She declined to co-operate, in theory, and sometimes in fact. She refused to sit on committees or to sign appeals, on the ground that women must not condone this tragic male-made mess, or accept the crumbs of power which men throw them occasionally from their hideous feast. Like Lysistrata, she withdrew.

In my judgment there is something old-fashioned about this extreme feminism; it dates back to her suffragette youth of the 1910's, when men kissed girls to distract them from wanting the vote, and very properly provoked her wrath. By the 1930's she had much less to complain of, and seems to keep on grumbling from habit. She complained, and rightly, that though women today have won admission into the professions and trades they usually encounter a male conspiracy when they try to get to the top. But she did not appreciate that the conspiracy is weakening yearly, and that before long women will be quite as powerful for good or evil as men. She was sensible about the past; about the present she was sometimes unreasonable. However, I speak as a man here, and as an elderly one. The best judges of her feminism are neither elderly men nor even elderly women, but young women. If they, if the students of Fernham, think that it expresses an existent grievance, they are right.

She felt herself to be not only a woman but a lady, and this gives a further twist to her social outlook. She made no bones about it. She was a lady, by birth and upbringing, and it was no use being cowardly about it, and pretending that her mother had turned a mangle, or that her father Sir Leslie had been a plasterer's mate. Working-class writers often mentioned their origns, and were respected for doing so. Very well; she would mention hers. And her snobbery—for she was a snob—has more courage in it than arrogance. It is connected with her insatiable honesty, and is not, like the snobbery of Clarissa Dalloway, bland and frilled and unconsciously sinking into the best arm-chair. It is more like the snobbery of Kitty when she goes to tea with the Robsons; it stands up like a target for anyone to aim at who wants to. In her introduction to *Life as we have known it* (a collection of biographies of working-class women edited by Margaret Llewellyn Davies) she faces the fire. "One could not be Mrs. Giles of Durham, because one's body had never stood at the wash-tub; one's hands had never wrung and scrubbed and chopped up whatever the meat is that makes a miner's supper." This is not disarming, and it is not intended to disarm. And if one said to her that she could after all find out what meat a miner does have for his supper if she took a little trouble, she would retort that this wouldn't help her to chop it up, and that it is not by knowing things but by doing things that one enters into the lives of people who do things. And she was not going to chop up meat. She would chop it badly, and waste her time. She was not going to wring and scrub when what she liked doing and could do was write. To murmurs of "Lucky lady you!" she replied, "I am a lady," and went on writing. "There aren't going to be no more ladies. 'Ear that?" She heard. Without rancour or surprise or alarm, she heard, and drove her pen the faster. For if, as seems probable, these particular creatures are to be extinguished, how important that the last of them should get down her impressions of the world and unify them into a book! If she didn't, no one else would. Mrs. Giles of Durham wouldn't. Mrs. Giles would write differently, and might write better, but she could not produce *The Waves*, or a life of Roger Fry.

There is an admirable hardness here, so far as hardness can be admirable. There is not much sympathy, and I do not think she was sympathetic. She could be charming to individuals, working-class and otherwise, but it was her curiosity and her honesty that motivated her. And we must remember that sympathy, for her, entailed a tremendous and exhausting process, not lightly to be entered on. It was not a half-crown or a kind word or a good deed or a philanthropic sermon or a godlike gesture; it was adding the sorrows of another to one's own. Half fancifully, but wholly seriously, she writes:

> But sympathy we cannot have. Wisest Fate says no. If her children, weighted as they already are with sorrow, were to take on them that burden too, adding in imagination other pains to their own, buildings would cease to rise; roads would peter out into grassy tracks; there would be an end of music and of painting; one great sigh alone would rise to Heaven, and the only attitudes for men and women would be those of horror and despair.

Here perhaps is the reason why she cannot be warmer and more human about Mrs. Giles of Durham.

This detachment from the working-classes and Labour reinforces the detachment caused by her feminism, and her attitude to society was in consequence aloof and angular. She was fascinated, she was unafraid, but she detested mateyness, and she would make no concessions to popular journalism, and the "let's all be friendly together" stunt. To the crowd—so far as such an entity exists—she was very jolly, but she handed out no bouquets to the middlemen who have arrogated to themselves the right of interpreting the crowd, and get paid for doing so in the daily press and on the wireless. These middlemen form after all a very small clique— larger than the Bloomsbury they so tirelessly denounce, but a mere drop in the ocean of humanity. And since it was a drop whose distinction was proportionate to its size, she saw no reason to conciliate it.

"And now to sum up," says Bernard in the last section of *The Waves*. That I cannot do, for reasons already given; the material is so rich and contradictory, and ours is not a good vintage year for judgments. I have gone from point to point as best I could, from her method of writing to her books, from her problems as a poet-novelist to her problems as a woman and as a lady. And I have tried to speak of her with the directness which she would wish, and which could alone honour her. But how are all the points to be combined? What is the pattern resultant? The best I can do is to quote Bernard again. "The illusion is upon me," he says, "that something adheres for a moment, has roundness, weight, depth, is completed. This, for the moment, seems to be her life." Bernard puts it well. But, as Rhoda indicated in that earlier quotation, these words are only similes, comparisons with physical substances, and what one wants is the thing that lies beneath the semblance of the thing; that alone satisfies, that alone makes the full statement.

Whatever the final pattern, I am sure it will not be a depressing one. Like all her friends, I miss her greatly—I knew her ever since she started writing. But this is a personal matter, and I am sure that there is no case for lamentation here, or for the obituary note. Virginia Woolf got through an immense amount of work, she gave acute pleasure in new ways, she pushed the light of the English language a little further against darkness. Those are facts. The epitaph of such an artist cannot be written by the vulgar-minded or by the lugubrious. They will try, indeed they have already tried, but their words make no sense. It is wiser, it is safer, to regard her career as a triumphant one. She triumphed over what are primly called "difficulties," and she also triumphed in the positive sense: she brought in the spoils. And sometimes it is as a row of little silver cups that I see her work gleaming. "These trophies," the inscription runs, "were won by the mind from matter, its enemy and its friend."

Note

1   See Adrian Stephen, *The Dreadnought Hoax*. See, still more, an unpublished paper which she herself once wrote for a Women's Institute, leaving it helpless with laughter.

Chapter 69

Louis MacNeice (1907–63)

"THE TOWER THAT ONCE" (1941)

BORN IN IRELAND AND EDUCATED in England where he would make a permanent home, MacNeice became widely regarded as a poet with his 1935 collection,
Poems. Although nominally part of the group of 1930s poets that Roy Campbell dispar-
agingly labeled "Macspaunday" – an amalgam of the names MacNeice, Stephen Spender,
W.H. Auden, and Cecil Day Lewis – MacNeice was never completely in sync with his
poetic peers. What he did share with the 1930s poets was an Oxford education, affiliations (albeit loose) with socialism, and a politically engaged poetics that aligned
documentary-style detail with traditional poetic forms and genres. *Autumn Journal*
(1939), the MacNeice poem that Woolf singles out for critique in "The Leaning Tower,"
demonstrates these principles as the poet interpolates his personal struggles on to the
desperate political morass that would lead to World War II. Defending his poetry and that
of his peers from Woolf's critique, in "The Tower That Once" MacNeice provides an
alternative literary history to Woolf's: situating his generation within a tradition of politically engaged poetry running throughout English letters. Despite this rancorous public
exchange between the two writers, MacNeice continued to admire Woolf's writing, and
toward the end of his career with the BBC (1941–63), he adapted her novel, *The Waves*,
for a radio production.

Louis MacNeice, "The Tower That Once," *Folios of New Writing* (Spring 1941): 37–41.

Mrs. Woolf, in her article *The Leaning Tower,* looks forward to a classless society which will
give to writers 'a mind no longer crippled, evasive, divided. They may inherit that unconsciousness which . . . is necessary if writers are to get beneath the surface, and to write
something that people remember when they are alone.' With this general aim or hope I
sympathize. 'Literature,' I would agree with her, 'is no one's private ground.' I find it, therefore, 'both inconsistent and unjust that she should dismiss not only so lightly, but so acidly—
as 'the embittered and futile tribe of scapegoat hunters'—that group of younger writers who
during the Thirties made it their business to stigmatize those all too present evils which
Mrs. Woolf herself considers evil and to open those doors which she herself wants opened.
She seems to understand these junior colleagues of hers no better than Yeats understood

Eliot. This mutual misunderstanding of the literary generations is one of the evils of our times; my own generation has too often been unjust to its immediate predecessors.

Mrs. Woolf's literary history is over-simplified. She writes of the social divisions of the nineteenth century: 'the nineteenth-century writer did not seek to change those divisions; he accepted them. He accepted them so completely that he became unconscious of them.' Confining ourselves to our own literature and leaving aside all foreigners—the Russians, for example, or Zola—we might ask her what about Shelley whom she herself has mentioned by name. Or what about Wordsworth whose early inspiration was 'Nature' admittedly but Nature harnessed to a revolutionary social doctrine? And even with the great Victorians 'All's well with the world' was not their most typical slogan; is *In Memoriam* a poem of placid or unconscious acceptance? 'Life was not going to change,' writes Mrs. Woolf; Tennyson said something different in *Locksley Hall*. And what about William Morris? Or Henry James, for whom (according to Mrs. Woolf) as for (according to her too) his predecessors the social barometer was Set Fair for ever? Mr. Spender put forward a different, but at least as plausible a view of James in *The Destructive Element*.

Mrs. Woolf assumes that a period of great social and political unrest is adverse to literature. I do not think she produces adequate evidence for this; we could counter with the Peloponnesian War, the factions of Florence in the time of Dante, the reign of Queen Elizabeth, the Franco-Prussian War; but, even if she is right, she should not attack my generation for being conditioned by its conditions. Do not let us be misled by her metaphor of the Tower. The point of this metaphor was that a certain group of young writers found themselves on a leaning tower; this presupposes that the rest of the world remained on the level. But it just didn't. The whole world in our time went more and more on the slant so that no mere abstract geometry or lyrical uplift could cure it. When Mrs. Woolf accuses the Thirties writers of 'flogging a dead or dying horse because a living horse, if flogged, would kick them off its back,' her point seems to me facile. No doubt we spent too much time in satirizing the Blimps, but some of those old dead horses—as this war shows every week—have a kick in them still. And the ruling class of the Thirties, the people above the Blimps, our especial *bête noir* or *cheval noir*, did manage to kick us into the jaws of destruction. But it remains to be seen who will be proved to have died; we'll hope it was the horse.

She proceeds to a surprising sentence: 'How can a writer who has no first-hand experience of a towerless, of a classless society create that society?' How can a larva with no first-hand experience of flight ever grow wings? On the premises implied in this sentence human society is incapable of willed or directed change. Because, quite apart from the intelligentsia and the privileged classes, there is nobody in the whole population of Great Britain who has had first-hand experience of that kind of society which nearly everybody needs. Mrs. Woolf is making the same mistake as some of the very writers she is attacking. For some of those writers were hamstrung by modesty. It all, they said to themselves, depends on the proletariat. And in a sense they were right. But they were wrong to assume that the proletariat itself knew where it was going or could get there by its own volition. These intellectuals tended to betray the proletariat by professing to take all their cues from it.

Mrs. Woolf deplores the 'didacticism' of the Thirties. But (1) if the world was such a mess as she admits, it was inevitable and right that writers should be didactic (compare the position of Euripides), (2) she assumes that this writing—especially the poetry—of the Thirties was solely and crudely didactic—which it was not. She makes an inept comparison between a morsel of Stephen Spender and a morsel of Wordsworth as exemplifying 'the difference between politician's poetry and poet's poetry': this ignores the fact that the great bulk of Wordsworth is pamphleteering and that Spender's poetry is pre-eminently the kind—to use her own words—'that people remember when they are alone.' Politician's poetry? Look at Spender's professedly political play, *Trial of a Judge*: it failed as a play just because it was not 'public' but rather a personal apologia; it displeased the Communists just because it sacrificed propaganda values to honesty.

It is often assumed by the undiscriminating—among whom for this occasion I must rank Mrs. Woolf—that all these writers of the Thirties were the slaves of Marx, or rather of Party Line Marxism. Marx was certainly a most powerful influence. But why? It was not because of his unworkable economics, it was not because of the pedantic jigsaw of his history, it was because he said: '*Our job is to change it*.' What called a poet like Spender to Marx was the same thing that called Shelley to Godwin and Rousseau. But some at least of these poets—in particular Auden and Spender—always recognized the truth of Thomas Mann's dictum: 'Karl Marx must read Friedrich Hölderlin.' Even an orthodox Communist Party critic, Christopher Caudwell, in his book *Illusion and Reality*, insisted (rightly) that poetry can never be reduced to political advertising, that its method is myth and that it must represent not any set of ideas which can be formulated by politicians or by scientists or by mere Reason and/or mere Will—it must represent something much deeper and wider which he calls the 'Communal Ego.' It is this Communal Ego with which Auden and Spender concerned themselves.

Politician's poetry? Yes, there was some of it; and some of it was bad. Rex Warner, for example, lost his touch when he turned from birds to polemics. Day Lewis's social satire cannot compare with his love lyrics. Auden and Isherwood's *On the Frontier* was worse than a flop. Mr. Edward Upward ruined his novel, *Journey to the Border*, with his use of the Deus ex Machina—i.e. 'the Workers'—at the end. But these mistakes are nothing to their achievements and it is grotesque to dismiss someone like Auden as a mere 'politician's poet' and an ineffectual one at that; was it not Auden who repudiated the Public Face in the Private Place? It is carrying the Nelson eye too far to pretend that Auden and Spender did not bring new life into English poetry and what was more—in spite of what Mrs. Woolf says about self-pity—a new spirit of hopefulness (see some of Spender's early lyrics). As for the novel, Mrs. Woolf suggests that, whereas her own generation could create objective character and colour, her successors can manage nothing but either autobiography or black and white cartoons. I would ask the reader—with no disrespect to *Mrs. Dalloway*, a book that I like very much—to compare Mrs. Woolf's 'Mrs. Dalloway' with Mr. Isherwood's 'Mr. Norris.'

Self-pity? Of course our work embodied some self-pity. But look at Mrs. Woolf's beloved nineteenth century. 'Anger, pity, scapegoat beating, excuse finding'—she intones against the poor lost Thirties; you find all those things—in full measure and running over—in the Romantic Revival and right down from *Manfred* or Keats' Odes through Tennyson and Swinburne and Rossetti to the death-wish of the Fin de Siècle and even to Mr. Prufrock. My generation at least put some salt in it. And we never, even at our most martyred, produced such a holocaust of self-pity as Shelley in *Adonais*.

Mrs. Woolf deplores our 'curious bastard language,' but I notice that in the next stage of society and poetry she looks forward to a 'pooling' of vocabularies and dialects. Just one more inconsistency. And Shakespeare wrote in a bastard language too.

This is no occasion to put forward a *Credo* of my own, but I would like to assure Mrs. Woolf (speaking for myself, but it is true of most of my colleagues) that I am not solely concerned with 'destruction.' Some destruction, yes; but not of all the people or all the values all the time. And I have no intention of recanting my past. Recantation is becoming too fashionable; I am sorry to see so much self-flagellation, so many *Peccavis*, going on on the literary Left. We may not have done all we could in the Thirties, but we did do something. We were right to throw mud at Mrs. Woolf's old horses and we were right to advocate social reconstruction and we were even right—in our more lyrical work—to give personal expression to our feelings of anxiety, horror and despair (for even despair can be fertile). As for the Leaning Tower, if Galileo had not had one at Pisa, he would not have discovered the truth about falling weights. We learned something of the sort from our tower too.

Chapter 70

Ralph Ellison (1914–94)

"RICHARD WRIGHT'S BLUES" (1945)

NAMED AFTER THE AMERICAN TRANSCENDENTALIST philosopher Ralph Waldo Emerson, Ellison was raised in Oklahoma City, one of the great American jazz cities in the 1920s and '30s. He trained as a trumpet player and pianist at Oklahoma City's Frederick Douglass School and at the Tuskegee Institute's renowned music program; while studying there in the 1930s, he became an appreciator of Alain Locke's New Negro Movement and an *aficionado* of modernist literature. Ellison frequently spoke of Eliot's *The Waste Land* as a groundbreaking work for him as an artist and intellectual. After leaving Tuskegee in 1936, he moved to Harlem in New York City to study sculpture and the visual arts. Richard Wright urged Ellison to start writing after Ellison had written a review of his work; Langston Hughes also encouraged the new-comer's writing talents. Ellison wrote reviews and columns for scholarly journals and publications including *Negro Quarterly*, *New Challenge*, *New Masses*, and *High Fidelity*; in 1938 Ellison worked for the Depression-era Federal Writers' Project, where his interests in American folk cultures intensified. *Invisible Man* (1952), which he began writing in 1947, won the National Book Award in 1953. Ellison's collected essays in *Shadow and Act* (1964) and *Going to the Territory* (1986) are the best illustration of his American, cosmopolitan, and modernist influences; the essays' subjects include Stephen Crane, Mark Twain, Mahalia Jackson, Ernest Hemingway, Henri Matisse, William Faulkner, Andre Malreaux, and Charlie Parker.

Ralph Ellison, "Richard Wright's Blues," *The Antioch Review* 3.2 (Summer 1945). Reprinted in *Shadow and Act*. New York: Random House, 1964. 77–80, 87–89, 91–94.

> *If anybody ask you*
> *who sing this song,*
> *Say it was ole [Black Boy]*
> *done been here and gone.*[1]

As a writer, Richard Wright has outlined for himself a dual role: to discover and depict the meaning of Negro experience; and to reveal to both Negroes and whites those problems of a psychological and emotional nature which arise between them when they strive for mutual understanding.

Now, in *Black Boy*, he has used his own life to probe what qualities of will, imagination and intellect are required of a Southern Negro in order to possess the meaning of his life in the United States. Wright is an important writer, perhaps the most articulate Negro American, and what he has to say is highly perceptive. Imagine Bigger Thomas projecting his own life in lucid prose, guided, say, by the insights of Marx and Freud, and you have an idea of this autobiography.

Published at a time when any sharply critical approach to Negro life has been dropped as a wartime expendable, it should do much to redefine the problem of the Negro and American Democracy. Its power can be observed in the shrill manner with which some professional "friends of the Negro people" have attempted to strangle the work in a noose of newsprint.

What in the tradition of literary autobiography is it like, this work described as a "great American autobiography"? As a non-white intellectual's statement of his relationship to Western culture, *Black Boy* recalls the conflicting pattern of identification and rejection found in Nehru's *Toward Freedom*. In its use of fictional techniques, its concern with criminality (sin) and the artistic sensibility, and in its author's judgment and rejection of the narrow world of his origin, it recalls Joyce's rejection of Dublin in *A Portrait of the Artist*. And as a psychological document of life under oppressive conditions, it recalls *The House of the Dead*, Dostoievsky's profound study of the humanity of Russian criminals.

Such works were perhaps Wright's literary guides, aiding him to endow his life's incidents with communicable significance; providing him with ways of seeing, feeling and describing his environment. These influences, however, were encountered only after these first years of Wright's life were past and were not part of the immediate folk culture into which he was born. In that culture the specific folk-art form which helped shape the writer's attitude toward his life and which embodied the impulse that contributes much to the quality and tone of his autobiography was the Negro blues. This would bear a word of explanation:

The blues is an impulse to keep the painful details and episodes of a brutal experience alive in one's aching consciousness, to finger its jagged grain, and to transcend it, not by the consolation of philosophy but by squeezing from it a near-tragic, near-comic lyricism. As a form, the blues is an autobiographical chronicle of personal catastrophe expressed lyrically. And certainly Wright's early childhood was crammed with catastrophic incidents. In a few short years his father deserted his mother, he knew intense hunger, he became a drunkard begging drinks from black stevedores in Memphis saloons; he had to flee Arkansas, where an uncle was lynched; he was forced to live with a fanatically religious grandmother in an atmosphere of constant bickering; he was lodged in an orphan asylum; he observed the suffering of his mother, who became a permanent invalid, while fighting off the blows of the poverty-stricken relatives with whom he had to live; he was cheated, beaten and kicked off jobs by white employees who disliked his eagerness to learn a trade; and to these objective circumstances must be added the subjective fact that Wright, with his sensitivity, extreme shyness and intelligence, was a problem child who rejected his family and was by them rejected.

Thus along with the themes, equivalent descriptions of milieu and the perspectives to be found in Joyce, Nehru, Dostoievsky, George Moore and Rousseau, *Black Boy* is filled with blues-tempered echoes of railroad trains, the names of Southern towns and cities, estrangements, fights and flights, deaths and disappointments, charged with physical and spiritual hungers and pain. And like a blues sung by such an artist as Bessie Smith, its lyrical prose evokes the paradoxical, almost surreal image of a black boy singing lustily as he probes his own grievous wound.

In *Black Boy*, two worlds have fused, two cultures merged, two impulses of Western man become coalesced. By discussing some of its cultural sources I hope to answer those critics who would make of the book a miracle and of its author a mystery. And while making no attempt to probe the mystery of the artist (who Hemingway says is "forged in injustice as a sword is forged"), I do hold that basically the prerequisites to the writing of *Black Boy* were, on the one hand, the microscopic degree of cultural freedom which Wright found in the South's stony injustice, and, on the other, the existence of a personality agitated to a state of almost manic restlessness. There were, of course, other factors, chiefly ideological; but these came later.

Wright speaks of his journey north as

> . . . taking a part of the South to transplant in alien soil, to see if it could grow differently, if it could drink of new and cool rains, bend in strange winds, respond to the warmth of other suns, and perhaps, to bloom . . . .

And just as Wright, the man, represents the blooming of the delinquent child of the autobiography, just so does *Black Boy* represent the flowering—cross-fertilized by pollen blown by the winds of strange cultures—of the humble blues lyric. There is, as in all acts of creation, a world of mystery in this, but there is also enough that is comprehensible for Americans to create the social atmosphere in which other black boys might freely bloom . . . .

Man cannot express that which does not exist—either in the form of dreams, ideas or realities—in his environment. Neither his thoughts nor his feelings, his sensibility nor his intellect are fixed, innate qualities. They are processes which arise out of the interpenetration of human instinct with environment, through the process called experience; each changing and being changed by the other. Negroes cannot possess many of the sentiments attributed to them because the same changes in environment which, through experience, enlarge man's intellect (and thus his capacity for still greater change) also modify his feelings; which in turn increase his sensibility, i.e., his sensitivity, to refinements of impression and subtleties of emotion. The extent of these changes depends upon the quality of political and cultural freedom in the environment.

Intelligence tests have measured the quick rise in intellect which takes place in Southern Negroes after moving north, but little attention has been paid to the mutations effected in their sensibilities. However, the two go hand in hand. Intellectual complexity is accompanied by emotional complexity; refinement of thought, by refinement of feeling. The movement north affects more than the Negro's wage scale, it affects his entire psychosomatic structure.

The rapidity of Negro intellectual growth in the North is due partially to objective factors present in the environment, to influences of the industrial city and to a greater political freedom. But there are also changes within the "inner world." In the North energies are released and given *intellectual* channelization—energies which in most Negroes in the South have been forced to take either a *physical* form or, as with potentially intellectual types like Wright, to be expressed as nervous tension, anxiety and hysteria. Which is nothing mysterious. The human organism responds to environmental stimuli by converting them into either physical and/or intellectual energy. And what is called hysteria is suppressed intellectual energy expressed physically.

The "physical" character of their expression makes for much of the difficulty in understanding American Negroes. Negro music and dances are frenziedly erotic; Negro religious ceremonies violently ecstatic; Negro speech strongly rhythmical and weighted with image and gesture. But there is more in this sensuousness than the unrestraint and insensitivity found in primitive cultures; nor is it simply the relatively spontaneous and undifferentiated responses of a people living in close contact with the soil. For despite Jim Crow, Negro life does not exist in a vacuum, but in the seething vortex of those tensions generated by the most highly industrialized of Western nations. The welfare of the most humble black Mississippi sharecropper is affected less by the flow of the seasons and the rhythm of natural events than by the fluctuations of the stock market; even though, as Wright states of his father, the share-cropper's memories, actions and emotions are shaped by his immediate contact with nature and the crude social relations of the South.

All of this makes the American Negro far different from the "simple" specimen for which he is taken. And the "physical" quality offered as evidence of his primitive simplicity is actu-ally the form of his complexity. The American Negro is a Western type whose social condi-tion creates a state which is almost the reverse of the cataleptic trance: Instead of his consciousness being lucid to the reality around it while the body is rigid, here it is the body which is alert, reacting to pressures which the constricting forces of Jim Crow block off from the transforming, concept-creating activity of the brain. The "eroticism" of Negro expression springs from much the same conflict as that displayed in the violent gesturing of a man who attempts to express a complicated concept with a limited vocabulary; thwarted ideational energy is converted into unsatisfactory pantomime, and his words are burdened with mean-ings they cannot convey. Here lies the source of the basic ambiguity of *Native Son*, wherein in order to translate Bigger's complicated feelings into universal ideas, Wright had to force into Bigger's consciousness concepts and ideas which his intellect could not formulate. Between Wright's skill and knowledge and the potentials of Bigger's mute feelings lay a thousand years of conscious culture. . . .

In discussing the inadequacies for democratic living typical of the education provided Negroes by the South, a Negro educator has coined the term *mis-education*. Within the ambit of the black family this takes the form of training the child away from curiosity and adventure, against reaching out for those activities lying beyond the borders of the black community. And when the child resists, the parent discourages him; first with the formula, "That there's for white folks. Colored can't have it," and finally with a beating.

It is not, then, the family and communal violence described by *Black Boy* that is unusual, but that Wright *recognized* and made no peace with its essential cruelty—even when, like a babe freshly emerged from the womb, he could not discern where his own personality ended and it began. Ordinarily both parent and child are protected against this cruelty—seeing it as love and finding subjective sanction for it in the spiritual authority of the Fifth Commandment, and on the secular level in the legal and extralegal structure of the Jim Crow system. The child who did not rebel, or who was unsuccessful in his rebellion, learned a masochistic submissiveness and a denial of the impulse toward Western culture when it stirred within him.

Why then have Southern whites, who claim to "know" the Negro, missed all this? Simply because they, too, are armored against the horror and the cruelty. Either they deny the Negro's humanity and feel no cause to measure his actions against civilized norms; or they protect themselves from their guilt in the Negro's condition and from their fear that their cooks might poison them, or that their nursemaids might strangle their infant charges, or that their field hands might do them violence, by attributing to them a superhuman capacity for love, kindliness and forgiveness. Nor does this in any way contradict their stereotyped conviction that all Negroes (meaning those with whom they have no contact) are given to the most animal behavior.

It is only when the individual, whether white or black, *rejects* the pattern that he awakens to the nightmare of his life. Perhaps much of the South's regressive character springs from the fact that many, jarred by some casual crisis into wakefulness, flee hysterically into the sleep of violence or the coma of apathy again. For the penalty of wakefulness is to encounter ever more violence and horror than the sensibilities can sustain unless translated into some form of social action. Perhaps the impassioned character so noticeable among those white Southern liberals so active in the Negro's cause is due to their sense of accumulated horror; their passion—like the violence in Faulkner's novels—is evidence of a profound spiritual vomiting.

This compulsion is even more active in Wright and the increasing number of Negroes who have said an irrevocable "no" to the Southern pattern. Wright learned that it is not enough merely to reject the white South, but that he had also to reject that part of the South which lay within. As a rebel he formulated that rejection negatively, because it was the negative face of the Negro community upon which he looked most often as a child. It is this he is contemplating when he writes:

> Whenever I thought of the essential bleakness of black life in America, I knew that Negroes had never been allowed to catch the full spirit of Western civilization, that they lived somehow in it but not of it. And when I brooded upon the cultural barrenness of black life, I wondered if clean, positive tenderness, love, honor, loyalty and the capacity to remember were native to man. I asked myself if these human qualities were not fostered, won, struggled and suffered for, preserved in ritual from one generation to another.

But far from implying that Negroes have no capacity for culture, as one critic interprets it, this is the strongest affirmation that they have. Wright is pointing out what should be obvious (especially to his Marxist critics) that Negro sensibility is socially and historically conditioned; that Western culture must be won, confronted like the animal in a Spanish bullfight, dominated by the red shawl of codified experience and brought heaving to its knees.

Wright knows perfectly well that Negro life is a by-product of Western civilization, and that in it, if only one possesses the humanity and humility to see, are to be discovered all those impulses, tendencies, life and cultural forms to be found elsewhere in Western society.

The problem arises because the special condition of Negroes in the United States, including the defensive character of Negro life itself (the "will toward organization" noted in the Western capitalist appears in the Negro as a will to camouflage, to dissimulate), so distorts these forms as to render their recognition as difficult as finding a wounded quail against the brown and yellow leaves of a Mississippi thicket—even the spilled blood blends with the background. Having himself been in the position of the quail—to expand the metaphor—Wright's wounds have told him both the question and the answer which every successful hunter must discover for himself: "Where would I hide if *I* were a wounded quail?" But perhaps that requires more sympathy with one's quarry than most hunters possess. Certainly it requires such a sensitivity to the shifting guises of humanity under pressure as to allow them to identify themselves with the human content, whatever its outer form; and even with those Southern Negroes to whom Paul Robeson's name is only a rolling sound in the fear-charged air.

Let us close with one final word about the blues: Their attraction lies in this, that they at once express both the agony of life and the possibility of conquering it through sheer toughness of spirit. They fall short of tragedy only in that they provide no solution, offer no scapegoat but the self. Nowhere in America today is there social or political action based upon the solid realities of Negro life depicted in *Black Boy*; perhaps that is why, with its refusal to offer solutions, it is like the blues. Yet in it thousands of Negroes will for the first time see their destiny in public print. Freed here of fear and the threat of violence, their lives have at last been organized, scaled down to possessable proportions. And in this lies Wright's most important achievement: He has converted the American Negro impulse toward self-annihilation and "going-under-ground" into a will to confront the world, to evaluate his experience honestly and throw his findings unashamedly into the guilty conscience of America.

Note

1   Signature formula used by blues singers at conclusion of song.

Chapter 71

H.D. (Hilda Doolittle) (1886–1961)

TRIBUTE TO FREUD (1956)

H ILDA DOOLITTLE WAS BORN IN Bethlehem, Pennsylvania and attended two of the state's distinguished schools, Bryn Mawr College, where she was a classmate of the modernist poet Marianne Moore, and the University of Pennsylvania, where she became acquainted with the modernist poets Ezra Pound and William Carlos Williams. In 1911, she moved to Europe and lived on the Continent for the duration of her life. In 1912 and early in her career as a poet, essayist, and fiction writer, H.D. became affiliated with the imagist movement led by Pound. The imagists sought to elevate poetry, to rescue it from the sentimental, flaccid, and alleged emotional dishonesty of the genteel poetic tradition. Imagist poetry would be spare, direct, precise in relation to the treatment of the poem's object or subject, and formally restrained. Pound was partially inspired by the elegant simplicity of the Japanese *haiku* and that poetic tradition's reliance on strict form and the juxtaposition of images, which were believed to represent a kind of snapshot of crystallized emotion and intellect. The imagist's ideal was to maintain the image's radiant possibility and not to over burden the image and its productive possibilities with unnecessary or ornate description. H.D.'s interest in classical cultures, ecstatic language, and her exploration of a feminist Hellenism would lead her away from strict adherence to Pound's poetic mission. H.D. began her analysis with Sigmund Freud in Vienna in 1933; she was 47 years old and the famous psychoanalyst was 77. *Tribute to Freud* was written ten years after her treatment with the famed doctor; she crafts her memories of her sessions and her process of examining dreams, family objects, classical and biblical symbols, memories and personal losses. Merrill Moore describes *Tribute to Freud* as a "poetic document" that depicts the spiritual transference between two individuals, H.D., the poet-analysand, and Freud, the "magician-analyst" ("Foreword," *Tribute to Freud* viii–ix). A collection of the doctor's and patient's letters are included in the book's appendix; they reveal the mutual respect each had for the other as an artist and unique practitioner of his and her respective crafts. H.D.'s majors works include *Sea Garden* (1916), *Hymen* (1921), *Heliodora and Other Poems* (1924), *Hippolytus Temporizes* (1927), *The Walls Do Not Fall* (1944), *Trilogy* (1946), her epical World War II poems, and *Helen in Egypt* (1961).

H.D. (Hilda Doolittle), *Tribute to Freud*. New York: American Book–Stratford Press, 1956. 14–18.

I only saw the Professor once more. It was summer again. French windows opened on a pleasant stretch of lawn. The Gods or the Goods were suitably arranged on ordered shelves. I was not alone with the Professor. He sat quiet, a little wistful it seemed, withdrawn. I was afraid then, as I had often been afraid, of impinging, disturbing his detachment, of draining his vitality. I had no choice in the matter, anyway. There were others present and the conversation was carried on in an ordered, conventional manner. Like the Gods or the Goods, we were seated in a pleasant circle; a conventionally correct yet superficially sustained ordered hospitality prevailed. There was a sense of outer security, at least no words were spoken to recall a devastatingly near past or to evoke an equivocal future. I was in Switzerland when soon after the announcement of a World at War the official London news bulletin announced that Dr. Sigmund Freud, who had opened up the field of the knowledge of the unconscious mind, the innovator or founder of the science of psychoanalysis, was dead.

I had originally written *had gone*, but I crossed it out deliberately. Yes, he was dead. I was not emotionally involved. The Professor was an old man. He was 83. The war was on us. I did not grieve for the Professor or think of him. He was spared so much. He had confined his researches to the living texture of wholesome as well as unwholesome thought, but contemporary thought, you might say. That is to say, he had brought the past into the present with his *the childhood of the individual is the childhood of the race*—or is it the other way round?—*the childhood of the race is the childhood of the individual.* In any case (whether or not, the converse also is true), he had opened up, among others, that particular field of the unconscious mind that went to prove that the traits and tendencies of obscure aboriginal tribes, as well as the shape and substance of the rituals of vanished civilizations, were still inherent in the human mind—the human psyche, if you will. But according to his theories the soul existed explicitly, or showed its form and shape in and through the medium of the mind, and the body, as affected by the mind's ecstasies or disorders. About the greater transcendental issues, we never argued. But there was an argument implicit in our very bones. We had come together in order to substantiate something. I did not know what. There was something that was beating in my brain; I do not say my heart—my brain. I wanted it to be let out. I wanted to free myself of repetitive thoughts and experiences—my own and those of many of my contemporaries. I did not specifically realize just what it was I wanted, but I knew that I, like most of the people I knew, in England, America and on the Continent of Europe, were drifting. We were drifting. Where? I did not know but at least I accepted the fact that we *were* drifting. At least, I knew this—I would (before the current of inevitable events swept me right into the main stream and so on to the cataract) stand aside, if I could (if it were not already too late), and take stock of my possessions. You might say that I had—yes, I had something that I specifically owned, I *owned* myself. I did not really, of course. My family, my friends and my circumstances owned me. But I *had* something. Say it was a narrow birch-bark canoe. The great forest of the unknown, the supernormal or supernatural, was all around and about us. With the current gathering force, I could at least pull in to the shallows before it was too late, take stock of my very modest possessions of mind and body, and ask the old Hermit who lived on the edge of this vast domain to talk to me, to tell me, if he would, how best to steer my course.

We touched lightly on some of the more abstruse transcendental problems, it is true, but we related them to the familiar family complex. Tendencies of thought and imagination, however, were not cut away, were not pruned even. My imagination wandered at will; my dreams were revealing, and many of them drew on classical or Biblical symbolism. Thoughts were things, to be collected, collated, analysed, shelved or resolved. Fragmentary ideas, apparently unrelated, were often found to be part of a special layer or stratum of thought and memory, therefore to belong together; these were sometimes skilfully pieced together like the exquisite Greek tear-jars and iridescent glass bowls and vases that gleamed in the dusk from the shelves of the cabinet that faced me where I stretched, propped up on the couch in the room in Berggasse 19, Wien IX. The dead were living in so far as they lived in memory or were recalled in dream.

GLOSSARY OF TERMS

Avant-garde: literally the "advanced guard" (of an army); though the term first appeared in the early nineteenth century, it was often used synonymously with "modern" regarding innovative forms, subject matter, and ideas in art, literature, and music.

Bauhaus: Germany, 1919–33; literally "house of building"; artists' collective and school that reacted against the prevailing taste for elaborate decorativeness, espousing beauty, simplicity, rationality, functionalism, and mass production to create a "total" work of art that would unify all arts; its leading practitioners and exponents were the architects and designers Walter Gropius and Ludwig Mies van der Rohe (the latter is commonly associated with the notion "less is more," a phrase from Robert Browning's 1855 poem, "Andrea del Sarto"), and the artists Josef Albers, Wassily Kandinsky, and Paul Klee; the Bauhaus was shut down under pressure from the Nazi regime.

Bloomsbury: the group of artists and intellectuals that would come to be known as the Bloomsbury Circle comprised the Cambridge University friends and associates of Virginia (Stephen) Woolf's brother, Thoby Stephen. These luminaries included the biographer Lytton Strachey, the economist John Maynard Keynes, the painters Duncan Grant and Clive Bell (Woolf's future brother-in-law), poet "Tom" T.S. Eliot, the art historian Roger Fry, the novelist E.M. Forster, and Leonard Woolf, whom Virginia married in 1912. Woolf began her professional apprenticeship writing book reviews and she and Leonard founded the Hogarth Press in 1917. This cutting-edge publishing house published the literary works of numerous modernist writers and visual artists, including Eliot, Katherine Mansfield, Robert Graves, Gertrude Stein, Christopher Isherwood, Dora Carrington, and Vanessa Bell. Roger Fry's collectivist Omega Workshops were a crucial addition to Bloomsbury's artistic culture. The workshops' artists aimed to incorporate modern design into everyday domestic life with their post-impressionist inspired textiles, household furnishings, glassworks, ceramics, murals, and children's toys.

Constructivism: an artistic movement that rejected "art for art's sake" in favor of its having a "practical," social purpose even though it was non-representational; originally associated with the Russian sculptor Vladimir Tatlin (1913), then with the German Bauhaus; after the Russian Revolution, it became a forerunner of socialist realism.

Cubism: an art form that broke and fragmented objects and human forms into abstract, angular blocks and planes, and presented several perspectives simultaneously; most commonly associated with Pablo Picasso and Georges Braque; flourished roughly 1907–21.

Dadaism: a cultural movement that, beginning during World War I in Zurich, Switzerland where Tristan Tzara, Jean Arp, and others were waiting out the war, peaked from 1916 to 1922; anti-bourgeois, anti-war, anti-nationalist, and anarchistic, it rejected prevailing standards in art, literature, and design; loss of the past made the present meaningless, if often funny; later associated with the bitterly anti-Nazi German expressionist artist George Grosz and became the basis for surrealism and street happenings.

Epistemology: the philosophical term for the study or theory of the basis of knowledge and understanding; it asks what knowledge is, how it's acquired, and how we know what we know; it is linked to perspectivism in art and literature.

Expressionism: an artistic movement that sought to impose and represent subjective feelings and experiences rather than objective or external reality; the results are often highly colorful, with unnatural figures or abstract designs; associated with George Grosz, Lionel Feininger, Oskar Kokoschka, Edvard Munch, and Wassily Kandinsky, 1905–20.

Fauvism: term derived from the French word for "wild beasts"; it was applied by the art critic Louis Vauxcelles in 1905 to denigrate the work of such artists as Henri Matisse, André Derain, and Maurice de Vlaminck; it grew out of pointillism, post-impressionism, and the more primitive and less naturalistic art of Paul Gauguin. The fauvists embraced the term as expressing the euphoria, vivid colors, rough brush strokes, and distorted forms of their work; it flourished 1905–08.

Futurism: an art form that celebrated modern technology and industry, the urban environment, speed, and war; represented vitality and chaos through dynamic and kaleidoscopic images of movement; primarily associated with the Italian Filippo Marinetti who launched it with his *Futurist Manifesto* (1909), which declared "We will glorify war – the world's only hygiene – militarism, patriotism, the destructive gesture of freedom-bringers, beautiful ideas worth dying for, and scorn for woman"; Hulme called it "the deification of the flux, the last efflorescence of impressionism"; it flourished in Italy 1910–14.

Imagism: a movement that, rejecting Victorian and Georgian poetry, espoused a new mode that, according to Ezra Pound, Hilda Doolittle (H.D.), and Richard Aldington, its main exponents, included:

1.   Direct treatment of the "thing" whether subjective or objective.
2.   To use absolutely no word that does not contribute to the presentation.
3.   As regarding rhythm: to compose in the sequence of the musical phrase, not in sequence of a metronome.

Impressionism: like fauvism, impressionism (a term derived from Claude Monet's painting, *Impression, Sunrise*, 1872) was originally used derisively by critics and subsequently embraced by the artists themselves; impressionist paintings, usually landscapes, sought to depict the luminosity of light and color; the movement thrived mainly in France, 1870–1900. In literature, writers like Ford and Conrad, for whom it expressed their rendering of reality, also seized upon the term.

Ontology: a branch of metaphysical inquiry involving the philosophical study of the nature of being, existence, and reality itself. In the modernist expressive arts, ontological inquiry frequently focuses on the relationship between the human subject and the world of objects, and between words and things. Ontology is closely related to epistemology, the metaphysical science of knowledge – the question of how and why we know what we know. "Thoughts without words . . . Can that be?" asks Bart Oliver, the Victorian rationalist in Virginia Woolf's novel *Between the Acts* (1941). This kind of ontological question reflects some modernist authors' self-reflexive concern with language, knowledge, meaning, and truth, and helps to explain modernist artists' and writers' philosophical investments in variable perspectives and points of view.

Orphism: Orphism, or Orphic Cubism (1910–13), is a term coined in 1912 by the French poet and art critic Guillaume Apollinaire, who also coined the word surrealism. In *Les peintres cubistes* (1913), Apollinaire describes orphism as "the art of painting new totalities with elements that the artist does not take from visual reality, but creates entirely by himself; he gives them a powerful reality. An Orphic painter's works should convey an untroubled aesthetic pleasure, but at the same time a meaningful structure and sublime significance." Orphism was an art movement that paved the path from cubism to abstraction.

Perspectivism: a philosophical view developed from a Friedrich Nietzsche aphorism: "In so far as the word 'knowledge' has any meaning, the world is knowable; but it is interpretable otherwise, it has no meaning behind it, but countless meanings. – 'Perspectivism'" (*The Will to Power*, trans. Walter Kaufmann, §481 [1883–88]). Descended from Nietzsche's denial of absolute, objective truth, Conrad's four Marlovian tales, Ford's *The Good Soldier*, Hemingway's *The Sun Also Rises*, Fitzgerald's *The Great Gatsby*, Faulkner's *The Sound and the Fury* and *As I Lay Dying* offer partial narrators (in both senses) who, by expressing their limited perspectives, yet reveal more than they intend or know.

Pictorialism: a movement begun in the mid-1880s by photographers who sought to turn their craft into an art by using techniques that shifted the emphasis from realistic representation to aesthetic achievement and emotional impact. Pictorialism occurred simultaneously with the sales of the first mass-produced cameras by Eastman Kodak (in 1888), which made photography accessible to millions of amateurs.

Pointillism: neo-impressionist art technique in which small distinct dots of color form an image; the term pointillism was coined by art critics in the late 1880s to ridicule the works of such artists as Henri-Edmond Cross, Georges Seurat, and Paul Signac, and, like impressionism, subsequently became used without its mocking connotation.

Post-impressionism: a term coined by the British artist and art critic Roger Fry to describe developments in French art since Manet and first used when he organized the 1910 London exhibition, "Manet and Post-Impressionism," which led Virginia Woolf to pronounce that "On or about December 1910 human character changed"; including such painters as Van Gogh, Gauguin, Seurat, and Odilon Redon, post-impressionists sought to make art more vivid, colorful, and geometric than had the impressionists.

Postmodernism: viewed variously as an extension of or rejection of modernism. In *Postmodernist Fiction*, Brian McHale distinguishes modernism (in which epistemological issues – the nature of understanding – predominate) from postmodernism (whose concerns are ontological: reality itself is mysterious and unstable).

Primitivism: the incorporation of Négritude (usually African, though also Pacific) culture and artifacts (sculpture, masks, fabrics, music, dance, myths, etc.) into modernist art; associated especially with Constantin Brancusi, Nancy Cunard, Paul Gauguin, Pablo Picasso, and Man Ray.

Russian formalism: movement of literary criticism focusing on the distinctive linguistic features of literary language. Developed in the 1910s and '20s by Russian scholars Viktor

Shklovsky, Roman Jakobson, Boris Tomashevsky, and Boris Eikhenbaum, Russian formalism concentrates analysis on the language of a literary work itself and, therefore, breaks from contextual or interpretive approaches in literary criticism that study an author's background, explore the work's historical context, or offer philosophical interpretations. Russian formalists believed in the autonomy of literary language – that it functions differently from everyday language and develops along evolutionary patterns of its own that are not dictated by historical events. Many of the Russian formalists were linguists and approached literature empirically using scientific methods of classification.

Stream of consciousness: term coined by William James in his *Principles of Psychology* (1890) to denote the flow of thoughts, impressions, and feelings experienced by a character and the narrative technique that represents them. Sometimes used interchangeably with "internal monologue."

Suprematism: influenced by cubism and the ideas of the Russian mystic-mathematician P.D. Ouspensky, who wrote of "a fourth dimension or a Fourth Way beyond the three to which our ordinary senses have access," Kasimir Malevich originated suprematism in 1915 based on fundamental geometric forms (mainly the square and circle). In his book *The Non-Objective World* (1927), Malevich described the inspiration for suprematism: "I felt only night within me and it was then that I conceived the new art, which I called Suprematism." After the Russian Revolution gave way to Stalinism in 1924, suprematism became more influential abroad than in Russia, impacting, for example, constructivism.

Surrealism: following on from late nineteenth-century symbolism and the psychoanalytic work of Freud and Jung, created art of the subconscious mind without logical comprehensibility; first Surrealist Manifesto issued in 1924 (second in 1929) by Louis Aragon, André Breton, and Philippe Soupault; its adherents included Hans Arp, Giorgio de Chirico, Salvador Dali, Marcel Duchamp, Max Ernst, René Magritte, Joan Miro, and Man Ray.

Symbolism: refers to the use of a word or image in a work of art meant to evoke extra-literal meanings. In contradistinction to mimesis, the symbol is a representation that points to something other or beyond that which it represents. The French poets who comprised the symbolist movement in the late nineteenth century – most notably Charles Baudelaire, Stéphane Mallarmé, Paul Verlaine, and Arthur Rimbaud – differentiated themselves from the realist writers by emphasizing the symbolic nature of representation in their works. In English literature, the British critic Arthur Symons and Irish poet W.B. Yeats defined symbolism as the quest for deeper spiritual truths in art beyond the language of quotidian reality.

Synthetism: an art movement begun in the 1880s and most associated with Paul Gauguin and Émile Bernard. Breaking with impressionist art and theory, synthetists emphasized painting's two-dimensionality through their use of flat patterns and strong outlines.

Unreliable narrator: a narrator who misconstrues the nature of reality and whose judgments are untrustworthy; the term at first seemed particularly apt for modernist narrators, but it turns out that all narrators are unreliable and partial (in both senses of that word), but unlike "realist" novelists, modernists tend to foreground and flaunt unreliability rather than try to hide it.

Vorticism: a sort of English futurism combined with cubism; tended to fear that humans would be displaced by machines; primarily associated with Wyndham Lewis, who edited the vorticist newspaper, *Blast*, and the sculptor Jacob Epstein, most famous for his robotic work, *The Rock Drill* (1913–14).

Bibliography of literary modernisms

Essential modernist literature (listed in order of writers' birth dates)

Henrik Ibsen (1828–1906), *An Enemy of the People* (1882).

Thomas Hardy (1840–1928), *Tess of the D'Urbervilles* (1891); *Jude the Obscure* (1895).

Henry James (1843–1916), *What Maisie Knew* (1897); *The Ambassadors* (1903).

Oscar Wilde (1854–1900), *The Picture of Dorian Gray* (1891).

George Bernard Shaw (1856–1950), *Man and Superman* (1903); *Major Barbara* (1905); *Heartbreak House* (1919).

Joseph Conrad (1857–1924), *The Nigger of the "Narcissus"* (1897); *Heart of Darkness* (1899); *Lord Jim* (1900).

Anton Chekhov (1860–1904), *The Cherry Orchard* (1904).

Rabindranath Tagore (1861–1941). *Gitanjali* (1910, translated as *Praise Songs* or *Song Offerings*); *Ghare Baire/ The Home and the World* (1916).

William Butler Yeats (1865–1939), *The Tower* (1928); *The Winding Stairs* (1929).

Luigi Pirandello (1867–1936), *Right You Are, If You Think You Are* (1917); *Six Characters in Search of an Author* (1921); *Tonight We Improvise* (1929).

Marcel Proust (1871–1922), *In Search of Lost Time* (1913–27).

Ford Madox Ford (1873–1939), *The Good Soldier* (1915).

Dorothy Richardson (1873–1957), *Pilgrimage* (1915–38, 1967).

Amy Lowell (1874–1925), *The Complete Poetical Works* (1925).

Gertrude Stein (1874–1946), *The Making of Americans: The Hersland Family* (1925); *Four Saints in Three Acts* (1929).

Thomas Mann (1875–1955), *Buddenbrooks* (1901); *Death in Venice* (1912); *The Magic Mountain* (1924); *Joseph and His Brothers* (1933–43).

Sherwood Anderson (1876–1941), *Winesburg, Ohio* (1919).

E.M. Forster (1879–1970), *A Passage to India* (1924).

Wallace Stevens (1879–1955), *Harmonium* (1922); *Ideas of Order* (1935); *The Man with the Blue Guitar and Other Poems* (1937).

Carl Van Vechten (1880–1964), *Firecrackers. A Realistic Novel* (1925); *Nigger Heaven* (1926).

James Joyce (1882–1941), *Dubliners* (1914); *A Portrait of the Artist as a Young Man* (1916); *Ulysses* (1922); *Finnegans Wake* (1939).

Virginia Woolf (1882–1941), *Mrs. Dalloway* (1925); *To the Lighthouse* (1927); *Between the Acts* (1941).

Franz Kafka (1883–1924), *The Trial* (1925); *The Castle* (1926).

D.H. Lawrence (1885–1930), *The Rainbow* (1915); *Women in Love* (1920).

Ezra Pound (1885–1972), *Hugh Selwyn Mauberley* (1919).

H.D. (Hilda Doolittle) (1886–1961), *Sea Garden* (1916); *Hymen* (1921).

Marianne Moore (1887–1972), *Poems* (1921); *Selected Poems* (1935).

T.S. Eliot (1888–1965), *Prufrock and Other Observations* (1917); *The Waste Land* (1922); *Four Quartets* (1936–42).

Katherine Mansfield (1888–1923), *The Garden Party and Other Stories* (1922).

Eugene O'Neill (1888–1953), *The Emperor Jones* (1924); *Strange Interlude* (1928).

Claude McKay (1889–1948), *Home to Harlem* (1928).

Katherine Anne Porter (1890–1980), *Pale Horse, Pale Rider* (1939).

Jean Rhys (1890–1979), *After Leaving Mr. Mackenzie* (1930); *Good Morning, Midnight* (1939).

Zora Neale Hurston (1891–1960), *Their Eyes Were Watching God* (1937).

Nella Larsen (1891–1964), *Passing* (1929).

Djuna Barnes (1892–1982), *Nightwood* (1936).

Edna St. Vincent Millay (1892–1950), *Renascence and Other Poems* (1917).

Elmer Rice (1892–1967), *The Adding Machine* (1923).

Jean Toomer (1894–1967), *Cane* (1923).

F. Scott Fitzgerald (1896–1940), *The Great Gatsby* (1925).

William Faulkner (1897–1962), *The Sound and the Fury* (1929); *As I Lay Dying* (1930); *Absalom, Absalom!* (1936).

Bertolt Brecht (1898–1956), *The Threepenny Opera* (1928).

Ernest Hemingway (1898–1961), *In Our Time* (1925); *The Sun Also Rises* (1926); *A Farewell to Arms* (1929); *For Whom the Bell Tolls* (1940).

Elizabeth Bowen (1899–1973), *The Last September* (1929).

Hart Crane (1899–1932), *The Bridge* (1930).

Langston Hughes (1902–67), *The Weary Blues* (1926).

Richard Wright (1908–60), *Native Son* (1940); *Black Boy* (1945).

Aimé Césaire (1913–2008), *Notebook of a Return to the Native Land* (1939).

Modernist collections and anthologies

Bender, Todd K., Nancy Armstrong, Sue M. Briggum, and Frank A. Knobloch, eds. *Modernism in Literature*. New York: Holt, Rinehart, 1977. Writings by modernists (loosely defined) from Thomas Hardy to Michael Ondaatje grouped into three categories: "Realism," "Expressionism," and "Impressionism." Seems designed for introduction to literature courses.

Brown, Judith. *Glamour in Six Dimensions: Modernism and the Radiance of Form*. Ithaca: Cornell UP, 2009.

Caws, Mary Ann, ed. *Manifesto: A Century of Isms*. Lincoln, NE and London: U of Nebraska P, 2001. An invaluable compilation of modernist literary and artistic manifestoes.

Deane, Patrick. *History in Our Hands: A Critical Anthology of Writings on Literature, Culture, and Politics from the 1930s*. London and Washington: Leicester UP, 1998. A comprehensive anthology of political and cultural writing – much of it out of print or otherwise inaccessible – from the 1930s, including a strong representation of writings by women. In an informative introduction, Deane notes his aim to uncover the multiplicity of alternative voices in this period, against the prevalent representation of the 1930s as the "Auden Generation."

Ellmann, Richard, and Charles Feidelson, Jr., eds. *The Modern Tradition: Backgrounds of Modern Literature*. New York: Oxford UP, 1965. Somewhat dated and unwieldy compendium of major statements on ideas, values, the human condition, aesthetics, religion, etc. from the eighteenth to the mid-twentieth centuries.

Eysteinsson, Astraudur, and Vivian Liska, eds. *Modernism*, 2 vols. Amsterdam: John Benjamins, 2007. Essays by 65 scholars examine aspects of literary modernism broadly understood; they treat individual texts; national literatures; other arts; cultural, social, philosophical, environmental, and political contexts; and such related issues as race and space, gender and fashion, technology and science.

Faulkner, Peter, ed. *A Modernist Reader: Modernism in England 1910–1930*. London: Batsford, 1986. Literary statements by 14 modernist writers (from James to Lawrence, including two "New Critics") on their aesthetic projects during the two central modernist decades; plus "A Chronology of Publications 1910–30."

Friedman, Alan Warren, ed. *Forms of Modern British Fiction*. Austin: U of Texas P, 1975. Essays by James C. Cowan, Avrom Fleishman, James Gindin, J. Hillis Miller, Charles Rossman, and John Unterecker on major modernist writers from Hardy to Beckett and Lawrence Durrell, plus a panel discussion featuring all the contributors.

Howe, Irving, ed. *Literary Modernism*. New York: Fawcett, 1967. Essays by major critics of literary modernism.

Kiely, Robert, ed. *Modernism Reconsidered*. Cambridge, MA: Harvard UP, 1983. Essays on generally overlooked modernist writers and writings, that question "received opinion about modernist theories and assumptions."

Kolocotroni, Vassiliki, Jane Goldman, and Olga Taxidou, eds. *Modernism: An Anthology of Sources and Documents*. Edinburgh: Edinburgh UP, 1998. Wide-ranging primary modernist readings that are mostly "short extracts from lengthy originals" with some brief statements included "in their volatile entirety." The anthology's three sections are "The Emergence of the Modern" (subdivided into "The modern in cultural, political and scientific thought" and "Modern aesthetics"), "The Avant-Garde" ("Formulations and declarations" and "Manifestos"), and "Modernists on the Modern" ("The 1910s and 1920s: The making of Modernist tradition" and "The 1930s: Modernist regroupings").

Levenson, Michael, ed. *The Cambridge Companion to Modernism*. Cambridge, UK and New York: Cambridge UP, 1999. Essays on metaphysics, culture, genres, politics, gender, the visual arts, and film.

Lief, Leonard, and James F. Light, eds. *The Modern Age: Literature*. 1969. New York: Holt, Rinehart, 1976. Wide-ranging, amorphous collection of primary texts grouped into three broad categories: "Influential Voices, 1848–1917"; "The Long Armistice, 1918–39"; and "Under the Volcano, 1939–76." Appendix offers introductions to literary genres generally; seems designed for introduction to literature courses.

Matthews, Steven, ed. *Modernism: A Sourcebook*. New York: Palgrave Macmillan, 2008. Documents for contextualizing modernist literary texts. Contains a substantial introduction laying out key events, movements, and literary and cultural issues of the time.

Rainey, Lawrence, ed. *Modernism: An Anthology*. Oxford and Malden, MA: Blackwell, 2005. Literary texts meant to represent the significant modernist writers by genres, though necessarily shortchanging fiction (it includes only short stories and short excerpts from novels) and drama.

Scott, Bonnie Kime, *et al.*, ed. *The Gender of Modernism: A Critical Anthology*. Bloomington: Indiana UP, 1990. A pioneering collection by and about female modernists (5 of the

26 writers included are men) that challenges the notion that modernism was "gendered masculine."

——. *Refiguring Modernism, vol. 1, Women of 1928; vol. 2, Postmodern Feminist Readings of Woolf, West, and Barnes*. Bloomington: Indiana UP, 1995. Revisionary anthology that brings together feminist criticism and modernist feminist writings.

Stromberg, Roland M., ed. *Realism, Naturalism, and Symbolism: Modes of Thought and Expression in Europe, 1848–1914*. New York: Harper, 1968. Statements (including some from literary texts) on European literary, artistic, and philosophic thought, subsumed under the titular rubric, between the revolutions of 1848 and the beginning of World War I.

Whitworth, Michael, ed. *Modernism: A Guide to Criticism*. Chichester: Wiley-Blackwell, 2006. A selection of key works of criticism on literary modernism, focusing on its relationship with other literary movements and cultural developments.

Annotated bibliography of literary modernist criticism

Armstrong, Tim. *Modernism: A Cultural History*. Cambridge, UK and Malden, MA: Polity, 2005. A broad and wide-ranging discussion of modernism as essentially situated in – and actively engaged with – its historical and cultural contexts. Examines the aesthetics of modernism, especially literary modernism, in connection with developments and reforms in other cultural spheres including politics, mass culture, science and technology, psychology and consciousness, and market culture.

Auerbach, Erich. *Mimesis: The Representation of Reality in Western Literature* (1953). Ed. and trans. Willard Trask. Princeton: Princeton UP, 2003. A classic of literary criticism that examines, in rich detail and wide scope, the history of representation and realism in the traditional canon of Western literature.

Baker, Houston A., Jr. *Modernism and the Harlem Renaissance*. Chicago: U of Chicago P, 1989. An examination of the inseparable nature of African American culture and politics in which Baker argues that modernity, for black Americans, was centrally concerned with the struggle for self-determination; the study examines the height of African American renaissance culture after World War I and into the early 1920s. Baker's harbingers of modern change are "Race Men" like Booker T. Washington, W.E.B. DuBois, and Charles Chesnutt. Black music, literature, and political discourse are "soundings," mobile expressive forms that contain and represent an oppressed and defiant people's "repository of spirit" and will to live, freely.

Beach, Joseph Warren. *The Twentieth Century Novel: Studies in Technique*. New York and London: Century, 1932. First major attempt to take the measure of the modern novel and to situate its major practitioners in relation to impressionism, post-impressionism, and expressionism.

Bergonzi, Bernard. *The Myth of Modernism and Twentieth Century Literature*. New York: St. Martin's, 1986. A collection of reprinted essays and reviews, with a helpful introduction; addresses as myth the notion that modernism was a totalizing and permanent revolution in literature.

Berman, Marshall. *All That is Solid Melts into Air: The Experience of Modernity*. London: Verso, 1983. Inspired by the student occupation of Columbia University in 1968, examines the experience of living within the perpetual struggles and contradictions of modernity, and looks to modernists of the nineteenth century (Goethe, Marx, Baudelaire, and a selection of Russian writers) to find possibilities for creative renewal in the flux of modernization which is alive and well on the streets of American and European cities.

——. "Why Modernism Still Matters." *Tikkun* 4.1 (January/February 1989): 11–14, 81–86. Re-examines *All That is Solid Melts into Air* (see above), and sees modernism still "alive and well" in the world's urban centers.

Booth, Wayne C. *The Rhetoric of Fiction*. Chicago: U of Chicago P, 1961. A brilliant analysis of narrative strategies and authorial "distance," but limited by Booth's moral absolutism and his stricture "that an author has an obligation to be as clear about his moral position as he possibly can be."

Bradbury, Malcolm, and James McFarlane, eds. *Modernism: A Guide to European Literature 1890–1930* (1976). New York: Penguin, 1991. Includes a long first chapter by the editors on "The Name and Nature of Modernism" and essays by various critics on modernism's cultural and intellectual climate, geography, and literary movements, plus its poetry, novels, and drama.

Bradshaw, David, ed. *A Concise Companion to Modernism*. Chichester: Wiley-Blackwell, 2002. A collection of essays that discuss the emergence of, and major developments in, twelve fields that shaped the intellectual milieu of Anglo-American modernism. Topics include evolution, eugenics, the influence of Nietzsche, physics, psychoanalysis, and anthropology.

Bradshaw, David, and Kevin J.H. Dettmar, eds. *A Companion to Modernist Literature and Culture*. Oxford and Malden, MA: Blackwell, 2006. Essays by different critics on modernism in various disciplines, on its movements and genres, on modern media, and brief readings of major modernist texts.

Bürger, Peter. *The Decline of Modernism*. University Park: Pennsylvania State UP, 1992. Examines the relationship between art and society from the emergence of bourgeois culture in the eighteenth century to the decline of modernism in the twentieth century.

Calinescu, Matei. *Five Faces of Modernity: Modernism, Avant-Garde, Decadence, Kitsch, Postmodernism* (1977). Durham: Duke UP, 1987. An impressive intellectual history of five key aesthetic concepts of modernity, including (if slightly confusingly) modernism and postmodernism. Curious treatment of Romanticism, which Calinescu rightly considers to have significantly impacted modernity, as essentially French, and his modernity is largely literary. Views modernist time as teleological: linear, progressive, and irreversible.

Childs, Peter. *Modernism* (2000). London and New York: Routledge, 2008. Examines the origins of the modernist movement in the writings of Darwin, Marx, Nietzsche, Freud, Saussure, and Einstein; the changes in literary and artistic genres; the writings of several major modernists; and the shift from modernism to postmodernism.

Diepeveen, Leonard. *The Difficulties of Modernism*. New York: Routledge, 2003. Discussion of how difficulty became an essential characteristic of the modernist aesthetic, and how its legacy continues to shape modern culture and literary criticism.

Douglas, Ann. *Terrible Honesty: Mongrel Manhattan in the 1920's*. New York: Farrar, Straus and Giroux, 1995. A cultural history of 1920s' Manhattan as the site of American modernism's formation. Douglas argues that this development was instigated by a matricidal impulse against the white, middle-class Victorian mother figure, and also examines the creative collaboration between white and black artists during this period as crucial to the formation of American modernist culture.

Eagleton, Terry. *Literary Theory: An Introduction*. Minneapolis: U of Minnesota P, 1983. First situates the rise of English studies during the modernist period within the context of a decline of established religion, new scientific discovery, social change (especially the entry of women into institutions of higher education), and new (and troubled) nationalism occasioned by World War I; then examines the major types of contemporary literary theory.

Empson, William. *Seven Types of Ambiguity* (1930). London: Chatto and Windus, 1949. An influential work of literary criticism that examines, through close readings, the variety of meanings in poetic language, and the ways they are apprehended by the reader.

Esty, Joshua. *A Shrinking Island: Modernism and National Culture in England*. Princeton: Princeton UP, 2004. Examines the "anthropological turn" of British modernist writing from 1930 to 1960, arguing that the late modernists of this period dealt with the decline of empire – and its sense of contraction – by deliberately shifting toward the insularity and particularity of English culture as a basis for renewal.

Eysteinsson, Astraudur. *The Concept of Modernism*. Ithaca: Cornell UP, 1990. Discusses the multiple, and sometimes contradictory, theoretical and critical forces that have contributed to the development of modernism as a literary and aesthetic concept.

Faulkner, Peter. *Modernism*. London: Methuen, 1977. A short introduction to a critical understanding of English literary modernism, with critical analysis of writings by Eliot, Woolf, Pound, Joyce, and Lawrence.

Frank, Joseph. "Spatial Form in Modern Literature." *The Widening Gyre: Crisis and Mastery in Modern Literature*. New Brunswick, NJ: Rutgers UP, 1963. 3–62. Working from Pound's definition of *image* as "that which presents an intellectual and emotional complex in an instant of time," this essay explores the modernist disruption of traditional narrative's method: progress through sequence of time. Frank discusses the employment of spatial form in modernist novels, drawing parallels with modern poetry and the plastic arts, to illustrate that they are meant to be apprehended as a whole – in a moment of time – rather than linearly.

Friedman, Alan. *The Turn of the Novel*. New York: Oxford UP, 1966. How the modern novel became psychological, unresolved, and open-ended.

Gay, Peter. *Modernism: The Lure of Heresy from Baudelaire to Beckett and Beyond*. New York and London: Norton, 2008. Sprawling treatment of conflicting forces, histories, personalities, and achievements of modernism, loosely defined by Pound's injunction to "Make it new" and covering the years from the early 1840s to the 1960s and beyond.

Gillies, Mary Ann, and Aurelea Mahood. *Modernist Literature: An Introduction*. Montreal and Kingston, Ont.: McGill-Queen's UP, 2007. An unusual introduction, with each chapter focusing on a literary genre, a major theme (e.g., "the New Woman," "Technology and War"), and a decade (from 1900 to 1940, plus a coda on the World War II years). Includes a modernist chronology and suggested further readings.

Gilroy, Paul. *The Black Atlantic: Modernity and Double Consciousness*. London: Verso, 1993. Gilroy's study examines formations of black identity, culture, and consciousness, and the hybrid or syncretic nature of each. He reads the ship as the vehicle that gives birth to modern black identity, from the Middle Passage and height of the slave trade, to black intellectuals' postwar exilic wanderings in Europe, Africa, the Caribbean, and beyond. Gilroy builds upon W.E.B. DuBois' notion of "double consciousness" to highlight black artists' and intellectuals' diasporic and transnational inclinations and the ways in which often brutal economic and political conditions influenced Black Atlantic people's literature, music and culture, and their strategies of survival and affiliation.

Gross, Harvey. *The Contrived Corridor: History and Fatality in Modern Literature*. Ann Arbor: U of Michigan P, 1971. In an age largely defined by a sense of crisis and cultural disorientation, certain writers (such as Adams, Eliot, Malraux, Mann, and Yeats) displayed a "heightened consciousness of history."

Gross, John, ed. *A TLS Companion: The Modern Movement*. London: Harvill, 1992. Collects *Times Literary Supplement* reviews of a dozen major modernist writers plus other pieces by modernists on modernism, including several written by T.S. Eliot and Virginia Woolf, who regularly contributed to the paper.

Gubar, Susan. *Racechanges: White Skin, Black Face in American Culture*. Oxford: Oxford UP, 1997. A wide-ranging critical analysis of the history and legacy of "racechanges," or cross-racial impersonations and imitations, in twentieth-century American art and popular culture.

Hanna, Julian. *Key Concepts in Modernist Literature*. Basingstoke, Hampshire and New York: Palgrave Macmillan, 2009. Useful introduction to the literature from 1900 to World War

II; the three major sections are Contexts (History, Politics, Culture), Literature, and Criticism.

Hughes, Robert. *The Shock of the New: The Hundred-Year History of Modern Art: Its Rise, Its Dazzling Achievement, Its Fall* (1980). New York: Thames and Hudson, 1991. Originally a 1980 BBC TV series of the same name; witty and insightful examination of the development of modern art since the Impressionists.

Kenner, Hugh. *A Homemade World: The American Modernist Writers*. New York: Knopf, 1975. How American modernist writers such as Faulkner, Fitzgerald, Hemingway, Moore, Stevens, and Williams reshaped fictional and poetic genres as well as "the American language."

——. *The Pound Era*. Berkeley: U of California P, 1973. Quirky tracking of Pound's work and life as key to the modernist period.

Kermode, Frank. *The Sense of an Ending: Studies in the Theory of Fiction*. London: Oxford UP, 1966. Explores "the apocalyptic spirit" from Plato and Augustine to millennial anxiety of the modernists, especially Eliot, Joyce, and Yeats, plus Beckett and Sartre. Views Joyce as the central, liberal figure within modernism.

Kiely, Robert, ed. *Modernism Reconsidered*. Essays by various critics of literary modernism.

Krutch, Joseph Wood. *The Modern Temper* (1929). New York: Harcourt, Brace, 1957. Influential study that locates in modernism a sense of despair, which Krutch attributes to the loss of belief in humanist values and their replacement with scientific materialism.

Levenson, Michael. *A Genealogy of Modernism: A Study of English Literary Doctrine, 1908–1922*. Cambridge, UK and New York: Cambridge UP, 1984. Traces the development of English modernism through its transitions and continual self-revisions during this period. Levenson focuses on Conrad, Ford, Pound, Lewis, and Eliot as representatives of successive literary movements in the time between Pound's arrival in London (1908) and publication of *The Waste Land* (1922).

Levin, Harry. "What was Modernism?" *Refractions: Essays in Comparative Literature*. New York: Oxford UP, 1966. Explores literary modernism's emphases on metamorphosis and migration – expressions of a keen awareness of time, of self, and of instability that characterized the early twentieth century.

Lyon, Janet. *Manifestoes: Provocations of the Modern*. Ithaca and London: Cornell UP, 1999. A history and theory of the manifesto, beginning with the Levellers and Diggers of seventeenth-century Britain. Examines the manifesto's role in the development of political modernity and avant-garde aesthetics.

McHale, Brian. *Postmodernist Fiction*. New York: Methuen, 1987. Wide-ranging study, especially strong on modern narrative theory.

Mahaffey, Vicki. *Modernist Literature: Challenging Fictions*. Malden, MA: Blackwell, 2007. Explores how modernist fiction can cultivate deliberate ethical engagement with culture, as its difficulties require readers to look beyond the surfaces of a text, to take greater responsibility for interpretive and ethical choices, and to challenge the sensibilities and "fictions" by which they live.

Matthews, Steven. *Modernism*. London: Hodder Arnold, 2004. Examines many of the major authors and texts of the modernist period, mapping literary alongside historical and social issues.

Meisel, Perry. *The Myth of the Modern: A Study in British Literature and Criticism after 1850*. New Haven: Yale UP, 1987. Examines modernism as a response to the sense of "belatedness" to literary tradition, which renders impossible the fundamental will to modernity – to "make it new." Revisits canonical modernist texts to demonstrate how they thematize and dramatize this paradoxical burden. Discerns a fundamental divide between two separate lines of high modernism: one originating in Eliot, who approaches this will to modernity as a straightforward quest, and the other in Joyce, who exemplifies a self-conscious and liberating awareness of its paradoxes.

Mellard, James M. *The Exploded Form: The Modernist Novel in America*. Urbana: U of Illinois P, 1980. A dialectical approach to the development of the modernist novel's form. Through study of representative novels, traces three distinct phases in this development: the *naïve*, in which modernist principles emerged through the unconscious practice of authors; the *critical*, during which these principles became consciously and intentionally applied; and the *sophisticated*, in which critical understanding is distinguished from belief in and adherence to these principles.

Miller, Tyrus. *Late Modernism: Politics, Fiction, and the Arts between the World Wars*. Berkeley: U of California P, 1999. Examines the interwar years as a distinct period during which "late modernist" writers challenged the earlier, high modernist aesthetic of formal mastery. Through particular focus on Lewis, Barnes, and Beckett, Miller situates the literary modernism of this time in its broader political and cultural contexts, including its engagement with the influences of film, radio, and advertising.

Nichols, Peter. *Modernisms: A Literary Guide* (1995). London: Macmillan, 2009. Argues for the rich diversity of modernism through examination of the writings of Baudelaire and Mallarmé, major modernist texts and movements, and African American modernism.

North, Michael. *Dialectic of Modernism*. Oxford: Oxford UP, 1994. Challenges the motives of the white avant-garde who embraced African and African American art and artists.

Perloff, Marjorie. *The Futurist Movement: Avant-Garde, Avant Guerre, and the Language of Rupture*. Chicago and London: U of Chicago P, 1986. With broad international scope, considers works by Pound, Marinetti, Picasso, and Khlebnikov, and traces simultaneous developments in futurist manifestoes, avant-garde art, and literature before and during World War I.

Quinones, Ricardo J. *Mapping Literary Modernism: Time and Development*. Princeton: Princeton UP, 1985. Major modernist writers, such as Eliot, Joyce, Lawrence, Mann, Proust, and Woolf, challenged the ethical and dynamic sense of time derived from the Renaissance. A key concept, "the paradox of time," explains how and why major modernists considered time to be effected through both objectively depicting events and their characters' subjective experiencing of them.

Schorer, Mark, ed. *Modern British Fiction*. New York: Oxford UP, 1961. Early essays on modern British fiction by major critics.

Scott-James, R.A. *Modernism and Romance*. New York and London: John Lane, 1908. One of the earliest works of literary criticism to use the word "modernism"; discusses the influence of "the scientific spirit" in such areas as psychology and philosophy in the twentieth century.

Surette, Leon. *The Birth of Modernism: Ezra Pound, T.S. Eliot, W.B. Yeats, and the Occult*. Montreal and Kingston, Ont.: McGill-Queen's UP, 1993. Argues that occult ideas significantly influenced the development of literary modernism, with particular focus on Pound and *The Cantos*.

Trilling, Lionel. "On the Modern Element in Modern Literature." *Varieties of Literary Experience*, ed. Stanley Burnshaw. New York: New York UP, 1962. Drawing significantly from his experience of teaching it, Trilling discusses his definition of "modern" literature, particularly its intensely personal demands on the reader.

Weber, Nicholas Fox. *The Bauhaus Group: Six Masters of Modernism*. New York: Knopf, 2009. A detailed group biography, with photographs and art reproductions, of six influential artists of the German art school: Gropius, Klee, Kandinsky, Mies van der Rohe, and Josef and Anni Albers.

Williams, Raymond. *Modern Tragedy*. Stanford: Stanford UP, 1966. Studies in modernist drama and fiction.

Wilson, Edmund. *Axel's Castle: A Study in the Imaginative Literature of 1870–1930* (1931). London: Fontana, 1979. The first major study of literary modernism, locating its roots in Romanticism and its first flowering in the aesthetics and irrationality of symbolism (Wilson's term for "modernism").

A sampling of multimedia resources for literary modernism

Modernism and Modernity (online journal): <muse.jhu.edu/journals/mod/>

MIA: Minneapolis Institute of Art's modernism site: http://www.artsmia.org/modernism/

MOMA (Museum of Modern Art, New York): http://www.moma.org/

Pompidou Center, Paris: http://www.centrepompidou.fr/en

Voice of the Shuttle (Modern British and American): http://vos.ucsb.edu/browse.asp?id=2747

The vorticists' Blast Manifesto: http://www.davidson.edu/academic/english/Little_Magazines/Blast/manifesto.html

Early cinema site: http://www.earlycinema.com/timeline/index.html

Little magazines

Davidson's little magazine site: http://sites.davidson.edu/littlemagazines/

Modernist journals project: http://dl.lib.brown.edu/mjp/

Modernist magazines project: http://www.modernistmagazines.com/

Albert Einstein: http://einstein.biz/

In Flanders Field Museum: http://www.inflandersfields.be/

The Imperial War Museum: http://www.iwm.org.uk/

Orlando: British Women Writers: http://www.cambridge.org/home/news/article/item6852081/?site_locale = en_GB

Sigmund Freud: http://www.freud.org.uk/

Magnus Hirschfeld Institute for Sexual Science: http://www.hirschfeld.in-berlin.de/institut/en/index1024_2.html

James Joyce

Ulysses "Seen" Comic: http://ulyssesseen.com/

Walking *Ulysses*: http://ulysses.bc.edu/

Virginia Woolf

Tate Modern's Bloomsbury site: http://www2.tate.org.uk/archivejourneys/bloomsburyhtml/

Words Fail Me, BBC Radio (audio): http://www.bbc.co.uk/archive/writers/12240.shtml

W.B. Yeats

The National Library of Ireland online Yeats exhibition: http://www.nli.ie/yeats/

Walter Benjamin

The Walter Benjamin Research Syndicate: http://www.wbenjamin.org/walterbenjamin.html
Susan Buck-Morse on Walter Benjamin's "The Work of Art in the Age of Mechanical
    Reproducibility" (video): http://video.google.com/videoplay?docid=-3659405701394
    697641#

Index

Milton, John: *Paradise Lost* 443, 468
modern novel 35
modern writers as literary critics 441–5
modernist aesthetics 18
Modernist Studies Association 400
Modernité 17, 25
Modigliani, Amedeo 146
Molière (Jean-Baptiste Poquelin) 217, 222
Moll, Albert 320–2, 324
Mondrian, Piet 146
Monet, Claude 38, 499, 500, 501
montage 8–9, 19–20, 22, 111–13, 116–17
Montaigne, Michel de 93, 178
Moore, G.E. 145; *Principia Ethica* 145
Moore, George 387, 389, 394–5; *A Drama in Muslin* 340; *Esther Waters* 340
Moore, Henry Spencer 38
Moore, Marianne 511
Moore, Merrill 556
Morel, Benedict-Augustin 303
Morrell, Lady Ottoline 485
Morris, William 295, 402, 547
Mosley, Oswald 466
Mozart, Wolfgang Amadeus 419, 542
Muhammad 439
Muslim/Mughal Empire 425, 428, 429
Mussolini, Benito 22, 146, 243, 257, 339, 340, 461, 477

NAACP 340, 359
Napoleon Bonaparte (1769–1821) 217, 254; Napoleonic Wars 524–5
Nashe, Thomas: as symbolist poet 462
nationalism (nineteenth century) 251–6, 341, 409–11
National Urban League 359
Native Americans 340
naturalism 4, 6
natural selection 345, 347
Nazism (National Socialism) 20, 136, 275–88, 296, 336; Nazi Academy for Public Health Service 294; Nazi Ministry of Propaganda 22
Négritude 3, 6, 8, 17, 100, 339, 389, 399
Negro question 293
Negro Zionism 337, 369
Nehru, Jawaharlal: *Toward Freedom* 551
Nerval, Gérard de 55
New Architecture 3
New Criticism 3
New Deal 104
New Dwelling 3
New Modernist Studies 399
New Negro Movement 339, 363–4, 366, 367, 368, 383
New Photography 3
New Woman 57, 62, 295, 297, 318, 327–9, 332
Newton, Isaac 234, 235, 236; Newtonian physics 194, 195

Nicholson, R.A. 427–8
Niebelung's Ring 182
Niermeyer, Oscar 401
Nietzsche, Friedrich 1, 2, 6–7, 145, 147, 151, 401, 413, 430; "Aphorism #477" 249–50; "The Antichrist" 153–8; *The Gay Science* 151–2; *Of the Use and Abuse of History* 188; *Thus Spoke Zarathustra* 152–3
nihilism 3, 155
Nobel Prize 339
Noh theatre 19, 114, 147
non-Euclidian geometry 194
novel as genre 441, 444, 451–5, 485–9, 506–8, 513–17
Nuremberg Tribunal 273

O'Casey, Sean 243
O'Flaherty, Liam 8; *The Informer* 8
O'Keefe, Georgia 297
O'Neill, Eugene 4
Oedipus complex 296, 307–11, 315, 316
Opportunity 316, 359
orientalism 36, 400, 425
orphism 3
Orwell, George 2, 424
Owen, Wilfred 241

Pais, Abraham 194
Pan-Africanism 402
Pan-Indian nationalism 401
Pankhurst, Sylvia 341
Parker, Charlie 9
Parnell, Charles Stewart 266–9, 496
Pascal, Blaise 155
Pater, Walter 18, 30, 33, 39; *The Renaissance* 30–2, 456, 496
Paty de Clam, Armand du 354–6, 357
Pauling, Linus 336
Pavlov, Ivan 111
Pearl Harbor 340
perception 43
Péret, Benjamin 439
Persian literature 425–8
perspectivism 3, 9, 195
Pétain, Philippe 104
Peter the Great 254
Picasso, Pablo 8, 9, 104, 146
Pirandello, Luigi 4, 8, 442; *Six Characters in Search of an Author* 8, 477–84
Pisaro, Michael 38
Planck, Max 235–6; Planck's constant 236
Plato 34; *The Dialogues* 508
plumbing 196
Poe, Edgar Allan 25; *The Man of the Crowd* 25, 27
poetry as genre 509–12
pointillism 19
Porter, Katherine Anne: "Pale Horse, Pale Rider" 199, 241
post-impressionism 3, 4, 5, 17